Broken

Fragmenting
Indigenous Families
1800–2000

Overlapping circles of extended family lie at the heart of the lives of most Aboriginal Australians. Networks of family relationships determine day-to-day activities and shape the course of destinies. From an early age Aboriginal Australians learn who belongs to whom, where they come from and how they should behave across a wide universe of kin. These are highly valued and integral components of Aboriginal cultural knowledge. And yet, these same familial systems have been the site of repeated attacks by successive waves of Australian governments, tearing at the very heart of Aboriginal family life.

Broken Circles tells the tragic history, from colonial times to the present, of the destruction of successive generations of Aboriginal families through the forced removal of children.

Anna Haebich has degrees in anthropology, history and fine arts. Her publications include the authoritative *For Their Own Good: Aborigines and Government in the South West of Western Australia 1900–1940*. Anna has taught and written widely in the area of indigenous studies and has worked for several indigenous political and cultural organisations. For the last fifteen years she has lived with a Nyungar family in Perth.

Anna travelled extensively across Australia while researching *Broken Circles*. She attended hearings of the National Inquiry into the Separation of Aboriginal Children from their Families and presented submissions. She also worked closely with various community groups on projects relating to the Stolen Generations.

Anna is currently a Curator of History at the Western Australian Museum.

Broken Circles

Fragmenting
Indigenous Families
1800–2000

Anna Haebich

FREMANTLE ARTS CENTRE PRESS

First published 2000 by
FREMANTLE ARTS CENTRE PRESS
25 Quarry Street, Fremantle
(PO Box 158, North Fremantle 6159)
Western Australia.
www.facp.iinet.net.au

Reprinted 2001.

Consultant Editors Janet Blagg and Ray Coffey.
Production Coordinator Cate Sutherland.
Cover Designer Becky Chilcott.

Typeset by Fremantle Arts Centre Press
and printed by South Wind Productions, Singapore.

National Library of Australia
Cataloguing-in-publication data

  Haebich, Anna.
  Broken circles: fragmenting indigenous families 1800–2000

  Bibliography.
  Includes index.
  ISBN 1 86368 305 4.

  1. Aborigines, Australian – Children – Government policy.
  2. Aborigines, Australian – Removal – Government policy.
  3. Aborigines, Australian – Treatment – History. I. Title.

The State of Western Australia has made an investment in this project
through ArtsWA in association with the Lotteries Commission.

Publication of this title was assisted by the Commonwealth Government
through the Australia Council, its arts funding and advisory body.

To my parents Bert and Ruth Haebich
who gave me the precious gift
of a warm and loving family

To my late sister Lynette McKell
who dedicated her short life
to caring for children in hospital

To my partner Darryl Kickett
who brought me into his family
and taught me to look at the world 'Nyungar way'

To the Johnson family
for their great courage and their passion for justice

CONTENTS

ACKNOWLEDGMENTS

Broken Circles owes its existence to the generosity of spirit of my family, friends and colleagues around Australia. In particular, Bill and Pauline Johnson had faith in my ability to write a history to honour the memory of their adoptive son Louis Johnson/Warren Braedon who was tragically murdered in Perth in 1991 'because he was black.'

The Louis Johnson Memorial Trust Fund magnanimously funded the research and writing of *Broken Circles*, which was supervised jointly by Dr Tom O'Regan, Director of the Centre for Research in Culture and Communication at Murdoch University, and Ann Martin, Head of the Aboriginal Education Unit at the University of New South Wales. The School of Humanities at Murdoch University provided administrative support and the Aboriginal Education Unit at the University of New South Wales provided backing for the project on the 'east coast.' Both institutions also assisted with funding. Invaluable advice on research directions, editorial assistance and emotional support were provided by the Project Advisory Committee: Darryl Kickett, Steve Mickler, Ann Martin, Tom O'Regan, Tim Rowse, Peter Read, Jackie Huggins, Jean Carter and Len Collard. Several other colleagues generously commented on draft chapters and provided additional information — Bain Attwood, Raymond Evans, Lyndall Ryan, MaryAnn Jebb, Sarah Yu, Julie Gough and Matt Trinca. Useful suggestions for research were made by Heather Goodall, Linda Briskman, Ros Kidd, Dave Palmer, Steve Kinnane, Lauren Marsh, Gus Bottrell, Robert Van Krieken, Richard Broome, Rosie Kerr, Nigel De Souza and Luke Brown. Vicki Fair, Christine Carter, Cynthia Lim and Jen Buchanan assisted with various research tasks and Jen also patiently transformed my unruly drafts into a presentable manuscript. The editors of Fremantle Arts Centre Press, Ray Coffey and Janet Blagg, advised on the final crafting of the book.

Publication of *Broken Circles* was assisted by the considerable generosity of JLV Industries, Pty Ltd.

As I travelled across the country researching and writing the book I met up with hundreds of people who selflessly supported and encouraged my work. I am deeply indebted to you all. I was fortunate to be able to attend many hearings of the Human Rights and Equal Opportunity Commission Inquiry into the Separation of Aboriginal and Torres Strait Islander Children from their Families. I would like to thank Sir Ronald Wilson, Michael Dodson, their hard working staff and the many Aboriginal and other people who appeared before the Inquiry for the valuable insights which informed my research. A highlight was the opportunity to work with the Kimberley Land Council in preparing their submission to the Inquiry. Staff at the National Archives in Canberra, Melbourne and Darwin, the State Archives of Queensland, Western Australia, Tasmania, New South Wales and South Australia, the Australian Institute of Aboriginal and Torres Strait Islander Studies and several government departments unstintingly assisted me in finding my way around their collections. In particular I would like to thank Ros Fraser, Kath Frankland, Andrew Wilson, Sue Beverley, Andrew Hall and Heather Shearer for their advice and friendship. Members of the Uniting, Lutheran and Catholic churches also assisted me with their records. I met with representatives of many organisations concerned with the forced removal of Aboriginal children including the Alice Springs Aboriginal Child Care Agency, the Victorian Aboriginal Child Care Agency, Secretariat of National Aboriginal and Islander Child Care, the Western Australian Aboriginal Legal Service, the Tasmanian Aboriginal Health Service, Link-Up New South Wales and the Federation of Aboriginal and Islander Research Association. I also attended the National Stolen Generations Conference in Alice Springs which brought together key Aboriginal players from around Australia. Some members of the Stolen Generations also shared their personal experiences with me, in particular, my friends Joylene Koolmatrie and the late Rob Riley, whose sudden death was a devastating confirmation of the effects of removal policies. In Alice Springs Brian White took the time to introduce me to members of Louis Johnson/Warren Braedon's family, and Kevin and Eric Braedon and Mary Williams generously provided background information about their family. Colin Clague, Bruce Alcorn, Denis Daniels, Dr Tom Gavranic and Muriel Cadd clarified aspects of recent government practice in the Northern Territory, Tasmania and Victoria.

Everywhere old and new friends and family members spent time with me and provided warmth and company: in Canberra, Uncle Bill and Aunty Glenda Humes, Peter Read and Jay Arthur; in Cootamundra Lesley Whitton; in Alice Springs Brian White, Sally Hodson, Tim Rowse, Jan and Georgia McKay, Kieran Finnane and Pastor and Mrs Gierus; in Darwin Andrea Williams, Des Kootii Raymond, Paul Roberts, Melissa Hasluck, Kate Ackerman, Kath Mills, Leon Morris and Sue Jackson, Lyn and Barry Kickett; in Hobart Julie Gough, Irene Schaffer, Dr Cassandra Pybus; in Adelaide Selima and Riley Omelzcuk, John Bowden, Anna and Stefan Omelzcuk, Andrew Wilson and family, Marge Turner, Lorna Goss, Ivy Nitschke, Garry Benson, Peter Bertani; in Sydney my sister Joan and her family, Derek, Rowena and Daniel Curtin, Ann Martin and family, Stephen Muecke and Pru Black, Ben Forshaw, Noel King, Neville Hind, Nola Farman and Anna Gibbs; in Brisbane my parents Bert and Ruth Haebich, my brother Bob Haebich, Kath Frankland and Geoff Farrer, Georgina Murray and Tom Bramble, Tony Kelly, Jenna and Daniel Maffe, Kay Saunders, John and Sue Brown, Chris Sayer and John Lucacs, Jackie Huggins, Pat Buckridge, Jim and Robin Walter; in Melbourne Lucy Ellam, Linda Briskman, Pat Grimshaw, Sonja Smallacombe; in Western Australia my family Darryl, Rikia, Latisha, Sunimah, Andrea, Tooda, Colleen, Kyron, little Tooda, Tina and all the Kicketts, the Morrisons, Julie Parsons, MaryAnn Jebb and Malcolm Albrook, Peter and Sarah Yu, Jimmy Chi and Glennys Allen, Helen Cattalini, Helen Greenacre, Jen Buchanan and Dave Palmer, Pat Dodson, June Oscar, Olive Knight, Grant Drage, Cynthia Dann, Pauline Kennedy, Father McMahon, my friends at Dadiri Sister Emily Cattalini, Father Reg, Edyr, Ledo and Rebekkah, my colleagues at Murdoch University, in particular, Steve Mickler, Tom O'Regan, Tony Buti, Alec McHoul, Lyn Dale, Peter Stuart and my colleagues at the Museum of Western Australia, in particular Matt Trinca and Ann Delroy.

ABBREVIATIONS

AAL	Aborigines Advancement League
AAPA	Australian Aborigines Progressive Association
AAM	Australian Aborigines Mission
ABM	Australian Board of Missions
ACA	Advisory Council of Aborigines (SA)
ACCA	Aboriginal Child Care Agency
AFA	Aborigines Friends Association (SA)
AFWV	Australian Federation of Women Voters
AIM	Australian Inland Mission
ALRC	Australian Law Reform Commission
APB	Aborigines Protection Board (NSW, SA, Vic)
APL	Aborigines Protection League (SA)
ASAPS	Anti-Slavery and Aborigines Protection Society
AWB	Aborigines Welfare Board (NSW, Vic)
BCL	British Commonwealth League
CAAC	Central Australian Aboriginal Congress
CAALAS	Central Australian Aboriginal Legal Aid Service
CLC	Central Land Council
CWD	Child Welfare Department (NSW)
CWPRB	Child Welfare and Public Relief Board (SA)
DAA	Department of Aboriginal Affairs (Federal)
DChW	Department of Child Welfare (WA)
DCW	Department of Community Welfare (WA)
DFW	Department of Family Welfare (Vic)
DNA	Department of Native Affairs (WA)
DNAO	Director of Native Affairs Office (Qld)
DNW	Department of Native Welfare (WA)
DSS	Department of Social Security (Federal)
FCAA	Federal Council for the Advancement of Aborigines
FCAATSI	Federal Council for the Advancement of Aborigines and Torres Strait Islanders

HREOC	Human Rights and Equal Opportunity Commission
NACC	National Aboriginal Consultative Committee
NTALA	Northern Territory Aboriginal Legal Aid
OCC	Office of Child Care (Federal)
RCIADIC	Royal Commission into Aboriginal Deaths in Custody
SCC	State Children's Council (SA)
SCD	State Children's Department
SNAICC	Secretariat of National Aboriginal and Islander Child Care
SWB	Social Welfare Branch
UAM	United Aborigines Mission
VAAL	Victorian Aborigines Advancement League
VACCA	Victorian Aboriginal Child Care Agency
VALS	Victorian Aboriginal Legal Service
WNPPA	Women's Non-Party Political Association (SA)
WSG	Women's Service Guild (WA)

INTRODUCTION

REMEMBERING BACK THROUGH THE HEART

To remember. From the Latin 'recordis', to pass back through the heart.

Eduardo Galeano[1]

Overlapping circles of extended family lie at the heart of the lives of most Aboriginal Australians. Networks of family relationships determine day-to-day activities and shape the course of destinies. From an early age Aboriginal Australians learn who belongs to whom, where they come from and how they should behave across a wide universe of kin. These are highly valued and integral components of Aboriginal cultural knowledge. And yet, these same familial systems have been the site of repeated attacks by successive waves of Australian governments, tearing at the very heart of Aboriginal family life. The tragic history of these relentless efforts to fragment Aboriginal families is the subject of this book.

Australia is a society which has placed immense value on the importance of the intact family as the building block of the nation and its emotional heartland. For non-Aboriginal families, bonds between parents and children have been considered sacrosanct and the experience of growing up within the circle of the family an inviolable right to be disrupted only through strictly controlled legal processes to protect the 'best interests' of the child. By contrast, Aboriginal families have been viewed as sites of physical and moral danger and neglect and the rights of parents and children to remain together denied. Official interventions into these families have taken the form of direct action through the forced removal of children from their homes and official campaigns to carve family networks into isolated nuclear family units, as well as officially condoned practices of discrimination and neglect which threatened the very survival of many families and communities.

During the late 1990s Australians were forced to acknowledge the discriminatory treatment of Aboriginal children and families as members of the Stolen Generations opened up their hearts and recounted their painful memories to the Human Rights and Equal Opportunity Commission Inquiry into the Forced Separation of Aboriginal and Torres Strait Islander Children from their Families. The Inquiry Report, *Bringing Them Home*,[2] and other recent publications[3] have begun to expose through the heart-wrenching stories of those who were removed the systematic nature of Aboriginal child removals across the Australian continent. This book pushes further. It endeavours to provide a comprehensive history of Aboriginal child removal in the various states and territories stretching from the early days of colonisation to the recent past. It locates this history within the broader context of official policies and practices in relation to Aboriginal families and communities and examines Aboriginal reactions to these interventions. Aboriginal child removal emerges as constituent with the processes of dispossession, depopulation and destruction of Aboriginal societies and cultures that began with colonisation and continue to affect Aboriginal communities to this day.

A wide range of questions concerning the removal of Aboriginal children and the fragmenting of Aboriginal families is addressed in these chapters[4] — many of them raised in public debate at the time of the Human Rights and Equal Opportunity Commission Inquiry. What were the various historical circumstances in which Aboriginal children were removed? Why were Aboriginal families targeted? Who advocated the removals and on what grounds? Which children were removed? Why were they removed? How many were removed? Who was involved in their removal? What was the machinery for removing and raising Aboriginal children? What were its goals? Were removal systems similar across the continent? How did they compare with the treatment of non-Aboriginal children separated from their families? What were the conditions of life for the children who were removed? What impact did this have on the children and on their families and communities? How did Aboriginal people react? Did any other Australians criticise the policy and practice of removal? On what grounds? How did Aboriginal child removal compare to the treatment of indigenous children in other countries? Not all these questions can be fully answered. For example, the inadequacies of the archival

14

records[5] mean that we can never know exactly how many children were taken away. Historian Peter Read has estimated that there were at least 50,000 'separations,' while the *Bringing Them Home* report has calculated that in the period between 1910 and 1970:

> between one in three and one in ten Indigenous children were forcibly removed from their families and communities ... In that time not one Indigenous family has escaped the effects of forcible removal.[6]

The book begins with a chapter anchored in the personal story of Louis Johnson/Warren Braedon. This story is linked to the broader historical circumstances of his removal in Alice Springs and his murder in Perth and serves as an introduction to changing policies from the 1970s to the 1990s. The next chapter turns the magnifying glass on the colony of Van Diemen's Land (Tasmania) and provides an idiosyncratic example of the treatment of Aboriginal children in the early years of colonisation. It also foreshadows the paucity of official policy in the treatment of Aboriginal children over time with the approaches and errors of this early period being adopted repeatedly by successive governments well into the twentieth century. Chapter Three explores the exclusion of Aboriginal families from the emerging Australian nation in the early twentieth century and the oppressive administrative and legislative systems that were set up to control them in both the wider community and in segregated institutions. Removal of 'mixed race' children to institutions to train them as menial farm and domestic servants became entrenched during this period, despite the move away from institutionalisation of children evident in child welfare practice at the time.

Chapter Four fixes attention on the system of removal as it operated in Western Australia and provides insights into differences between the treatment of Aboriginal and non-Aboriginal children and families by child welfare authorities. Chapter Five examines the resistance of Aboriginal parents to removal of their children and the few voices of protest raised by other Australians against this practice. The staff and machinery of the children's institutions and the experiences of the children kept in them are examined in Chapter Six.

The following two chapters explore the assimilation policies of the mid-twentieth century and official efforts by federal, state and territory governments to bring Aboriginal families into the 'Australian way of life' by dismantling the discriminatory systems of control and attempting to break the families into discrete nuclear units. Despite a new rhetoric endorsing the need for Aboriginal children to remain with their families, removals and institutionalisation of children continued alongside new programs of adoption and fostering of Aboriginal children and incarceration of Aboriginal youth by mainstream juvenile justice systems. Chapter Nine chronicles the political campaigns by Aboriginal people and their supporters during the early 1970s and 1980s to regain control of their children. These campaigns laid the ground work for the campaigns of the 1990s culminating in the 1996 Human Rights and Equal Opportunity Commission Inquiry. The chapter concludes with the courageous story of 'Nan and Pop' who devoted their lives to keeping children within their extended family circle.

The narratives and information gathered here take us deep into the shared history of Aboriginal and non-Aboriginal Australians. The text speaks to us of a past that lies at the very core of our nationhood, a past that we can no longer ignore. The wounds left by this destruction of Aboriginal families will continue to haunt our consciousness until we begin, as a nation, to grapple with it 'through our hearts' and create new visions and pathways to bridge the chasm between our people.

CHAPTER ONE

A BOY'S SHORT LIFE

Warren Braedon, son of Dawna Braedon, named by his adopted parents Louis St. John Johnson. He never knew his name, he never knew his mother, he never knew his family, he never knew his people, he never knew his country. Born Alice Springs, 4th January, 1973, murdered Perth, 4th January 1992 … because he was black. Returned to his family and his country 20th January, 1992, he has found his dreaming. 'Wrap me in the Mother Earth so I can nurture the land's rebirth, give me joy and give me song, carry the struggle wide and long.' (Kev Carmody) 'Beautiful, beautiful child now you are free, free, from this heartache and pain and misery … I wish I was with you right now, my beautiful child.' (Archie Roach)

Louis Johnson/Warren Braedon's epitaph at Alice Springs Cemetery

Three month old Warren Braedon was taken from his mother Dawna in Alice Springs in 1973 at a time of major political and administrative changes in the Northern Territory. The town's economy and social basis had diversified rapidly during the 1960s from a largely isolated and insular regional pastoral centre to embrace new industries, namely tourism, the establishment of a US intelligence base at nearby Pine Gap and associated service industries, and a growing public service presence. The town had its origins in the establishment of a telegraph station in 1871. Called Stuart until 1933, the tiny outpost served local pastoral stations. From the beginning there was conflict between settlers and the Arrernte, Luritja and Warlpiri peoples whose country was being colonised. The Aborigines' hunting and gathering economy was increasingly marginalised by the pastoral economy and pastoral land acquisitions dispossessed them of their lands. Buttressed by police and the Native Patrol Force, the settlers were able to inflict serious casualties and an estimated 500 to 1000 Aborigines were killed during the first three decades of white settlement.[1]

In order to survive, Aborigines were obliged to comply over a long period of time with government pacification and population control measures. These included food rationing at pastoral, mining and telegraph stations, and relocation of Aboriginal people to reserved areas and missions.[2] In these 'sanctuaries' Aborigines could at least hope to survive. Here also developed various areas of economic and social interdependency. Indigenous men and women became essential to the pastoral industry and hence the whole regional economy.[3] They also worked in mining, domestic service and mission industries. Rowse[4] describes a strategy of welfare colonialism, which sought to cut links between the generations by housing children separately from their families in dormitories on the missions and government settlements, and which accelerated in the region following the Second World War. Stuart also became a centre where Aborigines could get work, rations and medical treatment. Many simply had nowhere else to go. However, their presence created tensions with the townsfolk who relied on Aborigines for menial labour, but often viewed them with a mixture of resentment and disgust. Settler efforts to control Aborigines' presence around the town frequently clashed with Aborigines' determination to maintain their own ways of living which combined elements of traditional Aboriginal and European lifestyles.

In 1911 responsibility for the Northern Territory was transferred from South Australia to the federal government. The *Aboriginals Ordinance 1918* was modelled on legislation in Queensland and Western Australia. It embodied a policy of segregation and control under the guise of protection, implemented through restrictions on Aboriginal employment, mobility and family and personal matters. The 1918 Ordinance was administered locally by police officers who enforced the special laws and also issued welfare in the form of rations. The continuing influence of Social Darwinian assumptions within governments was no better instanced than by the conviction that little could be done to help 'full-bloods' apart from issuing rations to 'smooth the dying pillow.'[5] By contrast, while the 'full-bloods' were expected to become extinct through the operation of 'natural' evolutionary forces, the Aboriginals Department purposefully acted to limit the 'half-caste' population through strict controls over the women's sexual contacts and by removing and institutionalising their children. The Bungalow, opened in Stuart in 1914, acted as a government depot for some 'half-caste' children of Aboriginal women and mining and pastoral workers in Central Australia. Consisting of a few old iron huts next to the police station and the hotel, the Bungalow housed up to sixty children at a time during the 1920s. After a period of rudimentary schooling the children were sent out to work, under

Young residents outside the Bungalow's iron huts with Manager Mrs Standley and Assistant Topsy, Alice Springs, 1928.

(Courtesy of Department of Foreign Affairs and Trade and National Archives of Australia: A1200/19, L26062)

police control, as domestics, labourers and pastoral workers. Living conditions were deplorable and, despite exposés by the press in the southern states, continued virtually unchanged, until after a brief move to a site at Jay Creek outside the town in the late 1920s, the Bungalow was finally relocated to the site of the Old Telegraph Station in 1932.

National attention was focused on the region following reports of a punitive massacre of perhaps one hundred Warlpiri men, women and children at Coniston Station by police in 1928. The resulting public criticism prompted government inquiries and action which continued during the 1930s. As in other states at the time, these inquiries focused on the 'half-caste' problem. Under the Chief Protector of Aborigines, Dr Cecil Cook (appointed in 1927), the Aboriginals Department embraced the eugenicist policy of biological absorption, aimed at breeding out the 'mixed race' altogether, although federal authorities did endeavour to limit Cook's enthusiasm. Influenced by anthropologist A P Elkin, the *Aboriginals Ordinance 1939* adopted the policy of social assimilation of Aborigines and aimed to develop what were considered to be positive steps for change. Tribalised and semi-detribalised Aborigines were to be protected in special settlements which would, over generations, in the words of Federal Minister for the Interior, John McEwan, 'transform these people from a nomadic tribal state to take their place in a civilised community.'[6] In 1952 the Northern Territory Adminstrator clarified official policy on the 'removal of partly coloured children from Aboriginal camps' for assimilation into the Australian community:

> Those most easily assimilated are persons of mixed blood, provided that they are able to enjoy from an early and impressionable age the medical care, training, teaching and general living conditions available to the community at large.[7]

They were to be trained to assume full citizenship rights. With the exception of a small number of children of legally married 'half-castes' who could remain with their parents unless deemed to be 'neglected', 'half-caste' children in the Territory faced the likelihood of being removed from their families.

For seventy years Alice Springs had remained small, having only 400 white residents by the Second World War. The war boosted this number to 6000 — for the first time outnumbering Aborigines. This shift from the enforced interdependence of a small frontier population was accompanied by a growing sensitivity to gradations of racial descent and the observance of the strict caste barriers found in rural towns throughout Australia. A study of social relationships in Alice Springs in the mid-1940s found that the 'mixed race' population of 300, many of whom were graduates of the Bungalow, tended to stick together, to marry each other and to see themselves as a distinct group within the town.[8]

The *Welfare Ordinance 1953*, which repealed the 1918 Ordinance, attempted to introduce a welfare model for all regardless of race. However, it embodied the policy of assimilation of Aboriginal people in the Territory. The Ordinance turned on the category 'ward', which was determined by a person's lifestyle, their ability to manage their own affairs, standards of behaviour and personal associations. While ostensibly non-race specific, the only adults who could be declared 'wards' were people who could not vote, and of course in this period 'full-blood' Aborigines as a group — like children, prisoners, foreigners and the insane — did not have the vote. Tatz[9] argues that the law was meant to apply only to those needing 'guardianship' while they made the transition from traditional to 'assimilated' life. So from 1953 to 1964 the direct government control of Northern Territory Aboriginal people was carried out on the basis of declaring virtually all 'full-bloods' to be wards.[10] People of mixed descent no longer came under special welfare legislation. They were to be assimilated into

European society. The legal separation of people of mixed descent served to isolate them from their 'full-blood' kin at the same time as it endeavoured to force them into a society that did not accept them as equals. 'Mixed race' families in Alice Springs were pressured by government officials to

Government cottages for 'mixed race' families at The Gap on the outskirts of Alice Springs, 1958.
(Courtesy of Department of Foreign Affairs and Trade and National Archives of Australia: A1200/19, L25487)

move into austere cottages at the Gap on the outskirts of town. They were to dissociate themselves from their 'full-blood' kin in the camps who were directed to settle in the vicinity of the Bungalow.[11]

Despite stated intentions to assimilate 'mixed race' families into the wider Australian community, the administration persisted in treating them as a distinct group requiring special supervision and control. Their households were subjected to surveillance by Welfare Branch officers in their quest to transform them into nuclear families. Welfare efforts were focused on the women and children. Welfare officers carried:

> diaries in which they recorded salient notes on their clients' domestic habits. If a woman began to leave her children unattended, drink heavily, neglect the washing, or otherwise fail in her duties, the welfare officers warned her. After several warnings, the Welfare Branch would take the derelict family to court.[12]

The Welfare Branch could also intervene more directly by simply taking children who 'lived in remote areas or homes that were otherwise considered unsuitable' and placing them in institutions.[13]

Until 1964, when 'full-blood' Aborigines ceased by legal definition to automatically be wards, government authorities had sweeping legislative powers which enabled strict control over their movement and residency, through removal to reserves, the declaration of areas prohibited to unemployed Aborigines, and removal of their camps

Communal kitchen at Amoonguna, Alice Springs, c 1958.

(Courtesy of Department of Foreign Affairs and Trade and National Archives of Australia: A1200/19 L28237)

from the vicinity of towns. These powers were exercised on a regular basis through local police officers and Welfare Branch patrol officers appointed from the mid-1940s, who also carried out the removal of 'mixed race' children from their families and the moving of Aboriginal people to government and mission settlements to undergo the process of assimilation.

In Alice Springs the controlling of the movement and residency of 'full-blood' people, some of whom were locals and others visitors, was a constant theme of local town development. As was evident in the case of the famous painter Albert Namatjira, this control was invariably exerted to suit white prerogatives. During the 1950s Namatjira bought a block of land in the town, but was refused permission to build a house on it because it was assumed that his family would cause trouble and the value of adjacent houses would fall.[14] This theme continued through the 1960s. The major settlement at the Bungalow, with 300 residents, was closed to make way for tourism interests in 1961. The people were relocated to a new government settlement, Amoonguna, fourteen kilometres south-east of town.

Established in 1960, Amoonguna was to become a self-contained village for town and visiting Aborigines. Rationalised as a training ground and conceived by the government as

Communal housing at Amoonguna, Alice Springs, c 1958.

(Courtesy of Australian Institute of Aboriginal and Torres Strait Islander Studies, Hilliard. W1.CS)

producing westernised citizens who could live in houses and aspire to permanent work and a settled, urban life, the populating of Amoonguna relied on the fact that food ration distribution was concentrated there. A place beset with internal strife and resembling more the environment of a refugee camp or military barracks than the ideal 'white Australian lifestyle', the settlement proved a failure by the end of the decade and people largely moved off to sites closer to town once better wages, pensions and other social security payments became available. In any case, these 'assimilation' projects failed because people rejected the carceral regime which endeavoured to enforce institutional housing and living patterns, to prevent the use of alcohol, and to break the strength of residents' adherence to kinship structures, traditions of free movement and ties to country. The Welfare Branch's 1969 annual report commented:

> Detribalisation in the sense of surrender of their basic social organisation and social arrangements has not ... gone very far, and traditional institutions such as marriage patterns, and traditional attachment to particular geographical areas are still greatly respected.[15]

Indigenous living conditions deteriorated even further in and around Alice Springs from the introduction of drinking rights in 1964 and of the Pastoral Award in 1968, coinciding with the phasing out of restrictive legislation and special welfare measures. With the granting of the right to vote in federal elections to indigenous people in 1962, the 1953 Ordinance gave way to the *Social Welfare Ordinance 1964*, which removed all legal restrictions which had been, in effect, on the basis of Aboriginality. However as Aboriginal historian Barbara Cummings[16] notes, this Act was still aimed primarily at Aborigines. While it was officially directed at a wider range of persons 'the mechanics of the language' was derived from earlier, repealed legislation. Although definitions which could only apply to 'full-blood' Aborigines were removed from the statutes — and bureaucrats were required to deal with people on the basis of need rather than 'race' — in practice the legislation continued to apply mainly to Aborigines. The system had retained much of the personnel, administrative perspectives, values and rationalities of the assimilationist era of the 1950s, and local white populations continued to demand the enforcement of controls over the presence of Aborigines and their behaviour.

With the introduction of award wages for Aboriginal pastoral workers in 1968 and growing mechanisation of the industry pastoralists cut their work forces, leaving many indigenous pastoral workers unemployed. They and their families thereafter had to lead a precarious existence in town. Their presence was not welcomed by most white townspeople, who viewed the town camps and Aboriginal consumption of alcohol as well-established problems and deemed the government's action in liberalising controls over Aborigines' movement and access to alcohol as absurd and disastrous for all concerned.[17]

Some Aborigines had been able to earn cash wages in Alice Springs since the 1930s at least, largely through doing odd jobs and cleaning for the white townspeople and working on the town sanitary carts. In the hinterland they did stock work and domestic duties on the stations for minimal wages or rations. The inflow of cash increased dramatically as social security benefits were extended to all Aboriginal people during the 1960s. As Rowse[18] demonstrates, this served to further undermine administrative control. Old age and invalid pensions, available to Aborigines from 1960, were paid in the form of cash or rations. By the early 1970s, reforms in relation to Aborigines' eligibility for social security payments and to payment of wages on settlements meant that most Aboriginal adults on missions and settlements were receiving some cash. With Aboriginal consumption 'liberated' from rationing and the major reforms in social welfare legislation in 1964, the administration's strict control of Aborigines on settlements came to an end. This also made it more difficult for European authorities to monitor the presence of Aborigines in Alice Springs.

Among front-page headlines such as 'Police Discontent Grows: Human "Garbage Collectors' Claim"',[19] the following summaries of press articles from 1973 give an idea of the public representation of disorder amongst Aborigines at the time, a state which was widely attributed to the granting of drinking rights in the Territory. Many of these events related to intra-communal violence, suggesting an actual breakdown in internal Aboriginal social control mechanisms.

> Fifty-eight Aboriginal people charged with drunkenness are kept in jail an extra twenty-four hours awaiting the arrival of the magistrate.[20]

> Of sixty-seven court cases on Christmas Eve, fifty were for Aboriginal drunkenness.[21]

Aborigines reported fighting on Todd Street.[22]

Reports of continued brawls involving Aborigines in Alice Springs streets, camps and hotels.[23]

Five Aborigines charged with assaulting a former Alice Springs police officer are sentenced to two months hard labour, an Aboriginal man charged with indecently assaulting an Aboriginal woman is sentenced to three months hard labour. [24]

An Aboriginal man is on trial for poking a burning stick into an Aboriginal woman's face.[25]

Aboriginal women are reported fighting half naked in an Alice Springs hotel, one woman is sentenced to two weeks jail.[26]

Feature articles and an identikit photo of a 'part Aboriginal' suspected by police of the murder of a driver outside Alice Springs.[27]

Police are attacked by Aborigines with rocks at the Alice Springs Show after they arrest a group of Aborigines for drunkenness.[28]

An Aboriginal man assaults a barmaid who refused to serve him beer in an Alice Springs hotel.[29]

Three men, including a white man, are in hospital after three separate incidents involving Aborigines and violent behaviour, with stabbings.[30]

A drunken Aboriginal man is sentenced to fourteen days hard labour for stabbing another Aboriginal man.[31]

An Aboriginal man is accused of murdering an Aboriginal tracker.[32]

The further development of Alice Springs also contributed to deteriorating conditions for Aborigines. By the 1970s the Alice Springs population had reached 10,000 and this rapid residential growth saw the introduction of new facilities and services such as a drive-in theatre, ABC television, a commercial radio station, a swimming pool, hospital upgrading and a new high school. These developments affected established relationships between Aborigines and whites in several ways. As land was increasingly taken over for residential purposes — and its value grew — Aborigines were pressured by local authorities to move away from town or were squeezed into concentrated areas. Tourism's interest in presenting Alice Springs as a safe and clean holiday destination added to the pressure to get Aboriginal camps out of the centre of town. This was a familiar picture of the marginalising of indigenous campers in country towns such as Broome and Cairns — where tourism had no place for people who were not benefiting the town in some way. The touristic attractions of art, craft and corroborees aside, town camps were deemed undesirable. At the same time there was pressure to reduce the number of these camps, which struck against the Aboriginal tradition of distinct groups, based on geographic and linguistic affiliation, living largely independently of one another.

People camped in locations that were roughly aligned to their homelands; for example, people from areas south of the town would camp on its southern side. Moreover, the town, being the regional centre, meant that many were visitors for the purposes of medical treatment, holidays from pastoral work, court appearances, shopping and visiting relations. Jeff Collman[33] points out that indigenous camping arrangements were one strategy for resisting outside interference. They could be a temporary residential arrangement while seeking permanent work and they could free inhabitants from the intrusions of welfare agencies, allowing them to live in domestic groups outside welfare housing. They were also places where Aborigines could negotiate and endeavour to influence the social forces impinging on them. Camp residents had specific ways of organising and relating internally. To a large extent they preferred town camp dwelling to the restrictive life entailed in government settlements like Amoonguna, designed for assimilation. In the early 1970s there were some fifteen significant camps around Alice Springs on the Todd River banks and outskirts of town, with a total population 200–500 increasing to just under one thousand by the end of the decade.[34] The cores of these camps were the pensioners who, importantly, after gaining their pensions, no longer had to deal with the Welfare Branch. Other residents worked for stations. F Thornton describes the diverse make-up of the camps:

There are in fact many different groups, all with their own different needs: young educated people with their new expectations, old people that have spent most of their lives in station work, families with alcohol problems, mission people coming in to start to live European style for their children's sake and to get away from alcohol problems at home, and other people who come into town to drink.[35]

Conditions in these camps frequently provided a justification for Aboriginal child removal. Architects M Heppell and J Wigley[36] reported a lack of services, exposure to the elements, poor health and diet, police harassment, hostility from white people and an overall vicious cycle of deprivation, disputes and deaths. A report by the Central Australian Aboriginal Congress (CAAC) in 1976 described similar conditions:

> The majority of these people live in grossly overcrowded and sub-standard housing and few have even the barest facilities such as toilets. There is a large number of unemployed men not receiving any benefits and obviously the only method of survival is by sharing the limited income from pensions and the few relatives [sic]. The diet of these people is poor with concentrated or canned and prepared food. Most of the conditions are similar to fringe conditions in Africa and Asia. Most health workers recognise that the major difference in health between Aboriginal people and the white population is related to the vast difference in physical and social environment ... There can be no major improvements in health until people live in good houses, have adequate hygiene facilities and sufficient income to provide good food.[37]

While the CAAC saw the solution to camp dwellers' problems to lie in improved housing, hygiene, diet and employment, this did not mean the camps needed to be closed and the people moved from the town. Consultations between residents of the Mount Nancy camp and Heppell and Wigley during the 1970s showed that the campers wanted permanent, culturally appropriate dwellings in terms of architectural design and the layout of houses in the camps. They saw this as:

> an important element in having the town camp integrated into the township of Alice Springs and its members becoming recognised as permanent and responsible citizens. Housing would also ... give the community the residential security it had so long desired.[38]

Geoff Shaw, the director of Tangentyere Council — an organisation established to build houses and facilities on the camps — wrote that camp dwellers:

> would have stayed in the fringe camps if houses were built because they are community oriented and stick with their own mob ... Some

people write letters to the editor calling us campers a health hazard, bludgers and so on. They do this because they don't want to see us living in this town. Another thing is they want us right out of town. We've been fighting for years and years for a place to live, and we're going to keep fighting. White people want to get it through their thick heads.[39]

Articles in the *Centralian Advocate* of the period indicate the pressures on Aboriginal people. Responding to demands of white residents to close down the camps, the parish priest, Reverend Fr J F Clancy wrote sarcastically to the editor of the paper:

Perhaps you could install a few gas ovens, no longer required at German situations and get rid of the whole lot at one go.

The priest wrote that Amoonguna and Santa Teresa Mission were:

actual dumping grounds for the unwanted, former inhabitants of Alice Springs. It is no use ... to have these campers return to their homes. Alice Springs is their home! And one day they may demand it back.[40]

Calls for a heavy police crackdown on Aboriginal people were endorsed by the town magistrate in a most violent way. During a 1972 court case over a riot at Papunya settlement, magistrate G F Hall told police they should have 'opened both barrels' on the Aborigines.[41] Recurring themes in the local newspaper and talkback radio were hygiene, drunkenness, public safety and social order. Rising unemployment contributed to increases in rates of arrest for offences related to consumption of alcohol, which had been legally available since 1964. A Liquor Board Inquiry in 1973 was reported in the *Centralian Advocate* as having stated:

We are reluctant to say it but the scenes of drunkenness and degradation we found in and around the hotels, streets and creek beds in the town were far worse than anything we could have expected and can only be regarded as a disgrace to the town.

The paper went on to report:

The situation is due to in part 'deplorable conditions' of Aboriginal people living in the open in the riverbeds adjacent to town. While the creekbeds are said to be the traditional home of these people it was no excuse for allowing people black or white to camp indiscriminately in a town area.[42]

Neville Perkins, an executive officer of the Federal Council for the Advancement of Aborigines and Torres Strait Islanders (FCAATSI) had earlier, in 1971, recommended urgent government action to remedy what he described as a 'social scandal':

There will continue to be economic, social, legal and educational deprivations unless there are comprehensive social welfare programs, effectively sponsored by the Australian government, directed towards the plight of many Alice Springs Aborigines.[43]

The flooding of the town's court with people charged with drunkenness was a daily routine. David Parsons, a lawyer with the Central Australian Aboriginal Legal Aid Service, recalled his first impressions in early 1974 :

I walked past this line of Aboriginal people as I was on my way to court … assuming that everyone was lining up for an injection outside something like the Health Department, and I looked at the next building, assuming I'd got the wrong building, and no, it must have been the court house. So I walked back again and sure enough, it was the morning's list. There were 127 people, most of whom were charged with drunkenness.[44]

Many people ended up in gaol. The federal government moved to have public drunkenness decriminalised in 1973 and this was implemented in July the following year. But it was not long before townsfolk were demanding the reintroduction of drunkenness as an offence, arguing there had been a further breakdown in law and order.[45]

The health of indigenous people, particularly infants, came under the spotlight. Their drastic social circumstances are perhaps no better indicated than in the fact that Central Australia in the 1960s reportedly had the highest infant mortality rate in the world — one in four Aboriginal infants died.[46] At the same time the birth rate in the predominantly Aboriginal population in the Territory was 33.3 percent — compared with the national average of 20 percent.[47] Indeed there

Aboriginal babies fight to survive

Alice — the town of death

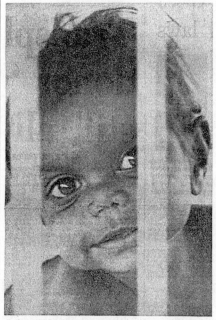

He plays peek-a-boo with the photographer through the bars of his cot at Alice Springs hospital. He seems one of the lucky ones. But like twins Sheila and Marlene (below) he's destined to return to the squalor and malnutrition which nearly killed him.

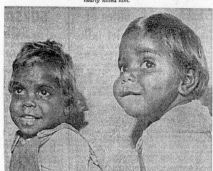

FROM PAGE ONE

There should be an establishment of 11 doctors. The hospital has just been lent a surgical registrar by the Americans at Pine Gap, but it is one resident medical officer short and another two are on leave.

300 p.c. staff turnover

The nursing establishment is 157 and the hospital is allowed 116 trained nursing staff. It has only 76 and another nine working part time.

The effectiveness of this limited nursing strength is cut by the fact that there is a yearly turnover of 300 per cent. Many of the nurses come here to work while they see the Centre. They leave in the summer when the dust blows and the sun burns. They leave when most children are sick and most nurses are needed.

Things will improve. The Ministers' fraternal has seen to that. In July, they wrote to the Prime Minister, the Ministers for Health, Interior and Aboriginal Affairs demanding action on "the scandalous waste of life."

They gave an ultimatum that unless assurances were given in a month they would make the letter public.

Bureaucracy was evidently bumble-footed, the month passed and the publicity was given.

Since then there have been top-level talks, questions in Parliament and an inspection of the hospital by the Minister for Health (Senator Sir Kenneth Anderson).

The Minister has said he viewed the matter "with utmost concern" and there are indications that accommodation will be bought so that convalescing children are no longer threatened by cross-infection.

Possibly work on the new $11.5 million hospital, planned to open in 1975, will be hurried along. And possibly staff will be increased to adequate levels by providing accommodation and salary incentives.

But, with these actions, will Mary's battle be over?

The answer is clearly no. It will be made easier and most likely the infant mortality rate will be cut. But no Australian should have an easy conscience until Mary's chances of survival equal those of a white child.

Her survival rests only partly on a well-equipped, well-staffed Alice Springs hospital.

Certainly, some of the blame must rest there: nursing procedures suffered because of the great strain put on the girls; red tape and the distance from Darwin probably hampered administration. In March, during a hearing on the proposed new hospital, the Federal Parliamentary Public Works Committee had been told of the extent of overcrowding. Could the new hospital have been built before this? Why were not more demountable wards provided?

Problem is 'out there'

However, it is not in The Alice that the major problem lies, but "out there" in the fringe camps, the stations, settlements and missions where the Aborigines live.

The basic fault lies not with the inadequate hospital and its dedicated, overworked staff but with the Australian society.

"If we had a 300-bed hospital, we could fill it tomorrow," a doctor told me. "As it is, we have over 10 per cent of Aboriginal children up to two-years-old in hospital all the time."

Children are brought in ill, many of them also suffering from malnutrition. They are treated and kept as long as possible — at the risk of cross-infection — to build up their strength before being sent back "out there".

Like Mary, many will return to the hospital again.

Professor George Maxwell professor of child health at Adelaide University, uses the analogy of evacuating men with battle fatigue from the war zone.

"We can rescue them but we cannot protect them from what they go back to — over-crowding, filth, lack of food, lack of opporunity.

"The major problem is that we have to drive those poor soldiers back to the bombs and the battle. It's not to certain death, but it is to danger."

Handicapped, if they live

Even if Aboriginal infants win this battle to stay alive, they may be severely handicapped in a war which is almost impossible to win: the war to live a reasonably satisfying life.

Dr. Kerry Kirke, who is chairman of the Institute for Aboriginal Development, has studied Aboriginal and toddler death and illness in Central Australia.

In his recently published doctoral thesis, he says: "It is clear that an enormous number of Aboriginal children die from apparently curable, if not preventable illnesses."

He goes on to list malnutrition as one of the principal health problems in Central Australia.

In this fat and lucky country, these Aboriginal children simply do not have enough proper food.

Aboriginal infant ill-health and mortality in Central Australia attracted widespread media attention during the early 1970s.

(Courtesy of Cameron Forbes and The *Age* Newspaper, The *Age* (Melbourne), 20.9.1971) appeared to be a crisis in Aboriginal parenting. F Thornton notes that the primary responsibility for child care fell on Aboriginal women:

> In both the traditional and the semi-traditional ways, the women are the ones responsible for children and for the family's welfare arranging for shelter, food, placement of children whose parents have died or are unable to care for them for short or long periods … Many women in the fringe camps and in households in the town area, are burdened with very heavy tribal and family responsibilities and are receiving little support.[48]

That many Aboriginal women in the early 1970s were finding it difficult to meet these demands is suggested by reported levels of drinking and violence in the camps referred to above and high rates of hospitalisation of children and infants.[49] Local missionaries pointed to the desperate need for special accommodation for mothers with sick children and facilities to train mothers in hygiene and the proper care of children who had been hospitalised.[50] In January 1973, the month Warren Braedon was born, the Federal Minister for Aboriginal Affairs, Gordon Bryant, threatened to sack public servants if 'something was not done about Aboriginal infant mortality.'[51]

From 1972 the new federal Labor government had set up the Department of Aboriginal Affairs and, following the adoption of the policy of self-determination, Aboriginal communities established self-managed organisations that were incorporated under federal legislation. These organisations, initially involved in health, legal aid, community government and land matters, were mainly funded by federal grants. In Alice Springs, in addition to community management councils, the major new corporations established in 1973 to service the region were the Central Australian Aboriginal Congress (CAAC), the Central Land Council (CLC), and the Central Australian Aboriginal Legal Aid Service (CAALAS). These organisations greatly increased the ability of Aboriginal people to negotiate change and development, to put funding agencies and mainstream welfare institutions at one remove, and to have more control over processes and decisions affecting them. Pat Miller, the director of Aboriginal Legal Aid in 1993, and whose father was a founder of the organisation, describes this:

The incorporation came through in 1973. Then they went about employing a lawyer, and it just sort of flowed from there, it just grew and grew and grew. As the demand grew, more and more people were aware that they could get legal advice and assistance, more and more people became aware of their rights, so right up to today people walk in the door demanding legal assistance and advice because they've come across injustice just across the street or out on a station, things like that.[52]

The Central Land Council began the work of organising the traditional land owners to make their claims under the Northern Territory *Aboriginal Land Rights Act 1976*. This Act was to progressively return lands to indigenous owners in Central Australia over the next two decades. In the town itself fourteen Aboriginal areas and campsites were granted leases by 1979, which provided security and enabled houses and ablution facilities to be built on them. However, many whites felt threatened by Aborigines' new-found power to advance their civil and indigenous rights. According to Collman,[53] organisations like CAALAS were labelled as 'radicals and southern stirrers' who were interfering in local customs and upsetting Aborigines, with the result that the town had become strife-torn. There was resentment at the town's growing reputation in the national and international media as a 'particularly troublesome place with regard to race relations.' Other changes to federal, territory and local government structures exacerbated tensions. Federal Labor's assertive policy-making in indigenous affairs, mandated by the 1967 referendum, conflicted with the Northern Territory Country-Liberal government's desire for more independence. The Territory had gained its own legislative assembly in 1974 and was pushing for full self-government. Federal intervention into Aboriginal circumstances in Alice Springs, particularly the funding of self-determining organisations, was seen as a federal unwillingness to delegate power over local issues. Collman argues that another reason for high racial tensions at this time was that:

'racial tension' ... is part of a long tradition in the Northern Territory whereby whites use Aborigines and their alleged problems as political resources in their own struggles for local power.[54]

Discrimination and exploitation were embedded in the town's social fabric — in public institutions, services and general attitudes. An Aboriginal field officer with CAALAS in 1975, Peter Rotumah, gives his impressions of this:

> The first one was the segregating, the categorising of Aboriginal people. The categorising of Aboriginal and European people in the hospital, and the segregating of Aboriginal people from Europeans in the hospital wards. The second was the general attitude — I suppose, of non-Aboriginal people to the people in the fringe-camps and the tribal people was 'Jack's all right as long as he stays in his place. If he moves out, then it's not his place to move out.'[55]

By 1975 community tensions had escalated to breaking point, leading to actual violence between whites and blacks, proposals for vigilante groups and intense lobbying of the federal government by local whites. A CAALAS lawyer recalled the fear of the time:

> ... we thought very seriously about arming ourselves, simply because there were vigilante squads being interviewed on the talkback radio up there about how they were arming themselves for the black invasion of Alice Springs ... Yes, it was a very aggressive, very nasty time when whites were being for the first time challenged by Aboriginal people who had spokespeople who were prepared to go to court and say, 'No, this isn't right,' and 'No, it can be done in a different way.'[56]

The early 1970s perhaps marked the peak of a period of particular neglect where mainstream welfare services could not attend to the scale of Aboriginal need, which left the familiar drastic and inhumane strategy of removal of children and incarceration of adults. By 1970 a Town Management Board, the precursor to the Alice Springs Town Council, endeavoured to deal with the camp issue differently. According to Donovan:

> In most instances suggestions brought before the Board urged the forcible removal of the camps from the proximity of the town. Yet the Board had not the power to ensure this. Ultimately in 1970 it determined that control was probably a more realistic option than outright prohibition and urged that the Welfare Branch should establish several camps equipped with basic services. Again the bureaucracy moved slowly, and it was not until March 1972 that the

government approved plans for two camping areas for Aborigines near Alice Springs that would also include basic services.[57]

The two camps selected for improvement were Charles Camp and Little Sisters Camp, both of which had a history of church involvement with residents, but improvement was done without proper dialogue with the residents, and without adequate funds. In the short term neither of these initiatives proved satisfactory.[58]

In 1973, when Warren Braedon was born, the situation appears to have been quite desperate for many Aborigines living in camps in the town. Town campers like Dawna Braedon and her family were under constant pressure to move out of the town area through a combination of heavy policing of drinking, public panics over health, and the removal of children by welfare authorities. The failure of local authorities and the Northern Territory administration to improve the campers' health and welfare problems appears to have owed more to the desire to simply remove the people from the town, than to any insurmountable practical factors. The rationale of the policy of assimilation was that Aborigines were to live like other Australians — in houses, as nuclear families, in regular employment and schooling. The method of enforcing this change was institutionalisation — the relocation of families to missions and government settlements and the removal of children. But as the CAAC statement above indicates, Aborigines were not opposed to living in houses per se. They were not, as a rule, opposed to using the sanitation systems suited to more sedentary populations. They did, however, resist the breaking-up of their extended families and restrictions on their freedom of movement and traditional cultural practices. Ways needed to be found to make the social technologies of sanitation, housing and health care adaptable to contemporary indigenous lifestyles and traditions. This was the thrust of CAAC's and Tangentyere's strategies. From the mid-1970s the implementation of these strategies started to take effect — too late however, to make a difference to Dawna Braedon's capacity to keep her family together.

REMOVING THE CHILDREN

The *Child Welfare Ordinance 1958* notionally applied to the general population of the Territory — that is, it was not an Aboriginal-specific ordinance. But indigenous children were predisposed to be by far the main population affected. Because indigenous people constituted the majority of disadvantaged and destitute people, their children were more likely to fit the criteria of 'neglected child' to official eyes than non-Aboriginal children as a whole. Indeed the Ordinance was used, in the mid-1960s at least, for purposes other than its objective of protecting the best interests of the child. As well as fitting in with enduring assimilationist perspectives that separating indigenous children from their cultural communities was desirable, removal was infinitely cheaper and easier for governments than embarking on the major social reconstruction programs that could have helped communities and families to recover stability and security. Perhaps even more significantly, the record of the treatment of indigenous people in Alice Springs reads less as a failure of cruel, misguided and miserly but 'well-intentioned' efforts at alleviation, than as a series of government and townsfolk campaigns to keep Aborigines out of town.

This is evident in the fact that following the removal of formal powers in 1964 to control Aboriginal movements, the Northern Territory government resorted to using the *Child Welfare Ordinance 1958* to limit the presence of Aborigines in Alice Springs. In 1965 the Director of Welfare, H Giese, in a letter to the Director of Health, outlined his proposals to use the ordinance to attempt to break up town camps:

> I propose so far as families with children are concerned, and where the children are obviously not regularly attending school to have the Children's Court commit the children to my care as neglected children, but this will not completely solve the problem because there are a number of families without children living in this area.[59]

In a particularly revealing document, Welfare Branch official, T C Lovegrove (signing for his superior, L N Penhall), reported to his Director on the operation of this tactic in 1966:

> Some children have been taken before the court and some [families] have been persuaded to leave Alice Springs upon being threatened that the provisions of the Child Welfare Ordinance will be used.[60]

After detailing cases where twenty-seven children were removed from the town with the deliberate intention of making their town-camping parents leave as well, Lovegrove continued:

Pressure will continue to be applied in accordance with your instructions. This will only go part of the way towards solving the problems of unsightly camps in the Alice Springs area and if there is a genuine desire to solve this problem persons outside of the Welfare Branch will have to co-operate by doing some hard thinking and hard acting on the problem.

Despite this open admission, three years later in 1969 Lovegrove, now Assistant Director, wrote to District Welfare Officers, in effect to caution them on the too overt use of the Ordinance as a means of removing town campers:

I think some members of the public are conscious of this and generally concerned. For the person viewing the situation from a distance this appears to be and often is the case and there have been a number of children prosecuted as 'Neglected' in these circumstances.[61]

But despite what Lovegrove claimed was genuine concern for the welfare of children by 'members of the public', he went on to reinforce the fact that the primary concern was to remove campers, for which the Ordinance was, in any case, not always effective:

This has the effect of removing the child from the situation but does not necessarily remove the rest of the family and it has no effect when there are no children involved. Furthermore, it must not be used automatically on families living in these conditions. The case must be one of severe and immediately irretrievable neglect. I suggest that it was never intended that this piece of legislation be used to solve the municipal problems of any township.[62]

Lovegrove revealed himself to be part of that same 'concerned' Alice Springs 'public'. Town campers should be shifted because:

[their] mode of living is substandard and aesthetically offensive to a majority of townspeople. This may be a valid complaint but I doubt if it is a violation of any law applicable to the town. If we are honest we will admit that this is our main complaint. (In using 'our' I am identifying myself as one of the townspeople of Alice Springs.)[63]

Lovegrove went on to advocate the introduction of appropriate and transparent legislation that would allow his department to deal effectively with the 'municipal problems' of offensive behaviour and concern about health threats instead of having to resort to child welfare legislation:

> There should be legislation to deal with it. If there is legislation then it should be put into effect. If it is inadequate or non-existent then the [Health] Department should be proposing legislation that will deal with the problem.[64]

The broad definition of 'neglect' in the *Child Welfare Ordinance 1958* was open to culturally biased or ethnocentric interpretation and application on the part of individual officers, the judiciary, police and medical professionals. Also, because there were no formal mechanisms for Aboriginal advice on what constituted neglect, child care circumstances that were culturally acceptable to Aborigines could be determined as unacceptable by non-Aboriginal officials working from the perspective of their ideals. Moreover, failure to recognise indigenous family arrangements and patterns of child care ensured that the alternative of placing children in the care of their extended families was rarely considered. That there were cases where the extended family was unable to provide the alternative care because whole families had become destitute points us to the larger political and economic contexts. The removal of children from their families was an administrative measure that reflected the failure of government to tackle what was obviously a social disaster of great proportions. Bureaucratic thinking and policy proceeded with the expectation that Aboriginal people were to adopt the standards of an ideal non-Aboriginal norm inherent to the assimilation vision. Not only was this profoundly ethnocentric, but it was a practical impossibility for the majority in Alice Springs after decades of impoverishment and exclusion from the resources and institutions of Australian society.

THE BRAEDON FAMILY

Warren Braedon was born in Alice Springs on 4 January 1973 to Dawna Braedon and Joe Johnson, Dawna a Luritja woman (of the Napajinpa skin group) and Joe an Arrernte man. Warren's Dreaming was the eagle from Titjikala.[65] The Arrernte peoples are the traditional owners of the Alice Springs region. The land on which the town stands is known as Mparntwe. The Arrernte language group comprises five or six major interrelated groups distinguished from each other by geographic territory and variations in dialect, customs and religious beliefs. The Luritja occupy country that mainly borders on that of the Western and Southern Arrernte, to the west and south of Alice Springs. A distinct language group from the Arrernte, the Luritja often intermarry with them and share some facets of ceremony and custom. Traditional Arrernte and Luritja societies are based on communal hunting and gathering. The main social and economic unit is the extended family, with each family living independently of each other on their separate estates. Families travelled within their estates for ceremonial and economic purposes, and

Warren Braedon's uncle Eric Braedon, Alice Springs, 1998.
(Courtesy of Eric Braedon)

congregated with others for larger ceremonies. Hagen[66] states that 'for the Aranda, law, convention and morality are intimately linked to the land through the actions of their ancestors.' These were autonomous, self-governing societies, with complex social and legal and spiritual systems. Just as rigid social and religious precepts and taboos governed the relations between groups and individuals within each group, so they also dictated the manner in which individuals and groups used the resources of the fragile environment.[67]

Dawna's father was an Arrernte man, Toby Braedon,[68] from Titjikala (Maryvale Station). Her mother was a Matuntara woman, Tilly,[69] from Tempe Downs. The couple had six children: Dorothy,[70] Dawna,[71] Valerie,[72] Raylene,[73] Ernest[74] and Eric.[75] These children produced at least twenty-four grandchildren between them — Warren's siblings and cousins. At his home in Little Sisters Camp in 1996 Eric, Dawna's brother, recalls:

My father used to work here and my sisters grew up here. He worked night and day, went out in this old truck, didn't work for money, just got tucker, to bring all my sisters up. He was one of the wise old men, he even knew everyone's Dreaming. They come and ask him. He knew everything.[76]

Eric's niece, Mary Williams, daughter of Dawna's sister Valerie, describes Toby's important role as an elder:

Everyone that forgot about their Dreaming, they'd come and he'd tell them, he told them all. Even Hermannsburg, you know how the missionaries made them not want to do that thing any more, they forgot that Dreaming, he could tell them their Dreaming. He'd just ask, 'Tell me what family group you're from,' and he'd just tell them, sing that story and all. He was really a wise old man, he knew everything. Any family group they just come and talk ... and he'd know, 'Oh you're from this country,' tell them.[77]

Eric states that Toby's cousin Max Stuart and son-in-law Casey Kenny are now the custodians of these Dreaming stories.[78]

Prior to the establishment of a sewerage system in the 1950s, local contractors employed Aboriginal people in sanitary and rubbish collection for the town. Some of those employed lived at Little Sisters Camp, including the Braedons. Little Sisters was used during the 1940s by sanitary workers servicing the town's wartime-inflated population.[79] Dawna's son, Kevin, describes Toby's work as a sewage truck driver:

Warren Braedon's brother Kevin Braedon, 2000.
(Courtesy of Kevin Braedon and Bill and Pauline Johnson)

Old grandfather, Toby, from here, when he was young he used to work here in town getting that, bucket of thing, shit carting, bring around the toilets getting that bucket in the lane way, driving. He had a licence for driving, working for something for one pound a day. That's when we was talking he was telling me that, this story, working and this old, what they used, bucket and they had this big trench to empty it at — take it back, come round, put it back in the same place, drive around. He did that for a long time when he was young.

His kids grew up with him. They went to school. Mum went to Telegraph station, Bungalow to school and come home again, didn't have to live there. She went to school and then she met up with Dad. Here. That's when they had me. He was from station, working out at Nappa Station, a stockman. That was his country.[80]

A former resident at Little Sisters described their lives:

We lived in humpies all in a line. The families there were all one big family, the fathers all worked hard and were working till they died. They didn't know what the dole was. The kids all went to Old Harley Sreet Primary (but not Dawna). We went to grade seven in those days. All the kids knew each other, went to same school. We all called uncles 'father' and they all helped look after the kids. We got meat, tripe from the old slaughter yards. We were poor and ragged but we shared everything. Our mothers didn't turn kids away, we shared everything.[81]

Toby lived to a very old age and died of pneumonia at the Hettie Perkins Hostel in 1992.

Eric Braedon was raised by his sisters, principally Dawna, who nursed him along with her own baby, Kevin:

When I was a new born baby we was sharing walytja [breast], we was both sharing, he was on this side and I was on this side. That happens a lot, it's Aboriginal way. So it was my sister that brought me up. So Dawna was sort of my mother too. As I got older she handed me to my mother's cousin and she brought me up, Phyllis Whistle. I call her mother. She brought me up from when I was a little boy.[82]

Dawna had grown up in Alice Springs camps with her parents. She gave birth to five children: Kevin,[83] who lives in Alice Springs, Vincent,[84] Ricky,[85] Jaclyn[86] and Warren. All except Kevin were taken away from her. She was sixteen when Kevin was born in Alice Springs Hospital in 1961, during a period when she was working as a housekeeper at Tempe Downs station. Kevin recalls these early years:

I grew up with Mother and Dad. They got separated, I was raised up by my grandfather [Toby Braedon], the one in the cemetery there, and from there I was raised up by my mother's young sister Valerie. From there she started looking after me. I was a little fella when I went to her and then I went to school out at Amoonguna. We were stopping out at there, went to school there first. Mum and

Dad went separate ways. From there Mum went out to Western Australia, she come back with Jaclyn and from there she had Ricky and they were taken away. Then she went back to Western Australia again. From there she come back here to Alice Springs that's where she had Louis.

She married out there [Western Australia], another man, from Derby and I heard he passed away. Used to go there by plane, flying over. When Mum came back when she had Louis she went back to the Aboriginal reserve [Amoonguna] seven miles out from here where I was. She started drinking again from there.[87]

Eric Braedon says that Dawna began drinking heavily when her children were taken from her. Ricky and Jaclyn were both removed from her custody and are presumed to have been adopted or fostered.[88] Another older son, Vincent, was apparently placed with an Aboriginal family in the late 1960s in Santa Teresa Mission. Only Kevin grew up within his extended family in Alice Springs, on pastoral stations, and at Amoonguna government settlement. He kept in contact with his mother and lived primarily with his aunt Valerie. In addition to English, Kevin speaks Luritja, Arrernte and Pitjantjatjara.

I went off working on the stations. I went with my uncle to Amburla Station [west of Alice Springs], a bit close, one day trip and back again. Working out there then. We had this cattle coming in from Queensland, all the little calves, for transport. Had to shift them bore to bore, riding horses. I was fourteen. Because I didn't want to really go to school, just wanted to go out bush. We had a cook and a Land Rover and trailer with everything on, spare saddles, bridles and some tin stuff, go bore to bore shifting all the calves. I was with family, working out there. I was learning hunting and how to, teaching me how to brand calves. I did that for six months straight just come in for weekend to Alice Springs and back out, do a bit of shopping, see family.[89]

This was 1975. After six months Kevin returned to Alice Springs and then went back to Amoonguna. Life at the government settlement was desolate for young men. Frustrated, he soon came into conflict with authorities.

I was working out on the reserve for long time. I was rubbish collecting, driving around in the tractor. I just went mad, rolled that drum of diesel rolled it down to the wall, started tipping it over, let all the diesel spill out and push it back again and strike a match and then just ... That's when they found out that I did it and went to court for it and they tried to sentence me to twelve months to some children's prison, Essington House, in Darwin. And so one of these old ladies, she's one of the welfare, came. She used to work out at Amoonguna, fighting, so she had to fight for me so they had to drop the sentence to six months, to spend six months at Darwin. They had to send me by plane, my first time. I was scared.[90]

When Kevin returned to Alice Springs, he lived in a camp and worked as a rubbish collector at Amoonguna. As people moved away from the settlement, Kevin went to stay with his grandfather and other relatives at Maryvale Station. During this time Kevin was taught about his grandfather's country.

I was stopping there for my grandfather, there's two grandfathers, one buried here and one buried out at Maryvale. I was stopping with him just like looking after him, working out there sitting down, just going out hunting and all, camping out and grandfather was showing me all these Dreaming sites you know, things. This rainbow snake they was marking it all the way. That's my grandfather's country out there. He was showing me where they going to make this outstation [Titjikala].[91]

In 1986 Dawna was admitted to hospital with a chronic neurological disorder, and lost the power of speech. At the time Kevin was staying with her and other family members at the Little Sisters Camp. The following year she was placed in Hettie Perkins Hostel. Kevin described Dawna's treatment by ambulance attendants:

That's when she had that stroke and she couldn't even move at all. She was lying there and this ambulance man come round there and they thought she was drunk because her eye was red. And like my grandfather and uncle they was talking to the ambulance driver, 'She's not drunk at all, she just had a stroke. Can't you see?' She was just lying down there so they had to put her in and, you know, to hospital. I don't know how long she spent in hospital there.[92]

Two years later, Kevin's younger brother Vincent was accidentally driven over and killed while he was camped just outside Santa Teresa

Mission. He left a wife and two boys.

> They were drinking too much and another bloke on the Toyota he
> didn't know that my young brother was in front asleep. So he took
> off and just runned over him. So he had to pass away too. He was
> lying on the ground in front of the Toyota.[93]

Tragically, details of these two incidents would be repeated in the
events surrounding Warren Braedon's death in Perth in 1991.

REMOVAL

Warren Braedon was committed to state custody in early 1973 under
the Northern Territory's *Child Welfare Ordinance 1958*, following an
application by the Department of Child Welfare to the Southern
District Children's Court. The Northern Territory government has, to
the time of writing, refused to release documents that would clarify the
precise steps that were taken in Warren's case. For instance, the official
grounds for his removal remain locked in his file. Legal correspondence held by the Johnson family indicates that Dawna had been
arrested for drunkenness on numerous occasions from 1971 to 1973,
and that two departmental reports provided 'very substantial grounds
for the Officer's belief that the mother has neglected her child
Warren.'[94] A Court Order was issued in Alice Springs to the effect that
Warren was 'a neglected child' and he was committed to the care of the
Director of Child Welfare.[95] As a 'State child' Warren would remain
under the Director's guardianship until the age of eighteen.[96]
Presumably Warren had then been placed in the Welfare Receiving
Home in Alice Springs. He was then sent to Dundas House, a receiving
institution in Darwin. It is not known whether the Department made
any effort to find care or placement for Warren in his extended family
or in any other Aboriginal family. Kevin explains that Dawna's
drinking, which began after the removal of Ricky and Jaclyn, was to
play an important role in the removal of her youngest child Warren —
removal which went ahead despite her objections and her persistent
refusal to give her permission for his adoption.

> She had her sister there, the one who look after me but she was too
> sick to look after Louis, so she started reporting to the welfare

because she had kids of her own and that's when welfare went round and had a talk with Mum there and they said, 'Oh, we have to take Louis away because you're drinking too much, you can't look after him.' She didn't say nothing, couldn't do anything, because there were some police there you know too. And from there they took Louis away. He was still a little baby. Then we didn't see him again.[97]

Mary Williams, who helped to raise Kevin, says:

Just that she had a drinking problem, that's all. But she was a good mother. Now [in the 1990s] it's all right, I was working with [a government organisation] … for four months and the last thing they do is take them off their mother, especially Aboriginal family they have to find a way of talking to the mother first, try and straighten things out. They don't want to do what they did before. They're trying to change that now. They wouldn't have talked to anyone, just taken him away, same with the other two children.[98]

ADOPTION

Warren Braedon was put up for adoption under the Northern Territory's *Adoption of Children Ordinance 1964.* This ordinance, like the Social Welfare and Child Welfare ordinances, did not have a special formal application to Aboriginal children but applied to children generally. Legal adoption of Aboriginal children was rare in the Northern Territory until the late 1950s. Prior to this children were placed in institutions or apprenticed to employers. During the 1950s and 1960s adoption and, to a lesser extent, fostering, were seen by many as the best means of assimilation into white society for babies and infants (older children were not as favoured by adoptive parents). In this way, the Ordinance's 'paramount consideration' of 'the best interests of the child' was axiomatic with an upbringing in a white home. As with the Child Welfare ordinances — and partly because of them, since state wards were often fed into the adoption process — Aboriginal children were far more likely to come under the adoption jurisdiction. Louis was a case of involuntary adoption in the strict sense. It is clear that Dawna did not give her consent to his adoption since the Director of Child Welfare was obliged to take action in the Northern Territory Supreme Court to have her consent dispensed with.[99]

The government resorted to promotional campaigns in the press and within churches, to attract prospective adoptive parents.[100] Non-Aboriginal couples were the targets of this program. Various factors precluded indigenous people from adopting any children, let alone those from their own community. Given the assimilationist intent of the adoption program, it was unlikely that children would be placed with Aboriginal applicants,[101] and the Ordinance's broad selection criteria for adoptive parents provided a ready way to exclude them.[102] Adoption in the western legal sense of transferring permanent custody conflicted with Aboriginal family systems and values and this may have deterred Aboriginal couples from applying. Without even considering the rationales of the departmental and judicial decision makers, the actual operation of both the Adoption and Social Welfare ordinances illustrates how government instruments, that are notionally egalitarian and universalist, can be structurally inequitable. Inequality of outcomes is virtually guaranteed because such policies and legislation cannot recognise either the existing cultural difference or the economic disparity that predispose certain populations to be disproportionately affected by them.

It was only from the late 1970s, through Aboriginal and welfare agency pressure, that major changes in policy and practice — to attend to cultural and economic difference — began. The Aboriginal child placement principle which guided these changes stated that Aboriginal children should remain within their family and community environments, and that removal of any Aboriginal children should be a last resort. It called for the recognition of indigenous customs relating to child care, the review of existing welfare practices and services, and the development of Aboriginal family support programs — all for the purpose of keeping the children within their natural families. Where removal was seen to be the only course of action, fostering and adoption should be within Aboriginal families only. Aboriginal advice to governments on adoption issues was to be formalised and Aboriginal services for families and child placement agencies were set up in all states.

These national developments were reflected in the Northern Territory government's child welfare reviews and reforms from 1978. They coincided with the Territory's change to self-government in 1978, and a determination to revamp the welfare system which had been the butt of public criticism from the early 1970s. The Department of Community Development was created with a Community Welfare

Division mandated to provide child and family services. In 1979 the report of the Martin Inquiry into welfare recommended the repeal of the Social Welfare Ordinance and the introduction of new legislation to promote individual, family and community welfare.[103] The Northern Territory *Community Welfare Act 1983* enshrined the Aboriginal Child Placement Principle: that is, 'the best interests' of Aboriginal children were met by allowing them to remain in their own families and communities — the first Australian legislation to do so.[104]

The shift in attitudes toward Aboriginal child adoptions is illustrated by a judgment on child custody handed down by the Northern Territory Supreme Court in 1976 that went in favour of the Aboriginal mother.[105] This was only two years after it had agreed to the legal adoption of Warren Braedon. The case involved the application to the Court by an American couple based in Alice Springs to dispense with the consent of the Aboriginal natural mother whose child they wished to adopt. The mother was represented by CAALAS. The two-year-old baby boy had been committed to the care of the Director of Child Welfare as a neglected child in May 1975. In the same month the baby was given to the American couple to foster. However, in this case the court did not grant the application. Justice Forster noted that Section 10 of the Adoption of Children Ordinance directed that the 'welfare and interests of the child be regarded as paramount'.

> The Judge considered that the only grounds on which he could dispense with consent would be if the advantages to the child of being adopted by the white foster parents amounted to special circumstances. While the foster parents could offer the child love and security within their family, the mother could offer him 'the love of his natural mother and an extended family in which, as he grows older, he will probably feel more at home than with a white family.' It was further found that the living conditions which the child would enjoy with his mother 'would, by European standards, be considerably less than those offered by the foster parents. However, by Aboriginal standards they are perfectly adequate.' The judge concluded that what was offered by the foster parents in a material, emotional, spiritual way was not superior to what the mother could offer and ordered that the child be returned to the mother's care.[106]

Forster was also critical of the way that staff of the Northern Territory Department of Social Welfare had handled the commital application to the Children's Court. They had failed to properly notify and explain their intentions to the boy's mother and as a result she was not able to attend the hearing and hence to represent her interests. He found that this constituted 'a denial of justice of a particularly serious kind.'[107] He also criticised their failure to provide the court with a report on the mother's present circumstances, that is, information that would support or otherwise the claim that she was incapable of caring for her son. As a result, the Department could not 'confirm or deny' the evidence presented by the mother's witnesses that the boy should be returned to her care. The Children's Court ruling was that the mother had neglected the baby, however, the judge was unable to find that she had persistently done so in the past or would do so in the future. On the other hand, it was evident that the mother had gone to great lengths to find her son and the judge was satisfied that she loved and wanted him.

The case was also significant for Justice Forster's recognition of the serious problems associated with cross-cultural adoptions. He expressed concern that if the boy grew up in a white family in America he would:

> undergo an identity crisis when he realises that he is different in appearance to the people who surround him. Quite apart from any racial problems which he may encounter in the United States he is likely to encounter problems arising within himself because of the very fact that his physical appearance is different.[108]

Forster accepted expert evidence that the child's best interest was served by having him remain with his mother and within his community. He found that although material conditions may have been less substantial than the foster parents could provide, they were nonetheless adequate and more than outweighed by the advantages of a loving and caring extended family, and of being a fully accepted member of an Aboriginal community. The CAALAS lawyer, Ross Howie, reflected on the significance of the decision:

> It challenged the assumptions of the way the system worked, because instead of Aboriginals being lined up in court and asked whether they pleaded guilty, and everybody nodding and being dealt with, people started having the rights that other Australian citizens have, and that is to have advice and to make decisions and

to fight cases and to be found not guilty. Similarly, not only the criminal justice system but the welfare system, which like all systems, I suppose, tended to make patronising decisions about people who didn't have much power, regardless of what their rights were or whether they ought to be heard about the matter. And one of the good things about the court's decision was that His Honour was critical of the magistrate and critical of the Welfare Department, and criticisms like that change how things happen.[109]

THE JOHNSONS

Bill and Pauline Johnson arrived in Australia from England in 1972. They were living at Nhulunbuy on the Gove Peninsula, Northern Territory, when they applied to adopt a child. They were told that it was easy to adopt an Aboriginal child but the government officer handling their enquiries, a Mr Taylor, advised them against it because 'they just cause trouble.' They responded that:

> one child is very much like another and we were happy to adopt an Aboriginal child as much as a white child. We didn't understand at that time what we were getting involved in. We didn't understand the damage that was done by cross-cultural adoption and the part that cross-cultural adoption played in the enforced assimilation policy that was still being practised at that time. So we did, as far as we were concerned, we did involve ourselves in a grave injustice to Aboriginal people and a grave injustice to Louis and his family, and obviously we recognise now, we have since apologised for the wrong that we caused and the injustice that we were involved in. Obviously that doesn't help Louis' family at all.[110]

The officer informed the Johnsons that they were on the official adoption list and that a baby who would not be 'too dark' would soon be available.[111]

The Johnsons first saw Warren at the receiving home, Dundas House, in Darwin in 1973. He was three months old and weighed twelve pounds. He was described to them as 'a hard to place child' and they were told that he had hearing problems and a heart condition, although subsequent medical tests showed that he was in perfect health. They were also informed that he had been declared a 'neglected child' by the Alice Springs Court and committed to the care of the Director of Child

Welfare. A month later the baby was handed to the couple on the understanding that they could adopt him. Bill recalled that:

When we were introduced to him he had above his cot the [name] 'baby Warren'. We said to the two nurses and the social worker who introduced us, he was just lying in the cot, 'Is that his real name because we will keep it.' They said, 'No, no, don't worry about that, that's just a name that the nurses have given him.'

I think that was one of the nastiest things about Louis' adoption — that Warren Braedon was actually his name. We found out when we took him back to Alice Springs for burial, and you know it wasn't sufficient for them to strip him of his family and all connections with his family but they even had to strip his name from him.[112]

Both twenty-eight years of age, Bill and Pauline were taken through the adoption process by the Department of Child Welfare. Dawna had not given her consent to the adoption and the Director of Child Welfare applied to the Supreme Court to have it dispensed with. The Department had told the Johnsons that the baby had been abandoned three times by his mother and that this was sufficient reason for him to be removed. Encouraging the couple to push ahead with the adoption, officials spoke of Warren's family, and indigenous people in general, in 'dismissive, almost derogatory terms.'[113] Bill and Pauline had him in their care for sixteen months before the order was made by the Supreme Court to dispense with Dawna's consent. In an emotional verbal submission to the Inquiry into the Separation of Aboriginal and Torres Strait Islander Children from their Families in 1996, Bill stated:

Louis Johnson/Warren Braedon
aged 10 months.
(Courtesy of Bill and Pauline Johnson)

so you can see that we participated in something that was doubly unjust, you know. To take a child away, to participate in an adoption that may be seen to be to the child's benefit, is one thing, but to actually participate in an adoption that was specifically against the mother's wishes is doubly unjust. Anyway in our ignorance — and that's the only justification, the only excuse we've got — that's what happened. Our reaction was, well his mother doesn't want him, we'll give him a good home and he is going to be advantaged rather then disadvantaged by the separation.

Why the hell couldn't they have placed him with an Aboriginal family or into an Aboriginal background? I don't know, because it did happen with [his brother] Vincent.[114]

Reflecting on their thinking at the time, Bill believes that had they looked more deeply into Warren's background and the adoption issue, they may have acted differently.

We were just blinded by the fact that we wanted a child. I don't believe that we considered Louis' mother's position objectively or even subjectively by putting ourselves in her position, and if we had taken the time to do so then we may have done that, and we should have come up with a different decision.[115]

Irrespective of the couple's desire to have Warren, they believed, and indeed they had been convinced by the Department, that they were doing the right thing by him. Indeed, they were led to believe that they were saving him from death, such was the departmental representation of his unseen mother. Giving the couple the child without Dawna's consent to an adoption should never have occurred in a legal state adoption. Furthermore, the Department should have been entirely responsible for handling any legal issues arising.[116]

In October 1973 the Johnsons moved to Sydney with the baby and in the following year they moved to Perth. The couple received a telegram on 27 August 1974 from their solicitor informing them that their application for the adoption order in the Northern Territory Supreme Court had been successful. The judge's grounds for dispensing with Dawna's consent were that he 'was satisfied that ... the mother had abandoned the child and had neglected the child.'[117] Under the conditions of the Adoption Ordinance Warren was renamed Louis St John Johnson and his birth certificate was altered to show the Johnsons as his natural parents. With Bill following work in the construction industry, the family moved back to the Northern Territory for a period, then to Sydney again, before returning to Perth to settle permanently in 1978.

The city to which the Johnsons brought young Louis in 1978 seemed to hold the promise of a better life for all. It was the fastest growing capital in the country, with a beautiful river and coastal setting and a strong economic base in the state's mineral resource wealth. Although Perth did not like to think of itself as a particularly discriminatory place, as having a 'race' problem in the sense of American or British cities, the reality for many indigenous people said otherwise. The statistics on incarceration of indigenous people alone demonstrate the gulf between the ideal of general prosperity and this reality. In 1981 the Aboriginal imprisonment rate in Western Australia was 1448 per 100,000 compared with 109 per 100,000 for non-Aborigines, the highest rate of Aboriginal incarceration, by far, of any state.[118] Moreover, by 1987 Aboriginal teenagers made up about sixty percent of the inmates of juvenile detention centres, while they comprised only four percent of the state's child population.[119] Of the ninety-nine cases of Aboriginal deaths in custody between 1980 and 1989 investigated by the Royal Commission into Aboriginal Deaths in Custody (RCIADIC), thirty-two occurred in Western Australia. The Equal Opportunity Commission (1989) and RCIADIC (1991) found that police harassment of Aborigines, and particularly Aboriginal youth, was a serious problem in Western Australia.[120]

In almost every other area of life too, indigenous people suffered massive inequalities. In 1981 Western Australian Aborigines had the second highest official rate of Aboriginal unemployment of any state at 30.9 percent, compared to the state's overall unemployment rate of 6.3 percent.[121] Their infant mortality rate in 1980 was 31.3 percent.[122] In 1984 over fifty-four percent of children in foster care placements in Western Australia were Aboriginal, while fifty-eight percent of children in residential child care establishments were Aboriginal.[123] Educational levels were also disastrous. In 1983 only forty-eight Aboriginal children in Western Australia made it into Year 12 high school, a retention rate of 4.5 percent.[124] By 1987 this had improved to 10.2 percent but was still far below the 57.1 percent for the total population.[125] In the south-west of the state only thirteen students reached Year 12 in 1988.[126] Indigenous dispossession in Western Australia was almost total. For example, in 1981, apart from land purchased as private citizens, the original inhabitants held freehold title to only thirty square kilometres out of a total land mass of two-and-a-half million square kilometres.[127] Lands were available as reserves and leases for Aboriginal use, but not ownership, and the vast majority of these were located in the northern and western regions of the state even though one third of the state's indigenous population lived in the capital and southern region.

Public attitudes towards Aboriginal people in Western Australia in the early 1980s were the most hostile of any state. The 1984 Australian National Opinion Poll survey of attitudes found that:

Fears and prejudices are much the same across Australia, but they are more pronounced in the West and the North.[128]

More Western Australians were strongly opposed to land rights (forty-three percent compared to only six percent strongly in favour) than in other states.[129] More believed that Aborigines received too much government assistance (sixty-nine percent),[130] and more were unable to nominate a single Aboriginal person they were 'particularly impressed with' (forty-nine percent).[131] Anti-land rights publicity campaigns by the mining industry and the Liberal Party in the mid-1980s did much to spread and harden such attitudes. This was only made worse by openly discriminatory actions by successive governments, notably the trampling on Aboriginal religion and sacred areas at Noonkanbah in 1980, the Harding Dam in 1984 and, from 1989, the Old Swan Brewery in Perth.

Since the 1950s, many Nyungar[132] families had moved into the metropolitan area from country towns seeking a better life, mainly in terms of employment, housing and schooling. This urban movement occurred because of a combination of assimilation policies and prejudice and exclusion in rural areas and a fall in employment due to the drop in rural labour demands. However, by the late 1970s, with the decrease in manufacturing industries, prospects of stable employment and job training declined for Nyungar families in Perth. Growing unemployment was particularly severe amongst youth. Sixty-three percent of Aborigines in Western Australia were under the age of twenty-four in 1986.[133] Economic deprivation and all the social problems associated with it, such as delinquency and substance abuse, were exacerbated by widespread prejudice and indifference in Perth society. This included a denial of Aboriginal cultural identity. The 1984 Western Australian Aboriginal Land Inquiry Commissioner put his finger on a particular white perception of Nyungar people:

There is a sense in which Europeans do not see Nyungars as being real Aborigines because they do not have the overt trappings of what Europeans have decided is a typical Aboriginal lifestyle. The Nyungars take a different view. Although they live in a European environment they retain a strong consciousness of their own identities as Nyungars. They draw a firm contrast between Nyungar and Wetjala (white fella) ways especially between Nyungar and Wetjala values.[134]

Both Coalition and Labor governments had failed to develop and implement appropriate programs to address the problems of Nyungar youth.[135] By the end of the 1980s they had become demonised in the Perth public domain by police, media and politicians. The Director of the Western Australian Aboriginal Legal Service Rob Riley stated in 1990:

You can imagine the effect this sort of reporting is having on young Aboriginal people around the city, going to school or work, or just walking down the street. It would be very difficult to feel positive about yourself or that other people were going to have a positive attitude toward you.[136]

Louis Johnson was not a Nyungar, nor was he poor. But he was young and Aboriginal. He had to go to school, to work, and of course 'just walk down the street' in the capital city of the state with the worst regard for its indigenous citizens.

LIFE IN PERTH

The Johnsons recall Louis having a happy early childhood. He was contented and 'didn't have a care in the world.'[137] In 1978 Louis started at St John's Catholic Primary School in Scarborough and later transferred to the Holy Rosary Primary School at Wembley. Even though these were happy years for the boy, the effects of racial prejudice were to increasingly affect Louis and indeed the whole family. Pauline had already been the butt of racist taunts from members of the public in Darwin and Perth who presumably thought that Louis was her son to an Aboriginal man. As she wheeled baby Louis along in his pram she was spat upon by men and verbally abused by women muttering that this 'shouldn't be allowed to happen' and by people in cars calling out 'boong' and 'nigger'.[138] As Bill reflects:

> We could see the prejudice that he was always meeting in those
> early years because you go out with an Aboriginal child, boy, youth
> and stand back, you can see the prejudice that they are meeting
> every day of their lives. It's either overt or it's covert, it's a raised
> eyebrow, it can be anything, people looking down their noses at
> kids. They can express it in many different ways.[139]

When Louis started at Newman College in Doubleview in 1986, at
the age of thirteen, he came to experience more unrelenting racism
because of his Aboriginality. The relative happiness of his primary
school years turned into increasing misery and hurt. This is evidenced
in a homework assignment in which he was asked to list his likes and
dislikes. 'I like most of the teachers, I like Brother Joe, I like the people
in the school office, I like science, maths, TD, English. I like the Year 9
girls, boy! I like the music class.'[140] For his dislikes, Louis wrote down
four boys' names who called him 'boong, petrol-sniffer, Abo and
nigger.' Pauline recalls that from this time she became increasingly
protective of Louis and exercised 'one hundred percent vigilance' to
protect him from harassment. It became evident that the other students
would often set Louis up to get him into trouble and that he would be
blamed and punished by the teachers. Finally the
Johnsons took him out of the school after an
older nun told Bill that Louis was the 'worst type
of native' and they placed him in a pre-appren-
ticeship welding course with the family
company JLV Industries in Myaree. The
Johnsons recall that, despite these set-backs,
Louis still loved to socialise with white people,
although he was quickly learning that many of
them did not feel the same way about him.[141]

*Louis Johnson/Warren
Braedon in Grade One, Perth.*
(Courtesy of Bill and Pauline
Johnson)

Like many other Aboriginal children
adopted into white families Louis' identity and
natural family became matters of great
importance and urgency to him at this time.
Bill later wrote that Louis was 'crying out for
information about the whereabouts and
identity of his natural family.'

The result of the adoption and the results of the isolation that Louis suffered from his natural family led to a great deal of grief and strife and loneliness for Louis in his teenage years and resulted in his abusing alcohol and getting into trouble with the police and all the time striving to find his own family.

All he wanted at that time was to meet them, find out who he was, who they were, then come back to Perth with us, finish his schooling, his apprenticeship, those types of things, but he just needed to touch base with them. It was very, very important at that time, for him to do that. In fact it was absolutely crucial that he did that and the way he was treated by those [Northern Territory Department of Community Welfare] was nothing short of disgraceful.[142]

At their teenage son's request the family went to Alice Springs in 1987 to attempt to find his natural family. Not knowing what to expect, Louis would say in anticipation, 'heartbreak or happiness'. They sought information from the Northern Territory Department of Community Development to no avail. Strict privacy laws still prevented the handing over of identifying information about parties to adoptions. The Northern Territory government maintains that prior to 1994, 'adoption legislation in the Northern Territory did not allow the release of identifying information to any person regardless of their stake in the adoption process.'[143]

Bill and Pauline remain extremely angry and bitter towards the Northern Territory government and its officials who refused to give Louis access to his records and through these, the possibility of being reunited with his family. As Bill recalls:

They gave him no help, no assistance, all they said to him in Alice Springs was we can't give you any information, just go to Darwin and see if they can tell you anything. We said that we know that his family is here, we know that you've got the family files, we know that he has got brothers and sisters because that's what we were told when we were adopting him. We said we believe that it's essential that he meets them, that he contacts them in some way for his own development. He needed that. They just absolutely refused to give us that information. Just blind bureaucracy.[144]

In Darwin they met with even more obstructiveness and indifference. Officials there told Louis to 'come back in seven years time

Louis Johnson/Warren Braedon aged 14 years on the Todd River, Alice Springs.
(Courtesy of Bill and Pauline Johnson)

when you are twenty-one and we might be able to do something for you.'[145] The Johnsons' pain was only made worse when they were told, after Louis' death, that the Northern Territory government officials were at least legally permitted to have told them, in 1987, that Louis' mother was still alive.[146] Louis' brother Kevin points to a photograph of Louis standing by the Todd River taken during that trip and laments that he and Dawna were living so close by. Bill believes that knowledge of his kin was essential to Louis' development and, as it tragically turned out, his survival.

In the midst of his emotional turmoil Louis continued to work at his father's factory. He also completed several solo flights toward his pilot's licence and took up painting. He displayed considerable artistic talent and, reflecting his desire to link with his people, he painted fine images of Aboriginal spirituality and dreaming themes. However, Louis was also getting deeper into trouble with the law.

Louis had been targeted by police routinely from the age of twelve when he first began to move around Perth without his parents. As a young Aboriginal man who was often alone and who could not handle even small amounts of alcohol, he was particularly vulnerable to police harassment. Louis was regularly stopped by police when driving the company utility, and finally had to display a card on the dashboard authorising him to use it. He was even accosted by police in the family home and had to prove he belonged there by referring the officers to a family portrait. He was ambushed by police while walking down the road near his home and only released when, fortunately, one officer recognised him — he was not one of the car thieves they had been lying in wait for.

Bill and Pauline Johnson were acutely aware that Louis' Aboriginality had marked him out for anyone to accuse, harass and deprive him of his liberty — police or otherwise — in the street, in shops, anywhere. They say his most vulnerable times were when he was on his own, out of sight of family and friends, and sometimes only momentarily. 'That's when it would happen. It's like children falling into backyard swimming pools. In the brief moments when they were not watched, suddenly they're in trouble or they're gone.'[147] While he had many friends, Louis did not go about in a group of young indigenous people, a factor which Bill and Pauline believe meant he was more vulnerable to opportunistic abuse — whether on his own or with others, he stood out.

In 1991 Louis was sentenced to twelve months gaol for a minor offence. The Johnsons appealed against this in the Supreme Court which quashed the sentence, on the grounds that it was excessively severe and did not fit the crime, and placed Louis on probation. That year the young man was also convicted of insulting a police officer and was put on probation for twelve months with a community service order. This conviction was unofficially cleared on appeal the following year, but after Louis' death. The court found that he had been provoked by a 'highly improper, uncalled for and provocative remark' made by the police sergeant.[148] Despite such harassment, Louis was quick to acknowledge that the police were not all the same. The Johnsons recalled his story of the constable at Central Station who responded angrily after the sergeant-in-charge told Louis, 'You know what your problem is, you're black,' and said to Louis, 'Listen, we're not all like that,' and gave him a cigarette.[149] In retrospect, the Johnsons believe, despite their vigilance and unconditional support for Louis, that without the personal experience of living as Aboriginal people, they could not impart to Louis the full repertoire of skills he needed to survive in a racist society — skills that would have been drummed into him from an early age in an Aboriginal family.[150]

UNSAFE STREETS

There was in fact a law and order hysteria gripping Perth at the time. From 1990 Perth's news media became increasingly preoccupied with juvenile and youth crime, which was presented as escalating to crisis proportions. Much of the coverage focused on Aboriginal youth, often in a discriminatory way. Although non-Aboriginal youths were also involved, Aboriginality was the only ethnicity identified in reports. The controversial police practice of pursuing stolen vehicles at high speeds in built-up areas resulted in over a dozen fatalities between 1990 and 1992. These deaths, and the sensationalising of burglaries and violent assaults — which in themselves were not unusual in a city of this size — were fodder for an extraordinary public campaign for severe penalties, organised by the populist talkback radio program, the Sattler File, on Radio 6PR. This radio program had significant advertising sponsorship from firms marketing home, car and personal security devices, all businesses that had obvious interests — converging with Howard Sattler's ratings quest — in the perception of rampant crime. The program was the publicity machine for a demonstration of up to 30,000 at Parliament House on 20 August 1991 — the 'Rally for Justice' — organised to pressure the government to simply incarcerate young offenders, and at which Sattler spoke. This was a complete rejection of the recommendations of the RCIADIC report released only three months earlier. Moreover, politicians and journalists simply took for granted the claims that youth crime was indeed spiralling out of control, and either failed to counter them or actively contributed to the myth for their own diverse purposes. The Sattler campaign's objectives were achieved in early February 1992 when the state Labor government caved in and pushed through parliament what were then the harshest juvenile crime laws in the country. At the same time Assistant Police Commissioner, Frank Zanetti, instructed police officers to adopt pro-active policing by targeting Aboriginal youth and he talked of introducing a youth curfew. This drew fire from the Human Rights and Equal Opportunity Commission which issued a 'challenge to official and unofficial policies contravening young people's human rights' in Western Australia.[151] Early in March the West Australian newspaper reported a 'series of inter-changes' between Human Rights Commissioner, Brian Burdekin, and Zanetti and the then Premier, Carmen Lawrence. Zanetti initially denied having issued the directive to police to 'harass young people who were on the street' while the Premier was reported as saying that she had 'seen no suggestion that they are doing it' (harassing offenders) despite a concurrent parliamentary inquiry that reported 'significant abuses of power by police against young people.'[152]

Subsequent research has shown that in the peak year of the crime hysteria, 1991, juvenile and youth crime rates did not increase, and possibly even *declined*. What did increase were public claims of increasing crime from demagogic media commentators such as Sattler, drum-beating politicians and police.[153] It was certainly the case that youth crime was a serious problem, but it had been for some time. Indigenous people had voiced their concerns about the problem and called for a range of solutions. The point here is that once the atmosphere of civil emergency took hold, so did demands for a single 'solution' — lock them up and throw away the key. This campaign relentlessly undermined public acceptance of progressive reforms in the areas of juvenile justice and indigenous rights and welfare in this period. Instead the campaign fostered wide support for harsher punitive measures and increased public hostility to indigenous rights and indifference to their circumstances. It worked to create a noxious public air of fear and malevolence toward Aboriginal youth in particular, of the kind conducive to racist thuggery and vigilantism, as Louis was to experience. Bill says:

> The amount of hysteria and hype and racism that was generated, particularly by people like Howard Sattler on the 6PR show created, I believe, the environment within which it was very easy for a couple of white people to murder Louis. If you cast your mind back to the 'Rally for Justice' outside Parliament House where fifteen or twenty thousand people were screaming for the death penalty to be brought back, there were actual photographs and effigies of Hal Jackson [magistrate] from the Children's Court being strung up.[154]

According to Bill the public atmosphere was so bad that Louis, who was not interested in following current affairs, told him in late 1991:

> 'Dad, it's just not safe to be out on the streets any more.' This is after he had been assaulted in Northbridge while sitting outside a cafe drinking with a couple of white girls, and he was assaulted because an Aboriginal kid, a black kid, had no right to be talking to white girls.[155]

MURDER

Around this time Louis made plans to return to Alice Springs to resume the search for his family. He would not, however, see his birthplace again. Only weeks after the attack in Northbridge Louis was brutally murdered by a different group of white youths.[156] At about three o'clock on the morning of 4 January 1992, his nineteenth birthday, Louis was walking home from a party in the affluent Perth suburb of North Beach. From the sequence of events established in court and in a coronial inquiry, it appears that he stopped to rest on the grass verge in North Beach Road, his legs protruding on to the road. Louis was seen by five white youths, three males and two females, passing by in a car. The two females and one of the males got out of the car further down the road, after which twenty-one-year-old Mark Wilder and the other male,[157] who was seventeen, returned in the car to watch from a short distance as another passing motorist, concerned for Louis' safety, stopped and moved the now sleeping young man fully on to the verge. After this man had driven off, the killers made their move. Louis was bashed and Wilder pulled his legs back on to the road. Then, urged on by Wilder in the passenger seat with 'Do it, do it,' the seventeen-year-old driver deliberately drove the car over Louis at high speed. The two then picked up the other three youths and returned with them to observe their victim, with the driver saying to the group, 'I got him, I am glad I got the black sod.' The killers and their friends sped off, leaving Louis for dead, with massive internal injuries including a shattered pelvis. A few hours later a passing cyclist came across him and called an ambulance. Before it arrived, Louis was still conscious enough to talk to the cyclist who, as a layperson, realised that Louis was seriously ill.

However, the ambulance attendants assumed, without making a proper examination, that Louis was not injured but had been sniffing petrol. They referred to him in casual and prejudicial terms to the cyclist. Instead of taking him to hospital, they took him home, telling his younger sister he was intoxicated, was not a hospital case, and should sleep it off in bed.[158] Bill and Pauline had left the house, for a business-related matter, before the ambulance arrived with Louis. Returning home around eight-thirty in the morning, and unaware of what had happened to him, they found Louis in bed and obviously ill. When the gravity of his condition became apparent, they called a second ambulance. His condition worsened and he lapsed into a coma just before the ambulance attendants arrived. His heart stopped while he was being carried on a stretcher to the ambulance.

In a taped confession to police after being arrested some days later the driver of the car admitted the racist motivation of his actions — 'because he was black'. He pleaded guilty to murder and was sentenced to seven years and nine months in prison. Wilder, who had described his victim as 'the black bastard,' pleaded not guilty to the charge of murder, but was found guilty and given a mandatory life sentence in September 1992. The other youths involved were not charged with any offences.

The Johnsons have come to further conclusions about the degree of premeditation and ideological motivation of the murderers, based on what Louis was able to tell them while he was still conscious and on other subsequent evidence. Before he slipped into the coma Louis had managed to tell Pauline that he had been attacked by 'Nazis'. Louis told her, 'He hit me so hard.'[159] Bill and Pauline therefore believe Louis saw and heard his attackers and was beaten up by one or more of the group — before or after the other motorist stopped, attended to him and departed — after which the killers drove the car over him. Moreover, his attackers gave him an impression of a particular brand of racist thug. The Johnsons are not convinced that the other three youths did not take more direct roles in the killing.

In a press article Bill is quoted regarding the affluent social background of the killers, and the global racist elements involved.

Louis died because there were five kids in a car, one of whom admitted he was a member of National Action [a fascist organisation]. He thought they could go out on a hunting party — like the pastoralists did many years ago in the Pilbara. These kids went to beat up or to kill a black person. Louis was the one that they met and killed. That's admitted. And we're not talking about deprived white kids who have had a lack of education. One of the two girls in the car went to one of the most expensive schools in Perth. You're talking about the mortgage-belt in the northern suburbs where this racist murder occurred, committed by middle-class kids. The other obscenity which really hurts me is that none of the kids had been in this country longer than November 1988. They're all English.[60]

Here was a deadly confluence of currents of British fascism and Australian racism.

The Coroner's report on the murder concluded that in their treatment of Louis the ambulance attendants had failed to follow a number of basic protocols, including failure to carry out a proper examination which would have detected Louis' major injuries. Coroner David McCann found that the operation of prejudicial stereotypes about Aborigines was indicated in the attendants' verbal communications with Louis and witnesses, and in written comments in the patient's records. There was no evidence to support the attendants' assumption that Louis had been sniffing petrol. The Coroner found that racial prejudice was a likely factor here.

> While witnesses have given evidence that the fact that Louis was of Aboriginal descent did not influence their decisions, the fact remains that within the general community there are prejudices against persons of Aboriginal descent. These prejudices manifest themselves in many ways. Some are seen in instances of personal abuse while some are expressed in physical attacks causing injury as revealed in the Supreme Court proceedings which arose as a result of Louis's death. The use of derogatory terms when referring to persons of Aboriginal descent is common in the workplace and in the privacy of homes. It would be difficult in the light of the present widespread attitude to persons of Aboriginal descent, to conclude that there were not at least some unconscious prejudices in the decision-making process.[161]

The Johnsons took legal action against the ambulance officers and the St John Ambulance Association for their failure to treat Louis properly and thereby contributing to his death. The case was eventually settled out of court on the basis of an agreement that the ambulance service deposit $25,000 into a trust established for the Braedon family, and that it institute improved training of officers and employment screening procedures to ensure that the negligence and prejudice accorded to Louis would not be repeated.

Even after his death, after the seemingly closing act of racial prejudice against him by the ambulance attendants, Louis was to suffer final posthumous discrimination. Although the Perth media had been preoccupied with youth and juvenile crime — had given incidents of car theft, assaults and robberies headline and lead story status — its treatment of Louis' vicious murder by a group of youths was subdued. It was not taken up as an instance of the alleged spiralling youth crime wave. Nor did media and public commentators express outrage on Louis' behalf, as a victim of crime, as they had for people assaulted and robbed or maimed and killed during police chases. His brutal murder was treated as a different kind of crime, one that failed to fit the actual, though unwritten, news agenda of innocent non-Aboriginal victims of Aboriginal lawlessness. The Sattler File's lack of interest in the killing was particularly conspicuous and revealing. Here was a cowardly and unprovoked attack on a citizen by a group of youths and juveniles, seemingly tailor-made for the Sattler theme of uncontrolled 'feral' teenagers roaming the streets. The relative lack of media interest in the murder of Louis Johnson in the days and weeks after it occurred, raised serious questions about the entire structure of news reporting in Perth, and about the role of the media in shaping public attitudes towards crime, Aboriginality and justice. It demonstrated the media's racial selectivity in marshalling public sympathy for victims of crime, its professional, journalistic incompetence in failing to test assertions and impressions against fact, and its failure to pay regard to the social consequences of sensationalism. It was only after the *Sunday Times* ran a front page story and feature on the killing in March 1992, and through the efforts of Bill and Pauline Johnson to make the public aware of its significance, that other mainstream media began to show more than a cursorily routine interest.[162] Later that year a feature in the *Australian Magazine*[163] and a television current affairs report finally drew out the significance of Louis' case that the majority of the local mainstream media had largely neglected.[164]

Vowing not to bury their beloved adopted son until they had fulfilled their promise to reunite him with his natural family, the grief-stricken Johnsons and friends took his body back to Alice Springs.

> We lodged it [the coffin] at a funeral parlour, and then began knocking on doors. This time we were very, very angry; we'd been polite before and followed the rules, and it had got us nowhere.[165]

Within hours a receptionist at the Central Australian Aboriginal Child Care Agency (ACCA) saw in Louis' photograph his resemblance to a local woman. ACCA worker Brian White conveyed to the Northern Territory Department of Community Development Bill Johnson's threat that 'unless they cooperated we'd call in the national media and hold a press conference over Louis' dead body.'[166] Fifteen minutes later the Department rang back with the information that Louis' mother, brother and ninety-year-old grandfather were living in Alice Springs. The following day many of Louis' relatives met the Johnsons at the ACCA office. Louis' brother Kevin recalled the day. He was at first under the impression he was going to meet his long lost brother:

> Brian [White] had to come round pick me up and tell me to come and meet up with Bill and Pauline and we went into this ACCA.

Sitting there, waiting there, I thought he was still alive you know. They told me later he got killed. I thought I was coming to meet him.[167]

Louis was buried at Alice Springs cemetery on 20 January 1992. Over a hundred of his relatives attended the funeral, including his invalid mother Dawna. This caused Bill to wonder why the Department could not have arranged for Louis to be left in the care of an obviously large and caring family back in 1973. Pauline Johnson says of her experience:

I personally felt ashamed because I had returned Louis to his own people dead. They had waited years for their son to come back. How can you look a hundred relatives in the face and say, 'I've got five photo albums to show you of your son?'[168]

The Johnsons have maintained a relationship with the Braedons after Louis' death, visiting them in Alice Springs, and Kevin has stayed with the Johnson family in Perth. Kevin is still waiting to be reunited with his other missing siblings as, together with the Johnsons, he continues to fight the red tape preventing him from learning their identities.

CHAPTER TWO

EXPERIMENTS IN CIVILISING

... she carried a little girl, who she still suckled ... [her] eyes had expression, and something of the spirituel which surprised us ... She appeared also to cherish her child much; and her care for her had that affectionate and gentle character which is exhibited among all races as the particular attribute of maternal tenderness.

M Peron anthropologist with Baudin's French sailing expedition in 1802.[1]

A MELANCHOLY TRANSACTION[2]

In May 1804 at Risdon Cove on the banks of the Derwent River in the colony of Van Diemen's Land a military party opened fire, without provocation, on a party of 300 Moomairremener people, killing an unknown number of men, women and children. From the site of the massacre the Government Surgeon, Dr Jacob Mountgarrett, collected several bodies for scientific dissection as well as a 'live specimen'. He wrote to the chaplain Reverend Robert Knopwood:

As you express a wish to be acquainted with some of the natives, if you dine with me tomorrow, you will oblige me by christening a fine native boy whom I have. Unfortunately, poor boy, his father and mother were both killed. He is about 2 years old. I likewise have the body of a man. If Mr Bowden wishes to see him dissected I will be happy for Aylwyn to see him with you tomorrow.[3]

The dissected corpses were subsequently packed in lime and remained in Mountgarrett's possession. The boy was baptised and renamed Robert Hobart May — May being the month of his capture —

and although Lieutenant Governor Collins ordered that he be returned to his people, he appears to have been kept in defiance of the order since he was listed in December the following year as having had the smallpox vaccination compulsory for colonists living in the 'settled' areas of Van Diemen's Land.[4]

This was the first officially recorded removal of an Aboriginal child in the colonial outpost. In many ways it was typical of those that followed across nineteenth-century colonial Australia and into the twentieth century. In addition to the violence experienced by the children there was the denial of Aboriginal humanity in the presumption of the colonists' prerogative to take and keep the children and to recast their identities to fit the culture of their new masters. There was also in this 'melancholy transaction' an intense curiosity about the nature of these indigenous 'specimens'. They were another puzzle in the bewildering human diversity revealed by global exploration, to be satisfied by drawing back the layers of skin and flesh of corpses on the dissecting table, collecting assemblages of body parts and experimenting with the potential of the children to become 'civilised' men and women.

HEARTS OF DARKNESS

The analysis of the treatment of indigenous children by colonists in the context of nineteenth-century Tasmania is not an esoteric historical exercise. On the contrary, it provides valuable insights into their treatment across colonial Australia and identifies many continuities and contradictions in policy and practice which endured in the twentieth century. The conventional view that the Tasmanian Aboriginal colonial experience was singular, having culminated in 'the complete destruction of a unique race,' has been discarded. The people were not exterminated and there are many commonalities with mainland colonial history. Van Diemen's Land was one of many 'Hearts of Darkness' in Australian colonial history — to paraphrase the title of Joseph Conrad's fictional account of colonialism in central Africa. Palawa[5] writer Greg Lehman states 'the experience of Aborigines in Tasmania foreshadowed what was to come elsewhere in Australia on many fronts.'[6] Lyndall Ryan[7] agrees, calling Van Diemen's Land the 'cradle of race relations in Australia.' It was not 'an aberrant case in the Australian context' but constituted the 'proving grounds of

European technology, warfare, culture and political economy which, emerging victorious in Tasmania, swept across the mainland as an expression of manifest destiny.' Ryan argues that the fiction of extermination there allowed mainland colonists to ignore the extent of Aboriginal depopulation in their own areas while the myths that the Tasmanians 'lost the will to live' or 'lacked the technical, cultural or moral means of confronting European invasion' conveniently expiated the guilt of whites.

Tasmania has a wealth of colonial archival records which provide insights into the experiences of Aboriginal children as documented by their colonial keepers. These are the precursors of the dossiers on individual Aborigines created by bureaucracies in the next century. George Augustus Robinson's journals, compiled by N J B Plomley, contain detailed information about the children's lives and relevant colonial policies and practices, as does Lyndall Ryan's history of the Tasmanian Aborigines. Henry Reynolds'[8] more recent reinterpretation of the Tasmanian wars provides a further valuable perspective. Together their work has done much to debunk old myths. These are all European narratives — as indeed is this chapter — and we can only imagine what the real feelings of the children were. This imbalance is being redressed by Palawa writers, artists and historians like Maykutenner (Vicki Matson-Green) whose research combines archival and oral histories to create a 'cultural and racial history [of] ... unbroken, continual survival.'[9]

The Australian colonies, along with New Zealand, North America and parts of South America were 'settler societies'[10] — immigrant fragments of metropolitan Europe set up in far distant places to meet European economic, penal and military needs. The emerging economies were based on the export to Europe of products extracted from a vast hinterland, largely through the labour of free settlers and convicts, and, to varying degrees, of the indigenous inhabitants. In colonies established in the densely settled areas of India and Africa, indigenous systems were able to sustain European capitalism as an imposition on their economies and way of life. Settler societies were located in relatively sparsely populated areas, the indigenous inhabitants were dispossessed of their lands and dispersed, and their cultures marginalised by a way of life that was self-consciously European.

These processes of dispossession and dispersal occurred on the moving frontiers of all Australian colonies. They were buttressed by doctrines of economic progress and cultural and racial superiority, an insatiable appetite for land, and the imperatives of economic survival, isolation and fears of aggressive Aboriginal retaliation. A particular brutality emerged, expressed in the merciless dislocation of many indigenous communities, the virtual enslavement of some of their members and terrible loss of life through violence, disease and starvation. The perceived extermination of Aboriginal people appeared to remove any impediments to the colonists' spread across the continent and endorsed their claims to be the rightful and legitimate owners of the land. As one colonist explained in 1858 in Victoria:

> It is the design of providence that the inferior races should pass away before the superior races ... since we have occupied the country, the aborigines must cease to occupy.[11]

Alongside these forces of destruction were glimmers of reason and compassion, of humanist beliefs in universality and the equality of all people, of Christian endeavours to protect indigenous people from the worst effects of colonialism enunciated by distant officials in London in directives to colonial governors and in the writings of some humanitarians and Christians in the colonies. This reflected Enlightenment beliefs in the possibility of what we now refer to as social engineering — that all individuals, including the criminal, the poor, the colonised and their children, could be taken from their 'barbarous' cultural environments and transformed into 'civilised beings'. Opinion on how to achieve this with Aborigines varied. Should they be employed in socially useful roles in colonial society? Did they need to be temporarily segregated to protect them from the vices of colonial society? Or should they be kept permanently apart to form enduring Aboriginal communities? These questions preoccupied administrators well into the twentieth century.

The powerful evangelical movements of the early nineteenth century guaranteed Christianity a central role in the 'civilising process'. This was evident in the Report of the 1837 British House of Commons Select Committee 'appointed to consider what Measures ought to be adopted with regard to the NATIVE INHABITANTS of Countries where BRITISH SETTLEMENTS are made.' In a section entitled 'Effects of Fair Dealing, combined with Christian Instruction, on Aborigines' the Committee argued that:

every tribe of mankind is accessible to this remedial process ... there is but one effectual means of imparting the blessings of civilization, and that is, the propagation of Christianity, together with the preservation, for the time to come, of the civil rights of the natives.[12]

The Committee indicated the modest goals of the 'civilising' experiment by quoting from the Governor of Canada concerning the conversion of the Mississagua and Chippeway Indian tribes:

they perceived the evils attendant upon their former ignorant wandering state; they began to work, which they never did before; they perceived the advantage of cultivating the soil; they totally gave up drinking, to which they had been strongly attached; they became industrious, sober and useful.[13]

Indigenous children were swept up in these tragic processes as their communities were dispossessed of their lands along the moving frontiers. They were killed and injured in violent confrontations. They died from the effects of introduced diseases and malnutrition. They were orphaned and left to survive on the fringes of colonial society. They were snatched from their parents' arms during raids and confrontations. Survivors were often forced into menial servitude with uncaring employers. This continued on through the nineteenth century, sanctioned in various ways by colonial authorities and eventually taken over by them. Children were also integral to the 'remedial process' of civilising and Christianising. In recommending the establishment of systems of protectorship for Aborigines in the colonies, the 1837 Report to the House of Commons pointed to the central place of indigenous children:

The education of the young will of course be among the foremost of the cares of the missionaries; and the Protectors should render every assistance in their power in advancing this all important part of any general scheme of improvement.[14]

In Australia this was to be carried out in isolation from Aboriginal adults in Christian institutions or the homes of colonists or even of supporters back 'Home' in Britain. Plomley states that this separation was of no ultimate advantage to the children:

on the one hand it deprived them of parental affection and the stability of the family, and made difficult or impossible cultural transmission; and on the other hand it did not give them any advantages in regard to their adopted European culture.[15]

In the short term the outcome of the 'civilising project' was frequently failure — young adults sank into oblivion on the fringes of colonial society, railed against the injustice of their treatment or returned to their families and Aboriginal ways of living — and early death. These outcomes prompted a deepening pessimism over the children's potential to change. This was further rationalised by race theories arguing that biological difference, not environment, determined individual ability and morality, and that it was futile to attempt to change members of a race so low on the 'Great Chain of Being'. The spreading dogma of Social Darwinism added a terrible, inexorable evolutionary dynamic. Aborigines were not only incapable of change, they were doomed to extinction. Indeed, 'civilisation' was constructed as a deadly force in itself, as one commentator observed, 'civilization ... has imposed on them the sad fate reserved for the inferior races ... In a near future we shall no longer have anything but a remembrance for them.'[16] In this way stereotypes of Aborigines served the interests of Europeans in colonising the land. Child removal was an integral part of Aborigines' experience of colonisation. It undermined Aboriginal culture and identity, threatened Aboriginal claims to sovereignty and to land and contributed to Aboriginal dislocation and depopulation in all colonies.

AN INDELIBLE STAIN UPON THE BRITISH GOVERNMENT[17]

How did these colonising processes evolve in the context of Van Diemen's Land? Between five and seven thousand indigenous inhabitants had been living in isolation for eight to ten thousand years when European sailing expeditions visited the coast between 1722 and 1802.[18] From the late eighteenth century coastal groups also encountered sealers sent to hunt the large seal colonies on islands in the Bass Strait by business entrepreneurs capitalising on the rich market for oil and fur in China and England. In 1802, a 'mixed rabble' of two hundred seamen and fugitives from the law were on the islands for the season. Sealing was an enterprise that linked hunting to capitalism. In the Bass Strait sealers abducted Aboriginal women and girls whose hunting and food-gathering skills and enforced sexual services proved central to the success of the enterprise.[19] In 1803–4 small convict outposts were established on the Derwent and Tamar rivers. During its first twenty years, development of the colony was hindered by the limited growth of its population[20] and its inability to become self-sufficient in food production. Faced by famine when their crops failed, local officials sent out armed convicts to shoot kangaroos which became the colonists' meat staple for several years.[21] In the hinterland escaped convicts and military deserters ranged largely outside the control of authorities and engaged in violent confrontations with Aborigines. These led to spiralling levels of brutal attack and counterattack, frequently characterised by sadistic practices perpetrated by convicts, soldiers and 'respectable' colonists, including the removal of Aboriginal body parts and the murder of infants and children by throwing them into fires or dashing out their brains.[22] By 1808 the intense conflict had led to the deaths of twenty colonists and one hundred Aborigines.[23] Ten years later the combined effects of violence and introduced disease had halved the original indigenous population.[24] Nevertheless, the colonists had possession of only fifteen percent of the land.

In 1818 Van Diemen's Land embarked on a period of major expansion. Regular transportation of convicts began with the cessation of the Napoleonic Wars and the colony was opened up to general migration. A new moneyed class of retired military personnel, sons of the landed gentry and colonial officials arrived, intent on setting up a viable pastoral industry on the vast stretches of land between Hobart in the south and Launceston in the north. With a reservoir of free convict labour and private capital, Van Diemen's Land was soon on the way to becoming 'a successful agricultural colony'.[25] The wave of invasion into Aboriginal hunting grounds heralded a dramatic escalation of conflict with Aborigines.

Plomley,[26] normally a careful commentator on events in Tasmanian history, commented angrily on the continuing land grab in the colony:

Whatever may be said or written about the relations between the settler and the Aborigines, there is no doubt that the only interest of the settlers was to hold on to the lands they had taken. Humanity was no more than the sugar in their words, no more than the publicity designed to allow them to proceed with their occupation of the land.

Many colonists unrepentantly declared their determination to be rid of the Aborigines.

We make no pompous display of Philanthropy — we say unequivo-cally — SELF DEFENCE IS THE FIRST LAW OF NATURE. THE GOVERNMENT MUST REMOVE THE NATIVES — IF NOT, THEY WILL BE HUNTED DOWN LIKE WILD BEASTS AND DESTROYED.[27]

Nevertheless, as Reynolds[28] points out, there was a deep ambivalence about the level of violence against Aborigines —'some applauded when the newspapers reported they had been butchered; others were appalled ... The newspapers conducted a vigorous, if sporadic, debate on the subject throughout the war years.' For their part, the Aborigines appeared determined to fight their enemies to the last. They used an effective campaign of guerilla warfare which exasperated and terrorised the colonists, burning huts, driving off cattle, spearing stock, raiding food stores and attacking and killing the colonists. In 1830 Jorgen Jorgenson, a much travelled explorer, wrote that Aborigines had 'inflicted severe and sanguinary castigation on the [colonists]' and that:

There [was] not a single instance on record shewing that savages [had] courted terms of peace from this civilised invader unless first humbled. At present the Aborigines of this island consider themselves our superiors in the art of war.[29]

What did the British government do to protect the rights of Aborigines during these killing times? Although the 1837 Select Committee claimed the 'strongest desire was felt by the Government at home, and responded to by the local Governor, to protect and conciliate them,'[30] Plomley contends that Britain thought Aborigines merely a distant 'natural feature capable of being pushed aside in much the same way as the bush was cleared for ploughing.'[31] The colonial historian James Bonwick reflecting back on these years during the 1870s, was damning of British government action:

It is undeniable that the British Government converted the island of Van Diemen's Land into what has been called a dust hole, for the reception of the moral rubbish and turpitude of Europe, without the least consideration of the question of the Aborigines. The authorities were pleased not only to seize and hold the island, without consultation of the will of the inhabitants, but actually, without their knowledge, and most certainly against their wishes, constituted them British subjects.[32]

Britain was well aware of the colonists' intentions to drive Aborigines from the island. An official committee in Hobart reported in 1830 that there was 'the strongest feeling amongst the settlers that so long as the natives have any land to traverse, so long will life and every thing valuable to them be kept in a state of jeopardy.'[33] The 1837 Report to the House of Commons contained a comment indicating British government compliance with this view at the time: 'though diminished to a very small number ... their remaining in their own country was deemed incompatible with the safety of the settlement.'[34]

This, then, was the situation confronting Colonel George Arthur, Governor of Van Diemen's Land from 1824 to 1836. Conservative, religious and an advocate of 'British imperialism and dictatorial government', Arthur also believed 'the aborigines had the right to live.'[35] In his handling of the conflict Arthur oscillated between military and conciliatory solutions. In 1828 he proposed a distant Aboriginal reserve on the north-east coast and then declared a state of martial law on the island and authorised 'roving parties' to scour the bush for Aborigines. In 1829 he appointed a committee of prominent colonists to advise him on the treatment of captured Aborigines and in the following year commandeered the infamous Black Line to flush out all Aborigines still at large in the 'settled districts'. The Black Line was a straggling, disconnected, military-style operation of 3000 colonists who spent six weeks trudging relentlessly through the bush at a cost of 30,000 pounds to capture only two Aborigines, one a small boy.

The toll of the Black War for both sides was severe. Reynolds[36] states that by the end of 1831, 175 Europeans had been killed and 200 wounded. The loss of land and resources, disruption of their way of life, the abduction of women and children, the killings and mutilations, starvation, and the cold hand of disease were disastrous for the Aborigines: when martial law was revoked in 1832 only an estimated 400 Aborigines were still alive. The complicity at all levels of colonial society was exposed in a statement in the *Hobart Town Gazette* in 1836 from an unidentified correspondent who demonstrated a surprising degree of sympathy for the Aborigines and showed that not all colonists endorsed what had happened. Perhaps this letter also reflected the pity that conquerors can afford to express for their vanquished foes.

> They have been murdered in cold blood. They have been shot in the woods, and hunted down as beasts of prey. Their women have been contaminated, and then had their throats cut, or been shot, by the British Residents, who would fain call themselves civilized people. The Government, too, by the common hangman sacrificed the lives of such of the aborigines as in retaliation destroyed their wholesale murderers, and the Government, to its shame to be recorded, in no one instance, on no single occasion, ever punished, or threatened to punish, the acknowledged murderers of the aboriginal inhabitants.[37]

Despite such noble sentiments, little was done to chastise the colonists for their acts of murder and, as Plomley noted, 'no persons suffered any but the slightest inconvenience at the hands of the law for any crime committed against the aborigines.'[38]

Already in 1830 there were official expressions of concern about the possibility of the total annihilation of the Aboriginal population. In that year Sir George Murray wrote from Downing Street to Governor Arthur:

> The great decrease which has of late years taken place in the amount of the aboriginal population, renders it not unreasonable to apprehend that the whole race of these people may at no distant period become extinct. But with whatever feelings such an event may be looked forward to ... by the settlers ... it is impossible not to contemplate such a result ... as one very difficult to be reconciled with feelings of humanity, or even with the principles of justice and sound policy; and the adoption of any line of conduct having for its avowed or secret object the extinction of the native race could not fail to leave an indelible stain on the character of the British government.[39]

In the same year Arthur attempted 'a negotiated settlement to the war'[40] through the agency of the 'Friendly Mission'. This consisted of small parties of Aborigines led by George Augustus Robinson, a bricklayer by trade with a limited education but a strong missionary fervour, who scoured the remote west and north-west coast for survivors of the Black War. Six expeditions were made between 1830 and 1834, and in all twenty-seven Aborigines accompanied Robinson. They provided invaluable bush skills and knowledge of the country as well as expertise in 'translation, negotiation and diplomacy' which were essential in persuading the survivors to come in. Reynolds argues that, having valiantly fought their 'patriotic war', the Aborigines knew they had to negotiate and that Robinson, on behalf of the government, entered into a form of treaty with them that promised:

In 'Conciliation' artist Benjamin Duterreau positions G A Robinson as the benevolent leader of a group of Tasmanian Aborigines, 1835.
(Courtesy of Tasmanian Museum and Art Gallery, AG 794)

> an end to hostilities and offering the hope of survival, protection from future attack, and such basic necessities as food, clothing and shelter. Robinson promised that their cultural tradition would be respected and — at the least — there would be frequent return visits to their homelands.[41]

From 1833 Wybalenna ('Black Men's Houses') on Flinders Island became home for two hundred survivors of the Black War. When they were moved to Oyster Cove south of Hobart in 1847 only forty-six remained.

The colonising processes advocated in the 1837 House of Commons Report were mirrored in a 'General Plan' for the amelioration of Aborigines developed by Robinson in 1829. Shaped by his reading on missions in the Pacific and New South Wales, and on penal institutions, and by the general climate of reforming zeal in the convict settlement,[42] the Plan would determine the structure of Wybalenna.

Indeed Aboriginal missions and government settlements across the Australian mainland into the twentieth century would echo this plan. The 'object to be obtained,' Robinson wrote, was 'the amelioration of the Aborigines of Van Diemen's Land,' and the means to achieve this were: '1. Civilisation; 2. Instruction in the principles of Christianity.'[43] The Aborigines were to become 'Christianised peasants'.[44] living together in a small village with a mission house, single and married huts on fenced allotments, a school which would double as a church, and garden plots. They would be trained to take on the 'habits of industry' — build their huts, tend their own gardens, catch fish (although fish eating was taboo for them) and learn to cook food in the European manner, and learn Christianity through 'public worship' and 'public schools' conducted in English.[45] The children were integral to Robinson's plan and he told Governor Arthur 'these children appear to be detained by providence as a foundation upon which the superstructure of your Excellency's benevolence is hereafter to be erected.'[46] The children were also essential to the Aborigines' endeavours to continue *their* cultural practices at Wybalenna.

With the Aboriginal survivors apparently safely corralled on Flinders Island and with 36,500 colonists on the mainland it seemed that the Tasmanian Aborigines had finally been vanquished. As their numbers dwindled, the fiction of their extermination spread, making them 'the most well known of the exterminated peoples [who] were often held up as symbols for them all.'[47] However, the people and their struggle continued on through the few surviving children at Wybalenna, and in families in isolated pockets on the mainland and on the Bass Strait islands where some sealers and Aboriginal women had settled and earned a living from mutton birding and wallaby hunting. Indeed, their descendants were central, both for the survival of the Tasmanian Aborigines and their future as a sovereign people. Reynolds identifies a striking 'continuity of principle, belief and rhetoric ... the fierce assertion of independence, the resistance to interference by government, the memory of past dispossession leading to claims to assistance and support by way of compensation,'[48] that was maintained through the nineteenth century into the modern land rights movement of the 1970s. A Palawa woman, Mrs F Gardiner, wrote in the *Launceston Examiner* in 1977, 'We are claiming land rights ... What is wrong with that? It is our ancestors calling from their graves. Claim what is rightfully yours.'[49]

What was the fate of Tasmanian Aboriginal children during these years of invasion and warfare? Like children in all war zones they suffered the pain of injury, disease and death and the loss of family, country, possessions and their familiar way of life. The survivors fended for themselves on the streets of towns like Launceston or were forcibly taken to be trained in farming and domestic duties in the homes of their enemies or in government institutions. A few lived with or worked for wealthy families in Hobart and back in England. Some were taken by their masters to mainland Australia where they married into local Aboriginal families or simply disappeared from the records. Others were forced to act as intermediaries between their captors and their own people. Most died young. The few who reached adulthood lived out their years in the narrow niche allotted to them by colonial society. The exceptions in this tragic story were the children growing up with their families in the relative isolation of the Bass Strait islands where, despite the harsh climate and living conditions, numbers of children had begun to increase during the 1820s.

Enforced separation from their families and unpaid work was the lot of many children of the poor in Britain and its colonies. The concept of 'childhood', with its associations of dependence, protection, segregation and delayed responsibilities, which spread through middle-class families in England from the late eighteenth century, had little relevance for these children. England had a long history of harsh treatment of its poor and destitute children.[50] In Tudor times they were apprenticed out or sent to work for employers in families in their local parish. They were transported to the American colonies to become live-in workers — the first batch of 100 children was sent to Virginia in 1619 — a forerunner of the child migrant schemes of the nineteenth and twentieth centuries. From 1703 destitute boys could be forced into apprenticeships in the navy and legislation passed in 1717 allowed for the penal transportation to the colonies of young people aged from fifteen to eighteen years. The extensive urban child poverty of early nineteenth-century industrial England left children particularly vulnerable to exploitation by employers and to the dangers of street life described in the novels of Charles Dickens. Official efforts to deal with this perceived social disorder focused on programs to transform children into useful workers through institutionalisation (in workhouses) and expanded systems of surveillance and imprisonment.

With escalating levels of child crime and growing labour needs in the Australian colonies, transportation of children as young as seven began in earnest. Between 1830 and 1842 some 5000 'youthful criminals' were transported and in 1834 Australia's first penal institution for boys — the infamous Point Puer (Latin for 'boy') at Port Arthur in Van Diemen's Land — was opened. Orphaned and abandoned children were gathered into institutions and then apprenticed out to employers to shield them from 'corrupting influences' and to transform them into 'good workers and wives who knew their station in life within basically exploitative working relationships.'[51] Conditions 'back home' were replicated in the colonies: harsh treatment was the norm in the institutions and the families the children were sent to work for.

Indigenous children were similarly treated. Abduction of children was an integral part of the system of slavery. Prior to the abolition of slavery in British colonies in 1838, large numbers of young boys, in particular, were forcibly taken by slavers from their homes in Africa to work on plantations in America. There, slave families were often forcibly broken up and the children sent away to other employers. In 1773 slaves in Massachusetts petitioned the Governor:

> Our children are also taken from us by force and sent many miles from us, we seldom or ever see them again, there to be made slaves for life which sometimes is vere short by Reson of Being dragged from their mothers Breast.[52]

The removal of orphaned children — but not children living with their families — from indigenous populations was an ancient political practice sanctioned by the British Empire.[53] However, from the early seventeenth century Catholic missionaries in Canada were removing Native American children from their families to educate them away from the influence of their parents. French Jesuits sent some children to live in family homes or convents in France or to boarding schools in Canada. Children were also taken in as workers by colonists.[54]

Although Australian Aborigines were to be guaranteed rights and protection as British subjects, the majority of child removals were effected outside of the law. The children were not always orphans and parental permission was rarely sought, although there were some instances where destitute parents left them with colonists. The children were of considerable benefit to colonists, providing free labour, companionship and even sexual services, and they brought valuable knowledge of the bush and local terrain as well as linguistic skills useful in mediating with local Aboriginal groups.[55] Colonial gendered lines of work were observed: the girls did domestic duties while the boys laboured outside. For some colonists, their presence created an illusion of the status conferred on wealthy slave owners and European aristocracy by their 'sable valets' and 'body servants', popular in eighteenth-century Europe. In return the children cost the colonists little to obtain and to keep: being 'part of the family' generally meant cheap clothes, little food and no pay. There were no controls over how they were treated and little likelihood of their masters and mistresses being taken to court for physical or sexual abuse. They could train, mould and discipline the children as they wished — indeed many believed that the workplace was the most appropriate site for training them — and, if there were any problems, they simply blamed the children's racial inheritance. Many children were completely dependent on their masters, having lost contact with their kin, culture and land. A few may have developed a sense of belonging and interdependence, especially those whose masters valued their skills and learned from them about Aboriginal culture. The psychological damage from internalising colonial ideas of race and negative stereotypes of Aborigines, the frequent sexual harassment, the harsh punishments meted out to them and the realisation of their inferior status in the family as they grew up were frequently expressed in rebellious behaviour, running away and early death. Meanwhile, surviving families mourned their loss and their inability to reproduce their culture through their children. This was the hidden side of the story of 'extermination'. While much was written of the infertility of Tasmanian Aboriginal women little was said about Aborigines' ability to survive as a distinct people without their children.

EARLY CHILD ABDUCTIONS

Abductions of Aboriginal children occurred from earliest contacts and continued until the 1830s when G A Robinson began his campaigns to round up the children and their families. The number of proclamations issued by governors in Van Diemen's Land between 1810 and 1818 suggests that abductions were widespread. Nevertheless, official intervention was only half-hearted. The children's services were invaluable to colonists who had few alternative sources of labour and in their homes the children learned of settler society while they cost the State nothing.

The sealers were the first to abduct female Aboriginal children. In some cases the assistance of the 'Tyrelore' — the Aboriginal name for the sealers' women — was negotiated through exchanges of goods in accordance with Aboriginal trading conventions. It was more often the case, however, that women and girls, some as young as eight, were forcibly abducted, subjected to horrific physical beatings to force them to work, raped and even murdered. Drummernerlooner (Jumbo) of the Cape Portland people told Robinson in 1830 how a group of men led by the sealer James Munro:

> ... rushed them at their fires and took six [females], that she was a little girl and could just crawl, said she had been with Munro ever since, said that the white men tie the black women to trees ... then they flog them very much ... much blood.[56]

Colonists on the mainland looked to Aboriginal children to meet their need for farm workers and domestic servants. Ryan[57] states that they believed they were saving the children from 'starvation and barbarism' and bestowing the benefits of a Christian and civilised life on them. This belief reflected contemporary stereotypes of hunters and gatherers as ignorant, lazy and wasteful in their use of resources and the conflation of Aboriginal pauperisation following colonisation with their conditions prior to contact. Perhaps colonists did save some children's lives. However, evidence suggests that most were simply taking children for their own self-interest and needs. D Davies[58] suggests that there was a strong sexual interest in young Aboriginal girls — reflecting the high sex imbalance in the colony (in 1830 non-Aboriginal women constituted only twenty-eight percent of the population of New South Wales and Van Diemen's Land) — and cites Reverend Knopwood who recorded that in 1813 and 1814 several girls 'were taken for prostitution amongst the sex-starved convicts.'[59] This may have also reflected the long history of sexual use of young girls in England and the flourishing trade in child prostitution in nineteenth-century England. There is evidence from other colonies that Aboriginal girls were taken by white men to avoid venereal infections that had spread amongst the women.[60] For a time the colonists, like the sealers, negotiated arrangements to 'borrow' the children from their parents in exchange for provisions.[61] However, most were abducted against their own and their parents' wishes. Ryan[62] states that by 1816 'kidnapping had become widespread' and in 1817 over fifty children were living with settlers. A cold-blooded vindictiveness often accompanied these abductions. Bonwick[63] described how a group of Aborigines visiting Hobart were given flour by colonists and then:

> in the merriment of the feast, some white monsters decoyed away and stole several of the children. At the discovery of the loss, the parents sought by passionate entreaties to procure the restitution of their offspring, but were met with brutal jests from the kidnappers. Returning in sorrow and rage to their hilly homes, no black was seen in the streets of the Christian savages for several years after.

Avoiding colonists and towns, hiding their children and training them to fear whites was one strategy for avoiding the abduction of children. Indeed this was repeated by Aborigines around Australia over the decades. Violent retaliation was more frequently the Aborigines' considered response in Van Diemen's Land. The link between child abductions and Aboriginal attacks on colonists was officially acknowledged and condemned, reflecting a mixture of humanitarian concern and pragmatic necessity to stop the violence impeding colonisation. In June 1814 Lieutenant Governor Davey issued a proclamation attributing Aboriginal hostility near the Coal River in the Richmond district to the 'robbery of their children' and expressing his 'utter indignation and abhorrence thereof.'[64] The proclamation continued:

> Let any man put his hand to his heart and ask which is the savage — the white man who robs the parent of his children, or the black man who boldly steps forward to prevent the injury, and recover his stolen offspring; the conclusion, alas! is too obvious.[65]

In 1819 Governor William Sorell wrote of the reported abduction of two children in the Plenty River district:

> This last Outrage is perhaps the most certain of all to excite in the Sufferers a strong Thirst for revenge against all White Men, and to incite the Natives to take Vengeance indiscriminately.[66]

He ordered that:

No person whatsoever will be allowed to retain possession of a native youth or child, unless it shall clearly be proved that the consent of the parents had been given; or that the child had been found in a state to demand shelter and protection, in which case the person into whose hands it may fall, is immediately to report the circumstance to the nearest magistrate or constable.

All native youths and children who shall be known to be with any settlers or stock-keepers, unless accounted for, will be removed to Hobart Town, where they will be supported and instructed at the charge and under the direction of the government.[67]

However, these pronouncements had little impact, indicating the value of the children to the settlers and the lack of strong government leadership. Most settlers disregarded the proclamations and kept the children. Only a small number were handed over to the care of Reverend Knopwood, who had twelve children in his home in Hobart by 1820.[68] No official action was taken as abductions continued during the escalating hostilities of the 1820s. When Governor Sorell left for England in 1824 he failed to even mention the matter in his report to his successor.

THE HORRORS OF WAR

In all the Australian colonies warfare struck indiscriminately across lines of age and gender in Aboriginal populations. Half of the Aborigines killed in the 1838 Myall Creek massacre in New South Wales were children, and two of the five survivors were girls aged seven who had been sexually assaulted.[69] In Van Diemen's Land many children living in the bush with their families simply disappeared during the escalating horror of the Black War.[70] To the harsh imperatives of guerilla warfare — the continuous movement, the need for absolute silence, the hunger and starvation due to disruption of regular hunting and gathering practices, the ban on fires for cooking and warmth and light at night so as to avoid detection — were added the trauma, injuries and deaths from violent confrontations. Lacklay (Jemmy) was only twelve years old when he witnessed the following attack on his family by soldiers and employees of the Van Diemen's Land Company near Quamby Bluff in the north-west of the island:

some soldiers surrounded our camp and fired their guns at us. A man and a woman were shot. The soldiers also killed the woman's young child. They beat his head with a stick.[71]

'Old Daddy,' a former stock-keeper for John Batman at Ben Lomond, recalled an ambush where a boy was killed with terrible brutality by soldiers:

A sergeant seized hold of a little boy, who attempted to rush by him in the darkness; and, exclaimed, 'You —, if you ain't mischievous now, you will be,' and swung him round by his feet against a tree, and dashed his brains out. Women were lying about still grasping their children amidst their dying torments.[72]

Many children were seriously injured. Toobelongeter of the Oyster Bay people was only five years old when her legs were broken during a raid near Little Swanport in 1825. She was maimed for life. She lived for two years with her captors at Swansea and was then handed to Dr Temple Pearson, Assistant District Surgeon and prominent landowner, who had her baptised and renamed Margaret Douglas Pearson.[73] The declaration of martial law in 1828 served to legitimate these atrocities.[74] In August 1829 Alexander Goldie — agriculturalist and employee of the Van Diemen's Land Company — and his men perpetrated a violent and unwarranted attack on two women and a four-year-old girl near Emu Bay. Passing near the site in 1830 Robinson recorded:

Passed where the woman was shot by Mr Goldie's party. This was a melancholy transaction! ... Two women were walking along the beach ... when one of the men shot the woman who had a child. The affection of the poor creature was very striking: seeing she was about to be shot, she turned her back to her executioner, placed her child between her legs and stooped down in order to save it. The ball went through the woman's body and when she fell another of the party ran up and chopped her on the neck. The other woman was secured and the child, and was harshly treated.[75]

The little girl was taken and handed over to Mrs Cameron, a shopkeeper in Launceston. She died soon afterwards.[76] Although Edward Curr, manager of the Van Diemen's Land Company, condemned the killing as murder and Goldie as 'a guilty accessory to the crime,' a magisterial inquiry into the killing concluded that the proclamation of martial law prohibited any committal for murder, a decision endorsed by the Solicitor General. The children's terror of being captured was painfully evident in the story recounted by surveyor John Wedge of a nine-year-old boy who escaped into the sea near Cape Grim after his family was ambushed in 1828. There he remained, safe from his captors, while he was buffeted by a heavy surf until finally he was 'washed on shore apparently lifeless.'[77]

WORKING FOR THE ENEMY

Captured youths were often forced to work for the 'enemy' as conciliatory ambassadors or mediators with their own people or as captors of Aboriginal groups still at large in the bush.[78] Nicermeric, captured by Edward Curr at Circular Head in 1829, was sent back to his people with the official message that 'our intentions were peaceable towards his tribe and drawing a distinction between ourselves and sealers.'[79] Others were sent out under Governor Arthur's instruction bearing illustrated boards showing 'the real wishes of the government towards them,' as well as the consequences of continued hostility.[80] The youths were also commandeered as guides by official and civilian 'roving parties' of appointed 'constables' and trusted convicts who from 1830 were paid bounties for captured Aborigines — five pounds for an adult and two pounds for a child — and rewarded with grants of land and convict servants.[81] The youths' bush skills and ability to communicate with Aborigines, or simply not to alarm them in a world where colonists shot them on sight, were integral in rounding up Aboriginal people. In 1828 Kickerterpoller led Gilbert Robertson's party in the capture of five Aborigines near Swanport, including the feared and elusive leader of the Stoney Creek people, Umarrah. The young men did not always cooperate: Constable Jorgenson reported that sixteen-year-old Mungo 'frankly confessed that he invariably led the roving parties astray when on the tracks of his countrymen.'[82] Others managed to escape and endeavoured to link up with their families. In 1830 Nicermeric escaped from John Wedge's roving party but was recaptured and sent to Launceston Gaol and then on to Wedge's property, Leighland. He escaped with another youth soon afterwards and remained at large until 1834 when he was found stealing a boat on the Leven River.[83] Lacklay was sixteen when he and Maulboyheenner (Timmy) were captured near Port Sorell in 1830 and sent to Leighland. He too escaped but was recaptured in 1831 and sent to Launceston Gaol.

Tragically, Arthur's conciliatory measure of using 'roving parties' to bring in the Aborigines resulted in further brutality against Aborigines. Between November 1828 and November 1830 the roving parties captured some twenty Aborigines and were directly responsible for the deaths of sixty others.[84] The captured were placed in the nearest secure holding places — gaols and asylums — and treated roughly. A boy of eleven held in the lunatic asylum at the colonial hospital in Hobart in 1829 was 'thrown down and had two of his teeth knocked out.'[85] At Richmond an Aboriginal woman grieving that her son had been sent out with a roving party was taunted by a sentry who 'repeatedly enquired for her piccaninny.' When she threw a stone at him in exasperation he responded by 'striking her a severe blow on the head with the butt-end of his musket.'[86]

WITH THE WHITE PEOPLE[87]

The fate of those children who survived as orphans and refugees in their own country — 'unfortunate creatures prowling about the country, friendless and homeless'[88] — was often a life on the streets or exploitation and servitude in the homes of colonists. Two-eleven-year old boys named Friday and Arthur lived, like Dickens' Artful Dodger, by their wits, picking the pockets of passers-by on the streets of Launceston and committing robberies for convicts and other criminals.[89] In the same town an eleven-year-old girl was left in 'the midst of a notorious nest of lowest description of men' since there was nowhere else for her to go.[90] In 1831 two girls aged sixteen and thirteen, both daughters of sealers, were imprisoned after they were found living on the streets of Launceston.[91]

By 1830, throughout the settled areas, an unknown number of Aboriginal children were living in the homes of prominent landowners and officials, publicans, shopkeepers and farmers. Some children were taken overseas as servants, including Kitty Hobart who travelled to Batavia in 1818 as the servant of a colonial official and Catherine Knopwood who sailed to England in 1820 as the servant of the captain's wife. Their fate is not known.[92] Estimates based on baptism records and official lists of Aboriginal children in the colonists' households collected by Plomley[93] suggest that as many as eighty-nine children may have been taken in between 1810 and 1836, although this certainly underestimates the extent of abductions. More than half were girls, indicating the demand for their domestic and possibly sexual services. Some were daughters of sealers[94] sent to work in Launceston — the sealers' nearest trading centre — as domestic servants and perhaps to be educated as well. This may have reflected British servant class traditions or perhaps the girls were sent away to protect them from the harsh island life. Boys appear to have been kept to work on the islands.

What happened to these children? Many died in the homes of their captors. This was, for example, the fate of the boy captured by Wedge on the beach in 1828. Named May Day — the date of his capture — he accompanied Wedge's roving parties and surveying expeditions, probably acting as a personal servant to Wedge. Wedge was teaching him to speak English and to read and write when he died of a pulmonary attack two years after his capture. Wedge recalled optimistically:

He was faithful, and became very attached to me; and I scarcely think, had his life been spared, that he would ever have returned to lead the uncivilised life from which he was rescued.[95]

The anomalous position of children like May Day in colonial society is evident in the following poignant anecdote from Wedge.

On one occasion, when in Hobart Town he was present at a mixed party of ladies and gentlemen. During the evening one of the gentlemen tried to persuade him to kiss a young lady in the room. He hesitated and said 'No good — no good,' meaning, 'not right.' But after being importuned for some time, he watched his opportunity, went behind the lady, and gently touched the neck, and then kissed his fingers.[96]

Many grew into unhappy and rebellious young people. Plomley and Henley[97] writes of a pattern of 'restlessness from the age of puberty, as they became a nuisance in the households in which they lived and where they lacked care and interest.' This is sadly reminiscent of descriptions of Aboriginal children fostered and adopted into white Australian families from the 1950s. Some colonists despaired at their charges' behaviour and pleaded with the officials to take them off their hands. In 1831 Dr Temple Pearson requested that his 'adopted' daughter Margaret Pearson — the girl crippled by a raid on her family in 1825 —

be sent away to the Aboriginal settlement. He claimed that his wife had:

> paid great attention to her instruction, but it appears she has of late become so exceedingly obstinate and perverse that Mrs P finds it impossible to keep her under restraint. An inclination to pilfer trifling articles has shewn itself and conscious of the impropriety of her conduct she endeavours constantly to screen herself by falsehood.[98]

Margaret died at Wybalenna in 1834 aged fifteen, probably of pneumonia. In that year, the daughter of a sealer living in John Wedge's home was also sent to Wybalenna after this letter of complaint to Hobart:

> I took charge of her under an idea that she would be rescued from the dreadful state of depravity which prevails amongst that class of people [the sealers] and that she would become a useful member of society. She has, of late, however, notwithstanding the very great pains taken with her by my sister turned out so incorrigibly bad in *every* respect, a drunkard, a thief, a prostitute, that I am induced to solicit that she may be allowed to join her mother at Flinders Island as the only step likely to save her from the extreme punishment of the law if she remains near those who contaminated her, an intercourse with whom it is quite impossible to prevent.[99]

Reflecting stereotypes of the time, colonists attributed the children's behaviour to their inherent 'barbarity,' expressed in an inability to learn new ways and an instinctual tendency to 'revert' to their former lifestyle.[100] Colonists also feared that the children would use their new skills against their masters — a common anxiety across the frontiers of colonial Australia. A combination of these sentiments was expressed in the following excerpt from the *Colonial Times* in 1826.

> Aboriginal natives, who are reared from their earliest years among us, if even they should be kept until they arrive at maturity, always evince a disposition to join their black brethren and when they do so, they carry with them the seeds of civilisation which they have sown in their own minds, and which they disseminate among their tribes, thereby rendering them more formidable by thus enlightening them — not that we are enemies to the civilisation of the blacks — far from it, but as by nature they are prone to enmity

against Europeans; any increase in knowledge is only stirring up the flame within their bosoms and by their becoming acquainted with our manners, they are less likely to be intimidated by us, as it is now clear that fear alone has kept them so harmless as they have been. Now they are in the possession of cutlasses, pistols, muskets, bayonets, &c., which they have learnt the use of by those who have been brought up (under the hope of ameliorating their condition) in civilised society.[101]

G A Robinson had drawn on preconceptions about the powerful sexual needs of Aboriginal young people to explain their behaviour when he observed that 'at puberty, the males have the avowed purpose of cohabiting with the other sex.'[102] Plomley[103] elaborates on this explanation and also suggests the emotional and sexual loneliness of the young people:

On reaching puberty they could not satisfy their sexual urges normally in the new environment and so they either ran away and joined the tribes or prostituted themselves with the convict servants, for which they gained the ill-will of their masters.

Bonwick[104] explained that most children were unhappy with their subordinate status: told that the Aboriginal way of life was inferior, that they were not the equals of whites, they rebelled against the long hours of unpaid work, the harsh punishments and strict controls over their behaviour. Bonwick quoted a colonist who wrote in 1818:

A poor native boy in a kitchen was worse than in a state of solitude, for he had constantly, the more so as he improved in facility, to lament a debasement which nature alone had stamped on him.[105]

Plomley[106] concluded: 'The children became little better than slaves, and were retained solely for their usefulness' and rather than assimilating, they had 'merely served to exacerbate relations.'

THE 'SOFT HAND OF CIVILISATION'[107]

Most of the children disappeared and, if they were recalled at all, their sad stories were used to buttress racist stereotypes about Aborigines. However, there were several narratives celebrating what seemed to the colonists to be successes in the 'civilising project' and these were widely discussed amongst them. It was also hoped that the 'success stories' would serve as instructive examples for Aborigines. These circulated in the colony and survived down to the present, although they never achieved the prominence of the narratives of racial extinction built around the lives of William Lanne and Truganini. While we have no record of the feelings of these children or their families, the narratives do provide valuable insights into both the course of their lives and colonial perspectives on their potential to become 'civilised'. They also influenced G A Robinson's 'civilising project', and he in turn helped to shape the narratives through his own writing and work, which would influence the lives of Aboriginal children in Tasmania and the mainland colonies during the nineteenth and twentieth centuries. The fact that, with one exception, the narratives did not have 'happy endings,' their subjects did not go on to lead long and productive lives, seemed to be lost on Robinson and his fellow colonists.

GEORGE VAN DIEMEN

The story of George Van Diemen is essentially that of an 'experiment in civilising' with a 'live specimen' in the 'laboratory' of the educated British middle-class home during the period when the great evangelical and anti-slavery movements swept through Britain. It was hoped that George's experiences would shed light on debates concerning the potential of all races to become civilised. Instead, like most of these children, the outcome was the tragic and early death of the 'subject'.

Born in 1812, Van Diemen was separated from the Big River people near New Norfolk at the age of six when workers found him and his baby brother hidden in the bush near the River Plenty. The baby was sent to a farm to be nursed but died soon afterwards and George was placed in the care of Reverend Knopwood in Hobart and christened and given his European name. In 1821 Governor Sorell agreed to send George to England despite the fact that another boy, William Thomas Derwent, had already died there. Sorell wrote to George's new guardian, William Kermode:

The experiment of instructing and civilising a boy of a race so little known, may attract the attention of some persons in your great liberated and enlightened town. I am happy of the occasion of trying it.[108]

The parties agreed that if the experiment proved successful the boy should complete his education before returning to the colony; if not, then Kermode was to send him back immediately.

From 1822 to 1825 George lived with Mr G Greatbatch of Southport in Lancashire. Greatbatch was a proponent of the popular 'dissenting ministry', and wrote fondly of his 'little sable friend', praising his ability to learn and his affectionate nature and sense of 'gratitude'.[109] In 1826 George was living with John Bradley of Liverpool who was impressed by his skills in arithmetic and his excellent memory, in particular his ability to recite the Psalms. In a statement redolent with the ideals of the Enlightenment, Bradley wrote that the experience had confirmed his opinion:

> That Man is in all parts of the Globe the same. Being a free agent, he may mould himself to excellence, or debase himself below the brutes, & that education, government and established customs are the principal causes of the distinctions among nations ... I believe the blacks will keep pace with the whites, for colour neither impairs the muscles nor enervates the heart.[110]

In November 1826, for an unknown reason, George returned to Van Diemen's Land. Reporting on George's accomplishments, Bradley requested that he be granted 'a portion of the land that gave him birth ... let the Native have what the voice of reason and equity adjudge to him, and not let power supersede this right.'[111] Back in Hobart Governor Arthur sent George to continue his education at Thomas Stone's School — he was to be an example to the other Aborigines. However, he died ten months after his return. He was only fifteen years old.

ROBERT OF MUDDY PLAINS

The narrative of Robert of Muddy Plains was constructed as a story of the success of the experiment of taking young children into colonist households. Robert was born in 1807 and reared from the age of eighteen months to the age of twenty-one in the home of Captain

McAulay of Muddy Plains. In a response to an official circular in 1829 requesting settlers to surrender young Aborigines in their employ to G A Robinson, Robert was described by his guardian as follows:

All that I can say of him is that he has been a faithful and trusty domestic to me and indeed I can with truth say that he is the best servant I have about me therefore I shall part with him with the greatest Regret for having him so very young and for the kind attention he has at all times paid to me I feel a parental regard for him. [Still] should his Excellency the Lt Governor think it right for me to part with him I am willing to comply with His desires.[112]

Robinson found Robert to be 'useful and intelligent'. He spoke excellent English, had 'acquired habits of industry', was capable of performing agricultural labour equal to anyone, was a good boatman and was of 'unreproachable character'.[113] Robinson perceived in the young man the way forward for his civilising project:

When I behold this man and contemplate the improvement which a life spent in social intercourse with rational creatures has accomplished on the rough image of a poor aborigine; when I compare him in his original rough and unhappy state with what he is capable of being when the soft hand of civilisation has lent a polish to his uncourteous mould; when I view him partaking of the same feelings, the same qualities and the same habits as any of us who call ourselves Christians, I no longer doubt the necessity which exists that as many of the aboriginal children as possible should be brought together and by a course of proper discipline taught to imbibe those impressions which through the assistance of Almighty God will ultimately lead to their general conversion.[114]

Robinson planned to use Robert as a 'model of civilisation' and to this end Governor Arthur granted him twenty acres of land on Bruny Island, along with farm implements, a boat, a cart and a bullock:

as an example of industry in one of their own race [which] may perhaps have the effect of gradually involving the Natives who frequent the establishment at Bruny Island to relinquish their wandering habits.[115]

However, Robert did not take up farming and instead accompanied

Robinson on his conciliatory expeditions. He died at the age of twenty-three at Launceston Hospital from the effects of the 'rigours' of one of these arduous expeditions and was given a Christian burial.

KICKERTERPOLLER

The story of Kickerterpoller — also known as Black Tom and Tom Birch — was presented as one of success, failure and redemption. It was the narrative of an Aboriginal man reared by whites who returned to the 'barbarism' of his people, thereby endorsing the view that the 'savage instincts'[116] continued under the thin veneer of civilisation and that environment of itself was not sufficient to bring about permanent change. It is also a tale of an Aboriginal man using skills learned from his white 'benefactors' to fight the colonists, a greatly feared prospect paralleled in other colonies in accounts of the lives of Tjedboro, son of Pemulway in New South Wales, and Jandamarra in the Kimberley.[117] In this instance the young man was finally redeemed and transformed into a faithful and trusty guide working against his own kind for the roving parties — a testimony for the colonists to the power of the civilising process.

Kickerterpoller was born in 1800 into the Poredareme band of the Oyster Bay people. He lived from the age of nine with Thomas Birch, owner of the properties Lovely Banks and Jericho near Richmond. Baptised as Thomas Birch in honour of his benefactor, Kickerterpoller was taught to read and write, became a Christian and spoke English as well as several Aboriginal languages.[118] His guardian described him as:

so good and useful a lad, so obliging and gentle, so honest and careful, and so thoroughly devoted to his master. He spoke English perfectly, and could read and write. In his attendance at church, and general deportment, he gave promise of true civilisation.[119]

At the age of twenty-two Kickerterpoller suddenly left to rejoin his people. Various explanations were put forward at the time for this. His guardian claimed he was enticed away by Musquito,[120] the notorious Sydney Aboriginal bushranger and leader of the Oyster Bay mob during the early 1820s. Others claimed variously that he was lured away by an Aboriginal girl or badly treated by his guardian.[121] Whatever the reason Kickerterpoller soon found that his people had been killed or were off fighting the colonists and he joined up with

Musquito. He was captured soon afterwards and imprisoned at the notorious hellhole, Macquarie Harbour, but managed to escape and for several years engaged in attacks on colonists.

While most colonists resented Kickerterpoller for his perceived betrayal and ingratitude, his few supporters recommended to Governor Arthur that, when captured, he should be attached as a guide to the roving parties. Recaptured in 1828, he was assigned to Gilbert Robertson's roving party and eventually redeemed himself in the eyes of the colonists. Such was Kickerterpoller's standing that Governor Arthur reportedly requested him to act as a negotiator with Aboriginal bands in the bush, to which Kickerterpoller responded, 'No! me like see you tell him yourself; he very soon spear me?'[122]

In August 1829 G A Robinson persuaded Arthur to send Kickerterpoller to Bruny Island as a 'stimulus' for other Aborigines. There he met his wife, Pagerly, of the Nuenone people. However, like Robert, he was then commandeered to join Robinson's expeditions, acting as his interpreter and guide. It seems the two did not always agree and that Kickerterpoller often diplomatically did what he could to help their captives.[123] Nevertheless Robinson gratefully recorded: 'He is a famous interpreter, and this is the stronghold on which I build my chief hopes.'[124] Following a particularly cold and wet expedition in 1832 Kickerterpoller died of dysentery at Emu Bay, just two years after Robert. He was twenty-six.

DOLLY DALRYMPLE

The colonial narrative of the life of Dolly Dalrymple, a revered matriarch and ancestor of many Palawa people, is exploited as an integral part of the tourist lore of Tasmania to this day. This tells of a 'civilised' 'half-caste' woman whose loyalty was to her colonial ancestors, who absorbed colonial ways to the point of fighting against Aborigines, became a devout Christian and, unlike the previous subjects, prospered and reared a large family.

Dolly was born between 1808 and 1810 to George Briggs, a sealer, and Wortemoeteyenner, daughter of Mannarlargenna, the prominent Aboriginal leader of north-western Van Diemen's Land. As a young girl she went to live with Dr Jacob Mountgarrett, by then a prominent landowner in the north.[125] There Dolly was baptised and educated and generally well treated by the family. A visitor described her as:

a fine child, remarkably handsome, of a copper colour, with rosy cheeks, large black eyes, their whites tinged with blue, long well-formed eyelashes, the teeth uncommonly white, the limbs admirably formed.[126]

She left Mountgarrett's at the age of fourteen, and four years later was reported to be living near Deloraine with Thomas Johnson, an ex-convict and stock-keeper, and their two children. In 1831 their home was attacked by Aborigines and, after her daughter was speared in the thigh, Dolly acted quickly to protect her children by firing back while her attackers tried to set fire to the house. This action brought Dolly lasting fame amongst the colonists as well as a reward of eight hectares of land from Governor Arthur.[127] Over the following years Dolly and her husband became owners of a house and two hotels near Latrobe and raised their thirteen children. A devoutly religious woman, Dolly had a hall for church services and a school built nearby. In 1841 she successfully petitioned the Governor to allow her mother to leave Wybalenna and spend her remaining years with her. Dolly died in 1864 aged fifty-two.

BEATING THE SWORD INTO A PLOUGHSHARE AND THE SPEAR INTO A PRUNING HOOK[128]

During the 1830s many of the surviving Aboriginal children in Tasmania experienced further disruption and dislocation, this time to a new way of life in dreary institutions where their lives were regimented and monitored to enforce the civilising goals. This shift to institutional regimes reflected the influence of convict processes of reform, following the arrival of thousands of convicts from 1818 and the upsurge of interest in missionary work with indigenous peoples in all British colonies. There was also Governor Arthur's determination to halt the bloodshed of the Black War and bring about a peaceful settlement and G A Robinson's personal zeal for the enterprise. This same shift occurred in the other colonies, mainly from the late nineteenth century, as governments took over the training of Aboriginal children to turn them into 'useful workers' and to protect them from unscrupulous employers.

Enlightenment ideas of surveillance, control and reform of society arrived in Van Diemen's Land with the convicts. Indeed the colony was essentially a reforming project aimed at transforming a host of petty criminals into 'possessive individualists driven by the belief that through work you could attain well-being.'[129] The project would be accomplished through internalising habits of self-discipline and a commitment to a sedentary way of life, fixed patterns of work as agricultural labourers or small-scale farmers, and a stable family life. Whether in penal institutions or in servitude with the colonists, convicts were subjected to reforming regimes of physical punishment, confinement, surveillance, regulation and indoctrination and, to a lesser extent, rewards and inducements. Citing Robert Van Krieken, K Pearce and S Doyle[130] linked these agendas to the embryonic child welfare system in the colony that was intent on replacing the perceived disorder and promiscuity amongst its young with values of 'discipline, obedience and submission'. These aims were similar to those of missionary civilising projects for indigenous populations that accompanied all British colonial efforts. The upsurge of 'spiritual and humanitarian sentiment' that reached its height in the 1830s hoped to produce:

> obedient, well-behaved, literate Christian Aborigines who would cheerfully accept employment as labourers and kitchen maids, who would marry one another [and] baptise their children.[131]

Officials failed to recognise that most Aborigines saw their own way of life as superior and would not willingly give it up for the colonists' vision of them as lowly menial labourers; they were also slow to realise that Aborigines could not be changed by example or by random efforts with individuals, considering that a whole state apparatus was necessary to enforce change on convicts. Early attempts, such as Macquarie's Native Institution at Parramatta and Smithies Wesleyan School in the Swan River Colony, had to be closed down after parents reclaimed their children. As an alternative Macquarie recommended that 'the few remaining Aborigines — just like the convicts — should be educated in isolation.'[132] To this end punitive and institutionalised regimes were introduced to induce Aborigines to take on the mantle of civilisation. Food was used as a tool to force them to settle down; removing the children served to keep families in line. People could be kept on isolated sites like islands and, from the end of the nineteenth century, legislation backed up by punitive measures enforced Aboriginal compliance.

The model of the isolated, regulated mission settlement guided Governor Arthur in the final stages of his conciliatory mission. With insufficient funds to attract a mission organisation to take on the task and with increasing pressure from his superiors to stop the war that was so impeding colonial progress, Arthur turned to the enthusiastic plans of G A Robinson. This reliance on the agency of the state, rather than voluntary and church organisations, to regulate 'problem populations' was characteristic of the colony throughout the nineteenth century. Arthur was convinced that Aborigines would only be safe on the islands and appeared to believe they would survive there. The fate of captured Aborigines kept on temporary island settlements during the 1820s should have alerted him to what would happen. The short-lived Bruny Island Aboriginal Establishment (1827–29) was a dismal failure plagued by disease, death and the defection of its Aboriginal inmates who refused to remain in 'a place of sickness'.[133] Not everyone agreed with Governor Arthur. Chief Justice John Lewis Pedder argued that the proposal was 'an unchristian attempt to destroy the whole race,' and that the people would pine away when taken from their lands:

> when they found their situation one of hopeless imprisonment, with bounds so narrow as to necessarily deprive them of those habits and customs which are the charms of their savage life.[134]

He advocated instead the approach used with Native Americans where parties negotiated a treaty, the people remained within set geographical boundaries and government representatives resided with them and protected their interests and those of local settlers.[135]

G A Robinson's first-hand knowledge of the terrible Aboriginal death toll should have raised serious questions in his mind about the wisdom of implementing his 'Great Plan'. However, he was a man with a strong belief in his own capacities to succeed where others had failed. Robinson had arrived in the colony in 1824. A devout member of the proselytising Wesleyan Society, he was soon consumed with the zeal to save the Aborigines from destruction and to share with them the 'message of God' and the 'beliefs of British civilisation'.[136] Robinson was a complex and contradictory man. His missionary fervour did not prevent him from investing his work with a strong element of commercialism. Lacking sufficient status and assets to be granted land as a right, he obtained land and cash from the government as a reward for his work with Aborigines and from the bounties paid for their capture. His work also gave him status and access to society otherwise denied to him. He was not a likeable man; pompous and self-promoting he cast himself, as have many other white 'middle men', as the sole authority on the Aborigines and strongly resented any challenges to this view.

In his personal diary Robinson wrote of Aborigines as 'fellow humans suffering grief and loss.' In 1830, after joining them in their anguish on learning of further Aboriginal deaths, he described them as 'Poor unbefriended and hapless people! I imagined myself an aborigine. I looked upon them as brethren, not as they have been maligned, savages.'[137] He also noted the Aborigines' love for their children: 'They are equally fond of their offspring and here the ties of nature must be acknowledged to weigh in a superior degree amongst these unhappy people.'[138] Nevertheless he advocated separation of the children from their parents:

> The evil derived from such a measure is more than counterbalanced by the good. Where children can be safely separated from parents without giving offence to the latter, they should doubtless be placed beneath the threshold and under the auspices of this asylum for the sole purposes of improvement. To the children of these unenlightened creatures we must first direct our whole study and attention ere we can expect to make any sensible progress towards the grand work now in contemplation. They are the main prop upon which our future exertions must rest and the only source from which we can expect to derive any solid advantages. The first stages of life when the habits and ideas are only in the bud and the mind is capable of receiving any impression that is duly enforced, is doubtless the season for inculcation and the only period when precept can be attended with a favourable effect.[139]

Having met with Robert and Kickerterpoller, Robinson was convinced of the children's ability to become 'civilised':

> God has given them the same portion of understanding as ourselves. Their organs of intellect are as capable of improvement, and I am moreover convinced that they would as readily acquire any of those attainments by which human nature is distinguished, provided they enjoyed the means that are necessary for their acquisition. Those who maintain that savages of this country are nearly akin to brutes themselves, or that they possess no faculties in

common with our own species, oppose the arguments to the dictates of humanity and common sense itself. Any man that is not born a fool is capable of becoming wise.[140]

Despite his close observation of Aboriginal life, Robinson, like his contemporaries, seemed to be incapable of discerning the realities of Aboriginal family life and kinship structures. They were obscured by the general absence of features of British middle-class family life. There were 'no fixed abodes, fields or flocks', no observable single family units or familiar gendered divisions of domestic labour. The absence of anything like a 'home' prevented a 'strategy of redemption through the household'[141] as was pursued in missions in Melanesia and Polynesia. Instead, 'radical intervention' in Aboriginal familial relations took the form of separation and placement of children in dormitories.

This then was the context for the establishment of the settlement at Wybalenna, where Aborigines lived in inhospitable conditions far from their homelands and separated from their children. Like other institutions across Australia it would prove 'an impossible exercise'.[142] This was due to the cumulative effects of inadequate funding, resources and staff and Aboriginal disease, death and resistance. Furthermore, while Robinson was determined to make Wybalenna into a self-supporting farming settlement, the Aborigines were equally determined to continue *their* cultural practices.

BRINGING IN THE CHILDREN

More than 180 Aborigines were brought in by the 'Friendly Missions' between 1830 and 1834 when Robinson claimed proudly (and mistakenly) that he had cleared all Aborigines from the colony. Unlike earlier officials, he was most earnest about gathering all the children together and placing them under the care of the state. In 1830 he told Governor Arthur, 'I shall endeavour to possess myself of as many children as I can safely procure, for the purpose of affording them the same advantages.'[143] Given the devastation of the tribes there was little that Aboriginal parents could do to stop this, although the action of the Oyster Bay Aborigines, who sent their children to stay with the more remote Big River Aborigines, suggests an effort to prevent their removal. While Robinson encountered little opposition from colonists to his endeavours to remove children from families still living in the bush, there was resistance from some with Aboriginal children in their 'employ'. This reflected self-interest and reliance on the children as well as ideas about the place of the Aboriginal children in colonial society. A similar conflict between colonists and government was repeated on the Queensland frontier early in the twentieth century.

Two of Robinson's major opponents were Gilbert Robertson and John Batman. Both men were colony-born, cultural 'hybrids' dedicated to the practicalities of carving out a permanent and profitable life in the colony. They believed that Aboriginal children should be trained in colonists' homes to be useful and faithful servants who, as young adults, would marry and reproduce a similar labour force for their masters. In this way Aborigines could be incorporated into a broader colonial framework of caste and class. These views would be echoed around the continent, particularly on the pastoral frontiers of northern Australia. By contrast, Governor Arthur and Robinson stood for Britain, Empire and the forces of civilisation in the colony. They joined British administrators and missionaries in advocating a state-controlled process of 'Christianising and civilising' the children who would grow up to live in segregated, self-supporting communities of their own.

Gilbert Robertson was a well-known personality in the colony. Editor of the *Colonist* and proprietor of the *New Colonist* he was of mixed race and West Indian by birth. He arrived in the colony in 1822, aged twenty-eight, to take up the position of Superintendent of the government farm at New Town. Six years later he was Chief Constable in charge of six roving parties of ten convicts each. He was political anathema to the very British Lady Franklin, wife of the Governor, who described him as 'a perfect miscreant, equally devoid of principle and feeling, a half cast of the West Indies, of great corporeal size and strength and of the most brutal countenance.'[144] He resented Robinson's appointment to lead the 'Friendly Mission' rather than a man of his own experience, and he protested angrily to Governor Arthur when Robinson commandeered the youth, Comentermina (Jack or John Woodburn) from one of his roving parties:

> I conceive that any person taking upon themselves to remove or detain him from me without both his consent and mine being first obtained might with right and justice come to my house and forcibly take away one or all of my children as suited their pleasure.[145]

Robinson interpreted this as an expression of envy at his greater powers and wrote in his journal that Robertson 'was an enemy of mine because he thought I had taken the work out of his hands.'[146] Comentermina died within a few months of arriving at Gun Carriage Island.

John Batman was in many ways Robinson's opposite. The son of a convict and married to a former convict, he was a skilled bushman who came to Van Diemen's Land from New South Wales in 1821 at the age of twenty. He had built up extensive land holdings near Ben Lomond in the northern mountainous areas, land which included grants for rounding up bushrangers and Aborigines.[147] With surveyor Wedge he planned to set up sheep and cattle properties at Port Phillip on the Australian mainland as well. Batman's biographer, James Bonwick, claims that he had friendly relations with Aborigines and showed fondness for the children and concern for the women.[148] Governor Arthur described him as 'one of the few who supposed that they [Aborigines] might be influenced by kindness.'[149] Nevertheless, the roving parties of convicts and Aborigines he brought with him from Sydney had several violent confrontations with local Aborigines, resulting on one occasion in fifteen Aboriginal deaths. They also rounded up considerable numbers to turn over to the authorities for bounty payments.

Batman openly defied Governor Arthur and Robinson by refusing to hand over two Aboriginal boys in his employ: Rolepana[150] (Benny Ben Lomond) and Lurnerminer[151] (John or Jack Allen), captured by Batman in 1828. He claimed that the boys were there with the consent of their parents, Rolepana's father who lived at Wybalenna and Lurnerminer's mother who travelled on Robinson's expeditions. He also demonstrated a strong proprietorial interest in the boys when he told Robinson that they were 'as much his property as his farm and that he had as much right to keep them as the government.'[152] Indeed, Batman was convinced that the best plan was to leave the children with colonists, who clothed and fed them at no expense to the government and raised them to become 'useful members of society'. In a series of letters to Govenor Arthur he 'pleaded hard for the retention of youths educated by settlers, and devoted to their service.'[153] Robinson's response to this opposition was vitriolic and he wrote of Batman in his journal in 1834, 'This is a bad and dangerous character. He married a prison woman. He has recently lost part of his nose from the bad disease.'[154] Batman left Van Diemen's Land for Port Phillip in 1835, accompanied by his wife and six daughters, his English servants, the Sydney Aborigines and the two Tasmanian boys. He made his famous 'treaty' with the Port Phillip Aborigines in the same year.[155] Ironically, after Batman's death in 1837, Rolepana and Lurnerminer went to work for Robinson, then Protector of Aborigines at the Port Phillip Protectorate.[156] Rolepana died there in 1842 and Lurnerminer returned to Tasmania to learn that his parents were dead. He settled at Wybalenna and then at Oyster Cove and died there of asthma in 1864.

Robinson was equally determined to take Aboriginal women and children living with sealers on the Bass Strait islands and between 1830 and 1837 made several expeditions to this effect. This official intervention into 'mixed race' families through the removal of women and children was unique in the Australian colonies at the time, although it would become common practice in all jurisdictions in the next century.[157] In 1830 seventy-four women, including Tasmanian and mainland Aboriginal women and Maori women, were living with sealers on Bass Strait islands.[158] With seals hunted to the point of extinction the seasonal visits of large numbers of men had stopped. The groups of men, women and children who remained earned a small cash income by hunting and selling mutton-bird meat, oil and feathers and wallaby skins in Launceston.[159]

The situation of the women and their responses to the chance of leaving with Robinson were varied. Some, like Emerenna who had lived with sealers from the age of ten and was now in a stable relationship with James Beeton, wanted to remain with the men who had originally forced them to go with them. While Plomley and Henley[160] are at a loss to explain such a preference, it may be that these women had few memories of any other way of life and found emotional fulfilment on the islands with their men. Institutional life at Wybalenna may not have been an appealing alternative and they may have worried over their own and their children's chances of survival there. Most, according to Robinson, were keen to leave and he wrote that their 'joy seemed unbounded and they sang and laughed.'[161]

Robinson was encouraged in his endeavours to bring in the women and children by his Aboriginal companions, in particular Mannarlargenna, who wanted his daughters to join him at Wybalenna; further, his ability to command the loyalty of the men he needed for his expeditions became linked to this outcome. His outrage at the accounts of enforced abductions, sexual and physical abuse, and allegations of abortion and killings of 'mixed race' children, was another impetus. For Robinson and many of his contemporaries, abortion and infanticide signified the violent and lawless life on the islands.[162] The extent to which the women actually practised these traditional methods of population control remains open to speculation. In his analysis of Aboriginal depopulation in eastern Australia, Butlin does link infanticide to 'black rejection of half-caste children' however he describes colonists' frequent reports of infanticide as 'highly prejudiced' and remains undecided as to whether infanticide increased in response to resource loss following white settlement or decreased in order to restore population levels.[163] It is possible that the colonists' preoccupation may have reflected middle-class concern over the extent of these practices amongst the lower classes in Britain and in the colonies. Benjamin Disraeli, novelist and future prime minister of England, had referred to the projection of this concern onto colonised people in his novel *Sybil: Or, the Two Nations*, originally published in 1845.

> Infanticide is practised as extensively and legally in England as it is on the banks of the Ganges; a circumstance which apparently has not yet engaged the attention for the Society for the Propagation of the Gospel in Foreign Parts.[164]

For Robinson, the small number of children he observed on the islands was sufficient proof of the extent of the practice. He explained that:

> Although the Tasmanian women were passionately fond of their children of their own blood, as a rule they detested those they bore to white men and frequently practised infanticide.[165]

Testimonies by some of the Aboriginal women endorsed this interpretation. Drummernerlooner told him in 1830: 'The black women kill them in their belly, beat their belly with their fist. Kill big boys; take them in the bush to kill them, men no see it; men angry.'[166] Others claimed that the sealers encouraged them to 'do these murders,' perhaps to ensure that they continued their work unimpeded.

Given the women's testimony, it seems that abortion and infanticide were practised to a limited extent, however, other factors certainly contributed to the small number of children on the islands. Sterility due to venereal disease was probably not a cause as rates of infection on the islands were reportedly low.[167] It is likely that environmental factors — the harsh rigours of island life, accidental injury and death, a restricted diet and susceptibility to introduced disease — contributed to low rates of fertility and high levels of spontaneous abortion, as well as maternal, infant and child mortality. These in turn produced a pattern of a small number of offspring with only a few couples having significant numbers of surviving children.[168]

Nevertheless, in contrast to the strife-torn Van Diemen's Land, numbers of children on the islands were increasing and an estimated sixty-nine first generation 'half-caste' children were born and survived between 1800 and 1830.[169] Contemporary descriptions of these children suggest a level of physical and mental health not observable amongst the casualties of war on the mainland. In 1828 Rosalie Hare wrote in the journal of her voyage to Circular Head:

I had one sweet little boy (belonging to a fisherman, his mother a native) on board the *Caroline* some days, and a more sensible child (considering he had until within half a year been on a desolate island called Preservation) I never saw in England. He was five years old, very tall and stout, and had black curly hair, his complexion was copper-coloured. He spoke English well. His dress was generally a shirt, pair of trousers buttoned at the knees and little kangaroo skin coat which we never could prevail on him to take off when he slept, nor would he sleep on a bed, preferring a mat on the bare deck.[170]

Robinson's determination to remove the women and children was met by an equally strong refusal by the sealers to part with them. Women were hidden in the bush or taken in boats to Sydney and even Mauritius. The sealers claimed, rather illogically, 'they would not let them go, that the government had no right to them and that they had as much right as the government to them.'[171] The more educated men took direct political action. In 1831 James Munro, spokesperson for the families, arrived in Hobart to put their case to Governor Arthur. He petitioned him for land on Preservation Island and for James Beeton's pregnant wife Emerenna[172] and daughter Lucy to be returned. Six-year-old John Briggs, son of George Briggs and Wortemoeteyenner, who had accompanied Munro, recited verses from the Bible before the Governor to show that children on the islands were being raised as Christians. Arthur and Munro came to an agreement: Munro's men would round up other Aboriginal women as long as their own women were returned. Robinson was incensed by this decision. Not only did it threaten his civilising mission but it seriously undermined his status with the Aboriginal men on Wybalenna, some of whom had already taken up with these women. At the same time it contributed to his sense of grievance and growing conviction that the authorities were working against him.[173] The sealers also took back their children. In 1832 the visiting Quaker missionary, James Backhouse, recorded the following removal of a girl by her father and the mother's grief at her loss:

> In the course of the day a sealer from Gun Carriage came and took away a child that he had by a native woman, now married to a man of her own nation on the settlements; he would not be persuaded to leave the little girl under the care of its mother who was greatly distressed at parting with it.[174]

Robinson's actions had an immediate devastating effect on the island populations. In 1837 only six Tasmanian Aboriginal women, four mainland women and a Maori–Tasmanian Aboriginal woman, along with twelve European men and sixteen children, were still living on Flinders Island and the Furneaux Group islands. Their numbers only began to recover in the 1840s.[175] Most of the women and children removed by Robinson to the settlements died.

INSTITUTIONAL LIFE

By 1835 Robinson had gathered up the majority of Aboriginal children in Van Diemen's Land from their parents and masters and mistresses and from the streets. They were placed in the Orphan School in Hobart, the dormitories at Wybalenna and a few went to work, with the Governor's permission, for prominent colonists. Some experienced all of these placements in a dizzying series of moves. Despite official assurances that Aboriginal culture would be respected, the removal of the children meant that the transmission of traditions was irrevocably disrupted. Subjected to the 'civilising process' in alien institutional settings, children learned the colonists' language, values, beliefs and notions of time, space and work. This further dislocation and separation of the children from their families seriously threatened the future of the Aborigines as a distinct people and culture. It also fanned beliefs that they were a 'dying race'.

COLD, COMFORTLESS AND ILL ARRANGED[176] — THE HOBART ORPHAN SCHOOL

As early as 1832 Governor Arthur approved a plan to remove boys aged between six and nine from Robinson's temporary island settlements to be educated in the Hobart Orphan School or placed in service with approved employers. The boys, Friday and Arthur, who Robinson collected from the streets of Launceston were amongst the first batch to be sent to the orphanage in August 1832.[177] Aboriginal girls and boys continued to be moved in and out of the orphanage over the next forty-seven years. Governor Arthur stipulated that in the case of children living with their families, parental consent for the move was required. The absence of recorded objections by the parents raises the question of why they would agree to this. Plomley[178] suggests they were persuaded both of the benefit of a 'European education' and that the children's 'future lay in an acceptance of European ways of life.' Perhaps they hoped to protect their children from the swathe of deaths on the island settlements. It is more likely that they were offered no real choice. Robinson later wrote that he had promised the Aborigines that their children would not be sent away and that they 'had a strong parental feeling and did not consent willingly to separation from their children.' The parents he encountered at Wybalenna were labouring under 'a mental affliction' from their loss.[179] The deep distress of one mother was evident in an altercation recorded by James Backhouse: 'One of the women on Preservation threw sticks at J Thornlow for mentioning an absent child — a boy at the New Town school.'[180]

The admissions to the Orphan School contrasted with practice in other colonies where children were typically sent to Aboriginal missions. This reflected the lack of missionary interest in Van Diemen's Land. Nevertheless it fitted with the 'civilising project' for Aboriginal children and also saved the expense of providing separate institutions for them. Located in New Town, on the outskirts of Hobart, the Orphan School was opened in 1830 to provide a 'school of industry, where labour as well as learning is taught' and to 'house, feed and educate the many destitute children.' Prior to this, such children were cared for by family friends, neighbours and designated civil officers.[181] From 1844 the Convict Department administered the orphanage and colonists complained that it was little more than 'an asylum or workhouse for lodging, maintaining and educating the children of convicts.'[182] The Orphan School took in children of convict women sent out to work, orphans, destitute or abandoned children and some whose parents were unable to provide for their education and care.[183] Once they were admitted it was difficult to get them back, as parents who negotiated 'temporary' placements in times of crisis soon learned.[184]

While it is impossible to obtain accurate figures due to the nature of the records,[185] it seems that as many as sixty-three Aboriginal children between the ages of three and sixteen were admitted to the orphanage. The majority were official admissions from the island settlements, suggesting a parallel with children of convicts who were officially placed there after arriving in the colony with their mothers or fathers. Aboriginal admissions fluctuated with changing policies on whether children should be accommodated in the orphanage or at Wybalenna.[186] Some were dumped there by guardians or employers who no longer wished to keep them — in 1832 Mrs Harriet Aylwyn admitted nine-year-old Mary Ann Robinson,[187] daughter of Tanganutura (Sarah or Tibb) who had been with her from the age of two.[188] Governor Franklin and his wife left their young charge Mathinna there when they left the colony in 1843. Some children of sealers were also admitted — John Smith requested the admission of his son after his mother was taken to Wybalenna in 1832.

Little is known about the Aboriginal children's experiences at the Orphan School. Certainly they were viewed as different administratively, since their names were recorded in red ink in the registers.[189] Given colonists' attitudes there is every likelihood that they were treated differently as well. For the children, recovering from the trauma of their war experiences, the loss of their families and the enforced separation, fearful of the colonists and coping with cultural and language differences, the dismal institutional life must have been alien and frightening. Conditions were Dickensian. Management was characterised by 'a state of turmoil due to poor management, numerous scandals and the internal machinations of its staff.'[190] The convict servants 'set a bad example' and the managers were little better — there were dismissals for improper conduct, including misappropriation of the children's food, the use of child and convict labour for their own financial interests, brutal punishment of the boys and sexual abuse of the girls.[191] Living conditions for the children were harsh even by contemporary standards; in 1839 the *Colonial Times* described the children's accommodation as:

> Cold, comfortless, and ill arranged upon a most mistaken parsimonious economy ... in one room we saw 5 little fellows blue and shivering with the cold, there was it is true a fireplace in the room, but no fire ... never did we see two hundred human beings, that exhibited so squalid an appearance, as did the majority of the Queen's orphans.[192]

The children washed in chilly stone rooms, the boy's dormitories accommodated eighty each and infants slept three to a bed.[193] The diet was monotonous and far less adequate than that provided at Wybalenna:[194]

> no other food than dry bread and weak tea, morning and evening; and for dinner a mess, made from the miserable quarter pound meat ... one quarter pound vegetables, broken bread and the occasional scraps of broken meat ... stewed together and seasoned with salt. On Sunday they got a suet of pudding extra.[195]

The drab uniforms, moleskins for boys and blue and white patterned dresses with a white pinafore for girls, were indicative of their intended stations in life as cheap servants for the colonists.[196]

The children's health suffered. In an era of general high child mortality, deaths exceeded those in the community outside. In 1835 five Aboriginal boys and three Aboriginal girls died. Epidemics swept through the crowded dormitories and, in 1843, fifty-six inmates died of scarlet fever.[197] In the 1850s mortality rates were eight times higher than for other children in the colony. The children were also reportedly shorter and lighter than those on the 'outside'. In 1848 the superintendent noted the senior boys had many 'bodily and mental infirmities' and some were 'literally Dwarfs for their age.'[198] The quality of education and training for the children was also poor. Religious instruction[199] formed an integral part of their learning, with church, daily prayers and religious instruction two afternoons a week. The monotonous daily routine consisted of rising at six am, spending half a day in school learning basic literacy — with eight classes running in one room — half a day learning a trade, then a brief time for play and back in bed by six pm.[200] In 1848 the Inspector of Schools registered his displeasure with the children's progress — they could not explain 'self-denial' or show on a map where Jamaica was and thought that Van Diemen's Land was in the northern hemisphere.[201] Their 'industrial training' consisted of doing jobs — baking, gardening, sewing and laundry. Staff combined correction, discipline, punishment, cruelty and degradation in their efforts to control and mould the children, who were flogged with whips, canes and even keys, and starved and shamed in front of their peers. The children responded by absconding, by disobedience, insolence and theft, or by withdrawing into themselves.[202] Two Aboriginal boys Joey Tamar and Teddy Flinders ran away repeatedly to the bush and were finally sent to Wybalenna by exasperated officials.[203] From the ages of twelve to eighteen children were sent to work in private homes under legally binding indentures setting out conditions for their proper care. However, there was no system of supervision and the children were 'at the mercy of their masters regarding food, clothing and housing.'[204] Many treated their charges cruelly and, rather than punishing employers, the courts often penalised the rebelling young workers by sending them to gaol or a reformatory.[205] Aboriginal children had also been sent out to work for settlers in this way during the 1830s and 1840s.

In 1878 the orphanage was closed in keeping with the broader shift in official practice in all colonies from institutionalisation of white children to a system of boarding out. However, on the mainland, institutionalisation of Aboriginal children was increasing. The Dickensian conditions at the Hobart Orphan School were mirrored in the Aboriginal children's dormitories operating in most states into the mid twentieth century. We are only beginning to come to terms with the effects of this way of life on Aboriginal children. The inner experience of these children stuck in an alien and debilitating environment can only be imagined. Bonwick[206] described them as 'sickly and depressed, and I wondered not at the terrible mortality that had thinned their numbers.' Nevertheless some managed to achieve even in this dismal atmosphere. In 1834 the school-master reported that the boys in his care showed 'fair intelligence'. Arthur and Friday, two years before 'sunk in the barbarous habits of their race,' had made 'considerable improvement' and could now read and write. He concluded that 'with some exceptions, the aboriginal children were not inferior in capacity to the European children in his charge.'[207] Indeed the boys educated at the Orphan School would emerge as the leaders of the next generation at Wybalenna. However, any sense of stability that the children may have developed was undermined as they were repeatedly shunted between the orphanage and Wybalenna by officials intent on promoting their own agendas of reform. Principal amongst these actors was G A Robinson who, as Commandant of Wybalenna from 1835 to 1839, insisted that the children be returned from the Orphan School to his care.

AN IMPOSSIBLE EXERCISE[208]

In 1835 only one hundred and twenty Aborigines, the bulk of the survivors outside the sealing groups, were still living at Wybalenna. The high death rate had generated a sense of 'general despondency ... so that [the Aborigines] were coming to wonder whether there was any future for them.' They spoke of Wybalenna as 'a place of sickness' and asked their captors 'what, do you mean to stay till all the black men are dead?'[209] Robinson arrived in this scene of tragedy full of optimism, convinced that he would succeed in transforming the fragmented community settlement into a prototype multipurpose institution.

Robinson's 1829 'General Plan' shaped the experiment in civilisation at Wybalenna. Plomley[210] claims that he had only a vague idea of what this meant in practice:

the idea of what made an Englishman and what a Christian were not very clear in his mind. He thought being a good Englishman ... meant living in a house, eating 'civilised' food, keeping himself clean and tidy, and giving up all his native customs; and he thought being a Christian meant an ability to repeat a number of so-called facts of religion and perhaps attain that state of bliss where he could read about these facts for himself in the Bible ... As for the women, Robinson clearly felt that their place was in the home.

Since children were to be 'the spearhead of his work and means of fulfilling his ideas,'[211] he demanded their immediate return from the Orphan School and within a year had eleven children aged from six to fifteen years under his care — Thomas, Davy and Peter Bruney, Adolphus, Teddy, Charley, Thomas Thompson, John Franklin, Bessy, Mary Ann Thompson and Mohonna. Robinson had often commented on the Aborigines' love for their children and he wrote in 1835:

In the course of my visits to the native huts I observed the king Wartenattelargenna and his consort watching with much anxiety their little Eliza, a female child of around 4 years of age who was afflicted in the bowels. They were much concerned and requested me to look at the child and send the doctor. I saw the surgeon afterwards who said that he would see the child, but he imagined it had eaten too much and which was the case. Mrs C [Clark] was much struck with the affection of the parents and the maternal tenderness of the mother and said it would be an example to many white persons.[212]

However, this awareness did not stop him from insisting that the children lived separately from their families.

The 'civilising process' at Wybalenna was haphazard — a confusion of regimentation, neglect, paternal concern and occasional deliberate cruelty that changed, along with the children's place of residence within the settlement and as they were shuffled between Wybalenna and the Orphan School, according to the whims of the settlement superintendents and available funding. Such was the confusion that for a time the only literate children were former inmates of the orphanage. Isolated from the inspectorial gaze of colonists in Hobart and with miserly levels of funding, conditions for the children at Wybalenna were often worse than at the orphanage. A report in 1837 stated that the boys' sleeping quarters in the catechist's cottage were cold and damp and that the girls, who lived with the storekeeper, slept on a wet brick floor. The children were grubby, their clothes tattered and their diet consisted only of flour, sugar and tea with the occasional bowl of soup.[213] No doubt there was some compensation for this dismal way of life for the children — as for the thousands who would follow them into similar institutions around the Australian continent — in the proximity of their parents and elders, and of the bush where they could sometimes lose themselves.

The children followed a monotonous daily timetable intended to grind concepts of time, regularity and order into their minds and bodies:

6.30am   rise and wash
7.00am   prayers and Bible readings with the catechist and his family
7.30am   breakfast with Robinson
8.00am   school starts
12.00   break for lunch and then back to school
3.30pm   free time then tea

6.00pm help the adults at the evening school
8.00pm return to the catechist's house for family worship
9.00pm bed time.[214]

Like other schools in the colony, Wybalenna followed the Bell System of Education.[215] Developed for 'mixed race' children in Madras, India, to produce 'good subjects, good men, good Christians,' this enabled a single teacher to control large numbers of children. More advanced students acted as class monitors and their work was diligently copied and repeated by the rest of the class. Children learned by memorising material and responding to questions in unison.[216] At Wybalenna the monitors included Robinson's sons and children from the Orphan School: Davy and Peter Bruney, Friday (now renamed Walter George Arthur in honour of the Governor), Mary Ann and Bessy. They also taught the adults. Robinson encouraged adult literacy hoping that the Aborigines would learn to read the Bible. However, according to an earlier superintendent their motives were more political — they were learning to write so that they could 'induce' their 'Governor Father in Hobart Town' to return them to 'their native land.'[217] Robinson wrote with pride of his Aboriginal child monitors:

I have seen at the evening school a child of nine years of age, son to Wymarrick ... perched upon the end of a table, teaching in English seven and eight adult aborigines of different tribes their letters and to whom they paid the strictest attention. I have seen a little girl of twelve years of age ... teaching in English her mother and other native women their letters.[218]

The students' progress was tested in oral examinations — which were also propaganda exercises — before settlement staff and invited guests. In 1838 young William Robinson's student Leonidas repeated 'the Lord's Prayer, the Collect, the names of the months and the days of the week, in addition to counting up to one hundred.' Neptune from Charles Robinson's class answered the following theological questions:

What will God do to this world by and by? Burn it.
What did God make us for? His own purpose.
Who are in heaven? God, angels, good men and Christ.
What do you love God for? God gives me everything.[219]

Several men had learned the alphabet and were able to read words of one syllable. The performance by the women and girls was not so impressive, suggesting that less effort was made in their education.

Clara reads — Daphne attempts to read — Emma attempts to read — Rose attempts to spell — Sophia attempts to spell — Sabina, imperfect in the alphabet — Henrietta, imperfect in the alphabet — Lucy, imperfect in the alphabet — and Wild Mary imperfect in the alphabet.[220]

The recorder observed that:

When the examination of the women resumed they appeared very sulky, and it was with some difficulty that they were induced to answer the questions proposed to them ... even the docile and amiable aborigines could stand only a certain amount.[221]

During 1837 the former orphanage boys produced a news sheet, the *Flinders Island Chronicle* with Thomas Bruney as 'Editor and Writer'. Since few Aborigines could read this may have been another exercise in public relations by Robinson to convince authorities that they could be civilised. Here is the *Chronicle*'s prospectus as set out by the young Thomas Bruney:[222]

THE ABORIGINAL
or
FLINDERS ISLAND CHRONICLE

The object of this journal is to promote Christianity, Civilisation, and Learning amongst the Aboriginal inhabitants at Flinders Island. The chronicle professes to be a brief but accurate register of events of the colony, Moral and Religious. This journal will be published weekly on Saturdays, the copies to be in Manuscript written exclusively by the Aborigines, the size half foolscap, and the price twopence. The Profits arising from the Sale of the journal to be divided equally among the writers, which, it is hoped, may induce emulation in writing, excite a desire for useful knowledge and promote Learning Generally. Proof sheets are to be submitted to the commandant for correction before publishing. Persons out of the colony may subscribe.

THOMAS BRUNEY.

In 1838 Robinson introduced training in vocational skills 'to fit [the children] for being useful members in society.'[223] This would become common practice for Aboriginal children's institutions well into the twentieth century. Peter Bruney was apprenticed to the local tailor, Thomas Bruney to the shoemaker and Augustus and Walter George Arthur to the shepherd. The literate graduates of the Orphan School also helped in Robinson's office while the girls worked as domestic servants for the staff and officers. The plan had only limited success since, according to Plomley,[224] the boys did not turn up regularly or apply themselves to their work. It is likely that, as in later programs in Aboriginal institutions, the 'training' was little more than monotonous and menial chores that were of scant interest to the children. Robinson, like others of his ilk before and after, also strove to transform the adults into settled domesticated farmers. There were strong parallels between efforts to 'produce domestic habits' amongst the women and the domestic training programs of the assimilationist drives during the 1950s. In 1834 two white women, hitherto glaringly absent from the record of events at the settlement, were employed to visit the Aboriginal huts each morning to instruct and supervise the women in cleaning, personal hygiene, laundry and sewing.[225] In an effort to introduce adults to practices of capitalism, such as the use of money, Robinson organised a regular market where the residents could buy and sell goods.

Robinson also endeavoured to wean the people from their love of hunting and their dances and ceremonies and already in 1836 had provided them with new European names. However, when he left in 1839 large numbers were still going out hunting, often for weeks at a time, and they continued to make their own traditional implements. Being able to live off the land in this way gave them considerable independence. Prior to Robinson's arrival ceremonies were conducted openly but in response to his opposition they were practised in secret. In other matters they strongly resisted any interference in their affairs, in particular Robinson's efforts to regularise sexual relationships through imposed monogamous marriages. One group of women threatened to take their dogs and go 'into the bush' after Robinson admonished them for not remaining with their 'husbands' and, intimidated by the strength of their response, he deemed it 'prudent not to go to extremities.'[226] The Aborigines strongly resisted orders to carry out chores which they considered were the responsibility of the convicts working at the settlement.

Plomley states this reflected a fundamental misunderstanding:

> The Aborigines had been induced to leave their native land by a promise that all their wants would be supplied and they expected this undertaking to be honoured ... Regular labour was certainly not part of the bargain, though they did not mind helping with odd jobs if they were treated properly.[227]

Reynolds[228] concludes that Aborigines at Wybalenna developed their own mix of Aboriginal and European ways. They were 'adept borrowers', were curious and interested in the new and had 'strategies to avoid those aspects of European life they didn't find appealing.' In short, they decided for themselves which aspects of Robinson's experiment they would take on.

The Aborigines' response was not the only problem frustrating Robinson's civilising project. It was also dogged by fundamental environmental, structural and operational flaws which inevitably undermined his ambitious plans. The climate was conducive to the fatal pulmonary disorders that so affected the adults and children and, due to the poor quality of the land, the geographic isolation and inadequate funding, chronic shortages of food and water resulted in nutritional disorders. The staff were 'inept, quarrelsome, cruel or useless officers who seemed more concerned with their own status than that of their Aboriginal charges,'[229] so that there was considerable dereliction of duty and neglect of Aborigines' needs. Tragically, these features were to characterise Aboriginal institutions around Australia into the mid twentieth century. The Aborigines' frequent resentful and rebellious behaviour towards staff, as well as apathy and despondency, are behaviours typically associated with institutionalisation and these feelings were driven on by the escalating deaths as Quaker surgeon, Dr George Storey, explained:

> The deaths at Flinders Island, and the attempts at civilising the aborigines, were consequent on each other. If left to themselves, to roam as they were wont, and undisturbed, they would have reared more children, and there would have been less mortality. The [move] to Flinders induced or developed an apathetic condition of the constitution, rendering him more susceptible to heats and chills ... inducing a peculiar disease in the thoracic viscera.[230]

During Robinson's period of command between October 1835 and February 1839, there were fifty-nine deaths — including twelve children — sixty-four percent due to pulmonary disease. The only children to be born and survive were Mathinna, Fanny Cochrane and Hannah, daughter of Henrietta.[231]

In 1838 Robinson announced his intention to take up the position of Chief Protector of Aborigines at the Port Phillip Protectorate on the Australian mainland. The deterioration in conditions during his absence on a trip to Sydney should have alerted him to the mayhem that would follow his departure. Staff quarrelled, the children's classes stopped and in desperation the chaplain, Reverend Thomas Dove, proclaimed publicly that the people would never come to anything at Wybalenna and should be distributed amongst the colonists on the Tasmanian mainland.[232] The children were also drawn into the conflicts surrounding Robinson's pending departure. Dove and Robinson quarrelled over the former orphanage girl, Mary Ann Thompson, after Dove smuggled her off the island to work as his wife's servant in Hobart. Robinson's response demonstrated a certain self-interest in the case. While he reported with concern that Dove's action had 'made a great impression on the mind' of Mary Ann's mother Harriet, he also noted his annoyance at the frustration of his own plans to take Mary Ann and her brother Thomas — the grandchildren of the leader Mannarlargenna whose culture he had pledged to respect — to Port Phillip as servants for his own household.[233]

Robinson also demonstrated his sycophantic attitude to colonial authority in his response to the visit of Governor Sir John and Lady Jane Franklin in 1838. Franklin was an explorer and naturalist of repute and he and his wife shared Robinson's interest in the Aborigines. Like Dr Mountgarrett at Risdon Cove in 1804, Lady Franklin acquired both live and dead 'specimens' from her visit.[234] At her request Robinson sent her an Aboriginal skull, the cranium of a man, Christopher, decapitated during post-mortem by the surgeon expressly for her. The man was probably Meterluerparrityer of the Ben Lomond people, formerly described by Robinson as 'a quiet, inoffensive man; a good husband and industrious.'[235] One of the adult students at Wybalenna in 1837, he was 'perfect in the alphabet' and to the question from his examiner: 'What must we do to be saved?' gave the answer, tragic in hindsight, 'Believe in the Lord Jesus Christ.'[236] Although Robinson was generally loth to let go of what he regarded as 'his children', he agreed to send two of them to live at Government House. Timme-menedic

(Adolphus), born in 1827 and captured at the age of six on the west coast, was escorted to his new home by the eminent natural scientist and publisher, John Gould and his wife. Robinson informed Lady Franklin that the boy was:

> somewhat volatile in disposition on which account his studies should not be prolix and I would recommend persuasion before coercion at the same time he should be kept under command … Active and athletic exercises would be conducive to health.[237]

Timme-menedic was set to work as a groom in the Governor's stables and was then apprenticed as a seaman on the government vessel the *Vansittart*. As a young man he signed on with a government ship and set sail for England, and nothing further is known of him.[238]

A portrait of young Mathinna at Government House in Hobart by Thomas Bock, 1842.
(Courtesy of Tasmanian Museum and Art Gallery, AG 290)

Mathinna, the five-year-old daughter of Wongerneep and Towterer ('Chief' of the Port Davey people, who died at Wybalenna in 1837) was also sent to Government House. In the following year her mother died. Mathinna appears to have been treated as an exotic 'pet' by the childless Lady Franklin. Contemporary descriptions of Mathinna — clad in red with her pet possum draped around her neck driving past in the Governor's carriage — were redolent of images of black slaves in the courtly surrounds of their masters. The following description of the contents of Lady Franklin's 'famous sanctum' at Government House suggests Mathinna's central place in her ladyship's scientific collection as well as the compatibility between 'collecting and domesticity'[239] at the time:

> snales [sic], toads, stuffed birds and animals, weapons of savagery, specimens of wood and stone fossils, and last but not least, a

juvenile lubra in bright scarlet being the staple articles of furniture.[240]

Mathinna's grief on being abandoned by the Franklins on their return to England was later described in the Hobart *Mercury*:

> Poor Mathinna was transferred sobbing and broken-hearted, from the tender care of one who had always proved far more than a mother to her, and the luxury and grandeur of government house, to a cold stretcher in the dormitory of the Queen's Asylum. She soon fell sick and was taken to a bed in the Hospital, she had no friends.[241]

Robinson not only failed to fulfil his verbal treaty with the Aborigines he had gathered together at Wybalenna, he then abandoned them to their fate while he pursued his own ambitions. He also robbed the establishment of fifteen of its most able residents who he took to Port Phillip as his personal attendants, including Pevay, Robert Timmy, Jemmy Smallboy, Jack Napoleon, Timninapareway, Truganini, Pagerly, Walter Arthur and his wife Mary Ann.[242] Once at Port Phillip, Robinson largely abandoned them to their fate. Most found work — Walter Arthur worked as a stockman on overland trips to Adelaide. However, Robert Timmy and Pevay[243] became the first men to be hanged in the new colony after a campaign of terror around Dandenong and Westernport, which ended in the revenge killing of two whalers alleged to have taken Truganini's sisters or to have killed her promised husband. Only five of the original party returned to Wybalenna. With the exception of Thomas Thompson, 'half-caste' son of Harriet (Watty), who may have stayed in Victoria, the remainder were dead.[244] In 1849 the Port Phillip Protectorate was abolished and three years later a financially comfortable and recently widowed George Augustus Robinson returned to England. In 1853 he married the daughter of a successful English artist and toured Europe for five years, eventually settling in Bath in 1859 where he died in 1866 at the age of seventy-eight.[245]

PENSIONERS OF THE STATE[246]

Robinson's departure from Wybalenna coincided with significant policy changes initiated by Governor Franklin which left the people there as little more than 'pensioners of the State.' From this time until its closure in 1847 conditions at Wybalenna were characterised by increasing staff incompetence and conflict, a bewildering change of commandants and other staff, Aboriginal deaths, and deteriorating conditions caused by an ever-dwindling budget. There was also evidence of a new assertiveness amongst the next generation of Aboriginal residents.

The new commandant, Malcolm Laing Smith (1839–41), formerly Police Magistrate at New Norfolk Plains, had none of Robinson's sympathy or understanding. He saw the people simply as 'a cheap source of labour' to develop the land he planned to lease on the other side of the island.[247] While in Robinson's time contact between residents and the sealing families was prohibited, now there was increased contact with sealer families and some of the men were employed at Wybalenna and even married Aboriginal women there. In 1839 a government inquiry concluded that the Aborigines were not responding to civilising influences and appeared to be 'doomed to extinction.'[248] A further inquiry two years later described Wybalenna as little more than 'a home for the indigent' with fifty-nine colonists caring for a like number of Aborigines: twenty-one men, twenty-three women and thirteen children.[249] Plomley notes that from this time any spending on Aborigines at Wybalenna was 'begrudged, it being held that the more quickly they died the better for the government purse.'[250]

Efforts to civilise the children had ceased with Robinson's departure. They now lived with their parents or soldiers and convicts employed at Wybalenna. In 1840 Reverend Dove reported that children with their parents experienced 'vitiating and debasing influences and were not controlled at all' while the others suffered 'incapacity and moral corruption.' To stop their 'moral and intellectual debasement' he recommended that they be placed in dormitories under his immediate control with a special fund to provide inducements for them to learn.[251] Dove viewed the parents' feelings for their children as 'more of the nature of an instinct than a principle' and therefore 'directed to no high or worthy end.'[252] An inquiry in 1841 recommended that the three orphans and other children of school age at Wybalenna should be sent to the Orphan School in Hobart.[253] The new Commandant, Dr Peter Fisher, formerly medical supervisor of convict hulks in England,[254] reported that parents were opposed to the plan but that he was determined to 'induce every willingness' on their part 'by explaining the advantages of the measure.' He added that no one would say it was preferable 'to bring up the children, some of them half-caste — in the wild habits of the Aborigines — to giving them the advantage of a civilised education.'[255] Implicit in this singling out of 'half-caste' children — presumably because of their British inheritance — is a reflection of emerging theories of race mixing. This view would become a major rationale for removal of children of Aborigines throughout Australia for the next hundred years. Eight children were subsequently sent to the Orphan School in the hope that they would 'lose their Aboriginal identity.'[256] Over the next six years children continued to be moved backwards and forwards between the orphanage and Wybalenna.

In 1842 the last family group to come out of the bush, a couple and their five sons, arrived at Wybalenna. Five years later all were dead save the youngest, William Lanne. He was destined to become the 'last' male Tasmanian Aborigine. In the same year Walter Arthur, his wife Mary Ann, Truganini, John Allen and David Bruney arrived back from Port Phillip. They were to became thorns in the side of the newly appointed Commandant, Dr Henry Jeanneret, formerly catechist at Point Puer at the Port Arthur penal establishment.[257] Jeanneret was determined to restore strict control and to halt increasing conflicts between factions of staff and Aborigines. In mid-1842 a further six children were sent off to the Orphan School despite the protests of their parents, who were concerned at the number of deaths there.[258] At the request of her parents and with the Governor's approval, Fanny Cochrane was sent to the Hobart home of the former catechist at Wybalenna, Robert Clark. He agreed to 'Feed, Clothe and Educate the child as I do my own'; however, ten months later she was returned to Flinders Island due to 'domestic matters'.[259]

From this time escalating conflict at Wybalenna engulfed all residents, including the children still living there. In late 1843 Jeanneret was dismissed from his post on the grounds of incompetent medical treatment of a soldier on the island. The Aborigines, who resented his heavy-handed management of the settlement, breathed a collective sigh of relief. He was replaced by surgeon Dr James Milligan, formerly attached to the Van Diemen's Land Company at Circular Head. Milligan arrived at the island with three children from the Orphan School.[260] In February 1844 Robert Clark, dismissed for incompetence five years earlier, was reinstated. Then the people at Wybalenna heard that Jeanneret was also to be reinstated, following his successful appeal to the Home Office against his dismissal. This was the final straw. In

February 1846 twenty-six-year-old Walter Arthur and his companions[261] forwarded a petition to Queen Victoria in an effort to prevent Jeanneret's return. The petition listed a host of grievances against his treatment of the people at Wybalenna. More significantly it also provided, as Henry Reynolds points out, 'the most important Aboriginal historical interpretation available for the colonial period anywhere in Australia.'[262]

Essentially, the petition argued that the Aborigines at Wybalenna were 'free people' who, after a protracted guerilla war, had negotiated a settlement, the terms of which were fresh in their minds. They had met their part of the agreement and expected the colonial government to do likewise. In short, they had rights that the government was duty bound to honour; they were not captives deserving only of scraps of charity. Reynolds interprets the petition as an instance of astute Aboriginal political agency. With its potential to propel the powerful humanitarian and missionary societies in Britain into action, it forced the British government to dismiss Jeanneret for a second time and influenced its decision to abandon Wybalenna, although the latter was not an outcome intended by Arthur.

Walter Arthur, at the centre of the petition, could be considered the culmination of Robinson's civilising dreams. From another perspective his story is a 'postmodern' narrative of personal reinvention and hybridity, of a man constantly changing himself in response to new challenges in his environment. Born in 1820 in the Ben Lomond tribe he became separated from his people and ended up as Friday, working on the streets of Launceston for convicts and other criminals. Removed to Wybalenna by Robinson he then lived at the Orphan School for two-and-a-half years from 1832 and was one of the boys commended for their abilities in learning. When Robinson took over as Commandant Arthur was returned to Wybalenna. There he assisted with religious services and taught in the school and, along with the other Orphan School boys, encouraged a 'Christian decorum' amongst his fellow residents.[263] His companion Thomas Bruney wrote in the *Flinders Island Chronicle* in 1838:

My friends, who was it wrote the ten Commandments? ... It was God that wrote those ten Commandments ... and there is ten of them which we must obey. It is certain that we must obey these laws. These are the laws which the Israelites obeyed, which they had obeyed in the wilderness.[264]

In 1838 Arthur married Mary Ann and in the following year the couple accompanied Robinson to Port Phillip. On their return Arthur emerged as an unofficial leader in the fight against the tyrannical rule of Dr Jeanneret. For his part Jeanneret saw Arthur as a bad influence on his 'more peaceable countrymen,' with the capacity to 'excite them to riot, and set [to] naught the authorities.'[265] Arthur was not simply a blank slate transformed by the civilising process — he was able to successfully synthesise Christianity and education with his Aboriginal identity. Reynolds[266] contrasts him with John Bungaree in the colony of New South Wales who publicly expressed his hatred of his Aboriginal legacy, and suggests that Arthur represents something different and 'more challenging' than Bungaree and Truganini: the death of both the 'primitive past' and the 'transcendence of colonisation'. Arthur's career 'pointed the way to the possibilities of the future rather than the past, the politics of rights rather than those of guilt.'

The interval between the posting of the petition and the dismissal of Jeanneret was a stressful time at Wybalenna. In June 1846 Mary Ann Arthur wrote to the Colonial Secretary to complain about Jeanneret's behaviour towards them:

> Dr. Jeanneret wants to make out my husband & myself very bad wicked people & talks plenty about putting us in jail & that he will hang us for helping to write the petition to the Queen from our country people. Dr Jeanneret does not like us for we do not like to be his slaves nor wish our poor Country to be treated badly or made slaves of.[267]

Mary Ann's letter had little effect and Jeanneret had Arthur imprisoned illegally in an effort to force him to renounce the petition. Jeanneret then accused Clark of mistreating the children and suspended him from duties.[268] The children who had been living with Clark were sent home to their parents. In March 1847 Jeanneret forwarded to the newly appointed Governor, Sir William Denison, a statement signed by the majority of the parents[269] listing cruelties allegedly perpetrated against the children by Clark. In the same month he reported that there were only forty-seven Aborigines at Wybalenna and five young 'half-castes', and that the children were in better health after being removed from Clark's cruelties. Plomley[270] suggests their improved health was probably due to the 'freedom of living with their parents.' The colonial government finally lost patience with Jeanneret

— Governor Denison himself described him as mad — and he was dismissed in May 1847. Clark resumed his duties and Milligan was reappointed as Commandant. However Jeanneret would not go quietly and he caused further havoc during the handover period.[271]

This sustained and intense conflict shows the dissolution of colonial authority at Wybalenna. It was probably also an outcome of the growing independence and assertiveness amongst the Aborigines there, influenced by a new young leadership with considerable experience and understanding of the colonists. While this conflict no doubt had detrimental effects on the children caught up in the crossfire, a positive outcome was that some were able to move home to their families. It is interesting to speculate how differently events may have turned out in Wybalenna had the children remained together in the establishment with their families and elders and the people permitted freedom of contact with the sealing community and the Tasmanian mainland. It might have seen the regeneration of the Tasmanian Aboriginal people and their culture which had to wait another century. Instead, once again the children were to be rounded up, sent far away from the islands and split up from each other. Indeed, around the Australian continent mission doors were being slammed shut and Aborigines abandoned to their fate.

WE HAD SOULS IN FLINDERS ... BUT WE HAVE NONE HERE[272]

By August 1847 arrangements were under way to move the Aborigines from Wybalenna to the site of a former female penitentiary at Oyster Cove that was closer to official supervision from Hobart and more economical to service. Milligan remained in charge with Clark as Catechist and Assistant Superintendent.[273] Forty-six Aborigines arrived at Oyster Cove in October — fourteen men, twenty-two women, five boys and five girls. Governor Denison ordered the immediate removal of the children to the Orphan School or to employment, under the same proviso as Governor Arthur — where it could be 'managed without in any way offending their parents.' The younger children — Moriarty, Adam aged seven, Billy Lanne aged eight, Hannah aged seven, Nannie aged ten, Martha aged twelve and Mathinna also aged twelve — were bundled off to the Orphan School. The eldest boy, Charley, was apprenticed to a farmer while George, the youngest, went to live with Mary Ann and Walter Arthur along with Mary Ann's sister, Fanny Cochrane, who was 'almost a woman'.[274] The intention was in part to send them away from persons who made them 'the unconscious instruments of fighting out their misunderstandings and criminations against each other.'[275] More importantly, they were to be trained to become part of the colonial society rather than a segregated Aboriginal community. In a statement, the sentiments of which would be repeated by administrators into the twentieth century, Denison wrote that the children would acquire:

> such a degree of education and useful training as may fit them for a residence amongst a community of Europeans here, after which the elder of the Aborigines are died off and the Aboriginal establishment necessarily closed.[276]

Thus Denison heralded the demise of the people. The elderly would die and the children would be cast adrift and eventually disappear into the wider colonial society. By positioning the adults as old and close to death when in fact their ages ranged from twenty-one to forty-eight,[277] Denison not only reflected the 'doomed race' theory — rapidly becoming the dominant discourse about Tasmanian Aborigines at the time — but also provided a justification for minimal expenditure at Oyster Cove. Why invest in institutional supports and services when the people were on the brink of extermination?

Governor Denison took a personal interest in the fate of the Aborigines. He wrote at the time, 'I felt it was due to the former owners of the soil that they should be carefully tended and kindly treated.'[278] He was also concerned about colonists' opinion and, when they expressed fears that the Aborigines would rampage across the country causing death and destruction, he assured them that they were now 'harmless creatures'. He visited the children at the Orphan School on several occasions and invited them with their parents to a Christmas party at his New Norfolk

'Tasmanian Aboriginals, Oyster Cove: "The Last of the Race"' From left to right — back: Tippo, Flora, Sophia; middle: Caroline, Bessy Clarke, Emma; front: Truganini, Patty, Wapperty.
(Courtesy of Mitchell Library, State Library of New South Wales)

123

residence where they were paraded as 'curiosities, the last specimens of a nearly extinct race'.[279]

After Denison's departure in 1855 — which coincided with the granting of self-government to the colony — Aboriginal policy was guided by the principles of 'minimal expenditure and neglect in the hope that [the Aborigines] would die out.'[280] Within the year expenditure was slashed by half. In a directive to be repeated in Victoria thirty years later, all 'able-bodied' people of mixed descent were instructed to leave and make their own way in the wider society. Aboriginal residents were also encouraged to find work locally. Mary Ann and Walter Arthur moved onto a fifteen acre grant adjacent to the Oyster Cove establishment and in 1856 petitioned the Governor for 'a Passholder Servant man, subject to existing regulations' to assist with farming the land.[281] The application was rejected. They were also employed at the Oyster Cove establishment and in 1859 Walter worked on a whaling ship for eighteen months. Three years later he drowned in the River Derwent when he fell from a boat on his way from Hobart to Oyster Cove.[282] In 1866 Mary Ann remarried a colonist, Adam Booker.

What happened to the children? In 1848 Fanny Cochrane was in service with the Dandridge family but was sent back to Oyster Cove for misbehaviour. In 1854 she married a local colonist, William Smith, and when she moved off the settlement was granted an annuity of twenty-four pounds, a sum made available for her support because she was Aboriginal. Nannie died at the Orphan School from inflammation of the lungs in 1849. Martha returned to Oyster Cove at the end of 1849 after repeated requests from her ageing parents for her return. She died in 1851, a year after her mother. In 1850 Hannah was placed in service on Flinders Island with Dr Smith, the former Superintendent at Wybalenna, and then disappeared from the records. Mathinna returned to Oyster Cove from the orphanage in 1851 and died in tragic circumstances some time later. The Hobart *Mercury* later luridly recounted her last moments:

> Too soon alas! She fell into the habits of the rest ... One night, however, Mathinna was missing; and although cooey after cooey resounded ... no tidings were heard of the lost girl. In the morning the search was continued, till at length the wanderer was found. The little wild girl, with the shell necklace, and the pet opossum — the scarlet coated, bare-headed beauty in the carriage — the protegee of

the noblewoman — the reclaimed daughter of a great Tasmanian chief, had died, abandoned by every virtue and drunk, in the river.

Moriarty died in 1852 at the Orphan School of inflammation of the lungs. Billy Lanne and Adam were discharged from the orphanage early in 1853 at Milligan's insistence, perhaps because he needed them to work for him at Oyster Cove. The Orphan School records described Adam as lively and 'quick of apprehension but mischievous' and Billy as 'obtuse but quiet and well behaved' and difficult to employ due to a 'natural obstinacy' — characteristics typically associated with institutionalisation. Both were apprenticed to a whaling ship in 1855. Adam later went to live with his half sister Fanny near Hamilton and died in 1857 at North West Bay. Billy regularly visited Walter and Mary Ann Arthur and spent his time between whaling ships and Oyster Cove where the old women fussed over him and called him a 'fine young man — plenty beard — plenty laugh — very good, that fellow,' and he in turn took care to protect their interests.[283] Billy Lanne died alone in Hobart in 1868. He was in his early thirties. In one more shameful episode of our colonial history his grave and body were desecrated in a fight for the skull and bones of the man known as the 'last male Tasmanian Aboriginal' — a valuable addition to a collector's cabinet or a scientist's laboratory.[284]

The twenty years of the Oyster Cove establishment constitute a dreary and disheartening chronicle of neglect, inadequate medical treatment and death, interpersonal conflict, pilfering by staff and Aboriginal resistance to authority. Proximity to white settlement brought further problems of sexual abuse of the women, open resentment and racism and a voyeuristic interest in the Aborigines' fate. Their despondency and sense of hopelessness were often relieved through the oblivion of alcohol. When Robinson visited in 1851 the people told him they wanted to return to Wybalenna as Oyster Cove was too unhealthy.[285] By 1869 so few were left that the government decided to close the establishment and subdivide the land. Mary Ann Arthur and Truganini were sent to stay with the Dandridges nearby. Mary Ann died there in 1871. Two years later the Dandridges moved with Truganini to Hobart. She died there in 1876 aged sixty-three.

With Truganini's death the fiction of the extinction of the Tasmanian Aborigines became firmly embedded in colonial consciousness. This suited the colonists' purposes, endorsing their claim to full entitlement to the land. At the same time they ignored the existence of the Aborigines' descendants and even denied their right to claim Aboriginal identity. Descendants of sealers and Aboriginal women on the Bass Strait islands were called 'islanders', rarely Aborigines or even 'half-castes'. This reflected nineteenth-century views of races as discrete entities or even species, so that 'mixed race' progeny were considered distinct from their 'pure race' ancestors.[286] A strange public debate, that centred on whether Fanny Cochrane Smith was Aboriginal and therefore entitled to receive her government annuity, provides insights into the political and economic significance of these positions. The side claiming that Fanny was not Aboriginal drew on a theory promulgated by Polish scientist and explorer Count Paul Strzelecki, who visited Van Diemen's Land in 1845. Endorsed by several international scientists, who claimed it as a 'law of nature,' the theory stated that once Aboriginal women had borne children to white men they could no longer give birth to children of Aboriginal men. Thus, since Fanny Cochrane Smith's mother, Tanganutura, had lived with sealers and borne children to them prior to her marriage to Nicermeric at Wybalenna, she could not have conceived a child with him and therefore Fanny's father must have been white. This view was opposed by critics of Strzelecki who believed that Fanny's parents were both Aboriginal and that *she*, not Truganini, was the 'last Tasmanian Aboriginal'.[287] Such an assertion seriously threatened the myth of a sterile dying race which could not adapt to British civilisation and which left no descendants. It is hardly surprising then that the myth of a barren Truganini — and even this is doubtful since it is now claimed that she had at least one child[288] — took precedence over that of a fecund Fanny Cochrane Smith.

MORE THAN A FEW 'EXTINCT' PEOPLES HAVE RETURNED TO HAUNT THE WESTERN IMAGINATION[289]

Of course the Tasmanian Aborigines were not extinct. Despite Robinson's determined efforts, small groups of white men and Aboriginal women and their children continued to live on the islands which they now looked on as home. Although the Aboriginality of their offspring was officially denied, the families followed a lifestyle which reflected a mixture of Aboriginal and European traditions — hunting and gathering food and trade goods, using Aboriginal remedies for illness and wounds, following a mixture of Aboriginal and Christian spiritual beliefs, running stock and gardens, building their own boats which they sailed between the islands, and entering into legal marriages and baptising their children. While some colonists saw the islanders as 'hale, rubicund fellows, hearty and joyous' and their children as 'sharp and intelligent',[290] others, recalling the former lawlessness of the islands, wished for their decline to 'remove the stigma of the disastrous conflict between black and white.'[291] However, despite hardships, their numbers steadily increased over the last half of the century[292] while populations in the institutions dwindled and died. A description from 1848 — 'the children by a European father and native mother are really handsome ... with rosy cheeks ... fine teeth, well-proportioned heads, and robust limbs'[293] — suggests a healthy generation of children on the islands.

Over the century the islanders' economic vulnerability grew as their land bases were increasingly threatened and their semi-nomadic hunting lifestyle came into conflict with agriculture and pastoralism. They also encountered government pressure, similar to that faced by Aborigines at Wybalenna, to take on a settled agricultural way of life. This, together with government refusal to provide adequate services for the families, left the islanders locked into a precarious life of harsh poverty, open to accusations of failing to care for their children and susceptible to the removal of their children by colonial authorities on the grounds of neglect. Some families made concerted efforts to obtain secure landholdings and services such as education for their children so they could continue their way of life. They believed they had a strong claim to the land.

Like their mothers, the daughters of the sealers and Aboriginal women were essential to the survival of the island communities keeping house and caring for the children, hunting and working on the boats used in sealing, fishing and for transport around the islands, and striving for improvements in their way of life.[294] Mary Ann Proctor, daughter of Pleenperenna and sister of Nancy Smith, applied for land on the basis of her Aboriginality, perhaps inspired by the example of G A Robinson's protege, Robert of Muddy Plains, who was granted land on Bruny Island. Her application was rejected on Robinson's advice that, since her father was white, she was not Aboriginal and the government was therefore under no obligation to help her. However, an application by her Aboriginal mother in 1837 to lease Gun Carriage Island was also rejected. Strong representations were made to the government by the families from 1846 as land on the islands was increasingly leased to colonists — amongst them Robinson's daugher and her husband — for sheep raising and farming.

The families also began to lobby for schools for their children. In the early days some children were taught by the sealer Thomas Tucker, an educated man who Jeanneret employed for a time at Wybalenna as 'dispenser, overseer, schoolmaster'. He later settled on Gun Carriage Island with his two Aboriginal wives. There he taught Lucy Beeton who was sent in 1843 to Launceston for further education. Lucy Beeton became a champion of schooling for the island children and demonstrated a strong commitment to maintaining a distinct island population. Her invitation to Truganini in 1872 to spend her remaining days on the islands with the Beetons also suggests a strong concern about the fate of the Tasmanian Aboriginal people generally. From the 1850s the Church of England took an interest in the families and played an intermediary advisory role between them and the government. This included successfully lobbying for the leasing of Badger Island to the Beeton family in 1857.[295] The Launceston parish's support for Lucy Beeton's petition to Governor Denison for a missionary teacher was less successful — it was refused as the island families were deemed not to be Aborigines. Beeton then set up a school and taught the children herself. The school was moved to Badger Island following the granting of the lease and she taught there for the next ten years. Following the death of her father in 1867 Beeton took on the family business and the school was closed. It was not until 1871, three years after the introduction of compulsory education in Tasmania, that two government teachers were appointed at Badger and Cape Barren islands with an enrolment of over sixty students, the majority Aboriginal.

As increasing white settlement forced the islanders out of their hunting grounds and destroyed many of the mutton-bird rookeries on which they depended for their livelihood, they were forced to look for new ways to survive. On Cape Barren Island they could apply for ninety-nine-year lease blocks and there was still some protection for mutton-birds. In 1881 a reserve of 6000 acres was gazetted for their use. There now began a new phase of outside intervention in their lives as they became the focus of a civilising agenda endorsed by the government and the church; this in spite of the following exceptional comment by the Anglican Bishop Montgomery in 1885:

Here are a fine sturdy independent race of men, rapidly increasing in numbers, the descendants of the Aboriginal inhabitants of Tasmania, to whom surely there is a great debt still owing.[296]

The families were to be rounded up, centralised in a small village on the reserve and turned into settled farmers, although they were skilled sailors and hunters. Since they needed a secure land base and access to mutton-birds and the sea, they had little choice but to accept. By 1896 the Cape Barren Island settlement had a population of 100 and its own post office, school and church. A period of even stricter control and enforced change now began, especially through the broad range of duties assigned to the schoolteacher who, with the police, represented the government on the island. Matters came to a head in 1895 when the teacher, Edward Stephens, fired over the heads of a group of islanders and threatened to 'shoot all the half-castes or any other castes, be damned if he wouldn't.'[297] Following his resignation the islanders sought to regain control over their affairs by forming their own association and printing their own newspaper. These initiatives were actively opposed by both government and church and soon collapsed. The situation deteriorated further: licence fees and controls over egg collection made mutton-birding less profitable and the rift between islanders and the church widened as its representatives continued their campaign to pressure the families to abandon communal living, hunting and seasonal work.

At the end of the century Tasmanians remained uncertain about how to classify the islanders. Reflecting contemporary stereotypes of Aborigines, Edward Stephens wrote that 'civilisation was irksome to them if not offensive … They are very improvident.' At the same time he denied their Tasmanian Aboriginal ancestry, acknowledging only the European, Maori and mainland Aboriginal legacy.[298] As the twentieth century progressed this ambiguity continued. Some referred to the islanders as 'half-castes' but, like Stephens, made no reference to their Tasmanian ancestry; others referred to them as islanders — a 'problem' community whose difficulties mirrored those of

Aboriginal residents of Cape Barren Island, 1911.
(Courtesy of Tasmanian Museum and Art Gallery, Q4430)

depressed communities everywhere. With their perilous economic situation and distinct cultural practices they constantly faced the prospect of accusations that they were neglecting their children and the very real threat of government intervention to 'rescue' them through removal to the Tasmanian mainland. Effectively, however, the entire Aboriginal community on the islands, like Aborigines on the Australian mainland, had been 'neglected' by government inaction and entrenched opposition to their efforts to survive and maintain their way of life. It was this neglect which created the potential for repeated removals of their children under the guise of being 'neglected' — a short-term cheaper solution than taking action to assist the community as a whole — and a continuation of nineteenth-century 'civilising' agendas to crush this different way of life and to absorb Aboriginal children into colonial society.

In summary, this chapter has foregrounded the experiences of Aboriginal children in the colonial history of Tasmania, their sufferings during the Tasmanian wars, abductions and virtual enslavement by uncaring masters, enforced separation from their people, their lonely lives in drab institutions, their ambiguous status in colonial society as they grew up and their early and often lonely deaths. There are other stories, of children surviving with their families in the harsh conditions of the Bass Strait islands and remote parts of the Tasmanian mainland, the ancestors of today's Palawa communities. What emerges is the central place of child removal in the Aboriginal experience of colonisation. Children were removed from earliest contacts and the practice continued on throughout the nineteenth century, sanctioned in various ways by colonial authorities and eventually taken over by them. Child removal was an integral part of the destructive forces of invasion and colonisation in Tasmania and the Australian mainland. It not only ruptured the transmission of culture and broke the children's connection to their traditional lands but it also effectively ensured the decline in size of Aboriginal populations. Authorities must have been aware of these disastrous consequences of child removal for the parent populations. Both the Aborigines and the colonists needed the children to meet their respective goals: the Tasmanian Aborigines needed them to ensure their survival as a sovereign people; the colonists to circumvent this outcome. Possession of the children indicated ownership of the future.

CHAPTER THREE

OF CITIZENS AND OUTCASTS

If you would openly admit that the purpose of your Aboriginal
Legislation has been, and is now, to exterminate the Aborigines so
completely so that not a trace of them or of their descendants
remains, we could describe you as brutal, but honest. But you dare
not admit openly that what you hope and wish for is our death! You
hypocritically claim that you are trying to 'protect' us; but your
modern policy of 'protection' (so-called) is killing us off just as
surely as the pioneer policy of giving us poisoned damper and
shooting us down like dingoes!

Aborigines Claim Citizen Rights, 1938[1]

Despite the upheavals of the 1890s economic depression, many
Australians entered the twentieth century with a new sense of
nationhood, dreams of economic prosperity and the trappings of
modern family life. Aboriginal Australians, however, faced a bleak
future of ongoing poverty and exclusion and escalating government
control and repression. Official policies actively encouraging the
removal and institutionalisation of 'mixed race' children threatened the
very survival of many families. This contrasted starkly with
government initiatives to forge a nation of efficient white citizens by
advocating and encouraging the intact family unit.

Why was this so? During the nineteenth century Aborigines had
posed mainly a physical impediment to the project of continental
colonisation. Now reduced to a 'remnant' population they fitted the
profile of a 'conquered people' and appeared to no longer present an
obstacle to official claims to the land and its resources. However, they
were anathema to the country's new modernising and nationalising
project. There was no place for them in the emerging Australian

nation. Instead, they were to be swept out of sight into remote 'gulags' or their 'mixed race' children absorbed into the lowest rungs of the colonial work force or kept permanently in segregated institutions.

Political, economic and humanitarian interests drove the move towards the exclusion of Aborigines from the rights and responsibilities of citizenship that were extended to other Australians and their inclusion under discriminatory bureaucratic regimes. Racial theories endorsed the view that they were incapable of becoming modern citizens and fanned fears of an internal racial threat in a desired White Australia. Existing colonial practice in dealing with indigenous and other 'problem' populations showed the way forward. Operating under the rubric of 'protection,' state and federal governments created expanding webs of legislative and bureaucratic controls that firmly enmeshed Aborigines in the field of 'reformative intentions and bungled operations of government'[2], thus setting directions that prevailed in Aboriginal affairs into the 1960s with serious consequences for Aboriginal families across the continent.

BELIEFS, DESIRES AND FEARS

Beliefs about Aborigines at the turn of century were shaped by a combination of race theories, powerful economic and political interests and white fears and desires for the new century. The nineteenth-century mania for calibrating human physical diversity deeply engraved notions of racial difference, fixing Aborigines in direct contrast to the norm of 'white civilised man' and promoting perceptions of Aboriginal cultures as biologically determined and incapable of adapting to change. They were 'Stone Age relics' — profoundly primitive, irredeemably barbaric and closer to primates and children than 'modern civilised man'. Social Darwinian theory promised the extinction of Aboriginal people through a ruthless but 'natural' struggle for the 'survival of the fittest' which no human agency could prevent. Racial conflicts abroad fed a growing pessimism about the ability of the races to survive together. In Britain emerging eugenic theories argued that the inevitable 'race struggle' posited by Social Darwinism was in fact essential for human progress, being 'the fiery crucible out of which comes the finer metal.'[3] As in colonial Tasmania, these views fitted neatly with the political and economic motives of powerful interest groups as well as the desires and fears of ordinary citizens. For the colonial enterprise these intersections served to:

> rationalise the hierarchies of privilege and profit, to consolidate the labour regimes of expanding capitalism, to provide the psychological scaffolding for the exploitative structures of colonial rule.[4]

These views encouraged a heroic vision of the colonial past and provided a way forward that would stamp, once and for all, white ownership and supremacy across the continent. They also promised the disappearance of the internal 'menace of colour,' leaving a White Australia based on 'racial unity, exclusiveness and sanctity' where 'whiteness' was the passage to citizenship and the relative power, privilege and responsibility this bestowed.[5] Such beliefs intensified with the move towards Australian federation and nationhood.

Of course this constellation of beliefs and desired outcomes was not unproblematic. There *were* voices of opposition concerned at the immorality of a nation built on the annihilation of a 'weaker race,' but many of these same individuals were just as 'sentimentally committed to the emergence of a White Australia, unsullied by any "inferior" racial strains.'[6] This is not to deny their 'genuine concern', rather, as historian Raymond Evans explains, this grew out of 'their conflicting desires to protect somehow the colonised and the colonisers whose interests were so diametrically opposed.'[7] This concern often

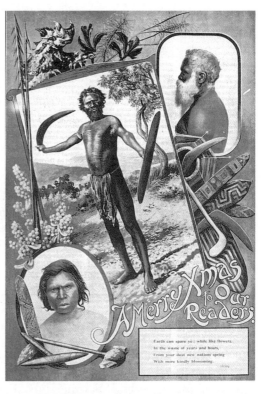

The 1904 Christmas edition of the Western Mail *combined themes of Aboriginal 'extinction' and nation building with a cheery seasonal greeting.*
(Courtesy of West Australian Newspapers)

prompted harsh solutions, including the separation of children from their families, as advocated in the following letter from a colonist to the New South Wales Board of Education in 1852:

> unless the connection between the old and young is completely severed — an act repugnant at first view to all — there is, I am convinced, no human power of civilizing or even perpetuating the race.[8]

It was evident to administrators in colonies with larger Aboriginal populations that the process of extinction would take time and that some intervention was required, if only to prevent further humanitarian concern or protests from white citizens objecting to this occurring in their very midst. Across the continent visions of 'smoothing the dying pillow' guided their designs for segregating the 'dying remnants' and providing in a minimal way for their physical care. However, in sweeping up the 'remnants' into centralised areas, administrators also had to consider the determination of powerful regional industrial groups to maintain exploitative systems of Aboriginal labour. This in turn had to be balanced against growing demands for intervention, by humanitarians and a largely self-interested labour movement, into alleged conditions of slavery in northern Australia involving the ruthless abduction of children. In 1869 the Queensland government had informed local magistrates that such cases could be dealt with under the Slave Act, but official apathy was such that no charges were ever laid.[9] By the turn of the century such inaction was no longer acceptable.

The growing presence in the late nineteenth century of Aboriginal people of mixed descent, many living in desperate circumstances, was a gnawing source of anxiety in the new nation. They were a visible reminder of the patterns of 'outright capture and rape, prostitution and concubinage' into which Aboriginal women had been drawn by the sexual desires of white men.[10] Their presence also threatened cherished notions of racial purity and fanned fears of 'European degeneration and moral decay' through race mixing.[11] They suggested to white Australians that 'the colour line was being broached in enormous proportions — and that the "mixed race" progeny were blurring the important colour and physiological distinctions between the racial groups.'[12] This growing concern was reflected in the expanding 'language of race'. The term 'half-caste' first appeared in the late eighteenth century and 'miscegenation' was introduced during the American Civil War to replace 'amalgamation' and thereby avoid confusion with political mergings. Refinements in degrees of race mixing were also expressed in terms such as 'quadroon' and 'octoroon.'

Bizarre scientific curiosity and controversy surrounded questions of the 'humanness' of the progeny of race mixing, and again there was the same fit between knowledge produced and desired political and economic outcomes. This was evident in exchanges during the American Civil War (1861–65) between abolitionists arguing that all races shared common human origins and could produce viable offspring with a rightful place in society, and slavers who maintained that races were separate species and that miscegenation produced degenerative offspring destined to remain forever separate, unequal and enslaved. Several intermediary opinions emerged: race mixing was a positive and inevitable process of merging and blending which produced distinct new social characteristics; fertility and vitality of offspring varied according to whether races were 'proximate' or 'distant' on the evolutionary ladder; all race mixing was degenerative or regressive and progeny died out after two or three generations; and the extreme but widely held view that race mixing led not only to human degeneration but to apocalyptic disaster. This view was promoted in the theories of the European theorist, Count Gobineau, who described race mixing as an 'inner poison' adulterating the pure blood of distinct races and leading to the eventual collapse of human civilisation.[13]

The mix of views in Australia about 'half-castes' and their future place in the nation was shaped by such 'learned' debates which also provided support for a range of brutal measures to control 'mixed race' populations. Not surprisingly there was considerable difference in opinion about their potential. Many believed that, because of their paternity 'half-castes' had the potential, if removed from Aboriginal environments at an early age, to benefit from a basic education and to enter the lower rungs of white society, although the possibility always remained that they would 'revert' to 'native ways.' Others were convinced that 'half-castes' were doubly defective since they inherited 'the vices of both races and the virtues of neither'.[14] It followed that they should be kept strictly segregated to prevent them from becoming 'a menace to our civilisation'.[15] The ongoing confusion was evident in the varied opinions about 'half-castes' expressed by witnesses to the South Australian 1913 Royal Commission on the Aborigines:

A 'first half-caste cross' is an improvement on the 'full-blood' and the second cross is 'better still.'

A 'half-caste ... is a better man than the blackfellow, I think it would be a disgrace if he were not.'

They are 'thrifty industrious fellow[s].'

They do not inherit the 'cunning of the black man' and the 'vices of the white man.'

'I don't know if they are any worse than the natives, but they are certainly no better.'

'From the moral point of view I should say that the result has been worse.'

'[They are] prolific but diseased ... I do not think there will be any third generations of half-castes.'[16]

There was a connective web between what the public saw, believed and wanted and the mutually reinforcing circles of superficial observations, preconceptions and vested interests. As 'half-caste' numbers in town fringe camps increased in the twentieth century their precarious circumstances often forced them into exploitative labour and sexual relationships with local whites, and into crime, violence and prostitution. Their growing presence also shocked local white residents formerly secure in their belief in the demise of the Aboriginal population. Casual observations of these conditions were swept up with settler understandings of Aboriginal society as inherently lawless and primitive, reflecting an inability to comprehend the complexities of Aboriginal social life and the integral role of family and kinship in its regulation.[17] They also made strong associations between poverty, idleness, nomadism, vagrancy, criminality, degeneracy and social chaos.[18] This in turn fanned white fears of racial violence and contamination of the alleged purity and racial superiority of a White Australia and drove white demands for strict race barriers and containment of 'mixed race' people.[19] Such views were widely endorsed by prominent officials. Archibald Meston, Protector of Aborigines for southern Queensland at the turn of the century, demanded:

a stop to the breeding of half-castes, a very undesirable element in any white population ... among whom the LAW of ATAVISM will assert itself in later years with unpleasant result.[20]

Distorted constructions of 'half-caste' families added weight to the need, indeed the imperative, to rescue 'mixed race' children 'for the good of everyone'. Widely held perceptions of Aboriginal society as devoid of binding familial relationships and emotions, and as barbaric in its treatment of women and children, were absorbed into the image of a 'primordial' unit consisting of 'a black woman living in comparative savagery' with her abandoned child, 'the offspring of a white man',[21] rejected by both white and black and living in a cultural limbo of disease, immorality and squalor. The potent mix of Aboriginality, poverty, illegitimacy and the absence of a protective patriarchal figure, positioned 'half-caste' children automatically as being 'children in need' and made them the inevitable target of special state intervention.[22] At the same time humanitarian opposition to unprecedented intrusion into the 'sacred' bonds between mother and child was assuaged. Alarm about weak and sickly progeny, immorality, prolific breeding and escalating 'mixed race' populations within a White Australia increased from the turn of the century, prompting calls for control of Aboriginal women's sexuality to strictly limit 'half-caste' numbers. We now know that by the turn of the century in southern Australia there were 'mixed race' families of several generations embedded in Aboriginal networks. Across the continent there were also mothers and children living with the children's fathers who were from various racial backgrounds or Aboriginal 'step-fathers' who took over the paternal role. Nevertheless the 'primordial model' provided an enduring image and rationale. Writing in his retirement in the early 1940s Western Australia's former Chief Protector of Aborigines, A O Neville, continued to use it to support removals of 'half-caste' children.

SKETCHES OF ABORIGINAL LIFE

While these popular representations contributed to emerging Aboriginal policy and practice they were only loosely connected to the realities of Aboriginal living conditions and lifestyles. This was to have long-term serious consequences for Aboriginal families around Australia. Indeed there was little available systematic knowledge to challenge widespread preconceptions of 'decline, disintegration, corruption and growing incoherence'.[23] At first glance colony census figures at the turn of the century appeared to reinforce views of a 'doomed race', providing estimates of only 60,000 to 80,610[24] survivors, out of an original Aboriginal population across the continent estimated at 1.25 million people by Noel Butlin, constituting less than two percent of the Australian population.[25] However, these survivors were distributed unevenly through rural and remote Australia, with large concentrations in frontier areas in northern, central and western Australia where, despite falling numbers, Aborigines often far outnumbered whites. For example, in 1901 they made up eighty percent of the Northern Territory population.[26] Census data and more recent genealogical and archival research show that in the longer colonised south the predominantly 'mixed race' populations were on the increase. The number of 'half-castes' in the south-west of Western Australia increased by sixty-five percent between 1891 and 1901 and made up almost sixty percent of the total Aboriginal population of 1529 in the region in 1901.[27] At Point McLeay Aboriginal Station in South Australia decreasing mortality and increasing fertility between 1900 and 1914 led to the highest average number of children per family in the long history of the settlement.[28] In Victoria the effect of high fertility rates — reflecting cultural practices of early marriage, high rates of remarriage, early initial child-bearing extending into middle age and a positive desire for children — was dampened by a low average life expectancy of forty years and alarmingly high infant and child mortality rates: between 1881 and 1925 a third of Koori[29] babies and children died.[30]

The few official reports of the period, while influenced by race ideologies and political and economic self-interest, nevertheless provide some first-hand observations of Aboriginal conditions. At the time, depictions of destitution and deviation from standards of life in the wider Australian community served to reinforce white stereotypes and fears and supplied a rationale for official intervention into Aboriginal family life through the introduction of legislative controls and enforced institutionalisation. In 1895 the Queensland government commissioned Archibald Meston to report on Aboriginal conditions in its far north and on the role of missions. Queensland had a reputation for extreme levels of violence against Aborigines, whose numbers had been slashed from an original population of 120,000 to 26,670 by 1901. Its agricultural, pastoral and marine industries, particularly in the north, were more dependent on Aboriginal labour than their counterparts in other states. Meston fitted the contours of 'Aboriginal expert' of the time — childhood associations with Aborigines in northern New South Wales, travel and exploratory expeditions in the outback, personal collections of ethnographic observations and artefacts, business interests in Queensland rural industries, a former seat in the Queensland Parliament and active membership of the Aborigines Protection Society in Brisbane.[31] While Meston was imbued with the race preconceptions of his day, he differed from majority views in acknowledging the injustice of treating Aborigines as 'trespassers' rather than the land's original owners and of governments

Archibald Meston, c 1900.
(Courtesy of John Oxley Library, 68274)

refusing to enter into treaties with them. Although he did not entirely discount the 'doomed race theory', he nevertheless criticised it as a subterfuge used by the strong to explain away crimes against the weak. Earlier in 1895 he had presented a treatise[32] to the Queensland government outlining a system of segregated supervised reserves to halt the Aborigines' decline and to preserve the race.

Over a four-month period Meston covered more than 5000 miles in far north Queensland travelling 'by steamer, whaleboat, dinghy, horse, and on foot' in the company of Gnootaringwan, an Aboriginal man from the Coen River region, and meeting with 2000 people from sixty-five language groups. He estimated that 20,000 Aborigines still lived in the region and that sixty percent had virtually no contact with whites.[33] Those between Newcastle Bay and Princess Charlotte Bay were healthy and well fed and, he conjectured, lived as they had '1,000 years ago'[34] apart from occasional visits from bêche-de-mer and pearl fishermen bartering flour and tobacco for women or seeking workers. However, the impact of economic development and violent dispossession in the area from Newcastle Bay north to Cape York had reduced the Aboriginal population from 3000 to 100 in the space of twenty years. Meston had little to say about pastoralist employers, although he said plenty later in his unpublished reports, but did refer to the cruel treatment of Aboriginal workers in marine industries and to the widespread practice of abducting Aboriginal children for slavery.

> Boys and girls are frequently taken from their parents and their
> tribes, and removed far off where they have no chance of returning;
> left helpless at the mercy of those who possessed them, white
> people responsible to no one and under no supervision by any
> proper authority ... Stringent legislation is required to prevent a
> continuation of abuses concerning the women and children.[35]

Meston sympathised with their plight. 'Scattered all over
Queensland' they fretted for the families they had lost and had few
prospects of finding suitable partners and starting families of their
own. In 1900 he reported a gathering of pastoral workers on the
outskirts of a town, cast adrift by their employers following the terrible
years of depression and drought of the 1890s. It was a desperate sight,
'a meeting of husbands and wives and relations who had been
separated for years' and, though 'chiefly clothed in rags, half-starved
and dejected,' they preferred to remain there together rather than
return to their employers.[36]

In the settled districts near government ration stations in the towns
and settlements of Kuranda, Atherton, Thornborough, Daintree and
Cardwell on the east coast, Meston encountered only scattered groups.
They had:

> lost their old habits and customs, abandoned their old hunting life,
> and descended gradually through various stages of degradation to a
> condition which is a reproach to our common humanity.[37]

He described the ravages of addiction to opium, often given to
Aborigines by white men to induce them to work, as a 'sad and
humiliating spectacle' and also referred to the prevalence of syphilis.[38]
However, in contrast to his peers he did not attribute this degradation
to any 'natural predatory or offensive proclivities on the part of the
blacks' but rather to the actions of 'unscrupulous and degraded
whites'.[39] The situation was not all bleak. Meston also encountered
examples of adaptation with Aborigines following lifestyles combining
hunting and gathering with paid work for local settlers and, while he
did not comment on numbers of children, an observer noted forty
'healthy looking piccaninnies' in the Cooktown camps in the following
year.[40] Everywhere the legacy of the murderous treatment of

Aborigines by Queensland's Native Mounted Police — a mounted force armed with repeating rifles, sabres and revolvers averaging between 200 and 250 non-Aboriginal and Aboriginal men which patrolled frontier regions in Queensland from 1848 into the first decade of the twentieth century[41] — impeded Meston's inquiries and the efforts of police to distribute rations as whole groups of Aborigines 'fled from their approach.'[42] Meston did not mention 'half-caste' numbers; however the Chief Protector of Aborigines reported in 1905 that there were few in the north and that most lived on missions.

> So far, they are apparently content to live, marry, and die there; their life is simple, happy, useful, and God-fearing; they marry amongst themselves and with the full-bloods.[43]

Meston also visited Queensland's six mission stations — Mapoon, Cape Bedford, Bloomfield River, Cape Grafton (Yarrabah), and Marie Yamba in the north and Deebing Creek in the south. He was highly critical of their overall management, the location and size of the reserves and the quality of the land which prevented them from ever becoming self-supporting. He also pointed to the failure of their work with the children who moved on and off the missions with their families as they pleased. He asked what would be the future of the young girls who would continue to marry 'primitive' men if no action was taken to keep them on the missions.

In Western Australia in 1901 and 1902, the Travelling Inspector for the Aborigines Department, G S Olivey, travelled thousands of kilometres through the eastern goldfields and the south-west collecting data on Aboriginal living conditions and employment.[44] As white settlement spread inland from the coast the south-west had experienced the same patterns of violence, depradation and dispossession as other longer settled areas of southern Australia. However, much of the interior still remained unalienated Crown land interspersed with sprawling sheep and cattle stations and dotted by only a small number of tiny rural centres. Starting from Esperance, Olivey visited these various stations and rural centres and, while he reported no Aborigines in some areas, his findings nevertheless differed significantly from Daisy Bates' lurid accounts of the 'dying remnants' in the Perth press of the day.[45] Olivey found a common pattern of mixed lifestyles based on paid work and hunting and gathering. At the stations and towns a core of workers was engaged in regular

A typical Aboriginal bush camp in the south-west of Western Australia in the early 1900s.
(Courtesy of Battye Library, 5323B/1442)

employment as station hands or labourers. A floating population of family members moved between camps on the stations or the outskirts of towns and more remote scattered camps in the bush where they hunted kangaroo and possum for food and skins for the cash market, sometimes in the company of white hunters, or lived off government rations. Some 'half-caste' families were purchasing their own blocks of land.[46] The camps consisted of family groups with a mix of Aborigines and 'half-castes' and some white men living with their Aboriginal wives. Olivey counted thirty-one people at the Esperance Station camp: twenty-two 'full bloods' and nine 'half-castes'. All children under fifteen were listed as 'half-caste' or 'quarter-caste'. There were eighty 'full bloods' and sixty 'half-castes' in the Katanning district and gatherings of up to two hundred people at Christmas were reported. In hindsight, analysis of genealogies collected by Daisy Bates at the Katanning camp in 1909 shows people related by close ties of kinship and with traditional ties to the area.[47] This challenges Bates' expressed view that the southern camps were a jumble of dispossessed 'remnants'. Chief Protector of Aborigines, Henry Prinsep, was left to report that some one hundred Aborigines lived in the environs of Perth. Many were employed — at Guildford they worked on the dairy farms and vineyards — and they camped here and there on uncleared land. There were also two hundred Aborigines (almost half of them children) living at New Norcia Mission and the Swan Native and Half Caste Mission in Perth.

While most Aborigines in Western Australia's south were self-supporting — in 1902 only twenty percent were on the ration lists and of these eighty percent were elderly or mothers with children — it is evident from departmental records that there was considerable economic distress. The significant proportion of women who were destitute — they made up a third of the ration list in 1902 — had serious implications for their children.[48] Families worked in a restricted economic niche and, with limited welfare support available to them, they were particularly vulnerable to the looming economic changes following the development of the wheatbelt after the turn of the century. The growing number of children provided an important labour resource as in all poor families, however, they, along with the elderly, were dependent on a limited number of adult providers. The cumulative impact of these stresses can be read in comments by government officials and others on numbers of 'half-caste' children in the camps and alarm about the conditions of squalor in which many were forced to live.

DIRECTIONS FOR ACTION

This then was the scene for the burst of activity in Aboriginal affairs around the turn of the century. What precedents guided the policies and practices developed by politicians and administrators to deal with these Aboriginal populations? As with Governor Arthur and G A Robinson in Van Diemen's Land they drew principally on missionary methods for 'civilising' indigenous peoples in the colonies and nineteenth-century practices for controlling white 'problem populations'. They saw in the model of the centralised institution an administratively efficient and economical solution to the perceived need to forcibly segregate Aborigines, to provide Aboriginal adults with a modicum of care to ease their 'passing away' and to submit 'mixed race' children to the 'civilising and Christianising' process. From the turn of the century governments around Australia adopted the policy of protection which enshrined contradictory but intersecting sets of philanthropic, ameliorative, punitive and even genocidal rationales, and which resulted in a convenient 'double speak' of stated humanitarian concern and agendas of segregation, assimilation, genocide and profound neglect. This mix seemed to enable everyone, from city humanitarian to brutal frontiersman, to feel comfortable with their stance and convinced that right was being done.

From its earliest days, Australian colonial policy had embraced the institutional mission model of centralising and segregating Aborigines and subjecting them to various strategies to turn them into settled agri-cultural workers. The imperative to isolate children from their elders and rigorously school them in the ways of the colonists was clearly expressed, for instance, by the Protector of Aborigines in South Australia in 1842:

> Our chief hope is decidedly in the children; and the complete success as far as regards their education and civilisation would be before us, if it were possible to remove them from the influence of their parents.[49]

The model was rarely challenged despite the fact that Wybalenna in Van Diemen's Land had succeeded only in hastening the deaths of its Aboriginal inmates. An exception was the missionary priest, Reverend Duncan McNab, who advocated in the 1870s that Queensland Aborigines should be educated and trained to live as independent homestead farmers and not 'merely preserved like cattle on a run'[50] — a view that his contemporaries dismissed as 'impractical and utopian'.[51] Nor was the model widely implemented during the nineteenth century, reflecting government parsimony and opposition from vested economic interests as well as deepening pessimism amongst some reformers about Aborigines' ability to change. Victoria was exceptional in having seven mission and government stations in the 1870s, although concerns were raised about residents becoming 'dependent paupers' and recommendations were made to expel 'half-caste' adults who were capable of supporting themselves outside.[52]

Policy in the colonies was also influenced by shifts in attitudes and practice abroad. In Britain the heady optimism of the abolitionists' call — 'Am I not a Man and Brother?' — in the 1830s had been dampened by the apparent 'failure' of freed slaves in British colonies to become 'industrious peasants'.[53] This contributed to a sense of despondency amongst some abolitionists concerning the capabilities of the 'black races' generally. Propaganda emanating from the southern states during the American Civil War also promoted a creed of inherent and permanent inferiority of 'black races' that appealed to many Britons. Following the rebellious and violent behaviour of colonial subjects and their masters in the Indian Mutiny in 1857–8 and the 1865 Jamaican uprising, Britain was also moving towards ever more forceful regimes of colonial control.

> British material prosperity, force of arms, Christian example and culture — all these clearly did not impress millions of subject people who instead clung tenaciously to their own cultures, shunning what the British knew to be superior institutions. That in itself was irredeemable proof, if more were needed, of the irredeemable

ignorance and savagery of the people concerned. What was needed, henceforth, was the smack of firm government rather than the seductions and blandishments of cultural persuasion.[54]

Late nineteenth-century British imperialism took on a brash arrogance celebrated in triumphant tales of military and geographical conquests and of white supremacy[55] and reflected in expanding, aggressive mission work with village communities in Africa, China and the Pacific. Children's dormitories and residential 'native schools' were the spearhead of this process as authorities determined to sunder links to the children's pagan past and to create new communities of 'civilised' Christians. The proliferation and apparent success of overseas missions provided both a depressing contrast and a beacon of hope for missionaries in Australia, who raised the question of adopting more forceful ways of inducing Aborigines to submit to change. Lieutenant Governor La Trobe had alluded to this in 1848 following the cessation of the Port Phillip Protectorate when he wrote of:

> the fundamental error in all previous schemes, namely, their premise that the native could be persuaded voluntarily to submit to guidance. Instead coercion should have been used.[56]

A possible legislative and administrative model was provided by the United States' Indian Act 1876 which allowed for the forced relocation and detention of Native Americans on designated reserves which were to be managed and controlled by a central federal government agency.

British treatment of its 'problem populations' at home provided a further precedent of enforced removal and detention. For a 'superior people' Britain had many problems of its own — social unrest, poverty, criminality, poor health — and British governments adopted harsh solutions for dealing with them. From 1834 the poor were forced into centralised workhouses, inscribed indelibly in the popular imagination by the novels of Charles Dickens, where they laboured for their keep and lived under regimes of regulation, surveillance and indoctrination intended to redirect their behaviour towards norms of middle-class respectability.[57] During the nineteenth century British children became the focus of a discourse causally linking social environment, moral disorder, criminal propensity and working-class threats to social stability. There was also geniune humanitarian concern about children in poverty-stricken urban areas and those exploited in the child labour market. This discourse provided a framework for the increasing regimentation of childhood through the introduction of compulsory education, controls over child labour and intrusion into working-class family life through removal of children to institutions for their 'own protection' and to be trained to become 'useful citizens'.

A distinct system of law for children and specialist institutions for their detention emerged, intended to prevent the 'contamination' of children by adults in prisons and to shield children of the 'deserving' poor from those of the 'dangerous classes' (a term commonly used by nineteenth century 'child rescuers'). Child offenders were now sent to reformatories, the new juvenile custodial institutions, while children deemed to be 'in danger of offending' — typically the neglected and orphaned — were sent to industrial schools.[58] The institutions were managed by religious and philanthropic organisations subsidised by government and their official aims were 'education and training for moral character and citizenship'.[59] More often the children's 'training' was little more than unpaid labour and they learned qualities of 'accepting and dutiful subservience' suited to their future as lowly rural and domestic servants. Between the ages of ten and fifteen children were apprenticed to employers to complete their 'education and training'. There was little screening of prospective employers and many children were cruelly treated.[60] Thus were laid the foundations of a system of child welfare in which 'care and protection' operated alongside social control and maintenance of social order so that 'child protection' came to mean:

> not only protection from 'bad' or 'irresponsible' parents, or from the evil influences of urban environments, but it also meant instilling in children the virtues of hard work, obedience to authority and the acceptance of their low status. This is clearly evident in the legislation which required the authorities to teach children under their care the skills of manual labour but never any skills in higher level occupations.[61]

Industrial schools were the model for Native American residential schools set up from the 1870s in the United States and Canada. They became a central instrument of assimilation policy and the ongoing process of 'the extermination of Indians *as Indians*'.[62] The schools were located off the reservations and, following persistent parental resistance, the United States government legislated in 1894 to forcibly remove the children from their families. In Canada the children lived in residential schools between the ages of five and fifteen. They could return to the reservations for two months each year but only with the approval of the local Indian agent. The high death tolls in the institutions meant that many never returned to their homes — an official report in 1902 estimated that fifty percent died as they passed through the system. Although the schools followed a mainstream curriculum, their goals were limited to preparing the children for a future life as farmers, housewives and 'effective emissaries' of Christian civilisation back on the reservations. Enfranchisement and citizenship were open to those who took up farming or a profession; however, this also meant that they ceased to be Indians in law. At its peak in Canada, one third of all Indian children aged between six and fifteen were living in residential schools. Although the schools consistently failed to realise official hopes of assimilation and in fact had a clearly negative impact on the children, many of whom became institutionalised and lived out their adult life as inmates of gaols and mental hospitals, the system continued to operate until the 1960s.[63]

In the Australian colonies there was also a strong move towards the introduction of legislative controls and institutionalisation of certain individuals for their own protection and benefit and in the interests of social control. There was already the powerful model of incarceration of Australia's convict populations and the removal of children from their convict mothers to 'orphanages'.[64] Although the workhouse model was never adopted for dealing with the white poor, many other 'problem populations' now faced the spectre of forced institutionalisation. Queensland was particularly zealous and passed legislation to incarcerate people with contagious diseases (venereal disease and leprosy in particular), the insane and alcoholics.[65] All colonies also passed legislation setting out procedures for the removal and institutionalisation of children: administrative boards, processes for identifying and classifying children, court committal procedures including definitions of 'neglect' and 'destitution,' management of institutions and supervision of apprenticeships. Industrial schools and reformatories, often in rural locations in keeping with contemporary views of the debilitating effect of city life on children, were established under private and government control. Welfare historians agree that the focus was on social control rather than protection, as managers worked to produce self-supporting, disciplined workers at minimal cost to the community through regimes of orderliness, discipline and deprivation.

The Australian colonies also found inspiration in these precedents for ways of dealing with their indigenous 'problem populations.' The systems of child removal and institutionalisation pointed a way forward for the perennial dream of effectively 'Christianising and civilising' Aboriginal children. 'Half-caste' children in particular appeared to closely fit the social profile of other child 'problem populations'. In the mainland colonies the basis of a legal and administrative framework began to emerge to enforce the removal, institutionalisation and apprenticing of Aboriginal children, rather than the haphazard process that had operated in Tasmania. This process went hand in hand with the undermining by the state of the structures and roles of Aboriginal family networks so as to break continuity between the generations and foster assimilation into white ways. There was considerable variation between the colonies (see Table One, pp 149–50). Statutes differed in terms of whether Aboriginal children were incorporated into mainstream legislation or whether special discriminatory legislation was passed. There were also differences in levels of intrusion into parental rights, powers to remove and retain children, and the nature of child placements. There were variations in where children were placed — in Aboriginal children's institutions, dormitories in multipurpose institutions, and mainstream children's homes. Most were eventually apprenticed out to employers under state control to complete the assimilation process. In this way the state took on the role of 'labour exchange'. Despite the apparent benefits to employers of state control of the Aboriginal child labour market, many vehemently objected to this outside intervention seeing it as a threat to the cheap labour they forced from the children.

The workhouse model, which closely fitted existing colonial models of centralising and segregating native peoples, influenced the development of the segregated multipurpose Aboriginal state and mission institutions from the end of the century.[66] Designed to contain families unwanted in the wider community and to provide services denied to them on the outside, institutions in some areas also provided a labour pool for local employers and played a reformatory role, particularly in relation to the children who were separated from their families and housed in dormitories in central compounds run by white staff. The threat of permanent incarceration in the institutions also acted as a significant instrument of social control for Aboriginal people on the outside, ensuring general compliance with official expectations of their behaviour.

TABLE ONE

NINETEENTH-CENTURY LEGISLATION AND INSTITUTIONS
FOR ABORIGINAL CHILDREN[243]

SOUTH AUSTRALIA

In 1844 the Protector of Aborigines became the legal guardian of Aboriginal children whose parents were deceased or unknown or who voluntarily surrendered their guardianship. The Protector could place these children in apprenticeships. These powers were not widely used.

From 1895 to 1911 Aboriginal children were removed under mainstream child welfare legislation.

Small residential Aboriginal schools operated in Adelaide from 1839 to 1853. The Poonindie Anglican Mission (1850–94) also took Aboriginal children. Point McLeay Mission and Point Pearce Mission (both opened in 1868) ran schools for Aboriginal children.

WESTERN AUSTRALIA

From 1844 it was an offence to remove Aboriginal girls from school or employment without official permission.

From 1874 managers of institutions for children of Aborigines could retain children voluntarily surrendered to them to the age of twenty-one and place them in service or apprenticeships without parental consent.

In 1886 a system of apprenticeship for Aboriginal children aged from six to twenty-one was introduced.

Several residential schools and children's homes were set up including Smithies Mission (1839–55), Fremantle and Guildford schools (1840–42), New Norcia Mission (opened 1846) Annesfield School (1852–71), Ellensbrook (1878–1917), Swan Native and Half-Caste Mission (1880s–1921), Beagle Bay Mission (opened 1890), Broome Orphanage (opened 1897).

VICTORIA

In 1860 a Board for the Protection of Aborigines was set up to supervise missions and government stations. Aboriginal schools were set up on the missions and stations.

In 1869 the Board was charged to provide for the 'care, custody and education of children of aboriginal people.'

From 1871 the Board could send 'neglected' Aboriginal children to live in dormitories on the missions and stations, apprentice them to employers, or place them with non-Aboriginal children in reformatory schools.

From 1886 the majority of 'half-castes' were barred from the missions and stations. 'Half-caste' children were apprenticed to employers or transferred to the care of the Department for Neglected Children.

Aboriginal schools were set up as part of the Port Phillip Protectorate (1838–49). From the 1860s the Board ran schools on the missions and stations: Ebenezer (1859–1904), Lake Hindmarsh (1859–1904), Lake Tyers (1861–1908), Ramahyuck (1862–1905), Framlingham (1865–90), Lake Condah (1867–1917), Coranderrk (1863–1923).

With the closure of the missions children were sent to mainstream child welfare institutions.

QUEENSLAND

Under the *Industrial and Reformatories Schools Act 1865* all children of Aboriginal and 'half-caste' mothers were deemed automatically to be 'neglected children' who could be removed and institutionalised to the age of twenty-one.

An Aboriginal school ran for a short period in Brisbane from 1838. Missions and government provided education for children on Fraser Island (1870s–1904), Durundur (1877–1905), Bowen (1878–1901), Bloomfield (1885–1902), Cape Bedford (opened 1886), Wujal Wujal (1886–1902), Marie Yamba (1888–1901), Mapoon (opened 1891), Yarrabah (opened 1891), Deebing Creek (1892–1902), Myora (1895–1906), Weipa (opened 1896), Barambah Home (opened 1899, renamed Cherbourg Settlement in 1932). The following institutions were declared reformatories or industrial schools: Deebing Creek (1895), Myora (1895), Mapoon (1901) and Yarrabah (1901).

NEW SOUTH WALES

The Aborigines Protection Board (1883) had no statutory authority over Aboriginal children. They were removed under mainstream child welfare legislation. However, the Board did have responsibility to 'train and teach the young, to fit them to take their places amongst the rest of the community' and, from the early 1890s, removed some children for 'educational purposes'.

The Native Institution for Aboriginal children at Parramatta operated for a short time from 1814. By the 1890s mission stations were operating at Cumeroongunja, Warangesda and Maloga. In 1893 a Girls Training Home was opened at Warangesda.

TASMANIA

There were no special measures for Aboriginal children. They could be removed under mainstream legislation.

Children were sent to the Hobart Orphan School, Wybalenna and Oyster Cove. Following the closure of Oyster Cove there were no separate Aboriginal institutions and children were sent to mainstream child welfare institutions.

NORTHERN TERRITORY

South Australia was responsible for Aboriginal Affairs in the Northern Territory from 1864 to 1911.

Dormitories were provided for Aboriginal children at Hermannsburg Mission (opened 1877) and the Daly River Mission (opened 1886).

For non-Aboriginal children in the mid nineteenth century, the pendulum had already begun to swing away from institutionalisation to family-based care. Government inquiries were showing that, contrary to earlier expectations, institutions were expensive and administratively cumbersome. They were found to be 'pernicious' environments where children were chronically undernourished, unhealthy, poorly educated and vulnerable to moral, psychological and physical abuse by unsupervised staff and other children. This acted very much against the children's 'best interests' and created a sense of personal worthlessness and shame, 'low intellects' and 'undeveloped' characters, and an inability to adjust to outside life. The matron of an industrial school told the South Australian Commission on the *Destitute Act* (1869–70) that children 'never grow up properly if you have a lot of them together. I would never have children of two or three years of age there … they never develop into anything.'[67] A government report in Victoria in 1872[68] concluded that institutions were:

> hurtful to children's health, intellect and preparation for working life, rendering them to sink into permanent pauperism and crime … [they] suffered morally and emotionally.[69]

Nor did the system work in the best interests of the state as it failed to produce reliable rural and domestic workers, 'virtuous and exemplary women and good mothers' and 'sound responsible families.'[70] Domestic servants from institutions in Britain had been found to be:

> sullen, short-tempered and incapable of initiative; they had no sense of private property and were allegedly given to pilfering … loneliness and a feeling that nobody cared for them outside made them wayward too.[71]

Rather than eradicating economic dependency and social disability, institutionalisation perpetuated the cycle of pauperisation from which the children had been originally removed. As 'institutionalised' adults they repeated the pattern of 'reckless parents' with destitute children who had to be rescued and provided for by the state.[72]

Social planners and reformers in Britain and Australia began to consider the alternative of a supervised and regulated system of 'boarding out' or fostering in private families as a less expensive and more effective way of caring for needy children. Prominent British 'child rescuer', Miss Florence Hill, wrote in *Children of the State*:

> The child placed in a family is under parental care; it becomes familiar with the duties and pleasures of family life; and it receives insensibly that training of the temper and affections which comes from living with persons of different ages and standing in different relations to it ... A highly important advantage to the boarding out system, and one wholly wanting in [industrial] schools, is that it weaves fresh home ties about the child, and creates an interest in his welfare among his foster relatives and a desire on his part not to lose their good opinion which, in his after life, are probably the most efficient safeguards from going astray with which he could be surrounded.[73]

In a supportive political and economic environment, and with an eye to reducing costs, boarding-out schemes were established for non-Aboriginal children in all Australian colonies from the 1870s through cooperation between the state and voluntary and religious organisations. In particular, the improved economic situation of many respectable working-class families meant there were sufficient suitable households to take in the children. A consequence was an overall decline in numbers of children in institutions into the 1890s in all colonies, although this system was limited mainly to 'less troublesome' children. Those with severe behavioural problems or physical and intellectual disabilities were deemed unsuited for family life and continued to be institutionalised.

The British child emigration schemes to Canada and Australia, which began in earnest from the 1870s, reflected the influence of the boarding-out movement. Thousands of mainly working-class children were shipped out of Britain and on arrival in their 'host countries' were placed in training institutions or sent out directly to work for families, often with no supervision to ensure they were properly cared for. In Australia the scheme operated until the 1960s. This *appeared* to be the most economical arrangement of all — for the cost of an outfit of travel clothes, a fare and maintenance at distribution centres, children could be completely removed from their families, all their former associations severed, and at the same time they could contribute to the building of the British Empire. The memoirs of British philanthropist Dr Barnado, who assisted in the removal of 20,000 children to Canada between 1882 and 1914, claim that, for Britain, the emigration scheme meant savings in government expenditure, less overcrowding in children's institutions, the relocation of workers not needed at home to a labour-hungry colony and, for the children, it brought 'unspeakable blessings'. It was only much later that the terrible costs for the children began to be acknowledged.[74]

As the century progressed there was a growing official opinion that, in the interests of the child and the community, non-Aboriginal children should be separated from their parents only as an absolute necessity. This was expressed in strong terms by the Lushington Departmental Committee in Britain in 1896:

> before a child should be taken from its home, before an order should be made for its compulsory detention in a school for a number of years, before it should be decided that the community are to be taxed for its maintenance — these are the three principal features of the system — it should be established in justice to the child and its parents, that such treatment is necessary for the child, and in justice to the community, that it is necessary for the public advantage. And by being necessary we mean that there should be a positive necessity of having to send a destitute person to a workhouse, and that nothing short of necessity can justify detention in one of these schools.[75]

The following judgment from a British wardship case in 1893 sheds some light on more enlightened views of the 'welfare of the child':

> the welfare of the child is not to be measured by money, or by physical comfort only. The word welfare must be taken in its widest sense. The moral and religious welfare of the child must be considered as well as its physical well-being. Nor can the ties of affection be disregarded.[76]

The keynote statement of an international conference held in the United States in 1909 maintained that:

> Home life is the highest and finest product of civilisation. Children

should not be deprived of it unless for urgent and compelling reasons.[77]

The 1913 Royal Commission into Neglected and Delinquent and Mentally-Deficient Children, prepared by Sir Charles Mackellar for the New South Wales government, advocated the following conclusions from the 1909 conference as a blueprint for child-care:

Home care — Children of worthy parents or deserving mothers should, as a rule, be kept with their parents at home.

Preventative work — The effort should be made to eradicate causes of dependency, such as disease and accident, and to substitute compensation and insurance for relief.

Home-finding — Homeless and neglected children, if normal, should be cared for in families, where practicable.

Cottage system — Institutions should be on the cottage plan with small units, as far as possible.

State inspection — The State should inspect the work of all agencies which care for dependent children.

Inspection of educational work — Educational work of institutions and agencies caring for dependent children should be supervised by State authorities.

Facts and records — Complete histories of dependent children, and their parents, based upon personal investigation and supervision, should be recorded for guidance of child-care agencies.

Physical care — Every needy child should receive the best medical and surgical attention, and be instructed in health and hygiene.[78]

These ideals shaped emerging state child welfare systems in all western countries from early in the twentieth century. However, these new directions had little effect on the treatment of indigenous children and families. In Australia and North America they became the responsibility of separate administrations with discriminatory powers to remove them from their families and place them in institutions. Indeed in Australia the scope and range of institutionalisation expanded into the twentieth century and a variety of institutional forms were adopted from small children's homes to compounds holding children within large multi-purpose government settlements or missions.

Why were institutions deemed essential for the management of Aboriginal populations in Australia? There were the established precedents of colonial practice and treatment of 'problem populations' at 'Home'. Race prejudices constructed Aborigines as a 'child race' needing constant 'parental' supervision and aligned them with those groups believed to require institutionalisation — the criminal, the insane, the unfit, the diseased and disabled. In particular, Aboriginal families were perceived as dangerous for the physical and moral well-being of their children. There were also widespread anxieties about race and gender reflected in government reports such as the New South Wales 1913 Royal Commission into Neglected and Delinquent and Mentally-Deficient Children which linked Aboriginal girls with sexual promiscuity, 'moral feeble-mindedness' and the need for reform through institutionalisation.[79] Aboriginal children were not being groomed for citizenship but were being trained to become docile, semi-enslaved and disenfranchised domestic and rural workers, either in the wider community or in permanently segregated Aboriginal communities. Institutionalisation fitted these goals. Assimilation in white middle-class family settings was not contemplated for them. Indeed there were few white families willing to take them in as the Chief Protector of Aborigines in Western Australia found in 1915 when he tried to place a 'half-caste' baby born to a white woman through the State Children's Department. No one would take the baby who was eventually sent to Moore River Native Settlement where it died soon after.[80] However, families were willing to take Aboriginal children in as servants. Apprenticing of the children by the state to employers as domestic servants and farm labourers continued into the 1950s, although this practice was dropped in relation to white children in most states by the 1920s. In this way white women in the home took on the role of training Aboriginal girls to become 'useful servants' and 'good wives'. As historian Heather Goodall points out, apprenticeships could lead to further institutionalisation when young people who rebelled against their employers or absconded were sentenced to terms in institutions such as Parramatta Girls Home, Long Bay Gaol or even psychiatric hospitals.[81]

Institutions provided convenient solutions for problems confronting planners, as well as excuses for not taking positive action. The native 'remnants' could be swept out of the way until they died out or found the strength to recover. Meanwhile nothing was done outside the institutions to improve Aboriginal living conditions and their treatment was characterised by abject neglect. Hiding Aborigines away in institutions and forging permanent segregated communities also met demands for a White Australia, while employers' interests could be accommodated, at least in part, by training 'half-caste' children to become part of a state-controlled labour force.

It was a tragic irony that when it suited governments, for financial or assimilationist reasons or in accordance with the local demand for labour, they could also choose to reverse the situation by forcing adult residents out of the institutions and leaving them to fend for themselves in a hostile white community.

MAKING WHITE CITIZENS AND ABORIGINAL OUTCASTS

From the late nineteenth century Australia was swept up in the drive to forge the diverse colonies into a modern nation — a rational, orderly and uniform society with a single system of law, unified by a homogeneous culture, a dominant language, a standardised history and collective loyalty.[82] Like other emerging nations of the period, Australia adopted strong interventionist strategies to ensure the development of an efficient and productive citizenry. In doing so governments followed the shift towards new processes of governing through political consent and social control: mass, free and compulsory education; hygiene improvement drives; and political enfranchising of labour and unions. Disciplinary networks spread throughout the society to shape populations into autonomous self-regulating citizens committed to national goals.[83] Through a whole 'package' of inducements and pressures centred on the modern nuclear family, Australian governments sought to entice, pressure and mould the populace into an efficient, healthy and loyal citizenry with all the attendant rights and responsibilities of civil, political and social citizenship[84]: the rights and freedoms of the individual to participate in political and social processes connected closely to the educational system and social services.

Australian constitutions contained no 'core positive notion of citizenship' and prior to the *Citizenship Act 1948*, Australian nationals were formally British subjects. Federal and state governments were left to clarify the details of citizenship in their designated spheres of jurisdiction through a complex web of legislative and administrative measures. Exclusionary clauses and procedures denied certain groups civil and political rights (and responsibilities) based on criteria of class, gender, and race. For example, in the colonies during the nineteenth century full citizenship was contingent on class and gender — only male property owners had the right to vote — and it was only at the end of the century that these franchise restrictions were lifted. From the late nineteenth century racial difference emerged as a major criterion of formal exclusion from citizenship. This was evident in the framework of laws and administrative procedures that grew up around the *Immigration Restriction Act 1901* which severely reduced the rights of non-Europeans and the special discriminatory statutes relating to Aborigines in state and federal jurisdictions. Indeed, the new Commonwealth government's legislative regime was 'dominated by the exclusion of "Aboriginal natives".'[85] This was evident in its action in 1902 of disenfranchising Aborigines at the same time as it demonstrated international leadership by enfranchising women.

These race-based exclusions were linked to the drive to subordinate racial, cultural and social minorities to the nation-building project of uniformity and unity under the hegemony of Anglo-Celtic settlement.[86] Just as the White Australia policy established government processes primarily to prevent entry, to deport and to deny rights of citizenship to Asians, so the exclusionary clauses of federal and state legislation promised to sweep away the internal menace of indigenous difference. Like similar groups in other emerging nations Aborigines were problematised, classified, graded and subjected to various discriminatory and often violent regimes to remove the perceived threat of their difference to the nation-building enterprise. Ironically these 'projects of homogeneity' actually generated further fragmentation and diversity within Aboriginal populations.[87] Gerald Sider writes that state power both destroys and generates cultural differentiation so that 'the historic career of ethnic peoples can ... be best understood in the context of forces that give people birth and simultaneously seek to take their lives.'[88] What place then did Aborigines have in the new nation? They were not to be permitted to maintain their autonomous societies but neither were they expected or allowed to become equal citizens. They were directed to the social and economic margins of White Australia where many lived a life of menial servitude in institutions or employers' homes. Others, made outcasts, maintained varying degrees of tradition and independence.

The modern nuclear family was the major site of state intervention for nation building as well as a goal towards which families should strive. This ideal was a self-regulatory unit — the father providing material comforts while the mother, working in tandem with various institutions, shaped her children, the nation's building blocks, into healthy, efficient citizens of the future. The family was enmeshed in a 'tutelary complex'[89] of laws and institutions moulding children into future loyal citizens and aligning them to the formal apparatus of government. In all this the mother's role as bearer and shaper of children was pivotal. This was expressed in the idealisation of mothers, state education and training of girls for motherhood and a host of government programs focused on the mother's agency within the family. It is simplistic to argue that this only brought oppression and subordination of women; rather it would appear that, as in the 1950s, change:

> created new forms of subjectivities or social agency. Women were provided with new responsibilities and powers, and the transformation of the family, effected by the intervention of various professional groups, was secured through the active participation of women.[90]

The family home was the focus of interventions by government working through a range of professional experts intent on building up the population and improving the health, morals and education of the nation. The health of infants and children was of particular concern. Advances were made through new infant and child protection measures and the creation of healthier living environments for families with improved housing, sanitary and water services and professional medical care. A consequence was a significant drop in infant mortality rates from 116 to 68 per 1000 live births between 1903 and 1914.[91] Efforts were also made to check both the declining national birth rate and the trend towards smaller middle-class families. Leading experts admonished couples to 'populate or perish':

> The future of the Commonwealth, and especially the possibility of maintaining a 'White Australia', depend on the question whether we should be able to people the vast areas of the continent which are capable of supporting a large population … patriotism dictates that the people of to-day should consider what these facts mean to the future.[92]

Indeed it was beholden on white women to exercise their new 'citizenship duties by patriotically having more children ... to populate the country with white babies.'[93] Various pro-natalist measures were introduced — medical surveillance of women's reproductive practices and prohibitions on abortion and artificial contraception, the official promotion of white motherhood and family life, and economic incentives for child-bearing, including the 1912 Federal Maternity Allowance — although little was done to reduce the high maternal death rate. These initiatives had little impact and the birth rate continued to decline. Under pressure from the growing union movement and in the interests of family welfare, governments also introduced measures to provide protection for workers and their families. These included the basic wage introduced in 1907 to ensure sufficient living conditions for a working husband, wife and three children, with welfare support and benefits such as old age and invalid pensions. The introduction of compulsory free state education for children aged six to fourteen from the 1870s was integral to the process of creating young citizens with a 'genuine popular nationalist enthusiasm'.[94] Centralised state education bureaucracies generated standardised professional teaching qualifications, curricula, texts, intelligence testing, age gradings and instructional materials. They promoted an all-embracing agenda for shaping future citizens in the ubiquitous primary schools, in cooperation with a myriad of connected socialising instruments from Sunday Schools to Boy Scout troops.[95]

An expanding child welfare system and the emerging children's courts promoted the family as the appropriate environment to reform potential 'inefficient citizens' with institutionalisation as a last resort. Authorities also began to move towards family maintenance in 'the best interests of the child' through direct financial support to selected needy families and probationary schemes allowing offending children to remain in their families under supervision. This fitted with women's improving economic status from the turn of the century as employment opportunities outside the home increased so that more families were better placed financially to keep their children.[96] Nineteenth-century practices of institutionalising and apprenticing needy children did continue in some jurisdictions due to economic and social imperatives, however increasingly only the most recalcitrant children and those requiring specialist care were institutionalised.[97] Certain childhood problems were now perceived to be hereditary in nature and impervious to environmental reforms alone. The development of eugenic and psychological practices fostered the development of systems of identifying and classifying 'unfit' children — the 'mentally defective' and 'delinquent,' in particular. Many of these children were placed in cottage homes or specialist institutions, along with children suffering from severe physical disabilities.

With these innovations came new levels of surveillance, monitoring and control of families through the expanding web of schools, children's courts, psychologists and other professionals involved in the development of scientific family and child management by the state. Increasing administrative regulation, statistical knowledge and dependence of families on state instrumentalities created an inter-meshing of state and family and of public and private arenas, described by J Donzelot as:

> a series of concentric circles around the child, the family circle, the circle of technicians, and the circle of social guardians. A paradoxical result of the liberalization of the family, of the emergence of children's rights, of a rebalancing of the man-woman relationship, the more these rights are proclaimed, the more the stranglehold of a tutelary authority tightens around the poor family.[98]

While vast sums of money and energy were committed to building up and moulding a White Australian citizenry, planning for Aborigines was moving in very different directions. They were to be excluded from the package of rights, benefits and responsibilities extended to white Australian families. Their families were not to be sites for forging strong productive citizens. They were officially discouraged from producing offspring — for example, Aboriginal women (along with Asian women) were deliberately excluded from the benefits of the maternity allowance. Their families were broken up and their children trained in state institutions. The Aborigines' situation from this time was unique within the Australian population. They were stripped of legal rights accorded to other 'British subjects' and subjected to special legal controls. In most jurisdictions their children could be removed without due court process and cause. They were denied access to benefits and services seen as rights by other Australians. Instead, separate Aboriginal administrations provided 'welfare' in the form of subsistence rations or through enforced institu-tionalisation. This was interpreted as special charity and further evidence of Aborigines' diminished self-regulatory capacity. Growing dependency on the state was the tragic outcome for many Aboriginal families. Others struggled against enormous odds to maintain some independence through their own work and traditions.

This discriminatory treatment of Aboriginal people was carried out under the flag of the policy of 'protection'. In a discussion of 'protection' in child welfare, Jan Carter suggests that it is an umbrella policy term which acts as a 'symbolic cement' for the organisation, while it subsumes a range of often conflicting ideologies and practices from, for example, humanitarian concern through to rigid social control.[99] This may reflect the relative powerlessness of the client group and its perceived relationship to the state, particularly under earlier, more repressive regimes of child welfare. Certainly, such 'conflicting views' operated under the policy of Aboriginal protection early in the twentieth century. A diverse range of policies was grouped together under the rubric 'protection'— segregation, assimilation and eugenic programs to 'breed out' Aboriginality altogether. Enforced through the expanding web of legislative and administrative controls, these were often simultaneously imposed within the various states and territories.[100] This confusion of meanings continues to influence public statements to this day — for example, that 'protection' was for Aborigines' 'own good' and that it was 'well meaning but misguided'. Confusion also remains as to how 'protection' of Aborigines differed from systems of governing white Australians, evident in assertions frequently made in public debate following the publication of the 1997 *Bringing Them Home* report that 'everyone was treated the same' and admonitions to judge the treatment of Aborigines 'in the context of the times'. In fact, these systems differed along a myriad of dimensions including the aims, nature and degree of state interventions, the consensus of the subject populations, and their capacity to influence objectives and outcomes and to protest at their treatment.

There was no single unified approach to the Aboriginal 'problem': in the carve up of jurisdictions between federal and state governments at Federation, Aborigines remained the responsibility of the states and this continued until the early 1970s — despite regular calls for federal control. Variations in policies of protection and outcomes across the continent reflected a complex mix of local demographic, economic and historical factors. These included the size of the Aboriginal and 'mixed race' populations, the ratio of black to white, gender balance in the white population, levels of frontier violence, reliance on Aboriginal labour and the nature of local labour relations, the 'muscle' of alliances of stakeholders and the stage of development of welfare services.[101] Rowse[102] reminds us of the many mediating factors surrounding the subjects of 'programmed experiment' in 'colonial encounters' which in turn influence the 'adoption of new technologies'.

It is not surprising that state governments developed quite different approaches to the problems facing them and that the very different states of Victoria and Queensland developed the most contrastive systems. Victoria adopted a policy of forced assimilation or ethnocide, merging 'mixed race' families into the wider community while 'full-blood' Aborigines were kept in centralised institutions. As historian Bain Attwood[103] points out, this was at the time 'an aberration in Australia-wide terms'. Queensland followed the more widely accepted policy of permanent segregation of Aborigines and 'half-castes' in closed institutions. These in turn provided models for states with similar profiles. In practice, all administrations slipped between policies of assimilation and segregation in accordance with changing political and economic pressures.

Yet, there *were* general trends in policy and practice. The imperative to change and adapt was directed at Aboriginal families and similar processes operated in the various states and territories to 'cast Aborigines outside the body politic'.[104] In most states separate legislative and administrative regimes created distinct Aboriginal 'problem populations'. They were provided with separate, inferior services, excluded from bureaucratic and statistical processes and, thereby, from the benefits of social policy planning and development. Aborigines were 'excluded from the key rights and privileges of citizenship while having its formal shell',[105] a shell that was essentially empty since Australian constitutions contained no core definitions of citizenship. Through a complex web of federal and state legislative and administrative measures Aborigines were denied rights in all core categories of citizenship — civil, political and social — and this formal exclusion was buttressed in various ways by 'less formal and cultural aspects of citizenship and community structures, practices and values'.[106] Aboriginal exclusion from citizenship was not exclusion simply due to ignorance or prejudices of the time. Rather it went:

> to the heart of the very idea of those qualities thought by the admin-istration to make up an Australian 'citizen'. These qualities were

negative. That is, the Australian citizen was thought to be simply a 'native born or naturalised' person who was not an 'aboriginal native.' It was the 'aboriginal native', in other words, who was the key boundary maker in Australia citizenship.[107]

Aborigines were also denied access to virtually all areas of power brokerage in the wider community, while at the same time their position as the indigenous landowners of the continent, with rights to social and cultural maintenance and self-governance, was denied. Disciplinary networks emanating from head offices of Aboriginal administrations through local police, employers and missionaries undertook surveillance and local control through enforcing the punitive legislation, skimming off 'unruly' elements to institutions and threatening to remove children from their families. Given such restrictions on Aboriginal rights as citizens, it follows that notions of 'assimilation' or 'merging' of Aborigines into the wider community had similarly circumscribed meanings at the time. In the case of institutional training for the children 'assimilation' meant preparation for a life of menial servitude at the bottom of the social hierarchy either in the institutions or in state-arranged employment outside.

In all jurisdictions white interests were accorded primacy over Aboriginal needs. Indeed, the powers of the Acts were so encompassing and the discretionary scope to make regulations so broad that individual public servants, responding to powerful interest groups, were able to shape policy and practice.[108] In this way economic interests in land and Aboriginal labour were advanced and race anxieties were assuaged. In many areas segregated Aboriginal communities provided a cheap and reliable state-regulated labour pool for agricultural and pastoral industries and a regular source of domestic workers.[109] As 'citizens without rights'[110], who were the responsibility of bureaucracies lacking accountability but with almost unlimited powers, Aborigines' lives became inextricably enmeshed in the optimism and failures of government.

While Aborigines were a state responsibility, the federal government still had a significant role to play. In relation to its federal territories it took over responsibility for the Northern Territory from South Australia in 1911, and in the same year transferred control of Aborigines in the Australian Capital Territory to the New South Wales Aborigines Protection Board. There was also an expectation amongst humanitarian organisations that it would monitor the states and, indeed, federal parliament provided a forum for complaint by Australian and British humanitarian groups. Although they were often protesting at conditions in the Northern Territory this did not dampen their enthusiasm for making Aboriginal affairs a federal responsibility.

Federal initiatives, in excluding Aborigines from the rights and responsibilities of citizenship in its statutes and administrative procedures and its endorsement of the White Australia policy, further encouraged a climate across the nation that was sympathetic to formal racialist interventions. While the Australian Constitution did not specifically exclude Aborigines from full citizenship it nevertheless excluded them from the census count and was interpreted as restricting the federal government from passing legislation relating to Aborigines outside the federal territories. Aborigines were excluded under other statutes from the federal franchise, the armed services and from access to social welfare benefits and the broader federal programs designed to improve the health and well-being of Australian citizens. These exclusions did not apply uniformly across Aboriginal Australia but were directed principally at Aborigines deemed by law to be the responsibility of the states. 'Quarter-castes' and the few 'half-castes' not embraced by state legal definitions were not always *formally* excluded, although they could be in practice if they were known to have received assistance from state departments. During the mid-1920s some effort was made by state and federal authorities to count numbers of 'half-castes' so that they could be included in calculations of federal grants to the states. There were also intersections between White Australia policy implementation and the lives of Aboriginal people, principally through the deportation of non-white husbands of Aboriginal women — Melanesian labourers in Queensland and Asian men across northern Australia. Their Aboriginal wives and families were left behind to fend for themselves and their children often grew up believing that their fathers had abandoned them.

FACILITATING ETHNOCIDE IN VICTORIA

By 1886 Victoria's original Koori population of 60,000 had dwindled to just over 800 people including 233 'half-castes,' seventy percent of whom were children.[111] The year saw a significant shift in Aboriginal policy in Victoria. Having endeavoured to gather all Aboriginal families into seven centralised, segregated institutions the government now set out to drive 'mixed race' families out and to force them by law into the wider community. The *Aborigines Protection Law Amendment Act 1886* was the first statute to legislate for the differential treatment of 'full-blood' and 'half-caste'. This took the form of a complex, arbitrary definition which forced all persons of 'mixed race' under thirty-four — that is, the younger people educated from the late 1860s — off the stations and missions, regardless of ties of kinship and country or need, and prohibited them from having any further contact with the people who remained behind. Regulations also allowed for the apprenticeship of children from the age of fourteen and the transfer of 'half-caste' orphans to industrial schools. Historian Michael Christie has dubbed this 'legal genocide' — ethnocide is another term — which complemented the physically destructive actions of earlier colonists and saw the 'culmination of a series of attempts to change the Aborigines, to divest them of their land and culture and have them adopt a Christian civilised British way of life.'[112]

What prompted this shift in policy? B Chesterman and B Galligan[113] state that it flew in the face of advice that families were better off in the missions and stations and that it was an initiative 'masterminded' by the Board for the Protection of Aborigines. Attwood[114] traces its emergence through debate from the 1860s about the 'Aboriginal problem'. Implicit in the policy was the conclusion reached by many colonists in the 1880s that 'Aborigines would disappear; Aborigines of mixed descent entering the European community would pass as whites, and the "full-blood" would die.' Its origins also lay in the 'general bourgeois ethos of individualism, economic self-help and moral improvement, and in an allied fear of pauperism.' The practical motivations for change were many: shortage of funds and hoped for financial savings; the influence of contemporary critiques of children's institutions, reflected in Board members' comments that the stations created dependency and that adults and children should be sent out to become independent 'useful workers',[115] and a determination to crush Aboriginal protest and unrest on the stations by dispersing 'troublesome half-castes'. Protest at Coranderrk Station proved a particular thorn in the Board's side as residents there fought 'a sophisticated political campaign to maintain the status quo,' to remain on the reserve and for better management.[116] Their leaders, Barak and Birdarak, walked the forty miles to Melbourne on countless occasions to represent their interests to politicians and prominent officials. In 1882 the following letter from the Coranderrk people appeared in the *Argus*:

> We have heard there is going to be very strict rules on the station
> and those rules will be too much for us, it seems we are going to be
> treated like slaves, far as we heard of it — We wish to ask those
> Managor of the station Did we steal anything out of the colony or
> murdered anyone or are we prisoners or convict. We should think
> we are all free as any white man of the colony.[117]

The 1886 Act set out to sweep Aboriginal identity away with the
stroke of a pen and to negate the government's special responsibilities
to its indigenous people which, outside of Australia, were a major
factor in colonial indigenous relations. Almost half the estimated 600
residents of the state's stations and missions, representing some forty
families and including 160 children, were forced out.[118] Kin networks
were broken up, community structures deliberately disorganised and
families pushed off their traditional lands into a hostile environment
without trades or capital, and with merely the promise of rations and
blankets when they were in dire straits. Their desperate situation was
compounded by the onset of the 1890s Depression. Most families tried
to remain together in fringe camps near the stations where they had
ties to family and land, knew the country for hunting and were known
to local employers. The skills they had learned at the stations fitted
them for an itinerant life as casual and seasonal rural labourers. As
with the Tasmanians, their Aboriginality, although denied officially,
was recognised locally and they were discriminated against as they
tried to find work, accommodation, send their children to school, and
access mainstream medical and welfare services, and were generally
prevented from exercising their rights.[119] The few who tried to take
their place in the wider community by denying their origins faced
other stresses. Acceptance by whites was elusive and a contemporary
observer wrote of one such man that 'being a half caste a lot of loafing
Aboriginals visited him too often, which in some measure kept his
nose to the grindstone.'[120] The lifestyle of the excluded 'half-caste' soon
came to resemble that of families who had always preferred to live off
the missions and stations. Eventually the Board had to admit defeat
and, in doing so, placed the blame squarely on the 'victims' of its
policies:

> It was thought [in 1886] that the half-castes would in time merge

into the rest of the population, and that they would be able to help themselves, but our experiences have not confirmed that expectation.[121]

In 1910 key provisions of the Act were extended to include 'half-castes' but the Board insisted on helping only those families who moved to its station at Lake Tyers.

The children who were apprenticed out to employers or sent to children's institutions were never to return to the stations or their families. Parents who protested had their rations stopped and were forced out of the stations. Dormitories on the missions and stations were gradually closed down and boys were sent to institutions such as the Salvation Army Farm at Bayswater and girls to domestic servant training homes. In 1900 the Board adopted a more streamlined method of getting children off the stations. On the basis of regulations passed in 1899[122] the Board decided to transfer all 'half-caste' children on stations to industrial schools to be trained in farm work and domestic service. It reported in 1902 that the children were 'happy in their new surroundings, and there seemed every likelihood of them becoming useful members of the community.'[123] The cumulative intentions of these actions were clearly stated by the manager of Lake Condah Station in the same report:

As the blacks are dying out, and the Board removes the half-caste boys and girls by handing them over to the Industrial Schools Department, finality is greatly facilitated, and will, doubtless, be attained within a few years.[124]

Expulsions from the missions and stations, continuing high mortality rates and the narrowing marriage pool — the Board opposed marriages between Aborigines and 'half-castes' — caused a dramatic drop in numbers in the institutions from 594 in 1884 to 252 in 1905. They were progressively closed, the land returned to the Crown for subdivision for farms and the missionaries and residents sent packing. The Board now determined to concentrate its remaining charges at Lake Tyers in eastern Gippsland, which was sufficiently remote and inaccessible for its purposes, and from 1924 this was its only staffed institution and the main focus of its work. Residents' lives there were so strictly regulated and controlled that most Kooris preferred to live outside.

In 1937 the Board Chairman agreed to attend the first Commonwealth–State Native Welfare Conference only as an observer on the grounds that his state had already 'solved the problem'.[125] He conveniently overlooked the hundreds of Koori families who had been edged off the path to citizenship because of their locally recognised Aboriginality and who were caught in the same precarious existence of extreme poverty as families in other states and treated in ways congruous with the more formal laws of exclusion enacted elsewhere. Indeed it could be argued that, as in Tasmania, government policies had caused entire communities to become 'neglected', initiating the familiar pattern of the removal of their children through mainstream channels by police and the children's courts on official grounds of 'neglect'. Again, as in the Tasmanian experience, it could be further argued that removing children under the guise of 'neglect' was a cheap alternative to taking real positive action to assist the communities as a whole. There were of course cases of real need, but lifestyle and white preconceptions predisposed the state to remove children, so that being Aboriginal could become:

a basic reason for a child's removal given the commonly held attitudes about Aboriginal responsibility and capacity to be competent. And the Aboriginal family ... would believe that this was the reason.[126]

Placed in mainstream systems of child welfare the children often lost contact not just with their families but with their Aboriginal identity as well. This circular process of neglect and removal attacked the very heart of Aboriginal family life.

'A PERMANENT HOME' — SEGREGATION IN QUEENSLAND

At the turn of the century Queensland had an Aboriginal population of 26,670 people. As Meston had found, a considerable number were living largely outside of white contact, others were employed in regional industries, and there was a 'mixed race' population estimated at 2300 people, seventy percent of whom were under sixteen years of age, with some families in the south stretching back over three generations and having had 'more or less close association for years past with Europeans'.[127] A range of white interest groups represented competing demands in relation to Aborigines: humanitarians demanding a stop to frontier violence and exploitation of Aboriginal labour and sexuality; employers objecting to outside interference in their exploitative work arrangements; missionaries keen to gather the dying remnants together and to work with 'half-caste' children; townspeople objecting to unsightly camps in their midst; developers wanting more land and resources. Authorities were also continually rapped over the knuckles by Britain on matters of race — Aboriginal, Melanesian and Asian. In 1883 the British government, unhappy with Queensland's treatment of Aborigines and fearing it was intent on exploiting a further source of cheap black labour, rejected the colony's proposal to annex southern New Guinea.[128] Allegations during the 1890s of slavery, and ongoing criticisms of its failure to protect Aboriginal women and children in employment, pointed to the likelihood of another public trouncing. Meston's proposal of an extensive system of centralised segregated Aboriginal reserves, outlined in his 1895 treatise and in his survey of Aboriginal conditions in the north published in the following year, appeared to provide a compromise solution which could appease all these demands.

The reserve system, Meston argued, could be made to work through strict legislative controls to force the removal and permanent segregation of Aboriginal families. With improved management and sufficient arable land the communities could become self-supporting. The target populations were to be destitute and diseased Aborigines near white settlements and children who would, for their own protection, be:

> collected to form a permanent home, and marry and beget children, and live happily free from all contact with the white race, except those placed in charge to see that order is established, their allotted food supplies distributed and teach them gardening and farming so as to make the reserves, as far as possible, if not altogether, self-supporting.[129]

Children were integral to the proposal. Meston was adamant that training and reform must start with the 'young savage,' the 'clear field and virgin soil', gradually guiding them forward through the stages of civilisation until, after three or four generations, all would settle in the agricultural stage, where they would be 'useful to themselves and to mankind'.[130] They would be taught basic literacy and numeracy, singing, the moral ethics of Christianity, systematic organisation of daily life with regular hours for work and rest, and habits of cleanliness and industry. Following accepted white gendered divisions of labour, instructors would train boys in horticultural and basic trades, while girls would learn housework, gardening and net and basket weaving. As young adults they would be encouraged to marry amongst themselves and to contribute to their keep through work on the reserve, hunting and the wages of selected men employed in seasonal work outside. Women would only be allowed to leave the reserve under exceptional circumstances. Drawing on G A Robinson's island settlement plans, Meston proposed a village layout of streets and squares, with the elderly housed in traditional style camps, the young men in timber huts, the girls in dormitories and married couples in their own huts with small plots of land to cultivate for their own needs. White superintendents and staff would run the reserves with 'Aboriginal constables' to assist in maintaining order.

A formal government response in 1897 by the Police Commissioner, W E Parry-Okeden,[131] a long-serving public servant and former district magistrate, endorsed Meston's proposals although it challenged his recommendations to disband the Native Police. Parry-Okeden recommended a firm legal framework with a system of police protectors to monitor employment and the introduction of minimum wages for all workers. He also advocated a system of segregated reserves, controls over Aboriginal movement and entry to towns, compulsory school attendance on missions for children aged six to twelve years and improved medical treatment. Meston and Parry-Okeden's proposals[132] formed the basis of a Bill introduced to the Queensland Parliament in 1897. The wording of the state's duties towards children and its broad powers to make regulations suggest the influence of earlier Victorian legislation. In introducing the Bill the Home Secretary, Sir Horace Tozer, stated optimistically:

I hope the result of this legislation will be to show the civilised world that however black may be the page of history in Queensland on account of the past, there is a bright page to be written, and that bright page will be written by the legislature in a determined effort to ameliorate the conditions of the aboriginals.[133]

The principles of the *Aboriginals Protection and Restriction of the Sale of*

Opium Bill 1897 (hereafter the 1897 Act), determined the government of Aboriginal populations in Queensland until the 1960s. The 1897 Act in turn was to shape legislation passed in Western Australia, South Australia and the Northern Territory from early in the twentieth century. In 1897 Parry-Okeden became the first Chief Protector of Aborigines in Queensland and Meston was appointed Protector in the south to oversee the implementation of the reserve system in southern and central Queensland.

The 1897 Act marked a significant move in official policy in Aboriginal affairs in Queensland and its punitive and restrictive clauses went much further than existing legislation anywhere else in Australia. Queensland now had a state-driven system of segregation, surveillance and control. Aborigines could be deported to reserves and missions and forcibly and permanently detained, and their freedoms and rights strictly curtailed. This was the realisation of what had long been desired by the white population and the consolidation of a whole tradition of colonial practice, mission endeavour and general treatment of 'problem' populations.

The 1897 Act established the Aborigines Department, headed by a Chief Protector of Aborigines, initially the Commissioner of Police; two northern and southern administrative regions each headed by a Protector (disbanded in 1905), and at the local level, police officers appointed as honorary protectors. All protectors exercised unprecedented controls over their charges' lives. These controls were built on and extended through amending legislation in 1901, 1927, 1928 and 1934. The *Aboriginal Preservation and Protection Act 1939–1965* which replaced the 1897 Act maintained and strengthened many of its original principles and practices. The many sweeping regulations passed by the Governor in Council meant that, as in Victoria, public servants rather than politicians shaped policy and practice in Aboriginal affairs. Combined with the absence of external monitoring, this meant that personal 'hobby-horses' of government officials, rather than parliamentary directives, frequently determined action. There was also considerable opportunity for arbitrary and even corrupt dealing at all levels. The 1897 Act applied to a broad range of people of Aboriginal descent. To the race and age-based definitions of the 1886 Victorian legislation were added qualifications of lifestyle, employment and residence. Those deemed to be 'aboriginals' for the purposes of the Act were: ·

(a) An aboriginal inhabitant of Queensland; or

(b) A half-caste who, at the commencement of this Act, is living with an aboriginal as wife, husband or child; or

(c) A half-caste who, otherwise than as wife, husband, or child habitually lives or associates with aboriginals; or

(d) A half-caste child whose age does not in the view of a protector exceed sixteen years.[134]

All came under the full force of the Act, although those in employment were exempted from the provision allowing removal to reserves under ministerial warrant. A 'half-caste' was defined as:

A person being the offspring of an aboriginal mother and other than aboriginal father.[135]

'Quarter-castes' were excluded from the Act. The distinctions between 'aboriginal' and 'half-caste' were intended to allow for some flexibility in the treatment of adult 'half-castes' — for example, those living a European lifestyle were excluded from the removal clause and could apply for exemption from the Act. The Act also distinguished between male and female 'half-castes' with females classified with 'aboriginals' in most clauses as a device to protect them in employment and to regulate their sexual contacts.[136] Torres Strait Islanders were subject to the Act from 1904 although it is not clear to what extent it was enforced. The view expressed by the Northern Protector in 1898, that Islanders were on a higher 'scale of civilisation' than Aborigines and therefore needed less protection, seems to have been widely endorsed. Certainly, official intervention in their lives was minimal compared to the treatment of Aborigines.[137]

While the Aborigines Department monitored race relations throughout the state, the major targets of its interventions were controls over employment, removal to institutions and the overall management of these institutions. Protectors controlled access to employment and conditions of employment and managed Aboriginal wages but the focus was less on protection of workers than regulation of employment and wages. In particular, the Department was determined to enforce a system of compulsory savings with wages paid to local protectors who banked the money and gave workers 'pocket money' to support themselves and their families. From 1919 all Aboriginal workers outside the reserves were forced to contribute to a general fund for the relief of all Aborigines and by 1935 the fund had accumulated almost 300 thousand pounds.[138] In this way Aborigines were forced to defray the costs of incarcerating the state's Aboriginal population while they were robbed of the money they needed to care for their own families. At the same time, as subsequent research has proven, fraud and corruption at all levels meant that hundreds of thousands of pounds were syphoned away from Aborigines to the pockets of individuals for their private use and to state coffers to support projects for the benefit of the wider community.[139]

Removal of Aborigines to institutions and the threat of removal were powerful instruments of social control used to modify behaviour, to defuse local trouble spots by getting rid of troublemakers, to force compliance with the aims of the Department and of vested white interests, and to regulate Aboriginal women's sexuality.[140] As historian Rosalind Kidd[141] points out, the Aborigines Department did not set out to enforce the segregation of all Aborigines in institutions although many whites may have hoped for this; there simply was not sufficient funding or manpower, and local employer interests had to be considered. From the beginning removal and institutionalisation were directed at children and displaced destitute populations in settled areas. The powers to remove were considerable. Adults and children could be removed by administrative decision of the minister, for virtually any reason; there was no court committal process and no right of appeal, and institutionalisation could be for the 'term of their natural lives.' A jumble of families from various areas were brought together in the institutions — the people at Fraser Island early in the 1900s came from twenty-five different localities. Queensland moved increasingly towards the ideal of permanent, segregated institutional communities in large sprawling complexes developed across the state, the expense of which was subsidised by deductions from Aboriginal wages and the work of Aboriginal inmates and missionaries. Segregation appeased white demands for separation of the races and the official determination to prevent further miscegenation, while centralisation allowed for economies in service provision and in maintenance of control. Queensland was the most extreme of the states in its drive to permanently segregate Aboriginal families in institutions and it only began to relinquish control with great reluctance from the 1970s.

These concerns shaped trends in removal over the years so that entire communities were often rounded up at a time. In contrast to other jurisdictions, the majority of children removed over the years in Queensland were accompanied by adults from their families or communities, although they were separated from them on arrival at the missions and government settlements. In its submission to the National Inquiry into the Separation of Aboriginal and Torres Strait Islander Children from their Families in 1996, the Queensland government stated that of an estimated total of 8912 Aborigines removed to institutions between 1908 and 1971, 2024 (twenty-three percent) were children. Of these children only 249 were not accompanied by adults.[142] No figures are available for removal of Torres Strait Islander children although there is evidence that some were removed with their families to institutions on the mainland.[143] The Queensland government offered no reason for these figures but no doubt the explanation lies in the state's strong commitment to the multipurpose institutional model and its vision of enduring, self-supporting, segregated Aboriginal communities. No separate Aboriginal children's institutions were ever established outside the mission and government settlements in Queensland.

The removal and institutionalisation of children were central to the work of the Aborigines Department and, initially at least, this was aligned to existing state child welfare practice. Aboriginal children were subject to two sets of legislation, the laws governing state children and the 1897 Act, although increasingly powers under the latter took precedence. Under the *Industrial and Reformatories Schools Act 1865* children of Aboriginal mothers were automatically deemed to be 'neglected' and magistrates could place them in institutions for a maximum of seven years and they could be sent out to service from the age of twelve. The 1897 Act streamlined the process by allowing for summary removal of any Aboriginal or 'half-caste' child to the age of sixteen without the involvement of the courts. Wide-ranging regulations could be passed in relation to the children's 'care, custody, and education'; to the transfer of orphaned or deserted 'half-caste' children to institutions and to the conditions for apprenticing children or placing them in service. A loophole created by the definition of 'Aboriginal' under the 1897 Act excluded 'half-caste' children not living with Aborigines and initially they were removed through court action under the 1865 Act. This anomaly was rectified in 1901 but the 1865 Act continued to be widely used until the discriminatory clause was repealed in 1906. Amendments passed in 1934 extended the scope of removal to include virtually any child of Aboriginal descent. Prior to this, 'quarter-caste' children were generally removed under child welfare legislation. In 1939 the Director of Native Affairs became legal guardian of children to the age of twenty-one, with the right to exercise all powers of guardianship in their interests or to transfer legal custody to those he deemed to be 'suitable persons.' This applied for the next twenty-six years. Requests to adopt, often made by the children's employers, were generally rejected because of the department's determination to transfer the children to its own institutions. John W Bleakley, Chief Protector of Aborigines from 1913 to 1942, told the South Australian Royal Commission in 1913 that his department had 'stretched the law' and allowed adoption of some children 'found' in camps for 'philanthropic' motives or in instances where the children's white fathers wished to adopt them.[144]

John W Bleakley, Chief Protector of Aborigines in Queensland from 1914 to 1941, 1928.

(Courtesy of Department of Transport and Regional Services and National Archives of Australia: A263/4, Album 1)

These laws gave administrators virtual carte blanche to treat the children as they wished, thereby making it effectively impossible to judge whether they were acting outside their legal powers or not. Children were removed for an extraordinary range of reasons, some being 'rescued' from reportedly unsavoury circumstances with white employers, and others simply because they were of Aboriginal descent. Included in a long list of children removed in north Queensland in the 1903 Annual Report of the Northern Protector of Aborigines[145] were the following:

> Half-caste twelve years, from Cloncurry, for alleged indecent practices. It was rather on account of the filthy surroundings in which this child has been living, and the treatment to which he has been subjected that I recommended the removal. His employer's wife puts this boy on a chain occasionally when he misbehaves himself.

> Half-caste, about thirteen years, lately in service at Normanton ...

for ten years past. Before leaving for Cooktown [her employer] asked permission from Protector Galbraith to send the girl to a neighbouring station ... but never mentioned or hinted anything concerning her condition. Permission having been refused, Dolly was accordingly handed over to the police who had her examined by a doctor, when she was found to be seven months pregnant ... Dolly was thereupon ordered to Yarrabah, but gave birth to a daughter soon after reaching Cooktown on her way south. The child died before the mother resumed her journey.

Half-caste female, about sixteen years, who has been travelling over the country as a boy, in the company of a stockman ... for eight years past.

Half-caste, about ten years, amongst the McIvor blacks. 'It is a pity to see her grow up in a camp. Could you not have her removed? I think it would be good for her if she could be taken away soon.'

Half-caste, five years, in good health and condition, living with her mother in the ... camp. 'She is fairly well looked after; but of late is inclined to visit the Chinese camps.'

Half-caste, about eight years. 'Given to ... about twelve months ago by ... of N ... Station. She has lately become unmanageable by her employers.'

Half-caste, twelve years, 'running wild' amongst the Charleston blacks.

Twelve years and eight years, two half-caste children, their reputed father ... in gaol, and mother dead.

A young half-caste boy, sentenced to two years at the Yarrabah Reformatory for breaking, entering, and stealing from a dwelling.

Half-caste, about seven years of age ... the manager of the station says 'the blacks knock this child about very much.'

Their parents had no right of appeal or redress. Bleakley told the South Australian Royal Commission in 1913 that under the 1897 Act every Aboriginal or 'half-caste' child was automatically a ward of the state and if there was any doubt the obligation was on the child or the parents to prove otherwise.[146] Thus the Department could take children whether they were neglected or not. Lighter coloured children living in Aboriginal camps were especially vulnerable. Bleakley stated that children with 'more white blood in them than black should be the care of the white man' and, while he acknowledged in this case the 'sentimental right' of their parents, he advocated that the children be removed before the age of three to the care of the State Children's Department.[147] The streaming of lighter children, and girls in particular, into the white community continued over the years and in the 1940s the Department was managing a file titled 'Almost white girls on settlements', referring to such girls already detained on government settlements.[148] According to Bleakley, 'half-caste' children should be left to live with and to marry their own kind according to their 'level of civilisation' rather than race. He also acknowledged that institutions produced young women with the 'confidence of little children. They do not know how to protect themselves.'[149] Girls were the major target group for removal — of 286 children admitted to Aboriginal institutions between 1897 and 1905, 171 were female[150] — reflecting departmental determination to protect them from sexual abuse by employers and to control their sexuality. 'Half-caste' girls were of particular concern to administrators and the Northern Protector wrote in 1902:

In the case of half-caste children, especially girls, already living in the camps it is desirable that these, where old enough, should be moved at once to the mission station or reformatory.[151]

Parents not only lived separately from their children in the large settlements, but they were often sent away from the institutions altogether, to work outside, for medical treatment, as a punishment or transferred elsewhere when an institution was closed down. There were considerable pressures on parents to voluntarily send their children to institutions to be educated. Sometimes this reflected opposition to the children's presence in local schools. A Miriam Vale farmer wrote to the Department in 1933 on behalf of one of his workers after the local police officer threatened to remove the whole family if the children continued to attend the local school. The father reported the following heated exchange between himself and the police officer:

if you don't keep them home to-morrow I will send you to the Mission. I said, you got no fault, the Law wont let you, he said I can make my own Law … I am not sending my children there while your black kids are going, so keep them home, I said, No I wont keep them home oh well he said, straight to the Mission you go.[152]

In his letter to the Department the farmer commented that the constable had 'a peculiar mental kink ... which makes him quite unfitted to be a constable in a district where aboriginals reside.'[153] Missionaries intent on achieving their goals of civilising and Christianising also 'enticed' families to send in their children. The children brought in government subsidies and gave missionaries some control over their parents and thereby access to a labour force to build up the mission.

Most children were placed in departmental industrial schools or residential dormitories on the large multipurpose government or mission run settlements where they attended school and were trained in rural and domestic work. Initially, some children in the south were sent to orphanages for white children but in 1900 Meston recommended that they be sent only to Aboriginal institutions where they could be kept at a fifth of the cost.[154] The practice was gradually phased out although some institutions continued to take in 'quarter-caste' children.[155] By 1905 the Aborigines Department had six missions in the north and two government institutions in the south, most registered as reformatories or industrial schools under the 1865 Act. There was a particular focus on educating the children and in 1902, 743 were attending schools at Cape Bedford, Mapoon, Yarrabah and Weipa missions in the north, and in the south eighty-eight were enrolled at schools at Fraser Island and Deebing Creek settlements and the Nudgee Orphanage for white children. Three hundred and forty Torres Strait Islander children were attending school.[156] For their work with the children the missions were paid two shillings and six pence per week per child, compared to the rate of seven shillings paid by the State Children's Department to its institutions. Missions were also provided with an initial grant for buildings and annual grants for rations and teachers' salaries.[157] This was paid out of the Department's modest annual budget: in 1903 the Department received 25,000 pounds to provide for 9293 Aboriginal people in its care. These rates were also low compared with the subsidies paid by the Aborigines Department for children placed in State Children's Department institutions — five shillings and ten pence per week to Nudgee Orphanage and up to six pounds a week to the Infants Home in Brisbane.[158] Although the Department was initially keen to send as many children as possible to Aboriginal missions and settlements, from 1905 the Chief Protector of

Aborigines began to advocate placement of lighter children in institutions for white children with the intention of 'improving their station in life' and to 'prevent inbreeding of half-castes with full-bloods'.[159] A comment by the Inspector of Orphanages that 'the question opened up by their admission is too wide a one to be dealt with under any existing orphanage arrangements' suggests opposition to accepting the children.[160] George A Ferguson, Director of the State Children's Department,[161] told the 1913 South Australian Royal Commission that his department had few such children and that while they endeavoured to place Protestant children with foster families, few white mothers were willing to take them as they felt the child's 'colour' reflected on them when they went out in public. Catholic children were sent directly to Catholic institutions.

Children in Aboriginal institutions, like Barambah settlement in the south, were sent out to work under departmental supervision as an integral part of their training and with the understanding that they would ultimately return there to marry and live out their lives.[162] This marked a significant step in state intervention in Aboriginal employment. Formerly unregulated, Aboriginal child labour was now controlled in terms of access, conditions and pay, with employers obliged to see to their education. Workers' wages were also to be paid into savings bank accounts supervised by the department.[163] From 1902 to 1906 girls in service in the south used the Aboriginal Girls' Home in West End for accommodation and as a refuge and meeting place while working in Brisbane. A Departmental Protectress inspected their conditions of employment until 1933 when this duty was transferred to the State Children's Department.[164] Nevertheless, the girls' vulnerability to sexual exploitation remained such that in 1913 Archbishop Donaldson noted, after a visit to Barambah, that 'over 90% came back pregnant to the white man'.[165] In consequence the government persistently demanded greater controls to regulate their sexuality.

TASMANIA

In many ways Tasmania paralleled Victoria — both had small predominantly 'mixed race' populations considered amenable to assimilation. However, Tasmania did not set up a separate Aboriginal administration to enforce change, although it did have statutes targeting the two hundred and fifty or so islanders living segregated lives on the Bass Strait islands, principally at the Cape Barren Island Reserve. Tasmanian governments simply refused to acknowledge the Aboriginality of the surviving 'mixed race' families, although locally they were constructed as being far from white, as a government official commented in 1900:

> These people are not English in character — the more you know of them the less English and the more native they are ... they can never be judged as we judge ourselves ... [they] should be firmly governed as an inferior race.[166]

While the islanders clung tenaciously to their hunting and gathering lifestyle and extended family networks, successive governments and missionaries continued to pressure them to assimilate. From 1908 the Flinders Island municipality joined the effort to enforce change and refused to assist them to develop a viable economic base, security of land tenure or to provide essential services.

The *Cape Barren Island Reserve Act 1912* endeavoured to force Aboriginal compliance by making occupancy of reserve land provisional on building houses and fencing and cultivating the land. However eight years later the Secretary of Lands was proposing to remove all the children to schools on the mainland. He was subsequently advised by the parliamentary draughtsman that this would be contrary to common law.[167] A 1922 report found, after examining Aboriginal reserve legislation on the Australian mainland, that the Tasmanian government simply did not have the necessary funding to make Cape Barren Island into a viable reserve. Instead a parliamentary committee in 1924 opted for increased supervision and control of reserve residents. Conditions mirrored those in the town reserves of mainland Australia — children were frequently ill and, as one resident put it, 'we always seemed to be making wreaths from little flowers.'[168] This contributed to pressures to remove the children to the Tasmanian mainland. In 1928 the head teacher of Cape Barren school was appointed special constable with police powers to remove children for neglect. A government report by A W Burbury[169] in the following year showed clearly that the 1912 Act was responsible for the destitution on the reserve and the islanders' failure to become economically self-sufficient. 'How they live is a mystery,' Burbury commented. Nevertheless, finding that many of the children were suffering from malnutrition, Burbury recommended their removal from the islands: 'Better that they should be taken young and innocent, rather than live to be turned out to a life of idleness and worse, on the Reservation.' The report also noted the islanders' continuing fierce sense of ownership of the land and their deep antipathy to whites: 'They hate whites, regarding themselves as having been supplanted and exploited by white men ... They say that the whites "took away their land."' Furthermore they believed they 'had a claim on the State' and that the 1912 Act constituted 'recognition of their claim that their country had been taken away from them by the whites.' A report by the Australian Board of Missions in 1931 recommended the dispersal of the people from the island and their absorption into society on the Tasmanian mainland. This prompted the comment from the President of the Australian Women's National League that this 'would be a dreadful thing.'[170] In 1937 the islanders presented a petition to the Tasmanian parliament in which they appealed for 'equal treatment with their white brethren in the matter of social service payments, and the right to travel, not to be pushed back by Cape Barren Island authorities.' In Parliament one speaker likened their treatment to the Jews in Germany.[171]

An unknown number of Aboriginal children were taken from their families on the islands and, as in Victoria, were absorbed into the mainstream child welfare system, placed in white foster families or in institutions like Ashley Boys Home at Deloraine. From 1935 they were removed under the *Infant Welfare Act 1935* which also allowed for a parent to be imprisoned for the criminal offence of neglecting a child. As in Victoria, the islanders were trapped in a vicious circle where their poverty and destitution put them at risk of losing their children while the government continued to refuse to provide appropriate family supports, a policy that fitted with government aims to force the families to assimilate and to clear the islands for white settlement and economic development.

NEW SOUTH WALES

New South Wales moved uneasily between models of forced dispersion of Aborigines into the wider community as in Victoria, and segregation in centralised institutions as in Queensland. This equivocation reflected the effort to accommodate local white demands for

Purfleet School was one of several segregated Aboriginal schools set up by the New South Wales government to provide segregated education for such children.

(Courtesy of New South Wales State Records, 4/8566 COD 423 8503)

Aboriginal labour and land, shrill cries for the expulsion of Aborigines from towns and entire regions, and Aboriginal resistance manifested in continual movement within and across their territories.[172] By the 1890s the state's original estimated population of 200,000 Aborigines[173] had fallen to between six and ten thousand people. Most were employed in seasonal work on farms and pastoral stations and lived a way of life similar to that described earlier in the south-west of Western Australia. These adaptations were soon to be undermined by the disastrous droughts and economic depression of the 1890s and strident white racism, leading to increasing numbers settling in segregated Aboriginal stations managed by the Aborigines Protection Board (APB). With the passing of the *Aborigines Protection Act 1909* the Board adopted a policy of dispersal similar to the Victorian model in order to break perceived dependency on government aid in the stations by forcing Aborigines to merge into the wider community. This would lead, the Board hoped, to the eventual 'withering away' of the communities.[174] However, at the beginning of the First World War there were still seventeen centralised managed stations and 170 unsupervised camps around the state. The former were controlled by white managers and committees of local white residents, and provided services that were refused to families in the wider community, in particular schooling for the children, under the direction of the Department of Public Instruction.[175] Some had dormitory accommodation where children were forced to live separately from their parents. The unsupervised camps comprised small blocks of unalienated Crown land lacking basic facilities where families lived when in employment or in order to escape surveillance by the Board and the threat of removal of their children. The Board endeavoured to maintain a balance between numbers in the stations and camps and local labour needs. In 1915, in response to the wartime demand for rural labour, all males of 'half-caste' descent or less who were over the age of eighteen were ordered off the stations and camps.

The removal of Aboriginal children was integral to the APB's policies. Initially children were removed through normal court committal proceedings under the *Neglected Children and Juvenile Offenders Act 1905.*

Children sent to live at the Bomaderry United Aborigines Mission Home, nd.
(Courtesy of New South Wales State Records, 4/8566 COD 423 8335)

In 1909 it gained full 'control and custody' of Aboriginal children and their education with the power to apprentice them from the ages of fourteen to eighteen. This legitimised the process of removals begun by the Board in the 1890s.[176] In the following year regulations were passed setting out conditions for apprenticeships — rates of pay, banking of wages and 'moral training' — and application forms for employers. Then in 1915, following complaints by the Board about difficulties proving 'neglect' when the children appeared in court 'decently clad or apparently looked after',[177] station managers and police were granted powers of summary removal to take children without the due court process. Parents had the right to appeal to the courts against removals but most chose to flee the stations with their children instead. While lighter skinned children and offending youths could be sent to mainstream homes and reformatories, the others were kept in station dormitories or sent to special Aboriginal children's homes. The United Aborigines Mission Home, opened at Bomaderry in 1908, took in infants and children under ten years of age. Board institutions opened from this time — Cootamundra Aboriginal Girls Home (1911) and Kinchela Aboriginal Boys Home (1918; moved to Kempsey in 1924) — followed the model of nineteenth-century industrial schools, training the children to become servile rural and domestic workers and then apprenticing them out to white employers. Although parents had the right to visit their children once a year, through arrangements with the local station manager,[178] problems of distance, lack of money to travel, official disapproval and resentment at this official interference in family life often prevented these visits.

By 1916, 700 children had been removed and a total of 1600 were taken between 1912 and 1938.[179] Girls aged between ten and fourteen years constituted seventy to eighty percent of the tally,[180] reflecting the APB's aims to mould them into useful domestic servants to meet the growing demand for their services from middle-class families in Sydney and country areas as white girls moved to alternative employment in factories and offices. The Board was also determined to isolate the girls from the influence of their families and to strictly control their sexuality and fertility and thereby to limit any increase in the state's 'mixed race' population. Aboriginal 'maids' were advertised in popular women's magazines. An article in the *Australian Women's Mirror* in 1940 carried the headline, 'Try An Abo Apprentice' and included a testimonial concerning a girl who had become 'one of the family and [was] worth three of the white maids we have employed.'[181] Board controls over the girls made them an attractive proposition to middle-class women anxious to secure reliable home help — they could be legally bound for up to four years under conditions set by the Board in accordance with employers' interests. This may have compensated employers who were unwittingly drawn into the broader process of training the girls and policing their morals. Between 1910 and the 1930s the Board apprenticed out 570 girls to various positions with more than 1200 employers in city and country areas in New South Wales. In any one year an estimated three to four hundred Aboriginal girls were apprenticed, constituting 1.5 percent of the state's domestic workforce.[182] There was no adequate Board supervision of their employment and living conditions and, given the private nature of the workplace in which they lived, it is hardly surprising that many girls experienced cruel and abusive treatment at the hands of their employers. Although apprenticeships officially ceased at the age of twenty-one, many young women had no alternative but to continue with domestic work and they spent their lives caring for white families but never for their own. The working girls' frequent pregnancies to white men, although not officially condoned, 'whitened' the Aboriginal population and continued the cycle of removal and loss as many of these children were taken from their mothers.[183]

During the 1920s and into the Depression years of the 1930s, numbers in camps near towns increased, prompting local curfews, refusal of services to Aborigines and renewed demands for their total expulsion and segregation. Aboriginal parents faced a terrible dilemma — their children were now excluded from most state schools but they were required by law to send them to school or face the threat of their being removed.[184] The segregated Aboriginal schools on some government stations provided a further point of surveillance and possible removal.

The children marked with black and white crosses in this photograph from the Daily Telegraph *were excluded from Woolbrook school in 1936 following protests from white parents.*

(Courtesy of *Daily Telegraph*, 30.7.1937)

Teachers were required to forward the following details on each child to the Aborigines Protection Board:

Does the child attend school regularly?

State average attendance during quarter ended.

Does the child come to school clean?

Does the child come to school with clothes in decent order and well-mended?

Does the child appear well fed and cared for?

State if the child can read and progress as compared with last report?[185]

Such treatment of family fostered the emergence of a strong Aboriginal protest movement during the mid-1920s. The Australian Aborigines Progressive Association (AAPA), officially launched in 1925, had a membership of five hundred Aborigines in northern New South Wales and Sydney. The AAPA called for 'liberty, freedom, the right to function and act in our own interest, as right thinking citizens,' and the return of Aboriginal land. It also attacked the system of removing and apprenticing Aboriginal children. In the late 1920s AAPA secretary Mrs Elizabeth McKenzie-Hatton, a non-Aboriginal woman, travelled the state in a bid to reunite families and apprentices. Shocked at APB inaction at the exploitative treatment of Aboriginal girls in domestic service, the AAPA established its own home for working girls in Homebush, a suburb of Sydney. Aboriginal leader Fred Maynard also endeavoured to obtain legal representation for a fifteen-year-old Aboriginal girl who had been raped by her employer, sent to Sydney where her baby died and then returned by the Board to her former employer. When his efforts were thwarted Maynard retorted that the Board 'insulted and degraded all Aboriginal people, and it aimed to exterminate the noble and ancient race of Australia.'[186]

This political action resulted in modifications to APB policy in regard to Aboriginal girls in domestic service, who were now to be allowed to return home at the end of their indentures. However, officials were instructed to maintain a close watch over them and to ensure that they married and set up respectable homes, otherwise they in turn would face the prospect of losing their children. This heralded a new approach of training the girls to be 'good mothers' within nuclear family units, and would become a hallmark of assimilation policies introduced across Australia in the 1950s.[187] In 1934, as white tempers rose in response to the growing Aboriginal presence in their towns, and in an effort to stop the growing Aboriginal political muscle in the state, the Board returned to its original policy of concentrating families in a small number of centralised, segregated, managed stations, geared to social control and surveillance, with the long-term aims of assimilating the families into the wider community.

WESTERN AUSTRALIA

The largest state by area, Western Australia at the turn of the century had an Aboriginal population of 24,000 which included 1000 'half-castes'. Aborigines made up just over one percent of its population and were widely distributed across the state. As in New South Wales, administrators simultaneously implemented policies of segregation and assimilation as they grappled with strident employer demands, white racism, Aboriginal intransigence and the grinding problems of limited funding and the tyrannies of distance. The result was a combination of profound neglect of Aboriginal needs and arbitrarily imposed authoritarian control and repression. A strong code of silence built on isolation and parochial networks of family and business interests kept the scandalous treatment of Aborigines in the state out of the national public eye.

The Western Australian *Aborigines Act 1905* was based closely on the Queensland 1897 Act. It established a similar administrative structure and controls over Aboriginal employment and sexual contact and powers to remove and institutionalise 'mixed race' children. Some controls were made even more restrictive — Aboriginal women had to have permission from the Chief Protector of Aborigines to marry non-Aboriginal men, or those men faced being charged with cohabitation; areas could be declared prohibited to unemployed Aborigines; the Chief Protector of Aborigines became the legal guardian of Aboriginal and 'half-caste' children; harsh penalties were introduced for offences against the Act. In the absence of proof to the contrary, a bench of Justices of the Peace could decide solely on the basis of the person's appearance whether or not they came under the Act, a practice which even the notoriously racialist southern American state of Virginia ruled to be legally unsound.[188] White interests dominated the implementation of the Act — the pastoral lobby successfully blocked government intervention in employment and refused to pay workers a basic cash wage; casual sexual contact remained outside the scope of the Act, leaving Aboriginal women and girls vulnerable to sexual exploitation and abuse; and whites in the south demanded the segregation of Aborigines from the towns and their exclusion from all town services including schooling for their children. Throughout the state geographical and social isolation and relations of patronage and protection with white employers provided a protective buffer zone for some Aboriginal families.

Of all the states (excepting the Northern Territory), Western Australia's system of removal and institutionalisation of Aboriginal children was the most separate from mainstream child welfare processes, and the most extreme in terms of powers to remove children. This reflected the relative infancy of child welfare in the state, the problems of huge distances which favoured measures that allowed children to be removed quickly by local officers, and the entrenched white racism which pervaded the state. The Chief Protector of Aborigines was the legal guardian of children up to the age of sixteen, extended to twenty-one in 1936. No definition of 'legal guardianship' was provided but under nineteenth-century common law it embraced the full range of rights and powers an adult could exercise in respect to the welfare and upbringing of a child. This was a very significant step away from mainstream practice. Normally, parental guardianship was only displaced following the death of the parent or by court order in the 'best interest' of the child. While legislation passed in 1844 in South Australia conferring guardianship on the Protector of Aborigines was hedged with qualifications on its application, there were no such limits on legal guardianship of Aboriginal children in Western Australia. Thus Chief Protectors were apparently acting within their legal rights when they allowed children's names to be changed and when they denied what was generally considered to be parents' *prima facie* right of access to their children. Furthermore, the notion of 'dwindling right' in legal guardianship, intended to ensure independence from authority for maturing young people, was not observed, particularly in the case of 'half-caste' girls who, as they matured, were subject to increasing control in order to regulate their sexuality.[189]

Amendments in 1911 to expedite removal of the main target group — 'half-caste' children — further undermined the rights of Aboriginal mothers. Although by law all mothers have custody of their illegitimate children, the *Aborigines Act Amendment Act 1911* stated that in the case of illegitimate 'half-caste' children the Chief Protector of Aborigines' powers of guardianship exceeded those of their Aboriginal mothers. Police regulations introduced in 1909 also expedited the removal of children by authorising police officers to act entirely on their own initiative to take children from their families and send them to institutions. The result was an arbitrary and largely unsupervised system, lacking legal guidelines and checks and balances to protect the best interest of the child and with no right of appeal or redress for parents.

The Aborigines Department in Western Australia had the leanest funding per capita of all Aboriginal administrations in Australia. This was not simply due to a struggling economy: even during the flush years of the 1890s gold rushes, West Australians had protested vehemently at the high allocations to be set aside for the Aborigines Protection Board under section 70 of the 1889 Constitution Act, until the British government agreed to its repeal in 1897.[190] This poor funding continued over the years. In 1933 Western Australia spent only £27,238 on its estimated Aboriginal population of 19,201 — a sum that was 'one-half of what New South Wales spent on half that number, and only a little more than South Australia expended on its 3,407 Aborigines.'[191] A consequence was parsimonious and negligent treatment of Aboriginal families. Conditions in missions in the north of the state and in the government settlements were typically deplorable. While the Aborigines Department and the missionaries battled over whether missions, like the government settlements, were to act as 'clearing houses' to train Aborigines to take their place in the outside world, or to create enduring segregated populations, the reality was that most trainees had difficulty fitting in on the outside and gravitated back to the institutions where they married and raised their own families. Families outside the missions and settlements lived in camps near towns, lacking even basic facilities; on stations and in the bush they battled to survive on seasonal work and rations of flour, tea and sugar. They faced the continual threat of being rounded up and sent to an institution.

Families lived under constant surveillance and were forced to observe strict barriers separating white and black. They were denied access to community services while they provided a valuable labour supply for local employers. Throughout the state children were excluded from state schools and for most the only chance of education lay in the institutions. Those in the camps grew up within indigenous networks largely outside the influence of the state and the formative influences of nation and the school. This had two significant consequences. Living in economic hardship and being raised according to Aboriginal family ways made them vulnerable to removal on the grounds of alleged neglect and bad parenting. For pastoral and some rural workers the protection of employers could prevent this from happening, but families camped in highly visible clusters near southern towns were particularly vulnerable to invasive actions by police. On the other hand, these children had the psychological benefit of growing up within the circle of their family while they also learned Aboriginal traditions and ways of living and remained part of an ongoing extended kin network, which was often located in traditional country. This in turn ensured continuity of local Aboriginal cultural practices, rights to land, and survival as a sovereign people. While this has been widely acknowledged in the case of pastoral areas, it was also the case in many other parts of the state, including the south-west where, despite popular white constructs of these families as living like 'poor whites' and having 'no culture', cultural maintenance and diversity remained strong over the years, in part because of the extreme exclusion and segregation of Aborigines from the wider community.

Under the control of the South Australian government from 1864 to 1911, Aborigines in the Northern Territory had been largely neglected and left to the whims of white vested interests — pastoralists, police, government officials and itinerant miners.[192] The legacy of this was:

> a potent brew of fear, resentment, guilt and economic self-interest [and] belief in white superiority [with] economic exploitation, social discrimination, and physical mistreatment ... all justified on the grounds that Aboriginal people were grossly inferior to the colonisers.[193]

At the turn of the century, the surviving population, estimates of which ranged wildly from 13,000 to 50,000,[194] formed a significant proportion of the Territory population. While those living in areas outside of white settlement were left more or less alone, elsewhere there was an ongoing history of rampant disease, violent dispossession and abduction of children for labour. Terrible loss of life occurred in regions taken up for pastoral stations — depopulation in the Victoria River region between 1880 and 1939 has been estimated at between eighty-six and ninety-six percent.[195] While some survivors worked on pastoral stations in their own country and were afforded some protection by their employers, they nevertheless became the property of their captors.

> Europeans could do virtually anything to Aborigines, and Aborigines had little, if any, redress ... There was great cruelty in these practices [and] this was no accident. They were the product of total power.[196]

The shortage of white workers throughout the Territory was a serious concern, making Aborigines a sought after, although denigrated and exploited, source of labour. By 1900 pastoralists were totally dependent on unwaged Aboriginal labour while 'refugee camps' in towns like Darwin and Alice Springs provided much needed casual and domestic labour. Hermannsburg Lutheran mission, opened in 1877 in Arrernte country near Alice Springs, was then the only functional mission in the Territory — Jesuit efforts in the Daly River region had been abandoned — and while it provided some protection from frontier violence, it also imposed rigid and spartan regimes on its charges.

There was also a serious shortage of white women and stable domestic family life in the Territory and, in consequence, largely unchecked sexual exploitation and abuse of Aboriginal women and girls. Aboriginal women were also sought out as sexual partners by Asian men. Racial mixes in the Top End were particularly diverse — Aboriginal and European, Chinese, Japanese, Malay and Filipino. Some strong and enduring relationships were established and a number of Asian men lived with their families. However, as is evident in Xavier Herbert's expansive novels on life in the Territory, permanent relations were increasingly frowned on, although covert casual sexual contact continued to be tolerated as 'a necessary evil' for the outlet of white — but not Asian — men's sexual urges. By 1913 the 'mixed race' population was estimated at three hundred, the majority living in Aboriginal camps where they were generally welcome and because most whites would have nothing to do with them.

The passing of the Aboriginals Ordinance 1911 marked the official shift in the Northern Territory from 'pacification and dispersal' to protection through authoritarian control. In the same year the federal government took over Aboriginal affairs and the seat of power moved to even more distant bureaucracies in the south with little under-standing of conditions in the Territory. The transfer of control prompted church and humanitarian groups to lobby for Aboriginal affairs in the states to be made a federal responsibility as well. While the Northern Territory ordinances of 1911 and 1918 were closely based on the Queensland and Western Australian models, their implementa-tion reflected local concerns. 'Full-bloods' were left largely to the control of pastoralists and missions, or to their own devices on large inviolable reserves until the 1950s. This reflected the inordinate power of the pastoralists as *the* major industry in a region experiencing serious difficulties establishing a viable and varied economy. Pastoralists would brook no interference in their system of Aboriginal labour and, like their counterparts in Western Australia, would not hear of a minimum cash wage for their workers.

The focus of the Northern Territory administration was almost exclusively on the 'coloured' population. It adopted a two-pronged approach: to control the size and composition of this population, largely though punitive controls over Aboriginal women, and to create a viable labour force, by removing 'mixed race' children from their

191

families to be trained in institutions in a 'hazy and barely articulated concept of economic assimilation'.[197] The majority of 'mixed race' women remained under the control and guardianship of the Chief Protector of Aborigines for life — they needed his permission to marry; he could send a woman of any age to an institution or out to work under any conditions, and he had guardianship of their children and could take them away for any reason. Nevertheless the 'mixed race' population continued to increase, due in part to an administration that failed to enforce these provisions in any systematic way. The Territory Welfare Branch was concerned to stream lighter skinned children into the white community through removal to white children's institutions and over the years adopted programs to move them out of the 'sin sodden north' altogether. The South Australian government cooperated by assisting with the care of children requiring extended medical treatment in Adelaide, and through the placement and supervision of children in foster homes and of working girls sent down from Alice Springs. Other 'mixed race' children were sent to special Aboriginal children's institutions in the Territory. By the First World War the Aborigines Department had two major training institutions — the Darwin Half-caste Home at Kahlin Compound (1913) and the Bungalow at Alice Springs (1914). Conditions at both were deplorable and attracted widespread public condemnation in the southern press over the years. Concern about the example of the 'immoral behaviour' of adults at Kahlin Compound prompted the removal in 1923 of the

girls and youngest boys to a three-bedroom suburban home outside the Compound. By 1927 forty-four girls were crammed within its walls. Despite the many colonial resonances of the Top End, the system for training the children was not the colonial model of India and South-East Asia where young 'mixed race' people were separated out and educated to form an elite intermediary between the 'native peoples' and their

A wire netting fence kept children at Darwin's Kahlin Compound penned in and strictly separated from the adults.

(Courtesy of Australian Institute of Aboriginal and Torres Strait Islander Studies, Wilson.E1.BW)

colonial rulers. The Territory system was intended to churn out a 'coolie class' of servile menial workers — domestic servants, station hands, agricultural labourers — suited to working in tropical conditions.

Children at Darwin's Kahlin Compound.
(Courtesy of Australian Institute of Aboriginal and Torres Strait Islander Studies, Wilson.E1.BW)

Relations between the government and missions early in the twentieth century were strained. The missions operated on shoestring budgets — the remote Roper River Mission, opened in 1908, received the meagre subsidy of three shillings a week per 'half-caste' child, and Hermannsburg, which refused to admit 'half-caste' children, missed out altogether. Each had their own particular squabbles with authorities: Roper River refused to send children out to work as instructed and endeavoured instead to form a permanent mission community;[198] missionaries at Hermannsburg continued to lock children in the dormitories overnight on the grounds that the children were:

> little spitfires, more like wild cats and discipline of any kind is hateful to them. Again the will of the stronger must rule and they learn the lesson of obedience, of diligence, of quiet behaviour under the silent protest of their wild nature.[199]

Nevertheless, following the positive recommendations of a report by Chief Protector of Aborigines Baldwin Spencer in 1913, the Commonwealth government invited church and mission societies to establish self-supporting industrial mission stations in the Territory, principally for the detention and training of 'half-caste' children. By the early 1930s seven missions were operating, most on the northern coast, providing a sanctuary from ongoing violence as well as dormitories for the education of over four hundred children.

In a report commissioned by the Commonwealth government in 1929 the Queensland Chief Protector of Aborigines, John Bleakley, exposed the federal government's dismal failure in fulfilling its duties to its Aboriginal population, estimated at 21,000. Bleakley was appalled at conditions in the children's homes and recommended their immediate closure. He urged that all illegitimate 'half-caste' children should be removed to mission dormitories to be trained for 'a useful place in the development of the Territory industries'. Bleakley did not advocate their permanent separation from 'full-blood' people, arguing that 'these people are happier amongst their own race'.[200] However, all light skinned children should be sent to institutions in South Australia where they could be 'given a reasonable chance of absorption into the white community to which they rightly belong,' and to keep them away from 'the dangers of the blood call.'[201] Bleakley was not opposed to the marriage of 'half-caste' and 'full-blood' but advocated marriage between persons on similar 'planes of civilisation'. He did however recommend stricter controls over sexual contact between Aboriginal women and white men as well as increased migration of white women to the Territory. Bleakley also took on the Territory pastoral industry. He noted the mutual dependence of Aborigines and pastoralists. While the industry employed eighty percent of the Aboriginal workforce in the Territory it was also 'absolutely dependent' on their labour and 'if they were removed, most of the holdings ... would have to be abandoned.'[202] He also referred to the sexual abuse of women and the exploitation of their 'half-caste' children as station workers. The pastoralists were united in opposing the education of these children on the grounds that it 'spoilt' them and made them 'cunning and cheeky'. To this Bleakley replied:

The trouble is probably that they become enlightened, and, as a result, dissatisfied with conditions. The right education, with improved working and living conditions, should make for better service.[203]

While the boys were kept on the stations many girls were sent off to the Darwin 'Half-caste' Home (reflected in ratios of fifty girls to twenty boys there at a time) where they were vulnerable to abuse by the many non-Aboriginal men in the town.

The Chief Protector of Aborigines, Dr Cecil Cook, vehemently opposed virtually all of Bleakley's proposals, including the shift from state to mission control of children's institutions and the proposal to send all 'mixed race' children out of the state. In this he was endorsed by his superiors in Canberra. He also publicly condemned the Queensland administration for leaving 'half-castes' to grow up as Aborigines. A committed conservative, Cook fretted over the growing 'mixed race' population and its potential to develop into 'a left-wing revolutionary element in Australia'.[204] Like his counterpart in Western Australia, A O Neville, he looked to environmental and eugenic solutions. He was a staunch advocate of institutionalisation of children — in 1931 he stated that it was official policy to collect 'all illegitimate half-castes male and female under the age of sixteen years for housing in institutions for educational purposes'[205] — as well as young single women, and even the sterilisation of mentally handicapped 'half-caste' children.[206] During the 1930s under his administration removals to Homes increased by over seventy percent,[207] prompting criticism in the press about the extent of removal, the treatment of the children, and of tiny babies being taken from their mothers. The Commonwealth was forced to review its policy and to issue placatory statements to the public:

Half-caste girls are brought into the homes as soon as possible after reaching an age when they can be separated from their native mothers. They are reared and educated under constant medical supervision. After completion of schooling, the girls are taught domestic work, sewing and making of clothes for themselves and trousers for men. When proficient these girls are released for employment in approved homes under strict conditions regarding general treatment, preservation of morality and general training as citizens.[208]

Cook was prepared to take drastic steps to stop the increase in the 'coloured' population and encouraged lighter skinned women to marry white men and in this way to 'breed out the colour'. He wrote in 1933:

Many such men would be prepared to marry half-caste females and make decent homes. Provided the girl has been reared to a moderately high standard there can be no objection to such a mating … Experience shows that the half-caste girl can, if properly brought up, easily be elevated to a standard where the fact of her marriage to a white will not contribute to his deterioration.[209]

Cook believed that this would have the positive effect of creating a race of workers with physical attributes suited to the harsh tropical climate:

> stamina, high resistance to the influences of tropical environment and the character of pigmentation which even in high dilution will serve to reduce the at present high incidence of Skin Cancer in blonde Europeans.[210]

These eugenic proposals prompted an outcry from critics in the south. Cook's interventions in Aboriginal life also helped to incite the development of a strong Aboriginal protest movement through the Northern Territory Half-Caste Association formed in Darwin in the 1930s.

There were other changes in the Territory during the 1930s. The Bungalow was moved to new premises and a short-lived Boys Home was opened at Pine Creek, a Catholic mission school and an Anglican children's home in Alice Springs, and a new Catholic mission at Port Keats. In 1934, despite his department's earlier decision, the Minister for the Interior advertised in the southern press for homes for fifty Territory 'mixed race' children with 'interested people in capital cities' to save them from their 'tragic fate'.[211] An unknown number were sent south to church institutions and private families but it was not until the 1950s that this practice was formalised. A 1936 ruling that 'half-caste' children were to follow the mainstream educational curriculum and moves to send selected children interstate for secondary education promised improved education for children in institutions. However, due largely to the entrenched opposition of the powerful pastoralist lobby, there were few changes for children growing up outside the towns and the missions. Cook endeavoured in vain to force pastoralists to train and pay 'half-caste' boys on their properties, arguing that existing conditions contravened the League of Nations Convention on Slavery, of which Australia was a signatory, and that this was fodder for communist influences. Nothing had changed by the end of the decade. A census at Victoria River Downs Station in 1939 revealed a dying population — mothers dying in childbirth, children dying within their first year of life, low rates of fertility with many adults never having children, removals of 'mixed race' children, especially girls and instances of communicable disease — all related to exploitation, deplorable living conditions and malnutrition.[212] Even the pastoralists had to acknowledge the threat to their future labour supply and some, but by no means all, began to acknowledge the importance of providing adequate levels of health care, nutrition and accommodation for their workers.[213] The late 1930s also saw the beginning of a major shift in policy in the Northern Territory, dubbed the 'New Deal' after the New Deal introduced in the United States in 1933 by President Roosevelt to counter the effects of the Great Depression. However, the federal government did not follow the example of the United States' Indian Reorganisation Act 1934 — also known as the Indian New Deal — which abandoned the policy of assimilation in favour of a policy of sovereignty aimed at enabling Native Americans to run their own affairs. The Aboriginal 'New Deal' was a full-blown program of economic and social assimilation:

> to entitle [Aborigines] by right and by qualifications to the ordinary rights of citizenship and enable them to share with us the opportunities that are available in their own native land.[214]

Although this New Deal was interrupted by the war, the policy of assimilation would dominate Aboriginal policy across Australia in the 1950s and 1960s.

South Australia

At the turn of the century South Australia had an Aboriginal population of 4000 Aborigines and 820 'half-castes' with ongoing frontier conditions in its remote north and an established, largely 'mixed race', population in the south. Its framing legislation, the *Aborigines Act 1911*, was based on that of Queensland and Western Australia and in frontier regions it followed the example of segregated mission communities for populations undergoing rapid social change. In the south it resembled New South Wales as it alternated between concentrating populations in institutions and forcing them out into the wider community. Introducing the Aborigines Bill 1911 to Parliament the Premier. John Verran, explained the urgent need for new legislation to enable the government to concentrate Aborigines in centralised institutions:

it was becoming more and more urgently necessary, for their own sakes, to keep them away from the towns, and where and when such was found expedient — again for their own benefit — to require them to live in certain localities, and on special reservations ... On reservations there would be safeguards which would keep them away from the bad influence which now followed their being scattered throughout the country and townships.[215]

A question in Parliament concerning the situation of 'half-castes' drew the following comment from the Chief Protector of Aborigines, W G South:

In my opinion, all half-caste and quarter-caste children, especially girls, should be considered wards of the state, and should not be left in the blacks camps after they reach the age of six years ... It seems to me ridiculous to bring up a lot of practically white people in blacks camps and on mission stations in idleness, actually (if unintentionally) making them and their children, dependents on the state and private charity.[216]

Aboriginal children in institutional care in Adelaide, 1911. From the Annual Report of the Protector of Aborigines in South Australia, 1911.

(Courtesy of Andrew Wilson, State Records Aboriginal Project Officer, State Records of South Australia)

Not all South Australians agreed. In a letter to the Chief Protector of Aborigines in 1910, the editor of the *Renmark Pioneer* described the removal of two local boys as 'an outrage' and 'a grave miscarriage of the intentions of provisions made for the protection of the aborigines of this State.' Their mother, who had 'suffered several seizures since the abduction of her children,' also wrote, stating that the children had been taken 'under false pretences' and 'were never neglected'.[217]

While the Bill was passed with only minor amendments, its provisions were not rigorously implemented, prompting the Honorary Secretary of the Aborigines Friends Association, J H Sexton, to comment in 1933 that 'some of the finest features of our legislation remain inoperative … what we really need is good practical application.'[218] The legislation appears to have been used principally to manage the 'mixed race' communities at Point Pearce and Point McLeay Aboriginal Stations in the south, to supervise reserves and to create an administrative structure to work cooperatively with the State Children's Council (SCC). Although the Chief Protector of Aborigines had legal guardianship of Aboriginal children, these powers were not used and, instead, most children continued to be dealt with under the *State Children's Act 1895*. Two years before the passing of the Act the SCC had formally accepted a central role in assisting to:

> prevent the growth of a race that would rapidly increase in numbers, attain a maturity without education or religion and become a menace to the morals and health of the community. The Council feels that no consideration … should be permitted to block the way of the protection and elevation of these unfortunate children.[219]

Three years later the SCC reported to the Protector of Aborigines that 'the result so far has justified the course adopted, and has made the Council more anxious to proceed.'[220]

During the State's 1913 Royal Commission on the Aborigines, the SCC Secretary, James Gray, and William Garnett, Protector of Aborigines for the south, outlined a cooperative system of surveillance, selection and removal of children involving the SCC, police, courts and the Aborigines Department. On hearing of a neglected child the SCC or Aborigines Department would request a police report on the matter via the Commissioner of Police and this would determine subsequent action. If the report confirmed neglect then the police would take the matter to court to seek committal of the child to the care of the SCC.[221] Children tagged for removal were not always 'neglected' and in 1912 the Chief Protector wrote of an illegitimate 'quarter-caste' girl at Point McLeay:

> Although the girl is fairly well cared for, I consider that she should

not be reared amongst the Aborigines, and would respectfully suggest that the matter be referred to the State Children's Council with a view to her being brought under their control.[222]

In the following year he ordered the immediate removal from a camp at Bordertown of two children who were 'white, with blue eyes, and one has auburn hair'.[223] James Gray told the Royal Commission that the police and courts were not always cooperative. Some police officers sympathised with the Aboriginal mothers and others were 'afraid ... of violence on the part of the Aborigines which could lead to disaster'. Many magistrates were of the opinion that the 1895 Act did not apply to Aboriginal children and adopted the 'disposition' that 'an aboriginal child should be bought up in a wurley.'[224] The SCC and the Aborigines Department along with other experts were united in calling for greater powers to remove all 'half-caste' children. Gray[225] was particularly anxious to remove girls as they 'go to destruction in the camps.' Most Aboriginal parents objected strongly. Susie Wilson of Mount Searle[226] told the Royal Commission, 'We would like our children to go to school, but we do not want them to go too far away.' Matthew Kropinyeri, a prominent member of the Point McLeay community, was more conciliatory:

> I would suggest that the children be taken in hand on leaving school by the State and taught to become useful and independent members of society, allowing them an interval of such time as the State may consider necessary to visit their parents during the year.[227]

If committed, children were sent on to the receiving depot at the Edwardstown Industrial School to be scrubbed up and taught the 'rudiments of civilisation'. They were then placed in the same way as white children — younger children to foster families to attend school, older children in apprenticeships or industrial or probationary schools and only under special circumstances to reformatories. These placements were all funded at the same rates as white children.[228] In 1914 fifty-four children of Aboriginal descent were under SCC care — thirty-nine in service or foster care in the country, nine in homes in Adelaide, two in industrial schools, three in probationary schools and one in a maternity home.[229] Looking forward to mid twentieth-century assimilation policies, Gray[230] told the Royal Commission of the important influence of the European home on Aboriginal children but said that he encountered strong prejudice from foster families:

It is difficult to find homes for the natives when they are young, and it is almost equally difficult to find homes for them when they are of the age for going into service.

He added that it was always easier to dispose of girls of 'any nationality'. Gray also mentioned that in endeavouring to place children according to their religious denomination, as required under the 1895 Act, the SCC had adopted the practice where the religion was not known of declaring every seventh child Catholic and the rest Protestant in accordance with the ratio of religious adherence in the wider population. In addition to these SCC placements a total of 390 children in 1912 were living in dormitories or with their families at Point Pearce, Point McLeay, Koonibba Lutheran Mission near Denial Bay on the west coast and Killalpaninna Lutheran Mission near Marree in the north-east of the state in Diyiri country.[231] These institutions were the target of loud complaints from Chief Protector Garnett that there was 'too much charity' and not enough 'thrift and industry'[232] and that the children were too much with their parents and under their influence. He strongly recommended that his department take over their management.

The recommendations of the Royal Commission[233] had more in common with the early Victorian legislation than the Queensland and Western Australian Acts. They outlined the same processes of segregating 'full bloods' and forcibly merging 'half-castes' through expulsion of adults from the stations and increased removal and institutionalisation of the children:

Aboriginal parents have strong natural affection for their children, but in some cases the best interests of the child are sacrificed by the manner in which they are brought up. For this reason we think the board should have power to take control of such children, or other children — at the desire of the parents — at the age of ten and place them where they deem best, giving the parents such access as may be thought desirable.[234]

The Advisory Council of Aborigines (ACA), set up in 1918 on the recommendation of the Royal Commission, was a mix of citizens and government officials and more closely resembled boards in Victoria and New South Wales than the departmental structures operating in Queensland and Western Australia. The position of Chief Protector of Aborigines continued. The ACA and the Chief Protector were united on many issues, including calls for increased removals of children and for the building of special Aboriginal children's homes. However, while the ACA favoured the model of the Koonibba Children's Home — a dormitory within the mission where children remained in contact with their families — the Chief Protector advocated the complete isolation of children from their families. The fact that no funding for children's homes was forthcoming may indicate the role that advisory bodies could play in dampening bureaucratic 'enthusiasms'. A wave of United Aborigines Mission work during the 1920s saw the establishment of a children's home at Oodnadatta (1924) which was moved to Quorn in 1927 and became the Colebrook Children's Home, one of the few institutions remembered with affection by many of its former inmates.[235] In 1923, in order to accelerate removals, significant amendments were passed allowing the Protector of Aborigines to transfer his legal guardianship of Aboriginal children to the SCC without going through the normal court processes. However, public opposition to this proposed intervention into Aboriginal family life was such that the amendments were shelved although they were not formally repealed.

ABORIGINAL FAMILIES SURVIVING

Aboriginal people faced a bleak future in the early twentieth century. Despite the tragic lessons of Van Diemen's Land where dispossession of families from their land, forced separation of parents and children, and regimes of institutionalisation and control had served only to hasten the deaths of Aboriginal people, these very same processes were being adopted across the continent, now with strict legislative powers to enforce compliance by Aborigines. Powerful negative perceptions of Aboriginal families held by most white Australians served to endorse the escalating practice of removing and institutionalising their children. Aboriginal mothers were constructed as contrastive to the cherished image of chaste and loving white mothers and came to signify sexual promiscuity, maternal neglect, violence and contamination, and were deemed a danger to themselves, their children and to whites. Aboriginal families were seen as contaminating environments — sites of physical and moral danger where children were subjected to barbaric practices of bodily mutilation, child betrothal to old men, polygamous marriage, violence, sexual abuse and prostitution. At the same time they were sites of 'lack' and neglect where children learned little that was useful for their adult lives and where poverty and disease were rife. The 'sacred bonds of family' and the 'best interests of the child' had little meaning in this context. In contrast to the integral role of middle-class white families and mothers in shaping 'rising generations' of white citizens, Aboriginal families and mothers were deliberately excluded and their functions and structures progressively undermined. The state intervened in the most personal family processes in ways that would never have been tolerated for white families.

The tragic impact on Aboriginal mothers was poignantly expressed in the Link-Up (New South Wales) submission to the 1996 National Inquiry into the Separation of Aboriginal and Torres Strait Islander Children from their Families:

> Our mothers inevitably say that they didn't want to hurt us. But we also realise that here is where our mothers were hurt most deeply. Here is where they were shamed and humiliated — they were deprived of the opportunity to participate in growing up the next generation. They were made to feel failures; unworthy of loving and caring for their own children; they were denied participation in the future of their community.

We will never know exactly how many children were removed. The *Bringing Them Home* report [237] states:

> It is not possible to state with any precision how many children were forcibly removed, even if that enquiry is confined to those removed officially. Many records have not survived. Others fail to record the children's Aboriginality.

The report noted that removals were more extensive in some areas than others and that the intensity of interventions varied across time and that children of mixed descent were particularly vulnerable. It concluded 'with confidence' that 'not one Indigenous family has escaped the effects of forcible removal' and that:

> nationally ... between one in three and one in ten Indigenous

children were forcibly removed from their families and communities in the period from approximately 1910 to 1970.

Removal and relocation of children and families to segregated institutions and the forced dispersal of certain adults and families from settlements continued nineteenth-century patterns of breaking up family and community networks. The transmission of skills and knowledge between the generations was disrupted and children in the institutions were subjected to the normalising processes of institutional life and cut off from their families, their country and their Aboriginal identity. This was particularly so in the Children's Homes where there was virtually no contact with their Aboriginal past. In the multipurpose institutions children often had some contact with Aboriginal ways through the resident adults. Conditions in the institutions were frequently worse than in the camps, with serious long-term effects on the children's health and learning. The children were also excluded from the advances in education, child welfare and medical care extended to non-Aboriginal children in the wider community. The result was the creation of workers with a narrow range of skills that were superseded daily by technological advances, who lacked educational skills to shift to new employment niches, and who were vulnerable to abusive and exploitative employers. Discriminatory controls over the children's choices of employment, working conditions and wages kept them segregated from the rest of the Australian workforce and locked them into a state of chronic poverty and economic dependancy. Without proper parenting many were unable to develop the ability to establish and maintain family relationships and they found themselves trapped in the same cycle of removal and loss of their own children.

The breaking up of Aboriginal families and family structures along with controls over Aboriginal women's sexuality were integral strategies in the state's drive to stop the reproduction of Aboriginal diversity. Anti-natalist measures adopted to minimise increase in the 'mixed race' population were a reverse image of steps taken to encourage white women to bear children. They took the form of the policing of virtually all areas of women's lives — employment, sexual contacts, marriage, guardianship of their children — as well as denial of the economic incentives offered to white mothers to encourage child-bearing, propaganda challenging their role even to bear and raise children, and shocking neglect of maternal health. At the same time nothing was done to prevent the alarming rates of infant, child and maternal deaths. During the 1930s, evidence that 'mixed race' populations had continued to increase despite these interventions, led to the adoption of 'genocidal eugenics' in Western Australia and the Northern Territory, in the form of state-arranged 'marriages' to breed out Aboriginal physical characteristics. In 1937 alarm about the 'mixed race' population — which had more than doubled nationally from just under 10,000 in 1911 to almost 24,000 by 1937[238] — was such that the federal meeting of Aboriginal administrators endorsed a policy of biological absorption. These measures — anti-natalist propaganda, refusal of family benefits, the lack of medical attention and care — were being employed in European countries at the time to prevent the reproduction of unwanted racial groups, reaching their most extreme form in Nazi Germany programs of compulsory sterilisation and abortions of women deemed racially and eugenically inferior, and culminating in the mass extermination drives to annihilate 'unworthy life' in its borders.[239]

Various factors prevented wholesale removal of Aboriginal families and children — limited finances, local labour needs, the spasmodic nature of white community demands for their removal and Aboriginal resistance. Families that remained outside the institutions occupied various marginal sites in camps on the edge of towns, on pastoral stations and in the bush. For many their main point of contact with the wider community was in the work place, across the shop counter or at the front desk of the local police station. They were rendered invisible to the wider community through formal and informal barriers governing all areas of social life which kept black and white strictly segregated. They lived under varying degrees of control and surveil-lance by administrators, police and local whites. Aborigines in small camps adjacent to towns were under constant surveillance, while families working on pastoral stations lived under the regime of pastoral bosses.

Most Aboriginal families were forced to live in desperate conditions with chronic poor health, shockingly high infant and child mortality rates and low life expectancy. The cumulative effects of poorly paid work, constant surveillance, punishment for behaviours considered acceptable for whites, controls preventing families from moving freely around what they saw as their own land, the continual prospect of having a family member taken away possibly forever with no right to protest and knowing that there was little possibility of changing the system, all made for stressful and anxious lives. Government policies and dereliction of the duty of care to these families meant that in camps across Australia Aboriginal parents and children all lived with the constant threat of being separated from each other simply for being of Aboriginal descent, for living in conditions that were set in train by profound state neglect, or for being raised in ways that did not fit with dominant white concepts of 'good parenting'. Is it any wonder that Aboriginal families turned inwards to each other and erected their own 'cultural fences' in their struggle to survive? Many of the children who remained with their families grew up virtually outside of the reach of state agencies of social control, and were reared according to Aboriginal ways within the circle of extended kin networks. In consequence, there was considerable continuity of Aboriginal family life and traditions, even in areas of close white settlement in southern Australia.

The claim by some in the Stolen Generations debate that Aboriginal and white children in state care were treated equally or that the treatment of Aboriginal children and families simply reflected broader policies and practices of the times is patently false. Unless we are willing simply to excuse and overlook earlier racist behaviours in our history we have to face up to this shameful past when, because of their race, Aboriginal families and children were left to survive in deplorable conditions while the lot of other Australians was dramatically enhanced by direct government action to build up a nation of healthy and efficient white citizens. The *Bringing Them Home* report pointed out that according to the Convention on the Prevention and Punishment of the Crime of Genocide 1948, ratified by Australia in 1949, the forced removal of Aboriginal children constituted a 'crime against humanity' tantamount to genocide:

> the predominant aim of indigenous child removals was the absorption or assimilation of the children into the wider, non-indigenous community so that their unique cultural values and ethnic identities would disappear, giving way to models of culture. Removal of children with this objective in mind is genocide because it aims to destroy the 'cultural unit' which the Convention is concerned to preserve. The inquiry found that, while usually authorised by law, forced removal violated fundamental common law rights enjoyed by other Australians.[240]

In a paper published in 1999, international genocide analyst Colin Tatz presented compelling evidence of genocidal actions perpetrated against Australian Aborigines under *all* sections of the UN definition being:

> any of the following acts committed with intent to destroy, in whole or in part, a national ethnical, or racial or religious group:
>
> a. killing members of the group;
> b. causing bodily or mental harm to members of the group;
> c. deliberately inflicting on the group conditions of life calculated to bring about its physical destruction in whole or in part;
> e. imposing measures intended to prevent birth within the group;
> f. forcibly transferring children of the group to another group.[241]

Tatz urged Australians to acknowledge the 'causal chains' in our history that help to 'explain the degradation, disease and premature dying over these past two hundred years'; chains that began with:

> the incursions of settlers, the destruction of environments, the 'rough work', the genocidal impulses of the squatters, the segregation–protection era of reserves, settlements and missions, the legislation which always proclaimed itself to be for 'the physical, mental and social welfare' of the people, the dismissal of Aboriginal values and their evaluation as less than human, the creation of chronic dependency, and the (continuing) practice of institutionalisation.[242]

That Aboriginal people and their cultures were not eradicated by the relentless onslaught of these forces was due in large part to their dogged resistance and determination to survive. Government stinginess and official inertia also prevented the necessary investment of ongoing high levels of energy, time and finance. Perhaps officials were lulled into complacency by their strategies of assimilation and segregation which rendered Aborigines invisible by hiding them in the Australian equivalent of refugee camps, ghettoes or apartheid homelands.

CHAPTER FOUR

SPECIAL TREATMENT[1] WESTERN AUSTRALIAN STYLE

The burst of public debate on the Stolen Generations in the mid-1990s and my research for this book inevitably brought me to reflect on my own writing on Aboriginal history in Western Australia. I was at first concerned that, while I had written extensively about removal policies and practices and how they affected Nyungar people, I had woven this together with the whole range of oppressive actions carried out by the regime of control operating at the time. I wondered had I been remiss in not singling out the system more definitively? Had I devalued what had happened to Aboriginal children and families? Looking back over the historical records, I came to appreciate that, while it is essential to analyse removal and institutionalisation of Aboriginal children as a distinct system, it is equally important to insert this in broader historical contexts and to locate it as one of several pressing concerns in the myriad of responsibilities handled routinely by Aboriginal administrations. How *did* these processes operate within an adminstration where officers juggled a host of projects against stringent budgets, adjudicated conflicting demands of powerful alliances in the wider community against the needs of Aboriginal families and at the same time endeavoured to meet their own agendas and concerns?

A look at the working out of these processes in the administration of Aboriginal affairs in Western Australia from 1900 to 1940 provides important insights into these questions that have relevance across the country. Legislative and adminstrative powers allowed for quite extraordinary interventions into Aboriginal families by departmental officers and vested interest groups. Local features of geography, history, demography and economy frequently pushed officers to extremes in their treatment of Aboriginal families. At the same time the system allowed for abject neglect of the needs of these families. Analysis of the machinery for removing and raising Aboriginal children in Western Australia also contributes to our understanding of a question fundamental to public debate on the issue of Australia's Stolen Generations — what were the differences in the treatment of Aboriginal and non-Aboriginal children taken from their families by the state? It also introduces new insights into the profound question of who was responsible for this fragmenting of Aboriginal families.

KEEPING THE LID ON PANDORA'S BOX

When Western Australia was granted self-government in 1889 it was isolated, vast in area, small in population, parochial, patriarchal and very British. Run by a small elite of established colonial landed and commercial families, this was a society where people knew their place and were constantly reminded of it, where people showed their best face, but everyone knew their secrets. The 'Cinderella state', which had struggled economically since its foundation, was riding the crest of recent pastoral expansion and gold discoveries in the Kimberley and Pilbara regions and was on the verge of the tumultuous eastern goldfields boom. While the rest of Australia was devastated by economic depression and droughts during the 1890s, Western Australia experienced a period of unprecedented economic prosperity and development, population growth and social change, reminiscent of the Victorian gold rushes forty years earlier. With these changes came new ideas of universal suffrage, party politics, organised labour, a White Australia and Australian federation — a proposal initially not welcomed in the parochial west, geographically isolated as it was from the proposed centres of federal power. Many West Australians remained ambivalent about federalism. Many newcomers who made fortunes, and those who lost all, chose to remain in the west. The former created new economic and political alliances, some buttressing, others challenging the stranglehold of the established families on power and wealth. Unemployed diggers took advantage of the government's generous land and financial incentives to settle families on the land and thereby to build a viable local wheat industry in the south of the state. Western Australia celebrated its entry into the twentieth century with 'a powerful impulse' to assert the 'dignity of the ordinary man through a new Australian social order.'[2] The new progressivist spirit was evident in a range of legislation relating to health, child welfare, local government, urban services and employment which emulated enlightened advances in the other states.

Western Australia had a significant Aboriginal population — estimated at 24,000 at the turn of the century. Their treatment constituted a Pandora's box of troubles and secrets which colonial leaders strove to contain and prevent from flying out into the public domain. Historian Neville Green's[3] aphorism 'They came, they saw, they took' aptly describes the exploitative and often violent nature of the expanding pearling, pastoral and mining frontiers in the north from the 1860s, and the 'reign of terror' and death by parties of police and colonists which continued in the Kimberleys into the early twentieth century. Such exploits had left the colony embroiled in a welter of denials and cover-ups of atrocities and abusive treatment of Aborigines.

British government disapproval of the situation was clearly expressed in legislation passed from the 1870s to regulate Aboriginal employment and in the decision, enacted in the 1889 Constitution, to retain control of Aboriginal affairs and to oblige the state to set aside at least one percent of its annual revenue for Aborigines. The response of the newly formed colonial government revealed both the wisdom of this decision and the ruthlessness of local interest groups. The pastoral lobby used its control in both houses of parliament to protect its own economic concerns by passing unprecedented discriminatory legislation to ensure a stable Aboriginal work force and to stop cattle killing and other Aboriginal 'depredations'. Legislation included the reintroduction of whipping of Aboriginal men and boys — abolished for the general population in Australia from the 1870s — and extraordinary gaol terms of up to five years for breach of employment contracts compared to three months under the Master and Servants Act, which now excluded Aboriginal workers. The incidence of convictions for absconding does not appear to have been high — Peter Biskup notes thirty-five between 1900 and 1904 — and many Aborigines were simply rounded up by the police and returned to their employers.[4] Far more were arrested for stock killing and other actions seen as impeding the advance of progress in the north. With a paramilitary police force backing pastoral interests, it is hardly surprising that Aboriginal imprisonment rates soared to levels far higher than in any other colony from the 1880s.[5] Between 1841 and 1907 over 5000 Aborigines were gaoled in Australia's only Aboriginal gaol, Rottnest Island Prison off the Perth coast, by all accounts a hellhole of death by disease, execution, abuse and overcrowding — an Australian gulag with hundreds of unmarked graves as testimony to the brutality there. Hundreds of others were crowded into local prisons in the northern towns of Derby, Wyndham and Roebourne. In 1900 Aboriginal prisoners were predominantly male and seventeen percent were under the age of twenty-one.[6] In 1904 the Roth Royal Commission found evidence of boys as young as six years being brought in as witnesses (typically against family members) or charged with cattle killing. Although police were paid for their transportation and keep, young boys often arrived in town half starved and in neck chains. Sentencing depended on the whim of the local bench and, in the case of Halls Creek, was punitive and arbitrary: a ten-year-old boy sentenced to six months hard labour for cattle killing; a boy of fifteen sentenced to ten months gaol for killing a goat; eight children aged from fourteen to sixteen sentenced to two years hard labour for cattle killing.[7] High rates of institutionalisation and incarceration of Aboriginal adults and juveniles continued throughout the century.

There was alarming evidence of abusive treatment of Aboriginal children in employment and tolerance of this by authorities. During his unsuccessful attempt to establish a mission near the town of Carnarvon in the mid-1880s Reverend J B (John) Gribble witnessed horrific acts of child capture and exploitation. One man 'tore a boy away from his mother … The next day the boy was put aboard a cutter in spite of [his mother's] screams and struggles.'[8] Employers signed up children as young as five as servants for periods of up to two years and treated them like slaves, while girls as young as eight were sexually abused. Children attempting to escape were punished mercilessly. Two boys were stock-whipped over a distance of thirty miles back to their employer's station and on arrival were tied up and whipped 'until the second lash was worn out.' For this their employer was fined a total of six pounds by the local magistrate.[9] Legislation passed in the early 1870s to prevent the sexual abuse of Aboriginal women by pearling crews, to outlaw 'black-birding' — the notorious practice of kidnapping Aboriginal men, women and children and forcing them to work on pearling luggers — and to provide some protection for Aboriginal child workers was largely overlooked by authorities and employers alike. An Aboriginal apprenticeship scheme set up in the *Aborigines Protection Act 1886* operated to protect employer interests rather than the children.[10] The 1904 Royal Commission into Aboriginal conditions in Western Australia, found that employers in the pearling industry were binding children as young as ten in apprenticeships lasting in some cases up to the age of twenty-one, thereby avoiding a prohibition on employing Aborigines for terms of over twelve months set out in the *Pearl Shell Fishery Regulation Act 1873.* A resident magistrate also explained to Roth that:

> The child is bound and can be reached by law and punished, but the person to whom the child is bound is apparently responsible to nobody. Even the Chief Protector is obliged to admit the injustice of a system where, taking a concrete case, a child of tender years may be indentured to a mistress as a domestic up to 21 years of age, and receives neither education nor payment in return for the services rendered.[11]

Incidents of violent child capture continued in the Kimberley. It was common practice following killings of Aborigines in the east Kimberley for pastoralists to claim any surviving children as station workers. White retribution for Aboriginal violence was merciless to adult and child alike. Following an Aboriginal attack on Jerry and Patsy Durack in 1901, three boys aged sixteen and twelve and two girls aged twelve were rounded up and forced to trek in chains two hundred kilometres to Wyndham where one of the boys was found guilty of shooting Patsy and sentenced to death. There was also ongoing sexual abuse of young girls, as evidenced in 1896 when two men were charged in the Wyndham court with sexual contact with four girls, two under the age of twelve. They were found guilty of the charges, suggesting some local disapproval of such practices.[12]

Reverend Gribble's experiences demonstrated the high personal cost of breaching colonial 'codes of silence'. 'Self-righteous, out-spoken, tactless, humourless, obsessive and enormously courageous',[13] Gribble relentlessly accused pearlers and pastoralists of slavery in the Western Australian press, in his book *Dark Deeds in a Sunny Land,* in letters to the Aborigines Protection Society in Britain and in addresses to audiences in the eastern states. For his trouble he was driven out of Carnarvon, physically assaulted, vilified in the Perth press, rejected by his own church and finally bundled out of the state by police under the cover of darkness. From the late 1880s more diplomatic but no less critical missionaries arrived in the Kimberley region, following on the wave of missionary endeavour sweeping the British Empire at the time. The pioneering work of Reverend Duncan McNab, who arrived from Queensland in 1884, laid the foundation for a strong Catholic mission presence in the region, beginning with the establishment of Beagle Bay

Mission in 1890. The Anglicans, led by the son of Bishop Matthew Hale, the founder of Poonindie Mission in South Australia, faced strong Aboriginal resistance to their efforts to set up a mission at Forrest River in 1897, and it was not until 1913 that Gribble's eldest son, Ernest, succeeded in laying the foundations of Forrest River Mission. The missionaries, committed to spiritual conversion and physical preservation of the Aboriginal 'remnants' through strict segregation of the 'hunted and harassed', added the third dimension to Charles Rowley's[14] 'triangle of tension' of settler, government agent and missionary in the Kimberley.

Smarting at the British government's 'slur' on the state's reputation by its refusal to hand over control of Aboriginal Affairs and alarmed at the escalating financial commitment stipulated in the *Constitution Act 1889* — with the gold rushes it rose to 16,956 pounds in 1897 — parliamentarians vociferously demanded the repeal of the relevant sections of the constitution. The *Aborigines Act 1897* shifted the locus of policy making from the Colonial Office in London to the state parliament in Perth, although West Australians continued to remain sensitive to, and influenced by, British opinion. Political struggles between powerful local stakeholders who, like their earlier counterparts in London, were invariably male and white, now permeated and shaped the policy-making process. A central core of employers, landowners and public officials had expanded to include church and missionary groups; government departments, in particular the newly created Aborigines Department; and potentially included a range of politicians, political parties and voters, in particular, the welter of small land-holders in the south. For the time being establishment interests continued to dominate Aboriginal domains. The Aborigines Department, established in 1897, was more show than substance: it was small, unimportant, underfunded, and powerless to do more than distribute rations and, in its early years, operated under the eagle eye of Premier John Forrest. The first Chief Protector of Aborigines was a close personal friend of the premier and a member of Perth 'society'. A product of privilege in colonial India and Britain, Henry Prinsep combined public service duties with artistic pursuits and a life of domestic harmony and doting parenthood. Unimpressive in his public duties, he had no previous experience in Aboriginal administration and little to recommend him for the position apart from a guarantee that he would pose no challenge to powerful elites.[15]

Prinsep was inevitably drawn into responding to interest groups in the north. Pastoralists in the north-west were alarmed at the drain of Aboriginal workers from stations to the mining fields where many earned good money for their work in place of the pastoralists' hand-outs. Pastoralists' sympathisers on the fields included James Isdell, a future travelling inspector of the Aborigines Department, who wrote in 1900 to Prinsep from Nullagine of the 'disgraceful' conditions and immoral conduct, with Aboriginal girls becoming prostitutes and boys 'the biggest rogues and thieves'.[16] He advised immediate action to reassert control over Aboriginal labour and to ensure a reliable 'reserve army' of Aboriginal pastoral workers. Pastoralists also demanded stricter regulation of sexual contacts between Aboriginal women and 'lower orders' of white men and Asian pearling crews. This was expressed in terms of the need to protect whites from physical and moral contamination, to maintain boundaries between the races and to halt Aborigines' growing economic independence through women's earnings from prostitution. No doubt it also reflected pastoralists' intentions to maintain covert patterns of sexual contact on their own properties. Isdell also demanded the removal of 'half-caste' children who, 'growing up with the blacks and having some of the intelligence of the whites', would become 'extremely dangerous' as adults.[17] Prinsep responded by arguing for encompassing laws of control and containment, similar to those in the 1897 Queensland Act, but these met initially with Forrest's opposition and, following Forrest's move to federal parliament in 1901, a lack of interest from a stream of rapidly changing ministers.

Despite clear evidence of abusive treatment of Aboriginal children on the northern frontier and his legal obligation to 'provide for the custody, maintenance and education of children of Aborigines', Prinsep took no action in this direction, choosing instead to focus on an issue closer to his heart and closer to home — the situation of the 'near white' children in the south, some of whom were living in difficult economic straits in town fringe camps. Lacking legal powers to forcibly remove the children he hoped to persuade their parents to send them to institutions where they could learn to become:

> useful workers with merely such an amount of reading, writing, and numbers as to be of service to them in their positions as humble labourers, the position which they cannot hope to rise from for at least two or three generations.[18]

He was concerned that, once having left their families they should never return to them as they would revert 'to a more evil, because educated, barbarism than before'.[19] In his 1902 Annual Report[20] Prinsep wrote that the children would be a 'special point' of attention during the year and he hoped to build up numbers from the 122 already in missions. However, he quickly found that the 'natural affections of the black mothers ... stood much in my way.'[21] A doting father himself, he could not have been immune to the distress in the letter sent to him in 1902:

I am afraid that [my wife] will cimit suicide if the boy is not back soon for she is good for nothing only cry day and night ... I have as much love for my dear wife and childrens as you have for yours ... so if you have any feeling at all please send the boy back as quick as you can it did not take long for him to go but it takes a long time for him to come back.[22]

Frustrated in his efforts, Prinsep worked timidly around the edges of the problems confronting his administration, until the Pandora's box was burst open as a deliberate ploy by new labour interests struggling to wrest power from the establishment. Growing local outrage in the face of allegations of Aboriginal slavery in the pastoral industry, made locally and in the new federal parliament, and in the British press, prompted the appointment in 1904 of a Royal Commission to enquire into Aboriginal conditions in Western Australia. Above all it was intended to clear the state's name. Led by Dr Walter Roth, Chief Protector of Aborigines in Queensland, the inquiry focused on the north of the state and delivered a report damning of government policy and administration and of the treatment of Aborigines by Asian pearling crews, and exonerating pastoralists of the charges of ill-treatment of Aboriginal workers. Roth reiterated Prinsep's concerns about 'drunkenness and prostitution and consequent loathsome disease' along the Kimberley coast and expressed alarm about the growing 'half-caste' population. Decrying the lack of power to remove 'half-caste' children, he recommended that the Chief Protector of Aborigines be made legal guardian of all Aboriginal and 'half-caste' children to the age of eighteen and that all institutions for Aboriginal children be brought under his control with children working to state school standards and subjected to regular departmental inspection.

Roth's report brought forth a stream of abuse from conservative politicians, pastoralists and government officers, all of whom seemed to believe themselves to be above criticism. Nevertheless, legislators closely followed Roth's recommendations in drafting the 1905 Aborigines Bill, which proved to be remarkably similar to the Queensland 1897 Act. Debate on the Bill was intense and characterised by conflict between pastoral and labour interests over Aboriginal employment, with Labor members intent on freeing up jobs for their members and the pastoralists determined to maintain existing arrangements. Nevertheless, both were agreed on the need to strictly limit grants of land to Aborigines, to control sexual contact and to remove 'half-caste' children — 'the white man's child'. There was also broad agreement amongst parliamentarians on minimising financial cost, maximising control of Aborigines and protecting white interests. The resulting legislation was a loosely stitched together jumble of self-interest and overlapping and contradictory policies of protection, segregation, assimilation, reform and unprecedented wide-ranging duties and powers open to various interpretations and responses and encompassing diverse Aboriginal populations.

A STRANGE WAY OF DOING THINGS

Outwardly the Aborigines Department had many of the trappings of other new bureaucracies established in Western Australia at the time to deal with social issues and other 'problem populations' and it *appeared* to bring Aborigines into the ambit of modern systems of care and welfare. Nevertheless the administration remained profoundly colonial in nature. Unlike the colonies of British India and Africa, where structured bureaucratic systems of rule were grafted onto existing indigenous hierarchical systems, the Australian legacy was of a settler society. This consisted of a sparse colonising population scattered across a vast area, encountering indigenous societies characterised by relatively egalitarian systems of power and government and conditional patterns of leadership grounded in kinship networks and religious knowledge.[23] What emerged here was a loose system of administering indigenous communities through local government officers, typically the police, and in some areas authorised employers and missionaries, acting on formal instructions issued from a central administration, and often in accordance with dominant local white concerns. In contrast to colonial India and Africa, where certain indigenous elite groups were able to cooperate with their colonisers in designated areas of government and thereby protect and advance their own interests, there were no areas of governance open to indigenous Australians apart from complicity in the murderous activities of the native troopers in 'dispersing' populations in eastern Australia and the tokenistic appointments of Aboriginal 'kings', as worthless as the official breastplates presented to signify their status.[24]

The enduring colonial legacy was evident in the extreme power differential and degree of separation of the Aborigines Department from its target population. Aborigines had no role in its formation or execution of departmental duties and their societal values were ignored; their labour continued to be regulated through force and control; police, employers and missionaries remained central in executing its duties; and power remained concentrated in the hands of this small distant bureaucracy which zealously controlled information inflow and outflow. Despite, and perhaps because of, all this the administration did not always penetrate Aboriginal daily life, which often continued to be shaped by traditional institutions and power relations, while resistance to the Department's interventions remained strong and determined.[25] There was also a marked continuity with nineteenth-century institutional models of care and reform and this backwardness remained a feature of Aboriginal services. Such an administration raises serious questions of legitimacy when persons are governed in particular ways without their consent, with minimal accountability or guarantees to protect their human rights and without the necessary competence to formulate and implement appropriate policies and to provide effective services.

To hypothesise a bureaucratic process of sequences where goals are identified, translated into objectives and prioritised is 'the stuff of a perfect world in which there are no constraints in time, resources and knowledge. It is an ideal-type model which is never achieved.'[26] The process of governing or 'governmentality' — French philosopher Michel Foucault's term — is not a matter of implementing an 'idealized schema in the real by an act of will' but of negotiating and juggling a host of often conflicting 'strategies, techniques and procedures' through which a range of authorities seek to enact their programs of government in accordance with the 'materials and forces to hand ... the resistances and oppositions anticipated or encountered.'[27] The highly complex and conflict-ridden processes of governmentality involve assemblages of:

> diverse forces (legal, architectural, professional, administrative, financial, judgemental), techniques (notation, computation, calculation, examination, evaluation), devices (surveys and charts, systems of training, building forms) that promise to regulate

decisions and action of individuals, groups, organisations in relation to authoritative criteria.[28]

It is hardly surprising then that the 'eternal optimism' of governments in generating and implementing strategies to achieve objectives of good government frequently fail as these objectives are constantly undermined by the many interventions of vested interests.[29]

Nevertheless it is still useful to posit a more or less 'ideal-type model' to see just how far the Aborigines Department in Western Australia strayed from what has generally been considered an effective bureaucratic structure in the twentieth century. R Ripley and G Franklin[30] include the following as necessary features of a bureaucracy: clear policies and achievable goals; appropriate administrative structures and processes and sufficient resources to effectively plan, organise and link goals to clients; processes to monitor outcomes and provide public accountability; mechanisms to negotiate with vested interest groups inside and outside government to reach positive outcomes fitting with policy goals. The *Aborigines Act 1905* and the department it spawned were lacking in virtually all of these features.

The Aborigines Department's role was multifunctional, diverse and often conflicted between welfare and punitive control. Its duties of care to its charges were broad and included issuing rations, medical care and blankets to the sick and needy, establishing and operating institutions and reserves for Aborigines, and providing for the 'custody, education and maintenance of aboriginal children'.[31] Working with the police it also implemented special restrictions and controls over Aboriginal families and children: restrictions upon freedom of movement, place of residence, contacts with non-Aborigines, employment, marriage, access to alcohol, use of firearms, guardianship of children, and removal to institutions. These were backed up by a range of harsh penalties for breaches of the Act, including fines, imprisonment and removal to institutions imposed through police and courts, and corporal punishment and imprisonment within institutions imposed by departmental staff. The extensive powers to make regulations under the Act to facilitate administration of its duties and responsibilities, meant that the Department was able to steadily increase controls in all these areas with minimal parliamentary interference.

The Aborigines Department was unique amongst government agencies in having a clientele defined by race, association and cultural way of life. The *Aborigines Protection Act 1886* was the first statute in

Western Australia to introduce such distinctions and the 1905 Act built these into three major legal categories: (1) 'Aboriginal natives' — Aborigines of full descent and 'half-castes' (the offspring of an Aboriginal parent and a non-Aboriginal parent of any racial background or children of such persons) married to 'Aboriginal natives' or who associated with 'Aboriginal natives'; (2) 'half-castes' who did not associate with 'Aboriginal natives' and 'half-caste' children under sixteen irrespective of lifestyle and associations; and (3) Aborigines of a suitable degree of civilisation to qualify for exemption (see Table Two, pp 220–21). Although 'quarter-caste' children were meant to be excluded from the 1905 Act, the definition of 'half-caste' could be read to include them as well. These complex and clumsy classifications left considerable leeway for administrators in deciding who came under the umbrella of the Act. These classifications lumped together a wide range of people who would otherwise have been categorised by society in terms of non-racial or secular criteria — good/bad, sane/mad, comfortable/destitute, neglected/well cared for, employed/unemployed — and treated accordingly. For many, their only 'problem' was their race and culture, but, by being included under the definition, they were excluded from benefits, rights and responsibilities accorded to other Australians. Their needs were now centralised under one administration while non-Aboriginal people were provided for through hundreds of statutes and numerous bureaucracies. Other administrations were openly hostile to them and refused to help individuals or to cooperate with Aborigines Department programs. With the legal classifications sometimes conferring what could be seen as preferential treatment to 'half-castes' or 'quarter-castes' over so-called 'full bloods' — for example they were exempt from certain controls over employment — whiteness as status became introjected into some Aboriginal value systems, often driving a wedge between people of varying degrees of Aboriginal descent.

The administrative structure of the Department was also unique. It consisted of a small centralised head office run by the Chief Protector, operating at the local level through unpaid, part-time, honorary protectors — typically police officers, government officials, mission-aries and prominent private citizens, all male. Its major sites of control, in decreasing order, were institutions, missions, town camps, remote reserves and pastoral stations. Concerns for administrative economy and expediency dominated the administration and were behind its amalgamation with the Fisheries Department in 1908. There were few accountability measures to promote effective control and efficiency in

SUMMARY OF ABORIGINES ACT 1905
To 'make better provision for the better protection and care of the Aboriginal inhabitants of Western Australia.'

A. *ADMINISTRATION*

Aborigines Department made into a full government department under control of Chief Protector responsible to relevant Minister of the Crown; continued to operate through field system of honorary unpaid protectors at the local level; duties remained the same as under Act 5/1897; great increase in powers of the Chief Protector and local protectors; annual grant increased to 10,000 pounds; missions to come more directly under the control of the Department.

B. *APPLICATION OF THE ACT*

New definition of persons coming under the Act: Aborigines of the full descent (referred to as 'Aboriginal natives'); 'half-castes' (defined as persons with an Aboriginal parent on either side or children of such persons) who lived with an Aboriginal as wife or husband; other 'half-castes' who lived or regularly associated with 'Aboriginal natives'; and 'half-caste' children under the age of sixteen, irrespective of how they lived; clause included to allow Aborigines of a 'suitable degree of civilisation' to apply for exemption from the provisions of the Act.

C. *CONTROLS OVER EMPLOYMENT*

Employers obliged to apply to local protectors for agreements or single or general permits for right to employ any 'Aboriginal native' or 'half-caste' women, any 'Aboriginal native' men or any 'half-caste' males under the age of fourteen; employers and protectors to negotiate on working conditions, usually specified as sufficient rations, clothing and blankets and medical attention when necessary; protectors, in cooperation with the police, to supervise Aborigines in employment; protectors to initiate proceedings against employers or Aboriginal employees breaking terms of permits or agreements.

D. *CONTROLS OVER MOVEMENT*

Governor could declare 'prohibited areas' in which Aborigines not legally employed (that is, under permit from the local protector) could be arrested and removed at the Chief Protector's discretion; the Governor could declare Aboriginal reserves of up to 2000 acres in any magisterial district; provisions included (especially through regulations) for the establishment of segregated Aboriginal institutions on reserve land; the Minister could order the removal of Aborigines to any reserve or district without due process of court or appeal mechanism; police and justices of the peace could order Aborigines out of town; protectors and police could order Aborigines to move their camps from any area to another.

tasks, and to prevent exploitation of clients, leaving bureaucrats and their allies with considerable room to follow their own whims, fantasies, careerist drives and crusades of power and empire building, and encouraging the imposition of arbitrary powers. There was little accountability to the public with the only information outflow consisting of annual reports and budget statements to Parliament, and carefully worded press releases, while legislation imposed strict controls on contact between Aborigines and whites.

The use of police as protectors of Aborigines presented inherent problems for the administration and left Aborigines susceptible to manipulation by vested interests. As the agents of rural law enforcement, the police wielded considerable power, typically used to protect the interests of local elites. These were often inimical to those of Aborigines who were under no illusion about what 'protection' meant in this context. The roles of policing and protecting were in fundamental conflict and it was inevitable that the former should predominate. These protectors were also part of a police culture and hierarchy which advocated and rewarded policing rather than welfare duties, and displaying high levels of prejudice and discriminatory behaviour, including the condoning of unlawful killings of Aboriginal people in the Kimberley into the 1920s. The Aborigines Department had little hope of creating loyalties to *its* aims or even knowing whether police understood what was required of them: there was no training or preparation for the role and convoluted lines of communication through the Police Department to the Aborigines Department ensured social distance between the Chief Protector of Aborigines and individual officers. It was a considerable source of irritation to officers that, as policing in the white community became more professionalised and specialist, police duties to Aborigines actually increased and diversified. This also served to reinforce white attitudes associating Aborigines and criminality. The administrative structure also ensured that the system was never enforced in its entirety everywhere, leaving loopholes for Aborigines to manipulate as well as openings for police abuse and dereliction of duty, sometimes to the advantage of local Aborigines.

In addition to these structural impediments, the Department lacked sufficient resources to provide anything but minimal services to Aboriginal people. Its funding was a pittance compared to the sums spent on health, education and welfare for the state's non-Aboriginal citizens. It was also the first in line for government cutbacks in times of financial stress. This drastically affected all areas of administration. Workers at head office and in departmental institutions typically lacked relevant professional knowledge or training and were guided in their work by hearsay and racial stereotypes. Budgetary constraints prevented the development of a workable field service through, for example, the regular appointment of travelling inspectors directly responsible to the Department. Instead they were hired and fired according to available finance and numbered no more than one at a time when the Department of Fisheries boasted a field staff of seven. Financially strapped, and with Aborigines excluded from census counts, the Department had to rely entirely on amateurs — police, missionaries and institutional staff — and its office staff to collect and prepare statistical data. The priority was always to account for expenditure to Parliament rather than developing sets of useful social indicators for rational planning and development. In consequence the Department came to focus on surveillance and control of individuals and families. The instrument of rule became the personal dossier. From 1915 the Department developed a file and card system based on individuals and families, recording details on relief, blankets and clothing issued, any crimes and breaches of the Aborigines Act, family histories and departmental decisions relating to the subject's life. While these files resound with the voices of administrators, employers, missionaries and the police, those of their Aboriginal subjects are rarely heard. Ironically these files, despite their often unsavoury and insulting contents, have, in recent times, become a significant research resource for Aboriginal family historians.

Lack of resources was translated into services that were vastly inadequate but considered 'good enough' for Aborigines. Over the years these services diverged increasingly from those of mainstream programs. The latter were typically non-contributory, means-tested, cash-based benefit schemes available to families and individuals living in the community and, while not generous, they guaranteed minimal living standards for most Australians. Aborigines were carefully screened to distinguish the 'deserving' — the sick, elderly, women and children — from the 'undeserving' — principally unemployed Aboriginal men. The former were offered assistance in kind — rations and blankets — usually on the proviso that they relocated to segregated institutions where assistance could be centralised, provided economically and under strict surveillance. As far as possible all other services — medical attention, care of children, education, and even custodial care of juveniles — were delivered in the same multifunctional institutions. The Department also endeavoured to generate its own funding by emulating, albeit on a smaller scale, Queensland's obligatory contributory schemes for workers. This involved charging employers for access to Aboriginal labour and placing part of the wages of young people employed through the Department in trust accounts — an ironic term given that most never saw this money again — allegedly to provide for them in times of need rather than their relying on the Department. Further research is required to ascertain whether this money was expended by the Department on operational costs and special projects as occurred in Queensland. Savings were made in the institutions by forcing adults and children to work for their keep and, in a further terrible irony, by forcing some Aboriginal parents, whose children were taken from them by force, to contribute to the costs of their maintenance. Lack of funding and resources forced the Department, often against the preference of its administrators, into cooperative relationships with local agents. Police officers picked up 'half-caste' children, missions were subsidised at miserly rates to care for them, and pastoralists, who refused to pay wages to their workers, issued departmental rations to their dependents. In every case these relationships allowed for manipulation of the administration by local interests.

With little chance of expanding and developing along the lines of a typical bureaucracy, the Department turned to its wide-ranging controls and duties and became increasingly committed to concepts of social change through the force of the law. It treated its clients in ever more punitive ways, developing networks of control and surveillance and lobbying for ever increasing powers over an expanding web of people of Aboriginal descent. At each step it had to negotiate conflict and reach compromise outcomes with the demands of competing groups such as employers, missionaries, humanitarians and Aborigines. Most whites were convinced that the Department's role was to protect *their* interests: to prevent Aboriginal law-breaking; to maintain patterns of employment; to assist alliances of town people, organisations and government departments to enforce segregation of Aborigines; and to siphon off those Aborigines offending white sensibilities — from the criminal and diseased to the 'near white' children in the camps. Within this tangle there were a few who were prepared to stand up for Aborigines — the occasional employer acting to prevent removal of a loyal worker's children, and missionaries fighting local pastoralists for land for their 'flock' to live on. Following the passing of the 1905 Act, F Lyon Weiss started the Aborigines Amelioration Movement in Perth to act as a 'watchdog' of government. However, lacking a strong membership and political influence the Movement had disintegrated by 1908.[32] There was also William Harris, Aboriginal prospector and farmer from Morawa and future founder of the Native Union. In 1906, bearing letters of support from the mayors of Kalgoorlie and Leonora, he met with Chief Protector Prinsep and Premier Rason in an effort to force official recognition of the devastating conditions for Aborigines in the goldfields following the end of the economic boom. Nothing came of his efforts.[33]

While Harris was prepared to take on the government, most Aborigines adopted an attitude of apparent outward resignation to their arbitrary and often cruel treatment, while they manoeuvred within a narrow band of what constituted 'acceptable behaviours' to whites to ensure their own and their families' survival. Their strictly segregated camps created a circle of safety that both penned them in and allowed for continuity of old ways of being and doing. Within departmentally imposed limits, patterns of work were also negotiated to protect social and cultural traditions — working in family groups in the south, maintaining the Law and ceremonies in the pastoral off-seasons in the north and generally endeavouring to remain close to country and kin. Throughout the state Aboriginal knowledge of the bush provided some protection so that families could hide their 'half-caste' children and thereby sometimes escape the net of surveillance and removal.

Most Australians believe that the family is sacrosanct and that state intervention into family life occurs only in exceptional circumstances through a carefully monitored legal process that acts to protect family rights and children's 'best interests'. Many therefore found it difficult to accept the alarming claims of discriminatory treatment of Aboriginal families and children made in the 1997 *Bringing Them Home* report. Indeed, a fiery debate erupted over whether Aboriginal removals mirrored mainstream welfare treatment of needy and 'problem' children or whether they were race based and inherently discriminatory. This is an important issue which reflects directly on whether or not the Aboriginal Stolen Generations merit the specific measures of reparation recommended in the report. While undeniably there were common early influences and intersections between the two systems, a comparison of Western Australian child welfare statutes and the *Aborigines Act 1905* and their implementation, clearly shows that in this state they were profoundly different. They operated in isolation from each other from the first decade of the century to the 1950s when the responsibility for Aboriginal children began to be transferred to mainstream child welfare controls.

The systems were contrastive in terms of their role, administration, target groups, state and parental powers, rationales for and processes of removal, the nature of placements and the rights of the young adults.[34] The controls over Aboriginal children, embedded in the 1905 Act along with a host of other duties and powers, meant that their needs were frequently overlooked in the scramble to allocate scarce resources. They did not receive the specialist care provided for non-Aboriginal children by the State Children's Department (SCD) which, although small and under-funded, managed to keep up with professional developments. Aboriginal administrations remained insulated from advances in child welfare and education until the 1950s. Checks and balances built into the *State Children's Act 1907* to protect state wards from abuse and to ensure adequate living conditions were absent from the 1905 Act and its regulations, which granted total power over Aboriginal children to government officers and mission staff, were punitive in relation to the children and failed to specify criteria to protect their 'best interests'. This allowed for the development of abusive scenarios that would never have been tolerated for white children.

The SCD targeted children deemed to be neglected or abused by their families and also dealt with juveniles charged in the Children's Court. The majority of its charges were drawn from the Perth metropolitan area. The Aborigines Department could remove virtually any child of Aboriginal descent for any reason from anywhere in the state. While parental guardianship of white children was regarded as a sacred right which could only be annulled by the courts for good reason, the Chief Protector of Aborigines was the guardian of all illegitimate children of Aboriginal descent from birth — effectively the vast majority of children since the law did not recognise Aboriginal customary marriage. The removal of a child by the SCD usually began after authorities such as the police or schools informed the SCD of instances of possible neglect or abuse. An SCD officer then inspected the child's home and interviewed the family and arrangements were made either to improve the home situation or to remove the child to a government receiving home pending a court hearing, at which parents could present an argument for keeping their child. Court decisions on whether to commit children to the care of the state were guided by strict legal definitions of 'neglect' and 'abuse' and of what constituted the 'best interests' of the child. In the case of Aboriginal children there were no legal guidelines defining criteria and procedures for their removal — it was sufficient to be of Aboriginal descent and to come to the attention of the local police or the Aborigines Department. There was no process of notification and negotiation about their situation with the parents, no court committal process and no right of appeal, just the trauma of sudden loss as they were taken by police using their powers of summary removal. A former police officer described this horror in a letter to the *West Australian* following the publication of the *Bringing Them Home* report:

> The job of rounding up these children fell to the police ... In many cases Aboriginal women would hide their children and police would use trackers to find them. A police visit was feared because it meant one of two things: all the dogs would be shot or any half-caste child under twelve would be taken away.[35]

Since police rarely kept accurate records of who was taken and from whom during these 'round ups' many of those removed were subsequently unable to trace their families.

The SCD provided a range of alternatives to institutional care for children committed to its care: foster families, probation for juvenile offenders and, from the 1920s, financial supports to enable children to remain within their own families. Its institutions for child offenders and for disabled and older children deemed unsuited for fostering, while spartan and strict in their treatment of the children, were nevertheless ensured of adequate conditions by sufficient funding — set in 1907 at a minimum of seven shillings a week per child and adjusted with the economy over the years — regular inspections by SCD officers, and regulations establishing standards of diet, living quarters, medical and dental care, education to state school standards and limiting the range of chores that children could be ordered to carry out. From the age of fourteen they could be apprenticed out as rural or domestic workers under conditions set out in SCD regulations and enforced by regular inspections by its officers. Children were allowed some contact with their families and the aim for most was that they would be reunited with them. With the exception of the severely disabled and repeat offenders it was envisaged that as they moved towards adulthood they, like other white children, would begin to take on the rights, duties and responsibility of adult citizenship.

By contrast, there were no choices in the placement of Aboriginal children: they were all transported directly to dormitories in Aboriginal institutions where they could be detained indefinitely. This included Aboriginal juvenile offenders who, if they had been dealt with through the normal court system, would have been placed on probation or incarcerated for fixed terms. Conditions in these dormitories were typically appalling, reflecting low levels of funding which remained set at a maximum of ten pence a child per week until the 1930s, irregular inspections and minimal established standards of care for the children. They were to have no further contact with their families or their culture. The continued institutionalisation of Aboriginal children takes on a profound sadness when we recall from the previous chapter that authorities were well aware already in the nineteenth century of the damaging effects of institutional life. Official aims were less to improve their welfare than to sunder forever ties with their Aboriginality and to mould them into docile rural and domestic workers or to render them invisible in a White Australia while they lived under the yoke of the 1905 Act.

Institutionalisation remained the major option for Aboriginal children taken from their families in Western Australia for decades. It was widely believed that the children's attachments to their families and their former way of life could only be broken and their Aboriginal natures remoulded under strict institutional control in the way that problem white children needed the special discipline provided by these settings. There was no alternative place for them — white families would not take them in as foster children, and government policies prevented their being placed with Aboriginal families. It was not until the 1950s that welfare authorities began to place Aboriginal children in white families under adoption and fostering arrangements and not until the 1970s that they began to *consider* placements with Aboriginal families or care arrangements in the children's own families.

We can never know the exact number of children of Aboriginal descent removed from their families in Western Australia. While the Aborigines Department ran an efficient record system based on personal dossiers from the early 1920s, little accurate statistical data was collected. This reflected, in part, departmental reliance on police to collect data at the local level as well as problems of distance and mobility of Aboriginal groups. Missions and other institutions were required to send in reports of numbers of children subsidised by the Aborigines Department, but did not always enumerate children paid for by the mission or their parents. Furthermore, numbers were not reported in a regular or consistent fashion in the Aborigines Department annual reports. These provide only irregular estimates of 'children in missions' which do not include children in government settlements: 122 in 1902, 320 in 1911, 371 in 1918, and 500 in 1943 when 300 were also reported to be living in state institutions.[36]

The extent of removals can be surmised from the large number of institutions taking in Aboriginal children relative to the size of the Aboriginal population (see Table Three, pp 229–230). In 1996 the Western Australian government told the National Inquiry into the Separation of Aboriginal and Torres Strait Islander Children from their Families that there was 'not one' Aboriginal family in the state that had escaped the effects of removal policies.[37] The scanty records indicate that more girls were taken than boys, reflecting the demand for female domestic servants, concerns to control their sexuality and to protect them from sexual abuse, and the determination to transform them into good Christian wives and mothers. They also show that particular regions were targeted for mass removals at different times, for example the Kimberley in the first decade of the century. Nor can we provide exact answers to some demands to know the proportions of 'forcible removals' of Aboriginal children or of removals made on the basis of 'neglect or race'.[38] Such distinctions were simply not part of a system where police could ride into camps and grab children indiscriminately, then send them off to institutions without reference to any higher authority or legal process.

TABLE THREE

CHRONOLOGY OF ABORIGINAL CHILDREN'S INSTITUTIONS

(Multi-purpose government settlements, missions, children's homes; excluding child welfare institutions) providing care for Aboriginal children and youth in Western Australia from 1842–1960s

Smithies Mission, Perth	Wesleyan	1842–55
Anglican children's missions Perth	Anglican	1840s
New Norcia, Victoria Plains	Catholic	1846–70
Annesfield	Private	1852–c.71
Swan Native and Half-caste Mission, Perth	Anglican	1870–1921
Beagle Bay, West Kimberley	Catholic	1891–1976
Sunday Island, Kimberley	Private, UAM (1924–)	1898–1934
Ellensbrook, Busselton	Government	1899–17
Kalumburu (formerly Drysdale River), East Kimberley	Catholic	1907–75
Broome Convent, Broome	Catholic	1908–?
Dulhi Gunyah, Victoria Park	Australian Aborigines Mission	1909–17
Aboriginal Girls Home, Kalgoorlie	Salvation Army	1909–c.1930
Kunmunya (formerly Port George IV), Kimberley	Presbyterian	1910–?
Moola Bulla, East Kimberley	Government	1911–54
Lombadina, West Kimberley	Catholic	1911–85
St John of God Home for Native Girls (later Holy Child Orphanage), Broome	Catholic	1912–70
Forrest River, Kimberley	Anglican	1913–71
Carrolup Native Settlement, Katanning	Government	1915–22
Moore River, Mogumber	Government	1918–51
Mount Margaret, Goldfields	United Aborigines Mission	1921–75
La Grange, West Kimberley	Catholic	1924–85
Gnowangerup Mission	Australian Aborigines Mission	1926–73
East Perth Girls' Home (later Bennett House), East Perth	Government	1931–?
Sister Kate's Home, Queens Park	Anglican	1933–c.50
Warburton Ranges	United Aborigines Mission	1933–77

Derby Leprosarium	Government	1935–87
Roelands Mission Farm, near Bunbury	Interdenominational	1937–80s
Carrolup Native Settlement, Katanning	Government	1938–52
Kellerberrin	United Aborigines Mission	1939–?
Balgo, East Kimberley	Catholic	1939–80
Cosmo Newbery, Eastern Goldfields	Government	1940–80
United Aborigines Mission Cundelee, Goldfields	Australian Aboriginal Evengelical	1940–?
Norseman	Church of Christ	1942–c.75
AIM Mission, Halls Creek	Australian Inland Mission	1943–60
Saint Francis Xavier, Wandering	Catholic	1944–76
Carnarvon	Church of Christ	1946–?
Jigalong, Pilbara	Apostolic	1946–72
Tardun Agricultural School	Catholic	1948–1980
Rossmoyne Training Centre, Perth	Catholic	1948–80s?
Mowanjum, Kimberley	Presbyterian	1950–81
Alvan House, Mount Lawley	Government	1951–?
Mogumber, Wheatbelt	Methodist	1951–80
Geraldton Girls Home	Anglican	1952–?
Kurrawang, Goldfields	Brethren	1952–c.75
McDonald House,West Perth	Government	1952–72
Marribank, Katanning	Baptist	1952–70
Wongutha Mission Training Farm, Esperance	Interdenominational	1954–1970
Karalundi, Wiluna	Seventh Day Adventist	1954–85
Amy Bethel House,	United Aborigines Mission	1956–75
Riverton Hostel, Perth	Catholic	1956–72?
Riverdale, Nullagine	Government	1959?–?
Saint Joseph's Hostel, Derby	Catholic	1959–80s?
Charles Perkins Hostel, Halls Creek (formerly AIM mission)	Government	1960–?
Gnowangerup Agricultural School	Government	1960s–?
Moorgunya Hostel, Port Hedland	Government	1960s–?
Nabberu Hostel	Government	1960s–?
Nindeebai Hostel, Boulder	Government	1960s–?
Oolnayah Hostel, Marble Bar		1960s–?
St Michael's Mission Farm, Newdegate	Anglican	196?–?
Warramboo, Yalgoo	Government	1960s–?
Weerianna Hostel, Roebourne		1960s?–?
Maria Goretti Home	Catholic	1960s?–?
Cooindah Hostel, Mount Lawley	Methodist	
Kyarra Hostel, Cue	Government	1961?–?
Native Hostel, Onslow	Government	1962?–?
Gilliamia Hostel, Onslow	Government	1962?–?
Lake Grace Farm School, Wheatbelt	Anglican	1964–70
Fairhaven, Esperance	Church of Christ	1965–?
Esperance Home	Australian Aboriginal Evangelical	1966–?
Pallottine Boys Hostel, Albany	Catholic	1968–1978
Katakutu Home, Perth	Baptist	1969–?
Boulder Working Youths Hostel	Australian Aboriginal Evangelical	1971–?

In their study of governance, administration and development, Turner and Hulme[39] write that both policy making and implementation are permeated with 'politics and power rather than rational and technical matters'. The 'implementation phase' may be seen as 'an area in which those responsible for allocating resources are engaged in political relationships among themselves and with other actors intent on influencing that allocation.'[40] These processes are analysed in relation to the implementation of the 1905 Act in the major regions of Western Australia over different periods of time. The following questions are addressed: who were the actors and vested interest groups? What alliances of groups mobilised around perceived common interests? What was being contested? What strategies were adopted to achieve goals and what compromises were reached? What roles did the Aboriginal 'subjects' play? For certainly they, like all subjects of 'regimens of government', were never simply passive victims in the process. As Rose reminds us:

Human beings are not the unified subjects of some coherent regimen of government that produces persons in the form in which it dreams. On the contrary, they live their lives in a constant movement across different practices that subjectify them in different ways.[41]

We find the Aborigines Department manoeuvering along political 'fault lines' — avoiding action but, when pressures arose, responding by meeting the demands of the most powerful alliances. Pastoralists, politicians, rural businessmen and townspeople could combine in what E Hunter[42] describes as 'uneasy relationships of necessity', contesting control of Aboriginal labour, including sexual services, ownership of land, distribution of departmental rations and funds, and control over Aboriginal and 'half-caste' children. Aborigines had almost no control in any of these arenas. Their limited power lay in escape through their skills of physical survival in the bush, of rendering themselves invisible behind the barriers of caste and white race fears, and in establishing relations of patronage with significant white figures. When they did come to the attention of these interest groups, they were often dragged into the ambit of the Aborigines Department which allowed few to escape. Nevertheless, even here, departmental control might be attenuated by the inaction of unreliable local agents and the 'tyrannies of distance'.

The Department's initial thrust was in the north. Following the Roth Royal Commission there was considerable public pressure to 'clean up' the region through the implementation of the 1905 Act: regulating Aboriginal employment, controlling sexual contacts with Aboriginal women and dealing with the growing mixed-descent population. Powerful pastoral interests were keen to re-establish their regimes of Aboriginal employment in the wake of earlier criticisms and the new legislation. However, under Prinsep's continued leadership, the Department limped along and real change only came with new leadership at the helm.

The amalgamation of the departments of Fisheries and Aborigines in 1908 under the Chief Inspector of Fisheries and the new Chief Protector of Aborigines, Charles F Gale, placed a man with strong interests in the north in charge of Aboriginal affairs. Western Australian born, Gale was a former Gascoyne pastoralist and prospector turned career public servant with strong ties to pastoral and other landed interests. His views on Aborigines reflected this background. In 1882 he told the Fairbairn Inquiry into cattle killing in the Gascoyne that 'if the government shut their eyes for six months and let the settlers deal with the natives in their own way it would stop the depredations effectively,'[43] and it is likely that he was amongst those who drove Reverend Gribble out of the region in 1886. As head of the Royal Commission in 1908 into allegations of abusive treatment of Aborigines by members of the Canning Exploration Party, he exonerated members of all charges of cruelty and found 'slight foundation' for allegations of immorality.[44] He opposed payment of wages to Aboriginal workers and was determined to remove any impediments to pastoral development in the north. Under Gale's administration the Department's first institutions were established: the Lock hospitals on Dorre and Bernier islands off the Carnarvon coast, opened in 1908 for the treatment of Aboriginal men and women suffering from venereal disease, and Moola Bulla cattle station, opened in 1911 in the east Kimberley. Gale was dismissed in 1915 by a Labor government, probably because he was out of step with their ideas and policies.

Riding at Gale's side was a man of similar background and interests, the Aborigines Department's travelling inspector, James Isdell, a former Kimberley pastoralist and station manager and Pilbara prospector, storekeeper, mine manager and politician.[45] We have already encountered Isdell's mix of concern about the 'degraded' condition of Aborigines around the mining camps and his personal advocacy of pastoral interests. In further correspondence he promoted policies of Aboriginal segregation and containment to combat the spread of venereal disease in the north, demonstrating the trend at the time to link race, immorality, segregation, medicine, social orderliness

James Isdell, travelling inspector for the Kimberley from 1907 to 1909.
(Courtesy of Battye Library, BA368/6/1)

and health. In debate in the Legislative Assembly he proved a staunch opponent of race mixing, claiming 'we are talking about white Australia and we are cultivating a piebald one.'[46] He also advocated the removal of 'half-caste' children and told the Legislative Assembly in 1904 that leaving children with their Aboriginal mothers was not only 'wrong, unjust and a disgrace to the State', but 'maudlin sentiment ... They forget their children in twenty-four hours and as a rule [were] glad to be rid of them.'[47] Appointed travelling inspector in the Kimberley in 1907, Isdell inherited a field staff of resident magistrates, police officers and private gentlemen, including mission-aries at Beagle Bay and Forrest River, and the Broome Inspector of Pearl Fisheries. In this frontier region, official life and politics were tempered by the need to co-exist among the relatively small number of Europeans in the area and to respect local ways of managing 'the black'. Isdell worked within these constraints but rarely in the best interests of Aborigines.

KIMBERLEY ROUNDUPS

The Kimberley landscape has driven many visitors from the 'genteel' south to superlatives of romantic metaphor, encapsulating notions of remoteness, grandeur of nature, extremes of climate, human insignificance and magical and mysterious primitiveness. The usually reserved young Paul Hasluck left this impression of his first visit to the region in 1934 as reporter for the *West Australian* during the Moseley Royal Commission's tour of the Kimberley:

A vast, crumpled expanse of brown, red and yellow earth stretches below, like a discarded blanket flung without purpose into the sun and left in tumbled disorder ... In this unreal world very old and dead mountains, each with a coronet of red rock circling its bald head, sit around remote valleys. The long dry muddy beds of streams writhe in the torment of the sun. Those dull silver snakes, the Fitzroy and the Ord, sleep among the gorges; and here and there in their twinings are clasped the fertile station downs ... men moving in a land which seems to belong not to mankind, but to the sun, a land which is so vast and whose meaning is so hard to grasp that any idea of a Providence who had made the earth as a garden for the chosen beings to inhabit must be lost and men appear in its vastness in the proportions of ants who have strayed far from the nest.[48]

This was a frontier land of men, of white pioneers fighting nature and the 'natives', and bedding the native women. For newcomers it was a harsh and 'uncivilised' land with few white women or comforts of home which remained a long sea voyage away to the south. Following the end of the local mining boom of the 1880s, the region's main economies were pearling along the coast near the racially and culturally diverse township of Broome, and sheep and cattle rearing in vast pastoral stations throughout the east and west Kimberley, linked by small oases of white 'civilisation' at Derby, Wyndham, Fitzroy Crossing and Halls Creek. Aboriginal people played a significant role in all these domains: working in the pearling and pastoral industries, providing domestic and labouring services to townspeople, and contributing their labour to the expanding mission effort in the region. Outside these domains they struggled to survive in the face of depletion of traditional foods and were drawn into increasing dependence on introduced foodstuffs obtained as rations or through employment or ties to employed kin.

From 1907 to 1909 Travelling Inspector Isdell traversed the region, mapping for the administration in Perth an Aboriginal landscape of numbers, locations and conditions and endeavouring to impose the

Department's vision of orderly race relations in the north. In contrast to Hasluck's description, Isdell's diary entries and dispatches to Perth often resemble vignettes from a war zone. A seasoned bushman, he 'rode alone', watching warily for 'dangerous' Aborigines — not 'bush natives' but former Aboriginal prisoners and escapees. He was also on the lookout for 'half-caste' children. Isdell's diligence is evident in a diary entry in March 1909 which recorded his nervousness on encountering over 100 'bush natives' half a mile from the Margaret River; nevertheless he still managed to note the presence in the group of a three-year-old 'half-caste' girl.[49] Isdell's impressions on patrol only served to strengthen his commitment to the removal of 'half-caste' children and to stopping sexual contact between the races. In 1909 he wrote to Gale of 'half-caste women':

scattered throughout the north-west and Kimberleys ... some living with Aboriginal husbands, and some on stations without husbands, some of these women have children by white men and it is not a pleasant sight to see almost white half-castes living among Aborigines.[50]

He reported to Gale from Halls Creek after completing a major tour of the Kimberley:

People who have no knowledge of the surroundings of these youngsters in native camps, are fond of writing letters to the papers detailing the cruelty and harrowing grief of the mothers, their motives in writing may be perfectly sincere, but let them visit and reside for a while in the vicinity of these haunts in the far north where these youngsters are being reared, they would soon alter their opinions on the matter. To see the open indecency, immorality and hear the vile conversations ordinarily carried on, which these children listen to and repeat would convince them that separation is absolutely necessary if the future welfare of the youngsters is to be considered.

I am convinced that the short lived grief of the parent is of little consequence compared to the children's future. The half-caste is intellectually above the aborigine, and it is the duty of the State that they be given a chance to lead a better and purer life than their brothers. I would not hesitate for one moment to separate any half-caste from its aboriginal mother, no matter how frantic her momentary grief may be at the time. They soon forget their offspring.[51]

It was a bright spot for Isdell when he could enter in his diary:

I was glad to receive [Gale's] telegraphic instructions at Halls Creek to arrange for the transport of all half-castes to Beagle Bay Mission, it should have been done years ago.[52]

Of the various racial groups in the Kimberley apart from Aborigines, Asian men — Chinese, Japanese and 'Malay' (from the Philippines, Timor and Koepang, and other parts of what is now Malaysia and Indonesia), most of them involved in the pearling industry — were the lowest on the 'pecking order' and the most vulnerable to Isdell's inspectorial gaze. This was despite the long history of contact between coastal Aborigines and Asian fishermen to the immediate north and the several well-established 'mixed race' families living in the area. The pearling industry had a notorious reputation of blackbirding, high mortality rates and sexual abuse of Aboriginal women and girls, and the spread of venereal disease and leprosy was conveniently blamed on Asian crews. Legislation introduced in the early 1870s to protect Aboriginal workers and to prevent sexual contact with Aboriginal women was passed principally with them in mind. Asian men were constructed by whites as lustful, abusive to their women, and always ready to abandon Aboriginal wives and children for the 'call of home'. Children of mixed Asian and Aboriginal descent were doubly condemned. Anti-Asian racism and paranoia about Australia's security, enshrined in the White Australia policy, together with the avowed intention of white business interests, including some pastoralists, to drive Asians out of the pearling industry as managers and owners but to keep some as a cheap labour force, left hundreds of men in a very vulnerable situation.

Isdell took immediate steps to prevent Asian men from employing Aborigines and to stop them having sexual contact with Aboriginal women. The 1905 Act contained several measures to control sexual contacts, including earlier prohibitions on Aboriginal females boarding ships or being near creeks used by pearling crews and new provisions prohibiting non-Aboriginal males from cohabiting or travelling with Aboriginal females or being near their camps. The Solicitor General's ruling in 1908 that 'cohabitation' referred only to permanent de facto relations undermined efforts to stamp out casual sexual contacts. Isdell adopted another strategy to stop casual contact between Aboriginal women and Asian pearling crews pulling in to shore to pick up water, by recommending the closure of the northern coastline to their boats. Not surprisingly, the Pearlers Association, representing white business interests, supported this recommendation with the exception of boats under white masters, and in 1909 this was legislated for.[53] Under the 1905 Act de facto relationships of Asian men and Aboriginal women were unlawful and couples were instructed to marry or face prosecution. However, to marry they required the Chief Protector of Aborigines' permission and applications from Asian men were routinely knocked back to save mothers and children from the men's supposed 'immoral' influence. When couples continued to live together the men faced conviction, imprisonment and even deportation, in the process of which their Aboriginal wives and children were left abandoned. Ironically, this was the stereotyped outcome predicted by the Department. The Catholic church adopted a more measured approach in the case of Catholic Filipino men and early in the twentieth century married several couples who became the backbone of its missionary endeavours in Broome and Beagle Bay.

Isdell was far more conciliatory in his dealings with the powerful pastoral industry. It is not reading too much into the records to suggest a set of informal negotiations and pay-offs involving pastoralists and the Aborigines Department (represented by Isdell) which set the parameters for Aboriginal/pastoralist/government relations in the area up to the Second World War. Pastoralists were determined to maintain their hold on the cheap and reliable pool of Aboriginal male and female workers and 'reserve army' of seasonal labour. They vehemently opposed Aboriginal wage labour, arguing it would make the stations uneconomical and unworkable and would lead to mass sackings of Aboriginal workers. They were already supporting, reluctantly, their workers' family members — the elderly, the unemployable and the young — who the workers insisted on having with them but who were otherwise 'unnecessary' to the pastoral effort. The pastoralists also wanted a stop to attacks on their stock by 'dangerous' bands of Aborigines. Isdell endorsed these views and looked for ways to deal with the 'unnecessary' and the 'dangerous' which would fit both pastoralist and departmental interests. He was particularly concerned at the high rates of imprisonment for cattle-killing which he considered to be 'anything but a deterrent' and not only a major expense but also 'a terrible disgrace to the Government' with 'terrible harm' being done to the younger generations.[54] At the same time he realised that many Aborigines were starving and had few alternatives for survival.

Learning to be stockmen at Moola Bulla, c 1910–18.
(Courtesy of Battye Library, 68215P)

A series of compromises emerged. The pastoralists' existing employment arrangements continued, subject to the requirement of agreements and contracts under the 1905 Act. They were to be provided with government rations for workers' dependents and for workers as well during the off-season but otherwise would receive no other government services. Aborigines deemed to be 'unnecessary' or 'dangerous' would be siphoned off and contained within institutions. Isdell, Prinsep and Gale staunchly backed the establishment of the Lock hospitals which operated until 1917 and incarcerated a total of 800 Aborigines, the majority from the Pilbara, a quarter of whom died. Although they were established to deal with the panic about venereal disease in the north, the mechanics of the system ensured that local police and employer interests, to be rid of 'unnecessary' or 'dangerous' Aborigines, determined who was admitted, rather than medical conditions.[55] In the east Kimberley the Moola Bulla settlement served to remove such Aborigines from pastoral leases as well as to centralise groups living outside the influence of pastoralists, and also functioned as a ration depot to help prevent Aborigines killing stock.[56] The developing vision of Moola Bulla is evident in Isdell's reports of discussions with pastoralists and his own musings about the value of centralised native stations to protect white interests, get Aborigines to provide for their own needs through work, ensure a pool of trained workers for local employers by training children in stock and domestic work, keep unemployed Aborigines away from white centres, reduce costs of rationing and provide a cheap alternative to imprisonment.[57] Moola Bulla proved a spectacular success in reducing imprisonment rates. In 1910 ninety-seven Aboriginal prisoners were discharged from Wyndham Gaol and in the following year no Aboriginal prisoners were received.[58] The creation of the vast Marndoc Aboriginal Reserve in the north-west Kimberley in 1911 had similar motivations. While these developments may have suited 'the public, the Government and the pastoralists',[59] they held serious implications for Aboriginal families. Valued workers on pastoral stations were able to remain with their families and in their country, but in the long run *all* Kimberley Aborigines now lived under the threat of being 'creamed off' as 'unnecessary' due to injury or old age, or as 'dangerous' for a variety of behaviours and misdemeanours, and separated from their kin. However, most vulnerable of all were the 'half-caste' children.

Most 'half-caste' children on stations away from the coast came from unions between white station men and Aboriginal women. In contrast to attitudes to Asian men, there was considerable acceptance of white men's casual sexual contacts. The Solicitor General argued in 1900 that 'some allowance must be made for the utter lonely and monotonous existence which people living out in our never never country are called upon to face.'[60] This was evident during debate on the 1905 Act when pastoralists successfully moved to reduce the minimum fine for cohabitation from fifty pounds to five. However, there *was* growing condemnation of permanent relationships and official permission for marriage was rarely granted. The situation of 'half-caste' children on the stations was also ambivalent. Isdell was sympathetic to employer interests in 'half-caste' workers and recommended to the Chief Protector in 1909 that 'good' male workers over twelve years of age employed by respectable pastoralists should remain where they were. While he was prepared to assign girls over sixteen to employers for their 'own protection to prevent [their] being enticed away', he was determined to remove younger 'half-caste' girls to missions.[61] Isdell was keen to identify putative fathers to sue them for maintenance of children in institutions and this had the effect of alienating some who refused to acknowledge paternity. At the same time he objected to their involvement in the children's lives. A white father who wanted his son to be educated in Derby rather than Beagle Bay was informed that, since the boy was illegitimate, he had no legal parental rights and could do nothing without the mother's consent. Isdell in fact advised the Chief Protector not to recognise *any* white men's claims over 'half-caste' boys, claiming it was a ruse to secure the boys' services and to prevent their removal to missions.[62]

By 1913 six missions and an orphanage were operating in the Kimberley. The missionaries hoped to save the Aboriginal 'remnants' both physically and spiritually by segregating, protecting, Christianising and civilising them and forging them into enduring self-supporting mission communities. This was later spelt out by the Chief Protector of Aborigines during a visit to Forrest River Mission in 1928:

> Mr Gribble does not conceal the fact that in his opinion the future of the nation lies in marrying these boys and girls together in order that the population may go on increasing until he is able to settle them in village communities.[63]

Such aims brought missionaries into conflict with local employers and with the Aborigines Department, intent on supporting employers' demands for labour. At the same time missionaries had to comply with departmental directives in order to receive the grants of vast areas of land and various forms of assistance, including subsidies for children sent in by the Department, that were essential for their work. Other children came from Aboriginal families camped at the missions or were sent in by parents to be educated or protected from removal by police.

Beagle Bay Mission was the principal institution for 'half-caste' children in the Kimberley until 1921 when the Aborigines Department arranged for children from the east Kimberley to be sent to Forrest River Mission. Beagle Bay was established by French Trappist monks in 1890 and taken over in 1901 by the German-based Pallottine Order. In 1907 the Irish order, the St John of God sisters, arrived to educate the children. Located on Nyulnyul land, the early mission became a depot for local language groups — Nyulnyul, Nimanburr, Jabirrjabirr and Bardi — and for 'half-caste' children from across the Kimberley. Beagle Bay missionaries and church

A priest and his young charges at Beagle Bay Mission, early 1900s.
(Courtesy of Western Australian Museum)

authorities were not neutral in the process of removing the children. Historian Christine Choo[64] argues that not only did they actively encourage removals of children but that their views helped to shape broader policy and legislation in Western Australia. It would be naive to think they would be otherwise; after all, they had travelled far to work with the people and were personally committed to spreading their message and rescuing the children for a 'life with Christ'. Father Walter of Beagle Bay told the Roth Royal Commission:

> The children, both half-caste and black should be removed from the centres of vice such as Broome and other places and brought to this or any other institution which is working in the interests of the blacks.[65]

Missionaries *needed* a flock of young children — they were the 'putty' for creating a strong Christian community — and the government subsidies they brought with them. To this end they actively encouraged families and pressured the government to send in 'half-caste' children to their care. In 1906 Father Walter petitioned the Aborigines Department:

> many full-blood and half-caste children are roaming about Broome and other North-western towns, beginning the worst and most unhappy lives. If the police sent me only the most obvious cases, the number of children on the mission would be about 200.[66]

In the following year Bishop Gibney requested the removal to Beagle Bay of 'several hundred half-caste children' in the Kimberley who could be made into 'useful citizens'. Encouraged by Isdell's reports on numbers of 'half-caste' children, Chief Protector Gale instructed police officers and Isdell to round them up for removal to Beagle Bay. In 1908 Isdell wrote to Gale:

> I am indeed most anxious to have charge of [the children] and it is with feelings of gratification that I read your letter today, announcing the Home Minister's decision to have all the Kimberley children sent to missions. They urgently need the care of the Mission, for, surrounded as they are with vicious influences, they cannot but grow up immoral and criminal.[67]

Between 1907 and 1909 numbers of children at Beagle Bay increased from sixteen to ninety-four, constituting a third of all children in missions in the state, and indicating the strength of intention to institutionalise all 'half-caste' children in the Kimberley.[68] Government officials were optimistic that this would stop any further increase in numbers of 'half-castes', although missionaries looked to marriages between young people in their flock to build up enduring mission communities.

The 1905 Act granted the Kimberley police a range of new controls over Aborigines. They could drive them out of town, send women associating with Asian men to Beagle Bay under the stigma of being prostitutes, arrest white and Asian men living with Aboriginal women, escort Aborigines to Moola Bulla, and round up 'half-caste' children from the camps. The following summaries from the journal of Constable Johnston, on patrol in the vicinity of Beagle Bay on the Dampier Land Peninsula in 1909, illustrate how the old and new duties of the police were jumbled together and how the police maintained their role as the advance force of civilisation — riding into Aboriginal camps, arresting men, taking women and children to Beagle Bay, shooting Aborigines' dogs and assisting missionaries in maintaining order and building up their Aboriginal populations.

May: patrols of 'native' camps yielded one man and two women and a seven year 'half-caste' girl who were taken to Beagle Bay. During a 'daylight raid' on Emerian Point four men were arrested and seven women and a small boy were rounded up and taken to Beagle Bay. Five more men were arrested: one for deserting service in Broome, another for escaping from custody in Broome and the remainder for refusing to move away from the creeks after being ordered to do so by the police as required under the 1905 Act.

June–July: in the first week of June a total of twelve men were arrested and escorted from Beagle Bay to Broome. Patrols to check for Aborigines in contact with pearling boats in the creeks encountered only a few Aborigines. Twenty-two dogs were shot.

August: after receiving a report on the theft of eight loaves of bread from the Beagle Bay bakehouse police arrested a boy 'Arson' aged fourteen. Father Bischoff did not press charges and instead the boy spent several days in the police camp as punishment. Several futile attempts were made to capture Aboriginal adults and children by chasing them through the mangroves at Tappers Inlet and rough country at Chimney Rocks. The Reverend Mother from Beagle Bay requested police to 'hunt down' an elderly woman, five little girls and a boy who had escaped from Beagle Bay. Police assisted Aborigines to bury an Aboriginal woman. They also shot five dogs and took three indigent Aborigines to Beagle Bay. Police were patrolling the coast aboard the Beagle Bay lugger.[69]

The removal of children was a haphazard process and one that Isdell was determined to improve. He was well aware of the ruses used by Aboriginal families to keep their children and the advantages that their mobility and knowledge of the bush gave them over police. To this end in 1909 police were instructed to record names, sex, age, locality and living conditions for all 'half-caste' children encountered while on patrol and to maintain comprehensive lists for the travelling inspector's visits. They now also had the power to summarily remove 'half-caste' children over the age of eight years. Western Australia appears to be the only state which formally granted such unprecedented powers to police, although similar controls operated in the Northern Territory. Nevertheless there was some remaining confusion about the exact nature of powers to remove 'half-caste' children and in 1909 Gale wrote urgently to Isdell:

> Although you had my authority to remove such children to the different missions, I am rendering myself liable to prosecution for kidnapping by doing so, unless I have the consent of the maternal parent for the removal. My authority as guardian does not override parental authority, which rests entirely with the mother, as these children being illegitimate, the father has no control whatsoever over them.[70]

This was rectified by amending legislation in 1911 which granted the Chief Protector of Aborigines greater legal power over illegitimate 'half-caste' children than that of their Aboriginal mothers. Despite Isdell's indifference to the feelings of Aboriginal families, he complained to the the Chief Protector in 1909 at the inhumane treatment of 'half-caste' children transported to missions by the police, stating that he would 'have no party' with the practice of 'compelling these half caste children to walk to Wyndham in company with chained prisoners', and he insisted that a vehicle 'be provided irrespective of cost'.[71]

The position of travelling inspector was abolished in 1910 as an economy measure. Two years later another was appointed and this intermittent situation continued into the 1920s. Isdell remained in the Kimberley as an honorary protector of Aborigines at Turkey Creek and in 1916 he returned to more comfortable work as a storekeeper in the Pilbara. The patterns established during his time as travelling inspector remained accepted ways of working until the Second World War. Following the closure of the Lock hospitals in 1917 the departmental presence was represented by Moola Bulla, Marndoc Reserve and 'feeding depots' at La Grange and Violet Valley, as well as rationing from town police stations. Cooperation of police and other local protectors remained integral to the execution of departmental duties. The problems of distance and lack of police cooperation must have driven the staff at head office to tear their hair at times. In 1921, soon after declaring Forrest River Mission the depot for 'half-caste' children from the east Kimberley, the Chief Protector requested police assistance in transporting a small group of children from Fitzroy Crossing. Over the next twelve months the Chief Protector engaged in a frustrating ordeal with police intransigence, distance, geography and plain bad luck before the children were finally moved.

1921

June: the Chief Protector of Aborigines wrote to the Commissioner of Police requesting a police escort to transport ten 'half-caste' children aged between six and nine years from Fitzroy Crossing to Forrest River Mission travelling overland via Derby and by boat to Wyndham.

July: the Commissioner replied that the police had no time to take the children and recommended that they be sent to Moola Bulla and that staff there accompany them to Forrest River.

September: the Manager of Moola Bulla responded that the trip from Fitzroy Crossing to Derby was 247 miles compared to 352 miles via Moola Bulla. The Chief Protector repeated his request to the Commissioner for a police escort for the children.

October: the Commissioner instructed the Fitzroy Crossing police to escort the children.

November: the Fitzroy Crossing police replied that they were unable to do so and advised that the children be sent by mail coach instead. The Chief Protector agreed to this. The children were also booked on the state steamer the *Bambra* which was scheduled to arrive in Derby in January and the Chief Protector requested that the stewardess supervise them while they were on board.

December: the State Shipping Service informed the Chief Protector that it was not certain that the *Bambra* would sail north in January and that a stewardess would not be made available for the children. The Chief Protector offered a first class return ticket and a daily rate of ten shillings for a lady to escort the children from Derby to Wyndham. Derby police informed the Chief Protector that the children arrived in Derby on 19 December. The Chief Protector arranged to pay police for maintenance of the children and requested that some clothing be arranged as the children were almost naked.

1922
January: the State Shipping Service announced that the *Bambra* would not sail until February.

March: the Derby police informed the Chief Protector that the *Bambra* had left Derby suddenly due to bad weather and that the children were not on board and would be unable to leave until April.

May: Wyndham police informed the Chief Protector that the children had arrived and would remain at the station until Reverend Gribble arrived to escort them to the mission.[72]

Trapped in this bureaucratic nightmare were the young children. Sixty-two years later, one of them, Lily Johnson, recalled:

After a while we were put on the *Bambra*. We didn't know where we was going — we were so excited. But when we realised we were being taken further and further we knew we wouldn't see our parents any more. I didn't see my mother again until I got married and had children.[73]

Children continued to be sent from the east Kimberley to Forrest River Mission until 1930 when Moola Bulla was declared an institution for 'half-caste' children.

The inefficiencies of this system made it easy for police officers to neglect their duties and to overlook the needs of the children, however, the loopholes sometimes permitted creative manoeuvring by sympathetic parties as well. This is evident in the efforts of a police officer in the Pilbara town of Gascoyne Junction in 1923 to prevent the removal of two young girls from his district.

1923

June: the Chief Protector of Aborigines informed Constable H C Slater at Gascoyne Junction Police Station that it was 'pleasing ... that we have ... a constable who sees no difficulty in rationing the old people, a position we have tried to bring about for a considerable time' and requested details on 'half-caste' children on the ration lists. Fred Edwards, pastoralist, wrote to the Chief Protector asking whether, since the police were to begin sending local 'half-caste' children south, the older daughter of the three 'half-caste' children of an elderly Aboriginal man and his wife in his employ could be sent to work on Eudamullah Station. Constable Slater informed the Chief Protector that Edwards objected to the removal of the children, two girls aged thirteen and ten and a boy aged three years, because he was their father. He had treated their mother and her elderly blind husband poorly, turning them out to starve when she was last pregnant so that she lost the baby. Slater added, 'I do not see why any native woman should be made a convenience of.' He advised against sending the girl out to work and that Edwards should be prohibited from employing Aboriginal labour.

July: Slater recommended to the Chief Protector that the older girl should not be sent to Moore River Settlement until she turned sixteen. The Chief Protector instructed Slater to send all three children and a twelve-year-old 'half-caste' boy immediately. He explained, 'I am afraid if she remains with her parents she is liable to the usual way of such children when they attain the age of puberty, and it would be impossible for you to exercise constant supervision over the party. I think if you put it to her mother that it is in the child's interest that she should be educated and trained, she should be willing to give her consent, quite apart from the fact that I am the child's guardian and can remove her without the mother's consent.' Slater replied that he recommended against the girl's removal as she already had 'native ways' and so there was no use sending her away.

August: Slater informed the Chief Protector that the girl's Aboriginal father had died and he now recommended her removal to prevent her going astray. He suggested that she be sent with the twelve-year-old boy 'as they both belong to the one country and would be company for each other.' The girl's mother wanted the two younger children to remain with her until they were older. A file note to the Chief Protector advised that 'the necessity for removal of the male half caste is not nearly as essential as in the case of the female' and that if she was left 'any length of time she may develop the vices of her race and make it impossible to train her in such a manner as to be able to get her own living as a domestic.'

October: the Chief Protector instructed Slater that the three older children were to leave on the *Bambra*. The youngest boy could remain with his mother for the time being. Slater informed the Chief Protector that the Government Doctor had advised against the removal of the ten-year-old girl 'owing to physical and mental weakness.' He added that 'if the child leaves its mother she ... will probably die ... I would advise her remaining here.' The Chief Protector advised Slater to 'abide by the doctor's decision' and requested a copy of the medical report. The District Medical Officer subsequently informed the Chief Protector that Slater had brought the girl in to see him, saying she was very upset when her mother was not with her. Although he had found her to be 'slightly mentally deficient,' he was now in favour of removal as although 'it might upset her ... this new life might be a benefit to her. There is no reason she could not travel with a companion.' The Chief Protector advised his deputy that the older girl and boy were on their way to Moore River Settlement.[74]

Although Constable Slater appears to have succeeded in preventing the removal of one young girl from his police district, the older boy and girl sent to Moore River Settlement had no chance of returning home. In August 1924 the boy's father wrote to the Chief Protector inquiring after the children as his wife was fretting for her son and they had promised the girl's mother they would look out for her. Slater had told them the children would come back to visit them after twelve months and, although they had written to the children, they had heard nothing of them. The Deputy Chief Protector responded that both children had the measles and the boy had scabies as well and that they would write when they were better but that it would do them no good to go home for Christmas. After repeated requests for the children's return the Deputy Chief Protector simply noted that a visit 'would be the undoing of training [the children] have received' and asked how would they travel and who would pay the costs?[75]

The missions continued to provide, on shoestring budgets, for families living outside towns and stations and for 'half-caste' children removed from their families. Reflecting anti-papist attitudes in government and xenophobic wartime fears of Germans, Beagle Bay was increasingly overlooked as a depot for 'half-caste' children. Of forty-eight Kimberley children admitted to institutions between 1919 and 1925, only two were sent to Beagle Bay while twenty went to Forrest River Mission and the remainder to Moore River Native Settlement in the south.[76] From the early 1930s lighter skinned children were sent to Sister Kate's Home in Perth. Nita Marshall and another girl were picked up by police from La Grange south of Broome and while 'the police boy and the other police man sat on top of us two so we wouldn't jump out' the girls' mothers 'chased us up the track crying and screaming for us'. In Broome they were:

> put in the lock up. As if two little kids are going to be able to run away from Broome. They locked us up and we stayed in gaol for three days, till the boat came from Wyndham, and they put us there and took us to Perth.[77]

The Aborigines Department remained unwavering in its determination to remove 'half-caste' children 'for their own good'. In 1923 the Chief Protector expressed concern about the new generations coming of age 'procreating children' in the camps, and demanded their immediate removal.[78] Some local interests wanted the net widened and in 1922 the Resident Magistrate in Wyndham stated:

> I have always been of the opinion that *all* half caste children should be sent to an institution unless legally adopted by a white person ... All neglected full blooded native children should also be in an institution.[79]

There was also official concern about growing numbers of 'quarter-caste' children. In 1922 the Chief Protector insisted that one such girl be placed under the care of the State Children's Department:

> I have referred the matter of the child ... to the State Children's Department, as in my opinion such quarter caste children should, if possible, be brought up as white children. The Secretary states that

if this child is committed to the care of his Department as a neglected child, he will place her out at one of the institutions in the metropolitan area. I should think the fact that the girl, who is only quarter caste, is found in an aboriginal camp should be sufficient cause to treat her as a neglected child.[80]

The Department continued to strike a balance with pastoral employers. Relying on the 'civilising' and 'moral' influence of white women, the Chief Protector ruled in 1923 that employed girls could remain on stations only if a white woman was present.

The outcomes for Aborigines were neither simple nor clear cut. For example, 'half-caste' children on stations often grew up in deplorable conditions, subject to crushing work regimes and without schooling, yet they lived with their families, learned their cultural traditions in their own country and worked in an industry which carried considerable prestige amongst white and black in the Kimberley. Some children removed to institutions *did* grow up in better material conditions, attended school and were exposed to different ways of life and as adults became a vital part of the institution communities. But this was certainly not always the case and many children lived miserable lives of neglect while they were kept from their families and encouraged to reject Aboriginal ways.

Separate treatment

Initially the Aborigines Department took little action in the south of the state, responding instead, as we have seen, to political pressures to deal with matters in the north. Only a handful of children, most identified from police ration lists, were removed and placed in the New Norcia orphanages or in one of the several small children's homes taking in Aboriginal children. A comparison of the Anglican Swan Native and Half-caste Mission (SNHC Mission) and the Catholic New Norcia orphanages shows a clear bias in favour of funding the Anglican mission effort as well as differing models of institutional care. The SNHC Mission was funded at eighteen pounds per year per child or one shilling per day, which was equal to subsidies for institutions for white children, and operated along similar lines to orphanages for white children, and in fact, on reaching the age of seven, boys were transferred to the Swan Boys Orphanage. The children were

Boys at New Norcia Benedictine Mission, c 1910.
(Courtesy of Battye Library, 21605P)

apprenticed out to employers, boys from the age of fourteen as farm labourers for up to five years, starting on a wage of five shillings, and girls from the age of seventeen to twenty-one as domestic servants paid at one or two pounds a month. The subsidy for children at New Norcia was only two pounds and five shillings per child per annum, far less than that provided for the SNHC Mission. They were not apprenticed out but were put to work at the mission from the age of thirteen or fourteen and on reaching seventeen or eighteen were paid a small monthly wage and encouraged to marry and settle down as part of the mission community.[81] Chief Protector Gale's emerging vision for 'half-castes' in the south — permanent segregation in agricultural missions, where they would work the land, marry and raise their families — reflected the influence of the New Norcia model and the continued belief of child reformers in the regenerative power of nature and rural work and, perhaps, new eugenic programs for the institutionalisation of particular types of children.

There is evidence of increasing divergence from mainstream child welfare practice in the treatment of Aboriginal children, with mounting opposition to accommodating white and Aboriginal children together. In 1905 Aboriginal girls at the Salvation Army Industrial School in Collie were transferred to Kalgoorlie following representations that they were having a 'very bad effect' on white girls, despite denials of this by Salvation Army authorities. In 1910 the Aborigines Department issued instructions that the girls were to be moved away from the mining town and settled in agricultural areas where they would meet men 'of their own type'.[82] In 1909 the Solicitor General ruled that the *State Children's Act 1907* was not intended to apply to Aboriginal children and that in future they were not to be sent to State Children's Department (SCD) institutions but were to be cared for by the Aborigines Department. This ruling arose from the case of a twelve-year-old Aboriginal boy sentenced in Leonora to six years detention for stealing a bicycle. While there was no discussion about the severity of his sentence there was considerable disputation about where he should be placed. The SCD refused to send him to an industrial school, claiming he was the responsibility of the Aborigines Department and that 'the two races should be kept apart,' while the Department pointed out that the SCD had children's reformatories. In the end the boy was placed in service near Bunbury. Twelve months later he was found wandering and alone and was committed as a neglected child to the SCD. Again he was sent to the Aborigines Department which instructed the presiding magistrate to put him into service.[83] From this time a system of separate and discriminatory treatment of Aboriginal juvenile offenders developed. They were removed from their families under the 1905 Act and sent indefinitely to Aboriginal institutions. By contrast, white children appeared before the Children's Court and, depending on the nature of their crime and home circumstances, were returned on probation to their families or institutionalised for set periods.

CLEARING THE WHEATBELT

Despite tenuous beginnings the Aborigines Department was to have a far greater influence in the south than in any other region of the state, reflecting factors of proximity, geography, demographic spread, political alliances, labour needs and strict race barriers and attitudes. The majority of the state's population lived there and, in contrast to the north, the region was tamed, domesticated and white. It was a place of comfortable, respectable domestic life with the highest home ownership levels in Australia 'with all that meant in relation to employment and family life,' and its 'quality of education, church life and recreational life was splendid for many.'[84] Despite the strong labour and anti-war movement in Western Australia at the time, historian Tom Stannage states that residents of the wheatbelt were strongly patriotic and nationalistic, sending proportionately more volunteers to the First World War than other states and twice voting 'overwhelmingly in favour of conscription'.[85] The region was dotted with new towns servicing a hinterland of small family farms in a rapidly changing landscape, as the bush 'wilderness' was cleared to make way for a vision of rural peace and order. For the local Nyungar people, the clearing of the wheatbelt brought an initial increased demand for their labour and improved living conditions. In the long term, however, it brought a second wave of dispossession from the land. By 1914 most southern towns had fringe camps which provided a pool of Aboriginal seasonal workers for local farmers and domestic workers for the town. Strict 'caste barriers' backed by legal sanctions under the 1905 Act kept the growing numbers in the camps strictly segregated from white people and prevented them from using local town services such as hospitals and schools. However, their increasing visibility and proximity in the midst of a white population that had believed them doomed to extinction, and their poverty, which aroused fears of physical and moral contagion amongst whites, provoked demands for their complete removal.

While Australian troops fought overseas, Nyungar families were engaged in their own battle to remain in their traditional homelands and to attain a reasonable standard of living. Events in the town of Katanning were typical of the experiences of Nyungars in the years leading up to the war. The site of a traditional meeting place for local tribes and the centre of a prosperous farming district, Katanning attracted increasing numbers of Nyungars seeking work and the support of kin. With severe drought conditions, decreasing employment opportunities and widespread white settlement forcing them out of the bush, their numbers increased from forty in 1911 to over two hundred by 1914, most of them crowded together on a small Aboriginal reserve lacking toilet and rubbish services and running water. In 1912 conflict erupted when white Katanning parents, backed by the Education Department, demanded the expulsion of Nyungar children recently enrolled at the state school. A provision of the *Education Act 1893* allowed the Minister for Education to exclude children whose presence was deemed to be 'injurious' to the health, welfare and morality of other children. Their demands were framed in terms of race and fears of moral and physical contagion: one parent wrote to the *West Australian* objecting to the 'intermingling' of Aboriginal and white children as it would encourage 'the future mothers and fathers of this State in the belief that there [were] no differences between the races.'[86]

Aboriginal children were expelled from state schools throughout the wheatbelt from this time. Under the 1905 Act, the education of Aboriginal children was the responsibility of the Aborigines Department, however it refused to take any action. Although all children in Western Australia were required by law to attend school, no alternative facilities were provided, with the exception of Katanning where the Education Department reluctantly agreed to fund a special teacher. Aboriginal parents in the town of Beverley openly expressed their resentment at this treatment. In July 1912 the Secretary of the Beverley School

Annie Lock photographed in 1928 with children at Harding Soak in the Northern Territory.

(Courtesy of Department of Transport and Regional Services and National Archives of Australia: A263/4, Album 1)

Committee reported that Aboriginal parents were 'howling down at the reserve because the school had not started. They had congregated there for that reason and think they have been taken in.' Three months later the families were reportedly 'roaming the street and threatening to invade the government school.'[87]

In the same year, the former Matron of Dulhi Gunyah Children's Home in Perth,[88] Annie Lock, began itinerant mission work with Nyungar families camped in the Katanning district. The presence of a lone white woman embarking on such a task was certainly unusual for the times, although it fitted with the practices of the interdenominational Australian Aborigines Mission (AAM) to which Lock belonged. The AAM way of working was not an easy or romantic one. The typical procedure was to seek out camps, visit and preach to residents and then seek their endorsement and support to open a mission station in which the missionaries often lived in similar conditions and in close proximity to their 'flock'. The AAM's stated aims were the 'salvation of the native people, and incidentally to improve their social and economic conditions.' In achieving these aims the missionaries were totally reliant on government assistance, public donations, local support and their prayers because, as members of a faith mission, they received no financial support whatsoever from the AAM.[89] Lock herself preferred the 'lone calling' — she was not an easygoing woman and the strain of continual poor health and poverty led to problems with other missionaries and a life marked by controversy and antagonism to her work. What were Lock's qualifications for this difficult work? Born into a battling English migrant family of fourteen children in 1876 in the South Australian town of Riverton, she was 'called' to Aboriginal mission work in her early twenties. In 1901 she joined other trainee women missionaries enrolled at Angus College in Adelaide, studying the Bible, nursing and office work before joining the AAM in 1903. After six years of Aboriginal mission work in New South Wales, Lock took up the position of Matron at Dulhi Gunyah in 1909 before commencing her pioneering work at Katanning. She subsequently devoted the rest of her long life to Aboriginal mission work in the north of Western Australia and in central Australia and South Australia.[90]

Shortly before her move to Katanning in 1912, Lock wrote in a report on Dulhi Gunyah: 'In asking the Lord about the work he has pointed out to me what to do. I am going forward and his message to me is — "the Lord will send His angel with thee, and prosper thy way."'[91] Initially these spiritual assurances of success proved true. The AAM's intention to establish a small farming 'colony' and to instruct families in 'religion, hygiene and basic domestic skills' was endorsed at a town meeting by Nyungar spokesperson, Charles Hansen, and white town residents described it as 'very necessary work'.[92] In correspondence to her friends and supporters Lock recorded many generous charitable donations: 'The butcher has been very kind, giving meat for soup; several ladies have sent parcels of clothing; Mr G— has given milk; and several other donations in cash.'[93] She took over the issuing of rations and blankets from the police and nursed the many sick and dying who were barred from the local hospital and endeavoured to convert them in their last moments. The disastrous consequences of the deteriorating conditions in the camps were evident in the growing litany of deaths in her letters. In April and May 1914 Lock recorded: 'there has been much sickness, and several deaths. One week a child died, and the following week the mother passed away' — 'A young man passed away leaving a wife and four children' — 'We have had two deaths ... a little boy nine years old ... the other, an old man.'[94] Lock mourned with the people and described to her friends the many funerals she attended:

The children all dressed in white, followed the funeral, and sang

'Jesus loves me' and, when the coffin was lowered they sang, 'Safe in the Arms of Jesus,' and finished at the close by repeating the Lord's prayer.[95]

Writing of Lock's later work in central Australia, Bill Harney, author and field officer with the Northern Territory Aboriginal administration, claimed that while she was convinced of their need for her help, Aborigines saw her as needing their help: 'she was as the burrs on a blanket — a part of the black man's burden'.[96] There appear to be elements of both in her reception by Nyungar people. Lock recorded that families at Wagin took up a collection of two shillings and three pence for her and another group gave her a small gift, adding, 'It is a little gift, but we are so grateful for your help in time of sickness, and for looking after our children.'[97] On another occasion, following the death of their grandmother, two young men gave her one pound ten shillings with the words, 'Please accept the gift, as we feel so grateful to you for being so kind to Granny, and looking after her and keeping her so nice and clean.' Lock noted how 'dark people are not ungrateful for kindnesses shown'.[98]

Initially Nyungar families expressed surprise at Lock's interest in their children. A woman at Wagergarut near Wagin told her:

You must love us to have a little one of ours running after you. It seems so funny to have a white lady with us. It is the first time a white lady has done that.[99]

However as Lock's interest shifted to proprietorial interference and control, conflict with Nyungar parents became inevitable. Like the majority of her missionary contemporaries, Lock's 'first concern was for the children' and she was convinced of her right to:

get the children right away from their parents & teach them good moral, clean habits & right from wrong & also industries that will make them more useful and better citizen by & by.[100]

In her correspondence Lock frequently contrasted the children's 'dreadful experiences in camp life' with the 'rays of sunshine' she brought them.[101] In 1913 she wrote of her concerns for the children in the camps around Katanning:

There are a great number of girls here want protecting and caring for, many of them in a bad state of health. A Home for these girls is badly needed. They are not allowed to go to the Perth Home [Dulhi Gunyah] — it being too near the City. Then there are a number of boys (some very unruly), some orphan children.[102]

In the same year her efforts to take three children from their widower father who 'clung to them' brought her into conflict with local Aboriginal families and she was told by the Aborigines Department 'we cannot take them if they are cared for by the others.'[103] A father approached her and 'got very angry, and made all kinds of threats, being under the impression that I wanted to take his child from him,' while a mother wrote a letter of complaint to the Katanning police:

My children is going to school out here and the people are very nice to us. We could not get treated better ... I got a letter from Miss Lock. She told me to bring the children in at once or she would make me fetch them in. She must be the law maker and braker.[104]

Nevertheless in 1914 Lock reported that she had nine children staying with her in what she described grandiosely as 'the Home'.[105]

By 1914 the tempers of white residents in Katanning were at breaking point. Failing to understand the reasons behind the growing Nyungar presence, they accused Lock of wanting 'the whole of [the Nyungars] on the Great Southern Line dumped down here'.[106] For them the 'burning question' was how to stop breaches of the town race barriers by Nyungars collecting rations from the police, drawing water from taps on town residents' blocks, sending their children to the Aboriginal school and, with Lock's encouragement, endeavouring to get treatment at the government hospital. Town hysteria was expressed in fears of contamination of 'the morals of the youth of Katanning' and of attacks on white women who 'were afraid they would be interfered with by some black man'.[107] The Chief Protector of Aborigines, parliamentarians and the press were bombarded with deputations, petitions and letters from the townspeople threatening public 'indignation meetings' and inquiries 'instituted in the British parliament'.[108] Other towns joined in the protest and a meeting of seventy Mount Barker residents moved a motion requesting the Minister for Education:

to remove the black children from Mount Barker school. This horrible menace to the health and morals of young Australians admits of no further delays, and should not have been permitted for one moment.[109]

Nyungar leaders responded by endeavouring to impose law and order in the camps. In June 1914 leaders from Wagin, Katanning, Bunbury and Narrogin met in the town reserve to formulate rules for the camps and to appoint their own 'magistrates' and 'police' to enforce them. Lock was invited to the meeting to record the following decisions:

1. They must be good.

2. No loafers allowed on camp.

3. No gambling in the way of cards and 2-up allowed, they can have a game of cards at night when their work is done but not play for clothes or money.

4. All the men and women to be home from the town before dark or 6 o'clock and no drink allowed if they do get any drink they must not bring it into the camp and they must not make any noise or disturbance in town or on the reserve.

5. No native arms to be used to fight with and no guns and not even the wand [digging stick] the women use.

6. All young men must have their own camp and not loaf about on the old people and eat their rations but go and earn their own food and help the old ones.[110]

Historian Geoffrey Bolton[111] describes this meeting as an 'attempt to adapt the white man's institutions' but it also had much in common with the large tribal gatherings described by Jesse Hammond[112] where *Yoolins* (leaders) met to discuss alterations to rules and rituals. The meeting can be seen as a significant attempt by Nyungar leadership to regulate the impact of dramatic social change. Although the meeting aroused considerable discussion and some Nyungars even consulted a local solicitor about the new rules, they proved difficult to enforce and, in the end, were ineffectual.[113] Early in 1915 the townspeople took matters into their own hands and, after several hurried public meetings, the Aborigines were rounded up by the police and marched to a site on the Carrolup River. With only government rations issued

A O Neville, Chief Protector of Aborigines in Western Australia from 1915 to 1940.
(Courtesy of Mogumber Heritage Committee of the Wheatbelt Aboriginal Corporation, 105)

by Lock, and a little charitable support from relieved townspeople, the Nyungars set about creating yet another new home for their families.

The Labor government's return in November 1914 with a reduced majority contributed to its decision to take decisive action in the south, starting with the appointment of a strong and determined new leadership. R H Underwood, the new Minister in charge of Aboriginal Affairs, set a brash new tone of ruthless administrative economy and efficiency. His initiatives included cutbacks across the board, schemes to generate moneys from within the Department and measures to centralise services. In addressing the situation in the south, Underwood refused to consider the notion of separate services for Aborigines in the towns and immediately closed the Katanning Aboriginal school. The idea of forcing townspeople to share facilities with Nyungar families was not even contemplated. Instead, Underwood advocated further segregation in institutions under state control. The new Chief Protector of Aborigines appointed to work alongside Underwood was A O Neville. He was a break with tradition — neither a 'friendly amateur' nor an 'old chum' of the pastoral lobby but a British-born career public servant with an impressive track record of determined and energetic action in immigration but no previous experience of Aborigines. Neville adopted Underwood's initiatives as his own and these drove his administration, along with a determination to strictly implement the 1905 Act and a deep and abiding interest in the 'half-caste' problem, particularly in the south.

Much has been written of Neville's administration of Aboriginal affairs. He has been depicted variously as 'Mr Devil' the ruthless dictator, and as 'AON,' the benevolent but embattled public servant fighting valiantly for a neglected cause.[114] In fact, given the nature of the Department, the legislative powers he wielded and the social context in which he worked, he moved regularly between these two extremes. An ambitious and efficient administrator, his appointment as

Chief Protector essentially locked him into a career in Aboriginal affairs and closed him off from his colleagues and an advancing career up the public service ladder. These frustrations must have been compensated for by the powers and experiences afforded by his position which were quite outside the general realm of public service. There was also a level of public exposure and a place in Australian history that his colleagues could only dream of.

In his own words Neville was a man with a vision for his 'empire'; he saw himself as the personal guardian of all Aborigines in the state. His position was non-negotiable and he wrote from retirement in the early 1940s:

> The native must be helped in spite of himself! Even if a measure of discipline is necessary it must be applied, but it can be applied in such a way as to appear to be gentle persuasion ... the end in view will justify the means applied.[115]

His vision was the 'Native Settlement Scheme', a program of social engineering and segregation intended principally for Aborigines of mixed descent. The settlement scheme was hardly an original idea; it echoed Wybalenna in Van Diemen's Land and the plans sketched out by Archibald Meston in his 1895 report to the Queensland government. It grew out of Neville's own memories of missions and workhouses as the son of a country parson in Victorian England; directions already under way in the Department's scheme of removal, concentration and segregation at Moola Bulla; and the demands of wheatbelt residents to empty the town camps while also maintaining access to a cheap and reliable Aboriginal labour force. Again, it served white interests rather than Aboriginal needs. The settlements would act as 'clearing houses' — over two or three generations the older people would die off, the children would be trained, sent out and assimilated into the wider community and the institutions would no longer be needed. To this end the sick, elderly, unemployed and the children would be concentrated in isolated segregated farming settlements, providing a more economical solution to their care. Employed adults could remain outside but they and their children could be moved on any pretext to the settlements. As always, children were the crux of the scheme. Neville was convinced that separation from their parents was essential — 'until the children are taken ... and trained apart from their parents no real progress towards assimilation is to be expected.'[116] They would live separately from the adults and be trained as rural and domestic workers to be sent out under Departmental supervision to approved employers. In this way they would become 'useful workers instead of becoming a nuisance to the inhabitants of every town in which they are settled.'[117] Neville's optimistic adherence over the years to this model, in the face of the decline of the settlements into run-down institutions filled with institutionalised inmates, is striking but not exceptional for his times. Together with his peers, he attributed any problems to lack of funding and Aborigines' innate inferiority or inability to adapt. Repeatedly they looked to the next 'rising generation' of Aboriginal children removed from their families to prove the value and appropriateness of their schemes.

Neville endeavoured to enforce the full range of powers under the 1905 Act and sought to make the Chief Protector *the* source of wisdom and policy on Aboriginal matters. He developed his own knowledge and expertise through tours of the state and discussions with experts from other Aboriginal administrations and read extensively in history and ethnography. Lacking reliable statistical records, Neville's main instrument of rule became his knowledge of particular individuals recorded in his dossiers of personal files and cards. Neville's determination to impose his control across the various Aboriginal domains inevitably brought him into conflict with most stakeholders — politicians, missionaries, other government departments, employers and Aborigines. He remained in an uneasy truce with southern townspeople who looked to him to clear the camps on the slightest pretext.

Children at Carrolup Native Settlement, c 1918.
(Courtesy of Battye Library, 70720P)

The focus of Neville's early work was the establishment of settlements at Carrolup in 1915 and Moore River north of Perth in 1918.[118] His actions bore all the hallmarks of his administration — economy, efficiency and control. The settlements were set up on a shoestring budget; no additional moneys were provided and in fact, in 1916, funding fell to its lowest level in thirteen years. Economies made elsewhere provided the necessary funds, ration issue was centralised in the settlements and, with the exception of New Norcia, the children's missions were closed and the children transferred to the settlements. Using the full force of the law, Neville began to clear the town camps and build up the settlement populations. This led to complaints from Aboriginal families and their white supporters. In 1919 the *Geraldton Express*[119] launched the following attack on Neville over the removal of a local Aboriginal widow and her daughters to Moore River:

In wartime the Germans excited the horror of the world by deporting some French women from Lille. Here we have a Government of the day, under a British flag, banishing aboriginal women to a settlement 200 miles from their own country for no reason that appears either to sense or sentiment.

Letters to Neville from the widow's sons pledging to support their mother and sisters if they were returned proved of no avail. When Neville finally offered to release the mother she refused to be parted from her daughters. Five years later, with her daughters grown up, she agreed to leave. Her sons were instructed to pay for her train fare home.

At the settlements children lived in dormitories in a compound supervised by white staff. In 1916, following repeated absconding and rebellious behaviour, regulations were introduced granting sweeping powers to discipline children and adults. The school at Carrolup, not opened until 1917, did not follow the state curriculum but taught the basic 'Three Rs'. The children's vocational training consisted of doing jobs for the staff. The appointment of an untrained nurse in 1917 did little to staunch the ravages of disease and death that swept through a population surviving on a diet described by a visiting official in 1920 as 'Dickensian'.[120] In 1922 Carrolup was closed and the residents transferred to Moore River. In the same year the *Southern Districts Advocate*[121] printed the impressions of a Nyungar man, Phillip Morrison, of conditions at Moore River:

I see little boys and girls humpin' sugar bags full of gravel for long distances from the pits to the camp to make footpaths, instead of bein' at school. All our people up there reckon that place worse than bein' in gaol.

He also expressed his concern for the families remaining in the Katanning district:

> What about the little ones? They got no chance to get an education … What good of Mogumber to them? We can't let our children go there for schoolin'. Too far to go — anyhow only teach them to carry gravel and wood.

The Department increasingly took on the role of employment agency, sending trainees out to work when they reached the age of fourteen. Despite their limited training they were in constant demand as their wages and keep were low and domestic servants and live-in farm labourers were hard to find. The apprenticeship scheme remained integral to Neville's vision for the children over the years. A domestic service 'finishing school', the East Perth Girls Home, was opened in 1931 and in 1936 Neville was still requesting in his Annual Report that 'more of these young people be taken in hand by the department … they could be readily placed after a period of training.'[122]

Ruby Clinch, Nellie Lyndon, (?) Lyndon, Annie Sewell and Elsie Gardiner, East Perth Girls Home, 1930s.
(Courtesy Basil Gardiner)

As the population at Moore River continued to increase into the 1930s, conditions deteriorated rapidly. The 1934 Moseley Royal Commission described the settlement as a 'woeful spectacle': the buildings were overcrowded and vermin ridden, the children's diet lacked fresh fruit, vegetables, eggs and milk and their health had been seriously affected. The Commissioner concluded that in its present condition Moore River had 'no hope of success' in its work with the children.[123]

Mount Margaret Mission, opened in 1921 in the eastern goldfields by the Australian Aborigines Mission (AAM, United Aborigines Mission from 1929), became the centre of bitter ongoing struggles between police, townspeople, pastoralists and missionaries over the presence of Wongis[124] in the towns, their use of resources and services, their employment and the fate of their children. There was also escalating conflict between the mission founder, Reverend Rod Schenk, and Neville which developed into a showdown in the late 1930s that threatened the very survival of the mission. Schenk, called 'Old Hallelujah' by some of his Wongi flock,[125] arrived in Leonora in 1921. Born in Victoria in 1888 into a family of evangelical Christians, he undertook mission studies in Sydney and in 1919 began work with Aboriginal people in New South Wales. Inspired by pleas for workers in the eastern goldfields from a Perth correspondent in a Melbourne missionary newspaper, he joined the AAM and set off on his motorbike to begin what was to become a lifelong commitment.

The economy of the eastern goldfields rode precariously on a dwindling mining industry and a pastoral industry struggling to survive in the arid desert environment. A continuous trickle of Wongis moved into fringe camps near the towns of Laverton, Morgan and Leonora, surviving on bush foods, government handouts, scraps scavenged from miners' camps and meagre rations paid for work on local pastoral stations. After visiting the camps Schenk wrote to his future wife, Mysie, that the people looked 'half-starved'.[126] Schenk was appalled at white attitudes and their indiscriminate acts of cruelty against Wongis. He repeatedly heard them described as, 'The wildest laziest tribe I've ever seen,' and his expressed hopes to convert them prompted a 'Christian lady' to retort 'You might as well talk to that post.'[127] Police rode out daily to clear them from the towns, often at the end of a whip, galloping into camps, shooting dogs and frequently

Reverend and Mrs Schenk at Mount Margaret Mission, c 1930s.
(Courtesy of Battye Library, 70391P)

rounding up adults and 'half-caste' children for transportation to Moore River, the closest institution prior to the opening of the mission. This sent whole camps into hiding in the bush until it was deemed safe to move back into town. Despite this constant harassment the Wongis determinedly refused to leave the district. In 1921 fifteen adults and children transported from Leonora to Moore River escaped from the settlement and walked back to Menzies — a distance of nearly six hundred kilometres, in a straight line.[128] Quick thinking was often their only defence against losing their children. Schenk's daughter, Margaret Morgan, described how one man saved his daughter from the police:

Ada, when she was a baby her family was travelling in the open truck on the train to Kalgoorlie. That day the police decided to raid the trucks and turn them all out. Over the side went blanket rolls, billy cans and sugar bags filled with belongings. People took a flying leap out of the trucks as the police closed in. Gilyal, Ada's tribal father, standing below watched anxiously. Suddenly a four-gallon kerosene tin came hurtling through the air. He jumped quickly and caught it in mid-flight and breathed a sigh of relief as he put it gently on the ground. Baby Ada was inside the tin, covered with sugar bags.[129]

Although Schenk originally intended to work as an itinerant missionary ministering to the town camps, he quickly perceived the need for a permanent mission to act as a buffer between the pastoral stations, the town and the bush, and as a refuge from the 'Moore River Net'. This required official endorsement from the Aborigines Department as well as support in kind — land, rations, medical supplies, employment and a school and dormitories for the children. Initially this was not forthcoming. The Deputy Chief Protector in the early 1920s, E Copping, a former clerk with the Metropolitan Water Supply, Sewerage and Drainage Board,[130] refused Schenk's initial request for medical supplies and told him to push the people back into 'Spinifex country'. The AAM offered little financial or political assistance and, like Annie Lock at Katanning, Schenk depended on divine providence to survive. This was a precarious existence as Morgan recalled: 'When they asked God for funds Christian friends sent money in the post. That's how it worked. Missionaries never knew when or how their money would come to them.'[131] To ensure a regular flow of private donations over the years, Schenk developed an efficient 'propaganda machine' based on prayer letters, lecture tours and ideas such as the 'support system' where 'Christian friends sent regular support and prayed personally for a special child.'[132]

Schenk's vision for the mission was the eventual assimilation of Wongis and his catchcry was the 'Three Es — Evangelisation, Education and Environment.'[133] Outdated and unacceptable today, his approach was considered advanced in its time and Mount Margaret was held up by many as a 'model mission organisation'.[134] Profoundly evangelical in outlook, Schenk and his staff were vehemently opposed to Aboriginal religious beliefs and rituals which they described as the 'works of Satan'.[135] This created tensions for Wongis whose culture remained strong but who saw the value of the mission as a refuge where their children could escape Moore River and get some schooling. Traditional practices were driven underground. Children were warned by their parents that if they failed to follow Aboriginal Law 'a *Jinagarbil* might come from this way, or that, or it might be a policeman will come and you'll get caught ... He'll take you away, and we'll never see you again.'[136] Parents who worked for pastoralists in the district only saw their children in the Christmas holidays and many resented the missionaries' control over their children.

The missionaries adopted a practical and strictly gendered approach to developing work values and skills, providing the men with training and wages for sandalwood collecting, carpentry and stock work and training and paying the women for raffia work, spinning, weaving and domestic duties. Schenk's actions in encouraging workers to insist on wages from pastoralists and in endeavouring to identify fathers of 'half-caste' children made him a much hated man with local whites, who blamed him for the district's many 'Aboriginal woes'. He lived in a whirl of official inquiries initiated by police, townspeople and pastoralists, and of threats to close the mission down. Often his only consolation was found in prayer and the Bible verses he relied on for guidance in the conduct of his daily affairs such as 'The Lord will fight for you, and you shall hold your peace,' and '[They] have taken evil counsel against you ... it shall not stand, nor shall it come to pass.'[137]

Neville's resumption of control of Aboriginal affairs across the state in 1926 (from 1920 he was in charge of the north only) resulted initially in a leap forward in the mission's role in caring for and educating children. A school was opened, the Department began to send in subsidised 'half-caste' children and two years later children's dormitories were opened. The arrival in 1932 of the activist and writer

Mary Montgomery Bennett shifted the children's schooling from a program aimed at conversion, basic literacy in English and vocational skills, to an educational system using 'up-to-date methods and State School standards of skill and achievement'. Within two years the children were working to standards of the Education Department Correspondence School.[138] It was this program that truly distinguished Mount Margaret Mission and produced several Aboriginal 'firsts' in professions such as nursing and teaching.

This 'honeymoon' relationship between Neville and Schenk was short lived. Neville tolerated mission work by major churches operating under his control but disapproved of what he saw as the fanatical evangelism of the United Aborigines Mission (UAM), their perpetual calls for charity and their devotion to their own goals. There were also major differences in their goals for the children. Neville focused his attention on 'half-caste' children and advocated their total separation from family and culture to mould them into 'useful workers'. Schenk took in *all* Aboriginal children and insisted they remain in their home districts and in limited contact with their families. He was particularly opposed to children being sent far away to Moore River and refused to send his 'graduates' out to work in the 'corrupt world', encouraging them instead to marry and remain on the mission.

The breaking point came in 1932 when Mary Bennett declared war on the pastoral industry, the police, the Aborigines Department and Neville, using her many contacts in women's and humanitarian groups in Australia and in Britain to publicise her allegations of slavery in the pastoral industry and abusive treatment of Aboriginal women and children. Ironically, these allegations, in prompting the appointment of the Moseley Royal Commission, provided Neville with the opportunity to push through draconian controls and powers he had demanded from the late 1920s. Appearing before Moseley and a belligerent Neville at the Commission hearings in Perth, Bennett fearlessly repeated her claims of slavery in the pastoral industry and delivered a two-pronged attack on the treatment of Aboriginal women by their own men under tribal custom and their exploitation by white men. The police were given a 'verbal thrashing'[139] and the Aborigines Department condemned for its 'official smashing up of family life',[140] the deplorable conditions at Moore River and its failure to secure for Aborigines the 'three important safeguards ... one, education, two, medical services, three, the vote.'[141] When Moseley visited the goldfields Schenk faced a showdown with local employers. A neighbouring station manager claimed that:

> The Mission superintendent has ideas that natives are equal to white races ... [that] natives should eat with white men when working with us. 'They are our black brothers,' he says. The result is that it is difficult to keep natives working for station owners. They become discontented.[142]

Schenk responded that 'they hate the natives to be enlightened, not only because they want wages, but because they demand better treatment.'[143] He also pointed to the pastoralist's monopoly of the land, their refusal to allow the Wongi on to pastoral leases to hunt — a right clearly granted in state legislation — and their persistent opposition to 'granting land and education [to them], which are the main factors toward better conditions'.[144] He warned Moseley that if pastoralists succeeded in 'moving the missionaries on' then 'the public will know how the vested interests will use all their influence to crush a good work for the natives.'[145] In his report, Moseley had surprisingly little to say about the goldfields, focusing instead on conditions in the north and the 'half-caste' problem in the south. He nevertheless dismissed Bennett and Schenk's allegations of cruelty as unsubstantiated and attributed them to 'bad feelings between pastoralists and missionaries'.[146] Moseley recommended that the mission be relocated to an existing Aboriginal reserve to the east.

From this time Neville waged an all-out campaign to close the mission by reducing rations, opening an alternative ration depot in Laverton, stopping medical supplies, refusing permission for mission marriages and thwarting UAM initiatives to establish missions at Warburton and other centres in the state.[147] Meanwhile Schenk openly criticised the 'die out' and 'breed out' policies of the *Native Administration Act 1936* and Neville's extensive new powers. In his diary he wrote 'callous, hard men should not have arbitrary control over human beings.'[148] When Neville endeavoured to railroad regulations granting unprecedented controls over missions through Parliament in 1938, Schenk was one of his most vociferous critics. The final blow came in 1940 when, in the midst of terrible drought conditions, with reduced rations and many people starving, Neville opened a ration depot at Cosmo Newbery and ordered all Mount Margaret Aboriginal adults and children, including those attending school, to move there immediately, leaving the mission to function as a small institution for 'half-caste' children. Mount Margaret was only saved by Neville's retirement in the same year and the greater availability of work due to the war which enabled Aborigines to move more freely around the district once again. The mission never regained its former position. Many young people moved to Kalgoorlie during the war and the Department maintained the practice of using Mount Margaret as a 'half-caste' institution and continued to pressure Schenk to send the young people out to work. In 1942 the new Chief Protector of Aborigines, F I Bray, explained the need to separate the 'half-caste' children from other Aborigines:

> Their welfare is at stake and it is against our policy to allow them to live with the blacks. Their colour entitles them to special consideration, and they must each be given the opportunity of a better life under civilised conditions, therefore their removal is inevitable.[149]

This policy had the effect of promoting quite distinct populations of 'full-blood' and 'mixed race' Aborigines in the region. The continued existence of two institutions in such close proximity also led to unbecoming tussles over children. When the manager of Cosmo Newbery attempted to block the transfer of several 'half-caste' children to the Mission in 1941, Bray curtly reminded him:

> the welfare of these children is of more importance than the serenity of the Depot and whilst there may be a heartache or two and a disturbance of your quietude when the children are ultimately taken away, it is essential that they should be educated and trained to the economic advantage of the State. Many children have been taken from their mothers by my instructions, and I assure you that I have not taken them without the deepest sympathies to the feelings of their mothers. It is a painful duty but there can be no line of least resistance.[150]

THE FINAL SOLUTION: BLACK MUST GO WHITE

During the 1930s the situation of Nyungars in the south loomed as the worst nightmare of a White Australia — an expanding, poverty-stricken and disaffected 'coloured' population living right in its rural heartland. The Aborigines' growing visibility and poverty reflected, in part, the effect of sustained population growth from the turn of the century, although hardly to the extent of alarmist beat-ups in the local press. Their condition owed more to their precarious economic position as workers in a rural economy devastated by the combined effects of the international economic depression, bungled government agricultural planning and serious drought conditions.

Jack and his family, 1942.
(Courtesy of Axel Poignant Archive, Western Australian Art Gallery)

Thousands of Aboriginal men and women were thrown out of rural and domestic employment into town camps and onto Aborigines Department ration lists. In 1926, 326 Nyungars were receiving rations with only twenty-nine of these living outside of Moore River Settlement. In 1932 numbers peaked at 1273 with 892 rationed in the town camps. In the following year the Aborigines Department annual grant dropped to its lowest level in eight years, just 27,238 pounds.[151] While white male workers received an unemployment allowance of seven shillings a week during the Depression years, Nyungar men were issued weekly rations of flour, tea and sugar valued at two shillings and twopence, despite their protests and union support. At the height of the Depression, women's activist Miss Ada Bronham visited camps in the wheatbelt towns of Wagin and Brookton where she found sixty men, normally in employ on the farms, living with their families in 'beautifully clean' camps in small huts of 'kerosene tins flattened out, bags or hessian … which could not possibly be rainproof'. Food was 'a most pressing matter' — they could not hunt on the surrounding private land and one man told her that 'if a rabbit ran across the road, they could get it, but that was the only place where they could hunt.' Most had only a single change of clothes, few blankets and no bedding. Bromham told the 1934 Moseley Royal Commission, 'We are offering them no scope for development to provide for themselves a place in the State that they could fill with credit to themselves.'[152] Many town residents were alarmed by the reappearance of a presence they believed

In 1928 William Harris (centre) led
the first Aboriginal deputation to a
Western Australian Premier.
(Courtesy of West Australian Newspapers,
West Australian, 3.10.1928)

to have been eradicated and which assaulted their cherished ideals of a White Australia built on equal rights and a single living standard for all. Spreading fears of the racial violence that plagued the United States and of contamination through proximity to large numbers of Nyungars led to renewed demands for their total segregation. In letters to the press and the government southern residents angrily demanded the immediate removal of the families. As the perceived public custodian of Aborigines the pressure was on the Aborigines Department to act promptly and decisively.

However, the Department was virtually paralysed. The dramatic increase in Aboriginal unemployment coincided with the drastic funding cuts prompted by the Depression. Moore River was already overcrowded and overused, and many families stubbornly refused to move there from the camps, capitulating only when their rations were cut off and their families were starving. Some had hitherto lived independently of the Department, and Chief Protector Neville complained that they understood their legal status and strongly resented his control. A court ruling that children of 'half-caste' parents were not 'half-castes' under the 1905 Act meant that many Nyungar children were exempt from his guardianship. Neville continued to remove these children although he warned his superiors that he was exceeding his legal powers in doing so.[153] Growing public scrutiny of the Department by William Harris' Native Union and white activists such as Mary Bennett opened the possibility of public exposure of such illegal practices. During the late 1920s Neville was increasingly frustrated by criticisms of his department and opposition to his efforts to expand his legislative powers; Parliament had thrown out an amending Bill in 1929. Given the growing race hysteria in the wider community, he was forced to concede that his dreams of assimilating 'half-caste' children remained as elusive as ever. Thwarted at all turns, Neville began to look to radical biological solutions built on recent scientific 'advances' to make 'black go white'.[154]

From the turn of the century, many Western nations demonstrated an interest in the 'unholy alliance' of government and the 'science' of eugenics and adopted anti- and pro-natalist measures to manage the size and composition of their populations. Between 1907 and 1928 twenty-one states in the United States of America introduced laws for the compulsory medical sterilisation of various 'social misfits' — criminals, rapists, the feeble minded, imbeciles, drunkards, moral perverts, drug addicts and diseased and 'desperate' persons. Despite lobbying by powerful eugenic organisations, such laws were never introduced in Britain; however, anti-natalist laws allowing for the segregation of targeted groups in single sex institutions achieved similar outcomes. The 1913 Mental Deficiency Act, for example, locked away lower-class girls deemed to be sexually promiscuous.

Of the several European nations that adopted compulsory sterilisation laws, National Socialist Germany was the most extreme. Various races and classes — the Jews, Romanies, the feeble minded, the diseased, insane and handicapped — were marked for compulsory sterilisation and legal abortions, refused permission to marry and denied economic benefits for families. Females were typically targeted over men. Anti-natalism grew to nightmare proportions during the war years, culminating in programs aimed at the 'annihilation of unworthy life' as millions of men, women and children were executed. J Bock[155] contrasts these anti-natalist measures with the pro-natalist strategies — mainly economic benefits including tax incentives, bank loans and child allowances — introduced to encourage German couples to breed large families and increase the size and 'quality' of the German population. The *Lebensborn* program provided for babies born of 'racially valuable' German officers and women to be cared for in special maternity homes and adopted into high-ranking Nazi families. Children of 'Aryan appearance' in conquered territories such as Poland were abducted and transported to Germany to be reclaimed for the Fatherland through adoption into Nazi families.[156]

While most eugenicists were staunchly opposed to miscegenation on the grounds that it led to racial degeneration, scientific advances during the 1920s and fears of race violence on an international scale convinced some to reconsider their position. Simplistic race typologies and accounts of race mixing were undermined by Mendelian theories of genetic inheritance which pointed to the great complexity of the mechanics of inheritance and the universal nature of the materials of inheritance across the human species. In Britain prominent figures such as H G Wells and T S Eliot began to advocate a new world of racially 'homogenous' populations created through miscegenation and free of racial tensions and violence. Brazil offered a unique approach in its drive for national whiteness. With a population of former black slaves, indigenous people and the many 'mixed race' people resulting from an entrenched system of sexual exploitation by white males, it attempted to 'eliminate blacks and browns by pouring in white blood'.[157] This 'whitening ideology' drew on scientific race theory to support the view that the white race would prevail in miscegenation while at the same time it rejected claims of innate racial difference and degeneracy through race mixing. The mechanics of the process were seen as 'natural black attrition,' 'love' and the 'natural selection of the female species to choose a mate lighter in colour than herself'.[158] Theodore Roosevelt recorded the following comments from a Brazilian comparing the black ghettos of the United States of America with his own country's solution:

You of the United States are keeping the blacks as an entirely separate element, and you are not treating them in a way that fosters their self-respect. They will remain a menacing element in your civilisation, permanent, and perhaps even after a while a growing element. With us the question tends to disappear, because the blacks themselves tend to disappear and become absorbed.[159]

As we've already seen, Australian governments from the turn of the century had introduced various eugenic measures to encourage the growth of a healthy middle-class white nation: economic incentives, welfare benefits, healthier living environments and ideologies encouraging marriage and motherhood. By contrast Aboriginal families faced a range of anti-natalist practices and measures — official neglect and failure to intervene to halt declining populations, vastly inferior and inadequate services, legislative prohibitions on sexual contact and institutionalisation to separate Aboriginal men, women and children. From the 1920s organisations such as the National Council of Women and the Eugenic Society of Victoria advocated programs of compulsory sterilisation of 'mentally feeble' girls. During the Second World War Sydney businessman Lesley Owen Bailey set up the 'Hopewood Experiment' which involved the scientifically planned and monitored institutional care of sixty-eight white children with the aim of generating data for the 'eugenic engineering of the Australian population as a whole'.[160] In 1929 four eugenics-inspired Bills were placed before the Western Australian Parliament to allow the sterilisation of certain criminals, the sterilisation of Alsatian dogs, the identification and institutionalisation of 'mental defectives' and increased controls over Aboriginal marriage and sexual contacts. The Alsatian Dog Bill was the only legislation to be passed. During debate on the Mental Defectives Bill the issue of compulsory sterilisation of females was raised and staunchly supported by several members of parliament.[161] The 1929 Aborigines Bill seeking greater controls over Aboriginal marriages and sexual contacts was thrown out — not in the interest of Aboriginal rights, but by critics of Neville determined to thwart any further increase in his powers.

Neville's new vision wove together these pro- and anti-natalist strands of eugenic thought with recent revisions of scientific and anthropological knowledge about Aborigines and existing practices in Aboriginal legislation and administration. Physical anthropologists now classified the Aboriginal race as proto Caucasian and proximate to whites, signifying successful 'interbreeding' between black and white to produce 'viable offspring' with no possibility of 'atavism' (throwbacks) or 'degeneracy'.[162] The new policy did not require drastic new provisions or a major outlay of funding; rather it built on, refined and extended existing measures in the 1905 Act — definitions of who came under the Act, the Chief Protector's powers of guardianship over children and their removal to institutions, departmental controls over young adults, marriage and sexual contact and contacts between various 'castes' of Aborigines. Essentially Neville's vision was a program of racial and social engineering designed to erase all Aboriginal characteristics from a desired White Australia. Directed at Aborigines of mixed descent (Neville remained convinced that Aborigines of full descent were doomed to extinction), it was predicated on the removal and institutionalisation of 'mixed race' children. Indeed Neville later wrote:

It was the increasing numbers of near white children which finally turned the scales in giving the deciding answer to the question as to whether the coloureds should be encouraged to go back to the black, or be advanced to white status to be eventually assimilated into our race.[163]

Reared in government institutions to be white, young adults would be directed into state-approved marriages between progressively lighter 'castes' and whites so that over several generations Aboriginal physical features would be gradually bred out. Marriages and sexual contact between lighter and darker 'skins' would be prohibited by law, thereby stopping 'in-breeding' and the further development of a 'degenerate' 'mixed race' population who lacked the bearing of the 'uncontaminated black' and could only 'ape the white'.[164]

Chastened by the defeat of his 1929 Bill, and conscious of public horror of sexual contact between white and black, Neville trod carefully in promoting his vision. However, the policy of biological absorption was already shared by several prominent physical anthropologists, natural scientists, medical practitioners and administrators of the day, including Dr N B Tindale of the South Australian Museum, Dr Ralph Cilento, Director of Health in Queensland, and Dr Cecil Cook, Chief Protector of Aborigines in the Northern Territory. Like Neville they saw the policy as 'progressive' in relation to the prevailing racism of the times and, indeed, as the *only* solution to rampant white prejudice that was 'inherent and ineradicable'.[165] Cook had particular concerns about the balance of the races in the Territory and he wrote in 1931:

the preponderance of coloured races, the prominence of alien coloured blood and the scarcity of white females ... creates a position of incalculable future menace to purity of race in tropical Australia ... The Commonwealth has therefore endeavoured to elevate the Halfcaste to the standard of the white, with a view to his ultimate assimilation, encouraging the mating of white male and Halfcaste female, thereby gradually eliminating colour and reducing one contributory factor in the breeding of Halfcastes.[166]

There was also a generalised view that 'half-castes' actually desired whiteness and would welcome the scheme. Dr Cecil Bryan, a Perth medical practitioner with experience in the African native constabulary and the Indian civil service, told the Moseley Royal Commission in 1934:

274

Whether the black man ever wishes he had been born white may be a matter for argument, but there is no argument ... around the fact that every half-caste wishes he could get rid of the dash of colour within him ... By every artifice of which he is capable he tries to pass himself off as a full-blooded white, and the reason is obvious. As a known half-caste he is scorned by both whites and blacks ... Of all the outcasts in the world, of all the pariahs and untouchables, the half-caste fares the worst. And he fares the worst because he has too much of one colour and not enough of another. At bottom it is colour, and I do not hesitate ... to reiterate that statement and the similarly true statement that the greatest wish of the half-caste is to shed the last remnant of his colour and become wholly white. That is impossible ... But it is not impossible for his children, and next to making himself white the dearest wish of the half-caste is to see his children white so they can receive a fairer deal.[167]

It is incontestable that such notions, though powerful and enduring, were essentially *white* fantasies that legitimised *white* action. However, there were some 'half-castes' — institutionalised adults taught to desire whiteness, others hounded beyond endurance because of their colour — who fantasised a trouble-free 'white' existence for themselves and their children. There are well-known examples of people who hid their ancestry and 'passed' themselves as whites over the generations until the family's Aboriginal ancestry was forgotten and then rediscovered, usually with considerable joy and pride, by younger family members.[168]

The parallel policy of social assimilation, germinating in the writings of anthropologist A P Elkin and (Sir) Paul Hasluck at the time, had made little impact on the public. Even members of the Perth-based Australian Aborigines Amelioration Association (AAAA, of which Hasluck was a member), which took the radical — for the time — position of advocating an end to discriminatory legislation and segregation of 'mixed race' people and the introduction of measures to achieve their 'gradual reception' into the wider community[169], remained steeped in the racialist thinking of the time. An AAAA deputation in 1933 told the Minister for Aboriginal affairs:

All educationalists were agreed that the treatment of sub-normals should be mainly training and vocational education. If three or four thousand white people, sub-normals, were allowed to be neglected and untrained, they would constitute a tremendous menace to the welfare of the state, and that was what was actually happening in regard to the half-caste children of this state. They should be trained, and they will eventually become the hewers of wood and drawers of water for the white people, and in two generations the problem of the natives would be solved.[170]

The 1930s witnessed the outpouring of Aboriginal protest and despair at their treatment into the public domain, largely through submissions to the Moseley Royal Commission and letters to members of parliament read out during debate on the 1936 amending legislation. This action no doubt grew out of the earlier initiatives of the William Harris' Native Union (which folded when he died in 1931), mounting frustration amongst Aborigines at their treatment during the Depression years and the encouragement of supporters like Mary Bennett. They were unanimous in calling for freedom from the Act and chronicled the destruction of Aboriginal families under Neville's regime, in particular the abusive treatment of women and the removal of children and their abysmal treatment at Moore River settlement. The courage of those who spoke out should not be underestimated. Neville was an ever-present fixture at the Royal Commission hearings, asking questions alongside the Commissioner and doing his best to intimidate witnesses critical of his administration. No doubt he also scoured the written evidence and, through his personal knowledge, made informed guesses as to the identity of anonymous submissions. The consequences for the witnesses is not known, but there is every likelihood that they suffered for testifying.

In a ten-page letter to the Moseley Royal Commission, Aboriginal women of Broome called for 'freedom' and 'release' from the 'stigma' of the *Aborigines Act 1905*. They wrote:

Many of us have our own house and land ... We pay the rates ... we can read, write, sew, crochet, laundry and also make our own clothes, and for other people too, also do domestic work ... On that qualification alone we think we should not be classed as natives and kept in bondage by the Act.[171]

Departmental interference in their personal and family life was a major area of concern. Many local people had been sent as children to missions and this had meant the 'end of father and mother' for them. The women asked, 'Do you not realise the cruelty of this, would you white people like to think when you send your child to school that you would never see them again?' Because of the break-up of families, many old people were now living in a government ration camp on the outskirts of Broome with no one to care for them, no adequate shelter even in the wet season, and not even any soap to keep themselves clean. The Chief Protector's control over marriages had stopped many women from marrying the men of their choice, leaving them in an unenviable situation. If they continued their relationships they were branded as immoral and their children grew up illegitimate. Many women were left to rear 'fatherless' children with no financial support. The women alleged that police officers 'forced their way into our homes at any hour of the day and night and grossly insulted us knowing full well that we are helpless and too frightened to retaliate.'[172] If the women did not 'submit' to their demands for sexual favours, they were threatened with removal to a settlement or a mission. A woman from Mullewa described the terror of her family's removal to Moore River in 1930. Without any warning or explanation they were:

bundled into the police car ... [the police] didn't give us a chance to pack anything or have our tea ... We arrived at Mingenew at sun-down and they let me go to the shop to get some fruit and then they drove us to the police station and wanted to lock us all up in a cell. The children were hanging around their father screaming and I rushed off to see if I could get help but ... the policeman caught me and dragged me back to the cell ... we kept telling the children not to be frightened and they quietened down after a time. About a quarter to ten they started to the station ... we were told to get into the train and the policeman got in with us and sat up in the train with us until we got to Mogumber at daybreak next morning.[173]

Aboriginal pleas to the Royal Commission had little effect. In 1935 amending legislation was introduced to Parliament which proposed even greater powers than those Neville had sought in his 1929 Bill. The 1936 Bill enshrined the policy of biological absorption although little was said publicly about this. It also introduced new measures to promote departmental economic interests through contributory employers' medical schemes and greater controls over Aboriginal earnings. Some Aboriginal voices found their way into debates through letters read out by members of parliament. T Moore quoted a man who asked not to be identified: 'Now the Chief Protector wants guardianship over our children whether born in wedlock or not. Our children are our most sacred rights.'[174] Another member, W M Marshall, courageously argued against the Bill:

> We should not frame our legislation on the colour of the individual rather than on his intelligence and ambition. The Bill provides for roping in a native and then leaving it to him to get out. That is not calculated to enable him to rise or become a good citizen.[175]

However, more typical of debate was the speech by L Craig, replete with well-worn stereotypes and prejudices of the day:

> the worst feature is the growth of these people. It is typical of crossbreeds that they are rather prolific. One man told me he had working for him a half-caste man ... who had 16 children. His neighbour employed another man who had 10 children ... The most important aspect of the problem is that dealing with the female native ... We have a duty to these people. We contaminated their blood, and there is an obligation on us to see that the half-castes, at least, have an opportunity to earn a living. I refer particularly to the girls. We should take the girls away from their mothers when they reach a certain age and train them. They should be removed at as early an age as possible so that their removal will not be too much of a wrench to the mothers. I understand that up to the age of eight, nine or ten, half-caste children are capable of learning well at school. From then on to the age of puberty — and that is the dangerous time — they need to be taught other things, most important matters ... being sex questions and cleanliness. They should be given a reasonable education and trained to take their place as domestics in the homes of white people ... the native girl is a child of nature, and her character is not sufficiently strong to withstand the urge of nature.[176]

The major opposition to the Bill came from pastoralists acting as they did in 1929 to limit Neville's powers and to protect their own economic interests.

The policy of biological absorption was enshrined in the new *Aborigines Act Amendment (Native Administration Act) 1936*. What did this mean for the state's 'mixed race' populations? The definition of who came under the Act was extended to include children and young people of virtually any degree of Aboriginal descent, thereby bringing under departmental controls a whole range of 'near white' children formerly exempted from the Act. The Commissioner for Native Affairs now had legal guardianship of all legitimate children as well as illegitimate children and the period of guardianship was extended to twenty-one years of age. This meant that virtually any child of Aboriginal descent could be forcibly removed and placed in an institution. The Commissioner of Native Affairs, not their parents, controlled their lives until they reached the age of twenty-one. From this age any person of 'quarter-caste' descent or less was prohibited by law from associating with 'natives'. Thus they could be forced to live in the white community, although no measures were introduced to ensure their acceptance. All other adult 'natives' remained under the strict control of the Department of Native Affairs. Prohibitions on sexual contact were extended to include any act of sexual intercourse between 'natives' and others and the Commissioner's approval was required for all marriages. There were also harsher penalties for offences against the Act. Through these controls the Commissioner could ensure that parties married lighter rather than darker strains while prohibitions on the mixing of adult 'quarter-castes' with 'natives' obliged them to seek near-white marriage partners. In this way the 'mixed race' populations could be gradually bred out in accordance with the principles of biological absorption, thereby providing an ultimate solution to the problem.[177] Neville continued to promote his vision and at the 1937 federal meeting of heads of government departments he pushed through the following resolution endorsing biological absorption of 'mixed race' people:

That this Conference believes that the destiny of the native of Aboriginal origin, but not of the full-blood, lies in their ultimate absorption by the people of the Commonwealth and it therefore recommends that all efforts be directed to that end.[178]

In 1940 Neville retired and the drive to whiteness lapsed with the shift in public concern to the arena of war and the ensuing drain of resources and manpower to the war effort. Following the war, public exposure of Nazi eugenic-based race atrocities turned local attitudes against Neville's vision while, as we shall see, policies of social assimilation attracted growing support. Nevertheless his determination to 'make black go white' remained part of departmental practice until the end of the 1940s and left a painful legacy for the 'quarter-caste' children in Western Australia who were part of his experiment in social and biological engineering.

Sister Kate's Children's Home

'Her children shall rise up and call her blessed.' Proverbs 31:28

Sister Kate's letterhead

Sister Kate's Quarter Caste Children's Home, opened in 1933, was the site for implementing the first stages of grooming young, 'nearly-white' children for 'ultimate absorption' into the white community. The Home's aim was not, as some have suggested, to groom an educated 'mixed race' leadership, although this may have been an unintended outcome. While this certainly *was* the intention of special educational institutes for 'mixed race' children in colonial Africa, Asia and India, the principal aim of Sister Kate's was to *make the children white*. Selected according to criteria of corporeal whiteness, they were submitted to techniques of social engineering to make their minds white as well. As a former resident recalled, 'We went in Aboriginal and we came out white.'[179] The humanitarian rhetoric espoused by authorities at the Home masked these sinister aims and the associated violence to the children and their families, and all became inextricably linked in the fervent claim that this was 'for the children's own good'.

The founder of Sister Kate's was British-born Sister Kate Clutterbuck of the English Anglican order, Sisters of the Church, that was devoted to the education and care of children.[180] She had established Parkerville

Sister Kate and unidentified visitor with children from the Home, nd.
(Courtesy of Battye Library, 53990P)

Children's Home in 1903 and, at the age of seventy-three, embarked on the new challenge of mission work with 'quarter-caste' children. This was motivated in part by a falling out with the Anglican Board of Management of Parkerville which forced Sister Kate (as she was known) into retirement. She may also have been concerned about the future of the few 'quarter caste' children, being reared as white children, at the Parkerville Home whose presence there was opposed by some Home officials. In 1932 Sister Kate wrote to Neville suggesting the opening of an institution for such children — the 'most poorest and neglected children not those who have mothers who loved and care for them but those who are the most unwanted in the State'.[181] She offered to provide voluntary staff in return for a government subsidy for children sent in by the Department. Neville grabbed at the offer, seeing in it the opportunity to begin the biological absorption program, and he wrote back proposing a home for 'quarter-caste' children. The fiction that children at Sister Kate's were in between the white and black worlds and unwanted by their families was maintained over the years. In 1972 the Governor-General, Sir Paul Hasluck, a patron of the Home for many years, insensitively and mistakenly told a gathering of Sister Kate's children that the Home had been set up for children:

nobody wanted, governmentally or in private. Nobody wanted and nobody cared for them. They couldn't get into the ordinary orphanages, they couldn't even go back to the Aboriginal settlement. And these were the ones Sister Kate cared for ... people like Sister Kate ... just loved children. They just loved people who nobody else loved.[182]

But Sister Kate did not get the 'most unwanted children in the State but those with the palest skin'.[183]

Neville began by transferring from Moore River Settlement to Sister Kate's the children who were 'so very white and should have the benefit of the doubt, so to speak.'[184] He told the 1937 federal meeting in Canberra that in most cases their mothers were pregnant 'half-caste' domestic servants:

Our policy is to send them out into the white community, and if the girl comes back pregnant our rule is to keep her for two years. The child is then taken away from the mother and sometimes never sees her again. Thus these children grow up as whites, knowing nothing of their own environment. At the expiration of the period of two years the mother goes back to service. So that it really doesn't matter if she has half a dozen children.[185]

The 'scores of practically white children' that could now be moved legally from the camps, using the expanded powers of the 1936 Act, were 'entitled to different treatment from the natives in that they were quadroons, only their maternal grandmothers being black. Their fathers were white and their fathers and forebears of the same race as our own.'[186] Neville instructed the Superintendent at Moore River and local protectors to recommend children over the age of two years for placement at Sister Kate's on the basis of whiteness and he personally checked their suitability for admission. Departmental adherence to the selection criteria and absorptionist aims continued over the years and in 1947 the Acting Commissioner, C L McBeath, reminded Home authorities:

> The admittance of [the children] depends entirely on their colour, and I could not possibly agree that dark hued children be accommodated. As you know Sister Kate's Home was established for the education and training of quarter caste children, with the object of ultimate absorption into the community in the same manner of children who are inmates of white institutions.
>
> As you well realise, dark children could not possibly be absorbed as whites, therefore it is my wish that every care be taken in the admittance of children in order to ensure that they are fair enough to be regarded as white when the period of education and training has been completed, and the child placed in suitable employment.[187]

Children considered too 'dark' to 'possibly be absorbed as whites' were sent to Moore River. From the 1940s they were also sent to the new children's missions at Roelands near Bunbury, and Wandering. Head office gradually extended the Sister Kate's net and in 1946 protectors in pastoral areas in the north were instructed to record details of light-skinned youngsters for removal to Sister Kate's.[188] This surveillance and selection continued until the appointment of the new Commissioner, S G Middleton, in 1948 and the shift towards mainstreaming the care of Aboriginal children.

The sensitivity to physical signs of Aboriginality within the Home was also pronounced. After the 1937 summer holidays Sister Kate wrote: 'We have just returned from the beach and the children are as brown as berries. We must hope they will soon regain their usual colour.'[189] The demarcation between 'castes' was rigidly enforced. In 1949 the Superintendent of Sister Kate's, Horace J Minors, wrote to correct the headline 'Half castes happy in WA Home' in the latest *Women's Weekly*:

> There is not and never has been an aboriginal or half-caste child in this home. They are all quarter-castes. We are very sensitive of this line of demarcation. Those under our care have full citizenship rights on attaining the age of 21 years.[190]

Children who began to show 'signs of Aboriginality' — darkening skin, repeated misbehaviour, absconding or sullen attitudes — were sent to other departmental institutions or even to the girls reformatory, the Home of the Good Shepherd, in Leederville.[191]

While these children were to *become* white they were not sufficiently white to be funded at the same rates as white children. Departmental subsidies were insufficient for the more intensive care provided at the Home, and Sister Kate faced continual financial problems despite the children's contributions through their work, her own personal financial donations, generous private patronage from Perth's social and business elite and a bevy of voluntary female teachers, fund raisers, secretaries and workers. Sister Kate made liberal use of the press and information pamphlets to promote the Home in order to generate funding and, arguing that she was raising the children to become white citizens, lobbied the government for parity with white institutions. The latter received between seven and nine shillings a week per child while Aboriginal institutions received only three shillings. Despite Neville's support she succeeded only in having the subsidy raised to five shillings while that for white children was raised soon afterwards to fourteen shillings.[192] Lack of funding created problems in attracting sufficient qualified staff and this usually meant more work for the children and, on occasion, unfortunate appointments that rebounded on the treatment of the children. One woman recalled that some cottage mothers 'were a bit cruel. They wanted a job but they didn't care for kids. I think they just wanted a home.'[193]

The strategies of social engineering in the Home fitted with the aim of creating 'white minds' and for the first time brought innovative techniques used with white children into an Aboriginal institution in Western Australia. Sister Kate introduced the cottage home system she had pioneered at Parkerville instead of the large dormitories found in departmental institutions and missions. The cottages and cottage mothers were intended to closely resemble family life.

They were not large impersonal areas where youngsters would not feel the presence of a mother. But from the outset, Cottage Homes with Cottage mothers who would give something of the feeling of family to children who in many cases had never had the feeling of family before.[194]

Sister Kate was also influenced by the kindergarten movement in her endeavours to create an environment for children to grow to their full potential. She wrote in 1935 that her aims were to give the children:

> the best possible chance in life ... to give the children a happy childhood in happy circumstances and surroundings, not harassed by restriction and unnecessary rules they should lead the happy healthy life of normal childhood.[195]

This childhood was very English in nature with children's nursery rhymes, fairy stories, folk songs, maypole dancing at the annual fete, songs and training in good manners and etiquette. All of this linked the children to models of modern white Australian childhood and family life. Sister Kate also insisted that the children were to be integrated into the local (white) community and from the age of six they attended the Queens Park Primary School. In 1948 the first Sister Kate's children were enrolled at the local high school. The children were also treated at the local hospital and dental clinic and attended charitable events such as picnics and outings for underprivileged white children and orphans. Their diet was plain but superior by far to that provided in Moore River and religious training was sustained but not too doctrinaire. They were trained for menial labour and domestic work through daily chores, as in Moore River, and by the age of ten a Sister Kate's girl was an 'adept house keeper and child minder'.

It was equally central that the children's Aboriginality was completely erased. A former resident recalled a total blackout on all things Aboriginal at the Home:

> We were inculcated into a Christian religion and my Aboriginal culture and history was non-existent. That was completely irrelevant to our lifestyles at that stage. It was really an understatement to say that we were not taught anything about our Aboriginal

culture or history. The fact is that our Aboriginality was never mentioned, it was never a consideration.[196]

Contact with Aboriginal family members was strictly curtailed. Children were told they were orphans or abandoned by uncaring parents and some grew up not even knowing they were of Aboriginal descent.[197] Because of their upbringing some experienced deep feelings of shame on learning of their identity. Initially children were allowed limited contact with parents but as family bonds continued and even strengthened with separation, Home authorities became increasingly hostile to parental visits. In 1941 Sister Kate wrote to Commissioner Bray:

> The elder girls are inclined to make very much of their relatives, that is one of the difficulties, the mothers and relatives come to see the children and keep the remembrance always before the children that they belong to them ... Their relations write to them always keeping the tie between them. I think this is a real difficulty. Will the girl in service like it when her brown mother or aunt comes to see her? I think the relations are the real difficulty.[198]

Bray wrote back, 'They live as whites and their future lives would be along our own lines, therefore, it seems to me that severance of ties is inevitable,'[199] and he barred all parents from Sister Kate's annual fete. In 1944 he ruled that *only* mothers living according to white standards were to be allowed to write to their children and then only 'now and again'. But the family ties endured and in desperation Miss Lefroy, who took over the Home following Sister Kate's death in 1946, wrote to a friend in the country seeking ever younger children with no memories of Aboriginal family. 'There must be some,' she wrote, 'whose mothers have died or are no good, the younger the better.'[200] Despite often insurmountable problems — of distance, illiteracy, the attitude of Sister Kate's staff and rules such as having to book a month in advance to see a child — many parents persisted in trying to see their children.

Although Sister Kate's endeavoured to ignore the children's Aboriginality, it attracted constant attention from outsiders and even from some staff. The press headline in 1950, 'Native blood no hindrance to scholastic achievement' prompted a stern reply from Miss Lefroy that 'We never mention colour to our children ... They are extremely sensitive and (pathetically) anxious to merge into the white population.'[201] Some staff referred to the children as being 'basically flawed' by their Aboriginal ancestry.[202] The resulting confusion for some of the children was evident in school reports of their unhappiness, restlessness, indifference, cheeky behaviour, unwillingness to try and truanting, which typically came to a head when the children were sent out to work in 'apprenticeships' with white families. Aboriginal leader and former Sister Kate's resident Rob Riley[203] recalled that:

> The environment in the Home was quite a happy one and all the kids used to mix with each other as if it was one big happy family but the Home let the children down in a sense. It let the children down psychologically because it didn't bother to prepare them for the outside world. Everything was quite insulated in the Home. It was all happy-go-lucky but once you hit the outside world then it was a totally different sort of experience and the Home didn't create an awareness for kids.

Most of the young people were sent out to the country away from the temptations of city life and where employment as rural labourers and domestic servants was readily available. Employers were instructed to strictly supervise children and to treat them as one of the family. Wages were set at between two and four pounds a week, with most being banked on their behalf.[204]

When Sister Kate died her supporters claimed that she had lived to see the first generation of children 'take their places in life alongside their fellows in the fighting forces and in business,' and to see the girls marry 'nice white men' and become 'excellent wives and mothers'. The 'brave Experiment' had been a success.[205] There is another side to the story. A former Sister Kate's child recalled a feeling of vertigo on moving on from the Home:

> One of the greatest travesties ... is that they never prepared us for the fact that we had to one day leave the home and go into the outside world and deal with the fact that we were Aboriginal and how we would communicate with our own families and with the white community as Aboriginals. That is something that was very neglected by Sister Kate's and they basically just ignored the fact that we were Aboriginal. We were being brought up as whites and to live in a white society.[206]

The Home received many reports from employers of 'distressing signs of ingratitude',[207] impudence, laziness and of refusing to remain in the job. Many were homesick, accustomed to the institutional way of life and their close friendships with the other children, and they disliked and were frustrated by the monotonous work and the limited horizons open to them when they knew from school what could be achieved through apprenticeships and professional training. The girls especially hated servant work. They had absorbed white values and were not sufficiently 'humble' for the menial work they were required to do. They were 'culturally white' in a society that perceived them as Aboriginal.[208] With Sister Kate's largely closed to them as young adults, many were homeless. Some tried to find their families but the reunions were often difficult.[209] As 'quarter-castes,' once they reached the age of twenty-one they were also prohibited by law from having contact with Aboriginal people. This included their parents and extended families. Where were they to go?

Generalisations from the case of Western Australia to the other states and territories should be made with care. While its administration shared many features with them, local features of geography, isolation, history, demography and economy often pushed people to extreme responses. Aboriginal issues were and continue to be strongly contested and the nature of past administrations and ongoing power alliances have allowed for quite extraordinary interventions by vested interest groups. Nor are there any simple answers to the questions about systems of removal raised at the beginning of this chapter. Indeed new questions like 'Protection for whom?' continually emerge. Nevertheless, there is convincing evidence — which should be the cause of great concern and sorrow in our communities — that there were fundamental differences between the treatment of children removed by Aboriginal administrations in Western Australia and white children removed by child welfare authorities. Equally substantial evidence definitively erodes 'whig' arguments that removals of Aboriginal children were well-intended, benign and humanitarian, reflective of standards and practices of the time. Finally, in response to the question: 'Who was responsible?' there is the indelible impression of generalised white complicity at all levels, so that it seems naive in the extreme to point the 'accusing finger' solely at government.

CHAPTER FIVE

FIGHTING OVER THE CHILDREN

It is not always knowledge that is lacking. The educated general
public have always known what outrages have been committed and
are being committed in the name of Progress, Civilization,
Socialism, Democracy, and the Market ... It is not knowledge that
we lack. What is missing is the courage to understand what we
know and draw conclusions.

S Lindqvist, Exterminate All the Brutes[1]

Aboriginal families did not sit passively as their families were broken
up. In the song *Took the Children Away*, Koori singer-songwriter Archie
Roach tells how his father 'shaped up' to the welfare officers who came
for his children. Isobel Edwards' father confronted a Child Welfare
Inspector with 'a double-barrelled shotgun and told him "You lay your
hands on my kids ... and you'll get this."'[2] On learning that their
children had been taken to Carrolup Native Settlement while they
were away fighting overseas in the Second World War, men from the
Kickett family marched into the Superintendent's office in full army
uniform and carrying their army issue rifles and demanded the return
of their children at gunpoint.[3] However, since no one quite knew why,
when or how the children would be taken, most families adopted more
covert strategies — living on the fringes of rural communities, keeping
on the move, posting lookouts for strangers and camouflaging their
children by painting lighter-skinned ones with boot polish, hastily
hiding them in wheat bags and swags or sending them into the bush at
the approach of strangers. Some wrote letters of protest and anguish to
government departments, hoping to recover their children. As the
twentieth century progressed more joined together in public protest,
often with their non-Aboriginal supporters.

It would seem that the practice of removing Aboriginal children was condoned by most white Australians — if they thought of it at all. It fitted stereotypes of Aboriginal families and was endorsed by major social institutions such as the government, churches and the press. However, not all Australians were silent on the issue and the widely held perception that earlier generations did not care or that they fully endorsed official removal policies is misleading. Those who did speak out did so from various platforms — self-interest, a sense of decency and 'fair go,' humanitarian and Christian concern, feminist ideals about motherhood and the family. Here we examine some of these contestations over Aboriginal children, the participants, their motivations and their strategies. There are some Aboriginal voices, but rarely a child's

Vulnerable Aboriginal children often served as a point of contact between black and white.
(Courtesy of Battye Library, 4383B/74)

although their feelings are sometimes interpreted in the records of their keepers. The officers who actually took the children are typically silent. Most words are those of the powerful groups who set the systems in action and who have the most to explain. It is sobering to reflect that their shrill demands determined events while the pleas of Aboriginal parents fell on deaf ears.

THE LAMB DOES NOT EXPECT MERCY FROM THE WOLF[4]

The files and annual reports of the Queensland Aborigines Department from the turn of the century record a burst of removals of Aboriginal adults and children as the Department set about implementing the *Aborigines Protection and Restriction on the Sale of Opium Act 1897.* Annual reports list for public scrutiny the names of people removed and the reasons for their removal without concern for individual privacy. Those removed could be loosely classified as 'being a nuisance to white interests' — unemployed, unemployable, uncontrollable, insubordinate, immoral, aged and diseased adults — and children.[5] Scattered through the archives are the complaints, cries and laments of the children's parents. Their letters endeavoured to appeal to a common well of deep emotions shared by administrators as fellow human beings and as parents. We know that the appeals were invariably rejected, and we can only conjecture how those responsible felt when they read cries of pain like the following from an Aboriginal father in the north Queensland town of Bloomfield in 1901:

> I have nothing to work for, [my wife] is dead ... She died broken hearted, killed on that unlucky day when [our daughter] was arrested by [the police] and locked up in a cell ... dragged by animal force from her family and home, and forced from the arms of her weeping mother on a false charge of being neglected.[6]

How could the Protector of Aborigines in Brisbane refuse the plaintive plea of this Aboriginal mother from Taroom:

> I am writing to you about my little boy he has been taken away from me ... I would like to know if you would let him come back for he is only 3 year and ten months old and is too young to be taken from me if you would let me have him till he is eight years old I am quite able to look after him respectable and send him to school when he is old enough he has been sick for a good while and now he is getting well the police have taken him away.[7]

What of the painful inner conflict of feelings of love and shame expressed by this white father pleading to keep his children:

> I am ashamed to say I am the father of the children ... I wish to keep the children, and am in a position to educate them ... I am willing to make an affidavit that I am their father, but do not wish to further disgrace myself and relations by marrying the Gin, but should all else fail rather than have my children taken will do so.[8]

A series of emotional letters about the removal of a 'half-caste' teenage boy from the northern town of Cardwell expresses the terrible anguish of the mother and boy and his Aboriginal stepfather.[9] The letters were written in 1903 and 1904 by the town shire clerk and long-time resident William Craig on behalf of the boy's mother. In a letter to the Police Commissioner five years earlier, Craig had condemned the practice where local employers took Aboriginal children from their families claiming that 'family affection is their strongest feeling ...

[they] grieve and wail for months if [the child] dies or is taken away from them.'[10] Now he was writing to attack the government for what he saw as the same practice. In February 1903, following instructions from the Northern Protector of Aborigines, Walter Roth, to remove the boy to an industrial school to learn a trade, the Cardwell police placed the twelve year old in a police cell pending his removal to Yarrabah Mission. Locked in alone overnight the boy became hysterical and feverish and his mother had to be brought in to comfort him. The following day he was taken before the court and charged under the 1865 Act with being a neglected child because his mother was Aboriginal. Outside his mother threatened to 'kill herself by inflicting blood letting gashes and starving herself' if her son was taken. Craig protested angrily to the Aborigines Department:

It is an unassailable and incontestable fact that aboriginals treat all children ... with universal kindness, and the mother and her aboriginal husband are as endeared to the half-caste child equally as to the full blooded ... because it is the child of the mother and the family group. It is an act of impossibility to prove ill treatment in this or any similar case ... [she] had raised this child as her ancestors reared children for untold centuries ... it is her only child, and now after all the twelve years of trouble carrying him for miles herself and her husband, just when he is able to support himself and her and she is old and sickly she is to be deprived of him and suffer the mental agony of separation evidently forever or until death relieves her.[11]

Craig reported that the boy's Aboriginal stepfather had determined to find a way to take him off into the mountains and had told him, 'The government too much gammon, too much tell im lie, he all day want to steal im blackfellow piccaninny.' Informed by the police that the boy was to be returned to his parents, Craig managed to dissuade the stepfather from this action. The boy was eventually released and his family waited anxiously for what would happen next. They had to wait until November for what Craig called 'the final climax of the kidnapping'. On Roth's direct instructions the boy, quietened by lies that he was to be interviewed and then returned to his parents, was bundled on to a boat which immediately set sail for Yarrabah Mission. Craig wrote to the Home Secretary that this was nothing more than 'slavery and outright kidnapping'. Twelve months later Craig again wrote to the Department complaining about the boy's treatment at

Yarrabah, this 'mixture of Mission and Prison' where Aborigines lived in 'a state of chronic starvation'. An Aboriginal escapee had told them that the boy had stolen a 'bit of bread he was that hungry, and they punished and locked him up in solitary confinement.' Craig commented that 'it was to get treatment like this that the Qld. Govt. stole him from his mother and relations' and he included this plaintive plea from the boy's mother:

> Master you write im letter longa Govt. and tell im me too much cross [sorrowful] me cry all day longa my boy, you tell him quick fellow send im back longa me, me too much poor fellow.[12]

The final insult was when Craig's letter was forwarded to Roth for comment. 'I am sorry,' wrote Craig, 'that the Home Secretary should have thought fit to have forwarded the mother's prayer for mercy to you; the lamb does not expect mercy from the wolf.'

VESTED INTERESTS AND THE PATRIARCHAL STATE

While the families' cries went unheeded and largely unrecorded, a tug of war over Aboriginal children between powerful vested white interests filled hundreds of pages of official records and publications. The Aborigines Department's determination to take control of Aboriginal children contributed to a very public and acrimonious battle with employer interests early in the twentieth century, culminating in Roth's resignation and a compromise for both parties. This battle tellingly highlights differences in government responses to white and Aboriginal interests. The intensity reflected employer resistance to the government's determination to control Aboriginal employment generally in Queensland and the significance to employers of the children's skills and labour as station workers, domestic servants and boat hands. As historian Henry Reynolds notes:

> Though the Europeans constantly complained about 'unreliable,' 'unfaithful,' 'lazy' or 'stupid' servants it is clear that in a wide range of pursuits — from nursing children to breaking horses — Aboriginal labour was both irreplaceable and indispensable.[13]

As in colonial Van Diemen's Land, the children were a source of cheap reliable labour for employers who could not afford the wages demanded by white workers, especially in remote outback areas. They were more 'easily trained and disciplined' than Aboriginal adults and, removed from their families and homes, often became entirely dependent on their employers.[14] Indeed, employers looked on them as an 'investment' for which they would be rewarded by a lifetime of faithful service.[15] A northern pastoralist wrote in 1896:

> The early settlers usually try and get blacks out of the camp, say 8 or 10 years old, sometimes younger, and break them into station work. These get their clothes, tobacco, some few presents at times (but no money), and with a strict boss, who knows how to work them, prove valuable servants.[16]

Furthermore, employers could treat them more or less as they wished with little fear of condemnation or punishment.

The treatment of Aboriginal children was a matter of considerable concern across northern Australia in the late nineteenth century. In the Northern Territory there were official reports of kidnapping and sexual abuse of young girls by drovers overlanding cattle, of girls as young as eleven with venereal diseases contracted from white men, and of sexual interference with young house girls. A Bill modelled on the 1897 Queensland Act introduced in the South Australian Parliament in 1899 that sought, in part, to remedy these abuses was not passed despite considerable support for its provisions.[17] In north Queensland during the 1890s there were alarming allegations of Aboriginal child slavery. A controversial account of Queensland's Native Mounted Police, *The Black Police: A Story of Modern Australia* (1890), by English journalist Arthur Vogan, included a 'Slave Map of Australia' with much of northern Australia shaded to indicate areas of 'Worst forms of Slavery' or 'Milder forms of Aboriginal slavery.'[18] There was a strong awareness of labour issues generally in the colony in the wake of the emerging labour movement and the Great Strikes of the 1890s. The labour shortages of the 1890s and spreading ideas of a White Australia had sharpened resentment at cheap Aboriginal labour and, because white workers did not see Aborigines as equals, they advocated full pay for all in an effort to push Aborigines out and to secure employment for their own ranks. Determined to leave behind a reputation of brutal treatment of Aborigines, the Queensland government adopted a strong pro-active stance, as it set out to restructure Aboriginal employment relations, including Aboriginal child labour, in the state. The personal zeal of the Northern Protector of Aborigines, Walter Edmund Roth, to rescue the children from exploitative employers was also a significant factor.

Roth came from a distinguished Hungarian Jewish refugee family of physicians and intellectuals. Born in London in 1861 he followed two of his brothers to Australia in the late 1880s and in 1896 was appointed government medical officer at Normanton in north-west Queensland. Roth developed a strong interest in Aboriginal culture, perhaps influenced by an earlier working relationship with the famous scientist and ethnologist, Baldwin Spencer, and the work of his brother, Henry Ling Roth, author of a major history of the Tasmanian Aborigines. In keeping with scholarship of the times, Roth focused on collecting Aboriginal artefacts and recording discrete cultural practices and his several publications in the area earned him international acclaim.[19] Appointed Northern Protector of Aborigines in 1898, Roth became Queensland's Chief Protector of Aborigines in 1904. In the same year he gained national prominence when he headed the Royal Commission into Aborigines in Western Australia. Roth resigned during the political storm over his administration in 1906 and moved to British Guyana where he became a magistrate, contributed to the drafting of the Aboriginal Protection Ordinance there, and continued his ethnographic research.[20]

Roth represented a new form of 'Aboriginal expertise', combining professional training in science and medicine with amateur anthropological observation. Expertise based on personal proximity to Aborigines was increasingly downplayed outside the forum of parliamentary debate, much to the annoyance of former experts such as Archibald Meston whose application for the position of Northern Protector of Aborigines was overlooked in favour of Roth. An advocate of state intervention and segregation of Aborigines, Roth quoted the 'pre-eminent mid-nineteenth-century philosopher of progress' and social evolutionist, Herbert Spencer, in his 1904 Annual Report:

> the only forms of intercourse [between races] ... are those which are indispensable for the exchange of commodities ... No further privileges should be allowed to people of other races ... than is absolutely needful for the achievement of these ends.[21]

In the same report he also quoted comments by the Aboriginal Protector and Police Inspector for Normanton, Percy Galbraith, that 'it is not advisable that a race of half-caste and quadroon should grow up without religion and education, and continue their present life of more or less vagabondism.'[22] Roth's concern for Aboriginal children and women, but not for Aboriginal family units, reflected the racism and paternalism of the period, as well as his personal commitment to protection of

A poignant photograph of Aboriginal girls playing a traditional string game, probably taken by Walter Edmund Roth.
(Courtesy of Queensland Museum, EH2468)

children and his opposition to child labour.[23] However, like his contemporaries, his concern for white citizens often overshadowed Aboriginal interests. He commented in relation to the high levels of Aboriginal employment on pastoral stations in the Normanton district that:

> while I naturally like to see Aboriginals humanely treated and regularly employed, it seemed somewhat of a hardship that the work could not be given to the numerous deserving and unemployed Europeans.[24]

Describing the rampant spread of venereal diseases in the north in 1900 he wrote:

> Disease amongst the blacks is undoubtedly a source of danger to the whites … employers of black labour generally are either ignorant or callous of the risks they run.[25]

Nevertheless Roth was not fully imbued with the entrenched racism of the north. He attacked the White Australia policy and, while he was generally averse to employment of Aborigines by Asians, he

Walter Edmund Roth, Protector of Aborigines for north Queensland (1898–1903) and Chief Protector of Aborigines (1904–06).

(Courtesy of John Oxley Library)

asserted publicly that he would not 'conscientiously' oppose the practice solely on racial grounds.[26]

Described in the press as 'a big genial fellow, in the very midsummer of his manhood' with the 'modesty and frankness of a school boy',[27] Roth was a 'new chum' with limited political and administrative experience. He therefore made it his business to know his region thoroughly. From his base in Cooktown he travelled extensively — he was on the road eight months of the year — building up personal contacts and noting local evasions of the 1897 Act which he fearlessly exposed in his official reports. Rosalind Kidd observes that Roth was prepared to fight 'aggressively and publicly' against any foe and cites his action in exposing, to a federal Royal Commission on Commonwealth tariffs in 1905, the Queensland government's efforts to sabotage measures to halt the opium trade.[28] Historian Dawn May[29] states that 'from the beginning Roth showed a willingness to administer the Act far more rigorously than had been the intention of its creators.' This contrasted with the outlook of the colony's first Chief Protector of Aborigines, the Commissioner of Police, W E Parry-Okeden, who wrote 'I wish to cause as little friction as possible.' Roth's determination was especially evident in his actions to stamp out exploitation and abuse of Aboriginal women and children, to regulate Aboriginal employment and to 'rescue' children from their own families. In 1898 he told Parry-Okeden:

> Personally I am anxious to get all of these Cooktown Aborigines under the charge of the missionaries. It seems to me so discouraging to see all these little urchins running about the township, neglected and uncared for, and developing into nothing more than vagrants. I am confident that far more and lasting improvement can be made to their conditions if we can get hold of them when young.[30]

Roth was particularly proud of his efforts to rescue Aboriginal children and, indeed, he appeared to relish the conflict and turmoil he created. In 1904 on his way to Perth he told the Adelaide press:

One admission of the value of my work — if I may say so without being egotistical — is embraced in the receipt of so many complaints and petitions against my actions forwarded to the Government by Europeans. What better proof do you want?[31]

With ministerial backing Roth could afford to be cocky. He had strong support from the Home Secretary, Sir Horace Tozer, a man described by his contemporaries as 'stiff-necked where injustice is concerned'[32] and Tozer's successor, James Foxton, who believed that 'as a matter of strict morals our obligations to the Aboriginals ... are of a higher, more exacting nature than those we owe to our own ... We are the interlopers, not they.'[33] Subsequent Home Secretaries were less supportive, with disastrous consequences for Roth.

Roth had every reason to be alarmed about the unregulated employment of Aboriginal children in the north. While some employers claimed to have been 'given' children by their parents, the majority were taken and kept in employment under circumstances that were clearly illegal. Some agents recruiting labour for bêche-de-mer and pearling crews in the far north paid families 'commissions', of a bag of flour and a pound of tobacco valued at thirty shillings, and then returned the boys without any further wages after a season of back-breaking work. Roth was told by Reverend N Hey of Mapoon Mission that many young boys were never returned:

Bob was taken away by H— L—, a European, on 1st January 1898. This child was but a school boy at the time. His mother anxiously awaits his return. Harry, a child eleven years of age, was taken away three years ago. His parents also want him back, but, as the individual who removed him is unknown, his whereabouts cannot be traced.[34]

Pastoralists abducted children from camps to rear them as station workers. A Queensland pastoralist recorded in his memoirs how he obtained 'a young black boy':

While riding through the bush, I came upon the rear of the tribe of blacks ... Among them was a lad of about fourteen years ... I rode quickly after him, stopped and caught him by a strap around his waist which was his only garment, pulled him onto my horse and rode away. Kindness, plenty of good food and clothes soon made him a happy little nigger and he remained with me for years.[35]

An Aboriginal woman abducted as a child from a camp in the Gulf country recalled that families there felt powerless to act: 'There was nothing they could do, no one they could turn to for help. All they'd do was keep quiet about it. That's how it was.'[36] In 1905 Reverend Ernest Gribble, who worked as a missionary in Northern Queensland before moving to the Kimberley, visited Dunbar Station en route to Mitchell River Mission, and recorded the unsuccessful efforts of 'bush natives' to get back a 'half-caste' boy abducted from their camp along with six young women by 'a party of whites' in the previous year. On the night before Gribble's arrival, a group of men 'incited' by the boy's mother, had grabbed the boy from the station native quarters but were forced to abandon him after they were shot at by the station cook. Gribble left a stern letter for the manager demanding the return of the

boy and the women to their families. However, such was the arrogance of the manager that he merely gathered the 'station natives' together and burned the letter in front of them 'to show them that he did not fear us'.[37] Following complaints from Aboriginal parents, the Protector in Normanton informed Roth that some pastoralists were selling Aboriginal children 'as they would a horse, or a bullock'.[38] Employers like Jane Bardsley, who wrote to an acquaintance requesting 'a little Mary-mary ... to break in for housework,' were given Aboriginal children 'as a favour'.[39] Inspector Galbraith provided the following report on the process to Roth in 1903:

The loneliness and isolation experienced by many Aboriginal domestic servants is reflected in the face of this young woman in Brisbane, c 1900.
(Courtesy of John Oxley Library, 171823)

Settlers in outside districts who have plenty of myalls about their country are often importuned by town residents and others to bring them a boy or a girl. In due time the child arrives. How the children are separated from their parents is a subject of conjecture and surmise. Most people will tell you the child is better off with Europeans: in my opinion the contention is absurd. Most of the children will bolt (if old enough, and the distance not too great), and then they are termed ungrateful by *their owners*. This practice has been going on for years and with the exception of one or two cases personally known to me, without good results for the children: they change masters and mistresses, prostitution and disease follow, they can only speak pidgin English, and finally become pariahs amongst both whites and blacks.[40]

This movement of children between employers was a common occurrence. Not only were they cut off from their families and country but many ended up unemployed and alone. Reynolds provides the following example of a young boy called George who:

was taken away from Cooktown when a boy by a Mrs A—, and handed over to a Dr. H—, in Townsville, who subsequently handed him over to a man C—, a resident of Mackay. C—, left town two years ago for Brisbane and turned the boy adrift.[41]

This was especially painful for children who had been encouraged to feel that they were part of the family and whose members were the closest thing they knew to parents and siblings. This was often the case for girls who lived in the family home and cared for the children while attending to daily domestic tasks. Roth claimed that this was merely a ploy by employers to extract free labour:

Female children are engaged mostly as nurse girls, kept in a false position by being brought up as 'one of the family' — a fact which will probably account for their receiving no regular wages — and then when they get into trouble are no longer wanted, but packed off to shift for themselves as best they can.[42]

As Roth suggests, girls who became pregnant could expect the worst. A twenty-year-old girl who lived with Jane Bardsley and her family from the age of two was dispatched to Barambah after she gave birth to a baby who subsequently died. Her employer recorded the girl's terrible distress at the move:

> She was so upset at the idea of being sent away that as fast as I packed her clothes she took them out of the port and began to tear them ... At night ... she came in to us with a gun and asked us for a cartridge as she wanted to shoot herself ... She screamed hysterically, pleading not to be sent away as I was her mother ... when the time came to hand her over to the police she screamed and flung her arms around my neck and cried, 'Don't let them take me away, I won't do it again. I love you Missus, you are my mother.'[43]

We can only guess at the feelings of a young girl returned from London for health reasons by Mrs Christenson, wife of the owner of Lammermoor Station in north central Queensland and mother of 1930s activist Mary Bennett. In 1900 Mrs Christenson wrote to the Home Secretary, James Foxton, that the girl had been raised as 'an English child' and had learned 'clean habits and good manners' and 'loves her lessons and is wonderfully quick to learn — so much so that I believe her to be capable of being very highly educated.'[44] However, since the severe English winters had proved so trying for her health and the doctors advised that she could not survive another, she was being returned by passenger boat to Queensland and Mrs Christenson beseeched Foxton to send her to a good school to complete her education. Instead, within three weeks of her arrival in Brisbane, the girl was sent to the notorious Fraser Island settlement. There was no further mention of her in the records.[45] Her fate may have been that of many sent to the mission — disease and death. Raymond Evans writes that mission inmates were:

> ragged, sickly and malnourished [and] complained of being 'half starved' in 'a place where they are kept by the aid of the police' ... In large numbers [they] succumbed to disease, most notably Ankylostomiasis, a serious form of hookworm infection, resulting in progressive anaemia and often 'dysentery and death'.[46]

In 1904, Fraser Island was closed and the 117 surviving inmates were transported to Yarrabah where a similar fate awaited them. The superintendent there calculated in 1911 that of the original number only 'ten or so remain[ed]'.[47]

There are some instances in the records that suggest genuine affection for the children. What were the true feelings in the following triangle? In Parliament in 1901 Foxton[48] narrated the case of a wealthy childless woman in north Queensland who had 'adopted' a 'half-caste' girl at infancy and reared her as her daughter. During the woman's absence in the south for medical treatment her husband and servants plotted to get rid of the girl and, on the pretext of sending her to rejoin her 'mother'. they sent her instead to work as a family servant in Cairns. The 'mother' was reportedly 'very much cut up' when she learned what had happened and when the girl's employers refused to send her home she called on Foxton's assistance. He pursued the matter in the courts but after the Magistrate ordered the girl to return to her employer, Foxton had her declared a neglected child under the 1865 Act and she was sent to Yarrabah. After a suitable interval, she could decide if she wanted to return to her employers or to her 'adoptive' mother. A remarkable feature of this case was the Minister's preparedness to respond to the white 'mother's' pleas in contrast to those of Aboriginal mothers.

Life for most employed children was a round of unremitting chores, grinding poverty and loneliness. There was the ever-present threat of punishment, it being part of accepted bush lore that 'violence was necessary to discipline and civilise young black workers.'[49] One girl told police that her employer:

used to thrash me with a riding whip, and hit me in the face. Sometimes I was thrashed because I forgot to do something [I was] told to do, and sometimes I did not know what the thrashing was for.[50]

Children also faced the risk of sexual abuse. Roth reported instances of rapes of girls, some as young as six, which left them infected with venereal disease, permanently injured and, in some cases, dead. There was little chance of conviction for sexual abuse of Aboriginal minors under the Criminal Code as the Crown had to provide legal proof of age (the age of consent was set at fourteen) and few Aboriginal births were registered at that time.[51] It is hardly surprising that, despite their isolation, many children attempted to escape. Some succeeded and ended up in camps and missions but most were caught and returned to their employers with a sound thrashing. Some lived out their lives without ever marrying and having a family of their own. For female family servants there was often the expectation — a tradition in domestic service in nineteenth-century Britain — that they would sacrifice their hopes of marriage and family to devote themselves to caring for their employers' children and homes. In remote areas there were often no wives for Aboriginal pastoral workers who had been taken from their families at an early age and who were refused wives by local Aboriginal groups.[52]

Shocked by revelations of the conditions of Aboriginal child workers and guided by gendered concerns of the time, Roth determined to bring Aboriginal girls in particular under state protection and to transfer as many as possible to the care of the missions:

> It is far better to know that all such are ultimately legally married and protected by the missionaries, and, through them, by the State, than to realise that as soon as they get old enough to be tampered with by unscrupulous whites — the present normal condition of things — they are sent back to their camps as bad girls and left there to ultimate disease and ruin.[53]

In 1902 he set out his resolve to remove all 'half-caste' girls from Aboriginal camps and private employers:

> In the case of half-caste children, especially girls, already living in camps, it is desirable that these, where old enough, should be removed at once to the mission station or reformatory: on no account should they be allowed to go into private hands. The State takes upon itself the responsibility — a serious one to my mind — of taking such children from their aboriginal environments, but at the same time hands them over to the various missions and stations, which are now under direct Government supervision and control.[54]

To achieve his goals Roth had the legal machinery of the 1897 Act, the police, and the growing number of missions in the north. However, all three were problematical. The Act provided some control over access to Aboriginal employment through the system of compulsory permits to employ Aborigines issued by the police. Despite police resistance to this additional duty, permits were enforced in most districts and some employers who had reared workers since 'piccaninnies' lost them when they were deemed unsuitable employers by local police. Those who continued to employ child workers without permits could be fined. While the Act allowed for the removal of 'full-blood' children to missions, loopholes allowed some employers to escape the net. In working with the police, Roth encountered problems similar to those experienced by the Aborigines Department in Western Australia — deliberate obstruction, local loyalties and conflicts over the chain of command which the Police Commissioner and Roth's own Minister failed to untangle.[55] Relations were further complicated by fallout from the brutality of Queensland's Native Mounted Police which continued in the Gulf and parts of Cape York into the 1900s.[56] The new role of the police in implementing the 1897 Act was formalised with the appointment of the Commissioner of Police as Chief Protector of Aborigines from 1898 to 1904 and as Protector for all districts from 1904, and of police officers as protectors at the local level. Roth was not intimidated by surly police and in 1902 he publicly attacked officers who had employed Aboriginal trackers and their wives (who did all domestic work at the stations) without complying with the compulsory permit system and accused them of setting a bad example for other employers.[57]

In contrast to Archibald Meston in the south, Roth was staunchly pro-mission, reflecting perhaps a general administrative trend to prefer missions for work with Aborigines in contact situations. In 1900 and 1901 Yarrabah and Mapoon missions respectively were classified as industrial schools and reformatories for Aboriginal children and Aboriginal schools were opened at Weipa, Cape Bedford and in the Torres Strait. The Superintendent of Yarrabah, Reverend Ernest Gribble, agreed to this classification without consulting his executive, the Australian Board of Missions. Called on by the Board to explain his precipitous action he wrote:

> There are scores of children whom we wish to gather in … this being an industrial school for aboriginal children we can get them without any interference on the part of persons interested.[58]

Missionaries at Yarrabah actively participated in rounding up 'the little waifs and strays' — Roth's terminology. Gribble told sick and dying parents of the benefits of the mission for their children and trained 'the older Mission boys … for this particular kind of work, and parties of these young men … have brought several children to the station.'[59] Gribble's actions in separating children from their families prompted expressions of outrage in the local press from residents of nearby Cairns:

Powers have been extended to [Gribble] which should never be extended to anyone on this earth ... Gribble has torn children of tender years away from their parents and virtually held them in slavery while the grief stricken parents have gone on their unconsoled way ... it is left in the hands of the Rev Gribble to travel throughout this district and separate child and parents, brother and sister forever ... what excuse is to be put forward for the tyranny that is exercised?[60]

No doubt this reflected broader opposition to the missionary presence in the north, in particular, to the missionaries' condemnation of exploitative patterns of labour and sexual relations, their taking land wanted by locals, and their attracting Aboriginal workers and their families away from employers to meet their own needs for labourers and converts. Animosity to the missions was projected onto the Department and both became increasingly unpopular in the north.

Roth's interest in child workers formed part of a broader agenda to regulate Aboriginal employment. He recorded that he encountered 'extraordinary opposition' from local employers. This reflected peculiar regional features of north Queensland as well as more general concerns of employers to protect exploitative arrangements with Aboriginal workers. The north was characterised by a strong sense of regionalism, evident in the separatist movements of the 1890s, and an entrenched frontier mentality that believed firmly in 'progress and development' and 'chafed at [any] outside interference' in achieving these goals.[61] During the strikes of the 1890s, conservative governments had supported pastoral employers with a punitive backlash against strikers and unions. Now the government was endeavouring to smash long-established relations with Aboriginal workers and to intervene as a third party to regulate Aboriginal employment. As in Western Australia, Aborigines were a significant resource to employers in a range of industries — pastoral, marine, agricultural, domestic service and, to a lesser extent, mining — and were generally paid in kind rather than wages. The 'deep north' was also a place of entrenched racism with strict racial barriers and codes of silence about local discriminatory practices. In her study of violence on pastoral stations in the Northern Territory, anthropologist Deborah Bird Rose talks of 'conspiracies of silence' through which information was carefully managed. This was also noted by Vogan and other earlier commentators. The in-group of practical bushmen enforced silence through peer pressure and codes of mateship and by railing against and denigrating the work of 'sickly sentimentalists' and outsiders — missionaries, phil-anthropists, government men and anthropologists — so that 'would-be' protesters kept 'their dinkum opinions to themselves'. Aborigines were also silenced — they were killed, evidence of abuses against them was concealed and those who were acculturated and spoke English were labelled as untrustworthy, in contrast to 'real natives', so that 'there was no way they could represent their interests if they were in opposition to the interests of the bushmen who controlled them.'[62] Roth had no time for such practices and broke the codes of silence frequently and very publicly, thereby attracting further resentment and opposition. A contemporary observer commented:

It is hardly surprising that the residents of the colony who had lived under, and encouraged a system which, although degrading alike to Blacks and to Whites, had been the practised rule since the early days, would tamely follow the stringent provisions of the Act to be put into force without a protest.[63]

May notes that initially, at least, employers refused to see any advantages in the Department's efforts to shape a reliable, settled and committed paid work force:

It might have been expected that station owners would welcome government intervention in creating a well-disciplined work force, but this was not the case: employers bitterly resented the intrusion of a third party in their relations with their workers.[64]

Roth's zealous interventions to 'rescue' child workers provoked heated emotions. The owner of Lawn Hill Station claimed that Aborigines were 'being schooled to all kinds of trickery which will in a few years require harsh and severe treatment to control.'[65] Parties involved in the case where two girls aged ten and thirteen were removed from their white male guardians in Bloomfield drummed up considerable public sympathy for the men, despite reports that the girls were living in 'a regular brothel'.[66] The girls had been deemed neglected children under the 1865 Act and sent to live at Yarrabah until they reached the age of seventeen. A subsequent request from the older girl's guardian to marry or legally employ her suggested the nature of his interest in the girl, but this was overlooked in the rush to attack Roth. He was accused of 'officially vilifying men of high repute at government expense and of slandering residents',[67] and condemned for sending Catholic girls to an Anglican mission. When it became known that the older girl was to be married to a young Aboriginal man at Yarrabah, Roth was inundated with letters of complaint and the girl was questioned at length by missionaries, church dignitaries and even a police magistrate and politicians concerning her *real* intentions. Eventually Home Secretary Foxton was forced to explain:

> It became necessary to protect her from degradation quite irrespective of what denomination she might belong to ... She was simply sent to Yarrabah under the Reformatories Act in the interest of morality.[68]

Roth also received many emotional pleas from employers to keep children, among them some apparently genuine requests for exemption of their charges from the 1897 Act. Some employers manipulated the loophole where 'half-caste' children not living with Aborigines were excluded from removal under the Act, others simply flouted the rules, lied to local officials and hoped that their remote location and seclusion from prying eyes would avert official intervention.

In 1901, following a concerted campaign by Roth for amendments to the 1897 Act, the *Aborigines Protection and Restriction on the Sale of Opium Amending Act 1901*, known as 'Foxton and Roth's Act',[69] was passed by the Queensland Parliament. Debate on the Bill provided a public forum for the airing of grievances against Roth's interference in employment in the north and both Roth and Meston were brought in for questioning by members of the Legislative Council.[70] Much of Roth's response was devoted to his efforts to protect the children:

> What I consider is the most important of my duties — is to see to the removal of little half-caste and full-blooded aboriginal children from their present undesirable environments.[71]

Foxton succeeded in pushing through a range of major changes of general application but with direct relevance for Aboriginal children, as well as clauses relating specifically to them. The major thrust of the Bill related to state regulation of Aboriginal employment through the introduction of a minimum wage and working conditions for

Aboriginal workers, departmental management of Aboriginal property and wages, and strict controls over the movement of Aborigines by employers. These clauses were passed, although not without strong resistance from employer interests. One of Roth's opponents from north Queensland, Joe Lesina, described the measures as 'socialistic and revolutionary' and put the issue in the context of broader debates on labour relations:

> What right have they to interfere with me as an individual employing labour and expending capital? ... If the Government are going to father this principle in connection with aboriginals, we may come along and ask that they shall stand to that principle in connection with white men.[72]

Foxton told Parliament that special controls over employment of Aboriginal women and girls were central to the Bill and threatened to withdraw it, as he had done two years earlier, if these powers were reduced. These measures were augmented by other controls restricting entry to Aboriginal camps, controlling marriages involving Aboriginal women and non-Aboriginal men, and making fathers of 'half-caste' children liable to pay maintenance. To overcome the loophole used by employers to prevent removal of certain child employees, the definition of 'Aboriginal' was extended to include all 'half-caste' children under sixteen. Measures were also included to facilitate convictions for sexual assault of Aboriginal girls by shifting the onus of proof to the offender, who would be required to prove that the girl was above the legal age of consent of fourteen. This clause in particular prompted spirited debate which reflected a mixture of voyeurism, preconceptions about Aboriginal female sexuality, acceptance of sexual abuse which would not be tolerated for young white girls, as well as anger, revulsion, and a determination to put a stop to the practice. Following strenuous debate the measure was thrown out and replaced with a clause allowing medical proof that the girl had reached puberty as a defence against prosecution, effectively reducing the legal age of consent for some Aboriginal girls to below the age of fourteen.

Armed with these new powers Roth continued his fight in the north and, following his promotion in 1904, broadened his activity to the entire state. In 1902, together with Foxton and Lord Tennyson, Governor of South Australia, Roth was involved in a clandestine approach to the British Home Secretary, J Chamberlain, seeking his intervention to improve Aboriginal conditions. Lord Tennyson's dispatch included a 1901 report by Roth on conditions on the Queensland–Northern Territory border, containing allegations of rape of 'little undeveloped girls' and the unauthorised and unregulated movement of children across state borders. There was also a corroborating telegram from Foxton advocating border patrols and managed reserves and a copy of the 1901 amending legislation. In his letter, Tennyson asked the Home Secretary to write to the various Australian governments advocating Commonwealth control of Aboriginal affairs and calling for better protection and education of Aborigines and more reserves. He added, 'there is no doubt that any expression of sympathy with the black-fellows without entering into detail and however vague would have a great effect throughout Australia.' The Home Secretary's response was brief and final — in his opinion his intervention would 'serve no useful purpose and would in all probability give rise to feelings of irritation.'[73]

By 1903 Roth appeared to have modified his position by allowing the employment of girls on condition that they were legally employed and paid minimum wages set by the Department (part of this to be banked on her behalf by her employer), sent to school as required under the 1903 Education Act, regularly inspected by the Department (effectively excluding their employment in remote areas), and their morals safely guarded by their employers. In the following year he reported that the children's services were now 'appreciated' by their employers. No doubt Roth's shift reflected the mounting political opposition in the north, but it also fits with a growing tendency to negotiate deals between the Department and vested interests there, similar to those encountered in the Kimberley region of Western Australia. A file note in 1903 refers to requests from several stations to remove unwanted Aborigines and a 'deal' whereby pastoralists who employed a core of Aboriginal workers and maintained their dependants would not be required to take out permits or to meet legal obligations relating to wages and working conditions. On stations where the Department removed 'useless' old and young dependants, all legal employment requirements would be strictly enforced.[74] Nevertheless Roth continued to encounter opposition. He was obliged to remind police in the Gulf district who were not removing 'half-caste' children to the missions as instructed, that 'all such children are neglected; and can be treated as such and I ask again what action have you taken re this.'[75] Roth alleged that some employers were now dumping unwanted workers, and pregnant young women in particular, on the northern missions. He commented, 'The whole circumstances appear to be a sad comment on the illogical ideas of many European employers, that their black domestics are expected to remain single all their lives.'[76] In his 1903 Annual Report he continued:

With the general public the opinion appears to be gaining ground — though I am exerting my utmost to destroy it — that these institutions are being run for the convenience of employers, and afford them an easy means of obtaining or ridding themselves of their black labour. Mission stations are not registry offices for domestic servants, nor are they dumping grounds for blacks whose services their employers deem it inconvenient any longer to retain.[77]

Indeed, Evans argues that this was essentially how these institutions came to be viewed throughout Queensland — as ancillary to market forces and thus as social control mechanisms over Aboriginal workers.[78]

Roth and his administration were increasingly vilified in public meetings across the north and in statements to the press, petitions to Parliament and allegations made under the cover of parliamentary privilege. He was presented as a callous man who was creating 'ill feeling betwixt employer and employee on account of a few paltry shillings'.[79] His professional competence as a medical officer was also challenged. Mr Briggs of Gregory Downs Station claimed that a young man had died after Roth had refused to treat him because 'it was distasteful for him to go near the boy, and that it was not his duty.' Roth retorted that Briggs had reared the boy from infancy and had then turned him out after he was seriously injured in service, thereby 'disregard[ing] all moral and honourable obligations'. He denied even being asked to tend to the young man.[80] There were also demands to abolish the position of Chief Protector of Aborigines and to make police protectors responsible only to the Commissioner of Police. The public outcry following Roth's appointment as Chief Protector of Aborigines prompted him to tender his resignation but he withdrew it following a supportive deputation of some northern residents to the Minister for Lands. There were also wild allegations about Roth's personal behaviour and a petition was presented to Parliament demanding an inquiry into his administration on the grounds that he:

had been guilty of taking grossly indecent photographs, of conniving at immorality, of inhumane and unsatisfactory treatment, of making untruthful statements, of attacking the characters of respectable citizens, and of general unreliability and incapacity.[81]

The photographs referred to included shots of Aborigines having sexual intercourse, possibly taken as part of Roth's ethnological research.

Throughout these events Roth's ministers continued to repeat that all allegations had been investigated and were unfounded. Roth kept his silence. Finally, he could contain himself no longer and in 1905 documented his defence in a report that he made available to the press. In the report he claimed:

> I am well aware that the general opposition to my administration, and to myself personally, is mainly due to my interference with what has for many years past been considered a vested interest in the flesh and blood of the native.[82]

This created a furore in Parliament and members from the north renewed their attacks. Roth was blamed for the fraudulent mismanagement of working girls' savings accounts by the Protectress of Aborigines in Brisbane, Mrs Frew, that had led to her dismissal. But the *coup de grace* came when he was accused by Lesina of selling to the Sydney Museum, for the sum of four hundred pounds for personal gain, 2000 Aboriginal artefacts and 240 photographic plates which were allegedly the property of the Queensland government. Lesina demanded an official inquiry, cynically adding, 'if only to protect Roth's reputation'.[83] It is unclear whether Roth had the right to sell this collection although the Queensland government took no action against him. Nevertheless the writing was on the wall. Roth had to go. Early in 1906 he tendered his resignation. It was 'gracefully' accepted by his Minister[84] and Roth was replaced by a Chief Protector of Aborigines more in keeping with accepted traditions and less of an enthusiast for removals and segregation. The Secretary for Public Lands paid the following tribute to Roth:

> In the discharge of his duties it would be impossible in a country such as this to perform his work with any vigour or impartiality, and avoid making enemies. He had made enemies, but throughout

it all he was defended by his Minister; and, moreover, he had created in the community an active feeling of support in his favour which could not be ignored ... Dr Roth had been attacked in the strongest possible way ... more particularly during the last three years, and charges of a kind had been made which, if established would, if not make him a criminal, at all events damage him in the public eye, and stamp him as unfit to perform his duties. He had smarted under these attacks, as any one would ... He had been asked to answer the charges made, and he had done so in the most direct and strongest way. He answered the men who had been persistently attacking him for months, and in some cases years. Although the men who made the charges may be members of Parliament, it was a matter of public knowledge that, in a sense, some of them at least, were mere puppets, and were dancing to others who were pulling the wires.[85]

What was the legacy of Roth's administration? With his ministers he had irrevocably constructed the Department as the major body regulating and controlling conditions of Aboriginal employment, including the payment of wages for all Aboriginal workers. At the same time they had laid the foundations of the invidious employment 'contribution' scheme which deprived Aboriginal workers of their full wage entitlements and led to unfettered financial corruption of the accumulated moneys at all levels of government.[86] Despite Roth's efforts, his former opponents continued to manipulate the system to their own advantage and kidnapping of children from the camps continued into the 1920s.[87] Nevertheless, the system of child removal and mission institutional care in the north was now entrenched and Roth's action had set some enduring standards for Aboriginal child workers. In 1907 in Winton Mrs Norah Walsh, wife of the local police constable, was charged and found guilty of aggravated assault upon a seven-year-old girl whom she claimed to have 'adopted' in the previous year. The girl's body, hands and face were covered with scars, bruises, cuts and sores from being repeatedly hit by a cane, slapped and beaten. Mrs Walsh was accused of burning the girl's hand on the stove, beating her and then tying her hands behind her back and locking her in the wash house and making her pick up stones in the yard for hours on end for no apparent purpose. Mrs Walsh denied the charges but was found guilty and ordered to pay a fine and court costs totalling twenty pounds. Perhaps without Roth's exposure of such practices and his labelling of them as unacceptable this gross abuse of a young girl by the wife of a police officer may have gone unheeded. The full tragedy lay in the eventual outcome for the girl. She was not returned to her family but, in the same court on the following day, she was found guilty of being a neglected child and was sent to live in an unnamed industrial school.[88]

CONFLICT IN THE SOUTH

During the 1920s and 1930s the issue of removal of Aboriginal children was on the public agenda in the southern states. Attention was fanned by public outrage at specific incidents reported in the press, as well as the broader campaigns for reform during the interwar period by Aborigines and white sympathisers. These campaigns emerged in response to public revelations of alarming conditions and treatment of Aborigines, including massacres in northern and central Australia. Advances in scientific and anthropological research were also generating more positive views about racial difference and Aboriginal culture.

Political protest over Aboriginal issues had occurred spasmodically during the nineteenth and early twentieth centuries. We have already encountered some of these actions — for example, the petition from Aborigines at Wybalenna to Queen Victoria, the protests by residents of Coranderrk to the Victorian parliament, the public disclosures by Rev John Gribble in Western Australia, the writings of Arthur Vogan in Queensland and William Harris' appeals to politicians in Western Australia. However there was now a new vigour and unity of purpose in political action with a strong new Aboriginal leadership — men and women such as Jack Patten, William Ferguson, Fred Maynard, William Cooper, Pearl Gibbs, Margaret Tucker — and a spate of recently founded organisations promoting new ideas about Aboriginal welfare in national and international arenas. The aims, objectives and strategies of these organisations varied significantly. The conservative Aboriginal Fellowship Group drew together Christians interested in the welfare of Aborigines for 'Consideration Co-operation Fellowship and Prayer' and supported 'a just and constructive national policy'.[89] On the political left, the Communist Party Draft Program on Aborigines advocated 'equal rights for all Aboriginal people, as well as land for economic independence in remote areas and, if appropriate, for

political autonomy.'[90] Reform of systems of removal and institutionalisation of Aboriginal children was a particular concern of women's
organisations, which proclaimed that it was 'their duty to speak out on
behalf of "silent, suffering" Aboriginal women.'[91]

These initiatives paralleled the hard-fought campaigns of Aboriginal
activists and their organisations such as the Native Union in Western
Australia and the Australian Aborigines League and Australian
Aborigines' Progressive Association (AAPA) in Victoria and New
South Wales. They faced additional obstacles set by oppressive bureaucracies intent on controlling and silencing them. Nevertheless the
AAPA succeeded in exposing the inadequacies and injustices
perpetrated by the New South Wales Aborigines Protection Board and
organised the 'brilliantly symbolic plan' for the Day of Mourning held
in Sydney on 26 January 1938, the 150th anniversary of the landing of
the First Fleet at Sydney Cove.[92] The AAPA also targeted the issue of
the removal of Aboriginal children from their families objecting that
'girls of tender age are torn away from their parents ... and put to
service in an environment as near to slavery as it is possible to find.'[93]
In 1927 its president Fred Maynard wrote to the New South Wales
premier demanding that 'family life of Aboriginal people shall be held
sacred and free from invasion and interference and that the children
shall be left in the control of their parents.'[94]

In South Australia in the 1920s the issue of child removal
snowballed into a very public and heated battle between government
authorities and Aborigines and their supporters. The strength of the
public groundswell against removal practices as reported in the press
was not evident in other Australian states at the time. The reasons for
this are not clear, although it could reflect the legacy of the state's
colonial history which some have argued created a predisposition to
principled positions on political issues:

> there seems to be a prevailing atmosphere of puritanism ... reflected
> in the reserved and diligent behaviour of South Australians and the
> neat physical appearance of the city. South Australia's history is a
> strange combination of liberal thought and progressive reforms
> combined with often conservative and traditional attitudes and
> behaviour.[95]

The system of removal of Aboriginal children adopted in South
Australia from the turn of the century reflected this mix of sentiments,

combining a healthy professionalism and egalitarianism with a strain of parsimony and an imperative to assimilate. Although the Chief Protector of Aborigines was the legal guardian of Aboriginal and 'half-caste' children and could remove them summarily from their families, they were removed instead under the *State Children's Act 1895*, committed through the courts to the care of the State Children's Council (SCC) and placed in SCC institutions or foster families. Children sent in from the Northern Territory under arrangements with the Commonwealth government, also went to SCC placements. While the South Australian system of taking the children was less discriminatory and arbitrary than that of most other states, placement in SCC care typically meant greater emotional and cultural separation than that experienced by children sent to Aboriginal institutions.

South Australia boasted an organisational interest in Aboriginal issues. An Aboriginal leadership skilled in conventional methods of political protest had emerged from the schools and dormitories of Point McLeay and Point Pearce Aboriginal stations. Leaders included David Unaipon, a Ngarrindjeri man reared at Point McLeay who became a nationally recognised 'scholar, lecturer, preacher, author and musician as well as inventor'.[96] People at both stations had a long tradition of standing up for their rights. A visitor to Point McLeay in 1877 recorded Aboriginal men passing resolutions in the church and forwarding them to Adelaide for consideration.[97] In 1910 a deputation from Point Pearce campaigned against the proposed *Aborigines Bill 1911*. Letters of protest were frequently sent in to the Chief Protector of Aborigines and showed a level of confidence and political awareness not often seen in Aboriginal correspondence to officials at this time. Matthew Kropinyeri wrote the following letter from Point McLeay in 1912 after his request for assistance during a bout of illness was denied:

> Kindly permit me to express complete surprise and bewilderment at your suggestion to come to live at this Mission, after all the years of honest labour and endeavour to live a life independent of Missions … I should have written to you sooner but have awaited the result of Elections; and must tell you that your refusal makes it necessary for me to apply to our member Mr Peake even should I have to walk to Adelaide to see him.[98]

Some white citizens made a personal contribution to Aboriginal 'advancement,' through membership of the private organisations that founded Point McLeay and Point Pearce in the mid nineteenth century. Membership of Point McLeay's Aborigines Friends Association, established in 1858, included prominent political figures, such as the state governor, the mayor of Adelaide and several members of parliament, as well as mission, church and local businessmen and academics, and this ensured it the ear of Parliament.[99] The strong academic interest in Aboriginal physical anthropology in the halls of science and medicine at the University of Adelaide, one of Australia's first universities, opened in 1876, made it a foremost centre of Aboriginal research rivalled only by the University of Sydney which established a chair of anthropology in 1925. Academics such as the medical scientist and amateur anthropologist J B Cleland were considered national 'experts' and contributed to major forums such as the 1937 Conference of Commonwealth and State Aboriginal Authorities. In the early 1940s N B Tindale conducted his influential genealogical study of 'half-castes' in Australia which endorsed the policy of biological absorption.[100] Yet their forward thinking and academic rigour was expressed in 'scientific' solutions — in particular the policy of biological absorption — which were grounded in racialist thinking and interventionist in the extreme. Local women's organisations similarly hovered between liberal and conservative approaches. Although South Australia was the first Australian state to grant women the vote (in 1894), it was also the last to elect women representatives to Parliament. During the 1920s, the Women's Non-Party Political Association (WNPPA) joined with other women's organisations in the campaign for human rights for Aboriginal women as workers and as mothers. In 1929 its president, Constance Ternent Cooke, was appointed to the Advisory Council of Aborigines (ACA), the first such appointment in the state. At the same time the WNPPA angered some South Australians by advocating the permanent removal of 'light skinned' children from Aboriginal communities in the Northern Territory.

A major outburst of protest erupted over the passing of the *Aborigines (Training of Children) Act 1923*.[101] This Act was intended to expedite the removal of Aboriginal children to SCC control for educational and training purposes by allowing the Chief Protector of Aborigines to transfer his legal guardianship of Aboriginal and 'half-caste' children to the SCC. This meant that the children could be removed summarily and placed under SCC control without a court committal process. Legitimate children living with their parents could only be transferred from the age of fourteen and when they had achieved their Qualifying Certificate, but illegitimate children of any age could be transferred at any time.[102] In endorsing the Act, the Chief Protector of Aborigines and the ACA argued that it was more humane to remove children without the 'stigma and trauma' of the courts and that there was no erosion of parental rights. The 1923 Aborigines Department Report stated:

> the most urgent problem to be dealt with in our work for the aborigines is the better control and training of the rising generation, which consists principally of half-castes, quadroons and octoroons. This much-needed legislation ... should result in fitting the young to become self-supporting members of the community and an asset to the state.[103]

A train of events preceded the passing of the Act, beginning with the recommendations — reminiscent of earlier policies in Victoria — of the 1913 Royal Commission on the Aborigines to expel residents from Point McLeay, Point Pearce and Koonibba, and to transform the institutions into industrial schools for 'mixed race' children. The separation of Aboriginal children from their parents was pivotal to this scheme. The Professor of Physiology at the University of Adelaide, E C Stirling, told the Royal Commission, 'The more of these children you can take away from their parents and place under the care of the state, the better.'[104] The Secretary of the SCC claimed that children should be taken at birth: 'It was bad to be in a wurley for a week, fatal for a year.'[105] Point McLeay representative, Matthew Kropinyeri, presented a very different argument:

> In regard to the taking of our children in hand by the State to learn trades etc., our people would gladly embrace the opportunity of betterment ... but to be subjected to complete alienation from our children is to say the least an unequalled act of injustice, and no parent worthy of the name would either yield to or urge such a measure.[106]

While the Royal Commission acknowledged Aboriginal parents' 'strong natural affection for their children' it nevertheless recommended that the Aborigines Protection Board should take control of the children and at the age of ten 'place them where they deem best'.[107] The pressure for removals continued under the ACA, appointed in 1918 to administer Aboriginal affairs in South Australia. Two years later the new Chief Protector of Aborigines, William Garnett, former Superintendent of Point McLeay and Point Pearce, wrote 'I consider the most urgent problem ... is the better control and training of the rising generation.'[108]

Aboriginal parents vigorously opposed the 1923 Act, rightly seeing it as further unequal treatment of Aboriginal families before the law. In December 1923 three Point McLeay spokespeople and long-time residents, William Rankine, Leonard Campbell and John Stanley, visited Adelaide to present a 'memorial' to the Governor, demanding the repeal of the legislation which was causing families much 'heart-burning'. They told the press:

> We don't mind the Government taking them and training them. We want them to get on and be useful. But we want to feel we have full rights over them and that they are our own children ... We do not wish to be a burden on the State, but our children have never been state children and we don't want them to be. The people at Point McLeay would rather give up their mission station than sacrifice their children.[109]

The memorial was published in its entirety along with a set of condescending questions in 'pidgin English' about the 'early days and early ways' put to the trio by the reporter and the Aboriginal men's informative answers which were clearly expressed in perfect English. Written by N. Kropinyeri (possibly the Matthew Kropinyeri who appeared before the 1913 Royal Commission) the memorial roundly condemned the Act, likening the situation to a state of warfare between state instrumentalities and 'mother's love, its claims, its rights, its demands'. The memorial's extended militaristic metaphor no doubt reflected the enduring impact of wartime rhetoric and experience, Point McLeay having sent fourteen men to the front, four of whom died in combat.[110]

> The Bill has passed, legalising the Act of taking away the children from their parents. This Act, like a mysterious creature of ill omen is casting gloom over this our little mission home. Yes this Bill has passed at last, and the passing of it, provides food for serious consideration. And the first that presents itself to the mind, is the fact that, an Act, which, hitherto had been illegal, and I believe

punished by law, is now legal and supported by law as for instance in the past, anyone taking a child from its parents without their consent, will be liable to punishment by law. But today, any desiring to return and live with their parents, will be dealt with by the laws contained in the Act. Here we have a queer conglomeration of laws, through some unaccountable way, the wild cat of confusion, has effected or gained an entrance into the dovecote of legal harmony, and caused such utter confusion among the inmates, to such an extent, that some, if not all of them cannot with any degree of accuracy claim each their respective relationship either to the legal or illegal origin. However, this is not the matter on which I wish to write. It is a mother's love, its claims, its rights, its demands. Now it is understood that a refusal to comply with the demands of an ultimatum of one nation to another, is an acceptance of a condition of warfare whatever those conditions may lead to, so that the passing of that Bill is a declaration of war between right and wrong. And there is only one right, and only one wrong, which of the two contending parties is right? We will see presently. Mark well, the two forces, arrayed against each other. There stand the advocates and supporters of the Bill that has passed, strongly fortified, their guns of 'intellect' trained and ready for action, they represent 'Right.' There on the opposite and facing them is the rank of the enemy, strongly opposing the Bill, a very strange army, possessing no weapons of war, no intellectual powers, no Parliamentary eloquence, not a grain of science in the whole body, that makes the army of motherhood. The only piece of artillery that army possesses is the weapon called love. And thus equipped the army of motherhood has taken up their position in opposition to the Bill. The invader of those God given and therefore sacred dominions of mothers' love is its claims, its rights, its demands, a possession voted for them in the parliament of heaven, sealed with the image and superstition of His Majesty, whose name is 'Love.' This army also represents Right. Thus we see the two contending forces each striving for precedence in their claim of Right, and we ask, who is going to win the day? And the reply comes from the ranks of Intellect 'victory is ours' and rallying on their weapon of attack, intellect, they thunder forth their intellectual arguments again and again, propelled by the full force of scientific facts. Poor motherhood, how are you going to retain the beauties and glorious possession of motherhood, the right, the claims, the demands of love amid such fearful intellectual bombardments as this, and seeing that you are armed with the crude and primitive weapon love, the invention of which dates back in the past eternity. It is true, we are indeed poorly equipped, and we know not how we are going to fare in this fearful struggle, but — and just then, a thin spurt of smoke is seen issuing from the ranks of motherhood, and we knew that love, motherhood's weapon spoke, and that is its claims, its demands and its rights, in their threefold unity is speeding its unerring way to the ranks of the foe, bearing the seal, the hallmark, and the mandate of the majesty on high (the majesty of love). Hon Members (jurymen) — The question is asked, Who wins? The bar of eternal justice, truth and righteousness awaits your verdict! What says you?[111]

No immediate changes came from this appeal. However, the government could not ignore the general outcry early in the following year prompted by the removal under the 1923 Act of an Aboriginal baby from his mother at Point McLeay. In April the Adelaide *Sun* broke the story to its readers under the headline:[112]

'I WANT MY BABY!'
ABORIGINAL MOTHER'S PLAINTIVE CRY
STATE'S SHAMEFUL STEAL
ONE LAW FOR THE WHITE PEOPLE
ANOTHER FOR THE ABORIGINALS

Announcing that the family was taking legal action against the 'heartless Act of Parliament under which an aboriginal mother may ruthlessly have her babe stolen' the article argued:

The word 'stole' may sound a bit far-fetched, but by the time we have told the story of the heart-broken mother we are sure the word will not be considered out of place, especially by women who know the instincts of motherhood.[113]

A detailed background on the case was provided. In September 1923 the nineteen-year-old mother and her three-week-old baby moved to Point Macleay with her widowed mother and younger brother. They shared a small hut and lived off rations and money earned by her mother and sent in by her brothers, two of whom had fought in the War. One, a widower, had been seriously wounded and lived in England with his son. In February a female inspector from the SCC arrived unannounced; she told the mother that her baby and hut were 'dirty' and had to be cleaned up and that she must get a cot instead of lying with the baby on a mattress on the floor. No more was heard until April when the mother was informed by the mission superintendent and local police that the Chief Protector had ordered that she take her baby to hospital in Adelaide as he was 'dirty and neglected' and sick. Despite the family's protestations mother and baby were put on the train to Adelaide. On arrival an SCC representative met them and took the baby, claiming it was now a 'state baby'. The baby's grandmother told the press:

> I think a cruel wrong has been done to [us]. We only had one visit from the State lady and we got the bed as she told us. She never came back to see the bed but after a month had gone by the dear little baby was dragged away from his mother. We were never given a chance in a court of justice to say if we were right or wrong … Is there one law for the white people, and another for the black?[114]

Public concern over the incident was such that a popular sporting columnist congratulated the solicitor who had taken up the case and, observing that such an action against 'a white woman as respectable as this aboriginal girl would cause a cyclonic outburst of indignation,' called for 'a public indignation meeting' in Adelaide Town Hall. The columnist continued:

> What about the weather for Oakbank? Oh, I've forgotten all about the gee-gees since I have read about a young black gin who had her little piccaninny pinched … all my customers have been talking about it, and clean mad they are about it too … I want to know what the young black gin has done that her youngster should be taken away from its mother's breast, and stuck in some sort of institution, where it's sure to snuff it, as sure as God made little apples. Then the Government authorities should be hauled up on a murder charge.[115]

In June, shocked by the depth of public feeling, and fearing that, since Aborigines were so 'strongly opposed' to it, police would have to be called in to enforce the measure, the Chief Protector informally suspended the Act.[116] This demonstrated the effect of combined Aboriginal and public outrage. However, as the crisis abated the provisions were gradually reintroduced and were retained in consolidating legislation passed in 1934.

It was in the context of this sympathetic audience that an exceptional short novel about an Aboriginal mother's fight for her son was published. Written some twenty years earlier, *The Incredible Journey* was the work of Catherine Martin, daughter of Scottish migrants who settled in the Narracoorte district of South Australia, and writer of three other novels and locally published poetry and newspaper serials. Martin wrote in an introduction to the book that it was a 'true story'[117] related to her by 'one who knew the details at first hand'. The story had 'clung obstinately to [her] mind as one that must be told,' and aroused a strong feeling that 'to shirk the trouble of recording the story — though it might quite probably evoke but scant enthusiasm — felt like a sort of treachery.'[118] This documentary novel preceded by six years the publication of Katherine Susannah Prichard's novel *Coonardoo* cited as 'the first Australian work to sympathetically and fully realise an aborigine as the central character'.[119] While Prichard tackled the issue of sexual contact between Aboriginal women and white men, Martin presented a moving account of the 'heroic love and devotion of a black woman when robbed of her child'.[120] In doing so, Martin challenged negative stereotypes of Aboriginal women as mothers, endowing them instead with the idealised and essentialist attributes of motherhood generally reserved for white women:

> To those who have ears to hear, it is worth telling, that even among these people there have been those who were in a measure liberated from the thraldom of the lower nature. Iliapa and others have borne witness to this, with a selfless devotion akin to that of Saints, whose relics have been treasured to ward off disease, crime and sudden death.[121]

The novel is set amongst the Arrernte people of Central Australia and we follow the lives of Iliapa and her family to the point where, in the absence of her husband, Iliapa's son Alibaka is stolen in revenge by an older disappointed suitor and sold to a drunken white man who intends to capitalise on the boy's considerable skills as a jockey. We then accompany Iliapa and her kinswoman, Polde, on their heroic search for the boy which takes them across the Red Sand Desert to the township of Labalama. Through a combination of the women's wits, survival skills and mythical knowledge, Iliapa's maternal love which drives them inexorably on, Polde's audacious handling of white authority figures, and the agency of a lone white stockman, the mother, son and father are eventually reunited:

> When she felt the strong young arms of her boy around her, she cried for joy. They sat on the big gum log in the warm darkness, side by side, now talking, now silent. At times they began to say something and stopped short, saying, 'I forgot what I was going to tell you.' Then in the middle of a sentence they both would whisper: 'Ah, but I have you now — now all the long journey is over.'[122]

While nothing is known of the impact of the novel on contemporary reading audiences, it was ground-breaking in providing its readers with a sympathetic view of Aboriginal motherhood and the issue of the separation of Aboriginal children from their families.

Although the federal government took over control of Aboriginal affairs in the Northern Territory in 1911, South Australians maintained a lively interest in conditions there. Paradoxically, the Northern Territory had become for many southern Australians a 'heart of darkness' of evil deeds and depraved sexuality that demanded their redemptive interventions, as well as a romanticised pristine Aboriginal world to be protected from white intrusion. During 1924 South Australians were alarmed by descriptions in the press of the Bungalow, the institution for 'half-caste' children in Alice Springs, as 'A Place of Squalid Horror'.[123] Located next to a hotel and opposite the police station, the Bungalow, a galvanised iron shed, housed fifty babies and children in accommodation suitable for ten. The children slept three to a bunk or on the floor and during the day attended classes with Mrs Standley, the manager, and her Aboriginal assistant, Topsy, while the older children were hired out to local employers. Such living conditions were clearly unacceptable to some concerned citizens in the south: objections were raised in federal Parliament and letters of protest appeared in the southern press.[118] There was further outrage at a proposal by a deputation of WNPPA and church representatives to the South Australian government to remove all 'near white children' from central Australia to the south, to be raised by foster families. Members of the public registered their opposition to the severance of family ties that this would entail in a stream of letters to the press. 'Child lover' wrote of the special bond between all mothers and children:

Can a stranger love a child like its own mother? ... I think a home where they could be together would be better than boarding out. If we take a child from its mother, who loves it, we are as bad as the slave traders.[125]

The following letter appeared under the heading 'Pleas for the Mothers':

I tell Mrs Cooke and her friends there is no race of humanity on God's earth that are more affectionate towards their children than the blacks in Australia are, be it half-caste, quadroons or any other roons, or colour, or shade. They would rather die for their offspring than give them up and the whiter the child the greater the affection. On the other hand, the young would rather die than leave their mothers and their tribe and customs ... It would be most outrageous and cruel to separate the natives and their children, and it would be in violation of the proclamation read by Governor Hindmarsh, when he landed from the Buffalo.[126]

A former 'bush man', Alfred Giles wrote movingly of the children's anguish and pain:

The proposal is to drag these poor little creatures, not only from their own mothers, but from their own beloved country, and place them in an environment and climate absolutely foreign to them ... Added to this will be their natural but terrible grief at their separation from their relatives, as well as being debarred from their own free and glorious country and birth place, and the result will be to pine away and die or to escape.[127]

Giles reminded readers of the recent Point McLeay deputation which had:

bitterly protested ... about this very question of robbing parents of their children ... I know I shall not appeal in vain to the hundreds of my fellow-bushmen, who know the blacks and their habits intimately, to condemn the introduction of such methods as indicated by the deputation.

He asked readers to support the government's plan for a new children's home in Alice Springs where children could remain in contact with their families and grow up to make 'proper' marriages with their peers from the Bungalow and find useful employment in the pastoral industry.

The federal government was less amenable to such protestations than South Australian authorities. In 1926 it formalised a system with the South Australian government to send Northern Territory children to foster families or employment in the south under the supervision of the SCC and the ACA. Most working girls sent down were from Central Australia and their removal was intended, in part, to protect them from the expected influx of railway workers on the new line linking Alice Springs and Adelaide.[128] In 1929, five years after the federal government had assured the public that conditions at the Bungalow would be remedied, the Bleakley Report condemned the institution and recommended its immediate closure and the removal of all lighter children to Adelaide to be absorbed into the 'white community to which they rightly belong'.[129] Finally in 1932, following further public pressure, the children were moved to the Old Telegraph Station on the outskirts of the town. In the same year public indignation at allegations that babies were being taken from their 'frantic' mothers forced federal authorities to clarify for the public their policy on 'half-caste' removals. In a statement in the Canberra *Times* in October the minister responsible for Aboriginal Affairs in the Northern Territory explained that it was government practice to remove these children to institutions where they were educated and trained to enter 'industrial life' in the Northern Territory and to take on the full rights of citizenship.[130]

A radical alternative solution based on the twin principles of segregation and separate development also emerged in South Australia in the mid-1920s. This was of particular interest as it consciously linked the issues of Aboriginal land and removal of Aboriginal children. The driving force behind the proposal was the Aborigines Protection League (APL) established in South Australia in 1925, and one of several new humanitarian organisations that originated between the wars to promote the welfare of Aborigines. Its small but hardworking membership included Colonel J C Genders, an elderly Adelaide establishment figure, who wrote in the APL magazine, *Daylight*, 'There is not and never should be occasion for the Children to be taken away from their parents and farmed out among white people.'[131] Its founding president was Dr Herbert Basedow, a graduate of the University of Adelaide and a prominent medical doctor, geologist, anthropologist and member of parliament who took part in numerous expeditions into central and northern Australia. Briefly in 1911 he held the joint positions of Chief Protector and Chief Medical Inspector of Aborigines in the Northern Territory. During the 1920s he became a 'vigorous controversialist in the local press on behalf of Aboriginals'.[132] The League also had the support of several prominent Aboriginal leaders including David Unaipon, George Rankine, Mark Wilson and P Williams.

The APL was innovative in looking past contemporary abuses towards full Aboriginal autonomy. It advocated the creation of a self-governing, separate Aboriginal state in northern Australia 'with the view of saving the fast dying Aboriginal races and of redeeming as far as possible the mistakes (often well meant) we have made in our past treatment of them'.[133] This reflected concern, in the face of the growing incursion of development in the north, to find a solution where Aborigines could be protected while also contributing to their economic development. Historian Russell McGregor[134] writes that 'fundamentally, it was a proposal for the segregation of Aboriginals on large reserves on which they could "work out their own salvation" and, with government assistance, develop according to western economic imperatives'. But it also advocated Aboriginal self-government, preservation of customary law, return of sizeable areas of land to Aborigines and maintenance of Aboriginal family life. In its 'Proposed Aboriginal State Manifesto' the APL specifically linked the issue of removal of Aboriginal children to the need for a separate state:

When it is realised what the removal of these young children means, we shall find further argument for the creation of the proposed aboriginal state. They are taken from their country, their home, their parents, from environments where they should have an opportunity of settling down and marrying and they are placed in strange surroundings ... and not permitted to marry and unable to share in the national traditions which are held to be most powerful factors in creating character. Even with the greatest kindness from those in whose charge they are placed, what sense of loneliness, of exile, even of slavery must they not constantly feel? And what temptations must beset them? What is to become of them if, under these conditions, they live until they are 21 and regain their liberty?[135]

In the context of the recent public outcry about removals this paragraph holds a particular poignancy and appeal. By 1926 the APL had collected over one thousand signatures for a petition to federal Parliament and had made deputations to several federal and state politicians. In the following year APL representatives[136] presented a Petition for 'A Model Aboriginal State' with seven thousand signatures to the House of Representatives in Canberra.

DAUGHTERS OF THE NEWER EVE[137]

In various forums in southern Australia and in Britain during the interwar period Australian women's organisations waged a prolonged, although ultimately unsuccessful, battle for recognition of the rights of Aboriginal mothers and children. Their criticisms of Australian governments' treatment of Aborigines, particularly in relation to the breaking up of Aboriginal families, attracted widespread publicity and ensured that the issue of Aboriginal child removal remained on the public agenda during the early 1930s. Of the various movements advocating on behalf of Aborigines at the time their vision most reflected the influence of the 'internationalist, human rights and anti-slavery discourses' circulating within the League of Nations and British organisations such as the British Commonwealth League (BCL) and the Anti-Slavery and Aborigines Protection Society (ASAPS).[138] Australia's new independent status in the changing international contexts of the interwar period had opened the door for the entry of Australian women into national and international affairs, and for the adoption of a new feminist and internationalist critique of the treatment of Aboriginal women and children. The expanding organisa-tional network of women in Australia followed the international push for full citizenship rights for women of all nations.[139] Amongst their demands was the call for a 'caring, moral Commonwealth of Australia' — a 'civilised white community, responsible for the original owners of the land and for shaping a humane national policy for Aboriginal Australians', which recognised and made reparation for past and present mistreatment of its 'native people' and which welcomed them as citizens into a modern Australian nation.[140]

As a self-governing dominion in the British Empire, Australia was ceded full dominion status with responsibility for representing its own interests internationally. In 1920 it joined the League of Nations as a full member nation and, as a signatory to the League of Nations Covenant, pledged to promote peace, security and equality for all people and to secure 'fair and humane conditions of labour and treatment of native inhabitants in Territories under her control'.[141] In 1920 Australia assumed responsibility for the administration of New Guinea and for the well-being of its people as a mandated territory under League of Nations supervision. The League of Nations Slavery Convention 1926 took on a particular potency in the context of the centenary of the abolition of slavery in the British colonies in 1933. Drawing on the Covenant's definition of slavery, the BCL and women's organisations in Australia alleged that conditions 'akin to slavery' existed in most countries under white imperialist control, including Australia, and they called for the abolition of all forms of labour and sexual exploitation and the recognition of the rights of every woman 'in the ownership of her own person'.[142] The BCL also considered conditions of indigenous women in domestic service in British Commonwealth countries under this platform. These international discourses also drew attention to the rights of children, both in the context of ASAPS concern about child slavery, and in a more general 'overwhelming concern' about the well-being of children following the traumatic experiences of the First World War. In 1925 Australia became a signatory to the League of Nations Declaration of the Rights of the Child[143] which focused on children's need for special protection and priority care:

Men and women of all nations recognising that mankind owes to the Child the best that it has to give, declare and accept it as their duty that, beyond and above all considerations of race, nationality and creed:

I   THE CHILD must be given the means required for its normal development, both materially and spiritually.

II   THE CHILD that is hungry must be fed; the child that is sick must be nursed; the child that is backward must be helped; the delinquent child must be reclaimed; and the orphan and the waif must be sheltered and succoured.

III   THE CHILD must be the first to receive relief in times of distress.

IV   THE CHILD must be put in a position to earn a livelihood and must be protected against every form of exploitation.

V   THE CHILD must be brought up in the consciousness that its talents must be devoted to the services of its fellow-men.[144]

This contributed to feminists' public campaign for the rights of Aboriginal children and their mothers to remain together, for protection of Aboriginal children from abuse, and for their rights to citizenship through state education. The women's organisations were fully aware of the strategic power of attacking Australian governments' handling of Aboriginal issues in British forums, and from the mid-1920s the BCL conferences in London and ASAPS deputations and petitions provided major platforms for efforts to galvanise government action in Australia.

Through the peak national body, the Australian Federation of Women Voters, and its state affiliates including the Women's Service Guild in Western Australia, the Women's Non-Party Political Association in South Australia and the Woman Citizen's Movement in Victoria, a national platform was developed advocating significant new directions in the treatment of Aboriginal people. These included the review of all Aboriginal legislation and administrations; the transfer of state control to the federal government and the injection of federal funding; the granting of citizenship rights; the setting aside of inviolable Aboriginal reserve lands; paid employment; and the delivery of adequate welfare, education and health services to Aboriginal families. While many of these demands were shared by male-dominated humanitarian and church organisations, this was a distinctly feminist vision calling for the rights of 'person, motherhood and paid employment' for their 'less fortunate sisters' and, for their children, 'rights to family life, education and welfare'.[145] However, like their male counterparts, the women's organisations made little effort to consult with the subjects of their advocacy, in this case Aboriginal women, even those like Pearl Gibbs and Margaret Tucker who were prominent in Aboriginal political organisations at the time. These were white voices speaking out as members of a white Australian nation on behalf of Aboriginal women and children. Their advocacy formed part of a broader campaign to achieve equal participation for women in national development. The women's organisations positioned themselves in a dual role as advocates for these 'inarticulate' and 'suffering' women who were denied their fundamental human rights as British subjects, and as protectors to shield them from ruthless exploitation of their labour and sexuality by white and Aboriginal men.[146]

Membership of the organisations was made up of middle-class,

Anglo modern women. Their leadership was able to travel freely and to commit themselves to heavy schedules of conferences, lecture tours and political lobbying. For most, Aboriginal issues formed part of a broader feminist agenda and few were actively involved with Aboriginal women and children. Nevertheless, there were busy networks of correspondence across the continent which kept the women informed, and the 'power of the letter' shaped ideas and contributed to a more multifaceted and sympathetic perspective on Aboriginal family issues. Personal letters from women in the field — such as missionary Annie Lock, never a part of the feminist movement herself — related their own opinions and observations of their Aboriginal 'charges'. The following are excerpts from letters written by Lock to Mary Montgomery Bennett and Constance Ternent Cooke:

The natives say the white men round them up like bullocks and take young girls away, keep them one week, and sometimes send them back and sometimes kill them, and it makes them furious. They say, 'Why don't the white men leave the black girls alone? we no touch white girls and women.'
... the problem here is the children. If we could get a piece of country and get the children and train them while they are young and at the same time teach them usefulness, the girls to sew, cook, wash and clean, the boys to be horsemen, cowboys, shearers, and trades like making wood and tin cans and iron work, and to be useful at gardening and general work about a home, they would need good, firm, kind persons to train them and not to spoil them or make too much fuss of them. The only education they need is to read and write and do arithmetic, so that they may know the value of money and how to get change.[147]

... her mother carried her [child] nearly all the way over 26 miles to get her here for treatment, she was too weak & it overtaxed her heart & she collapsed on Monday morning at 2.30 ... we buried her by lantern and torch light, it was very sad, after the death ... the mother never spoke again only by signs with her hands & head. A week after she came up to me covered in white clay, she looked like a ghost all white from head to foot with only a little piece of blanket for a covering, she was dragging a branch after her & went all around my place to hunt away the spirit of the dead & any footmarks that may have been left.[148]

The work and writings of three significant women activists — Bennett, Cooke and Bessie Rischbieth — indicate the nature of the women's vision and the varying nature of their commitment to the cause of Aboriginal women and children. Bennett was well-off, widowed, childless and living in London when she began her, now widely recognised, campaign for Aboriginal rights in Australia. The daughter of a Queensland pastoralist, whose benevolent paternalism towards the Dalleburra people is recorded in her book, *Christenson of Lammermoor*, she had spent most of her life in the social circles of London. As an active member of the BCL and ASAPS, she helped to forge links with Australian organisations and to maintain a flow of information across the miles. In 1929 she wrote to Cooke of her meeting with Fernando, an Aboriginal man employed in London and then held in the Old Bailey on a charge of assault. Removed from his family at an early age he had told Bennett:

A good father is good but a good mother is above every other good. I was taken from my mother when I was little, but the thought of her has been the guiding star of my life.[149]

Bennett returned to live in Western Australia in 1930 and became actively involved with the Women's Service Guild (WSG) whose members included 'Perth's leading professional and socially prominent women'.[150] She visited missions in the Kimberley and Aboriginal camps in the south-west before eventually settling down, as we saw in Chapter Four, at the United Aborigines Mission at Mount Margaret where she devoted herself to teaching Aboriginal children.

Despite her years outside of Australia, Bennett had absorbed many prevailing preconceptions about Aborigines. She wrote of the 'contaminating' effects of 'civilisation' and entertained romantic views of pristine communities 'untouched by civilisation' — while also condemning practices such as child betrothal and polygamy. She was convinced that segregation was the Aborigines' only hope for survival and endorsed the notion of a model Aboriginal state. Her negative views of the effects of race-mixing are evident in the following excerpt from her account of a return visit to the Dalleburra people:

As for the baby it was the most complete contrast to all the full-blooded black children ... instead of glowing copper, its skin was sickly yellow, instead of the lively intelligence and concentration of aboriginal children, it had a vacant look, mean and complaining, and its mouth was pulled down in a whine.[151]

Nevertheless, Bennett did not endorse the punitive solutions of her peers. Her proposals, outlined in *The Australian Aboriginal as a Human Being*, were a mixture of stereotyped views, sympathy for the children and support for Aboriginal family life. She repeated the widely held view of 'half-caste' children abandoned by their fathers and left with mothers who were 'depraved by abuse' to grow up without the 'natural affections of family life' or the 'wholesome discipline of the public school'. However, she condemned institutionalisation as a solution, noting that the children seemed to 'lose all sentiment in the character' and when the girls were sent out to service they took up with 'any shams that come their way'.[152] In a letter written to Cooke in 1931 from Broome she denounced the dormitory system she had observed in the Kimberley, probably at Forrest River Mission:

The girls are taken from their parents and herded together in a squalid iron building; they grow up without root in their character, with lowered vitality and intelligence, and with a hardness which expresses itself in continual recrimination of 'you been steal such and such' — 'don't you tell lie' — 'I'll tell so and so' and endless fights. At puberty their escapades and cunning in hiding give cause for grave anxiety. But the girls are essentially as fine and responsive a lot as anyone could find anywhere. The initial evil is in the criminal presumptuousness which substitutes for the normally healthy life of the family, the system of a dead mechanism with a savage segregation of the sexes, and morbid inhibitions which do not fail to produce their crop of morbid reactions. The dormitory system is even more detrimental to native children than to white, for it is so utterly alien to them.[153]

The alternative, Bennett argued, was:

fellowship ... with their mother's people, the Aboriginal tribes, or, if these no longer exist, among other half-castes in Missions which do hold up an ideal of love and service. They need their homes, their families, and not to be interfered with.[154]

Bennett's expanding personal contacts with Aboriginal adults and children in her work and travels opened her eyes to the many human dimensions of Aboriginal circumstances. She developed a profound respect for traditional Aboriginal family life and wrote in 1931 of its central importance to Aboriginal society, supporting her views with quotes from the writings of anthropologist A R Radcliffe-Brown:

> the thing they live for is the sentiment of the family ... Working on their experience, the Australian natives were led to found their social structure on the family and its chief function of providing for the feeding and bringing up of the children, thence, working outwards from the particular to a social system which would unite individuals into groups and provide for collective action, they expanded the principle of family solidarity to include the whole tribe, and also surrounding tribes in 'an extensive and highly organised system of reciprocal obligations.' 'Relationships are traced without limit' so that every 'individual stands in some definite relationship to every person whom he meets in the course of his life.' There are never any orphans in wild tribes, for the children who lose their parents are adopted by members of the tribe who stand in that relationship to them ... the sense of solidarity in them is so strong that I have seen natives adopt half-castes, though they might not be related to them, and care for them with their own children.[155]

In the following year she told the press that Aboriginal women had 'neither human rights nor protection' and that 'slavery [was] in operation and there [was] white slave traffic in black women.' She attributed this directly to government policies:

> It pays the white man to dispossess the natives of their land wholesale ... The compulsion is dispossession and starvation reinforced by violence ... Other nationals are amazed at the mentality that regards the native race solely as cheap labour or slave labour to be used up and appoints police constables to dispose of them.[156]

As we have seen, Bennett's criticisms precipitated an acrimonious feud with the Chief Protector of Aborigines in Western Australia, A O Neville, as well as conflict with some of the state's women's organisations. In 1935 Bennett wrote to ASAPS in London that if the women's organisations were 'too smug and too self-seeking' to really fight for Aboriginal women's rights then 'I shall seek help outside wherever I can get it not forgetting Japan.'[157] Bennett's 1933 paper to the BCL Conference in London, entitled *The Aboriginal Mother in Western Australia*, attracted sensational publicity in London and Australia with headlines such as 'Slavery, Polygamy, Child-brides, Female Mutilation and Police Brutality.'[158] This paper is credited with forcing the appointment of the Moseley Royal Commission into the Condition and Treatment of Aborigines in Western Australia in 1934. In the paper Bennett linked Aboriginal women's precarious economic dependence to early death, starvation and enforced prostitution, and she called for immediate action to halt sexual abuse, associated births of 'half-caste' children, high infant mortality rates and the exclusion of expectant mothers from hospitals on the grounds that 'white people would resent their presence'. She wrote with emotion of the effect of removals on mothers and children:

> I know of aboriginal women who were hunted by the police to take their children to a remote Government settlement. Three women suffered an agony of fear, and the effects may still be seen in their children; I would refer particularly to one of my pupils, a nervy boy with a look of shock.[159]

In 1934 Bennett presented evidence to the Moseley Royal Commission as a representative of the WSG. Drawing on her experiences at Mount Margaret Mission, she argued that the mother–daughter bond was fundamental to processes of racial and cultural survival and successful 'self-regulated assimilation' of women of mixed descent into non-Aboriginal society:

> What Australia's aboriginal half-caste daughters need are their own mothers who love them, and their own homes among their own people, and teaching, until such time as they shall have attained legal and economic and political freedom, and meet white people on terms of equality.[160]

In a statement that was radical for her times, but that has a familiar ring at the turn of the twenty-first century, she linked removals to genocidal outcomes by quoting a social worker writing in the *Australian Board of Missions Review* in 1933:

> deportation by the Govt is one of the chief factors in causing the sure extinction of our native race ... Family life to the aborigines is

everything ... Such interference is fatal.[161]

She pointed the finger of blame at 'the white supplanters' who were 'too greedy and too mean to give [Aborigines] living areas in their own districts' and at her enemy, Neville, and his department:

> That the dept means well is presumed, but this does not justify inflicting such suffering as the splitting up of families always brings about, and it does not justify deportations of innocent people. No dept in the world can take the place of a child's mother and the Honourable Minister does not offer any valid justification for the official smashing up of native family and community life when he says —
>
> > The removal of half-caste children is a necessity for so many reasons that it seems futile to mention them.[162]

Bennett vividly evoked the fears and pain of the mothers and children:

> Many of these poor children are parted from their mothers, who are the only ones who really love them, and their hearts are starved for want of love, but first for years they suffer the misery of hunted animals, always running away from the police in the hope of hiding in the country which they know, among their own people, but always in fear that at any moment they may be torn away, never to see them again. They are captured at all ages, as infants in arms, perhaps not until they are grown up; they are not safe until they are dead.[163]

She also spoke of the joy when a little girl was returned to her people from Moore River Native Settlement after much pleading by her mother:

> Once we got north from Kalgoorlie the news ran along like wildfire, and at each station when the train pulled up, groups of natives collected to welcome the poor child back. In their joy at seeing her again they would stretch up and take my hand in theirs with such affectionate confidence. It was a triumphal journey.[164]

Finally, she told Commissioner Moseley:

Departmentalism is no substitute for mother love. I do most earnestly ask that the official smashing of native family life may be stopped, and that native families may be permitted to live where they wish within the law. The laws that are enough for the proper conduct of white communities should be enough for the proper conduct of native communities also. Our aim should be to raise the native camps into thriving self-respecting village communities, rather than to break them down materially by knocking their homes down, and spiritually by taking their children and women from them.[165]

Neville was present while Bennett gave her evidence and took the opportunity to cross-examine his accuser and to endeavour to undermine her credibility. The following excerpts show that Bennett was more than a match for Neville:

Neville: You are something of an idealist, and wish to bring about an ideal system all at once?

Bennett: I wish to treat other people like human beings. I do not put it higher than that.

Neville: Have you not been a little inconsistent? You spoke of the horrors of tribal rites and yet you infer that people who are subject to those rites should be left alone?

Bennett: I do not say they should be left alone, but they should be helped to establish communities of their own where they can live in their own homes. That would not mean splitting families or deporting them.[166]

Later Neville was forced to defend his own policies:

I say emphatically there are scores of children in the bush camps who should be taken away from whoever is looking after them and placed in a settlement ... If we are going to fit and train such children for the future they cannot be left as they are.[167]

Bennett and Miss Ada Bronham, representing the WSG and the Women's Christian Temperance Union, worked to ensure that for the first time in Western Australia a range of Aboriginal voices was heard at a Royal Commission. Nyungar witnesses were also inspired to come forward by the earlier protests of Nyungar spokesperson and founder of the Native Union, William Harris. Not surprisingly there were repeated references to Aboriginal children. Bronham had talked with Nyungar families living in camps in the southern towns of Wagin and Brookton and reported that they wanted a school. She commented, 'That struck us as rather good considering [they] were so short of so many things.'[168] Bennett read the following moving statement from Norman Harris, nephew of William Harris:

> Under the Aborigines Act every one of us is a prisoner in his own country. Any police officer can come along and take all of our children at any time, and we cannot object or we are committing an offence under the Act. A police officer deeming us to come under Clause 3, sends us off. If we refuse to go, we are forced to a settlement under Clause 55, and can be kept there under Clause 12. In many cases death alone ends our term of duress.[169]

Annie Morrison spoke out against the conditions in which her children were forced to live at Moore River Native Settlement:

> I have six children, three boys and three girls; they are given watery soup, no meat or vegetables or green fruit. Bread and fat is given for breakfast and tea. They have no warm clothes for winter. My children only have one blanket between three of them, winter and summer. I have been there and seen this.[170]

Sam Isaacs told how after five years at Moore River his sons were 'not well educated ... and not in good health', and he attacked Neville for his attitude to the children's families:

> I wanted to take the two eldest boys from the Moore River Settlement to spend the Christmas holidays with me. Mr Neville did not like the idea of my taking them to Margaret River. I asked why. He replied, 'Your father is living in a camp and is only an aboriginal.'[171]

David Nannup told the Commissioner that he had no idea why his children had been sent to Moore River:

> It was the Chief Protector of Aborigines who ordered the children to be sent to Moore River, but when I asked Mr Neville why he sent them there, he replied that he did not know anything about it ...

Nobody seemed to know, but when I pressed the matter, Mr Neville said it was the Child Welfare Department that was responsible ... I told Mr Neville ... 'It was not that department, it was you.'[172]

Little has been recorded about the life of Bennett's colleague in South Australia, Constance Ternent Cooke, apart from the fact that she was married to Adelaide University lecturer in Chemistry and son of a clergyman, William Ternent Cooke, had two children and lived in the wealthy Adelaide suburb of Kensington Gardens. Certainly she was sufficiently well off and unencumbered to lead a hectic public life as an activist for Aboriginal and women's issues in various organisations and honorary government appointments. Cooke was a member of the Advisory Council on Aborigines from 1929 to 1940 and the Aborigines Protection Board from 1940 to 1963,[173] president of the WNPPA and convenor of its Aboriginal Welfare Committee, a foundation member of APL and its vice-president for twenty years, a Justice of the Peace and member of a special panel of justices for the Juvenile Court.[174] In contrast to Bennett, Cooke worked principally from a governmental and organisational base which reflected both the more informed and open attitude to Aboriginal issues in Adelaide and her own more conservative position and social distance from Aboriginal people. As we have seen, in 1924 Cooke advocated the complete separation of 'half-caste' children in central Australia from their mothers, and their merging into white society. She told a meeting of ASAPS in London in 1927 that Aborigines were 'stone age remnants' and that anthropological evidence demonstrated that 'the gap between their civilisation and ours [was] too great to be bridged, and that segregation [was] the only hope for maintaining the race.'[175]

In Adelaide, Cooke promoted discussion and debate through public lectures, radio programs and study groups. During her 1927 visit to London she attended the BCL Conference, whose resolutions included a special section calling for equality for 'native peoples' and the care, protection and education of children of mixed parentage.[176] Cooke maintained an active involvement with ASAPS over the years and contributed to its sustained campaign to encourage reform in Australia through deputations and letters to federal and state governments. In 1930 she presented a paper, *The Status of Aboriginal Women*, to the Pan Pacific Women's Conference which surveyed their status according to 'domicile' and 'social standing' and summarised the various provisions relating to Aboriginal women under state and territory legislation. In contrast to Bennett's writings the paper was objective and distant — only one anecdote provided a glimpse into the nature of Cooke's personal experiences of Aboriginal women:

> Generally speaking the social standing of aboriginal or half-caste women may be defined as that of outcasts in white society. The first time that this was forcibly brought home to me was when I visited a far northern town in South Australia. At a social gathering in the galvanised iron hall, every person (i.e. white person) for miles around put in an appearance, for there is little class distinction among whites in the outback; as the fun was at its height I looked up and at the windows there was a sea of black faces looking in.[177]

Another active campaigner for Aboriginal rights during the 1920s and 1930s was Bessie Rischbieth. Childless, widowed, wealthy and living 'in style' in the upper-class Perth suburb of Peppermint Grove, she was also a committed international campaigner for 'social reform and the status of women', and for the education, care and welfare of children. She held office in a multiplicity of national and international organisations: she was President of the Women's Service Guild of Western Australia, honorary editor of its monthly journal *The Dawn*, founding president of the Australian Federation of Women Voters (AFWV), co-founder and foundation vice-president of the BCL, a board member of the International Alliance of Women for Suffrage and Equal Citizenship, and was actively involved in the International Women's Suffrage Alliance and the League of Nations. She was an intrepid traveller and 'the sight of Bessie Rischbieth stepping off the plane after one or another national and international conferences on equal citizenship remained a familiar one in Perth.'[178] Rischbieth was also a follower of theosophy which promoted, in addition to its more spiritual practices, racial tolerance and an international brotherhood regardless of racial distinction. By the 1920s the movement favoured 'not only imperial race reform but also Aboriginal advancement'.[179] Rischbieth was also well known in Perth circles for her advanced views on child welfare practice and her generosity in supporting facilities and services for child care.

With this background it is hardly surprising that Rischbieth supported the feminist Aboriginal platform. However, in contrast to Bennett, Aboriginal issues remained marginal to her overall commitment to the broader feminist agenda. Giving evidence at the

1928 Commonwealth Royal Commission on the Constitution, Rischbieth addressed national marriage and nationality laws but did not refer to Aboriginal rights. Until recently, her contributions to Aboriginal issues during the 1930s have been largely overlooked in historical accounts of her work.[180] Rischbieth may have preferred to forget her involvement after her acrimonious battle with Bennett in 1934 over what she saw as Bennett's 'national disloyalty' in her mounting attacks on Australia's 'anti-native complex'. Nevertheless, in the same year Rischbieth represented the AFWV at the Moseley Royal Commission. She advocated federal control of Aboriginal affairs arguing that Australia 'owe[d] a debt of reparation to the aborigines' and that there was an urgent need for consistency in legislation and practice across the states. She also addressed the rights of Aboriginal women and children. It was her conviction that 'Motherhood was a right ... and one ... the State had a duty to support.' She referred to removal of Aboriginal children as an example of Aboriginal women's lack of human rights and insisted that the reasons for removal went much 'deeper' than the charge of 'neglect'. The inference was that the government was removing Aboriginal children because it was a less expensive option than the system of support provided to keep white families together.[181] She called for an immediate investigation into the system of removal and institutionalisation of Aboriginal children. She also urged the government to adopt mainstream child welfare practice in dealing with Aboriginal children and to 'improve the system of dealing with the parents and their economic condition ... in order that they might keep their children.' Such views still have a surprisingly contemporary ring.

Despite their efforts, the overall impact of the women's actions on government practice was minimal. Historian Fiona Paisley states that the 1928 Royal Commission into the Constitution overlooked the feminist reconceptualisation of Australia as 'a caring and moral Commonwealth' and its imperative of better care for Aborigines in recognition of past wrongs. Instead it endorsed 'masculinist represen-tations of the "realities" of frontier Aboriginal administration in the states',[182] The women's testimony was subjected to harrowing interro-gation and omitted from the commissioners' summation of evidence. The Moseley Royal Commission ignored their recommendations for reform and adopted Neville's agenda of increased intervention in family life and greater removal and institutionalisation of children. Paisley writes that this final blow 'marked the end of the inter-war women's lobby. It never regained its momentum.'[183] Still, Neville continued his public denigration of Bennett:

> Mrs Montgomery Bennett is a cultivated woman and an excellent teacher, but suffers from ill health, at times severely. It is because of this fact that one is loath to take exception to any remarks she may make publicly ... The wrongs of the Native is an obsession with her.[184]

Bennett, equally determined and pugnacious, continued her campaign to restore the rights of Aboriginal families. In her 1957 publication, *Human Rights for Australian Aborigines*, she wrote:

> We robbed them of their land and their living resources together, and denied and destroyed their culture, without providing education to enable them to support themselves and their families and bring them into a different civilisation.[185]

With the more pressing and immediate problems of the war years the issue of the rights of Aboriginal children and mothers was shelved and eventually forgotten. Even Neville, writing from his retirement in 1947, appeared to have forgotten his earlier female foes and battles. He claimed that white women had failed Aboriginal women by not contributing to government inquiries or taking up positions in Aboriginal administrations and he referred only in passing to some limited organisational activity which he disparagingly described as based on 'exaggerated and inexact statements and faulty advice'.[186]

Following the publication of the *Bringing Them Home* report several conservative political leaders and intellectuals publicly asserted that removal practices were accepted practice in the past and that they went uncontested by earlier generations of Australians. Many members of the public uncritically accepted this claim. While not denying that many Australians did endorse the system or took little interest in what was happening to Aboriginal children, it is now clear that this blanket assertion is palpably false and that the issue was contested, albeit often in a patronising way, at various times in our past. Indeed, it is ludicrous and fallacious for politicians, with their day-to-day experience of negotiating compromise outcomes between vested interests, to blandly assert that a nation can adopt a unified stance on any issue, now or in the past. To privilege a single position which endorses past government action while obliterating the competing views of Aboriginal and other Australians is dishonest and undemocratic. Furthermore it is insulting to claim that white Australians who deeply value family life would have no qualms of conscience about breaking up families from the most disadvantaged section of the community simply because successive governments told them that this was 'for their own good'.

This raises the question of why the assertion has gained such wide currency in Australia. Certainly there is the matter of economic self-interest as governments seek to avoid massive compensation payouts by arguing that Aboriginal child removal was accepted practice and endorsed by previous generations of Australians. At a deeper level the answer may be found, as Fiona Paisley[187] suggests, in the strong defence in the present amongst many Anglo-Australians of the 'varying versions of assimilationism' which have powerfully shaped our society. Acknowledging a contested Aboriginal past profoundly challenges our comfortable and ingrained view of a 'homogenous past which unites "us all"'.[188] In this version of our past, experiences of Aboriginal people are erased through the inexorable processes of collective memory and forgetting, and the moulding influence of powerful national historical narratives which celebrate the achievements of 'settlers' and migrants in forging a nation out of an 'empty land'. In relation to the removal of Aboriginal children, Paisley argues that a contested past 'disturbs any easy either/or reading' of the motivations of non-Aboriginal 'men (and to a lesser extent women) officials, missionaries and others who formulated policy and/or participated in its administration'.[189] In the present, many Australians, including some of our political leaders, continue to endorse the goal of an assimilated way of life for all Australians and they are unwilling to consider the consequences and criticisms of past assimilationist policies and practices. It is easier to dismiss them, to forget the struggles and contests of the past and, by claiming that everyone agreed and tried to do their best, to bring about a comfortable sense of closure on the issue.

CHAPTER SIX

BROOMS, SPADES AND BIBLES[1]

Something else that never left my mind, my memory, was of a family of children being taken away and this little girl, she must have been about the same age as myself — suppose she might have been about six, as far as I can remember back — but I can still see that little person on the back of the mission truck with a little rag hat on, and she went away and we never seen her any more. She was crying, everyone was crying.

June Barker[2]

When we got to the mission, they told me that I'd have to have a wash ... they took me into this great big room ... they had a copper in there and ... I thought they were going to put me in this copper and boil me. The only time I'd seen boiling water was for puddings ... they scrubbed me with a scrubbing brush. It was hard. Then they cut all my hair. They cut my hair. That night, you know ... I didn't let anyone know, but I cried all night that night. I didn't want to stay there. I had beautiful long hair. I felt terrible ... the first night of going into the dormitory, the man comes along and he locks the door, with bars on the windows ... [I had] never been locked up before and I thought I was going to be in there forever.

Gertie Sambo[3]

In the many painful personal narratives told by members of the Stolen Generations there are always those heart-wrenching moments when the children were suddenly torn away from their families. Bundled into an official black car, they were driven off in a cloud of dust, their anguished faces peering out helplessly as their wailing mothers gradually disappeared from view. For most children this road ended at the gates of an institution. Here they began their new life. Exhausted and numb with grief and shock they were met by strangers who scrubbed them, roughly cut their hair and issued them with a drab set of clothes. This 're-grooming', to fit the children with institutional standards of dress and hygiene, was also intended to erase the outer vestiges of their former identity and individuality. As in other 'total institutions' such as prisons and mental asylums, this was the initial stage in a central process of re-creating each individual anew. The devastation experienced by adults stripped of their identity in this way has been represented in many films and novels — how much more traumatic were the experiences of these young and vulnerable children who did not understand what was happening to them or why, and who had no familiar cultural reference points to draw on apart from a terror instilled in them of this very fate by their families?

In most institutions the cut with the children's families and past was intended to be total. Many were told their parents were dead or did not want them and visits and correspondence were banned. A former resident of Cootamundra Aboriginal Girls Home claimed that family letters ended up in the 'garbage bin':

> And they were wondering why we didn't write. That was one way they stopped us keeping contact with our families. Then they had the hide to turn around and say, 'They don't love you. They don't care about you.'[4]

A former Yarrabah resident recalled the dizzying feeling of suddenly having no family, 'You got no parents. You got no parents to fight for ya. You just got to live. You got no mother ... father ... or relatives to stand by you.'[5] Children were often given new names and birth dates, making it virtually impossible for them ever to be reunited with their families. In some cases details were not recorded in the haste of removal, but, as in institutions for indigenous children in north America, the overall intent in renaming the children was assimilatory. European names undermined Aboriginality, blended the children nominally with other Australian children and linked them into western secular and Christian naming practices.[6] The children were also prohibited from speaking their own languages, a final onslaught on the membranous web linking them to family, culture and country. Literary analyst John Frow[7] concludes:

> in truth, these children [were] driven crazy, and part of their

craziness consist[ed] in the theft of the very language that would allow them to clarify and state the wrong done to them.

There is a genre of 'before and after' photographs of children taken for official purposes to document the narrative of successful transformation in these initial stages of institutionalisation.[8] These are found in various parts of the world and include nineteenth-century British working-class children, the 'Empire Children', children in former European colonies and indigenous children in North America and Australia. The children appear well scrubbed, adequately dressed and 'tamed', but a closer reading of their eyes and bodies tells of fear, blankness, withdrawal and the vertiginous feeling of having no past and few defences in a strange and alien new world. It is paradoxical, then, that while Aboriginal children felt so lonely and lost, they had in fact entered a whole new web of social relations, the institutional community of other children from near and far and their adult keepers. They had also become subjects of broader processes dedicated to the transformation of Aboriginal children — the carceral archipelago of institutions dotted across the continent and the extensive networks of bureaucracies, churches and mission and philanthropic societies committed to their reform. Here we examine these connections with the 'outside' and how they shaped the 'flavour' of the institutions; however, our primary focus is on the domestic reality in which the children were growing up and how this impacted on their lives.

INSTITUTIONAL CONTEXTS

As seen earlier, Aboriginal children were accommodated in a range of institutions — mainstream child welfare homes, Aboriginal children's homes and segregated living areas referred to as compounds or dormitories within larger multipurpose Aboriginal institutions. In some larger missions and settlements, particularly in northern Australia, children lived with their parents until they reached school age when they were transferred to the compound. Only a minority were allowed to grow up with their families. The type of institution reflected particular state and territory policies of the time. Victoria and Tasmania sent all children to child welfare institutions. New South Wales ran three major Aboriginal children's homes and provided dormitory accommodation on some managed stations. Western

Australia, Queensland and the Northern Territory opted principally for children's compounds within multipurpose state or mission institutions; and South Australia sent children to child welfare institutions, Aboriginal children's homes and missions. In all states, some very fair-skinned children were sent to child welfare homes. Jimmie Barker

The 'making do' accommodation of the UAM Mission at Oodnadatta in 1924.

(Courtesy of Australian Institute of Aboriginal and Torres Strait Islander Studies, UAM.1bw)

states that his people lumped all the institutional forms they had lived through into a single category — 'the mission' — a 'type of Aboriginal slang' signifying a common experience of 'negative memories of a repressive regime'.[9] Historian Charles Rowley agrees that all were variations of the same 'disruptive pattern of white settlement'.[10] The Aboriginal children's homes and the compounds can be similarly categorised together — certainly, from the point of view of the children, they had much in common.

The *Bringing Them Home* report[11] clearly demonstrates the commonality of children's institutional experience across Australia. In the Aboriginal children's homes and the compounds they were penned into segregated quarters where they lived, learned and worked in close proximity to their keepers while they had little or no contact with their families, other Aboriginal people or the outside world. They were subjected to a range of processes intended to transform them into the image of their 'captors'. The same dominant ideologies of white superiority shaped institutional goals of 'Christianising and civilising', the strategies adopted to achieve these goals and the very limited expectations held for the children. There were the same nominal motivations — the familiar rhetoric of 'rescue and reform' where the children were to be saved from the dangers and temptations of the outside world and Aboriginality erased and replaced with Christian values and traditions. New individualities were to be formed along with new social groupings of family, household and community. And there were the same preoccupations

The imposing Girls Dormitory at Barambah (Cherbourg) opened in 1928.
(Courtesy of John Oxley Library, 59630)

— economy, expediency, control and the grinding destitution of daily life peculiar to institutions everywhere. Child welfare institutions taking in Aboriginal children were similarly constructed, and embodied the same prejudices, while creating an even greater degree of separation from Aboriginal backgrounds and identities. Of course there *were* differences between the Aboriginal children's homes and the institutional compounds. While children in the compounds often had some, albeit strictly supervised, contact with adults and family in the adjacent Aboriginal camps, those in the children's homes were totally cut off from Aboriginal adults. Indeed children at the Bomaderry Infants Home 'were cut off from the rest of the world — we barely saw anybody.'[12] The homes dealt *only* with children and did not have to juggle their needs with other pressing problems of sick, elderly and unemployed adults. As young adults, their charges *had* to find their way in the world, while those from the compounds often married, moved to the institution camp or village and lived out their lives there.

In many ways institutional life was a microcosm of what the children could expect of their future lives as adults inside the institutions or outside in the wider community. The dynamics were not simply those of isolated rural or mining communities, as some have argued[13], although there were many parallels. There was only an outer resemblance to the organic image of the nineteenth-century Aboriginal mission, Ramahyuck, painted by historian Bain Attwood,[14] where all had their allotted tasks and duties in the 'whole machinery' of the place. Certainly duties were laid out and tasks enforced, but the institutions were riddled with peculiar tensions which created an underlying chaos and craziness evoked by Aboriginal writer Alexis Wright in *Plains of Promise*, a fictional account of life in an Aboriginal mission in the Queensland Gulf country. The frustration of staff and the resistance of their charges is evoked in the following excerpt from the novel. It is Saturday and the missionary Errol Jipp is mowing his lawn while the old people sit hopefully near the rations shed which is closed for the weekend.

> He is angry they are sitting there in the dirt in the heat. They always do it. Sit in the sun for nothing. He continues to mow ... Faster and faster — nothing will stop him. Red-faced with exhaustion he tries not to notice the old men. But he does. Errol Jipp's God keeps willing him to help the old ones ... But he won't go yet. He is sick of telling them. Let them sit there. Angrily he stays on his side of the dust bowl and mows on. They sit silently, separately, until midday. Then they get up and walk back again over the scorched dusty track. Empty-handed. Independence intact. Another successful protest against whiteman's time.[15]

The institutions were crisscrossed by barriers, separations and distances — social, spatial, linguistic, cultural, racial, gendered and bureaucratic — which created peculiarly high levels of stress, fear, hostility and stereotyping. Aboriginal writers Lilla Watson and Mary Graham argue that conflict is endemic in such systems so that participants are 'emotionally, psychologically and physically harmed and the fear which dominates this process leads to magnifications and distortions in the imagination.'[16]

Aboriginal institutions came under the direct control of small centralised state bureaucracies. Their policies, laws and processes set operational parameters, determined funding levels and provided a modest system of supervision. The institutions had no direct links with or responsibilities to any other state departments or agencies. This system was simplistic and skeletal compared to the complex administrative structures controlling Native American residential schools in the United States of America,

Kinchela Aboriginal Boys Home, opened in 1918.
(Courtesy of New South Wales State Records, 4/8566 COD 423 8806)

347

which facilitated professional inputs from specialist agencies in child welfare, health and education and allowed for closer external surveillance.[17] This reflected the benefits of federal government control and generous funding of Indian Affairs over the parochial and stingy state administrations in Australia. Aboriginal administrations were isolated, stagnant backwaters, cut off from professional and specialist practice in relation to children. The needs of children's institutions were treated as simply another expenditure item in a wide terrain of duties. In consequence, economy and expediency were invariably the primary considerations in planning. There were also serious flaws in the overall management and supervision of the institutions. Without formal training or instruction manuals to direct staff in their duties or regular inspections to ensure standards were met, institutions inevitably failed to meet even minimum standards of care. This raises serious questions about governments' failure to fulfil their 'duty of care' to Aboriginal children under their guardianship. Left largely to their own devices, and battling against often insurmountable odds, many institutions developed a pronounced 'them and us' attitude to government, most evident in the frequently strained relations between the state and missions.

MISSIONS

The *Bringing Them Home* report identified a strong 'symbiotic' relationship between government and missions: governments removed the children and the missions took them in. This was an acceptable compromise for both, although it went against the trend at the time towards secularisation of child welfare services. Choo[18] argues further that, through their 'encouragement and compliance', church agencies also contributed to emerging government policy and legislation. The continued role of the missions meant that the high operational costs of running large institutions, particularly in remote areas where most missions were located, could be reduced through a combination of low government subsidies (some missions received none at all), mission and church financial contributions, and zealous staff prepared to work in difficult conditions for low wages. The missions could not operate without state endorsement or official approval to enter Aboriginal camps and reserves, nor without resources, financial subsidies and the allocation of state land for mission bases. Children sent in by the government brought further subsidies and boosted mission numbers, enabling the working out of the central project of 'civilising and Christianising' Aboriginal children.

Nevertheless, relations between government and missions were often uneasy. In contrast to the relatively independent operation of the financially well-endowed missions in the Pacific, Africa and Asia, Aboriginal missions were kept on a tight rein. They were expected to conform to government policies and directives, regardless of what staff considered was in the best interests of their 'flock'. Dependent on the state for their survival, they reluctantly toed the line. Reflecting sectarian divisions in Australian society and government, authorities favoured mainstream Protestant missions which they expected would conform to official expectations. Nevertheless there were always conflicts over agendas and aims. Which children should be 'rescued'? Did their future lie outside in the wider community or in segregated institutions? Which Aboriginal traditions should be allowed and which should be stamped out? How much effort and funding should be devoted to Aboriginal children? There was a multitude of responses to these questions and considerable disagreement between governments and missions over the years.

Indeed there was considerable difference of opinion between state and territory administrations over mission involvement. Queensland Chief Protector of Aborigines, John Bleakley, welcomed the missions and wrote in his report to the federal government on conditions in the Northern Territory in 1929:

the cost of management is less and the missions can obtain the kind of workers who undertake the work from missionary, and not mercenary motives and is likely to have more sympathy with the people.[19]

By contrast, the Northern Territory Chief Protector, Dr Cecil Cook, was openly antagonistic:

missionaries appear to be working in a maze. Their controlling bodies are, for the most part, unaware of local conditions and unfamiliar with the aboriginal problem. They vest little authority in their local officer but, on the other hand give him very inadequate instructions. Each newcomer appears to evolve for himself a plan of campaign ... Every change of staff disorganises the existing policy, if any, so eventually a status quo is reached, which involves the continuance of minor routines and nothing more. Conscientious adherence to this routine is a conspicuous feature of several missions, but the ultimate objective of the missions' purpose is not known and conflict of opinion was evident [during inspections] as to what should be done.[20]

The Chief Protector of Aborigines in Western Australia, A O Neville, himself the son of an Anglican cleric, was perhaps the missions' harshest critic. In retirement he wrote, 'I sometimes wondered whether the missions were needed for the blacks — to convert them to Christianity, or the blacks for the missions — to create a job for someone.'[21] He recalled that his first visit to a Kimberley mission 'shocked me beyond measure. Ye Gods! were these the romantic fields — the "spicy breezes" — I had dreamed of?'[22] Soon after his appointment funding for Catholic missions was withdrawn and children's missions in the south were closed and replaced by state settlements. From the late 1920s Neville became embroiled in open feuds with missionaries who refused to send children out to work as directed; who interfered in local marriage systems, resulting in conflict and violence in the mission communities; and, in the case of the Anglican Forrest River Mission in the far north Kimberley, inflicted inhumane punishments and tolerated terrible living conditions for their charges. In 1938 Neville launched an all-out attack on missions in the state, with allegations of physical and sexual abuse by mission staff, of staff fighting and drinking alcohol and even the shooting of an inmate by a missionary during an attempted 'escape'. He endeavoured to push through draconian new powers to regulate the operation of the missions, which his Minister was forced to defend in the face of an outcry from missions and churches:

> We claim that the natives are first and foremost a charge upon the State, whoever may subsequently be delegated more directly to handle them, and our duty is to ensure that the job is efficiently undertaken by those best qualified to do it.[23]

A mission counterattack levelled similar allegations about conditions in government settlements and, in the face of mounting public opposition, the proposed regulations were dropped. Despite Neville's retirement in 1940 relations remained strained until the appointment of Commissioner Middleton in 1948, who advocated cooperation and transferred the remaining government institutions to mission control or closed them down. Writing with the benefit of hindsight, Rowley observes that whether institutions were under mission or state control really made little difference in the end:

> the mission settlement inevitably became like the government settlement ... Both exhibited the tensions and irritations of the closed isolated institution where the staff dominate the clients.[24]

Missionaries have been typically portrayed in broad sweeping brushstrokes — saintly and all-suffering agents of God and civilisation, well-meaning but eccentric and irritating proselytisers or 'racist agents of imperialism'.[25] In fact, they were a diverse range of individuals with varying denominational and cultural backgrounds and often conflicting perspectives on Aboriginal issues and relations with the state and other colonising enterprises. The Aboriginal mission field encompassed a range of churches and mission societies. While the major denominations were represented, their energies were directed to the more exotic and 'successful' missions overseas and in the Torres Strait. A former missionary, Patricia Harrison, recalled that Aboriginal missions 'were very poorly supported by church people — perhaps an indication of the general disregard for Aboriginal people.'[26] The gap was filled in part by overseas missionaries such as the German Moravians, German and American Lutherans, Spanish Benedictines, Austrian Jesuits, French Trappists, German Pallottines, Italian Passionists and the Irish Sisters of Saint John of God. Their organisational and personal networks spread awareness of Aborigines well beyond the shores of Australia. There were also openings for more peripheral evangelical organisations: the Australian Inland Mission, United Aborigines Mission, the Brethren and the Seventh Day Adventists.

While 'missionary' conjures up the image of an intrepid white man in the company of 'dark savages', Australian mission endeavour included a considerable but, until recently, largely unacknowledged contribution by white women and Aboriginal and Islander men and women. With the worldwide feminisation of mission work during the nineteenth century, white middle-class women had come to dominate in mission fields around the world. They typically assumed the roles of caring for the children and young people and of introducing women to western ways of child-rearing and family life. Their very presence was deemed a civilising influence[27] as they re-created an atmosphere of Christian family life and provided models of domesticity and feminine behaviour for Aboriginal girls and women. The belief that Christianity improved the lives of 'heathen' women was deeply ingrained in missionary thinking around the world. Women in the Indian subcontinent were portrayed as 'victims of barbaric cultural customs from which they needed help to escape', and schools run by some women missionaries encouraged a new 'feminist' consciousness in local women and produced the first Indian women professionals.[28] Endeavours in Australia followed more conservative models of self-sacrificing 'good wives and mothers' devoted to the Christian faith and the family.

Ironically, women missionaries had to struggle within their own patriarchal hierarchies for status and recognition of their contributions and they were sometimes ridiculed for their work by the outside world. United Aborigines Mission (UAM) worker Annie Lock was exceptional in being called on to fill demanding roles negotiating between state and local stake holders on behalf of Aboriginal interests. Most women missionaries played a more conventional and submissive role. Nailon[29] argues that this approach, of working in an 'inconspicuous way through daily relationships between people', enabled Catholic nuns at Beagle Bay Mission to establish close working relationships with their charges. Anthropologist Dianne Bell observed that nuns working with Tiwi women on Bathurst Island provided a vision of womanhood that was both new and familiar to Tiwi women:

> Like the Fathers they professed celibacy. Unlike some white women they undertook any task necessary for survival. They maintained an independence of spirit. Unlike missionaries' wives who passed on information to their husbands, the nuns could be trusted with women's secrets. They provided a cultural analogue to the Tiwi gender-based separation of tasks.[30]

Aboriginal and Islander men and women played a significant role as workers and as role models for mission charges albeit, like white women, from the edges of mission authority structures. Some were brought in from outside. In north Queensland, South Sea Islander, Willie Ambyn, and Aborigine, Pompo Katechewan, worked beside Reverend John Gribble in establishing Yarrabah Mission in the early

1890s.[31] At the Anglican Lockhart Mission, Torres Strait Islander men and women taught and preached to Aborigines providing 'great practical help' and an 'example ... of untold benefit'.[32] Missions also sought recruits from local communities, often focusing on children as the 'plastic wax'[33] from which to create a 'fifth column' of workers to win converts to Christianity. Some

Reverend James Noble, nd.
(Courtesy of Battye Library, 4383B–102)

Aboriginal missionaries had been taken as children and educated in white institutions and were able to rise to more significant positions within the family of the church. Born in the Gulf country in Queensland, James Noble was educated at Scone Grammar School and then worked as a missionary with his wife Angelina at Yarrabah, Mitchell River and Forrest River missions. He became the first ordained Anglican Aboriginal minister.[34] In 1939 Bishop Rabile of Broome established the Native Sisters, an Aboriginal order of nuns, with novices selected from girls reared at Beagle Bay who were accustomed to communal life and religious devotions. The choice of apostolate — the new Pallottine mission at Balgo in remote desert country near the Northern Territory border — was unfortunate and the order soon ceased. Concern for the 'hopeless outlook' of Aboriginal youth motivated Kathleen Jones to join the Anglican Church Army and to return to work with the children at Moore River where she had herself grown up.[35] The tensions that Aboriginal mission workers could experience working in this way with their own people were described by Connie Nungulla McDonald[36] who grew up and worked at Forrest River Mission:

> Unfortunately, my people, especially the dormitory girls, did not take kindly to my becoming a member of the mission staff because this meant I ceased to be one of them. To me, of course, this was not

true. I was still Connie McDonald, the same girl who had left the mission two years earlier for Alice Springs. They feared that I would become flash and not want to associate with them any more, and they assumed that because I had had a little more education, it would set me apart from them.

THE OUTSIDE WORLD

Institutional populations looking outwards frequently saw themselves as separate from and in opposition to local white and Aboriginal communities. Staff in particular, perhaps reflecting their own feelings of difference and isolation, often saw the institution as a small friendly pocket in a hostile, dangerous and immoral hinterland. But the institutions *were* part of the local social landscape and, while not always welcome, they were linked to local communities through ties with police, medical officers, employers, local parishes, suppliers and businesses. Open hostility often characterised relations between institutions and local economic interests competing for cheap land and Aboriginal labour. At Yarrabah, Reverend Ernest Gribble, who took over from his father John who died soon after establishing the mission, frustrated efforts to take over mission land by strategically establishing Aboriginal residential outposts across the reserve. During the 1930s missionaries at Doomadgee were ostracised by local whites when they disrupted an exploitative labour system involving pastoral employers and government officers, by pressing for proper rates of pay for Aboriginal workers and encouraging them to work at the mission instead.[37] The xenophobia and hysteria of the war years led to extreme punitive treatment of German Lutheran and Catholic missionaries who were accused of espionage and interned, and strenuous efforts were made to close the missions down altogether. In May 1942 the Hopevale Lutheran Mission was evacuated without notice, the mission site and crops levelled, and Aboriginal residents were trucked hundreds of miles south to Palm Island and Woorabinda where sixty of them died soon afterwards.[38] Institutions in more closely settled areas, such as Barambah Aboriginal Settlement in south-eastern Queensland and Carrolup and Moore River Native Settlements in the south of Western Australia, rode an uneasy line between begrudging acceptance by white communities and outbursts of racism grounded in their fears about threats to health, and law and order from proximity to large numbers of Aborigines. Children were generally kept strictly segregated from the outside; however, those at Sister Kate's in Perth attended the local state school and at holiday times could be selected to go home with a Perth family. According to testimony collected by the Aboriginal Legal Service in Western Australia in 1995, these largely unsupervised arrangements led in some instances to physical and sexual abuse of the children. Other outings showed children how they were regarded by outsiders. A woman who lived at the Dulhi Gunyah Children's Home in Perth recalled:

> When we had to go down to church we marched in twos with a lady on the side. Some of the white girls used to be cheeky — they used to sing out when they saw the girls marching along: 'All the niggers in navy blue.' Some of those girls used to come to church too, you know, they were church people. They used to poke tongues out and cheek the Aboriginal girls.[39]

While the Australian public was generally uninterested in the institutions there was nevertheless widespread awareness of their existence and their work with the children. This public knowledge was strictly controlled through government censorship of information, controls over staff, restrictions on visitors, harassment of persons speaking out, and officially orchestrated imagery and propaganda in government publications and the press. Major Queensland newspapers routinely reported on the round of life at Barambah and the achievements of its inmates under white tutelage.[40] Ironically, given their assimilatory goals, government institutions often used Aboriginal cultural performances such as spear throwing and corroborees to entertain official guests and to create 'good public relations':

> Journalists 'investigating' conditions at Moore River were invariably impressed by the colourful spectacle of a staged corroboree. These command performances often formed part of a lengthy concert programme of skits, songs and dances.[41]

Institutions also produced a significant literature devoted to justifying and shoring up their existence, in particular through requests for further funding, a sphere of continuous endeavour for missionaries desperate to persuade the wider community to donate funds, labour, support and prayers. This literature had its own conventions:

Missionaries seek to confirm the purpose and sincerity of their efforts, yet need to present a sufficiently grim picture of heathen conditions and the struggle of evangelisation to promote more support from home — but always with enough glimmers of success to encourage enthusiasm.[42]

To this end, accounts of the 'rescue' and conversion of children proved 'a master stroke of strategy', these 'tiny bits of human salvage' gave 'compelling persuasive power to mission propaganda'.[43] The UAM imperative that missionaries be self-supporting meant that they were obliged to devote a considerable part of their working and furlough time to fundraising. Mission newsletters and magazines, public lectures, addresses to mission conferences, lantern slide evenings, concerts, visits to congregations accompanied by their young charges, and exhibitions of their work were all opportunities to extol the fruits of their labour and to recount instances of success which glossed over the disarray of much of their work. Annie Lock wrote in the UAM magazine, *Australian Aborigines' Advocate*, of children at Sunday Island Mission in the Kimberley who 'sang hymns, and one girlie preached a sermon in English on John 3:16'.[44] A little girl at Katanning in the south of Western Australia would 'gather the children together and hold a service, Laura acting

the part of Teacher or Missionary.'[45] Yarrabah circulated its own newsletter, *The Aboriginal News*, and its annual reports to the Australian Board of Missions (ABM) were published. The contents of the 1909 report are instructive: there are ten and a half pages on staff, agricultural and other industrial activities and requests for specific items including an organ for the mission church, and only one page devoted to the children, with no reference at all to the adults.[46] This fitted the vision of

Images used by UAM missionaries in fundraising public lectures, 1930–40.
(Courtesy of Australian Institute of Aboriginal and Torres Strait Islander Studies, UAM 1bw)

successful mission work — material progress, donations well used, growing self-sufficiency leading to reduced financial support, an increasing settled civilised mission population and evidence of conversions. In addition to this public material, many women missionaries were inveterate letter writers, keeping in touch with distant friends and soliciting funds and support through Christian and other women's networks at home and abroad.

WHO WAS LOOKING AFTER THE CHILDREN?

Given their existence, in hindsight what the institutions needed was caring staff, preferably Aboriginal, with specialist skills and a commitment to working with Aboriginal children with their different cultural and social backgrounds, the trauma of separation from their families and the fear and resentment of their new status and their white keepers. In truth it seemed that nobody really knew what to do or what skills and qualifications were required, as a former staff member at Moore River acknowledged:

357

I think everyone was completely ignorant about how to handle the situation ... certainly the government didn't know how to handle it. They were suddenly stuck with a race of people who was here, who was not supposed to be here.[47]

The institutions provided the example of formal authority figures — Superintendents, Managers, Matrons, Instructors, Children's Assistants — with largely supervisory, administrative and disciplinary duties. Writing in 1895, Archibald Meston outlined the qualities of the ideal type of superintendent (sounding remarkably like himself) to oversee the successful establishment and operation of Aboriginal institutions — a man with a 'strong physique' who could 'stand apart ... with the absolute authority to order work to be done, tolerating no disobedience, always kind, dignified and firm; stern and severe if necessary.'[48] The 1909 Yarrabah ABM Report listed the following ideal staff qualities for matrons:

A woman who could lead others, firm and fair, tactful and jolly, sympathetic and patient, 'with no nerves' and above all an intense love for the girls and their Master and with 'God's own commonsense' is the sort we need for our work. And there is a field of usefulness and interest which such a woman would go far to find surpassed.[49]

Even these limited ideals were seldom realised as work conditions and community attitudes made it impossible to attract suitably qualified and experienced staff. Sister Eileen Heath, Anglican deaconess at Moore River from 1935, recalled that 'anybody could apply for a job, and anybody could get it. Whether they had any training or experience or not, it didn't make any difference.'[50] This should have been a matter of concern to authorities responsible for the children given the vast powers of staff over their charges. Aboriginal activist William Ferguson told a Select Committee in New South Wales in 1937 that superintendents and managers wielded powers:

greater than any other public servant in Australia. I say that no public officer, no magistrate, or no other man, I do not believe the King of England, has power under British law to try a man ... or woman, find them guilty and sentence them without giving them a fair and open trial and without producing any evidence to convict.[51]

While no one would deny that there were kind and noble staff, it is also the case, as John Harris[52] points out in his history of Aboriginal missions in Australia, that these sweeping powers encouraged 'more authoritarian, domineering people or the missions tended to attract this kind of person ... Somehow having control over people's lives changed them.'

Through their largely unpaid and forced labour, Aboriginal residents also played a significant role in the operation of the institutions and in keeping running costs at a minimum. The children also spent long hours doing chores, often at the expense of their schooling and leisure time. Colebrook Children's Home had a staff of two and a shoestring budget and the thirty children living there carried out most of the daily tasks, as former resident Nancy Barnes recalls:

> We all had to help in the work of the Home — we each made our own bed but one child was responsible for the overall appearance of the dormitory ... We took turns in sweeping out the dormitory and mopping. The girls did baby duty, looking after the babies and feeding them. The boys were responsible for wood chopping, bringing in the wood, and filling up the boilers on the stoves. We all helped in the kitchen and dining room, setting up the tables, washing up, wiping down tables, sweeping out the dining room ... Kitchen duties were helping the older girls do the vegetables, cutting bread, making sandwiches the night before school.[53]

Many staff in both state and mission institutions came from a religious background and had a shared zeal for mission work with Aboriginal people. Although they were employed on government stations, Charles and Elsie Burrage 'shared the strong feeling that it was a good thing to go to a different race and bring the light of the Gospel and help them physically too.'[54] Indeed in their roles as manager, matron and teacher they were expected to fulfil a 'missionary-like role' by improving the Aborigines 'mode of living', raising 'the moral and social tone' exercising 'sympathetic discipline' and so on.[55]

In selecting superintendents for state institutions preference was given to persons with previous experience working in institutions, with other 'native peoples' or in the army, or with a background in cattle raising and agriculture. Aboriginal writer Jack Davis provided the following description of Arthur J Neal, Superintendent of Moore River settlement during the 1920s:

> Superintendent Neal had been given his position because of his experience with the native people in South Africa during the Boer War and he had a colonial mentality ... Neal was a product of the *Boy's Own* mentality ... He was around five-foot-ten and military in appearance, with an upright stance, square shoulders, no middle age spread, and a severe angular face, adorned by a handlebar moustache waxed to a point at each end. When it trembled, the moustache signalled the depth of emotion behind his generally passive face, and its twitching was usually the first indication of his displeasure. He invariably wore light-grey or khaki trousers, supported at the waist by a wide brown belt reminiscent of an army webbing belt.[56]

Nepotism and patronage were evident in the selection of superintendents in southern Queensland during Meston's term as Southern Protector of Aborigines. He appointed his son Harold as Superintendent of Fraser Island in 1897 and Harold's brother-in-law Albert Tronson, a former grocer's clerk, as Superintendent of Durundur in 1901. From 1905 to 1906 Tronson was Superintendent of Barambah. While there he was investigated on several counts of defrauding settlement property which were dismissed due to insufficient evidence. He was subsequently found to have misused his authority for his own benefit by sending Aboriginal workers to labour on land selected by his wife near the settlement. The extensive improvements to the property included '80 acres of corn ... 20 acres of other land on which the scrub had been fallen or the trees ringbarked; a hardwood house and another house in the course of construction.' Meanwhile cultivation at Barambah remained minimal. Although Tronson resigned from his position he was not charged with any offence or ordered to recover materials and goods used on his selection, although just two months earlier two Aboriginal residents had been jailed for six months for stealing dogs.[57]

A track record of incompetence was no bar to appointment. L R Samut, Superintendent of Kahlin Compound in Darwin from 1934 to 1937, lost his position as government clerk in 1928 due to his unsatisfactory performance and was then found negligent in fulfilling his duties as gaol guard in the Northern Territory Prisons Branch.[58]

Evidence of mental instability and inordinately punitive and authoritarian rule were no bar either. Reverend Ernest Gribble was left to run Yarrabah and then Forrest River Mission between 1893 and 1928, despite his known debilitating bouts of depression and mental exhaustion, his despotic treatment of staff — at Yarrabah he seized a staff member who questioned his authority 'by the neck and the seat of his pants and dropped him over the edge of the verandah to the ground'[59] — and his frequently inhumane treatment of his Aboriginal charges, documented in a report by anthropologist A P Elkin to the ABM, which prompted Gribble's resignation in 1928. He was subsequently appointed Anglican Chaplain at Palm Island from 1930 to 1957. His son John 'Jack' Gribble was left in charge of Forrest River until 1930 when he was dismissed following reports of floggings and degrading punishments of children and sexual offences by staff at the mission. He then went on to work with Aborigines in the Northern Territory.[60] An inquiry in 1935 into allegations concerning the manager of Kinchela Aboriginal Boys Home led only to a reprimand in a private letter and to warnings that:

> He must not be drunk on duty. He must no longer use a stockwhip on the boys, nor tie them up. He was not to use dietary punishments. He had to keep a punishment register and he was no longer allowed to send the boys out to labour on local farms.[61]

He was later transferred to Cumeroongunja Aboriginal Station.

While farm assistants and mechanics had to be qualified and experienced, there were no such requirements to work with the children, apart from whiteness and the appropriate gender. Queensland governments did endeavour to appoint qualified schoolteachers, but this was the exception. The anthropologist N B Tindale reported in 1940 that he had found children in institutions in the south being taught by a 'soldier, ship's mate, pastry cook [and] manager's daughter.'[62] A former nursing assistant at Moore River, Joy Mort recalled:

> I was out of work. I used to read the daily papers to look for a job, a suitable kind of job. I wasn't trained in anything in particular. I looked up the newspaper [and saw] 'Nursing Assistant wanted by Native Affairs' so I applied. I wasn't asked for any qualifications, just 'When would you like to start?' 'As soon as possible' I said. 'Can you be on the train tomorrow? You'll escort an Aboriginal

woman up with you.' We got on the train together and went up there. There were no qualifications wanted.[63]

In keeping with constructions of femininity of the time, white women generally took on the roles of caring for the children and young people,[64] although men often looked after the older boys. The women were wives or daughters of male staff or single missionaries and nuns, who rarely had any experience of children apart from their own family domestic backgrounds. The expectation that they would be role models for dormitory girls meant strict controls over their own dress and codes of behaviour. Contacts with men were strictly circumscribed and friendships with Aboriginal men were unthinkable. Although Ernest Gribble devoted his life to working with Aboriginal people, he reacted with horror when his sister Ethel married an Aboriginal man at Yarrabah whom she had loved in secret for many years. Her name was subsequently scrubbed from the mission records.[65]

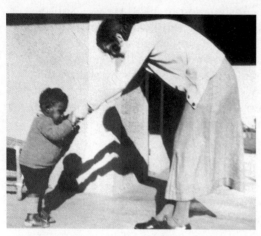

Female workers often took over the maternal role from Aboriginal mothers.
Colebrook Home, Quorn, South Australia, 1936.
(Courtesy of Australian Institute of Aboriginal and Torres Strait Islander Studies, UAM.1bw)

The women carried out conventional female roles while male staff organised, led, administered and worked with the Aboriginal men. The many demands on their time were recalled by Reverend Alfred Dyer of Oenpelli Mission:

> Mrs Dyer cooked, fed and clothed the growing family with what stores they had. She did all the medical work and started a small school with eleven children speaking five languages. Her sewing machine was often going until 10 pm ... Once when she was working in the garden, Dyer heard one of the Aboriginal women say: 'Is she a white woman? She makes her hands like ours.' He

went on to say: 'So as she cooked and worked with them they began to wash their babies and be uplifted by her love. Soon they were calling her, 'Mother.' Truly God gave me a good partner. It would have been an impossible task on my own.'[66]

Their relationships with Aboriginal mothers and children were ambiguous and fraught with potential hostilities. They were breaking bonds between mothers and their children by taking over the maternal role, and they were agents of change, intent on disrupting Aboriginal gender relations in their bid to 'save' the women from what they saw as the immorality and brutality of their lives. Depending on individual staff personalities and commitment to their work, these tensions could be aggravated or smoothed over. The missionaries who ran Colebrook Home in South Australia from 1927 to 1952, Ruby Hyde and Delia Rutter, were remembered with affection by former resident Nancy Barnes: 'We were very fortunate in having these two women ... They were dedicated, committed; they lived for the children, who became their family.'[67] Similarly, many children at Moore River and at St Mary's Hostel at Alice Springs grew to love Sister Eileen Heath. Connie Nungulla McDonald remembered:

Moore River Native Settlement, 1930s.

(Courtesy of Mogumber Heritage Committee of the Wheatbelt Aboriginal Corporation, 667)

I always felt at ease with Sister Eileen and had no trouble speaking openly with her. She accepted that some of us were rebels (including me!) and saw her task as being to direct that rebellion rather than to crush it. She was a strict and efficient missionary, who was mother, friend, confidante and spiritual leader all rolled into one. She was quietly spoken, sensitive to the racism that surrounded us and always telling us that we should hold our heads up in adversity and be proud of not only who we were but of what we were. Her quiet sense of humour must have helped her cope with many difficult situations.[68]

For some children, like Alicia Adams who was raised in a 'church home', there was also an inherent confusion in these relationships:

I never knew I had a mother or a father. I just thought Mum [matron] was my mum, you know my white mum and I thought all the ladies were my real aunties, because they were all white and I really loved them you know, each one of them.

Looking back, many former child inmates acknowledge the ties binding them and their female carers. Monica Mushiwun, who was raised by the nuns at Daly River Mission, stated:

Today we still have feelings for them because for many reasons that was the only way we learnt to communicate with white Australians. All that time we spent with them we learnt more about Europeans and their society in this world.[69]

Agnes Palmer had similar memories of mission staff at Santa Teresa Catholic Mission south-east of Alice Springs:

The image that I had of the priests and the nuns and the brothers was that they were people who were there who cared for us, who looked after us, who educated us. I accepted that, but looking back you could find out all the pain, the hurtful stories. You appreciate them for what they've done, but then you still feel anger — angry at myself that it happened, for being led.[70]

Aboriginal and Islander women and men working as dormitory attendants and in the cookhouse and laundry, like dormitory mother and father, Maudie Mulgal and Butchan in the early days of Cape Bedford (later Hopevale) Lutheran Mission, were also remembered with deep affection.[71] The children's memories of the Aboriginal 'police' appointed to maintain discipline in some larger institutions were more conflicted. This reflected the contradictory nature of these positions in the institutional structure. The 'police' were in many ways typical of institutional 'trusties' who gain 'kicks' from their powers over their peers and yet are also victims of the system. Inmate resentment is frequently directed at them rather than at the holders of real authority, while these same figures look down on them and often treat them with contempt.[72] Historian Susan Maushart[73] states that

Aboriginal police at Moore River saw themselves more positively as Aboriginal men who were imposing justice and discipline. The memories of boys at Moore River show a curious mix of fear, contempt, admiration and even gratitude to them. Some recalled that they looked up to the police as Aboriginal role models and believed in hindsight that they had imposed valuable lessons in discipline. Others bitterly resented the punishments they meted out.

Aboriginal women's work was significant in the operation of large institutions like Moore River Native Settlement.

(Courtesy of Mogumber Heritage Committee of the Wheatbelt Aboriginal Corporation, 839)

Staff operated in very trying conditions and this could impact negatively on their work with the children. They were called on to fill a multiplicity of roles and worked long and exhausting hours for low pay. Depending on the size of the institution, the matron could be called on to fill the roles of teacher, nurse and children's assistant. Queensland institutions, designed to develop into permanent segregated communities, built up quite large staff numbers with store-keepers, medical staff and supervisors for settlement industries. By the 1930s Barambah had fourteen permanent white staff; however the settlement population had also expanded and the ratio of staff to inmates had changed little from the 1905 figure of one staff member for every seventy-eight inmates.[74] The federal government made no pretence of even trying to maintain acceptable numbers of supervisory staff. When activist Mary Bennett visited Kahlin Compound in Darwin in 1930 she found two white staff in charge of seventy children, 120 young working men and women, and eighty adults, many of them sick and elderly.[75] At Forrest River Mission in the 1930s one matron was responsible for seventy girls aged from six to twenty years.[76] Staff living conditions, although better than those of their charges, were spartan. Like the children, they had to contend with the isolation and loneliness and the stresses of being thrown together with strangers in a remote place with all the power struggles, favouritisms, attractions and jealousies, bureaucratic regulations and personal antagonisms as well as the division between staff and inmates, reinforced by race fears and boundaries. There were also the tensions of living in cross-cultural situations with people undergoing rapid social change, and of leading a life marginal to both white and Aboriginal communities, with accompanying feelings of loss of identity and homesickness. The climate in the remote north brought threats of tropical disease, childhood illnesses, complications during pregnancy, debility and death. Indeed, their own children were a particular cause of concern for staff. How could they be protected from the epidemics that swept through the communities? Iris Wiley, a UAM missionary at Swan Reach in South Australia, protected her children from the ravages of whooping cough and tuberculosis in the Aboriginal camp by only allowing them to play with Aboriginal children in the precincts of the mission house.[77] There were also concerns about allowing the children to mix with Aboriginal children. Charles and Elsie Burrage's children played with the reserve children but:

> always felt a difference, the difference between the dark children and ourselves, and when I come to think about it I realise how it was emphasised by our parents all the time. It had to be. There had to be a line always: what you do and what they do.[78]

Given such conditions one wonders why anyone would agree to work in these institutions. In the absence of any critical survey of workers' opinions we are left to read carefully between the lines of the records. Research by sociologist Dave Palmer[79] into youth workers involved with Nyungar youth in Perth during the early 1990s, suggests possible motivations for workers in institutions earlier in the century. He identified a number of motivations grounded in complex attitudinal views of Aboriginal people that were adopted and abandoned and even held simultaneously over the youth workers' period of employment: the drive to 'rescue and reform' whether motivated by impulses of Christianity, social justice or guilt; Christian renunciation of the world and self-sacrifice; economic and personal advantage; the desire to contain and control Aborigines; escape from the conventions of white society; and an attraction to the exotic, the Other, the primitive.

Many women staff were motivated by the drive to 'rescue and

reform' the children and would have agreed with the sentiments expressed by Sister Lloyd, a Wesleyan missionary in New Guinea:

I thought ... it was worth a lifetime to help shield the lives of little children growing up, and the prospect of that would help me to bear the climate, separation, and what else towards this end.[80]

Many genuinely loved the children and, like UAM missionary Iris Wiley, were aware of the importance of this caring attitude:

unless you can really love those people and go and sit with them you might as well stop home because they sense whether you can touch them or love them or whatever.[81]

Patricia Gregory, who taught at Forrest River Mission in the 1940s, wrote of her strong affection for the children (although Connie Nungulla McDonald points out that her attitude was exceptional):

I am beginning to realise the difficulties here, but also the opportunities. I love the children, and long to be able to make their lives a little better than their parents can hope for. Why shouldn't they become an independent and flourishing community? If only we white Australians realised the debt we owe them and really made an effort to help them instead of salving our consciences by doling out rations of tea and flour and dreadful-looking clothes we wouldn't be seen dead in ourselves.[82]

Despite strong feelings for the children, few workers were immune from the sense of white superiority or the hard unbending determination and arrogance that often accompanied the mission of 'rescue and reform'. The founder of Bathurst Island Mission, Bishop Gsell, expressed this in a triumphant passage in his memoirs:

Indeed there would seem to be only one hope for these people. Us! Contacts with civilisation! With the help and intelligent persuasion of the white man ..., the aboriginal can unloosen the vice that grips him and the yoke that has held him in slavery for thousands of years, the yoke that atrophies him even before he is born.[83]

Annie Lock devoted her life to working with Aboriginal women and children and fearlessly condemned those who refused to acknowledge their 'essential humanity' and endeavoured to keep them 'in ignorance so they can bounce & drive them just as they please'.[84] Nevertheless Lock's biographer, Catherine Bishop, writes:

> [Lock's] confidence in the superiority of Western civilisation and her hierarchical view of society indicate the extent to which she was more a supporter of white Australia than a threat to it.[85]

Lock remained convinced throughout her life that 'intelligent' Aborigines — her term for those who accepted Christian ways — saw her work in a positive light, and were grateful to her for guiding them out of the darkness. Bishop observes that:

> She contrasted the children's 'dreadful experiences in camp life' with the 'rays of sunshine' she apparently brought into their lives by caring for them herself. At Ooldea in particular, she criticised Aboriginal mothers for being 'very careless with their babies [who] were sleeping cosy in my arms & cried when their mothers took them, they carry them so uncomfortable [sic].'[86]

Lock responded angrily to a father who physically attacked her after she chastised his daughter for being late for breakfast. She reported that he 'came in & struck me & every time I spoke to him he struck me again ... & he bruised the left side of my face very much.' She demanded that the girl be removed to teach her father a lesson.[87]

Christian renunciation of the world and self-sacrifice were also powerful motivations for many missionaries. They saw themselves as quasi-martyrs devoted to hard work, dispensing with the luxuries of life and even welcoming wretched conditions and difficulties as part of their lot. Neville wrote scathingly of this inclination:

> I have seen earnest, humble workers walking with God, on the poverty line because their very humility and submission to some archaic system kept them in subjection ... a form of self-immolation as unnecessary as it is ineffective.[88]

Koori historian James Miller points out that a consequence was that they were equally prepared to accept intolerable conditions for their Aboriginal charges:

The missionaries accepted this poor state of things too readily. To them poverty was a test of their own faith in God, but to the Kooris it meant they had to continue to rely on government and private charity.[89]

The outlook of fundamentalist religious groups could create a punitive and frightening way of life for Aboriginal children in their care. A survey by A L West[90] of staff at the interdenominational Roelands Mission, near Bunbury during the 1940s and 1950s, presents an alarming picture of a subculture of social misfits finding personal refuge from outside worldliness and united by their devotion to fundamentalist religion, a profoundly chiliastic outlook and an evangelical drive. The children were forced to spend long hours in church and at prayer and were frightened by 'fire and brimstone' prophecies about the end of the world. The missionaries' sober and dour attitude to life was reflected in a lack of warmth to the children — the Superintendent never greeted them or chatted with them — and their treatment of them as 'miniature adults' who had to work even on holidays, often at needless chores since idleness was the 'work of the Devil'. Their prudery and beliefs that Aboriginal children were easily sexually stimulated underlay rules prohibiting married couples from public displays of affection and male missionaries from appearing in public without a shirt. The staff had no prior training in working with children or managing an institution. No meetings were held to plan and assess their work and staff blindly followed the instructions of their Superintendent, the mission council in Perth and the promptings of the Holy Spirit. The children were the victims in this system. Staff demands on their time often prevented them from attending to their studies or participating in sporting and other activities. They inevitably absorbed the missionaries' views even while they resented them. The strict codes of behaviour and all-encompassing definitions of 'sin' created enduring feelings of guilt and frustration for them as young adults living in the outside world.

Economic and personal advantage may seem unlikely motivations for working in these institutions given staff conditions. Nevertheless there were perks for the majority of staff who, lacking qualifications and experience, would have been hard pressed to find other than menial work elsewhere. Northern Territory Chief Protector of Aborigines Cecil Cook made this point in his description of mission staff as:

individuals of low intelligence and poor capacity, who find missionary work an avenue of employment agreeable to them. It offers them a livelihood which their personal ability and merit could not elsewhere attain, it affords the idle and incompetent a safe and comfortable existence.[91]

Few could have enjoyed elsewhere the status and power they lorded over their Aboriginal charges. Women staff were relieved of the drudgery of domestic tasks by Aboriginal workers. Ivy Sam recalled that at Palm Island in the 1920s:

They didn't do a thing in those days, European ladies. Girls looked after their babies. Washed their clothes, ironed, cleaned, cooked. So they really lived a ladies life you know. They couldn't even go down to the boat, collect their mail or carry their parcels up. They had these old Aboriginal men to do all that.[92]

Economic insecurity and inbuilt prejudices caused some staff to openly resist any encroachment on their work by Aboriginal inmates, thereby keeping them in perpetual dependency and bondage. A 1932 official Queensland report noted:

There is a feeling of antagonism amongst some of the staff of the Settlements to any scheme which will give the aboriginal any official recognition. That such antagonism is borne of jealousy or fear of being supplanted is undoubted.[93]

In some institutions misappropriation of goods, equipment and money by staff for their own economic gain appears to have been endemic. Historian Thom Blake[94] states that the many reported incidents of corruption at Barambah were 'a fraction of the total number' and that all former residents he interviewed were convinced that they had been 'defrauded' by staff and could recall dismissals of particular superintendents for misappropriation of settlement funds.

Whatever their motivations for working at the institutions, most staff were dismayed as their initial enthusiasm was ground down by the difficulties and demands of their work and their charges' often sullen and rebellious behaviour. A teacher at Moore River told a departmental official in 1940:

I started with ideals and hopes for success in the training of the half-caste children, but with so much interruption and lack of understanding I feel my work is at a standstill.[95]

At Moore River the result was a profound neglect and even indifference towards the children, in turn reflecting the attitude of an apathetic administration:

most staff were not particularly hostile at all — at least not to the children. They were simply indifferent. There were notable exceptions, of course. At least one Superintendent had violently sadistic tendencies, and there was no lack of staff who took occasional satisfaction in humiliating their captives ... The real story of their mistreatment is one of passive neglect: of an administration that simply couldn't be bothered to provide more than survival strictly demanded. In fact, most of the evil committed at Moore River was committed in the name of nothing more exalted — or more dastardly — than bureaucratic expedience.[96]

In his analysis of Aboriginal institutions, Jeremy Long[97] found that staff often shifted their focus to 'physical' rather than 'human results', concentrating on the job at hand and overlooking the complex human needs of their charges. Progress in building programs, for example, could take on a special significance as tangible evidence to the outside world of institutional advance and commitment to the children. Staff also moved on with monotonous regularity — Palm Island had eleven superintendents between 1931 and 1953.[98] A third of the thirty-nine missionaries at Roelands between 1941 and 1957 lasted less than one year.[99] Problems finding replacements meant that services such as teaching could grind to a halt. Gertie Sambo noted how staff turnovers contributed to the children's feelings of insecurity:

when people stayed for a while the kids got really attached to them and then when they went it was really hard. Well, we had no more mother and father and good people, they'd get attached to them. It really hurt, especially with the little kids.[100]

By contrast Nancy Barnes recalled that 'the success' of Colebrook Home was 'because of the continuity and stability of these two Christian women [Matron Hyde and Sister Rutter] ... it was more of a home with two people who were always there — two parent figures.'[101]

Looking back on their experiences, some staff would no doubt have sympathised with the regrets expressed by a female teacher from a Native American residential school:

> I entered the Service believing implicitly in the Bureau's wise and honourable aims. Disillusionment came slowly ... I saw sick and overworked children. And I did nothing. I was cowardly and acquiescent.[102]

The serious mental strain experienced by staff can be inferred from revelations of often extreme levels of violence and cruelty to inmates. In 1906 the matron at Myora reformatory on Stradbroke Island flogged a child to death. In 1926 a young man at Moore River was tarred and feathered by the superintendent for a minor misdemeanour. Several superintendents had nervous breakdowns, the most notorious of which resulted in the tragic shooting and arson spree by the Superintendent of Palm Island, Robert Henry Curry, in 1930. Former resident Marnie Kennedy[103] recalled that Curry went berserk, setting fire to his own home — thereby killing his son and daughter inside — and the home of the settlement doctor, whom he shot along with his wife. He then burned down the main settlement so that the 'whole island was lit up bright as day', while the three hundred dormitory children ran around 'screaming and crying in panic and terror and afraid we were next to be burnt'. Order was finally restored when Curry was shot on the orders of white officers by an Aboriginal resident who was subsequently arrested and imprisoned for three months before being found not guilty of the charge of shooting in self-defence.[104] The traumatised children, many of whom were fond of Curry, were told by the police that 'the mad dog was dead.' Kennedy writes that 'To this day, fifty years later, I can still see all us kids outside the dormitory crying and the police around us.'[105]

Official files and reports demonstrate that the chaos of the institutions left openings at all levels for impropriety and abuse. This is corroborated by the findings of the *Bringing Them Home* report, which exposed widespread physical, sexual and emotional abuse of Aboriginal children in institutions. In his history of the Canadian Indian residential school system J R Miller[106] identified similar abuses perpetrated by a range of males, and some females, including institution staff, clergy and visitors from local parishes, medical doctors and older children. He attributed this not simply to the agency of particular aberrant individuals, but to a connective web which encouraged the development of 'general environment[s] of violence, sexual and otherwise'. He described a system of staffing identical to that in Aboriginal institutions: poorly trained workers in demanding and stressful jobs operating without proper supervision or support, with rapid turnovers in staff and frequently irrational behaviours amongst those who remained. Miller argues that this constituted a hothouse for disaster, for regimes of unpredictable and unjustified physical violence, punishments and sexual advances; arbitrary attacks in hidden places and a generalised atmosphere of fear — who would be next? This was compounded by the culpability of those in authority who failed to act on complaints by children, excused 'slips' in staff behaviour and thereby allowed the gradual slide into more serious abuses. Meanwhile, children's feelings of powerlessness and their fear of staff escalated and they withdrew into silence. Despite official disbelief, denial and cover-ups, internal reports and inquiries sometimes forced authorities into action. However, to avoid scandal most chose to act informally, seeking resignations from the worker or, in the case of religious orders, advising cold showers, prayers and a transfer out of the district, often — tragically for the children — to similar institutions.

Our hope is in the children

The children thrown together in these institutions were from a variety of backgrounds. Some came from stable families within the institutions or on the outside, others from situations of extreme poverty and social breakdown. There were children from remote traditional communities and those from 'settled' areas of major cultural dislocation. Their experiences of separation from their families also varied. In remote frontier areas some parents placed their children in missions to protect them from violence and sexual abuse. The Kuku-Yalnji people of far north Queensland, for example, used the Lutheran mission camp in their territory during the 1890s as a safe haven for their young girls.[107] Aborigines at Koonibba Lutheran Mission in South Australia supported the building of a dormitory for their children in 1914 to prevent their removal by the government while they were away working.[108] Some children were brought in for medical care and stayed on:

My mother and brother came too ... she was thinking, 'Might be these white people can make him better, because we don't know much about medicine.' And she took him to get some more. True too! After a while he got better ... they said, 'This little girl can go to school, and we teach her to read and write, and to sew.' So I stopped in the dormitory.[109]

Many other families hid their children from the missionaries, as Ernest Gribble found out when he visited a camp in north Queensland:

At first little notice was taken of me, the people being busy questioning the two boys while I stood a little apart. Presently one man asked Harry who I was, and on his saying quietly the one word 'Missionary' the effect was wonderful to behold, the women gave me one look full of fear, then clasping their children tightly, vanished; the men stood their ground, but looked as if they'd like the ground to open and swallow either me or themselves.

Gribble subsequently learned the reason for the hostile reception. Aborigines for miles around had heard of the mission, he wrote, and the idea was 'among them that we intend taking their children forcibly from them'.[110]

Forced removal by government authorities was the most common scenario, often after long periods of fearful hiding from authorities. In a very few cases mothers accompanied their children:

My mother was Emma Lily Mita ... She had three children when she arrived at Yarrabah ... She decided to come. That's my mother. Some of the other ladies who left their children in the bush and ran away, they had all the intention to come back and pick them up when things quietened down but like all babies they cried. So they were picked up by the police.[111]

Children were also moved between institutions. Following its closure in 1904, all Fraser Island residents were sent to Yarrabah and when Western Australia's southern children's missions were closed the children were transferred to Carrolup and Moore River. In New South Wales young children were routinely moved from the Bomaderry Home to Cootamundra or Kinchela. All babies born at leprosariums were sent away immediately to prevent contagion. Children who repeatedly misbehaved could also be transferred to another institution as punishment. They were also separated from their families already living in the institutions. From the age of ten all Yarrabah children were transferred from the camp to the dormitory to ensure regular school attendance and to 'prevent the camp natives taking them off at all hours for corroborees,' despite elders' objections that the children were 'getting too much like the white fellow.'[112] At Forrest River Mission parents who would not send their children to the dormitories were refused rations. School age children at Barambah not already living in the compound could remain with their parents but could be transferred on any pretext.[113]

The majority of children came with some experience of Aboriginal society — a varying mix of traditional ways of doing things and of European practices filtered through Aboriginal custom. Even very young children arrived with Aboriginal ways of perceiving, constructing and interacting with the world instilled in them through early socialising processes. Many had absorbed their parents' feelings about and responses to white people. Their new masters and mistresses had an arrogant blindness about this background which we, in hindsight, can see created insurmountable problems for their 'civilising and Christianising' quest. They could see no rational social order in the camps but only chaos, immorality and debauchery. For them the children were as empty slates whose earlier life experiences meant nothing. 'The children are as plastic wax under our hands and we can mould them at will,' wrote the Wesleyan Bishop of New Guinea in the 1890s.[114] Cut off from the expanding insights of psychological research, they remained unaware of the very early absorption of culture and identity and the indelible nature of this learning.

> The political identity of the body is usually learned unconsciously, effortlessly, and very early — it is said within a few months of life British infants have learned to hold their eyebrows in a raised position ... What is 'remembered' in the body is well remembered. It is not possible to compel a person to unlearn the riding of a bike, or to take out the knowledge of a song residing in the fingertips, or to undo the memory of antibodies or self-replication without directly entering, altering, injuring the body itself.[115]

The French historian of cultural manners Pierre Bordieu drives home the point about the ineradicable nature of this 'hidden pedagogy':

The principles embodied in this way are placed beyond the grasp of consciousness, and hence cannot be touched by voluntary, deliberate transformation, cannot even be made explicit; nothing seems more ineffable, more incommunicable, more inimitable, and therefore more precious, than the values given body, *made* body by the transubstantiation achieved by the hidden pedagogy, capable of instilling a whole cosmology, an ethic, a metaphysic, a political philosophy, through injunctions as insignificant as 'stand up straight' or 'don't hold your knife in your left hand.'[116]

While the determination to stop children from speaking Aboriginal languages, including varieties of Kriol, suggests an appreciation of the links between language, culture and identity, there was little comprehension of the very complex and subtle nature of these linkages and the detrimental effects of insisting that all children adopt standard English. The children's new masters had their own views about appropriate forms of pedagogy for Aboriginal children. As non-reflective amateurs and out of touch with contemporary trends, they were left to draw on their own experiences of a Christian upbringing and education. For most this was based on the premise of 'man's inherent sinfulness' and the injunction of 'he who spares the rod, ruins the child,' fortified by beliefs that Aboriginal children were steeped in evil and needed to be morally purified. They were predisposed to adopt rigid and punitive regimens and punishments to break the children's self-will and transform them into humble, self-denying and God-fearing servants.

It was argued that the institutions, like reformatories for working-class children, were the most appropriate settings for training Aboriginal children for their future life. Literature dating from the late nineteenth century showed that institutional life crushed children into institutionalised individuals suited as adults to life in institutions and to surviving in the controlled environments of live-in domestic servants and farm labourers. In the institutions the children could also be rigidly separated from all Aboriginal influences while, day in day out, they were enveloped in non-Aboriginal values and behaviours and taught to fear and condemn their own people and their ways. Their minds, bodies and spirits were invaded, controlled, disciplined, regulated, monitored and policed.

Yet, while everything on the surface, or at least in official reports, seemed ordered and directed at these goals, there was always a gap, some slippage between intentions and outcomes, that is an inherent and inevitable part of all regimes designed to mould human behaviour. Staff could be influenced by the values and behaviours of their charges, as Sister Clare Ahern acknowledged in her work with Aboriginal people in the Kimberley:

> We recalled that even though we had come as teachers or pastoral workers to minister to this community, the reverse also happened. We had been ministered to as well. Daily we had entered into the mysteries of another culture and felt privileged for that opportunity.[117]

There were the perennial problems of lack of money, staff, resources and professionalism, ensuring that nothing could ever be carried out properly. Goals were continually thwarted so that what was meant to be an introduction to a European way of life turned out to be a way of life that was peculiar to institutions inhabited by Aboriginal children and not preparation for living in the wider community.

Sewing class, Moore River Native Settlement.
(Courtesy of Battye Library, 12231P)

How did the children respond to life in the institutions? The 1997 *Bringing Them Home* report shows that they reacted to their situation in a variety of ways, from complete withdrawal to astonishing survival within a disempowering system. International research provides further insights into the diversity of these responses. Research from North America suggests that children who are shifted suddenly between divergent cognitive systems can experience 'a breakdown in the ability to think at all ... to predict, to plan, to choose, to put things first, to keep [their] wits about [them],' and they can only respond by withdrawing into themselves.[118] The physical and psychological exhaustion experienced by Native American children in residential schools was powerfully expressed in the following blistering indictment by Florence Patterson, an experienced public health nurse who conducted a major survey of Indian health conditions for the American Red Cross at the request of the Commissioner of Indian Affairs in 1922:

> This program combined with the strain of bells, bugles, and horns, forming in line five or six times each day, and the mental struggle to combat physical fatigue, could not fail to be exhausting, and the effects are apparent in every group of boarding school pupils and in marked contrast to the freedom and alertness of the pupils in the day schools. One gained the impression that the boarding school child must endure real torture by being continually 'bottled up' and that somehow he never enjoyed the freedom of being a perfectly natural child. One longed to sweep aside his repressions and to find the child. As a small child he had undergone a terrific shock in adjusting himself to the school life and routine so different from any previous experience in his life.[119]

Recent research[120] into the effects of war and political violence on children identifies a range of responses from withdrawal to resilience, and suggests that a major factor in shaping survival is a stable, positive and comfortable family life prior to and during calamity. Even memories of a happy family can be empowering for children uprooted from their homes. James Miller has alluded to this factor:

> My mother ... knew twelve years of family life before she went into the homes, but my Aunt Jean was institutionalised as a baby and knew no family life. The scars for her were much deeper.[121]

Uprooted children who are able to create stable and supportive relationships with adults and peer groups are also more likely to adjust. Those from economically and socially stressed families where social disintegration pushes parents beyond endurance, and those who are uprooted before the age of five, are least able to form meaningful relationships with adults or peers and are the most likely to develop acute symptoms approximating post-traumatic stress disorder:

> depression, psychic numbing, feelings of helplessness, anxiety, fear, instability, agitation, low self-esteem, paranoia, confusion, inflexi-

bility and suicidal feelings ... the child may also experience sleep disturbances, hyper vigilance, loss of concentration, loss of memory and psychosomatic disorders.[122]

This sorry list is echoed in the findings of the *Bringing Them Home* report and in evidence presented to the National Inquiry into the Separation of Aboriginal and Torres Strait Islander Children from Their Families by various psychologists and Aboriginal organisations such as Link-Up and the Western Australian Aboriginal Legal Service.

THE DIDACTIC LANDSCAPE[123]

The similarity in overall layout and landscaping of the Aboriginal children's homes and the compounds in the multipurpose missions and government settlements is striking — the children's dormitories, various functional buildings (chapels, dining rooms, classrooms, kitchen, showers and other ablution facilities) and staff accommodation are all neatly cordoned off from the outside Aboriginal and white worlds. The resemblance to other institutional landscapes such as boarding schools, asylums and prisons is equally strong. Historian Mark Finnane[124] terms this particular design, placement, and grouping of buildings with its strict separation of functional areas, style of surrounding gardens and outer walled boundaries, the 'architecture of incarceration'. This architecture is not only intended to ensure maximum surveillance and control of inmates by staff but is an integral component of the reforming and disciplinary processes of institutions, expressing a constellation of meanings about space, time, movement, social relationships and the body, intended to be absorbed through the various senses into the self.

The didactic landscape of the children's institutions expressed the valuing of white over black and undermined meanings integral to Aborigines' sense of self. Familiar Aboriginal circular and non-linear forms, spatial arrangements, social groupings and ordered landscapes were replaced by western architectural forms dominated by symmetry, lines, corners, rectangles, squares and rows, all alien ways of dividing up space and of reshaping nature into 'tamed' cultural and economic environments suited to the European lifestyle. Aboriginal ways were locked out of the institutions through outside boundaries, the separation of compound from camp, and the strict rules and surveillance controlling passage between 'inside' and 'outside'. Where contact with Aboriginal adults was allowed — for example, compound children might be allowed to visit families on weekends — it was organised by white staff and strictly monitored. The design and exteriors of buildings such as the imposing Cootamundra Girls Home, a former hospital, and the barrack-like buildings of Yarrabah, also contained civilising messages. The 'architecture of neglect' evident in the squalid run-down facilities at most institutions also sent messages to the children, particularly when they compared their dormitories to the staff homes they had to clean. The placement of buildings within the compound — the prominence of the church, the Superintendent's home, the single female staff quarters, the functional areas of kitchen, laundry and bakehouse, the white family home and its gendered separation of work — provided further lessons in power, social order, hierarchies of gender and race and the division and compartmentalisation of work. They also spoke of white preconceptions about Aboriginal children, for example, belief in their sexual precocity expressed in the strict segregation of teenage girls and boys. While exteriors *may* have seemed an improvement on Aboriginal camps, conditions inside often were not and they suggested economic stringencies, inferiority and neglect. Conditions were generally vastly inferior to even the most spartan child welfare institutions, which were governed by official standards determining space, hygiene and sanitation to ensure healthy living conditions. Aboriginal children lived in seriously overcrowded, unhygienic, uncomfortable and unhealthy environments.

Just as prisoners move through areas in the prison according to their custodial stage, so Aboriginal children were moved through the various spaces within a compound over time. A former resident of Barambah compound, Ruth Hegarty,[125] described this process:

> The thing about it was the structure of the place. Your whole life was mapped out for you. Say you were in the babies dormitory, you turned five, your mother had no chance of keeping you. If she wanted to keep you the choice wasn't hers until she married and moved out of the dormitory. Your mother was sent out to work and you were packed off to the girls' dormitory.
>
> You stayed there until you turned fourteen when you were sent to work even if you were in the middle of your school year ... When you came home from work from holidays, you were never allowed to go to the camp, you had to stay in the dormitory. Girls who got

pregnant while out working were put in the mothers' dormitory. I left the dormitory when I was twenty-one to get married.[126]

As in prisons, movement between buildings was controlled by rules and often involved marching in lines from one functional area to another. Indeed everything was governed by the overarching regimentation of space and time fundamental to creating the human 'working machine'. Wadjularbinna recalled this ordering of life at Doomadgee Mission:

> You all lined up, you all had a bath in line, you all walked to such and such a place and you were in senior, intermediate and junior groups and kindy groups, and you all had your areas and your little jobs to do and your tasks to do and it all had to be, and they had senior girls marching you off to do something and then making sure you're back at this time. To me, looking back, it was like a concentration camp and it's got really bad memories for me.[127]

Timetables and regimens have a long tradition in Aboriginal institutions, the earliest recorded examples being those at the Parramatta Native School in 1827 which reflected the organisation of boarding schools of the day though it was probably 'sterner than most.'[128] The strict daily timetable followed at Forrest River Mission between 1915 and 1935, recorded by a visitor to the mission in 1916, was fairly typical of Aboriginal institutional life (see Table Four, p 382). Timetabling operated at several levels — the overall seasonal and daily round of activities at the institution; the particular regimens of school, dormitory, meals, chores and prayer — with loud bells, verbal reminders and punishments forcing western concepts of time and order into the children's bodies and minds. June Barker describes the language of the bell:

> Your life was governed by the bell. The first bell would go of a morning, you would have to go down to the treatment room: that's where you would get your cod-liver oil and your eyes done every day ... The bell would then ring for school; the bell would ring for rations; a mournful bell would ring for the funerals; and if there was an Inspector coming up from Sydney, Mr Smithers, the bell would ring with a really important sound. You got to know the different sounds in the bell.[129]

TABLE FOUR

DAILY TIMETABLE AT FORREST RIVER MISSION, 1915–35

4.30 am.	Rising bell. Boys called by Mrs Sherwin and girls by Mrs Noble. Blankets hung to air.
5.15 am.	All dormitory boys and girls attend Chapel. The adults separated from pupils by wire netting.
5.45 am.	Staff breakfast in common room.
6.35 am.	Breakfast for Aboriginals; adults in kitchen, boys and girls in their dormitories and bush people in the camp.
7.00 am.	Triangle bell rung for work parade. All line up to be allocated the morning work.
10.30 am.	Bell rung for 'knock off'. Workers given tin discs as a food and tobacco tokens.
11.00 am.	Morning tea for staff.
11.30 am.	School for pupils; adults present tokens for rewards.
12.45 pm.	School ends.
1.00 pm.	Staff lunch and rest.
2.30 pm.	Chapel bell — staff intercessions.
3.00 pm.	Work bell —work parade and job allocation.
5.00 pm.	Knock off bell. Camp adults get evening meal of two pieces of damper.
5.30 pm.	Evensong. Boys and girls line up for service as in morning.
6.00 pm.	Dormitory children given a meal of damper.
6.30 pm.	Staff dinner, followed by gramophone records. Boys and girls heard holding separate 'corroborees'.
8.00 pm.	Pupils say evening prayers to 'La-La' for sending the missionaries and minding them all day, then put to bed on dirt floor with individual blankets. Staff say prayers in common room and then retire.

(From a letter by G K Freeman, *WA Church News*, March 1916 cited in Green 1995, p 114.)

The dormitory, the meal and the classroom were sites integral to the civilising project. They provided daily lessons and fulfilled other agendas such as weaning children from parental influence; disrupting Aboriginal conventions of initiation and marriage for the young people; ensuring attendance at school, church and chores, and allowing for strict surveillance through proximity to white staff. Experiences of inferiority and powerlessness, of grinding control and grim strategies of survival, were also learned in these environments. With such an introduction to 'civilisation' it is little wonder that many children looked for solace in memories of their Aboriginal past, while others absorbed the negative messages about Aboriginal people to the extent that they determined to blend themselves irrevocably into the white world.

THE DORMITORY

'Dormitory' could refer to single-purpose sleeping quarters like the former hospital wards at Cootamundra, the dingy huts at Moore River or the imposing two storey multipurpose building at Barambah. The Barambah dormitory expanded from an original single bough shed to segregated huts and then dormitories for boys, girls and single mothers and their children, to the new girls dormitory opened in 1925 with upstairs sleeping quarters, kitchen, dining room, pantry, storeroom, dressing rooms and sewing rooms. Its significance in institutional life was symbolised by the grand opening ceremony attended by over twenty politicians who were entertained by the settlement brass band, demonstrations of spear throwing and a special meal cooked by the girls. In 1927 a separate babies home and mothers quarters were erected and a new boys dormitory was completed in the following year. It followed that as more space became available more children were admitted to the compound from outside and from the settlement village. The percentage of children at Barambah in the dormitories

A children's dormitory at Moore River Native Settlement, c 1930.

(Courtesy of Mogumber Heritage Committee of the Wheatbelt Aboriginal Corporation, 378)

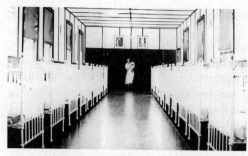

The new babies' dormitory at Moore River Native Settlement, opened in 1938.

(Courtesy of Mogumber Heritage Committee of the Wheatbelt Aboriginal Corporation, 378)

increased from three percent in 1910 to over twenty-two percent in 1933, with sixty-six percent of children aged between five and fourteen housed there.[130]

At night dormitories became 'holding pens', with children locked in to prevent escapes and to reduce the supervisory work of the staff. A voluntary worker recorded the following dismal treatment of children at Carrolup Native Settlement:

> They are locked up like fowls after an early tea every night, winter and summer — no light, no fire, no recreation at all — just an animal existence ... I have never seen kiddies with such dull, unhappy eyes, hang-dog expression and surly looks. It is a veritable prison to them.[131]

Connie Nungulla McDonald observed that security in the girls dormitory at Forrest River was more like a prison than a children's home:

> [It was] completely closed in with fencing wire. The main door was made of such solid iron that a prisoner from Long Bay would not have been able to open it by himself. Then there was the outside verandah door, and another one south of the building. All of these doors were locked from the outside with big heavy padlocks to form an elaborate fortification to protect the girls from 'danger' and 'temptation'.[132]

Jack Davis described the younger boys' fear and distress during the long dark nights at Moore River and how the older ones tried to console them:

> they might wake up crying from a bad dream or fleas biting them, and an older boy would then comfort them and gently make them lie down. Early in the night we would get them out of bed and help them to the toilet ... Then we would lead them back, half asleep, to their beds, tumble them in and cover them up ... In the morning we would get the younger kids out of bed and take them, with their pants dragging, to the slow torture of freezing water and brick-hard lumps of soap ... Then it was a slow trek back to stack the rugs and

pat the mattress lumps flat, for a military inspection by Superintendent Neal or the matron.[133]

Relations between the children were not always so cooperative and fights could easily break out during the long lonely nights. Jack Davis recalls fights over the few good mattresses and blankets in his dormitory:

if you were lucky enough to have a good mattress you guarded it zealously and had to be prepared to fight for it. Blankets too were apt to roam, and when yours did you would have to search every bed until you found it.
'Hey that's mine!' you would exclaim.
'If it's yours, how did it get on my bed?'
And then a fight would follow. You had to scrap, or slap, to get back anything you lost. That meant you had to fight for everything — with one exception. The fleas were shared equally by everybody, without question.[134]

Elsie Roughsey's memories of life in the dormitory at Mornington Island Mission were of 'unhappy times ... if girls would fight with me, I'd fight back. I had my older sister on my side. I'd be unhappy if we quarrelled.'[135]

Conditions in the dormitories were remarkably similar across the continent. They were often no improvement on Aboriginal camps and were frequently worse. Sister Eileen Heath roundly condemned conditions at Moore River:

The sanitation in the dormitories was absolutely appalling. The staff went in and they'd say, 'I'll have to have a cigarette before I go in.' There were no toilets there at all, there were just sanitary buckets which were emptied each morning. They were very dimly lit, cyclone beds, no sheets of course, blankets, bug-ridden. When anybody special was coming to the settlement, we had a stock of sheets which were put on the beds so that if anybody wanted to go into the dormitories to have a look they got the impression that the children always had sheets on their beds.[136]

In the early days at Barambah children slept on the ground with just a blanket to cover them. Moola Bulla Native Settlement in the east Kimberley, opened in 1911, had no dormitory until the 1930s and children slept on the ground and huddled under the manager's house during the rain.[137] Aboriginal oral historian Bill Rosser recorded Fred

Clay's memories of conditions at Palm Island:

> 'When I first went to Palm there was only an old slab building for the boys dormitory. It was just bush timber, stuck in the ground. It had gaps of about three inches ... and a corrugated iron roof. There was lime on an earth floor.'
>
> No doubt this was to keep down vermin which would have flourished under such poor and humid conditions. Nevertheless I asked, 'Didn't it burn your feet?'
>
> 'No.' he replied, 'I think they used to treat it because they had a lime burner on the island at the time.'
>
> 'You mean ... that you were all kept in this — this enclosure made out of bush timber and an earth floor?'
>
> 'Mmmn,' Fred reflected, 'And benches around the walls for beds. They were about three high. I remember the first night in the dormitory, the bugs got me regardless of the lime. It was hell!'[138]

With no privacy, personal space or property of their own, and their awareness of the inferiority of their living conditions, it is difficult to understand how the children could have been expected to develop positive feelings of self-worth and pride. Ruth Hegarty found that children at Barambah 'owned nothing, everything was company property'. Clothing was kept in one room and each morning children donned 'what was handed' to them. She also discovered that jealousies between the children meant:

> It was no good having anything nice. I deliberately went without socks and shoes in the winter although I had them. My mum bought them for me but I wouldn't wear them because the others would chuck off at me.[139]

Some children were issued an institutional uniform — girls at Beagle Bay were dressed in blue gingham and the boys in khaki,[140] and at Yarrabah boys wore sulus (wrap-around lengths of cloth) and the girls voluminous high-necked smocks. Most wore drab, uncomfortable, ill-fitting second-hand clothes or hastily sewn garments made of cheap cloth and even flour bags.

Children responded by creating their own amusements and even 'subcultures' in the dormitories, characterised by particular patterns of behaviour, ritual and even language. Older girls at Barambah in the late 1930s spoke a 'secret' language amongst themselves referred to as 'dormitory talk'[141] which provided a sense of ownership of something and, through exclusion of others, created the feeling of having some control over their situation. Some older children also informed the others about Aboriginal culture. Wadjularbinna recalled that children at Doomadgee were:

> very fortunate that there were some teenage girls already taken in by their parents and they'd kept the culture alive in the dormitory. They told us stories, they kept us in the kinship system; they kept that alive. And the older girls, as they grew up they were marrying — the boys were in the other dormitory — but they were marrying the straight skin, the way they were supposed to marry. The missionaries didn't realise that it was still going on and it wasn't until much later on that they started to penetrate the system and it was starting to go haywire. Our culture was intact, but we had to do it really sneaky, don't let the missionaries know.[142]

While there were few resources for the children, in many places they were nevertheless forced to labour to keep what they did have meticulously clean. At all institutions a major part of the girls' time was devoted to cleaning the dormitory and adjacent facilities. Each day at Barambah they made the beds, cleaned and polished the floors in the sleeping quarters, swept and scrubbed the dining room, kitchen, bathroom, laundry and verandah twice a day and regularly cleaned all walls, windows and doors. Visitors, like the journalist who commented in 1936 'these buildings are worth seeing ... spotlessly clean and well managed,' interpreted these clean surfaces as evidence of institutional success.[143] Looking back on her years in the dormitory at Mornington Island Elsie Roughsey came to the following conclusions:

> As years passed I became much grown up. I understand the real true life of the mission and the dormitory ... I could feel myself in a huge paddock where the place is fenced in. You cannot go too far. If you do, there is trouble. All kind of foolish punishment you have to pay for getting bit too far away where the marks have been measured ... that is enough, and no more further.[144]

THE MEAL

In all societies the meal is a significant social event. In describing its importance in Aboriginal camp life Rowse[145] suggests a set of images

The children's dining room at Moore River Native Settlement, c 1930.

(Courtesy of Mogumber Heritage Committee of the Wheatbelt Aboriginal Corporation, 368, 420)

that most Australian families would aspire to — the varieties of foods, the preliminary preparation, the cooking and presentation, the pleasure of eating together and the associated sharing of food, playing out of social relationships and the experience of sociability and interaction with kin. Institutional meals contrast in virtually every way with these images. For the Aboriginal children meals became yet another site of emptiness — physical and emotional — a tangible experience reinforcing feelings of worthlessness and rejection with the meagre and monotonous food providing another contrast for many with memories of the warmth of home. They noted the contrast with the food served to staff — children at Moore River thought the staff 'lived like lords' — and the little hypocrisies when they were served treats when special visitors arrived.

The meal was a site of regimentation and control with assigned chores, bells, line-ups, mass seating, and surveillance and suppression of sociability and spontaneity. Conditions in the dining rooms further reinforced feelings of worthlessness. Children at Moore River ate in a dingy dining room described as follows by a visiting official:

> The windows were indescribably filthy and choked with all manner of food scraps of food-stuffs. The kitchen floor was dirty … One girl was found sleeping in a blanket in the dining room and the girls had their clothes hanging around the walls.[146]

They ate in silence under the watchful eye of the Aboriginal police who ruled 'by the strap'.[147] With no cutlery they were obliged to eat with their hands. In 1945 a departing army regiment stationed at the settlement during the war donated knives and forks for the dining room, but a year later a departmental officer reported:

> Children at breakfast time were pushing food into their mouths from broken and buckled plates … The attendant in charge of the kitchen said that lack of culinary utensils and other facilities made it impossible to serve any variety of food, particularly second courses of sweets.[148]

Former resident of the Retta Dixon Home in Darwin, Barbara Cummings, described similar degrading treatment:

Ethel [Buckle] remembers having 'just tins, jam tins for our plates, jam tins for our tea or cocoa.' When plates were made available they were supplied in insufficient quantities and the children ate two to a plate, generally with their fingers. This ensured the faster they ate the more they got and Nellie Cummings recalls, 'We used to watch each other like hawks.' Some of the older girls, according to Hilda Muir, used to hide the few forks, plates, cups and spoons whenever they were fortunate enough to obtain them, thus ensuring they would have some utensils for their next meal.[149]

Food could also become a punishment as former Moore River inmate Eric Conway recalled:

The tracker would hold you while the grown-up would force that spinach down your throat, 'cause kids just didn't like spinach — especially the way it was cooked those days, just boiled in a copper. None of us liked it, but oh we used to eat it and swallow it and just sit there and say nothing.[150]

Donations of food could create a sense of shame in the children as a woman who grew up at Dulhi Gunyah Children's Home recalled:

There used to be a tea room somewhere by the Grand Theatre. They used to give us cakes, the broken cakes. And when it was harvest festival time, fruit would be donated. We used to have Egg Sunday, too, they'd pack eggs into the boxes and that was supposed to be a treat. Missionaries used to take us to church and on this platform out the front were all these things. Everyone used to be looking at us, you know. That's how we used to live in there, in that home.[151]

The frequent references to food, eating, hunger and deprivation in memories and accounts of institutional life everywhere — who could forget the gruel scene in Dickens' novel *Oliver Twist*? — highlight the symbolic significance of food to all inmates. Aboriginal oral history and autobiography is replete with such memories. A woman who arrived at Yarrabah in 1911 was greeted by the question:

You want a cuppa tea? Yes, please. You want something to eat? I said, whatya got? Treacle and bread. Oh, no thank you, I don't eat rubbish like that. You don't talk smart, tomorrow you'll be hungry, You'll eat anything. It's a hungry place. Next day I was hungry all right. I had to eat anything after that.[152]

These are some typical meals dished up around the 1920s and 1930s in Aboriginal children's institutions across Australia:

breakfast was porridge and two pieces of bread. You could pick up the porridge in your hand or cut it with a knife … The bread used to be mildewy … Lunch was bread and treacle, sometimes hot soup.[153]

Breakfast was pretty well the same fare day after day: bread and fat, with golden syrup or blackjack (treacle) for occasional variation. Lunch was pea soup, or soup with an odd spud or onion floating in it, but, like Oliver's gruel, very thin and watery. Tea was a repeat of breakfast.[154]

We were living mainly on corn porridge. Sometimes they would put potato in it. Sometimes when they got fish, they put it into the porridge as well. We had to eat it like that. In the morning we would have porridge, tea and a slice of bread. The same kind of food for lunch and tea. Sometimes we would have meat, but not very often.[155]

It is hardly surprising that the children were chronically hungry. Ruth Hegarty recalled, 'I was always hungry. I was never full. We were always looking for something to eat.'[156] Inmates referred to the early days at Yarrabah as 'starvation times' with 'too much prayer and not enough tucker'.[157]

In contrast to child welfare institutions, there was generally no set dietary scale for the children. This reflected the generally inadequate rations provided by governments around Australia, commented on by anthropologist N B Tindale in 1941:

It must be remembered that in many parts of Australia dietic care of Aborigines and half-castes is still confined to the provision of small amounts of tea, flour, sugar or treacle sufficient to keep the recipient alive. One result is that such folk show little of the joy of living, never, in fact, being properly alive.[158]

Official efforts in 1920 to bring the dietary scale at Moore River and Carrolup up to mainstream standards were actually opposed by superintendents on the grounds that they 'would be better fed than white children at boarding school' and that it would 'be a waste of rate payers' money'.[159] Superintendent Ernest Mitchell wrote in 1921:

> it is wasteful and foolish to provide these children with food they would never eat had the Department not taken them into its keeping, and will never have as a regular diet after they leave the settlement.[160]

Of particular concern was the lack of a special diet for babies. A former staff member at Moore River told the 1934 Moseley Royal Commission that on 'many occasions' he had seen 'babies drinking tea without milk from the bottles as no milk was available'.[161] Interference by staff could further reduce the quality and quantity of food reaching the children. In Queensland the Government Storekeeper regularly sent inferior stores to institutions arguing that they were 'good enough for Aborigines' and staff then cut out the best of what was sent for themselves.[162] Together with strict economies this meant that there was often a serious gap between official accounts of what was offered and what children received. Food was often prepared in insanitary conditions. A visiting departmental official provided the following report on the baking of bread for inmates at Moore River in the 1940s:

> The bakehouse is appalling from every point of view. Before you approach the door you are welcomed by a stench from ground contaminated by recently removed refuse, which had evidently been allowed to gather ... Windows are broken with bags hanging over them, the oven itself looks very like a quarry inside ... The actual bread tins resemble a pile of scrap tin.[163]

As late as 1974 a report in the *Medical Journal of Australia* stated:

> it seems on the whole the diet of nomads under average conditions is better than that provided on settlements and missions.[164]

The poor diet had serious consequences for the children's health, leaving them vulnerable to infections and epidemics of disease. During the first medical and dental inspection of children at Moore River in 1936 medical officers reported epidemic levels of pneumonia, measles and septic sores and dental officers performed 129 extractions.[165]

Chronic hunger was frequently the cause of misbehaviour and

consequent punishment. The children fought over food, bartered what they could and frequently stole food as well. The musical *Bran Nue Dae* opens with a scene in the Rossmoyne Pallottine Aboriginal Hostel in Perth as a group of boys raid the tuckshop and stuff their shirts with bars of Cherry Ripe and bottles of Coca Cola. The 'leader', Willie, mimics the German priest, Benedictus, who is in charge of the hostel:

WILLIE   Yah it is gut to eat at der Lord's table. First we haff made
             un inwentory ov der spoils.
             [He holds the black book up.]
             Den ve haff to partake of der fruits ov our labours.
             Thankyou Lord.

ALL   Thankyou Lord!

PETER   Und dis is for all der starfing kids in der vorld.
             [He bites a Cherry Ripe]

DARRYL Like us bro, us blackies starving.

WILLIE   Und den der liquid refreshments to make it efen bedder!

ALL   Ya, ya![166]

When the theft is discovered Willie is thrown out of the hostel by Benedictus who berates him: 'You are a rotten abble in der barrel. You are a blot on der mission and a stain on der celebration of life.'[167] Well-known Aboriginal tenor, Harold Blair, who lived at Purga Mission near Ipswich from the mid 1920s, had similar memories of raids on the kitchen pantry at Purga Mission:

three of us tried to raid the kitchen pantry. Being the smallest … I passed the food down as fast as I could … when we had taken a fair share of the little that was there, I put my hand down on my mate's shoulder as I prepared to jump off. I thought to myself, 'Gee, his shoulder can't be that big' and then I found myself looking directly into the eyes of the Camp Superintendent … That was the end of our extra food … but at least I had a warm bottom to take to bed that night.[168]

Wadjularbinna told how starving children at Doomadgee raided the rubbish bins and were then punished for their troubles:

I was still a little kid — and I used to go to the slop tin … to see if there was any food for all the kids as they were lined up outside ... The missionaries had their left-over foods — apple and orange peel — all in a tin that was just under the window ... for the pigs ... we were eating like raw potato peel and pumpkin seed and orange and apple peel and all out of the slop tin, you know, and we couldn't get water to wash it. But we were hungry, you know, we'd just wipe it on our clothes and just eat it. And one day I was caught by Mr Potter and he put me in the rubbish, slop, upside down ... He got me and he put me in the bin, in the slop tin, and my pride was hurt because I had the slops all over me. I got a flogging for it; he flogged me for being in that slop tin, with a plaited greenhide that they used to hit us with.[169]

Bush food that the children were sometimes able to gather took on particular meanings and significance. It not only eased hunger pangs and provided a break from a monotonous diet but also linked the children to earlier memories. Connie Nungulla McDonald recalled the joy of occasional trips into the bush with the Aboriginal adults at Forrest River Mission:

The only time our meals were varied was when we went walkabout. Bush food was delicious! The meat would be kangaroo, goanna, fish, turtle and eel. For fruit and vegetables there would be yams, wild tomatoes, wild cucumber and lily roots. For sweets, we enjoyed wild figs, honey (called sugar bag), various berries and wild potatoes but they were very sweet and were eaten raw as they disintegrated when cooked.[170]

Jack Davis described the pleasures of hunting in the bush with the other boys on the odd times that they were allowed out by staff:

We would leave the settlement say at eight o'clock in the morning and come home at dusk that night, and of course we'd get a roo or a rabbit or whatever and take salt with us, a billy can of water, and we would go hunting, we would just go out and hunt and eat and bring some meat back to the camp for the older people.[171]

THE CLASSROOM

Most Aboriginal institutions ran their own schools; even some of the children's homes were forced to do so due to opposition from white parents to the presence of Aboriginal children in state schools.

Characterised by serious overcrowding and lack of resources and taught by unqualified staff, it was hardly surprising that most Aboriginal children made little headway in their schooling. Again there was an overemphasis on regimentation and control. Together with limited expectations about the children's ability, this encouraged a pattern of rigid discipline at the expense of their real learning needs. While departmental officials interpreted high enrolments, school building programs and evidence of discipline, order and diligence in the schools as evidence of success, some professional educators saw things differently. In 1917 the District Inspector for the Queensland Department of Public Instruction wrote of the school at Barambah:

> If the object of the school is to keep the children quiet, and out of mischief during the daytime and to train them to be lazy with as much incidental teaching as a teacher can give 117 children in five different classes in an overcrowded room with less floor space than four square feet per child, it is a success, but if the aim is to cultivate their intelligence, to give exercise to their self activity, to train them to be industrious and self reliant with a fair knowledge of their class work when leaving, *the school is a failure*.[172]

In Native American residential schools a special 'curriculum of civilisation' with subjects on citizenship and government prepared the students to take on the mantle of citizenship as adults.[173] By contrast, Aboriginal children were taught basic literacy and numeracy usually only to third or fourth grade, in anticipation of their becoming disenfranchised rural and domestic workers, or inmates of institutions. This left them ill-equipped to find their way as adults in a changing world and confined them to a narrow employment niche. In a self-fulfilling cycle the children were labelled as 'failures' and blamed for their situation and this in turn reinforced the teachers' preconceptions and shaped how they taught the children. Managers at Kinchela believed 'the boys' intelligence to be typically and naturally low; even those who did well at school were often described in the Home as 'dull' or 'subnormal'.[174] Jimmie Barker recalled that teachers at Brewarrina Reserve:

> hammer[ed] our inferiority into us all day and every day ... I learned that because I was black or partly coloured, there is no place in Australia for me ... that an Aboriginal ... was mentally and physically inferior to all others.[175]

This cycle proved very resistant to change. The advent of intelligence testing of Aboriginal children during the 1920s and 1930s initially only boosted these ideas and practices. Even the anthropologist A P Elkin concluded, after surveying the results of tests by S D Porteus, that Aborigines lacked 'the "ethnic" capacity' to become civilised.[176] One of the pioneers in reassessing these negative preconceptions was anthropologist M F Ashley Montague, who wrote in 1938:

I am fairly convinced were [an Aboriginal] afforded the proper opportunities he could attain such a degree of development, and become in time a useful and desirable citizen of any State. What evidence that would bear a moment's critical examination has ever been produced to the contrary?[177]

Such a perspective was light years away from the outlook of most staff in Aboriginal institutions and it was only after the Second World War that a trickle-down effect on the quality of Aboriginal education began.

At the Barambah school the size of classes and teacher–student ratios continually exceeded state regulations. Between 1910 and 1924 enrolments doubled from ninety to 180. Staff–student ratios were more than three times approved levels for white schools and with inadequate classroom accommodation, children spilled out onto verandahs and classes were held outside under the trees. These conditions contributed to a rapid turnover in teachers, and problems replacing them meant that the schools were often closed down. The children's progress was painfully slow — most took eight years to reach Grade Four. Motivated by a mixture of prejudice and alarm at standards in the school, staff refused to enrol their own children and separate classrooms were provided for them.[178] In the 1930s the headmaster introduced a special curriculum based on the state curriculum but taking into account the difference in 'environment and ability' between Aboriginal and white children and the children's future, which lay with the 'labouring class' and not in the 'commercial and academic world'. To this end they were taught how to speak correctly, write letters, read for recreational purposes, and deal with money. They also studied geography to build up 'a general knowledge of Australia'; 'Civics and Morals' to encourage them 'in paths of honesty, industry, thrift, care of personal and public property, and recognition of respect due to officials and guardians'; hygiene to ensure 'habits of personal cleanliness and cleanliness of home and settlement generally'; and history to promote 'the qualities of courage, perseverance' and 'facing [of] difficulties'.[179]

Conditions in classrooms in Western Australian government institutions were even worse. Moola Bulla had no school at all prior to 1929 when the storekeeper's wife was appointed as a teacher. With increasing numbers of 'half-caste' children arriving in the late 1930s, Presbyterian missionaries Reverend and Mrs Hovenden set up a school; however it was closed during the war and many of the children transferred to Beagle Bay. The school was reopened in 1950 but four years later the settlement was sold to pastoral interests and the residents trucked off to the towns of Halls Creek and Fitzroy Crossing. There was no professional educational input at the Moore River school. Sister Eileen Heath recalled that:

> The teachers were not Education Department teachers. They were not trained teachers. We had two teachers most of the time, about 150 children, and the highest grade that they would have achieved would have been Grade Four. There was a constant turnover of teachers and the children didn't complete the normal education. I felt that a lot of the children there and the people had so much good in them and so much could have been done if they were given the right opportunities.[180]

A former student, Vincent Lambadgee, claimed ruefully, 'We learned hardly anything ... More or less little bit of spelling or arithmetic ... I could barely spell 'cat' when I left.'[181] These sentiments were echoed by another former student:

> A lot of us boys were interested in schooling but they couldn't teach us any schooling. They never had the teachers, never had the paper, never had the pencils, never had the space.[182]

A special curriculum prepared for the Moore River school in 1926 by the state psychologist, Miss E T Stoneman, demonstrated professional expectations of Aboriginal children in Western Australia. Stoneman believed that most children were not capable of going beyond Grade Three and recommended a practical approach devoted to the following subjects:

a. the building of a shack
b. the making of a bed

c. the making of a fire
d. cooking
e. simple pottery
f. making coarse soap for camp use
g. nose drill
h. disposal of waste
i. simple laundry exercises
j. use of knife and fork and spoon
k. how to clear and set a table, wash dishes
l. how to sweep a room, beat a carpet
m. how to prepare soil for seeds.[183]

Mount Margaret Mission was an exception in the state's shocking history of Aboriginal schooling. Combining the state curriculum with innovative teaching techniques, the school made 'remarkable achievements ... in literacy and numeracy.'[184] The founder of the mission, Reverend Schenk, wrote in his booklet, *The Educability of the Native*, in 1935:

Those who teach the Aborigines very soon discover that they are no whit behind any other race in mental capacity, and that they can master the lessons that the white children learn quite as quickly and completely as they can.[185]

All institutions provided some form of 'vocational training' for the children. This focused less on developing practical skills to enable them to compete successfully on the labour market, than on inculcating the work ethic and habits of industry and self-regulation. Anthropologist Barry Morris argues that this:

stress on self-regulation was an attempt to inculcate a regime of rational and calculating behaviour which is closely associated with cultural notions of possessive individualism within the wider society ... work was never simply instrumental but associated with the acquisition of a regime of ordered conduct.[186]

Lack of resources and instructors meant that training consisted largely of chores — work that should have been done by their adult keepers. In this way the children contributed to the economical operation of the institutions by minimising staff workloads and helping to keep staff numbers down.

Chores began at an early age outside of and during school hours, often leading to a conflict between work and schooling. The 1909 Yarrabah Australian Board of Missions Report noted that 'the large amount of domestic duties which fall on the girls rather detracts from their education, but many are good scholars.'[187] Victoria Archibald remembered how at Cootamundra:

> If the matron wanted something done, she would come straight down there and take the oldest girl out of the school to come up and do something ... I learned to read and write, but not that much, because you had your mind two ways there. The teacher was trying to teach you, but you'd be wondering when the matron was coming down.[188]

Her account of the girls' round of chores before school leaves the reader wondering how they could even stay awake in class:

> About half past five, six o'clock we'd start by getting our water for scrubbing, washing, bathing. That had to be carried from a dam down the bottom of the hill. We carried it in kerosene tins ... And then that bathroom had to be cleaned up. The other girls that were scrubbing the floor, there were about six rows of beds and you'd push those beds back and each girl on her hands and knees would do a strip. You couldn't just slosh it out ... If the matron saw it a little bit not bright, she'd make you go back right over it again ... We had to get that done, plus have our bath and get out ready for breakfast ... But then all the beds had to be put back in a row again, neat. You'd turn around and take your buckets out, rinse them out, turn them upside down with your cloth and your scrubbing brush and your soap standing alongside, and the matron would come out and inspect it before you could go in for breakfast ... As soon as the breakfast was over, then we had to turn around and clean up again and straighten up. The big girls would get the big tablecloths, take them off and fold them, and we had to stand to attention till the matron came out and she'd inspect us all to see if we were all right and clean, then the big girls would go about their work again and the little ones would line up. After breakfast the girls had to scrub the breakfast-room floor and put the tables back again ... You'd have to be working all the time. There was no let-up.[189]

Training was strictly gendered and targeted at rural and domestic labour inside or outside the institution. The skills for both were remarkably similar. Girls at Barambah were trained for domestic service outside — laundry, baking, sewing, knitting, gardening and hygiene, and in all 'the feminine accomplishments' needed for institutional life — laundry, baking, sewing, gardening and cleanliness. Girls cleaning staff homes experienced first hand the chasm between conditions here and their own way of life. In the novel *Plains of Promise*, Alexis Wright describes one girl looking around a kitchen she has been sent to clean:

Girls were trained as domestic workers and boys as farm labourers.
Cooking classes at Colebrook Home, Quorn, 1940.
(Courtesy of Australian Institute of Aboriginal and Torres Strait Islander Studies, UAM 1bw)

> She knew that in her whole life she would never have a house like this. So clean. With special cups to serve tea to guests. She would simply go on living the way the rest of the community lived.[190]

Boys carried out all the usual outdoor male tasks. However, Bruce Ellis recalled that at Kinchela they had to do all the domestic work as well:

> Most of the mundane work in the home was done by the boys. We mowed the lawns, milked the cows, made butter, cultivated the vegetable garden, took care of 150 hens, cleaned the cooking utensils and we cleaned the living quarters of the staff and the dormitories. The very young had to pick up litter around the place. These jobs were rotated every month.[191]

The children's work was often futile and meaningless. Jack Davis[192] was sent to Moore River by his father to learn about farming and

> imagined that he would be taught to set up a team of horses and drive a harvester or a plough. Tractors were the future and I had hoped that we might be taken to see one and perhaps learn to drive it.

Instead he was assigned to a gang of boys clearing the scrub:

> pick[ing] roots and stab[bing] zamia palms with a crowbar ... There
> was really only enough work for two people, but there were about
> eight in the gang ... Mr Hedge, the overseer, was very frustrated
> because there was nothing to do, and no equipment to do it with
> anyway ... Sometimes he would say, 'Do a bit more. Put a bit more
> effort into it.' We would reply, 'Righto, we'll put our backs into it.'
> But we never did. There was no point or purpose.

An inquiry into acts of 'sexual deviancy', allegedly perpetrated by
boys at Kinchela in 1943, estimated that the boys spent up to four
hours after school each day washing and scrubbing and carrying out
other menial tasks. The inquiry report observed that they 'demonstrated a noticeable tendency ... to sit on their haunches motionless
and silent'.[193] It concluded that the
boys were overworked and bored
and that 'sexual deviation' was
largely the product of the
environment in which they were
forced to live.

*Trainees in the piggery at the Aboriginal
Training Farm, Cherbourg, 1940s.*
(Courtesy of Queensland Museum, EH443)

As they grew older, children
were increasingly drawn into the
general work of the institution
until at the age of twelve or
thirteen they were sent to work
outside. Looking back on their
experiences at Kinchela, Bruce
Ellis admitted that 'doing the jobs
taught us boys that we had to
work for a living and that nothing
was free'.[194] while Richard Murray
commented wryly:

> It was a training school, but as for getting any training, I couldn't
> see it, 'cause no one was skilled in anything, no trades. If we'd had
> training in something, I suppose there wouldn't have been so much
> unemployment amongst the blacks.[195]

There was little time for rest and recreation. With few toys and games
or even sporting equipment the children had to make their own

amusements. Yet even here their time could be absorbed into the civilising project as they were encouraged to join various religious, musical and military style groups. The Church Lads Brigade at Yarrabah adopted military organisation and terminology to instruct the boys in British middle-class values of 'sobriety, thrift, self-help, punctuality [and] obedience'.[196] The Queensland Secretary for Health and Home Affairs in 1946 was more interested in boys' bodily posture and wrote that Boy Scouts training and drill would transform their 'slouching aboriginal gait' into 'an upright and manly posture'.[197] Discussing the operation of Boy Scouts groups in Native American residential schools in Canada, Miller[198] notes the irony of encouraging the boys to join an organisation steeped in the 'Romance of Empire' which promoted the ethos of white imperialism and militarism and taught its members imagined bush survival skills of colonised peoples, while at the same time the boys were taught to abandon the traditional skills of their own people. Such sensitivities were overlooked in a re-enactment of first contacts between whites and Aborigines at Palm Island during the Boy Scouts' 'Australian Family Robinson' jamboree in Queensland in 1936. White scouts from four Australian states disembarking from their boats on the beach were met by the settlement Aboriginal Boy Scouts troop painted in red, black and yellow ochre and brandishing spears.[199] Despite such ironies, many children enjoyed the relief from monotony that membership in these groups provided. Elkin Burrunga of Mowanjum near Derby in Western Australia recalled with relish the fanfare and celebration when the mission Girl Guides won competitions against other Guides and the enjoyment she gained from the trips away and the friendships she made outside her small community.[200]

HEALTHY BODIES AND MINDS

A further aspect of the reform process was the determination to erase any Aboriginal notions about the body and its care that the children may have absorbed,[201] and to train the children instead in the rigid processes of institutional hygiene and morality. Lack of resources to achieve these goals was compounded by ingrained white preconceptions about Aboriginal bodies expressed in a series of conceptual dualities — civilised/primitive, white/black, moral/depraved, clean/dirty, healthy/diseased. These often found expression in fears of contagion which encouraged controlling and punitive regimes. Pressures on the children to adopt institutional standards of personal hygiene were considerable, although they were very difficult to achieve given the dearth of ablution facilities, soap, towels, toiletries and clothing. Most institutions were unhealthy environments with alarmingly high rates of sickness and death — newcomers brought in disease and contagion, epidemics swept through the dormitories, buildings were unsanitary and poorly ventilated, the grounds were littered with safety hazards causing high accident rates, and minimal medical, dental, dietary and optical services were provided. The rare medical examinations could be a terrifying ordeal for the children. Marnie Kennedy recalled that at Palm Island:

> We were examined for VD, leprosy, cancer and any other disease that was going around. The VD examination was very frightening to us. We could hear kids screaming and when they came out they would tell us not to go in as they used a hot needle on us.[202]

In Western Australia in the 1950s an officer of the Aborigines Department claimed that children in missions would have received better medical attention had they remained with their parents since as pupils in state schools they would have received:

> at least one, and probably more, routine medical inspections by school doctors. The native child living in a mission has to my knowledge, no such advantage, and, if suffering from some defect, it is probable that it will pass unnoticed, with a consequent retardation of the child's progress and a worsening of the defect.[203]

Evidence gathered by Thom Blake[204] on conditions at Barambah explodes the notion that institutions were 'havens of health'. Into the 1920s deaths exceeded births, disease was widespread and between 1916 and 1925 one third of babies born there did not survive infancy. While officials of the period explained this in terms of racialist stereotypes of Aborigines as physically weak, inferior, susceptible to disease and fatalistic in the face of death, Blake identified contributory environmental factors including insanitary conditions — drinking water was pumped directly from a creek and there was no sewage system — and malnutrition and epidemics of childhood diseases and other contagions such as influenza. Population decline only began to be arrested during the late 1920s, following the introduction of sanitation, but extreme overcrowding and poor diet continued. In 1936 Dr A Jefferies Turner, Director of Infant Welfare and a leading

Queensland paediatrician, wrote of children in the compound:

> the physical condition of these children is deplorable. I am accustomed to the sight of ill-nourished children all over Queensland, but only as a minority or as isolated instances. Never before have I seen a whole classroom in which the majority, if not all, of the children were ill-nourished. These children have been ill-fed. I do not mean by this that they do not get enough to eat, but that their food is not such as to conduce to good health and physical development. I was not surprised to learn that they showed very poor resistance to disease, and that the condition of their teeth is very bad.[205]

Blake concludes that rather than improving health, conditions in the institutions exacerbated disease so that children were more susceptible and more likely to become seriously ill and, furthermore, that conditions were worse than in bush camps outside. In fact, conditions constituted a form of 'passive violence' by the state.[206] Such conditions were mirrored in institutions around Australia. Of 346 deaths recorded at Moore River settlement between 1918 and 1952, forty-two percent were children aged between one and five years. The major causes of death were bronchial-related disease and gastroenteritis.[207]

In place of resources to ensure good health there were endless inspections of bodies. The matron at Barambah checked children at the parade ground each morning before school and offending children had their ears soundly boxed. Lice inspections could lead to shaved heads, dreaded by girls and accompanied by floods of tears. Indeed Aboriginal girls' bodies were always a particular focus of concern in the institutions. This reflected in part a determination to impose Western standards of femininity, modesty and submission in appearance, posture, gesture and comportment, appropriate to their future station in life as domestic servants, wives and mothers.[208] This also

Woorabinda girls dormitory.
(Courtesy of Queensland Department of Aboriginal and Torres Strait Islander Policy and Development, QSA 62/91530NA, A/58935)

followed broader social programs directed at shaping white family life through indoctrination and control of white women. It was also directed at controlling Aboriginal female reproduction and family life by enforcing sexual purity and engraving a strict code of Christian sexual morality into their minds and bodies. Again this reflected powerful white imaginings about Aboriginal sexual precocity and traditional sexual practices. Pastor Kaibel of Hermannsburg enunciated these fantasies in rationalising the practice of locking up girls in the mission dormitories:

> the low intellectual status of the native … his utter rottenness in things sexual … (this action was essential) else they would swarm about all night and their mixing with parents and adults … would procure the direst results. No white man has any conception, not even the most wicked white, what depths of infamy these blacks are steeped in.[209]

Missionaries in particular were also determined to stop the girls from being incorporated into Aboriginal betrothal and marital practices. Aboriginal ways and physical characteristics were also denigrated by staff. Some girls in the more isolated children's homes grew up thinking that they were white and were shocked to learn of their Aboriginality. Alicia Adams thought she was 'different' from the other girls at Cootamundra:

> Yes I actually did, and I said to myself, 'These people are different, they're dark,' and I thought I was white you see. I said, 'I wonder why they're so dark?' I was looking at my sister Sally and thought, 'Dear she's really black' and you know, I was really confused. I looked at my skin, and I thought, 'I look brown like them too,' but I said, 'Oh no, I'm white … And I was real hurt because I didn't want to be brown, you know, I wanted to be white.'[210]

How were the girls instructed in these new ways? There was the example of their white female carers, the codes they set for the girls and their fiery determination to protect them from moral danger. In *Plains of Promise* Alexis Wright[211] indicates that the girls had other less 'worthy' models as well:

> Grace and Joan Chapel are beautiful, tall and slender, and their dark skin shines as though it has an all-over wax and polish. They are sophisticated, they read the *Women's Weekly* and they shave their

legs like film stars. Their legs are perfect and beautiful. Ivy Koopundi is fanatical in her desire to be like them and imagines there are similarities to herself whenever she chances a glance as they sit and gossip with the other girls in the dormitory ... Grace and Joan even act like film stars. Like those in movies about the killer women tribes in the Amazon jungle.

There were also the unspoken horrors hinted at in prayers, Bible classes, church and Sunday School of the consequences of an immoral life spent with 'low white men' and the 'barbaric' practices of Aboriginal men. At the same time there was total silence on all matters to do with the purpose and meaning of sex. The girls were forbidden to talk about their bodies. Ruth Hegarty recalled that:

It was dirty to talk about any part of your body. If you named the name you were dirty or talking dirty and you'd get punished for it ... Pregnant was a word you didn't use. If you noticed someone getting fat and said they were having a baby, 'you talk dirty' was the reply.[212]

The staff concentrated on separating the girls from temptation by keeping them under constant surveillance and control, and imposing strict rules on all contact with Aborigines in the camps. Courtship became an elaborate affair reminiscent of the traditions of Victorian England, requiring staff permission and constant watchfulness. Nellie Sheridan recalled meetings between young people at Barambah:

Three o'clock in the afternoon till five o'clock we could sit down outside and talk to the boys. The boys used to come down from the camp here, some had girlfriends and we used to sit down outside. Five o'clock the bell would ring and that gate in front of the dormitory used to be locked with a key. We had no reason for that: we wondered why we were treated the way we were. We never knew. It was just their rules, it was just the dormitory rules.[213]

Separated from their mothers and other Aboriginal women, the girls could not learn about Aboriginal ways of understanding female sexuality and of controlling conception. A frequent consequence of this repression and enforced ignorance was unexpected pregnancy, especially when the girls went out to work as domestic servants.[214] A further legacy was often an enduring sense of bodily shame. There were also the feelings of confusion as girls became aware of white sexual imaginings about them and as they realised that, simply by virtue of their Aboriginality, they could never achieve the standards of female whiteness they had been encouraged to desire.

LUX IN TENEBRIS — LIGHT IN DER DARKNESS[215]

The teaching of Christian beliefs and values was also an important part of the 'civilising project.' The central tenets of 'love of neighbour, compassion, forgiveness, reconciliation, work as prayer [and] morality independent of merely cultural convenience'[216] often became scrambled in the process. Lutheran missionary H Poland wrote in the *Church News* in 1889:

> We keep revising the Bible stories and they must surely derive some benefit from them; but some of them get them terribly mixed up ... Of course Podaigo and Kakural, in particular, are amazingly expert in family relationships of the various biblical characters. For such connections seem important to the blacks.[217]

Ernest Gribble recorded some amusing and telling adaptations of hymns and prayers by children at Yarrabah:

> At first we used the simplest hymns possible, 'Shall We Gather at the River?' being one of the first taught. I found, however, that the children had got hold of the second verse wrongly, and instead of singing, 'We will walk and worship for ever,' had it 'We will work and wash-up for ever.' In the Lord's Prayer, too, we found that the lads had learnt the petition 'And lead us not into temptation,' as 'Lead us not into the plantation.' Several had been punished from time to time for pilfering from the plantation.[218]

However, there were more serious aspects. While missionaries advocated Christian compassion and an end to all forms of victimisation, abuse and prejudice, many unfortunately repeated these patterns in their own work with the children. Indeed D Capps[219] argues that 'old-fashioned' Christian child-rearing practices could act to legitimate physical abuse by adults. The Biblical directive to break children's innate 'wayward will' and draw them to conformity with God through physical chastisement followed by a show of love, could be taken as a mandate to inflict violent punishment. Furthermore, some religious messages can be intimidating and frightening for children: fears of committing unpardonable sins, of lacking in faith, of apocalyptic events and of simply not being a good enough Christian to be saved. Selective interpretations of Biblical texts could also act to reinforce race prejudices and stereotypes.

While Aboriginal children conformed outwardly, many were troubled by inner confusion, conflicts between beliefs of their parents and the church, and the sheer exhaustion of their often excessive religious duties. Jean Beggs, who spent her early childhood in the Bomaderry Infants Home expresses some of this confusion and pain:

Bomaderry home was dominated with religion ... If we saw someone wearing lipstick we had to pray, because it was considered worldly, wicked and sinful — that was the type of fear we grew up in ... I remember being terrified of going into the dark. I was so scared that I would bump into Jesus and I would know him by the nail prints in his hand.[220]

The teachings shaped her views of Aboriginal people as well:

Besides that kind of religious fear, I had fear of Aborigines, knowing that they were evil, wicked. [I was] not understanding black, but only relating it to sin and drinking and cruelness.[221]

Wadjularbinna recalls her struggles to reconcile her parents' beliefs and the teachings of missionaries at Doomadgee:

My parents were allowed to visit me every Sunday, if they came to church ... They used to try and come every Sunday because they wanted to sit under the tree with us for about an hour and talk. I looked forward to that and they'd drum things into me and tell me that missionary's wrong, he's saying wrong, you know. And that was really bad for me, it was conflict going on in my head all the time. Dadda was killing a parrot to make a headband for a dance, for a ceremony ... And I just cried this Sunday when they took me for a walk. I said to my dad, 'Don't kill that. Jesus won't love you if you kill that bird.' My mother just turned around and walked over to me and she shook me, 'Hey,' she said, 'Missionary tell you another story; that's not good for us, that what missionary tell you. This is your way. Mamma and Dadda's way. This is our way and we been do this for a long time.'
We had to be home by five o'clock and I'd go to bed and I'd just

cry my eyes out because I didn't know who was who and who was right and what was going on. I loved my parents and I knew their way was right and their way was my way, but it was really hard for me to take. I'd go home and the missionaries would tell me something else — that my parents are just 'heathens' and they've got to learn this Christian way.[222]

John Harris[223] notes that while many children had positive memories, especially of the joyous religious celebrations and the rituals of baptism and confirmation, the majority recalled an 'excessive emphasis on religious instruction'.

Alongside this religious training there typically ran a powerful condemnation of Aboriginal practices and a determination to break the transmission of cultural traditions and knowledge between the generations. Through this work with the children the entire social system could be undermined and eventually replaced by a Christian community.

The handing on of the cultural tradition, assumed by ignorant sectarians to be of the devil, was deliberately and cruelly prevented … the missionaries' determination to promote Christian monogamy and marriage explains why even in the 1960s girls on some mission stations would be kept in lock-up dormitories until marriage; and the power of the missionary could be asserted in choosing a good Christian husband.[224]

While there were some notable exceptions to this outlook, such as the Presbyterian missions of Kunmunya in the Kimberley and Ernabella in South Australia, the fundamentalist UAM missionaries labelled Aboriginal traditions the 'work of Satan'. Elkin reported after a visit to Mount Margaret in 1930 that Schenk 'regarded all Aboriginal custom and belief as 'works of darkness'.[225] Even those European missionaries who recorded religious practices often condemned initiation, betrothal and polygamy as diabolical, barbaric, lewd and dangerous. Children were directed towards the model of the monogamous Christian nuclear family instead. 'The nomadic family group is the antithesis of the Christian family' wrote one missionary. Bishop F X Gsell wrote proudly of his efforts in this direction at Bathurst Island Mission in his book, *Bishop With 150 Wives*. Having worked for ten years with the adults and gained no converts he determined to work through the children, to influence them towards the settled mission life before they entered the rites of passage into adulthood — initiation for boys and marriage for girls. After he succeeded in persuading several boys to be baptised he hit on the idea of bartering goods with the girls' future husbands and families for controlling rights over them. In this way, between 1921 to 1938, Gsell won over 150 girls to the mission (hence the title of the book) who were educated, married to young mission men, settled in their own gardens and raised their children as Christians. They were also recruited to go out into surrounding communities to create the 'nucleus of a Christian community'. Gsell congratulated himself on his work:

> The wretched little slave of former days has become an accomplished young girl who may accept a husband who is a Christian youth. No longer is she forced to be the chattel of a degraded old man.[226]

Anthropologist Dianne Bell[227] notes that while Gsell undoubtedly changed Tiwi society on Bathurst Island he did not succeed in breaking down gender and marital relations. In fact, even the girls Gsell claimed to have 'saved' had not made completely free choices in marriage partners, but 'selected' boys to whom they had been tentatively promised by a relative or who were in the proper marital relationship to them.

TEACHING THEM 'THROUGH THEIR SKINS'

Former residents of all types of institutions, from boarding schools to prisons, invariably recall instances of punishment for seemingly trivial misdemeanours, often arbitrarily administered — a sudden whack across the head for no apparent reason — and hence more terrifying. They rarely recall examples of rewards for tasks well done. Such is the nature of institutional life. Punishment of young bodies is a powerful tool for manipulating young minds and was for many years an integral part of pedagogical processes, especially for boys. The body has a peculiar openness and what is learned through it, whether in pleasure or pain, 'is deeply embedded ... learned unconsciously, effortlessly and very early and with great difficulty lost.'[228] In Aboriginal children's institutions such practices were endorsed by a conception of Aboriginal corporeal nature, and indeed of colonised people and black races generally, as brutish, animalistic and child-like. This legitimated brutal punitive disciplinary treatment by whites: it was widely believed that, like animals, Aboriginal people were 'trained' most effectively through regular harsh physical punishment or threat. Thus the civilising project was often far from civilised in its implementation. Historian Ann McGrath[229] observes 'it was an uncomfortable contradiction for brutal punishment, essentially "uncivilised", to be employed as a means of "civilising" Aborigines.' The levels of violence and force in records of punishments and as recalled by members of the Stolen Generations, suggests an uneasy balance in the institutions with staff lacking authority and respect from the children and incapable of directing them by any other means than through force.

Embedded in the wider system of legal controls and prohibitions for all citizens, Aboriginal institutions also had their own 'separate system of law, discipline and punishment' with 'specific laws, policies, confinements and punishment designed to facilitate cultural and physical dispossession'.[230] Many of these powers were contained in Regulations to the various Aboriginal Acts. Regulations passed in Western Australia in 1918 to ensure compliance of Aborigines living at Moore River and Carrolup indicate the extent of powers to punish and the nature of misdemeanours, many of which were unique to Aboriginal institutions:

> Inmates are to work as directed, if they persistently refuse the Superintendent may withhold supplies or expel them.

> The Superintendent may inflict summary punishment by confinement for up to fourteen days for misconduct, neglect of duty, insubordination or breach of regulation.

> The Superintendent may inflict corporal punishment on any inmate under sixteen guilty of an offence against the regulations or for leaving or attempting to leave without permission.[231]

Institutional staff also defined further misdemeanours and administered forms of punishment not formally sanctioned by law. These misdemeanours were often trivial in nature and the punishments out of all proportion to the 'crime'. In 1918 the Superintendent of Carrolup, W J Fryer, was reprimanded in the Katanning Police Court after he admitted chaining a girl to a bed by the neck for three days to prevent her from leaving the settlement.[232] The Matron's Log for the Senior Girls Home at Yarrabah provides the following comprehensive list of punishable misdemeanours:

rudeness, disrespect, reluctant attitudes towards duties, half heartedness, disobedience, obstinacy, laziness, lack of enthusiasm, despicable, bad, and sullen spirits, naughtiness, running away, missing school, threats of violence, ridiculously babyish behaviour, disregarding rules such as visiting the married people's homes or talking to boys, insolence, dirty habits, impertinence and fighting amongst themselves.[233]

At Palm Island boys were 'imprisoned' for waving to girls and on one occasion a thirteen-year-old was locked up for wearing sandshoes.[234] Monty Pryor was imprisoned and then thrown off the island after he refused to address his friend, the son of the settlement doctor, as 'Master':

He was no master of mine ... He called me by my name, so why shouldn't I call him by his? He said 'you go back and apologise.' And I said 'I won't.' I did seven day's jail with bread and water over that.
A couple of weeks later I was dumped over on the mainland. Just left there with nowhere to go or what to do. Luckily the publican over there was a friend of my father and that's how I got from one place to another.[235]

Girls were also imprisoned, as Marnie Kennedy recalls:

[The matron] knew how to dish out punishment for the least little thing. I was thrown in jail for singing a song called 'Who said I was a bum?' I didn't know the matron was doing the rounds of the dormitory, and she heard me. All she said was 'come with me' and she shoved me in jail for the night. I was given a bag of beans to crack until nine o'clock, and no supper. I tried eating the beans but they were hard and dry. I was very frightened and hungry and cried myself to sleep. I was let out next morning after a lovely breakfast of dry bread and water.[236]

Most institutions had a special detention room — at Cootamundra it was the former hospital morgue — and other contained spaces, such as cupboards, where the children were routinely locked up as punishment. Shortly after his appointment as Commissioner of Native Affairs in 1948, Stanley Middleton was shown the 'boob' at Moore River settlement:

One of the buildings was introduced to me as being 'the boob.' I knew, because I'm a country Queenslander, what was meant by 'boob' — it was prison. I said, 'What have you got this for?' 'Oh,' he said, 'we lock them up.' I said, 'Why?' 'Oh,' he said, 'if they've done anything they shouldn't we put them in here for the night.' But I said, 'On what authority?' 'Oh,' he said, 'I'm the Superintendent.'[237]

There were also cruel and humiliating beatings. Dick Roughsey recalled that at Mornington Island:

If a boy was caught stealing another's clothes, or fruit and vegetables from the garden, he got a good hiding. The boy to be punished was laid face-down on the table and held by four men while he was belted on the bare bottom about fifteen times with a piece of rubber from an old car inner tube. I can still remember the blisters on my bottom.[238]

At Yarrabah a senior girl regarded by the matron as lazy, disobedient and obstinate, was whipped after she refused to attend church.[239] Marnie Kennedy recalled beltings by the matron at Palm Island:

One of the many beltings I remember well: I did some small wrong and was cuffed over the ears so hard that it dropped me. My ears rang all night and I cried all night. Most of us kids copped this kind of treatment.[240]

Parents living in the institutions sometimes retaliated on behalf of their children, usually with serious consequences for their own liberty. In 1940 a Moore River inmate was sent to prison after he attacked the superintendent for thrashing his son.[241]

Brutal punishments continued into the 1960s. At Doomadgee twelve fourteen-year-old girls were physically beaten by their parents on the superintendent's instructions and several had their heads shaved after they ran away from the dormitory because they 'could no longer suffer the discipline'.[242] Charles Rowley wrote of floggings still inflicted on Aboriginal residents at the Hopevale Lutheran mission during the 1960s, including:

… a case of flogging of a man and a girl there, allegedly by the superintendent. The minister responsible for Aboriginal Affairs stated that the 'caning' was administered by 'tribal elders.' This had to be nonsense except as a good example of the working of the 'trusty' system on the Queensland settlements.[243]

The Federal Council for the Advancement of Aborigines (FCAA) had taken up this case where the twenty-one-year-old man and sixteen-year-old girl were punished for flouting mission orders not to court each other — the man had received twelve lashes, administered by the missionary head E Kernick, and was then placed in gaol in Cooktown for seven days and sent on to Palm Island. The missionary also ordered that the girl should be whipped and have her head shaved. A subsequent inquiry, appointed after concerted lobbying by the FCAA and its supporters, found that the missionary's actions were 'inexcusable' and caused considerable embarrassment to the Queensland government in exposing the authoritarian powers of its so-called protection legislation.[244]

In addition to corporal punishment, imprisonment and solitary confinement, there were punishments based on various forms of deprivation, public humiliation and the assigning of meaningless arduous tasks. At Yarrabah, public shaming included the publishing of names of those reprimanded or punished in the *Aboriginal News*, being made to kneel or stand in public for long periods, public beatings, and the cutting and shaving of inmates' hair.[245] Dormitory girls who fell pregnant were denied a proper ceremony and were put through 'ragtime weddings' in front of the other inmates with their heads shaved and dressed in rags.[246] Some were exiled to Palm Island.

Rebellion and resistance, expressing the children's resentment and desperation, were frequently behind behaviours eliciting punishment. 'Absconding' was a serious and often dangerous instance of this. On the outside, children were vulnerable to a host of dangers, as well as bringing problems for those who helped them, and when they were caught they were punished severely. Nevertheless children ran away repeatedly. Fifteen-year-old Laura Dinah escaped from Carrolup on numerous occasions over a twelve-month period between 1918 and 1919 and was imprisoned for a total of sixty-four days.[247] Former Moore River residents had strong memories of girls running away:

A lot of the girls used to want to get away from there. Some of them jumped a train to go to Perth. They used to take them back and lock them up but they'd do it again. They were the ones who couldn't settle, or just wanted to get out and see what life was about I suppose.[248]

If the girls ran away they were tracked by the trackers, apprehended and brought back again and locked up in the place we called 'the boob', which was a small galvanised iron building with no proper facilities either for washing or for toilet. Their food was taken to them. They had no exercise and they were left for varying periods according to their misdemeanours.[249]

As in all institutional communities the children developed ways of subverting surveillance and punishments. Information networks about staff and institutional activities were integral to this, as Morris[250] observes:

Intelligence about those in authority and covert communication networks are essential if some measure of prediction and anticipation of possible responses or likely actions of those in authority are to be mediated or avoided. Rather than compliance with institutional authority, what was produced was covert, collective information that was used to place limits on the manager's control. This also generated an oppositional sense of identity.

Nor could the children be kept under constant surveillance — there were inevitably places where they could isolate activities from the view of their keepers and intersecting spaces where Aboriginal and white ways met. This was particularly so in the large institutions where children might visit the camps on weekends, watch corroborees and absorb in various ways Aboriginal traditions and knowledge and a positive consciousness of Aboriginal difference. Jack Davis' visits to adults in the camp at Moore River introduced him to Aboriginal culture and shaped his commitment as an adult to writing and political activism. Within very narrow bounds, there was also some room for negotiating outcomes with disciplinarians. The role of the older girls, whose work and cooperation were integral to the smooth functioning of the compounds, may explain the following outcomes at Yarrabah. In 1908 the matron at Yarrabah resigned following what she termed the 'despicable' behaviour of four girls during roll call but withdrew her resignation after the girls apologised to her. In the same year Ernest Gribble decided, following the 'open honesty of the confession' to him by a girl who was to be severely punished by Matron for breaking a cup at tea-time 'in a temper', that her behaviour necessitated only 'earnest words of reproof'.[251]

During debate on the Stolen Generations during the mid-1990s a frequent assertion by conservative leaders like Federal Minister for Aboriginal and Torres Strait Islanders, Senator John Herron, was that Aboriginal children benefited from the experience of being removed from their families. This despite repudiation of such views by the voluminous reports of the Royal Commission into Aboriginal Deaths in Custody (1991), the *Bringing Them Home* Report (1997) of the Human Rights and Equal Opportunity Commission Inquiry into the Separation of Aboriginal and Torres Strait Islander Children from their Families and submissions to these inquiries by Aboriginal organisations such as the Western Australian Aboriginal Legal Service (1995). The Royal Commission into Aboriginal Deaths in Custody exposed the tragic end in prison for some of the people in its finding that nineteen of its thirty-two case studies had been removed from their families. The hundreds of personal histories collected by the Western Australian Aboriginal Legal Service from those who grew up in institutions referred again and again to the problems they experienced trying to live 'on the outside':

> Most said they simply did not have the life skills to cope. On top of this many had no home to speak of, nowhere to go and no job. Some had so much trouble surviving outside the institution they ended up going back time and time again although they despised the place. At the same time they were dealing with the stresses of trying to live in society, without having any of that society's life skills. They were culturally adrift in a society that was endemically racist toward them.[252]

The *Bringing Them Home* report[253] provided a depressing list of enduring effects of institutionalisation on Aboriginal children separated from their families. They experienced problems in physical, social, intellectual and emotional development manifested in learning problems, difficulties in forming social relationships, antisocial behaviour, lack of personal identity, emotional disorders and feelings of alienation. As adults they experienced breakdown of family relationships, high levels of unemployment, substance abuse, imprisonment, poor health and mental disorders. There were also the devastating effects of a system that denigrated Aboriginal ways and encouraged the children to identify with white people and then sent them out into a world where they were looked down on for being Aboriginal. They were left to search for an identity in 'the very world they had been denied: the shadowy and disparaged world of Aboriginality'.[254]

Nevertheless, within the many accounts of removal and institutionalisation which the Stolen Generations have recounted to the Australian public there are also profound insights into the strength of the human spirit to survive and find worth in the darkest of worlds and to salvage some happiness from a deprived and hurtful childhood. The pain of growing up without the love of her parents remained strong in Lizzy Dalgetty's memories of life at Moore River:

> What I didn't like about it, I didn't have any love from my own parents. You know, being taken away like that, lot of kids have had love from their parents if they had of stayed, and would have felt more better inside if they were with their own parents. We didn't because we didn't have somebody to love us, sort of business. If you'd been loved, I think it would have been a different story, but we had nobody to love us. We had to just find our own way out, most of us, in the world without love.[255]

In South Australia, Lewis O'Brien regretted the sort of outlook and preparation for life that the institutional experience gave him:

> Institutionalisation teaches you to suppress all emotions. You don't learn all the natural things you learn in ordinary life. In the end what it does teach you — you don't do nothing because you'll get whacked. You learn by these lessons of being slapped and hit and told you're a nasty little boy.[256]

Margaret Brusnahan's memories were of being repeatedly told that she was 'bad, wicked, I was told that I would end up in gaol before I was twenty-one', and of cruel punishments. 'I was locked in broom cupboards and made to kneel on split peas with my hands on my head.' Through all this she demonstrated an indomitable courage and spirit:

> I'd always hold my own, even though I knew what I'd get at the end of it. You thought it would cripple you for life, but it didn't cripple your tongue. There was just that little mechanism in me that makes me go further.
> There's a lot of pain in having fingers, legs broken. But it takes a lot longer to repair spirits, minds. That takes a whole lifetime. When

you're adult and you can't accept that anybody loves you, that's because some other part of you has been broken.[257]

Connie Nungulla McDonald was inspired by the example of the older Aboriginal people she met while she was growing up in the Forrest River Mission dormitory:

The mission Aborigines gave me an example of dependability and education and the tribal Aborigines taught me to be me.

The period during the war when we were without missionaries had been a happy time. Observing my people taught me that we were capable of running our own lives. It gave me a glimpse of what life must have been before the *gudiyars* [white people] came. I emerged with more faith in myself and in my people and with a capacity to look on the missionaries as less god-like than I had been led to believe. They taught me to understand what it meant to be fully human … Having a rebellious nature enabled me to see more clearly what the government system was doing to us and to realise that some of the missionaries treated us like animals or convicts.[258]

There were also special lifelong and life-sustaining friendships formed between the children in the dormitories as Ruth Hegarty recalled:

It drew us together. We became sisters. We are all sisters, always have been. We looked about for one another. Even when we were married, we kept together … We had a bond.[259]

For Connie Ellement it was this same love and friendship that enabled her to survive:

I realise now my biggest gain was to experience the powerful and fine force of love between children collected together over such a long period of time and in such large numbers. This love and caring between children which pulled us through together is also what enabled me to survive.[260]

CHAPTER SEVEN

VISIONS OF ASSIMILATION

Images of 'assimilation' and 'the Fifties' are linked inextricably. If 'the Fifties' evokes images of 'complacency, conformity [and] a kind of cosy comfortableness' and of an Australia that was 'either static, complacent and monocultural, or ... prosperous, unified and satisfyingly middle class',[1] then 'assimilation' speaks of the road that was to lead all Australians, regardless of class, ethnicity or race, to the destination where these homely images converged — the modern suburban family home. Here, Australian families could settle, safe from the traumas of earlier economic insecurities and the upheaval of war, into a dream of domestic contentment and comforting sameness. But, if we look past the 'cosy comfortableness' evoked by 'the Fifties', we see dreamers tossing uneasily, haunted by Cold War fears of global atomic annihilation and more local concerns about threats to a 'White Australia', erosion of the social and moral order and the pressures of maintaining the image of domestic bliss and material prosperity. Similarly, if we look closely at the road to this dream we see it was often a rocky one which could lead those pushed onto it to unanticipated destinations.

From the 1950s the policy of assimilation was adopted by governments across Australia as the road to take the nation's estimated 80,000 Aboriginal people out of the institutions, pastoral stations, camping reserves and fringe camps and into modern suburban family life. This was due in part to federal government efforts to lead the states away from parochial concerns in dealing with Aborigines, towards new international standards of human rights. Humanitarian and Aboriginal organisations were agitating for reform and, overall, the public was more sympathetic to change. This reflected a postwar shift away from racialist explanations of social inequality and a rejection of social systems based on racism and colonialism that was expressed in the new vision of a 'global human family' free from racial differences and conflict. In these contexts, the policy of social assimilation of Aborigines — a concept reaching back into the nineteenth century and raised seriously during the 1930s as an alternative to existing race-based policies — appeared both natural and inevitable. Many Australian leaders were gripped by the image of intact modern Aboriginal families living in comfort in neat suburban homes with Dad at work, the kids at school and Mum in the kitchen. Assimilationists assumed that this 'Australian dream'[2] was an 'Aboriginal dream' as well and were supremely confident that their plans were 'for the good of all'.

Many Aboriginal people were more than ready for *positive* changes to their legal status and living conditions. From the 1920s Aboriginal protesters had been calling for full citizenship rights, equal standards of living and equal pay for equal work, although not an end to their cultural way of life. To the political agitation for citizenship were added new expectations generated by Aborigines' wartime experiences. Everywhere the rigid systems of administrative control of Aborigines had weakened as resources and staff were redirected to the war effort. At the same time dislocation and separation of families increased with mass movement across northern Australia. Institutions in and around Darwin were evacuated and women and children sent south where many had their first 'close-up' experience of conventional urban life. Children from Croker Island had the traumatic ordeal of walking overland to Pine Creek to be trucked to Alice Springs and then on to Adelaide where they were hived off to institutions and family billets in New South Wales and Victoria. In the Kimberley, women and children were evacuated from Broome to Beagle Bay and 'trouble-makers' from the missions were sent off to provide much needed labour on the pastoral stations. Aborigines at Forrest River Mission were left behind to run their own affairs.[3] Settlements in Queensland, New South Wales and southern Western Australia were emptied as workers were commandeered for wartime labour demands. Aborigines in the armed services experienced new, liberating ways of interacting with their white peers, many of whom learned a new respect and affection for the Aboriginal 'diggers'. In southern Australia Aboriginal families experienced a new level of economic prosperity with domestic and rural workers in full-time employment and on full pay, and the promise of access to social security benefits. New employment opportunities in factories attracted many families to a new way of life in the city. For many Aborigines legal prohibitions on access to alcohol became a potent symbol of their continued oppression. In remote areas where Aborigines were still paid in rations, equal wages was becoming the catchcry. By the end of the war discontented pastoral workers across the Pilbara in Western Australia were out on strike and their complaints were spilling over into their general treatment by government as well. One striker commented, 'We are just waking up to the Government laws against us. Just because our colour is black we have not the right to go where we want.'[4]

However, despite all these changes the end of the war brought a frustrating 'return to the mat'. Most families were forced back into conditions of extreme poverty and escalating unemployment, often with large numbers of dependent children. Race barriers were reasserted and families found they were once again outcasts in their own country. Administrative controls were also put back into place. Rather than developing on Aboriginal initiatives, administrators regrouped, reasserted their former powers and embarked on the new battle to enforce Aboriginal assimilation. In some ways this task echoed the earlier efforts to reform working-class families into responsible citizens through a package of economic, educational, medical and environmental programs centred on the modern nuclear family. This family unit now became the goal for Aborigines to strive towards and the unit of government intervention. However, in the case of the 1950s assimilation program, funding and political will were insufficient to bring about real improvements for Aboriginal families. Punitive controls continued — including removal of children — along with Aboriginal resistance to the breaking up of their extended family networks and the threat to their survival as a distinct people and culture. Postwar visions of racial tolerance and equality inspired a renewed burst of political protest against this ongoing oppression, by Aborigines and their supporters who were linked into expanding state and national organisations. Tensions between administrators and Aborigines escalated, despite the similarity of their stated goals of citizenship and social and economic equality, and governments lost the opportunity to negotiate a common ground. Instead, these organisations developed into a powerful oppositional force.

The lives of Aboriginal children in the deplorable town camps and run-down institutional dormitories remained a long way from official imaginings of assimilated family life and a far cry from the realities, dreams and hopes of other young Australians. Many white children were growing up in an atmosphere of stable family life, surrounded by unprecedented levels of material comfort. They were the focus of sustained pedagogical and commercial interest by a myriad of institutions intent on channelling them into conventional pathways of school, career, marriage and parenthood and into habits of self-centred consumerism. 'Teenagers' were now constructed as a separate social category requiring special monitoring and assistance, and were targeted as consumers by the burgeoning teen market. While Aboriginal children and youth may have looked longingly at new consumer items, they were, overall, marginal to these broader social processes. However, they *were* the focus of the intent gaze of Aboriginal administrators, who continued to view children as the solution to the 'Aboriginal problem'.

The forced separation of children from their families continued; in fact removals appear to have increased, although the statistics are unreliable. After years of neglect of Aboriginal schooling, authorities now looked to education as the socialising, moralising and normalising force to break the 'cycle of poverty' and to give children 'the will, as well as the means, to organise their lives within a project of self-betterment through diligence, application, and commitment to work, family and society'.[5] To this end many children were separated from their families for prolonged periods, living with white supervisors in hostels and 'boarding schools' and with white families or relatives in town. Families were also drawn into the ambit of mainstream systems of child welfare and juvenile justice. In one respect, the extension of Aboriginal legal rights and the alignment of 'Aboriginal welfare' with mainstream agencies restrained summary removals of children and gave parents more say. However, given Aboriginal disadvantage, destitution and cultural patterns of parenting, families were more likely to be condemned by mainstream standards, and the children deemed to be 'neglected', 'delinquent' or 'criminal', than non-Aboriginal children as a whole, contributing to ongoing high levels of separation of Aboriginal children from their families. Many children were now placed in white foster families, adopted by white couples or placed in mainstream child welfare or juvenile detention centres.

New imaginings

The assimilated urban Aboriginal family was one of several official images of Aborigines presented to an increasingly interested

Australian nation from the 1950s. Aborigines were now on the agenda. Public preoccupation with the tragic experiences of minority groups in Europe during the war had stimulated a general interest in issues of race and the situation of Australia's Aboriginal minority in particular. This was reinforced by official campaigns to promote racial tolerance in keeping with new international standards and media reports of Aboriginal political protest against ongoing oppression and inequality. Despite government determination to maintain a virtual monopoly over the 'production of public meaning about Aboriginal affairs',[6] other voices began to enter the public forum, generating increasingly complex and often contradictory understandings about Aborigines and imaginings about their 'rightful' place in Australian society. Startling images of Aboriginal families living in desperate conditions in remote Australia and in southern town fringe camps revived earlier calls for stricter segregation *and* for the acceleration of official assimilation programs, reflecting divided community opinion. Similar contradictory responses were evoked by the tragic narrative of overwhelming psychological tension, degradation and early death experienced by Aborigines 'trapped between two cultures'. These themes reverberated through many 1950s cultural productions — the feature film, *Jedda*, press coverage of the 'rise and fall' of Arrente artist, Albert Namatjira, and artist Arthur Boyd's *Bride Series*.[7] Sanitised press photographs of smiling Aboriginal children separated from their families inspired offers from white families to take them in as an ultimate stage in the assimilation process, a step which appeared to contradict official aims of creating Aboriginal nuclear families. This was symptomatic of divided official and public opinion on how best to achieve assimilation — through the old practice of removing children from their families or by transforming the unit of mother, father and children as a whole.

THE DREAM

Assimilation was the theme of a series of pamphlets[8] — *Our Aborigines* (1957), *Assimilation of Our Aborigines* (1958), *Fringe Dwellers* (1959), *The Skills of Our Aborigines* (1960), *One People* (1961) and *The Aborigines and You* (1963) — published by the federal Minister for Territories, ostensibly for the 'celebration of National Aboriginal Day'. These pamphlets represented a major shift from earlier official images of 'family-less' children in segregated institutions, to a new language and imagery of assimilated, intact Aboriginal families. While presented as celebrating achievements made, they were in fact constructed representations of assimilationist *goals* for Aborigines — many of the 'family shots' were staged using inmates from the Retta Dixon Children's Home in Darwin[9] — published as a propaganda exercise to convince Australians to support assimilation and to provide a positive image of race relations overseas. A lesson of the war years was the value of propaganda in manipulating public opinion and this remained an integral tool of governing during the fifties, sixties and beyond. A further lesson was the mobilising power of federalism: there was hope amongst Aboriginal and humanitarian organisations that federal intervention could bring about real change for Aboriginal people. This hope was to be thwarted by a lack of real commitment by the federal government and resistance by the states to surrendering control.

The Minister for Territories with responsibility for Aboriginal affairs from 1951 to 1963 was (Sir) Paul Hasluck. He was a long-time public advocate of assimilation through his journalistic writing for the *West Australian* newspaper in the 1930s[10], and in public speeches during the 1950s which he published in the press and privately under the title *Native Welfare in Australia*.[11] During the 1950s he set the parameters of official assimilation policy. He was convinced that it was an inevitable process that was already under way in the face of 'the crumbling away of aboriginal society and culture' and that Aborigines 'at all stages of progress from the primitive to the fully civilised' would eventually come to 'live like us'.[12] In essence Hasluck's vision was a 'doctrine of nationhood'[13] which:

> turned its back on the past and proposed a new beginning in the form of an affluent, classless, monocultural society: the poor would forget their former privations; migrants would forget Europe; and the Aborigines would forget their past. In return, all would enjoy the 'Australian way of life.'[14]

This also reflected Hasluck's 'liberalism of inclusion',[15] grounded in a concept of nationhood which viewed racial or culturally distinct entities within the nation to be dangerous — a version of liberalism which continues to have wide appeal. The cooperation of state governments and all white Australians was essential in the process of assimilation, and Hasluck took on the task of persuading the states to adopt this vision. To this end the meeting of Commonwealth and State ministers of Aboriginal Affairs which Hasluck convened in Canberra in 1951 issued a statement that 'social barriers' to assimilation must be overcome and 'it behoves all sections of the community to cooperate in the ultimate assimilation of our native people.'[16] In a climate of greater 'sympathy and interest' but 'much less knowledge and understanding' about Aborigines (Hasluck's words),[17] and of national aspirations for peaceful uniformity, images of Aboriginal domesticity and conformity had the power to appeal to audiences entranced by their own dreams of suburban family life and gripped by a genuine popular altruism — however misguided.

Hasluck was equally determined to counter any criticisms of the legal status and political rights of Aborigines in the global climate of concern over race issues following the Second World War. His experience as a diplomat in the Department of External Affairs — he assisted in formulating the Charter of the United Nations in 1945 and planning the first meeting of the United Nations Assembly in Geneva during 1946–48 — had alerted him to the role of government as 'custodian of the national reputation' and shaped his commitment to creating 'good global citizen[s] while maintaining the Australian "way of life".'[18] Indeed, Australia was obliged, through its membership of the United Nations and as signatory to its covenants, and its mandate over the territory of New Guinea, to remove all race-based, discriminatory legislation and practice in keeping with new intellectual currents on race enshrined in the United Nations Charter 1945, the Universal Declaration of Human Rights 1948, UNESCO anti-race statements 1950–51 and other international covenants into the 1960s. In this climate it was inevitable that local events such as the punitive treatment of strikers at the Berrimah compound on the outskirts of Darwin in 1951 by the Director of Native Affairs, culminating in the exile of the strike leader Fred Waters (Nadpur) to the isolated Aboriginal reserve Haast Bluff 1250 kilometres south of Darwin, would draw adverse comment overseas and at home, causing considerable embarrassment for Hasluck's administration.[19] It was also incumbent on the Australian government to support decolonisation and the rights of colonised peoples to physical and cultural survival and self-determination. Although Australia endeavoured to distinguish the situation of its indigenous peoples from those swept up in the decolonisation movement, many overseas leaders were not convinced. Australia's argument to the 1961 Commonwealth Prime

Ministers' Conference that South Africa's apartheid system was 'a matter of domestic jurisdiction for South Africa and thus not the business of other Commonwealth Prime Ministers',[20] brought adverse attention from African and Asian Commonwealth countries. In the same year the Ghana mission to the United Nations threatened to place the Aboriginal question on the agenda of the General Assembly. There were regular reports critical of the Australian government in the press of decolonising African countries.[21] In October 1961 Australia was embarrassed by accusations of genocide made in the United Nations by Nikita Krushchev, then General Secretary of the Soviet Union, and his call for the 'complete and final liberation of all peoples from colonial oppression'.[22] The Moscow press reported that Kruschev had:

pointed to the eternal shame that rested on the ruling class of Australia for the extermination of the Aborigines ... His reference had brought home that, in the sphere of modern international policies, Australia's prestige may ultimately depend as much, if not more, on her treatment of Aborigines.[23]

Australian governments were slow to acknowledge that the Aboriginal issue was no longer a purely domestic matter. Nevertheless, behind closed doors there was also considerable hostility and paranoia about international criticism. Hasluck was convinced that the Communist Party of Australia was using the race issue to provoke social conflict within Australia and to tarnish its image abroad. In 1963 he told the Native Welfare Council meeting — the annual meetings of state and federal Ministers of Aboriginal Affairs convened by Hasluck — of a 'definite planned campaign by both International Communism and by the Australian Communist Party' to paint Australia as:

one of the Western powers [that] can be discredited internationally so that the African and Asian nations will get a picture of us as a country full of racial antagonism and racial prejudices, and generally, in the international sphere, to lessen our influence and to besmirch our name.[24]

His chagrin can be imagined when he was informed that the *New Times*, a Moscow weekly published in eight languages, had used material depicting conditions in New South Wales Aboriginal fringe

Images from the federal government pamphlet, Fringe Dwellers *(1959) portray the steps from 'Stone Age' Aborigines to modern citizens.*

camps from his pamphlet, *One People*, to attack the treatment of Aborigines in Australia.[25]

In 1961 Hasluck's pamphlets were ruled to be 'thoroughly unsuitable for overseas readers' by the Department of External Affairs because of their muddled explanations of official policy, misleading facts and failure to inform readers about Aborigines' legal status and political rights.[26] Nevertheless, they continued to be distributed widely within Australia as part of Hasluck's campaign to change domestic opinion on Aboriginal issues. Their perceived strategic importance is reflected in their highly constructed layout, text and imagery of modernity. They are imbued with notions of a receding Aboriginal past and an assimilated future with the modern family as the vehicle and destination, and children as the focal point of change. *Fringe Dwellers* is replete with contrasts of the old and the new. Images of fringe camps, Aboriginal elders, traditional life, segregation, poverty and an absence of white people are juxtaposed with modern homes, urban life, nuclear families, hygiene, youthfulness, gendered family roles, white visitors, men working outside the home and white professionals such as teachers and nurses. Two-thirds of the images are of children and captions underscore their significance: 'The programme of assimilation throughout Australia concentrates particularly on children. For many of them, and in due course for their children, hopes for assimilation are high.'[27] There are also direct messages for white Australian and overseas audiences about shifting race attitudes leading to the 'trend ... towards helping the fringe dwellers to find their rightful place in the wider world'.[28] The cover of *One People* shows children of various cultural and racial backgrounds clustered around a globe of the world, suggesting the 'global nuclear family' sharing space and sameness and a unity achieved through education. The imagery in *The Aborigines and You* provides a straightforward visual narrative progression of 'stone age man to citizen', climaxing in images of Aboriginal and white Australians working amicably together. It directly addresses the Australian public with instructions for 'What you can do':

> offer friendship and a helping hand if they need it; guide them in their personal and social problems; assist them with the education of their children; help them to get and keep jobs; show them how to budget their income; influence the attitude of other Australians towards them; encourage a pride in their aboriginal ancestry; make them feel welcome in the community where they belong.[29]

The final shot is of a baby in a bath — the naked raw material on which the whole process rests.

State governments also had their own publications, put out with an eye to impressing white readers, but directed principally at persuading Aboriginal audiences that the 'Australian dream' was for them as well. James Miller[30] has described the New South Wales government magazine *Dawn* (*New Dawn* from 1966), distributed free of charge to Aboriginal families throughout the state, as an 'instrument of social engineering' peddling assimilationist propaganda through its imagery, cover pages, special features and editorials. An issue in 1956 attempted to persuade Aboriginal readers of the validity of the government's fostering program:

> Modern thought on the question of the placement of dependent children recognises that the best substitute for a child's home, is a

foster home … in view of the fact that many wards in the Board's care are of light caste, efforts were made late in 1955 to secure foster homes for these amongst white people. Furthermore this was regarded as being a positive step in implementing the Board's policy of assimilation.[31]

An unintended effect of the magazine was that some families were able to identify and trace children held in the Bomaderry, Cootamundra and Kinchela homes through its photographs. In 1964, following the lifting of legal prohibitions on alcohol in the south, the Western Australian government embarked on an educational campaign to inform Aborigines and the public of Aborigines' new citizenship rights and responsibilities and to get across the message that this meant more than just 'the right to drink'.[32] Publications included an instructional 'how to' primer, *Western Australian Citizens*,[33] with illustrations optimistically depicting Aborigines living in conventional nuclear suburban homes, surrounded by consumer goods, wearing fashionable clothes and generally acting as citizens — voting, working, drinking in hotels and seeking police assistance in upholding

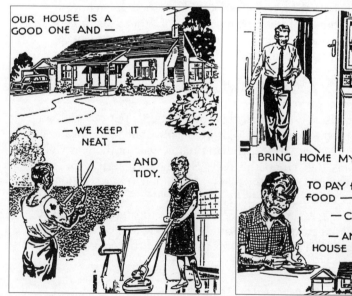

Selling assimilation to Aboriginal people.
(West Australian Citizens, nd, courtesy of Aboriginal Affairs Department, Western Australia)

their rights. A film series on suburban life included a cartoon segment where people carrying flagons of wine tumbled out of cars into a suburban house which suddenly exploded while a prim voice warned, 'Loud parties will cause trouble.'[34]

Hasluck's pamphlets appeared to be achieving some change as white residents in many country towns became actively involved in philanthropic projects to promote assimilation. However, hard-core race attitudes and town 'caste barriers' proved resistant to change. Hasluck himself fought to overcome such resistance — from 1953 he waged a war of words with officials in the Northern Territory Administration to secure housing for 'good' Aboriginal families in the new suburbs of Alice Springs.[35] Aboriginal living conditions also lagged far behind the comfortable depictions of family life in the pamphlets. However, white audiences believed the images and were convinced that the opportunity was there for all Aborigines to achieve these ideals if they wanted to. It followed that individual Aborigines were at fault. This view became widespread in the community and was apparently absorbed by some Aborigines as well, quoted in official publications as saying, 'We can do equally well if we really try — and get into it.'[36] Popular imagined narratives spread through the wider community where the decision to take the assimilation road and to reach its destination was seen to come down solely to a matter of individual decision and willpower:

A grinning friend is at the door, he holds flagons of wine … This is the test a settled aboriginal must face. The ordeals of building a new life … His impulse is to cry 'Come in!' His tribal ethic of hospitality demands it.

If he says those words it will be the start of a party. Before the night is out 20 people will be drunk in his house.

And he would like a party.

But he cannot afford to hesitate.

'No!' he shouts and slams the door.

He must do that. Otherwise his whole status, all he has fought for for years comes into peril.

That, in essence, is the basic problem of the aboriginal as he tries to adapt to life in a white community in the process officially known as 'assimilation.'[37]

During the late 1950s audiences across southern Australia were shocked by footage filmed[38] in 1957 by Western Australian Independent Liberal politician, Bill Grayden, showing injured, diseased and emaciated Aboriginal children and adults from the Warburton Ranges area in the Central Reserve. Screened in public forums, these images provoked a national outcry about Aboriginal conditions in the interior — apparently tolerated by the Western Australian and federal governments — and concern about the future of these communities and the vast reserve lands they inhabited. Debate also hinted at the connections between growing white incursions into these lands, and policies of assimilation and relocation of families and forced separation of children. These were matters of considerable concern for a nation that had just survived a war that many believed had been caused by 'the treatment of minorities and the oppression, or neglect, of little people too weak to stand up for themselves and always at the mercy of larger communities or greater Governments.'[39] These controversies proved an inspiration for protest action in southern Australia by established political organisations such as the Communist Party of Australia and newly formed groups such as the Aborigines Advancement League, formed in Melbourne in response to the issue. Aboriginal child removal was also located in the context of new international debates about the rights of children. However all this failed to provoke positive action by the Western Australian or federal governments to improve conditions for the people or to protect their lands.

The Ngaanyatjara people depicted in the film were living on a 'last frontier'. In contact from the 1930s with missionaries from the United Aborigines Mission (UAM) who established an outpost in the Warburton Ranges, their country and adjacent regions were now targeted by international scientific and military forces for atomic weapons testing and military and weather surveillance, and by multi-national mining companies. In 1955 the Western Australian government excised four million acres from the Central Reserve for mineral exploration. In August the following year the Australian government announced the first atomic tests at Maralinga in Central Australia.[40] Bill Grayden, who travelled through the area in 1953 and 1955, was alarmed at the possible impact of these changes and by rumours that the Department of Native Welfare (DNW) intended to curtail mission services and to truck all school-age children four hundred miles away to Cosmo Newbery, a former Aboriginal correctional institution handed over to the UAM in 1954, to be trained for employment in the local pastoral industry.[41] Late in 1956, in an emotional speech to Parliament,[42] Grayden successfully moved for the appointment of a select committee to inquire into the situation. He devoted particular attention to the plight of the children and, for the first time in a Western Australian parliament, quoted sections in support of the rights of Aboriginal families from the United Nations Universal Declaration of Human Rights 1947 which guaranteed protection for the integrity of family and of 'motherhood and childhood' and for the rights of parents to determine their children's way of life.[43] In this way, Grayden reminded his colleagues of Australia's obligations as a member of the United Nations and as a signatory to the Declaration. He also drew the remote Ngaanyatjara people into the international spotlight on the rights of children and family which had emerged in response to the traumatic wartime experiences of child evacuees, orphans and refugees.

Contemporary psychological research, in particular that carried out by Dr John Bowlby[44] for the World Health Organisation, highlighted the deleterious effects of maternal deprivation and institutionalisation on traumatised children, and emphasised the integral role of the family as the natural and fundamental unit of society. Grayden could have also referred to the United Nations Convention on the Prevention and Punishment of the Crime of Genocide 1948 whose definition of 'genocide' — a term coined at the end of the war to refer to attempts to 'obliterate an entire race or to place it in subjection' — included 'forcibly transferring children of one group to another group'. In 1948 in Nuremberg, fourteen Nazi officials stood trial for 'crimes against humanity and war crimes' including 'kidnapping' children in occupied territories for 'Germanisation' in German institutions, foster homes and adoptive families with the intention to 'strengthen the German nation ... at the expense of other nations and groups by imposing Nazi and German characteristics upon individuals selected therefrom ... and by the extermination of "undesirable" racial elements.'[45] Indeed, four years after Grayden's impassioned speech the lawyer representing Nazi war criminal Adolf Eichmann in his final address to the court in Jerusalem compared 'Hitler's massacre of the Jews to the extermination of the aborigines in Australia'.[46]

The Report of the Select Committee (chaired by Grayden) fully vindicated his concerns. It found that it was 'hard to visualise that any people, anywhere in the world, could be more in need of assistance', that the people lacked 'even the most basic necessities of life' and that 'malnutrition and blindness and disease, abortion and infanticide and burns and other injuries [were] commonplace.'[47] The Report devoted particular attention to the rights of the families, claiming that the detention of children in mission dormitories 'savour[ed] of a form of duress' since the majority were only placed there by their parents to save them from starvation. It queried how, given the absence of a common language, parents could have given missionaries their 'informed consent' to keep their children as required by the DNW from 1951. The Report[48] condemned the proposal to leave parents to raise babies in an inhospitable area with no help and then to take them at school age to a place 'they could never hope to visit' as 'an unpardonable violation of human rights' that was 'unthinkable from a human point of view'. It added that this would be particularly cruel given the strong emotional bonds between mothers and children created by constant physical contact and companionship and that separation would be 'intolerable' for children with no experience of outside life and they would only become 'lost souls.' The solution, seemingly radical to some West Australians but fitting with the policy of assimilation, was for the state to accept full responsibility for the well-being of these people, in particular, to improve living conditions so that parents could adequately 'support all the children born to them'. This could be achieved by establishing a fully resourced pastoral station with all necessary medical, educational and training services.[49] Parliament endorsed the recommendation but, already financially burdened by the costs of a program of administrative reform, made this conditional on Commonwealth funding to compensate the Ngaanyatjara people for disruption to their way of life through its incursions into the Central Reserve. The Western Australian government's approach to the Commonwealth met with an immediate curt refusal on the grounds that the matter was a 'State responsibility',[50] despite its evident contribution to the problem. This pattern of demands by the Western Australian government for funding for Aboriginal projects and federal knock-backs, which stretched back into the war years, would remain an integral part of state/federal relations into the early 1970s.

This major setback was followed by a series of humiliating public rebuttals of Grayden's Report during the early months of 1957. After a flying visit to the Warburton area, Adelaide journalist and newspaper proprietor, Rupert Murdoch, reported that the findings were 'hopelessly exaggerated' and that 'the natives were in fine shape and had profited much from the controlled intrusion of the white man into this area'.[51] Subsequent government, medical and anthropological expeditions also found 'no evidence to support the claim that natives [were] suffering from wholesale starvation, disease or physical neglect.'[52] The DNW representative attempted to deflect criticism by claiming that UAM 'rice Christianity' encouraged families to settle down and draw rations at the mission and that they were ready 'to sacrifice the independence of their traditional life if given the opportunity.'[53] Dr Ronald Berndt[54] of the anthropology department at the University of Western Australia, a former student of A P Elkin, reported that there was 'no severe or consistent food shortage or general starvation' amongst the Ngaanyatjara people. However, he echoed more general criticisms by anthropologists of the policy of assimilation when he asked, 'Do we want all of the traditional Aboriginal life to be eradicated?'[55] While he acknowledged that change was 'inevitable' he called for it to be 'guided in a scientific fashion' so that the people could become 'active and responsible citizens of this country, contributing something to our national culture instead of just becoming darker imitations of ourselves'.

The Department subsequently advised Labor Premier A R G Hawke that Grayden's film footage was based on an isolated case, although similar accounts from adjacent parts of the Central Reserve suggested that increasing white intrusion was indeed having a serious impact on local conditions.[56] Grayden later attributed this to a capacity amongst officials and experts to tolerate deplorable living conditions for Aboriginal people when they should have been improving conditions to enable families to remain together.[57] He touched on the heart of a complex issue — the nature and extent of government responsibility for physical welfare and protection from disturbance on Aboriginal reserves. With important political issues at stake it seemed these could be disregarded. In the context of the paranoia and fears of Cold War detente, Australian governments would not tolerate *any* hint of criticism of weapons testing in the Central Reserves, and labelled concerns raised about possible effects on Aboriginal communities as 'communist inspired attack[s] on British and Australian defences'.[58]Indeed Grayden was berated in an editorial in Murdoch's Perth *Sunday Times* for providing evidence for:

Communists and colour-conscious fanatics of several countries in our near North and at the United Nations ... to smear the good name of this country and its people in areas where we are trying desperately to create firm friendship.[59]

Mining exploration was already causing dissension between government, Aborigines and missionaries in north Queensland and in 1958 the Queensland government granted an eighty-four year lease covering ninety-three percent of the land originally reserved for the Mapoon, Aurukun and Weipa communities to Comalco to mine bauxite.[60] The connection between land, mining interests and assimilation of Aborigines was spelled out in the press by Murdoch:

> Great companies like International Nickel of Canada are watching for and have prospects of finding some of the world's most vast mineral deposits in this very area [Central Reserves]. If this comes to pass, action will have to be taken to protect these primitive but totally unprepared people, and to gradually set them up as fully self-supporting citizens capable of taking their place in the country as a whole.[61]

It was in order to vindicate his report that Grayden conducted the public screenings and lectures and in 1957 published his own account of the controversy entitled *Adam and Atoms*. He was supported in his efforts by Victorian Aboriginal activist and member of the Council for Aboriginal Rights (Victoria), Pastor Doug Nicholls. At an address in Perth Nicholls, referring to Aboriginal contributions to the war effort, told his audience, 'We were wanted then, why should we be neglected now?' and suggested that 'instead of bringing out 10,000 Hungarians [refugees] we should be looking after our own people.'[62] The powerful impact of the film was expressed by a Narrogin resident in a letter to the DNW:

> I must say that I was appalled at the absolute indifference shown by responsible people in high places to the shocking conditions of these unfortunate human beings. It is doubtful if Hitler could have produced worse human wrecks out of his concentration camps as these original Australians.[63]

In Melbourne the film aroused intense interest amongst a new vanguard of activists. The Australian People's Assembly for Human Rights had already addressed atomic testing, mining and Aborigines through its Commission on Aborigines, and advocated land rights for tribal peoples with 'legal ownership of all land and minerals and other resources'.[64] This reflected new intellectual constructions of race, the interest in social justice and human rights provoked by international debates, and the experiences of postwar European migrants escaping fascism and the Holocaust. A member of the Jewish Council to Combat Fascism and Anti-Semitism told the 1957 Board of Inquiry into the Aborigines Act of 1928 in Victoria that:

> as a member of the Jewish people who have known persecution over the ages, I feel it is my duty to help such people as the Australian Aborigines, who have been denied any rights and opportunities.[65]

American black singer Paul Robeson drew a parallel between conditions for Aborigines and his own people after he saw Grayden's film at a private screening organised by Aboriginal activist Faith Bandler during his 1958 Australian concert tour. Faith Bandler later recalled Robeson's deep emotional response to the film:

> 'The tears started to stream down his face'; but when the film showed thirsty children waiting for water, his sorrow turned to anger. Flinging down the black cap he had taken to wearing on his head for warmth, he swore aloud that he would return to Australia and help bring attention to the appalling conditions in which the aborigines lived.[66]

Robeson subsequently told a large peace gathering in Sydney: 'There's no such thing as a 'backward' human being, ... there is only a society which says they are backward'.

There was also a new willingness to listen to Aboriginal people. In 1951, following government efforts to put down Aboriginal strikes at Bagot and Berrimah reserves in the Northern Territory, the All-Australian Trade Union Congress was addressed by Joe McGinness of the Darwin Half-Caste Association who demanded 'full citizenship rights for part Aborigines' and 'the right to survival as a race, their right to be treated as human beings and not as outcasts from the human family'.[67] Grayden's public screenings prompted letters critical of the Western Australian government from unions, Aboriginal and women's organisations, churches, private citizens, university students and overseas correspondents. In a letter to the *West Australian* newspaper in June 1958 prominent activist and member of the Council for Aboriginal Rights, Jessie Street attacked assimilation in no uncertain terms:

> One incontestable fact, that has emerged over the last 200 years is that the aborigines prefer their own way of life to ours. They have demonstrated that they prefer poverty and death to the loss of their freedom and independence.
>
> Many policies of dealing with the aborigines have been tried without success. But the policy of co-operation in helping them to develop and improve their own conditions, while they lead their own way of life has not yet been tried.[68]

The screenings have also been credited with inspiring the formation of the first Aborigines Advancement League in Victoria (VAAL). Aborigines Advancement Leagues were subsequently formed in all capital cities. In 1958 their representatives met with the Sydney-based Aboriginal-Australian Fellowship to form the Federal Council of Aboriginal Advancement (FCAA; Federal Council for the Advancement of Aboriginal and Torres Strait Islanders — FCAATSI — from 1964) that developed into a powerful leftist national umbrella organisation representing state Aboriginal organisations with a program of helping 'the Aboriginal people of Australia become self-reliant, self-supporting members of the community'.[69] Attwood and Markus state that its program emphasised 'the rights of citizenship rather than Aboriginal rights, although it was to call for special rights on the grounds of Aboriginal disadvantage'.[70] Its members included prominent Aboriginal leaders Doug Nicholls, Joe McGinness and Kath Walker (Oodgeroo Noonucal) and non-Aboriginal leaders Stan Davey and Labor MHR Gordon Bryant. The FCAA demanded the repeal of discriminatory laws and practices and the 'right to integrate into mainstream society'. However, it was critical of assimilation policy and at its inaugural conference in 1958 Herbert Groves was reported as saying:

> What does assimilation imply? Certainly citizenship and equal status — so far, so good; but also the disappearance of Aboriginals

as a separate cultural group, and ultimately their physical absorption by the European part of the population ... We feel that the word 'integration' implies a truer definition of our aims and objects.[71]

Five years later Stan Davey, Secretary of the FCAA and Secretary of the VAAL, published a pamphlet entitled *Genesis or Genocide? The Aboriginal Assimilation Policy* which outlined objections to assimilation on the following grounds: the continuing inferior legal status imposed on Aboriginal people, the threat to their identity, the inability to achieve stated aims and the failure to meet international standards in dealing with an indigenous minority. He asked readers who condemned 'elimination by extermination' as implemented in Germany and Czarist and Communist Russia whether this should be 'condoned in Australia because of a different method in achieving the objective?'[72]

The Western Australian government responded with a ministerial clampdown on all communication between DNW officers and the local press and public.[73] Little changed on the ground for the Ngaanyatjara people, apart from the appointment of a DNW officer to patrol the area and alarming rumours of a proposal to throw open 40,000 square miles of the Central Reserve for pastoral purposes. The federal government continued to refuse to fund any improvements. On the positive side, the children were not removed and in 1958 sixty-five were living with their families in the Warburton Mission camp and ninety-one children were housed in its dormitories.[74] In the same year, in response to evidence of deteriorating conditions in the region, Grayden success-fully pushed for the appointment of a further special committee. The 1958 Special Committee on Native Matters, chaired by DNW officer Frank Gare, who was appointed Director of the department in 1962, was directed to inquire into general conditions of Aborigines, as well as the costs of Aboriginal administration and federal financial assistance. In its report[75] the Committee discussed at some length the issue of removal of Aboriginal children from their families, again with reference to human rights covenants and international research on children and the family, and to a significant new reference in the International Labour Organisation Convention 1957 to the rights of indigenous peoples to 'benefit on an equal footing from the rights and opportunities which national laws or regulations grant to any other elements of the population'.[76] Echoing late nineteenth-century reformers, the Committee cited evidence that compulsory segregation of Aboriginal children in institutions had not fitted the children for an independent way of life in the wider community but created 'self-perpetuating segregation' as well as loss of identity and self-esteem:

> The child's dignity and pride in his cultural background are shattered and he is left in a state of bewilderment which leads him to regard the white man's way as something imposed on him and hence views him with suspicion and distrust. This insecurity in early life leads in adolescence to defiance and hostility.[77]

Although the report concluded that positive change came only when a group was 'encouraged and assisted to make its own way in the general community, adopting its social and economic standards as it goes', the Committee could not escape the powerful grip of the model of 'institution' as 'apparatus of assimilation'.[78] Nor could their political colleagues — MLA Stan Lapham, a member of Grayden's 1957 Select Committee, appeared to have learned nothing from the experience when he enthusiastically repeated in Parliament the worn-out, disproved adage that:

> the native problem could be solved in twenty years if young children were separated from their parents and taught the white man's way of life in mission institutions.[79]

Lapham was subsequently attacked by the Aborigines Advancement League in its pamphlet *Smoke Signals* for his ignorance of Dr Bowlby's findings that:

> the remedy is not to remove the child but to improve the conditions of the family ... Family welfare and child welfare are two sides of a single coin and must be planned together. A child care service should be first and foremost a service giving skilled help to parents.[80]

The report's recommendations tinkered at the edges of the process — only children over the age of six should be admitted to institutions; they should be accommodated in cottages rather than dormitories, taught elements of tribal law, and be allowed 'reasonable contact' with their parents.[81] A significant recommendation was that, apart from court committal cases, admission to institutions should be on a voluntary basis. In keeping with new social explanations of economic and social disadvantage, the report stated optimistically that:

The so-called 'native problem' is ... essentially one of a depressed section of the community rather than a question of race or colour. The factor of colour may well accentuate the social problem in that it may render the natives more easily distinguishable from the whites.[82]

It echoed Hasluck's view of assimilation in recommending a new focus on citizenship and 'advancement':

The solution ... lies in making real citizens of these people, first on a legal level and then by improvement of their education, housing, economic and other social conditions.[83]

The report estimated the cost of these improvements at 2,398,600 pounds, a vast sum far beyond the state's resources that could only be met by the federal government and which the writers of the report were well aware would not be forthcoming. The report was also disingenuous in claiming that the impetus for change rested ultimately with the Aboriginal individual:

If he is to be acceptable to white society — and without this there can be no future for him — his mode of living and his whole outlook on life must undergo a complete transformation ... In short, while retaining the more desirable elements of his own culture, he must live as we live and generally conform to the requirements of white civilisation.[84]

ANOTHER DREAM

Smiling faces of Aboriginal children frequently beamed out from the pages of southern newspapers during the 1950s and 60s. These were images of children with white people — nurses, foster and adoptive parents, kindly citizens — in white domains — the city, the beach, the zoo, motor boats, hospitals and suburban homes. With no hint of their families or homes the message was that they were 'available' and their smiling faces promised readers that they would be better off and

Fun at the beach

About 150 aboriginal children from such places at Townsville, Yarrabah (Queensland) and Deniliquin — in Melbourne for the holidays· under the Harold Blair Aboriginal Children's Project — enjoyed a day at ·Frankston beach on Sunday last week. These youngsters are all set for a trip in Mr. Norm Sheppard's powerboat. Many had boat trips until the weather got rough — and the trio at left were certainly having plenty of fun in the shallows. (Photos by Rawdon Sthradher, 781-1552.)

Newspapers also promoted the Harold Blair Aboriginal Children's Project.
(Courtesy of *Standard* [Frankston] 27.1.1971)

happier assimilated into a white world. Perhaps the best known of these 'sanitised' images is the film footage *Dreams Do Come True* showing two toddlers and a nineteen-year-old girl from Croker Island in their adoptive parents' Melbourne family mansion. Their adoptive father, proprietor of W A Deutscher Production Engineers, told the press that 'the way to solve the native problem was to bring [the children] into the homes of white people so that they could be thoroughly acclimatised'.[85] This appeared to run counter to the federal government's message of assimilation through intact Aboriginal families, and reflected ongoing views of Aboriginal families as limiting environments for children and attachment to conventional practices of child removal. Indeed many Australians were convinced that the optimum road to assimilation lay in the bosom of the white Australian family — a further example of misguided public humanitarianism at the time. The support of state and even federal authorities for adoptions and other placements of Aboriginal children with white families demonstrates a continuing official commitment to such views as well. This may have reflected official pessimism about effecting real change in Aboriginal families, given the lack of resources and the families' resistance; here was the comfortable established option of endeavouring to effect change by rearing the 'rising generations' in isolation from their Aboriginal families.

During the 1960s the Melbourne press was replete with images of Aboriginal children visiting Melbourne under the sponsorship of the

Harold Blair Aboriginal Children's Project, a voluntary scheme bringing children from Queensland, New South Wales and even Darwin to spend their Christmas holidays in the 'big smoke'. The project organisers were dependent on the press for publicity to attract billets, raise funds and generate positive community support. The press in turn gloried in the personal charisma of Harold Blair — an outstanding Aboriginal individual whose abilities provided confirmation to whites of the validity of their intentions — and the 'irresistible' shots of smiling Aboriginal children. Australia's first nationally recognised Aboriginal tenor, Blair grew up at Purga Mission in Queensland and as a young man lived with a white family in Melbourne while he studied singing at the Conservatorium before marrying a white woman and settling in Melbourne. Blair explained the simple reasoning behind the Project:

For many years I searched for a solution for a way to help the children. My own experience of living with a European family while studying singing in Melbourne taught me a great deal. I came to the conclusion that if holidays with European families could be organised for the children they would benefit in the same way.[86]

These 'educational holidays' commenced in 1962 with the cooperation of the Queensland government and by 1974 had accommodated over 2000 children from northern and country Australia. These placements frequently led to requests by Melbourne families to foster and even adopt the children.

Newspaper readers were soon accustomed to the annual photos of the Blair Project children enjoying themselves with headlines such as 'Fun at the beach'[87] and 'Kim's happy ... And her family thinks she's great.'[88] There were also testimonials of the joys of host families who took in children. Mrs Edna Lyall told reporters, 'You don't know what you're missing till you've had one,' and her youngest daughter Pam added:

I think Laverne wished she could stay. She was a lot of fun and although she had beautiful hair, she always washed it and combed it to make it go straight like mine. If people had an Aboriginal child over for holidays, they would always want one.

Mrs Lyall added — indicating how Laverne spent at least some of her time — 'She was terrific with younger children ... and she always offered to help with the washing up. She loved helping me. I only wish I could have kept her.'[89] Readers' preconceptions about Aboriginal homes as emotionally and materially barren were appealed to in headlines contrasting them to the comforts of Melbourne:

'Back to reality go the children'[90]

'A group of Aboriginal children flew out of Tullamarine yesterday to go back home to their humpies at Bourke in NSW'[91]

The Project's publicity brochure read:

Australian Aboriginal children — defenceless — rarely well fed — battle from the beginning. Only in isolated cases are they given the opportunity to face adulthood as healthy, prepared people.[92]

Project organiser, Molly Pettett, told the public, 'It's love they need so badly'.[93] Reports of the Project's fundraising activities also set the children up as objects of charity with stories of young white girls organising events — talent quests, motor trials, mini muscle men competitions, baby shows — which culminated in the annual Junior Miss Victoria Quest. There were many claims from Project organisers as to how the children benefited from their experience:

It was thrilling to hear of the change in the children's attitude ... and later when we visited Cherbourg we were struck by the number of aboriginal mothers who used the word 'miracle' to describe the difference in their children ... our staid old Melbourne was regarded almost as 'the promised land'.[94]

Harold Blair told the press in 1970 that some of the children had taken up 'good positions' and when asked if the experience was unsettling for them responded, 'Of course it unsettles you. Why not be taken out of the reserves? Otherwise it's just living. This is the new thinking.'[95]

However, it was not all plain sailing as the project became increasingly out of step with the times. Already in 1963 the Victorian Aborigines Welfare Board was critical of the scheme in official correspondence with the Queensland Department of Native Affairs. The Board argued that the scheme's view of assimilation was 'outmoded' and expressed concern about the fate of the children and the lack of consideration of parental rights. The issue of family rights no doubt lay behind a tense meeting between Blair and 1500 'angry faces' at Cherbourg in 1967. We have only Blair's recollection of the outcome of this meeting: 'I didn't spare a punch,' he recalled. 'When I finished they gave me a standing ovation.'[96] There was also criticism in Melbourne from Aborigines Advancement League spokesperson, Bruce McGuiness, who claimed that the holidays were potentially psychologically damaging for children who came from 'the bank of a river, rubbish tip, aboriginal reserve or anywhere that is on the fringes of white society. It is a way of life denied to them in their day-to-day existence.'[97] Columnist Elizabeth Riddell claimed that the project brought 'more kudos for the white hosts than actual benefit for the child' and, referring to the worsening economic position of Victorian Aboriginal families, told her readers:

> If anyone really does want a black child for a holiday there are an ever-increasing number of them living in the big cities now, their families having been forced out of the country areas by the rural recession. A big savings in train fares, too.[98]

SETTING THE PACE FOR CHANGE

The closed doors of parochial state rule of Aboriginal populations had been forced open by the combined onslaught of all these various forces — Aboriginal activists and their supporters, well-intended but often paternalistic white 'do-gooders', vested interests, and national and international political, humanitarian and economic pressures to change. Quite simply, Aboriginal affairs was now a matter of national and international importance which could no longer be left to 'bumbling' parochial state administrations. From the early 1950s federal authorities had been moving to set a new pace for change, through the policy of assimilation and through ways of governing Aboriginal populations that were more in line with conventional bureaucratic processes and that fitted with international conventions on human rights. Hasluck led the charge, introducing significant changes in federal administration and attempting to provide leadership for the states, while conceding their right to make their own legal decisions through their own administrations. The process of change proved to be highly problematic. The states resisted intervention into what they saw as their domain of jurisdiction, although at the same time they looked to the federal government for the vast sums needed to improve Aboriginal conditions. Aboriginal and humanitarian groups demanded that the federal government take over responsibility for Aboriginal affairs completely from the states. Through all this the Menzies Liberal government endeavoured to maintain its role of leadership to the states, encouraging change through example and precedent rather than through any major shift in political or administrative responsibilities or funding arrangements.

FEDERAL INTERVENTION

In 1951 (the same year in which his government endeavoured to outlaw the Communist Party of Australia) Prime Minister (Sir) Robert Menzies told the states that, in view of Australia's international obligations towards Aborigines, they must work together with Commonwealth agencies. This was a significant shift. Humanitarians calling for this from early in the century had met with stiff resistance from state and federal governments. The broad climate of government after the war was more favourable generally to the extension of federal intervention into state affairs. This was evident in joint state/federal arrangements such as Hasluck's own Native Welfare Council, the State Housing Agreement, the Australian Universities Commission and the Australian Agricultural Council, all of which served as precedents for Nugget Coombs and others in establishing the first national Aboriginal administrative body — the Council for Aboriginal Affairs.[99] New taxation arrangements from 1942 whereby the Commonwealth took over collection of income tax gave it considerable leverage over the states, and there was a related trend towards greater interdependence in policy-making in areas outside Commonwealth jurisdiction.[100] Wartime imperatives established the precedent of expanded federal involvement, and massive postwar reconstruction programs ensured a continued strong federal presence. Peacetime measures to ensure comfortable living environments for citizens and to build up a 'healthy virile and great people' through improvements to the infrastructure of roads, services, schools, hospitals and so on; the building, maintenance and servicing of homes, and the expansion of the national social security system, all rested on massive levels of federal funding, planning and expertise. These measures managed to keep pace with the demands of a population rapidly expanding through natural increase and immigration, and ensured a rising standard of living and led to the highest private home ownership rates in the world by the mid-1960s.

However, the federal government was not prepared to take over the monumental planning and funding exercise of developing housing and infrastructure for Aboriginal families and, while the states pushed for greater funding for their initiatives, they were equally unwilling to relinquish their control. During the 1930s A P Elkin proposed the compromise position of 'parallelism' in Aboriginal affairs. That is, the Commonwealth would cover much of the costs and the states would 'converge' their policies with the Commonwealth into a 'national goal'.[101] This view was also espoused by Hasluck. He saw the federal role as leading and coordinating the states and providing the necessary financial assistance, and, while he sought 'one objective and one policy,' he did not expect 'one administrative practice'.[102] His government colleagues generally agreed with him on all points bar the central issue of finance.

Hasluck responded to Menzies' plea for cooperation in 1951 by announcing a national meeting of Commonwealth and State ministers to be held in the same year. Victoria and Tasmania declined to attend on the grounds that their states had too few Aboriginal people. On the agenda were the issues of citizenship, access to federal social service benefits, health, education, employment, missions and the franchise. The meeting achieved several significant outcomes — assimilation was placed squarely on the national agenda (in the same year the federal and South Australian governments adopted it as official policy) and a broad definition was agreed to; existing legislation for Aborigines was acknowledged to be discriminatory in nature and in need of reform; and participants agreed to a new focus on Aboriginal family welfare and on the need for programs of 'education for living in the European community'.[103] There was also talk of increased federal funding. However none of these agreements was binding and, after the initial excitement, the states continued on their own paths. The decision to meet annually as the Native Welfare Council to provide 'regular consultation and exchange of views on common problems' was not adhered to by the states and the Council did not meet again until 1961. This left Hasluck's plans for state and federal cooperation in limbo. In frustration he concentrated his energies on developing the Northern

Territory as a model of assimilation for all and on promoting his model of 'orthodox' assimilation through the government pamphlets discussed earlier as well as dissemination of his many policy statements and political speeches. When meetings of the Native Welfare Council resumed he again pushed for national acceptance of his model and in 1961 delegates produced the following 'common objective':

The policy of assimilation means in the view of all Australian governments that all aborigines and part-aborigines are expected eventually to attain the same manner of living as other Australians and to live as members of a single Australian community enjoying the same rights and privileges, accepting the same responsibilities, observing the same customs and influenced by the same beliefs, hopes and loyalties as other Australians.[104]

Two years later Hasluck was appointed Minister for External Affairs. In the same year, the Native Welfare Council began to unpick this definition to accommodate mounting pressures for a more positive policy of Aboriginal integration.

In adopting assimilation, Australia overlooked valuable lessons from the administration of Native American affairs in the United States. With the passing of the Indian Reorganisation Act 1934 the United States government had officially abandoned its policy of assimilation. After seventy years of programs to transform the 'average American Indian' into prototype white Americans, the government had acknowledged the enduring significance of Native American cultures and their powerful role in determining values and behaviours. Under the guidance of the Commissioner of the Bureau of Indian Affairs, John Collier, it initiated a policy of sovereignty aimed at assisting Native Americans to run their own affairs and offering them a place as 'American citizens with systems of belief and affiliations quite different from those of the majority, so long as all were equal before the law'.[105] The Native American residential school system survived this major shift in policy, testimony to the resilience of institutions and their sponsors to change.

Aboriginal people and their supporters were not directly involved in the national meetings, despite their growing public voice and the development of a tentative national platform by the FCAA as early as 1958. At its inaugural meeting in that year the FCAA adopted a platform of 'Five Basic Principles':[106]

Principle 1: Equal citizenship rights with other Australian citizens for aborigines ...

Principle 2: All aborigines to have a standard of living adequate for health and well-being, including food, clothing, housing and medical care not less than for other Australians ...

Principle 3: All aborigines to receive equal pay for equal work and the same industrial protection as other Australians.

Principle 4: Education for detribalised aborigines to be free and compulsory.

Principle 5: The absolute retention of all remaining reserves, with native communal or individual ownership.[107]

The meeting also resolved that under 'no circumstances should young children be separated from their parents by transfer to distant schools where their parents in the normal course of events have no access to them,'[108] and that 'children [were] not to be taken away from parents or natural guardians except in accordance with existing Children's Welfare legislation.'[108] By the mid-1960s the Five Principles had been shaped into a catchcry calling for:

LEGISLATIVE REFORM

EQUAL WAGES

EMPLOYMENT OPPORTUNITIES

EDUCATIONAL OPPORTUNITIES

LAND RIGHTS [110]

Instead of negotiating with the FCAA over points of common ground between these principles and the broad goals of assimilation, the 1963 Native Welfare Council meeting painted Aborigines and their supporters as 'Communist dupes' and proposed 'reds under the bed' fight-back strategies instead. This was seriously out of touch with the climate of sympathetic media and international interest in Aboriginal protest. It was only gradually that the federal government began to realise that it would have to work *with* Aborigines to negotiate an equitable future.

Federal authorities were also working to repeal their own discriminatory legislation and practice as part of the drive to extend citizenship to Aboriginal people and to provide a model of change for the states. Indeed, during the 1960s the Attorney General's Department progressively reviewed all federal and state legislation and pushed for the repeal of race-based provisions to meet conditions of the United Nations International Convention on Civil and Political Rights 1966.

The least problematic initiative — the extension of the franchise to all Aborigines[111] — was also a potent symbolic act guaranteed to appease the government's critics. Ironically, its advent is the least remembered. Indeed 'the right to vote' is widely assumed to have been granted as the result of the 1967 Referendum. In 1962, acting on the recommendations of its Select Committee on Aboriginal Voting Rights, the federal government extended the franchise to all Aborigines. In South Australia, Victoria, Tasmania and New South Wales Aboriginal people already had the right to vote in state elections. Western Australia and Queensland followed suit in 1963 and 1965 respectively.[112]

Initiatives begun in the 1940s to remove discriminatory measures that denied Aboriginal people, with the exception of certain 'half-castes', access to federal welfare benefits for widows, the aged, sick, unemployed and families, were accelerated. However, access qualifications based on race, lifestyle or place of residence[113] continued into the 1960s and it was not until the early 1970s that all benefits were fully available to all Aboriginal people. Since the Department of Social Security initially delegated powers to Aboriginal administrations to distribute what benefits were available, funds flowed principally to them, and in some cases to employers, and were often used to oblige the ideals of assimilation in contradiction to the interests of the Aboriginal families who should have received the money. Lack of supervision created opportunities for mismanagement and abuse of moneys by some employers, and Stevens[114] reported cases of pastoralists paying Aboriginal workers out of pension money.

The states had welcomed this financial arrangement. By using these benefits as public revenue they were able to cut back on rationing, which gradually became a 'thing of the past', and to improve facilities and services on missions, government settlements and pastoral stations.[115] In 1964 social security benefits provided up to forty percent of mission incomes in the Northern Territory (almost the same as Welfare Branch subsidies) and on pastoral stations social security money far outweighed Welfare Branch payments.[116] Systems of distribution of benefits to families varied across the states. By 1960 direct payments of pensions and the maternity allowance were being made across New South Wales and Victoria; elsewhere this 'privilege' depended on the client's 'ability to handle money wisely and to manage his own affairs'.[117] During the 1960s the Department of Social Security introduced measures to gradually extend uniform practice and to deliver benefits directly to their clients rather than to intermediaries.

Negotiations over child endowment raise serious questions about the morality of state and mission interests laying claim to these benefits to develop their own activities while paying lip-service to policies of assimilation of families and family welfare. In the Senate in 1950 the Liberal government stated that child endowment was intended to:

> ease the burden of the mother of the family. It relieves her at least of some of the fear that adversity may prevent her from giving to her children that adequate support which they deserve and which she desires to provide.[118]

In the same year Prime Minister Menzies explained that child endowment was to provide:

> practical encouragement and aid for those who have the responsibility and privilege of caring for their families. It operates on the principle that, by relieving the economic pressures on parents, their children will have better opportunities. It is, in effect, a redistribution of the national income to achieve that end. It is the great desire of the government to assist families ... we regard the family unit as the cornerstone of Australian life and the key to our national progress.[119]

The states controlled the distribution of child endowment, set at five shillings for the first child and ten shillings for each other child. In Western Australia a strict system of control and surveillance of families emerged which had the effect of increasing the threat of separation of children from their families. During the early 1940s representations were made to the Department of Native Affairs (DNA) by various organisations that child endowment money was being 'wasted' by Aboriginal families and they demanded that payments be made through supervised departmental channels.[120] In 1943 Prime Minister John Curtin took time off from the demands of the War to write to the Western Australian Premier Willcock about similar allegations. The DNA responded by requesting Commonwealth funding for staff to supervise distribution to the 100 families in the south that it deemed 'incapable parents' and therefore ineligible to receive direct payments. In a confidential note to the state treasurer the Commissioner for Native Affairs added that the appointments would also allow greater supervision and disciplining of Aboriginal workers and families generally.[121] When funding was not forthcoming the DNA adopted a loose system of distribution through orders on local storekeepers supervised by the police. They were also to ensure that parents did not purchase 'tobacco, cigarettes, face powder, cordials, ice-cream, adult clothing, periodicals or luxury items', and that children benefited and family standards of living improved. Police exercised a similar surveillance over families receiving cash payments.[122] The Commissioner for Native Affairs reported in 1946 that parents objected strongly to this system of control, adding ominously that 'there are various ways to deal with them such as the removal of their children to missions and settlements.'[123] When distribution was taken over by DNA field staff appointed in the late 1940s, child endowment applications were used to build up dossiers of information on individual families and their progress towards an assimilated way of life.[124] Supervision of individual payments was terminated in the south in 1950 on the grounds that it was 'a most iniquitous and inequitable deal' that families were denied benefits when they paid taxes and that with insufficient staff the system was open to abuse by shopkeepers, police and Aborigines. Furthermore, it had done little to stop the few cases of child neglect which would be better met 'by lodging applications for the children to be placed in the care of the State'.[125]

In the case of families on remote pastoral stations, authorities relied on the cooperation of employers in distributing child endowment to mothers. In 1960 the Minister for Social Services stated that payments were being made in this way on forty-six properties across Australia. Shirley Andrews, Secretary for the Council for Aboriginal Rights commented:

It is quite impossible for the authorities to supervise such a system adequately. Child endowment payments have been made in this manner for some years and it is common knowledge that money has been misappropriated in some cases and mishandled in many.[126]

Indeed, two years earlier in the Kimberley region of Western Australia the Department of Native Welfare District Officer reported that some stations were issuing payments in the form of goods 'which should be *given* normally' (my emphasis) while others objected to issuing cash because they were fearful this would 'weaken' their 'somewhat proprietary interest' in their workers.[127]

Child endowment moneys remained vital to the expansion of institutional facilities in most states and the Northern Territory and thereby to the continued removal and institutionalisation of Aboriginal children — in express contradiction to stated policies of keeping children with their families. In 1945–46 twelve Northern Territory missions received a total of 28,152 pounds in child endowment moneys for 1057 children in their care.[128] Two years later the Northern Territory Director of Native Affairs raised the issue of how to ensure that money granted to missions was used for the 'education, health and general betterment of aboriginal children'. He listed as appropriate expenditure many items which his administration would normally have funded — 'the establishment of schools, dormitories, hospital and clinics, the pre-natal and post-natal care of mothers, the equipping of training centres in art and crafts and the provision of an adequate and balanced diet'.[129] Even given this broad brief he found while on a tour of the missions during the year that:

apart from Hermannsburg, Groote Eylandt and Bathurst Island missions very little children's education and welfare work is being undertaken. In the light of existing conditions, no officer of the Native Affairs Branch could conscientiously certify to the Department of Social Security that endowment paid to the other missions [is] being applied in accordance with the requirements of the Child Endowment Act. On the other hand, in the absence of returns from the missions (which they are not obliged to furnish) and of a definition of legitimate activities which may be made a charge to child endowment, such officers could not recommend the cessation of payments.[130]

A subsequent report from the DSS found that moneys were being spent principally on building programs and the children's diet, medical care and education. It concluded:

A genuine effort is being made to afford improved conditions for the native children, and consequently it may be asserted that child endowment is being applied for the purpose for which it was intended.[131]

In Queensland child endowment also went in bulk payments to missions and settlements with little reaching the mothers. Kidd[132] states that in 1952, after desperate pleas from Presbyterian missions for more funds, child endowment revenue was used for 'administration and to feed starving adults and children'. Furthermore these moneys were used to pay for capital ventures including a total of 11,000 pounds from Palm Island Settlement child endowment funds on a transit hostel for Aborigines and land near Townsville in 1954 and 1957.

By 1967 the last remaining vestiges of formal discriminatory federal legislation were to be found in the Australian Constitution of 1901 — section 127 which excluded Aborigines from being counted in the national census and section 51(26) which prevented the federal government from making special laws for Aboriginal people living outside of the Federal territories. In the same year a federal referendum proposing the repeal of these sections received a resounding ninety percent 'Yes' vote from the Australian public. Section 127 was subsequently repealed and section 51(26) was amended. For most Australians the 1967 referendum represents a watershed in Aboriginal affairs, leading to the granting of citizenship rights and the triumphal transfer of Aboriginal affairs from the states to the federal government. As Attwood and Markus[133] point out, this was not in fact the case — the process of extending rights had already begun across the nation and the states remained firmly in control of their Aboriginal populations for some years after the referendum.

The Holt government had only begrudgingly called the 1967 referendum, despite a stated commitment to legislative reform, the recommendations of the Joint Committee of Constitutional Review in 1959 to amend the constitution, and sustained lobbying from the 1950s by the FCAA. It did so, Attwood and Markus argue, not to initiate major change, but with the intention of 'maintaining the status quo, shoring up the government's position at home, and bolstering Australia's image abroad'.[134] This is consistent with what we have already seen of federal action at the time — a commitment to make changes necessary to protect Australia from accusations of racial discrimination in international forums and a willingness to set the lead for the states but not to take over from them the task or expense of administering Aboriginal affairs.

The government was also responding to a groundswell of public opinion that condemned the exclusionary sections of the constitution as discriminatory. This groundswell grew out of the hard work of Aboriginal organisations like the FCAA building on the public's postwar sympathetic support for the extension of rights to Aborigines. FCAATSI and its supporters deliberately harnessed the constitutional amendments to a broad platform of reform built around federal responsibility for Aboriginal affairs. Attwood and Markus[135] note that this strategy was not only pivotal in the success of the referendum but also contributed to the myths surrounding its significance. Faith Bandler, director of FCAATSI's campaign in New South Wales, told the press that following the amendments 'the Federal Government [would] take formal responsibility for Aborigines.'[136] Parliamentarian and foundation member of the Victorian Aborigines Advancement League, Gordon Bryant, stated that 'the Referendum would not solve everything, but it would be a start on a national problem'.[137] A 1962 FCAA petition for the referendum positioned the sections as 'racial discrimination that should be removed'. It advocated federal control and uniform national laws and listed existing 'variations and inconsistencies' in laws across the states and territories in a table of 'Rights enjoyed by Aborigines in settlements and reserves' under the headings 'voting rights', 'marry freely', 'control own children', 'move freely', 'own property freely', 'receive award wages', and 'alcohol allowed'. The petition added that while the federal government had no power to make such laws, it had to 'defend in the United Nations and other International bodies the varied assortment of Rights and Restrictions practised by the States'.[138] In a speech launching the petition in Sydney in 1962 Kath Walker (Oodgeroo Noonucal) attacked the policy of assimilation on the grounds that it 'means the swallowing up by a majority group of a minority group ... the keynote should be full citizenship rights and integration *not* assimilation'.[139]

The referendum did open the way for an assertive Commonwealth role in Aboriginal affairs through its new intention to legislate for

Aborigines and through improved planning based on detailed national census information about Aboriginal conditions. It also held out the promise of increased funding to the states. However this was not its immediate effect. The Holt government staunchly resisted taking any major steps in policy and administration and left the states to administer Aboriginal affairs, although it established the Aboriginal Advisory Council in 1967. Together with the Office of Aboriginal Affairs, the Council initiated research into Aboriginal conditions and advised on the adminstrative and executive machinery to implement policies and to develop links betwen Aborigines and government. Council members like Nugget Coombs gradually reached the conclusion that many Aborigines did not want to become assimilated.[140] Community expectation generated by the referendum of a strong federal role in Aboriginal affairs could not be ignored. This provided the authority for the Australian Labor Party platform in 1972 that, if elected, it would 'assume responsibility for Aborigines and Islanders accorded to it by the Referendum of 1967'.[141]

THE GREAT EXPERIMENT

The apparent certainty of the oft-quoted Commonwealth definitions of assimilation overlay a host of shifting understandings of its meaning and mode of implementation amongst policy makers, the public and Aboriginal people. Rowse[142] describes it as a 'policy doctrine' that 'elude[s] consensual definition', with many remaining questions about when it began, when it ended and its 'essential and definitive practices'. As with earlier protection policies this confusion meant that a heterogeneous range of practices, both old and new, were subsumed and sanctioned under its name. The concept of assimilation was not new. It was evident, as we have seen in earlier chapters, in early colonial practice shaped by Enlightenment notions of 'universal man' and later nation-building projects intent on creating a uniform Australia. It was evident in the social engineering projects of the 1920s and 1930s, and in the concept of biological assimilation, adopted as national policy at the 1937 meeting of Commonwealth and State authorities. What was new was the pronounced intention to abandon race-based policies and practice and to endeavour to create a place for Aborigines within mainstream Australia. Furthermore, assimilation programs were to be directed at families — not just children — and the goal was middle-class family life, not just menial servitude on the lowest rungs of the working class. This breathed a new respectability and sense of purpose into the project of Aboriginal assimilation, despite the ongoing inherent cultural arrogance enshrined in the policy.

There was still considerable confusion at all levels as to what 'assimilation' meant. Rowley claims that Elkin adopted the term in 1939 as a 'counter to the set of ideas for which the current term was "absorption".' However this attempt to distinguish the policies had little impact on the public or the press, and absorption — with its associations of 'cultural liquidation' and the 'gradual loss of biological differences (especially skin colour) through miscegenation' — was often used interchangeably with 'assimilation'.[143] The principal architects of the assimilation policy, Elkin[144] and Hasluck, agreed that it was a process of 'advancement, uplift and civilising' through wider social, economic and cultural reform and the training and preparation of individuals leading to full citizenship for all. While both were determined to abandon earlier qualifications of race, neither could fully escape beliefs that 'imbued people with social and cultural characteristics on the basis of blood'.[145] However, there were also major points of disagreement between them.[146] Hasluck, in particular, retained a view of Aboriginality as something that Aborigines should work themselves away from. Elkin remained 'ambiguous and ambivalent about who could be granted [full citizenship] and when',[147] but he staunchly maintained that while:

full-blooded Aborigines will become literate and educated, skilled and more gifted to play parts in our economic life, they will remain in the foreseeable future Aborigines in their social and kin relationships and in their appreciation of values.[148]

Hasluck, the pragmatic administrator, could not afford intellectual uncertainties — all Aborigines, including those living a traditional way of life in remotest Australia, were to adopt the Australian way of life. Hasluck told the Native Welfare Council in 1963 that change was inevitable:

their tribal culture will be destroyed. We do not want to destroy it precipitately but if they are to become fully civilised, fully assimilated people they will be no longer living a tribal life, they will be living like other Australians.[149]

Within the federal bureacracy senior officials in the Department of External Affairs worried that such views could be interpreted on the international stage as advocating 'cultural genocide [as] a prerequisite for full assimilation into the non-Aboriginal community'.[150] Consequently, official government definitions of assimilation changed over time. In 1965 the National Welfare Council sought to appease criticisms that the policy 'sought the destruction of Aboriginal culture' by inserting the element of choice into the opening gambit:

> The policy of assimilation seeks that all Aborigines and part-Aborigines will choose to attain a similar manner and standard of living to that of other Australians and live as members of a single Australian community enjoying the same rights and privileges, accepting the same responsibilities and influence by the same hopes and loyalties as other Australians.[151]

There were also serious 'internal contradictions' and 'moral incoherencies' in the policy. Anthropologist W E H Stanner wrote in 1964: 'Our intentions are now so benevolent that we find it difficult to see that they are still fundamentally dictatorial.'[142]

The states also had their own positions reflecting what they perceived as their local Aboriginal 'problems'. Western Australian delegates told the 1963 national meeting that Aboriginal communities who 'have their own tribal culture very strongly developed' should be 'encouraged to retain it.' Some missions had their own dissenting views.[153] In 1965 the Pallottines at Tardun Children's Mission in Western Australia stated:

> We use the term 'integrate' ... in preference to 'assimilation' ... 'Integration' implies the existence of two separate systems which must be moulded to an homogenous whole at the same time retaining their individual entity. 'Assimilation' ... means the absorption of one of the elements, in this case the natives, and their ultimate disappearance.[154]

Charles Rowley[155] oberved that many officers in Aboriginal administrations interpreted assimilation as a 'means of the disappearance of the Aborigines' and a licence to force them to 'live like the white man' and they used their considerable powers to push Aboriginal families to this end.

What *were* Aborigines to aspire to? They were to abandon their rich cultural heritage and to forgive and forget generations of discriminatory treatment. The final goal was the suburban family home with occupants living as discrete nuclear families, mixing with neighbours and work mates, attending school, working for wages in the mainstream labour market, consuming their earnings according to 'non-Indigenous notions of domestic order' and with the capacity to act as citizens with attendant rights, freedoms and responsibilities.[156] However, as Rowley pointed out at the time, given Aborigines' profound 'resentment and suspicion' of whites, and their value systems that were 'directly opposed to those of middle-class Australians', the 'call to take the white man on as his model' could only serve to increase resentment.[157] Then there was the question of the acceptance of 'assimilated' Aborigines by their suburban white neighbours. An analysis of the efforts by middle-class Jewish families to assimilate into nineteenth-century German society by Zygmont Bauman[158] concludes that assimilation is a 'no win game' that can

Official photographs of (Sir) Paul Hasluck and other officials inspecting Aboriginal homes, schools and other facilities presented assimilation as a controlled, orderly and, above all, succesful process of change.

(Courtesy of Department of Foreign Affairs and Trade and National Archives of Australia: A1200/19, L28019; A1200/19, L28015)

never lead to unconditional acceptance by the dominant group. Instead, it produces a 'community of assimilants', outsiders to the society they aspire to and to their own people. Aboriginal people attempting to move into the wider community were 'stigmatised' by their appearance, while they were often branded as 'traitors' by their own people. Their struggles to conform were compounded since few could escape the cycle of desperate poverty and acquire the trappings of respectable middle-class life or learn the intricacies of its values and behaviours.[159]

Occupation of a conventional family home was the 'hall mark of an assimilated Aborigine'[160] — its location, layout, contents, daily tasks and maintenance tasks were all lessons in assimilation.[161] The family home was also a 'political need', both symbolising government assistance to Aborigines and showing that they could indeed be assimilated.[162] The modern nuclear family was both a vehicle and goal of the assimilation project. Instead of imposing change by taking Aboriginal children out of the family to institutions, Aboriginal populations would now be subjected to modern forms of governance through the family, in ways reminiscent of the 'package' for white families at the turn of the century, to re-form them into nuclear units and their children into efficient citizens. The new focus on shaping Aboriginal families into conventional nuclear units and drawing them into mainstream family management schemes meant increased monitoring and surveillance. This shift reflected both new understandings of Aboriginal difference and abilities to adjust to change and a powerful postwar discourse that placed the intact family and the mother–child bond at the centre of the psychological well-being of the entire nation. Children needed the security of conventional family life and maternal love to ensure their development in the values, conduct and skills of citizenship. The role of government was to provide environments for families to thrive and prosper and supportive mechanisms to prevent family breakdown. Working in tandem with the family and supported by government and citizen initiatives were a host of institutions, among them schools, churches, children's and youth organisations. The objective of these processes was 'intellectual stimulation and consistent, affectionate relationships with their parents'. [163] The lack of any of these was a sign of parental inadequacy or irresponsibility.

How could governments induce Aborigines to adopt these ways? There was general agreement on the principal steps towards full civil, political and social citizenship — the removal of statutory and administrative restrictions; the development of a functional infrastructure for

Aboriginal families and improved living conditions to white standards; access to mainstream services (health, child welfare, education, housing, hygiene, vocational training and employment); and the breaking down of social barriers between Aborigines and whites. Authorities were adamant that there could be no 'assembly-line approach' to assimilation. The Northern Territory Director of Welfare stated that policies had to consider diverse groups from the 'sophisticated' to the 'primitive' and had to treat Aboriginal people as 'individuals'.[164] The Victorian Aborigines Welfare Board — the most advanced state administration in terms of its philosophy on assimilation — argued that it was 'unjust to treat unequals equally' and that circumstances required different processes in terms of needs, capacities, interests, weight of responsibility and so on.[165] Thus, while some Aborigines would be awarded full citizenship rights, the 'situation' of others would require that they remain subject to 'beneficial' legislative controls, albeit on a temporary basis, and undergo special training in assimilation until their 'capacity and advancement removed the need for it'.[166] As they reached parity with white Australians they would take on all the rights and responsibilities of citizenship and live within the ambit of the institutions of Australian society which in turn would continue the assimilation process over the generations. Ideally, this process was not to be conducted on the lines of race but 'on the need of the individuals for special care and assistance in the transitional stage'.[167] In practice, decisions on who was to be included or excluded in assimilation projects were often arbitrarily made on the basis of established practice and expediency according to criteria of lifestyle, residence and race, and the process encouraged the continued growth of personal dossiers and surveillance by government officers.

There was a perception that the task of assimilation would vary between what Rowley later termed 'colonial' and 'settled' Australia. 'Colonial' Australia was seen as a multiracial society based on exploitation of Aboriginal labour where Aborigines had retained a strong traditional identity and cultural roots. 'Settled' Australia had pockets of fringe dwellers excluded from white society except as a reserve labour supply, whose lives were similar to those of other underprivileged peoples around the world. They were seen as 'outcasts' who had 'lost their culture' and 'been forced to adopt "distorted" or "pathological" versions of general Australian, white culture.'[168] Most administrators agreed that assimilation appeared to be a natural and salutary outcome for them —

a simple matter of opening the door and inviting them all in.

The 'apparatus of assimilation'[169] grew out of existing practice and resources. Its instruments remained legal controls, surveillance, punishment and tutelage of families, and removal of children to segregated institutions as administrators repeated the old hope that institutions would function as 'clearing houses'. Aborigines would be drawn into full membership of the wider community through a contradictory process of 'curtailing their rights' and then, as they proved themselves worthy, gradually extending to them the rights of citizenship.[170]

The gradual transfer of Aboriginal child welfare tasks to mainstream departments (not completed until the early 1970s) — carried out in accordance with the policy ideal of assimilation — brought children into the ambit of concepts and practices in professional child care and family management and brought new assimilatory forces to bear on them. Removals increasingly followed conventional processes involving child care professionals and children's courts, and various new placements were offered, from cottage homes and hostels through to fostering and adoption in white families. Cultural difference was frequently overlooked in these arrangements, and psychologists and social workers seemed to be more willing to intervene to remove Aboriginal children than to apply preventive casework models to build up their families. This was reflected in official reports of increasing removals and continuing disparities between removals of Aboriginal and other children. Thus, the assimilation ideals in relation to removals were effectively a failure. Panics about juvenile delinquency in the 1950s were extended to include Aboriginal youth who were increasingly dealt with through the juvenile courts. As we saw in the Blair Holiday Project, children were also expected to act as ambassadors of change within their own families and they became a visible gauge to the outside world of their own family's success or failure in achieving assimilation.

ASSIMILATION IN THE NORTHERN TERRITORY

Hasluck intended assimilation in the Northern Territory as a model of process for all Australian governments and a vision of progress for government critics at home and abroad. The *Welfare Ordinance 1953* enshrined a policy of assimilation through family welfare and reversed former legislation by assuming the goal of full citizenship for all. This was anticipated by amendments to the Aboriginals Ordinance exempting all 'half-castes' — a victory for the campaign for citizenship rights by the Australian Half-Caste Progressive Association in Darwin.[171] This marked a significant shift from the administration's previous focus on institutions for 'half-caste' children. However, since the cultural

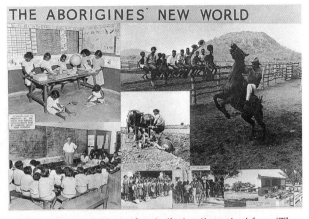

THE ABORIGINES' NEW WORLD

Official representations of assimilation 'in action' from 'The Exhibition of Aboriginal Life', Sydney, 1953.
(Courtesy of Department of Foreign Affairs and Trade and National Archives of Australia: 1200/19, L15354)

background of Northern Territory Aborigines varied from 'the most primitive to the nearly assimilated' the policy was to be implemented 'according to the individual needs of the clients'.[172] Those deemed incapable of exercising the rights and responsibilities of citizenship and in need of 'special care and assistance' could be declared 'wards' and placed under special protective laws administered by the new Welfare Branch. Once they showed that they could live an independent assimilated way of life, wardships would be revoked and they would then have full citizenship rights. This attempt to deal with people on the basis of need rather than race was undermined by federal parliamentarians who, concerned that whites could be lumped together with Aborigines, pushed through a compromise clause that 'anybody who was entitled to vote could not normally be declared a "ward".' This meant that, since Aborigines of full descent could not vote, only they were eligible for ward status and 'special treatment'.[173] Thus assimilation was to be applied principally through the grid of race despite Hasluck's stated intentions. Colin Macleod, who started as a patrol officer with the new Welfare Branch in 1955, described the system as:

> legalistic sleight of hand. Almost all full-blooded Aboriginals were to be gazetted in a register that was maintained by staff of the Welfare Branch ... Neither race nor colour could be used as criteria;

in theory gazettal depended on a person's lifestyle. One wonders who the drafters thought they were fooling.[174]

These changes were not welcomed by most white Territorians. In 1959 a group of prominent citizens claimed that granting citizenship to Aboriginal people was tantamount to 'writing their death sentence', prompting the Aborigines Advancement League in Victoria to respond that 'without citizenship rights aboriginal families had been broken up, children scattered and men and women debauched,' and calling for 'guaranteed security of family and home' and the recognition of citizenship as 'an inherent birthright for all aboriginals'.[175]

Existing practices of tutelage through protective controls and institutionalisation, formerly used principally to shape 'mixed race' children into workers, continued, not only for these children, but also in measures for the 'care, protection and tutelage' of wards and 'to assist [their] advancement in civilisation'.[176] A 'vital component' of the process was the goal of 'conventional, middle-class family life'. Other aims were to inculcate habits of 'steady work' and a 'sense of financial responsibility'.[177] Aborigines of mixed descent, formerly the focus of Northern Territory administrative rule were now to be treated in the same way as white families, although in practice the Welfare Board maintained surveillance over them through its 'network of intelligence'.[178] Their exclusion took a load off the administration but left the families to survive largely without assistance and unable to benefit from the dramatic increase in funding for Aboriginal affairs after years of miserly neglect. The focus also shifted to include 'full-blood' children. While powers of legal guardianship over *all* children were removed under the 1953 Ordinance, Aboriginal children under fourteen could still be removed by administrative decision and 'mixed race' children with parental permission.

In 1960 the compilation of a Register of Wards listing 15,277 Aborigines was completed and implementation of assimilation programs began in earnest. In response to political pressure from the south, Albert Namatjira was left off the Register, one of only six 'full-bloods', all men, not to be declared wards. The official position was that the only future for all wards was to discard their traditional way of life and become fully participating members of the Australian community. This would be achieved by removing them to government settlements and missions to improve their physical health and hygiene, educate their children, train adults to work and introduce families to settled Western domestic life. Pastoral stations were also subsidised to train Aborigines on their properties. While the focus would 'necessarily' be on younger Aborigines, officials stipulated there should be no separation as 'family life is strong in these people.'[179] The *Wards Employment Ordinance 1959* underscored the integral place of employment in the program of assimilation and the government's determination to develop in wards 'a sense of responsibility, and not idleness and profligacy'.[180] An Employment and Advisory Board was set up to recommend training and employment conditions for wards, to be implemented by the Welfare Branch and with the right to impose penalties on offending employers. Ironically, prior to 1963 the major employers of Aboriginal labour in the Northern Territory — the Welfare Branch and missions — were not bound to comply and even then the missions claimed they could not abide by the new standards and were not pushed to do so. Nor was inspection of pastoral stations sufficient to ensure that set standards of employment and training were met and few employers were penalised for failing to meet them.

Under Director of Welfare Harry Giese, appointed in 1954, the Welfare Branch developed rapidly. Staffing levels doubled from sixty-four in 1953 to 128 three years later.[181] The budget which grew from 166,000 pounds in 1954–55 to 1.2 million pounds in 1962–63 was devoted to developing an expanding network of institutions, and, in particular, to creating facilities to attract white staff. The system of tutelage through institutions was supervised through a network of Welfare Branch patrol officers. Based on the patrol model used in Papua New Guinea,[182] this incorporated the principle of governing in the interests of the indigenous people while also extending government influence and exercising a general supervision over local conditions and social relations.[183] In 1950 the use of police as protectors in the Northern Territory formally ceased.[184] Trained at the Australian School of Pacific Administration in Sydney and spending a good part of their time in the field, some patrol (later welfare) officers developed more sympathetic understandings of Aboriginal people. Former officer, Ted Evans, recalled his experiences in Arnhem Land:

I was spending my days in the company of Aboriginal people in their natural relaxed environment and was thereby almost unconsciously absorbing the fundamental elements of the traditional world and its meaning.[185]

This brought new tensions to their role as they negotiated conflicts between the interests of economic developers and the people, and the aims of encouraging continued occupation of traditional lands and of concentrating people in permanent settlements for assimilation into Australian society.[186] At the same time there were too few patrol officers to inspect and report on conditions on pastoral stations, missions and government settlements. The grafting of the new branch on to the former DNA also meant some continuity of structure, staff, attitudes and practices. Furthermore, the Welfare Branch's varied functions in dealing with education, employment, health and so on created overload, and action was often taken in a knowledge vacuum. The channelling of all moneys for these various functions through the one administration also prompted white complaints of excessive expenditure on Aboriginal affairs.[187]

By the early 1960s, in the face of mounting pressure from critics of assimilation, the federal government had begun to move towards adopting a policy of integration. In 1964 Colin Tatz, who had just completed a highly critical analysis of assimilation in the Northern Territory for his doctoral thesis, outlined in the *Age* newspaper a series of major legislative changes in the Territory indicative of this change of direction. The *Social Welfare Ordinance 1964* set out to remove all remaining restrictions on the full exercise of citizenship by Aborigines, although prohibited areas, the Director's power to remove and detain wards and the exclusion of non-Aborigines from reserves were retained, along with the right to maintain training of selected children in mission homes. Further legislation would improve wages and employment conditions and abolish all liquor restrictions.[188] The new Social Welfare Branch would focus on providing welfare to all persons in need of assistance irrespective of race, while functions of Aboriginal education and health were to be handed over to the relevant departments. Nevertheless, like earlier legislation, the Ordinance in practice was still directed primarily at Aborigines. The mechanics of its language also derived from the repealed legislation and the new administration was grafted on to the old Welfare Branch.

This combination of appearance of change and continuity of practice was evident in broader changes in the Northern Territory at the time. Although a new period of economic development and rapid population growth promised a prosperous modern society and an end to frontier thinking and practices, these advances were grafted on to the drive to take over remaining Aboriginal lands and ongoing discriminatory treatment of Aboriginal people.

ASSIMILATING ABORIGINAL COMMUNITIES

Between 1954 and 1972 the Branch oversaw a process of removal of Aboriginal people from their homelands and their enforced concentration in residential settlements, missions, and pastoral stations, the new transition points on the path to assimilation. The settlement sites were chosen for their proximity to their target populations and served to centralise and control Aboriginal residence. While never completely effective, this also served to keep them away from the towns. At the same time, government, missions and pastoralists continued to benefit from their cheap labour and minimal living conditions.[189] Settlements and missions also provided medical services and training for children and adults in community and conventional family living. Children in particular were being prepared for life in a 'wider community than the tribe'.[190] This notion of channelling residents out of the settlements coexisted with the contradictory 'assumption of permanence' and provision of 'experience and training in community living', so that in the end residents would form 'normal rural communities'.[191] Within this system, various manipulations of rationing formed a major part of 'training for citizenship' to shift Aborigines towards adherence to the norms of the 'Australian way of life' — earning their own living in a cash economy and living as suburban nuclear families.[192] However, while these strategies undermined some traditions and familial relations, they did not introduce Aborigines to the practices of conventional modern families but to a way of life which had little in common with that of other Australians.[193]

Rowse[194] provides a detailed analysis of the bumpy road to assimilation in Central Australian settlements during this period. In the late 1940s the majority of Aborigines in Central Australia — ninety percent — lived in the hinterland outside the town of Alice Springs. They became the target of the 'assimilation apparatus' and numbers of Aborigines concentrated in remote missions, government settlements and pastoral stations in the region increased from 1561 in 1950 to 4037 in 1970. They were to be trained to live like other Australians, whether they remained in their remote communities or moved to work in urban centres such as Alice Springs.[195] In these large institutional communities the government followed a policy predicated on working with indigenous kinship as part of the move towards assimilation and yet, as Rowse shows us, the effect was often disruptive of these patterns while it also failed to induct Aborigines into assimilated life. On the settlements children lived with their families, but they remained 'civilisation's spearhead'[196] and the focus of staff devotion was on their care and education. This served to undermine familial bonds and contributed to the development of 'substitute mothering regimes'. [197] Nor were mothers learning western maternal tasks. Over half the children's school day was devoted to tasks normally carried out in the conventional Australian family home — washing, dressing, playing and undressing[198] — and prepared meals were provided, in part to ensure the children's attendance. While the birth rate steadily increased, infant mortality in Central Australia had become the highest in world — 200 out of every 1000 live births — as babies died from gastroenteritis, respiratory and other diseases associated with poor living conditions, malnutrition and inadequate standards of child care and hygiene.[199] During the early 1970s there was a growing realisation that good mothering was essential to children's health and that substitute forms did 'nothing to cure the real "illness" or the mother's condition, whether the fault of her lifestyle or her diet.'[200]

Training and work on the settlements and missions were similarly problematic. Aborigines were trained for institutional tasks rather than the outside employment market. The combination of payment for work in rations and artificially low cash wages and the denial of access to unemployment benefits 'plunged thousands of settlement residents into poverty.'[201] The abysmal poverty gave a surreal quality to questions constantly raised by officials — 'Were parents willing to look after their families? Did they have the dietary knowledge to do so competently?'[202] Nor did Aborigines learn to settle down in conventional dwellings and adopt domestic life. Indeed, despite official propaganda, little housing was provided apart from transitional 'homes' for the few, and these were unsuited to the climate and lacked the facilities of conventional housing. Provision of even basic housing could bring increased surveillance and control of family life as authorities sought to impose standards of assimilated domestic behaviour. Aboriginal resistance to these interventions was strong — dwellings were adapted to Aboriginal ways and some families showed no interest in using them at all.

The assimilation project failed to shape these Aborigines into efficient citizens exercising 'the right to sell labour in the best market, the right to make decisions on purely personal matters, the right to enjoy social privileges and the right to have some say in matters affecting [their] life and living conditions.'[203] At the same time it turned many Aboriginal residents into opponents rather than partners in change as resentment built up at their continued exclusion from decision-making about their own lives. Administrators failed to appreciate the potential of the 'indigenous domain'[204] to persist in the face of these efforts. Hasluck later admitted, 'We did not see clearly the ways in which the individual is bound by membership of a family or a group.'[205] Former patrol officer Jeremy Long[206] described how Aborigines shaped introduced goods to meet their own cultural imperatives so that, for example, the more assured food supply at settlements contributed to an expanding ritual and ceremonial life. Marjorie Gartrell, a former settlement nurse, observed that Aborigines had little interest in money or even the food offered — 'the sum total of the material holds we had over them' — jeopardising the whole basis of the project of change. This was compounded by growing disillusionment and frustration of staff who reportedly were 'drift[ing] along and perform[ing] essential duties only in a half-hearted manner. The Aboriginal is quick to appreciate this situation.'[207]

In the town of Alice Springs the focus of government action was to move 'part-Aboriginal' families into new houses provided by the Northern Territory Administration and to train them to adopt conventional, middle-class, domestic family life. Welfare Branch officers were to ensure that Aboriginal men became 'good workers and in-resident fathers', the women 'good mothers and housekeepers'[208] and that the children were cared for and sent to school. By 1971 many of the 1850 Aborigines in Alice Springs were living in government housing, although a 'large minority' still lived in fringe camps.[209] However, few lived in conventional nuclear family units. This reflected both ongoing adherence to Aboriginal family patterns and the unintended consequences of government interventions which facilitated the development of matrifocal families, the continued removal of 'mixed race' children and continuity of a fringe-dwelling way of life. Various factors favoured matrifocal family life. The main source of employment for Aboriginal men was seasonal work in the pastoral industry, but with the new insistence on regular school attendance, many women chose to remain behind since at the stations they faced the prospect of having their children taken by the Welfare Branch to be educated in institutions back in town. Women in Alice Springs could also become financially independent by working as domestic servants and by means of child endowment and single parent's supporting benefits introduced in 1974. The actions of some Welfare Branch officers also facilitated the development of matrifocal families. Critical of the behaviour of some husbands they encouraged the women 'to apply for pensions, live without men, and independently support their families'.[210] Women who took this path and moved into conventional housing were regularly inspected by Welfare Branch staff and those who met standards of housekeeping and child care were rewarded by ongoing welfare support. Those who failed in their domestic duties were warned and if nothing changed their children were taken to court and made wards of the state. This undue interference encouraged some women to return to a fringe-dwelling way of life where the possibility of interventions by white officials was minimised, although it did not eradicate the prospect of having children removed.

THE MOST HATED TASK[211]

Removals of children of mixed descent resumed in the postwar period. In the early 1950s, 357 children — the majority of 'mixed race' children in the Northern Territory — were in mission institutions or the isolated island 'half-caste' missions.[212] They constituted over sixty percent of the estimated 583 Northern Territory children removed from their families between 1932 and 1952. It remained official policy that 'the part aborigine becomes absorbed in the population of the Territory therefore he must commence to be absorbed from his infancy.'[213] Official statements and statistics demonstrate that children were being removed through a combination of the ideals of assimilation and the perceived need to rescue them from poor living conditions or harm from tribal law — rationales which seem to have been closely entwined in the minds of officials of the day. At the time there were expressions of public concern at government removal practices as one senior official observed:

The presence of such children [in native camps] is decried, though a benevolent Government, acting entirely in the interests of the individual, is criticised severely when the chid is removed for upbringing and education.[214]

However, the initial impetus for a shift away from what former patrol officer Colin Macleod described as 'well-meaning callousness' and the 'taking away of children purely for ideological reasons'[215] came from within the administration.

In 1949 a comprehensive check was made on the numbers and ages of 'half-caste' children on pastoral stations, and children who had been overlooked during the war years were collected and placed in institutions. Ted Evans made an emotional report to the Government Secretary concerning his trip to remove children from Wave Hill Station. He stated that he had observed:

> distressing scenes the like of which I wish never to experience again. The engines of the 'plane are not stopped … and the noise combined with the strangeness of an aircraft only accentuated the grief and fear of the children, resulting in near-hysteria in two of them. I am quite convinced that news of my actions at Wave Hill preceded me to the other stations resulting in the children being taken away prior to my arrival.[216]

He recommended that where possible children should not be taken from their mothers before the age of six and that an itinerant female officer should be appointed to visit mothers to assist in the 'gentler removal' of their children.[217] The Government Secretary responded to Evans' report with the comment that he could not 'imagine any practice which is more likely to involve the government in criticism for violation of the present day conception of "human rights".'[218] He noted that, despite the Director of Native Affairs' powers of legal guardianship over Aboriginal children, he had been unable to identify any documents recording ministerial approval of the removal policy, apart from a 1931 statement by the Minister for Home Affairs advising that officers were to 'collect half-castes and train them in institutions to enable them eventually to take their places in the ordinary life of the community,' and that 'half-caste girls [were] to be brought into homes as soon as possible after reaching an age where they can be separated from their mothers.' He noted further that it was Branch practice to 'remove the children from their native mothers as soon after birth as is reasonably possible.'[219]

The uncertainties identified in official policy prompted high level discussions among senior bureacrats to define current removal policy in the context of assimilation. The Northern Territory Administrator, F J Wise, prepared the following detailed statement on the policy of assimilation operating in the Northern Territory. This clearly sets out how officials of the time defined what constituted the 'welfare' of a 'half-caste' child.

The basis of Commonwealth policy on native welfare is gradual assimilation of coloured people into the Australian community. Those most easily assimilated are persons of mixed blood, provided that they are able to enjoy from an early and impressionable age the medical care, training, teaching and general living conditions available to the community at large.

Assimilation of full-bloods will of course be difficult and slow but partly coloured people have inherited qualities and instincts which, if developed in a better environment, will make the task of assimilation relatively easy and quick, even of those born in aboriginal camps and under nomadic conditions.

Objections will no doubt be made against the policy from time to time on humanitarian grounds. As a general rule, mothers and their children should not be separated, and in a white community, a mother's right to the control and care of her child may be overruled only for very grave reasons and after the most careful enquiry ... the determining factor is, I believe, the welfare of a child and consequently the welfare of the community.

These considerations apply to the practice of removing partly coloured children from their aboriginal mothers.

On reaching adolescence, partly coloured persons living in native camps show a tendency to break away from their environment. Their colour and temperament are obstacles to their easy assimilation into the black community, but it is then too late for them to benefit by the training in habits of work and conduct, which would give them a secure place in the white community. Hence they can be easily exploited, and are unable to command a living wage or to reach the standard of hygiene or behaviour normal to a healthy and law-abiding community.

The partly coloured person who remains in a native camp is said to be the cause of constant trouble. He is apt to break laws and customs particularly those of marriage and become as much a misfit in the tribe as he would be in the white community.

Unless his future is taken in hand at an early age, therefore, the partly coloured person is destined to become an outcast from all communities, acceptable neither to the black nor to the white.

The aboriginal mother is notably devoted to her child, irrespective of his colour, during the first few years of his life but the attachment weakens as the child grows older. There is likely, therefore, to be a much stronger opposition to the removal of the child under 4 or 5 years of age.

The whole question is a difficult and delicate one but it seems clear that partly coloured children should continue to be removed. It is essential, however, that the removal be effected in such a way as to cause a minimum of distress and hardship.[220]

This statement is imbued with ongoing preconceptions about 'half-castes' as quintessential 'outsiders' in both Aboriginal and white society and this then becomes the reason to remove children 'for their own welfare and that of the community' so that they do not become 'outcast[s] from all communities'. To this end Wise endorsed the continued removal of 'half-caste' children from Aboriginal camps. He also added that, in future, only children over the age of four considered to be neglected or in need of medical care or whose mothers had given their consent should be removed.[221] This indicates some concern for the children's living conditions and for maternal rights. Hasluck approved all but the proposed age limit, claiming that 'the younger the child is at the time of removal the better for the child.'[222] This went against contemporary theories of child development and international human rights which stated that, especially in the early years of life, the best interests of the child were served by remaining in the family with the mother. This suggests ongoing wilful ignorance at the highest levels of professional practice and a leaning towards precedent. Hasluck provided a 'doctored' version of Wise's statement to the Australian Association for the United Nations later in 1961 in which he highlighted the link between removal, education and assimilation policy:

the policy has been that, where half-caste children are found living in the camps of full-blood natives, they should, if possible, be removed to better care so that they have a better opportunity for education. The theory behind this is that, if the half-caste child remains with the bush tribe, he will grow up to have neither the full satisfaction in life which the tribal native has nor the opportunity to

471

advance to any other status ... The purpose of this action taken is to serve the interests of the children and to give them the chance of living at a better standard of life.[223]

In October 1951 Aboriginal child removal in the Northern Territory emerged as a public issue when Dr Charles Duguid, President of the Aborigines Advancement League in Adelaide, launched a heated attack in the southern press on 'the most hated task' of patrol officers — the 'cruel' practice of taking 'half-caste' babies as young as three months of age from their mothers. He asked why, when the federal government now planned to educate all 'full-bloods', even on pastoral stations, it should continue to separate 'half-caste' and 'full-blood' and why it did not leave all children to grow up with their mothers?[224] A representative of the Department of Territories was reported in the press as saying that the government 'regard[ed] the interest of the child as paramount ... [and] would hate to think what would happen to the children in many cases if they were left with the tribes' as 'half-caste' children were not recognised by the tribe and had little chance of survival if not removed.[225] However, internal correspondence in response to Duguid's allegations describes a different scenario. Rather than rejecting the children, 'native mothers' had to be 'educated' by patrol officers over a two year period of 'the advantages to be gained by the children [from removal] and the disadvantage of allowing them to remain in the camp.' Only then in some cases were children handed over 'in a spirit of understanding, appreciation and cooperation' and field officers were able to maintain 'harmonious relations with the full-blood aborigines in their districts'.[226] Revised procedures for removals were issued in 1952 restricting removals 'to children who were neglected or in need of medical care or whose removal was expressly requested by the mother. The interests of the child were to be paramount.'[227]

Colin Macleod recalls that these events precipitated an overall shift in practice in removals:

Thereafter patrol officers were asked to look out for part-coloured children who were not fully integrated into a family or tribal structure, and make a humanitarian assessment of the child's future ... While the word 'counselling' was not used this was, in effect what occurred.[228]

Long states that this led in turn to an immediate decrease in removals from eighteen children in 1950 to twenty-one between 1951 and 1953.[229]

Official statistics highlight the fact that the reasons for child removals had more to do with white interests than the welfare of the children. Indeed the very fact that it was principally 'mixed race' children who were removed suggests this: they were widely believed to be more readily assimilated and authorities bowed to pastoralists' insistence that they leave 'full-blood' children to become part of their work force. The statistics show an uneven distribution of the 263 boys and 320 girls removed between 1932 and 1952 in accordance with employment and mission interests — the Darwin Half-caste Home intake was over seventy percent girls, reflecting the demands of the town domestic servant market, as well as the perceived threat of sexual abuse of the girls. Colin Macleod suggests that the latter was of particular concern to officials:

Young part-coloured girls became playthings of the outback, to be used and swapped like currency ... Back in Darwin, some of my friends and occasionally the press were critical of the Welfare Branch taking away children. But what if the mother was barely out of puberty, with no way of independently looking after herself, let alone her child? What if the mother was under the influence of some dissolute itinerant stockman? Young girls were becoming mothers way before they were old enough to be good mothers, in conditions of unspeakable squalor and cruelty.[230]

This distinction between the genders was evident in Macleod's assessment of a boy for removal in 1957:

If this child had been a girl I would possibly recommend it. In this case I am hesitant, as I often wonder if the pain of separation is worth it in a lad's case.[231]

In contrast to the Top End, the Children's Home in Alice Springs took in sixty percent boys for training for the hinterland pastoral industry. Intakes of boys and girls in the island institutions which hoped to create settled family communities were more equal. The age distribution of removal was also suggestive. There was no blanket spread as could be expected if children were being rescued from neglect and destitution; instead two-thirds of the children were aged between five and twelve years, fifteen percent aged one to four years and only one percent were aged between thirteen and eighteen years.[232] It might be suggested that mothers were left to do the hard work of rearing babies and toddlers — a notoriously expensive and time-consuming task in an institutional setting — and then the children were taken and trained to be sent out to work at an early age.

In 1949 the Northern Territory embarked on what appeared to be an ambitious and progressive program to make state schooling available to *all* Aboriginal children and to increasingly enforce attendance. Some 'mixed race' children were already attending mission schools and twenty-five percent, including those in Homes in Darwin and Alice Springs, were enrolled in state primary schools where they reportedly experienced no problems, as long as they started in their early years and 'came from homes conducted in the manner of Europeans.'[233] Few went on to secondary schooling. No 'full-blood' children were enrolled in state schools, although a proportion attended mission schools. In 1953 an Inter-Departmental Committee recommended the establishment of small schools with certified teachers on the larger pastoral stations. When employers objected that the children would not learn stock work and that they would abandon the stations they were assured that the school year and curriculum would be built around the needs of the pastoral industry and that the aim was to create permanent Aboriginal communities on the stations. Although the proposal was abandoned due to lack of funding, several station schools were established in cooperation with pastoralists. Due to these initiatives numbers of children attending school increased from 900 in 1951 to 2300 in 1956.[234]

From 1953 the Northern Territory took tentative steps towards mainstreaming Aboriginal child removals. The *Welfare Ordinance 1953* repealed legal guardianship of Aboriginal children but allowed that 'full blood' children could be taken to the age of fourteen with the Administrator's approval and 'mixed race' children with permission from their parents. No court committal process was required. This racial divide meant that old ways persisted. It remained 'normal procedure' to:

> remove coloured children from their native environment and place them in an institution when they are of school-going or even at a later age. Where the children are illegitimate and born in a town

they are removed to an institution providing the mother is agreeable.[235]

From 1953 'mixed race' children were also dealt with by the State Children's Council, a voluntary body formed in 1930 with responsibility for neglected and destitute children in the Territory. By 1958 almost one hundred such children were under its care. The growing confusion in arrangements between the Council and the Welfare Board was resolved by the *Child Welfare Ordinance 1958*[236] which consolidated child welfare services and brought them in line with standards and procedures in the states.

From 1959 welfare officers were required to assess whether a child was capable of being assimilated, whether the child and parents wanted to 'make the break', and if the child would lead a 'more contented, happy and fuller life, if removal occurs, than if he is left where he is'.[237] Colin Macleod states that 'Many children were assessed on the guidelines and were judged to be better off staying where they were. Many, also, were not.' He goes on to claim that 'never ... were children taken from families with a mother and a father. They were always from young and unprotected single mothers, often young girls between 10 and 13 with no family member to properly care for them.'[238] While this may be the substance of his memories — he states that he never personally removed any children — this does not tally with the many histories recounted by witnesses in the Northern Territory to the 1996 Inquiry into the Separation of Aboriginal and Torres Strait Islander Children from their Families. Nor does it fit with accounts discussed earlier of patrol officers 'counselling' Aboriginal mothers over long periods to avoid creating conflict with Aboriginal communities through removals of children.

During the 1950s there were four Aboriginal children's institutions in the Northern Territory — the island mission homes, Croker Island and Garden Point, and the town-based homes, Retta Dixon[239] in Darwin and St Mary's Hostel in Alice Springs. In a 1954 survey the Acting Director of Native Affairs, R K McCaffery, singled out the Australian Inland Mission's (AIM) Retta Dixon Home for harsh criticism. He described it as:

> a most undesirable environment for children ... the staff are ... quite unfitted to undertake the care of these children ... Superficially the Home is carrying out a necessary task ... however, ... more harm is

being done to the individual in the Home over the years, and the activities of the Home should be curtailed ... I have no hesitation in stating that the Home in its present location and form is a failure, and the children are merely benefiting to the extent that they are clothed, fed and are receiving some form of education. The only other contribution to their upbringing is perhaps the religious training given by the staff which to my mind is made to play far too much important a part in their formative years and is far too restrictive.[240]

McCaffery recommended its immediate closure and the transfer of the children to Croker Island and Garden Point. He also recommended the gradual closure of these Homes as well and their conversion to 'out-posts' for the assimilation of wards, and the establishment of a hostel in Darwin to accommodate 'mixed race' children. It says little for Canberra's attention to the advice of local administrators and to the custodial care of the children that the only action taken was to approve a loan to the AIM to build a new establishment on Bagot Aboriginal Reserve. Opened in 1961 by Hasluck, the new Home was the first in the Northern Territory to provide cottage-style accommodation. The aim was to recreate a family home atmosphere for up to eighty children; however, former resident Barbara Cummings[241] recalled a very unhomelike atmosphere where staff 'continued to enforce the methods of control previously established, such as its central food system, its regimental ordering and its system of discipline.' In fact it meant even more scrutiny by white staff, who were continually present in the cottages whereas in the dormitories children had been able to 'chatter among themselves at night, or until the doors were unlocked in the morning.' Child welfare historian Donella Jaggs[242] argues convincingly that the 'family atmosphere' of cottage homes is a myth. Rather, children are forced to negotiate complex emotional relationships with cottage 'parents', other children, their own parents and siblings and often holiday hosts, while the 'freedom and disorder of family life' is replaced by highly disciplined living standards and controls, educational aspirations and notions of morality.

While the mainstreaming of Aboriginal 'welfare' during the 1960s did bring 'half-caste' children, in particular, under the ambit of more regulated and professional systems of child welfare and juvenile justice, separations nevertheless continued as families were subjected to conventional standards of parenting and living conditions. By the

1970s the Aboriginal Children's Homes had been closed and children were placed in mainstream institutions or foster homes. In 1974 four hundred Aboriginal children were living with white foster families or in institutions in the Northern Territory.[243]

SENDING THE CHILDREN SOUTH

In the early 1950s government and mission representatives embarked on a joint scheme that revived earlier practices of sending selected 'mixed race' children out of the Territory to be educated and, hopefully, assimilated into white communities in the south. Motivated in part by economy and expediency — there was not enough accommodation in existing institutions or quality education and training for all — it was also an admission of the extent of racism in north. To be assimilated the children had to be sent away to environments which were not 'conscious of the colour problem in the same way as the Northern Territory' and where they would have the 'fuller opportunity to live a normal and well-conducted life than is available in the Northern Territory'.[244] Assimilation remained the goal and the scheme was 'part of the government's overall welfare program and, in particular, its policy to promote the advancement and ultimately the complete assimilation of the part-coloured peoples of the Northern Territory.'[245] In 1952 Hasluck wrote that the scheme would focus on 'lighter-coloured children who have no strong family ties' and who could 'pass as European or readily fit into a European way of life and may find it easier to do so in the South'.[246] Three years later he explained to mission authorities, alarmed at the possible effect of the scheme on their operations, that this did not mean:

wholesale removal of every part-coloured child from the Territory. We do not aim to depopulate the Territory in that way nor do we wish to force every child into the same mould.[247]

The aim was 'to give them a fuller opportunity to live a normal, well-conducted life.' Each would be dealt with on an individual basis so that some children would remain in the Northern Territory, others would go south at an early age to be 'brought up with complete separation and little knowledge of their Territory background', while others sent for secondary education and training could return or

St Francis Home at Semaphore in South Australia was the destination for many Aboriginal boys sent down from the Northern Territory.
(Courtesy of Department of Foreign Affairs and Trade and National Archives of Australia: A1200/19, L13764)

choose to remain permanently in the south. While the preference was for adoption into private homes many would have to be placed in 'established child orphanages'.[248]

To this end advertisements were placed in church magazines, such as AIM's *Evangel*, seeking Christian congregations to adopt or foster children. Prominent church boarding schools were asked to sponsor Aboriginal students. In 1958 the Chair of the Australian Board of Missions wrote to Anglican schools in the southern states suggesting that they accept a Northern Territory child as a 'community service' to allow the child 'controlled entry into ordinary life in Australia as a means of helping forward the assimilation of the Aboriginal people'.[249] Children would be selected by the Director of Welfare and government subsidies of up to three hundred pounds per year plus child endowment would be provided. The schools responded by offering places for seven boys and sixteen girls and raised the issue of whether the government would be prepared to meet the full costs of schooling. By 1959 some two hundred and fifty Northern Territory children were living in foster families, institutions and boarding schools in South Australia, Victoria, New South Wales and Queensland.[250] An unknown number were sent out of the Territory during the 1960s. Children were also sent south on holidays and social worker John Tomlinson estimated that altogether more than one thousand Aboriginal children were sent out of the Territory between 1964 and 1974, most of them 'staying longer than they were supposed to'.[251]

Many of the children were selected from the Aboriginal Children's Homes. Barbara Cummings was one of the Retta Dixon girls sent south and she recalls that from the children's point of view selection criteria were 'so vague' that no one could subsequently explain why they had been chosen; however they rightly intuited that it was based largely on good 'school reports' and light 'skin colour'.[252] She recalled that staff treated the selected children as 'the chosen ones' while those who remained behind felt 'second-rate' although they didn't understand what it was that they lacked. Some girls refused to go but Cummings recalled:

> for myself, I was eager to go south for education but the educational advantages were not uppermost in my mind. I simply wanted to be selected so that I could get all the good things that came with that lifestyle ... it also meant for me, an escape from the restrictions imposed by the Home — to see the picture shows that the other children at school saw.[253]

While the mothers' written permission was officially required, one mother claimed she was 'totally unaware that her daughter had been sent' until she received a letter from her. Indeed Cummings is adamant that few mothers knew their legal rights. Many had grown up in institutions and assumed that their children were 'state wards' and that they had to do as the Welfare Branch instructed. No one advised them to the contrary. Inevitably, some temporary foster arrangements led on to requests for permanent legal adoption. Some adoptions did occur and one mother stated that she consented because she wanted her child 'to have the best'. In the case of older children their wishes were taken into account and one girl who rejected adoption recalled, 'it might have been different if I didn't have a mother. I think the family ties are too strong to be adopted.'[254]

Processes for selecting host families varied according to the nature of the placement — 'billets' could be arranged by local church parishes while applications to foster and adopt children were dealt with by the Welfare Branch and officers of the Department of Social Security (DSS) or the state Aboriginal administration. In the case of foster and adoption applications the Branch preferred to arrange a 'trial period' and, if host families decided to go ahead, DSS social workers would investigate further and make recommendations. This practice was roundly condemned in 1959 by Northern Territory Administrator, J Archer:

When you are dealing with human beings it is a field where compromise is rarely justified. The responsibility we have is to the children ... I do not favour the compromise of a 'trial period'. We cannot gamble with the children as stakes; where we agree to fostering arrangements it should only be in circumstances where we are convinced that the arrangement is in the best interest of the children.[255]

DSS assistance with placements and supervision ceased in 1959 due to staff shortages and the Branch was forced to carry out its own inspections through specially appointed staff in South Australia and the Aborigines Welfare Board (AWB) in Victoria, with intermittent visits by Northern Territory Branch staff.[256] In 1963 the AWB complained that inspections were 'insufficient' and its staff were having to deal with problems without necessary background information.[257] In 1959 the welfare officer in Adelaide, Sister Eileen Heath, an Anglican missionary with a respected track record at Moore River Native Settlement and St Mary's Anglican Home in Alice Springs, visited forty-two children — fourteen in foster homes and the remainder in eleven different institutions.[258] She interviewed both children and adults, inspected living conditions and commented on the children's appearance, health, schooling and general social adjustment. Her reports[259] perceptively described the children's situations:

Mrs Y has 4 boys in her family and was moved to do something to assist the little coloured girl and to treat her as her own daughter. She has taken out an Insurance policy, opened a school bank a/c and placed X in a hospital benefits scheme. She gets much pleasure in sewing pretty frocks for X and is well intentioned towards her but is obviously feeling her way and not quite certain of herself in dealing with X, who is inclined at times to be moody. Mrs Y has a rather unprepossessing appearance and her home was very mediocre. X has probably been placed in a home within her social level, but it is not likely that she will develop socially or culturally in this environment.[260]

Sister Eileen[261] found that few foster families had any previous contact with Aborigines and were motivated by 'a sentimental rather than a realistic attitude'. She also questioned what would be the children's future when they left the foster homes, and recommended that the Welfare Branch should send south only 'very light skinned' children or adolescents who had shown a 'desire to obtain a higher education and better living standards ... [and] definite moral stability and independence.'

The children who went south through the system had varied experiences. On the positive side, Cummings writes that some former Retta Dixon girls found their new life liberating after their experiences in institutions. One girl recalled the 'freedom and the food' — 'I could eat all I wanted, go to bed when I wanted, have my bath when I wanted. Not go to bed like when the bell rang in the Home.'[262] Others experienced problems adjusting to their new way of life, some found it worthwhile but stated that had they been able to go home for holidays they would have been less homesick and would have been able to stay on and complete their studies. On the negative side, the general lack of support and the arbitrary supervision of placements meant that some children had unhappy and even abusive experiences. Many claimed that they were treated as a 'form of cheap labour'. One girl lived in constant fear of physical and sexual abuse by her preacher foster father and despite police intervention following an altercation with him, nothing was done on her behalf. Cummings writes that this was an 'indictment on the system of selection of foster homes and the subsequent supervision of children'.[263] Another girl had three foster placements before she was returned to Retta Dixon where her behaviour was seen as a 'bad influence on other children' and she was eventually sent to Parramatta Girls Home in New South Wales. The experience of the few girls sent to reformatories in the south was devastating. A girl sent to an institution in Melbourne recalled that her life there was marked by violence and exposure to 'girls from the streets of Melbourne', physically exhausting work in the laundry and arbitrary punishment often inflicted by a ring of white girls for the staff.[264] It is impossible to say how many remained in the south although it would appear from Cummings' account that many returned to the Northern Territory and to their Aboriginal families. Little is known about the achievements of these children — how many finished high school, took on apprenticeships, found labouring, factory or domestic work or simply dropped out of the system. It appears that only a small number went on to tertiary studies, where some found the pressure too great, while a distinguished few managed to achieve academic and public success.[265]

CHAPTER EIGHT

MAKING NUCLEAR FAMILIES

The federal rally call to assimilation prompted varying responses from state governments hitherto accustomed to governing Aboriginal populations according to their own parochial interests and concerns. New South Wales, Western Australia and South Australia claimed to already be on the path; Victoria and Tasmania had few formal barriers to assimilation and only Queensland openly resisted the closure of its large segregated settlements. Local factors such as established practice, vested interests, Aboriginal population size and distribution, and available funding shaped how states channelled Aboriginal populations towards civil, political and social citizenship through the 'assimilation package'. This package involved dismantling statutory and administrative regimes, transforming Aboriginal families through improved living conditions, providing access to mainstream services — in particular schooling for the children — and breaking down the barriers of race. Everywhere the removal of children for schooling or on the grounds of 'neglect' continued as an integral part of the assimilation process. In contrast to the Northern Territory, the focus in all states was on 'mixed race' Aboriginal communities in 'settled' areas where, as one official put it, assimilation seemed a 'far more natural process and outcome'.[1] This reflected contemporary perceptions that these people had 'lost their culture' and hence were amenable to change and that white communities would be more receptive to 'lighter skinned' Aborigines in their midst. The families were also closer to head office and to the urban lifestyles they were to emulate. Importantly, with the declining demand for Aboriginal casual and seasonal rural workers from the early 1950s, authorities could expect correspondingly diminished opposition from rural employer groups and Aboriginal families looking for work. Remote pastoral areas such as Western Australia's Kimberley region were an exception, where employers successfully thwarted change until the early 1970s.

THE ASSIMILATION PACKAGE

The dismantling of the oppressive legislative and administrative regimes underpinned the move to extend full citizenship to Aboriginal people. It was also a very public statement of government intent to the Australian people and to international observers, which to this day remains the most widely acknowledged aspect of the assimilation package. Nevertheless, it was a drawn-out process occurring over a twenty-year period, challenged by bureaucratic adherence to practices of tutelage and protection, by the opposition of pastoralists determined to maintain exploitative employment arrangements, and by white residents opposed to Aboriginal families moving into towns and using local services. In all states inadequate funding was a major obstacle to change.

The states did not follow the Northern Territory example of blanket exclusion of Aborigines of mixed descent. Early experiments offered citizenship for the few while maintaining strict controls over the mass of Aboriginal populations. In 1943 New South Wales introduced exemption certificates — already legislated for in Western Australia, South Australia, the Northern Territory and Queensland — to enable 'the more advanced aborigines ... to establish themselves as citizens of the state in the full sense of the word'.[2] In the following year Western Australia introduced Citizenship Certificates to confer 'state citizenship' on selected Aborigines who could demonstrate that they had abandoned extended family networks for respectable, conventional (nuclear) family life.[3] While this promised full access to State and Commonwealth benefits and services, recipients remained under official surveillance and faced the constant threat of having these new rights revoked. Certain categories of persons were also earmarked for automatic exemption — the *Native Administration Act Amendment Act 1954* in Western Australia exempted all persons who had served in the armed forces — while others, as in Queensland's 'assisted persons' classification in the *Aboriginal and Torres Strait Islander Affairs Act 1965* were specifically singled out to remain under restrictive controls. It was only from the early 1960s that *all* states began to move towards the blanket repeal of *all* discriminatory legal restrictions for *all* Aborigines.

Victoria had taken decisive action in 1957, New South Wales and South Australia followed in 1963 and Western Australia in 1964 and 1972. In 1966 most Aborigines in Western Australia were still designated 'natives' and only 3641 (including 1524 children) had been granted 'citizenship' — less than seventeen percent of the state's estimated Aboriginal population of 21,890.[4] Despite Queensland's protestations, following Hasluck's national meeting in 1951, that the move to citizenship rights 'already existed' there, the process did not really begin until 1965.[5] In 1972 the federal government introduced a legal definition of Aboriginality, subsequently adopted in all jurisdictions, which moved away from imposed racial categories to criteria of self-identity, Aboriginal descent and recognised membership of the Aboriginal community.

The states also moved slowly towards more conventional and professional ways of governing Aborigines. The practice of using police as local agents was progressively abandoned and they were replaced by field staff directly responsible to the administration. Nevertheless politicians and the public continued to look to police to regulate Aboriginal behaviour, and discriminatory methods of law enforcement continued in most areas. Police could also be called on to assist in family interventions through surveillance, arrests and child removal. Qualified and trained staff, including anthropologists and social workers, were appointed but many former staff remained and along with them old attitudes and practices. Following Northern Territory initiatives, Western Australia transformed its archaic administration into a decentralised field system based on Papua New Guinean models with a former high ranking officer from Papua New Guinea, S G Middleton, as Director of Native Affairs.[6] A dramatic increase in staffing levels followed and by 1967 the Department of Native Welfare had 112 employees — thirty-one at head office and eighty-one in the field. Steps were also taken to draw Aborigines into the administrative process. Western Australia appointed two Aboriginal clerical assistants in 1949 and in 1966 the New South Wales Aborigines Protection Board employed two Aboriginal welfare officers. Aborigines were also appointed to state advisory boards in New South Wales (1943), Victoria (1959) and South Australia (1963). While administrators paid lip-service to moving from a 'dole, control and punitive' function to 'general family welfare' based on the provision of welfare benefits, schooling, employment, training and housing, the actual outcome was often, as we shall see, greater surveillance and intervention into Aboriginal family life. Increased funding led to some improvement in the quality and range of services but these remained far behind mainstream standards and the absence of reliable statistical data continued to plague planning and service delivery. By the early 1970s, functions such as education and housing had been transferred to relevant government departments, and most administrations were amalgamated with state child and family welfare agencies. This left only small specialist state departments to provide a liaison and advisory role in designated areas such as Aboriginal land.

This mainstreaming exposed many families to aggressively assimilationist service programs in government departments at the same time as authorities were moving towards official policies of Aboriginal self-determination. While there was a *stated* move away from institutional control, New South Wales, Queensland and South Australia clung tenaciously to their managed stations, missions and settlements which, as in the Northern Territory, were envisioned as training posts for assimilation or self-sufficient rural communities. In Western Australia missions continued in remote areas and the closure of all government settlements was followed by the opening of a welter of institutions for the education of children. Thus institutionalisation retained its integral place in assimilating Aborigines and was only gradually phased out in most states. This was also the case in North America. Canadian historian John Milloy[7] notes that the closure of residential schools in Canada was a 'difficult and slow' process which lasted from the 1940s into the 1980s as authorities sought to link communities into mainstream schooling and to overcome the resistance of the churches, many of which sought to maintain and even expand residential education. What proved even 'more critical' in the Canadian experience was the struggle with the effects of past assimilation polices:

> broken communities, dysfunctional families, and their 'neglected' children. Those children had become in the post-war years, a significant portion of the residential school population, giving a new purpose to the schools as elements of an expanding post-war welfare system. That new purpose prolonged the life of the residential schools.

Research in Australia suggests a parallel in some states between closure of Aboriginal institutions and increased incarceration of

Aboriginal adults — in particular women — in prisons and Aboriginal youth in juvenile detention centres.[8] This was a consequence of the shift away from the practice of punishing 'troublemakers' by sending them to Aboriginal institutions to dealing with them through the courts. It was also related to the rise in convictions for alcohol-related offences following the granting of 'drinking rights' in all states, which Eggleston attributed to the response of police officers to the more open consumption of alcohol by Aborigines whose 'drinking habits had been excessive previously' rather than an overall significant increase in drinking.[9]

The above changes in legislation, administration and provision of services converged in efforts in all states to re-form Aboriginal families and communities according to the ideals of the 'Australian way of life'. A whole range of family residential areas — government settlements, missions, managed stations, reserve camps in and near towns, and urban housing settlements — now became focal points for control and pedagogical reform. In turn, Aboriginal families were drawn into a diversity of new areas — education, welfare, legal, employment and the media — all potentially facilitating the process of Aboriginal assimilation. All families were to adopt conventional practices relating to schooling, housing, cleanliness, hygiene, work, consumption and settled urban living. Governments initially focused on schooling for children and family housing, which were seen to be inextricably linked. While education of children was the major plank for reform, there was also a new interest in training Aboriginal adults to take on the responsibilities of citizenship and parenthood. This reflected new trends in psychology and sociology promoting 'a new confidence in the malleability or educability of adults [and] in the potential to resocialise adult citizens to suit the purposes of the state, using the tool of these emerging disciplines to educate or persuade.'[10] Women were subjected to often rigorous regimes of training in housework, hygiene and economic management of the home, while men were pressured to support their families through employment in a shrinking rural labour market. As had proved the case with Native Americans under earlier assimilation policies, the 'ruthless benevolence and the benevolent ruthlessness' of officials on and off reserves often had the unintended effect of widening the gap between Aborigines and whites and of uniting Aboriginal families in hostility against outsiders.[11] Official efforts to find alternative work were limited and, with decreasing rural employment, many families were drawn into growing dependence on welfare benefits. In addition to native welfare officers, a host of new government agents began to converge on Aboriginal families, the majority armed with negative preconceptions about Aborigines. At the same time new openings emerged that Aborigines could endeavour to manipulate for their own ends.

Schooling for Aboriginal children appeared the least problematic area of reform — the expertise, facilities and services were already there in state education departments. The task was to negotiate their support (and that of white parents) to ensure equal education for Aboriginal children in state schools and Aboriginal children's institutions and to introduce schooling for children in remote areas, particularly on pastoral stations. Many Aboriginal parents had been calling for years for equal education for their children, believing, as one mother put it, that this would help overcome the 'hardships of young people ... [and] bring about acceptance amongst themselves and take away lots of fears of being accepted in the community.'[12] While education departments now admitted Aboriginal children into the classrooms, conditions were hardly welcoming for them, or, indeed, for the many new migrant children enrolled during the 1950s. Schools were under-resourced, overcrowded, conservative in outlook and methodology, highly disciplined and regimented. Teaching programs took no account of cultural difference, ignoring the children's linguistic backgrounds and delivering classes only in conventional English.[13] The very real difficulties encountered by many Aboriginal children encouraged the establishment of Aboriginal preschools to bridge the gap between home and school, as in the Head Start programs in the United States of America. At the same time efforts began to expand Aboriginal participation in secondary and tertiary education and vocational training. There were costs for Aboriginal families in this new access to mainstream education. Schooling disrupted seasonal mobility for work in rural areas and families who failed to send their children to school could have them removed. Families in remote areas often had little contact with their children sent in for schooling and there were those officials who saw the resulting break between the generations as 'the main benefit of distant schooling'.[14] In the classrooms the powerful assimilatory forces of state education worked to replace Aboriginal values with those of mainstream society. The testing of Aboriginal children according to mainstream standards, without consideration of cultural difference or earlier educational disadvantage, also led to many being mistakenly classified as intellectually handicapped or retarded.

Housing was a potent and visible sign of Aboriginal assimilation and a powerful instrument of transforming behaviour which inevitably influenced family life. However, the cost of providing conventional housing for the thousands of Aboriginal families still living in makeshift huts and shacks far exceeded the budgets of state administrations, and plans to move families into rural towns were potentially explosive. Nevertheless the impetus was there to improve the living conditions of families who, as the 1948 Western Australian Bateman Report[15] put it, 'continued to live in filthy squalid humpies' after 120 years of white settlement. Faced by low budgets and convinced of the need for staged training of Aboriginal families, administrators developed 'transitional housing' programs beginning with inexpensive basic shelters and shared ablution facilities on reserves. As families approximated white models and practices and as conventional housing became available they were transferred to homes scattered through government housing estates in towns — referred to as 'pepper potting' or 'salt and pepper housing' in New South Wales and Western Australia

Shifts in Aboriginal housing in Western Australia under the assimilation policy.
Moora Aboriginal Reserve, c 1960.
(Courtesy of Battye Library, BA368/6/251)

Before and after, Darkan, c 1959.
(Courtesy of Battye Library, 86069P; 86068P)

488

respectively. The stages were accompanied by 'social education' in conventional home life. Welfare officers monitored mothers to ensure good housekeeping and hygiene, conventional familial living arrangements, appropriate furnishings, careful budgeting, prudent saving and so on. As the New South Wales Aborigines Welfare Board put it, 'Training for assimilation begins in the home.'[16] Many Aboriginal families faced fierce white opposition to their presence in town. Indeed this made the move to town impossible in some rural areas and Aboriginal families were offered alternative housing in the city. Housing programs lagged seriously behind family needs as administrators grappled with the problems of insufficient funding, planning and expertise. This *should* have been provided by federal contributions in the nature of postwar projects to develop infrastructure and housing for other Australian families. Its absence raises serious and profoundly important questions about government failure to meet fiduciary obligations to Aboriginal families, and about the ethics of child removals from 'neglectful' Aboriginal home environments when it was impossible for families to meet new standards expected under the assimilation policy.

Aboriginal reserve housing, Western Australia.
(Courtesy of Battye Library, BA368/6/3156)

Despite claims of a move to new forms of family welfare, removals of Aboriginal children continued and, as we shall see, increased in some states from the 1950s. This reflected, in part, the very real problems facing many Aboriginal families that brought them to the attention of authorities, including the loss of extended family

One of four houses for Aboriginal families in Narrogin, c 1959.
(Courtesy of Battye Library, 86064P)

networks for those relocated to urban areas and the disruption caused as legal prohibitions on alcohol were removed. Factors internal to Aboriginal administrations played a significant role: entrenched attitudes about Aboriginal families, adherence to old systems of removal, departmental investments in institutional networks and the slow pace of legislative reform. Frustrated and embarrassed by delays in meeting political objectives for the assimilation package, administrators could easily scapegoat Aboriginal families for retarding the children's progress, and endeavour to accelerate assimilation by transferring them to environments seen to be more conducive to taking on the mantle of responsible citizenship. A further significant factor was the growing cooperation between Aboriginal and child welfare authorities, culminating in the amalgamation of functions in all states by the early 1970s. This move was hardly surprising given their shared histories of working with economically deprived families and children, and in all states they had already cooperated in the removal of 'lighter' children of Aboriginal descent. Aboriginal authorities had much to learn from the professional practice of child welfare practitioners. By the early 1970s all cases were being dealt with through the courts under mainstream child welfare legislation. At the same time state justice systems took over responsibility for dealing with Aboriginal juvenile offenders.

However, this apparent legal equality often still resulted in unequal treatment of Aboriginal families. This reflected the rigorous enforcement of standards of middle-class family life by staff in Aboriginal administrations intent on imposing assimilationist goals and by child welfare staff working from models which took no account of cultural difference. Adoption and fostering, long used by child welfare authorities, were taken on board by Aboriginal departments who initially ran their own systems in tandem with those of child welfare. As a result, this not only increased Aboriginal children's chances of removal but also meant that once removed and placed in this way they were embedded in white domains where they were not always welcome, and they were often separated permanently from any contact with Aboriginal people. Aboriginal youths were also swept up in the growing concern amongst child welfare authorities about Australia's new 'youth problem' and alarm about the threat to social and moral order from 'the world of gangs, and bodgies and widgies, and wayward girls'.[17] Widespread public 'moral panics' had led to the adoption of a range of new legislative and administrative measures ·

promoting policing and institutionalisation of youth as well as informal activities to usefully structure their leisure time.[18] All of these factors caused heightened stresses for Aboriginal children. They were under constant scrutiny for signs that they and their families were conforming to expected imposed norms, their stability and security was constantly under threat, and they were expected to act as ambassadors of assimilation even within their own families.

These tensions are painfully evident in the novel *The Fringe Dwellers* by Nene Gare, wife of former Western Australian Commissioner of Native Affairs, Frank Gare. *The Fringe Dwellers* recounts the bitter-sweet life of a young Aboriginal woman, Trilby Comeaway, and the clash between what she learned in the mission where she grew up and the life she experiences when she returns to live with her family. The expectation is powerfully present that young people like Trilby would feel compelled to remodel their families and to carve out a new life for themselves. The pain and tensions that this creates for them and their families drive the plot and the novel's eventual tragic outcome. The extent to which Trilby has internalised resentment of her own people becomes evident in her verbal attack on her parents in their camp on the town reserve:

Pigs live better than we do. I tell you I hate white people because they lump us all together and never give one of us a chance to leave all this behind. And I hate coloured people more, because most of them don't want a chance. They like living like pigs, damn them.[19]

When Trilby finally succeeds in persuading her family to move to a house in town they enter a new world of tensions generated by the minutiae of small town prejudice, misguided charity and their own family upheavals. Trilby has her own inner turmoils. She is attracted to the young man Phyllix but is unwilling to marry him and abandon her dreams of a better life in the city. The story climaxes with the accidental death of Trilby's baby to Phyllix and her desperate attempt to flee to the city, away from her family and her fate. The novel ends with her wrapped protectively in Phyllix's embrace as he begs her to stay with him. She nods but inside she is thinking:

She wanted to tell Phyllix what she knew he most wanted to hear — that she would stay not for a while, but for always. And she could not. The thing that lived in her heart would not let her. So long as she had youth and strength and pride, so long would she seek to escape this life.[20]

The assimilation package also included measures intended to break down entrenched racial barriers in the community. In most states this involved coopting white community members to contribute to woefully under-resourced government projects in their towns. Overall there was a strong positive public response. In Melbourne during the late 1950s there was a surge of activity so that 'every [Aboriginal] city household ... had the experience with white do-gooders, whether kindly, neurotic, dishonest, religious or political reformers.'[21] In New South Wales the Aborigines Welfare Board encouraged the formation of assimilation committees in country towns to assist in programs to overcome Aboriginal poverty, poor education and white ignorance. The predominantly white membership of these committees included communists, Christians and liberal businessmen and professionals who were often forced to confront fellow white residents opposed to the growing Aboriginal presence in town.[22] This alliance attests to the strong attraction of assimilation as a policy ideal to the Australian public at the time. There was also geniune concern at Aboriginal living conditions. A former member of the Armidale Association for the Assimilation of Aborigines recalled that 'to ignore the situation, to close our eyes to the way the people were living — *that* would have been wrong.'[23] Arguing that 'full assimilation can be attained only by community effort and that committees of local citizens are an expression of community interest,'[24] the Department of Native Welfare in Western Australia established town Native Welfare Committees coordinated by a Native Welfare Council which also provided advice to the Department. In line with federal initiatives to educate the wider community, South Australia joined the United Churches Social Reform Board in 1963 in a 'programme of education for assimilation' — including public meetings, ministerial speeches and pamphlets explaining the intentions of new legislation passed in the same year.

Independent organisations representing a variety of community interests also contributed. The Save the Children Fund assisted children on reserves in New South Wales and Victoria by establishing preschool facilities and working to reduce infant mortality.[25] Abschol, set up in 1953 by the Australian Union of Students, lobbied for improvements in Aboriginal education and provided scholarships to encourage Aboriginal tertiary enrolments. In 1955 in Melbourne the

National Convention of Apex Clubs agreed on a plan of action for its 120 member clubs to work with local Aboriginal communities. This plan advocated steps to reduce racial prejudice and to develop trust between white and Aboriginal communities; to assist with housing, education and employment of Aboriginal families; to lobby government for positive change, and to encourage all Apex members to become personally committed to working towards these goals. Surveys of local conditions were undertaken in consultation with government authorities and, in most cases, identified improved housing on reserves, health and education as priorities for action.[26] Using their own funds and labour, the Albany Apex club in southern Western Australia built several simple galvanised iron huts at the Albany and Mount Barker reserves and encouraged local women's organisations to visit families to give 'lessons in nutrition; how to budget; how to sew; how to treat children and elderly people who were sick; how to take advantage of medical services and medicines; how to allow children to attend school and the need for them to go regularly and to do homework and to study.'[27] At the same time government agencies were lobbied to install running water and electricity. One Apex member recalled that relations with government authorities were not always easy:

> There was little inducement offered ... and continuous pressure had to be maintained to get anything from them as they considered the service groups etc. to be dangerous amateurs interfering where they had no right. In fact, it was still necessary for [volunteers] to call at the Police Station to be approved before they could go onto the reserve.[28]

Responses to these efforts varied. In 1958, Jack Horner, writer and biographer of Aboriginal leader Jack Ferguson, commented that 'the idea of donating a home for a good family was well-meaning and popular, full of whitefella notions that by changing the environment you change the human being.'[29] However, in retrospect an Armidale Aboriginal woman observed of the efforts of the local Association for Assimilation:

> some people say a lot against the assimilation but I just wonder if these people went through what we went through. You wouldn't knock anyone that was tryin' to help yer. I know they done a lot, the

people of Armidale, th' assimilation people, it was all voluntary, they gave a lot of their time.[30]

Despite these good intentions, overall white resistance to the presence of Aborigines in towns remained strong. Writing of 1950s rural New South Wales anthropologist Ruth Fink described how central powerful white cliques directed caste barriers against all Aborigines, including the few aspiring to live an assimilated way of life. Fink described the dampening effect on social change:

> So long as the white community imposes a caste barrier upon part-Aborigines, one cannot expect much change … for the fact of being rejected is one of the main determinants of their behaviour. While the caste barrier remains, few of the darker people have any incentive to assimilate themselves, and they prefer to make the best of their lot.[31]

Aboriginal political protest and local outbursts of frustration, as well as growing Aboriginal economic power in towns through access to social security benefits, contributed to the reluctant acceptance of the Aboriginal presence in towns. South Australia's initiative in passing the *Prohibition of Discrimination Act 1966* provided another avenue for breaking down barriers of race. By the late 1960s the federal government had formally abandoned assimilation for integration, however the integration policy had little currency in government circles or with members of the wider community, who continued to insist that Aboriginal people should live like all other Australians. There was also a growing perception that Aborigines were receiving special benefits and privileges and this perceived 'unequal treatment' provoked considerable resentment from white Australians.

ASSIMILATION IN ACTION

TASMANIA

In the immediate postwar period in Tasmania, the language of assimilation permeated proposals to deal with the 'problem' of the approximately four hundred Aborigines on the Bass Strait islands. A government inquiry in 1945 advocated the 'total absorption of the half-castes into the white population' and recommended offering 'homes and employment ... to families in various part of the State as an inducement for them to leave [the islands].'[32] The *Cape Barren Island Act 1945* reiterated earlier hopes of turning the islanders into settled agri-culturalists. In 1947 in Melbourne the *Truth* newspaper[33] reported that the families on Cape Barren Island were living on federal social benefits and money earned from hunting; levels of health, education and nutrition were poor; there were strong divisions between Aborigines and whites, and it advocated the removal of all the children to 'boarding schools':

> Educated and equipped to take their place as equals in society; removed from the evil of in-breeding and the bleak environments of Cape Barren Island, these children would be absorbed into the community, eventually to be married and become decent and respected citizens. In a few generations, all traces of their obscure ancestry would be eradicated. They would be proud of Australia. Australia would be proud of them. Posterity demands that something constructive be done immediately.

As the fifties progressed Tasmania was gradually drawn into federal initiatives and in 1959 the Chief Secretary instructed government departments to work with the Commonwealth 'with a view to investi-gating the whole half caste population and examining the desirability of pursuing a policy of assimilation as proposed by the Commonwealth'.[34] In 1961 the first Tasmanian representative attended the national meeting of the Native Welfare Council. Despite continued official resistance to classifying islanders as 'Aborigines', the government showed strong interest in tapping into federal funding for Aboriginal housing and health available to the states from the early 1970s.

Families continued to suffer under these policies. In 1951 the Cape Barren Island reserve was closed and many families were relocated to substandard housing in Launceston where they faced 'racial hatred, prejudice and rejection'.[35] There was also the threat of removal of their children because of their disadvantaged lifestyle. In the 1960s child welfare staff were assigned to assist such families to adopt a conven-tional suburban life. A former social worker recalled that they were initially pigeon-holed as 'multi problem families' with no recognition of cultural difference and as a consequence were vulnerable to official intervention.[36] Children were removed as 'neglected' children through mainstream child welfare processes while parents could be charged with neglecting their children and imprisoned and this could result in the removal of any remaining children.[37] In this way whole families could be torn apart, as one woman recalled in evidence to the National Inquiry into the Separation of Aboriginal and Torres Strait Islander Children from their Families :

> Welfare just took the lot, no reason — just took us. They took mum and dad to court for no reason. But there was no neglect. We was happy kids, you know. We just — we lived in the bush all our lives. ... We were always fed and happy there.[38]

Although it was official policy for all such children to be kept in contact with their families this was not always enforced in the case of Aboriginal children. A former foster child told the Inquiry:

> My foster family and the Welfare Officer said to me I shouldn't get in touch with my natural family because they were not 'any good'.[39]

Schooling was also used as a way to pressure children and families to move to the Tasmanian mainland. In 1967 the Director of Education threatened to close the school on Cape Barren Island. Government scholarships and other forms of assistance were offered to encourage families to send their children away for secondary education and vocational training. In 1969 an estimated forty island children were being educated on the mainland, at least half of them through private arrangements.[40] As more families publicly reclaimed their Aboriginal identity child welfare authorities found they had more Aboriginal children under their control than had been assumed.[41]

Visits by Aboriginal protest leaders such as Pastor Doug Nicholls and Bob Maza and the establishment of a branch of Abschol in Hobart in the late 1960s ushered in a period of significant political action by Tasmanian Aborigines and their supporters. In 1969 work began on identifying people of Tasmanian Aboriginal descent and this developed into a major genealogical project which had identified three thousand descendants by 1973.[42] In 1971 Abschol organised a conference which was attended by two hundred people from all over Tasmania and the islands. A significant resolution from the meeting was that 'we do not wish the Tasmanian Government to attempt to dilute and breed out our people and our cultural heritage.'[43] In the same year, Aborigines signed a petition against the policy of removal of children from the islands. In the following year Abschol called for an enquiry into Aboriginal affairs, including the policy of forced removal of children. The Social Welfare Department denied allegations of discrimination against Aboriginal families and claimed that Abschol was acting on hearsay 'from which grossly inaccurate inferences have been drawn.' When Abschol approached the Commonwealth for an inquiry the Department responded 'there is no policy to get them off the Island. The decision to move rests with the family. The right of the individual to take this choice is respected, no coercion or inducements are proffered.'[44] From 1973 the Aborigines Information Service provided legal representation for families in cases of neglect and juvenile justice and this curbed rates of removals. During the early 1970s the Tasmanian government began to draw on Commonwealth funding to provide special programs to relieve Aboriginal economic and social deprivation. Child welfare practice was also changing. A 1978 report to the Director of Community Welfare stated :

the punitive nature of welfare delivery has tempered in recent years and welfare personnel, recognising the trauma for children removed from their familial and cultural environment, are loth to take such action unless as a last resort.[45]

In its submission to the Inquiry into the Separation of Aboriginal Children from their Families in 1995 the Tasmanian government stated that 'how much the idea of assimilation influenced the practical administration of mainstream legislation and policy as it related to the Aboriginal community cannot be easily quantified,' but admitted that Aborigines were vulnerable to such interventions as were all disadvantaged groups.[46] In oral evidence it stated 'there is evidence of [child welfare legislation] being used as an active mechanism in support of the then assimilation policy.'[47] Aboriginal leader Michael Mansell told the Inquiry that children were removed:

in the hope that it [the government] could get rid once and for all of the problem of who owned the land in Tasmania, because the argument went, if there are no Aborigines in Tasmania and we are able to disperse them, prevent them from identifying as Aboriginal, then there can be no claims from any other group but whites that Tasmania is owned by Tasmanians, that is by white people. And it seems to us that the explanation as to why Tasmania systematically tried to break up Aboriginal communities relates solely to the question of who owns the land.[48]

VICTORIA

Like Tasmania, Victoria did not have the entrenched legislative controls or institutional networks of the states with larger Aboriginal populations. However, it did have hundreds of families living in desperate conditions in town camps. The population, estimated at between 1350 and 2260,[49] over half of whom were children, lived in extended family networks with continuing strong regional allegiances despite a growing drift to urban centres in search of employment and housing. The 1957 Board of Inquiry into the Aborigines Act of 1928[50] identified a 'sprinkling' of people who lived in houses, sent their children to school and 'generally lived up to their responsibilities as citizens'; however, it found that most families lived in 'squalor'. In the town of Mooroopna, fifty-nine adults and one hundred and seven children lived on the shire rubbish tip in humpies made of 'old timber, flattened kerosene tins and hessian'. The Inquiry noted that many of these children were 'dirty, undernourished and neglected and very irregular in attendance at school' and that, following its visit, local police had rounded up twenty-four of the younger children who were subsequently committed to the care of the Children's Welfare Department.[51] In keeping with new social explanations of Aboriginal disadvantage and the assimilationist platform, the Inquiry report pointed out that such circumstances were:

the product of existing conditions rather than any strict biological disability and that, basically, they have the capacity to live and maintain themselves and their families according to the general standards of the Victorian community[52]

To remedy the situation the report recommended the adoption of the policy of assimilation and the establishment of an Aborigines Welfare Board (AWB) to implement programs to promote economic progress and improved living conditions for families and to educate and train the young. The report also recommended the dispersal of the

186 Aborigines still living at Lake Tyers. It would be the task of the new Superintendent of Aboriginal Welfare and his officers to endeavour 'by personal contact to inspire in [Aboriginal people] a determination to better their lot, and that of their children'. They were to supervise families rehoused in town, liaise with local authorities on their behalf, assist them to find work, and supervise them in employment. In relation to Aboriginal children they would:

> maintain contact with school teachers and attendance officers to ensure regular attendance ... and prevent the employment of children of school age on seasonal and other work. [They] should be ... 'authorised person[s]' under the Children's Welfare Act to take action in the interest of children who require the protection of that Act.[53]

Legislation passed in 1957–58 repealed most remaining legislative restrictions and established the AWB (1957–69) with professional welfare staff to implement a policy promoting 'the moral, intellectual and physical welfare of the Aborigines with a view to their assimilation into the general community'.[54] The Board's efforts to intervene in Aboriginal family and community life often foundered in the face of sustained Aboriginal resistance or indifference. A police report to the 1957 Board of Inquiry noted that 'possibly Aboriginal people have no desire to be absorbed into the general community and are quite content to live with their own people among the freedom and comfort of their own social standards.'[55] Anthropologist Diane Barwick found that Aborigines in Melbourne in the early 1960s were following a path of 'economic absorption without assimilation' and that movement of families from camps to the city in search of work and better living conditions had not led to their dispersal into the wider community. Rather, their growing presence had brought greater contact amongst Aborigines through frequent visiting between households and social and political activities. Participation in these networks provided friendship, emotional security and a sense of belonging. By comparison, white society and white people 'simply [weren't] very interesting'.[56] Furthermore, assimilation implied recognition of Aboriginal inferiority, which naturally lowered self-esteem. A consequence was, as the 1959 AWB report noted, that there were many Aborigines in Melbourne who could 'pass as whites and become assimilated' but chose not to.[57]

Several Board initiatives were frustrated. Moves to close Lake Tyers in the early 1960s drew strong protests and the Board was forced to adopt a compromise whereby it pushed residents to leave while agreeing to maintain the land as a permanent Aboriginal reserve.

Families who left Lake Tyers experienced considerable difficulty in adjusting to their new way of life, often with tragic consequences, as one woman recalled in evidence to the National Inquiry into the Separation of Aboriginal and Torres Strait Islander Children from their Families:

> ... we went to Ararat and lived there for quite a while ... And [my parents] are sort of thinking it's a new world. We can cope. But unbeknown to them they couldn't cope. I mean they weren't taught how to manage money or even to live in white society, because all they only knew was how to live the way they had lived at Lake Tyers ... then I think it was in 1970 the government sort of stepped in and said, you know, the problems were there and mum and dad couldn't look after the kids. And they ended up taking the kids — the three of them — away.[58]

Limited Board resources plagued efforts to enforce school attendance and to overcome impediments due to their home conditions. How could real headway be made without adequate housing? Children also faced an education system which did not take into account their Aboriginality but treated them as 'a facet of its work in the education of the culturally deprived or handicapped child'.[59] In 1973 the Aborigines Advancement League claimed that hundreds of Aboriginal school children all over Australia were being classified as 'mentally retarded' by doctors when there was 'absolutely nothing wrong with them'.[60]

For some decades prior to the 1950s the removal and placement of Aboriginal children had been left largely to mainstream child welfare authorities and from 1957 the Board no longer had any special powers over them. Aboriginal children were removed under the *Child Welfare Act 1954* although the Board could instruct police to remove children and advise on their placement and eventual return to their own families. Thus it did not have the same investment in the process as the other states (with the exception of Tasmania) and it adopted a more critical position on child removal. Although limited by low staff levels and funding, it endeavoured to direct its energies to family welfare —

education, child care, health and housing. It called for facilities for the temporary care of children to relieve family crises rather than long-term institutionalisation. In 1966 the Board claimed to have:

always recognised the strength of family ties and stressed the importance of keeping children with their parents, of re-uniting children with their parents. Staff are loth to initiate action which may result in the removal of a child from his parents by court action.[61]

Nevertheless, social worker Linda Briskman[62] states tentatively that there was a steady increase in removals in Victoria during the 1950s and in numbers of Aboriginal children being declared state wards — seventy in 1958, the majority in institutions. The Board noted in 1966 that 'Aboriginal children are much more likely to become State Wards. A very high proportion of these children come into care as State Wards at some time in their lives.'[63] In the previous year it had linked this to official 'concern about standards of child care amongst Aborigines'.[64] The dominant role of voluntary organisations in placements of Aboriginal child wards meant that children were distributed across a wide range of organisations, institutions and foster families.[65] Prior to the passing of the *Child Welfare Act 1954* there was no external regulation of the non-government sector and unsupervised private agencies continued to organise some Aboriginal adoptions into the 1960s. A consequence was that children could disappear into the system and lose all contact with Aboriginal people. Some grew up unaware of their Aboriginal origins. The Board also assisted in the supervision of interstate placements of Aboriginal children by Northern Territory and Queensland authorities, a loose arrangement which often came to grief. This was put on a more formal footing at the 1963 meeting of the Native Welfare Council which moved that Victorian authorities were to be fully informed of all transfers to 'ensure that immediate assistance might be available in the event of a breakdown of arrangements'.[66]

NEW SOUTH WALES

By the late 1940s there were an estimated ten thousand Aborigines in New South Wales. Half were residents of government stations and supervised reserves, the rest lived independently of the Aborigines

Aboriginal housing at Green Hill near Kempsey, 1950s.
(Courtesy of Department of Foreign Affairs and Trade and National Archives of Australia: A1200/19, L32036)

Welfare Board but many nonetheless were covered by its laws. There was a growing move to the major cities but many families preferred to remain in the country if they could find employment, housing and schooling for their children.[67] As in Victoria children formed a significant part of the population — forty-five percent at the end of the War — and this exacerbated the families' increasingly precarious economic situation. In 1940 New South Wales adopted the policy of assimilation encouraged by Elkin, a regular adviser to the government on Aboriginal issues. This was expressed in the *Aborigines Protection (Amendment) Acts 1940, 1943*. The newly formed AWB laid out a seven-point program of assimilation to:

> inculcate the habit of self-help, to keep Aborigines occupied, to deal with youth, to apprentice outstanding talent, to select suitable families for removal from stations into the white community, to find employment for people away from the reserves, and to encourage local white people to become interested in Aboriginal matters.[68]

Historian Peter Read notes that these proposals were little more than 'a refinement of the continuing much older policy of dispersal' and that there was 'nothing particularly new' apart from the proposal to move families into town. Nevertheless, this 'pillar of assimilation' was to have profound consequences:

> The 'carrot' of a town house would reinforce the 'stick' of reserve and camp clearance. In effect, the re-housing scheme provided the

means to solve the hitherto intractable problem of where to put people expelled from the reserves.[69]

Rehousing in town was done despite known objections from Aboriginal people outlined during parliamentary debates:

What the aborigines are seeking and what the bill does not give them is the same social, political and economic rights as those enjoyed by other races ... The Bill is the reverse of what the aborigines ask for. It does not give them the liberty that they require and it does not improve their conditions.[70]

Responsibility for twenty-six segregated schools on the managed stations was transferred to the Education Department and all children off the stations were encouraged to attend state schools, with the promise of assistance for necessitous families. However, regulations allowing principals to refuse to enrol Aboriginal children were not withdrawn until 1972, and opposition from town residents could still lead to the removal of Aboriginal children or the opening of segregated classrooms.

Following the War the assimilation project began in earnest. As in the Northern Territory, the focus of the Board's efforts was its 'managed stations' supervised by government appointed managers and which provided some services denied to Aborigines in the local towns such as accommodation for families and schooling for their children. They were to act as 're-education stations' for 'unassimilated' families who would gradually be transferred, along with families from town fringe camps, to conventional housing in town under the surveillance of AWB staff according to the 'pepper pot' policy, intended to prevent the development of urban ghettoes. Transfer to town typically meant further dislocation and separation from country and kin. The duties of station managers as set out in the Board's 1958 Annual Report were to promote:

Aboriginal housing at Tingha, New South Wales, 1950s.
(Courtesy of New South Wales State Records, 4/8566 COD 423 8506, 9173)

the moral and social welfare of residents by encouraging them to acquire habits of thrift and personal hygiene and a pride in their homes and surroundings, so that eventually they may reach that standard where they could, if they so desired, remove themselves from the Board's supervision and occupy, with credit, a niche in the community.[71]

They could also see to the removal of Aboriginal children from their families. One woman told the National Inquiry into the Separation of Aboriginal and Torres Strait Islander Children from their Families how in 1952:

the manager from Burnt Bridge Mission came to our home with a policeman. I could hear him saying to Mum, 'I am taking the two girls and placing them in Cootamundra Home.' My father was saying, 'What right have you?' The manager said he can do what he likes.[72]

Managers typically found little to encourage them in this task of assimilation. One recalled that his actual duties consisted of responding to 'endless knocks on the door' and 'demands [by Aboriginal residents] for more action to control the station'.[73] He found that most adults had received little education and children only completed fourth grade.[74] His wife, the matron, whose duties included training the mothers in nutrition, faced stubborn resistance and comments such as, 'Well I'm healthy. I grew up all right.'[75] Residents openly resented AWB interference in their lives, claiming that 'all the Board ever does is take our kids away from us'.[76] Indeed, the intrusive inspection of homes was a particular point of complaint on all stations. One woman recalled that her house was inspected each Friday and threats made to 'take the children away if the house was not clean and tidy'.[77] The same manager reported that Aborigines on his station were not interested in assimilation.[78] They simply wanted to remain together as a group and sought 'only citizenship rights' which one resident explained as follows — 'Well, there's a pie shop in X and they won't serve us. Why?'[79] In the opinion of this manager, the policy of assimilation was 'doomed to failure ... [and] can only mean maintaining of the group in a state of unrest, dissatisfaction and despair'.[80] Anthropologist Marie Reay[81] shared this view:

Mission people have no desire to be like a white person. White people are thought to be snobs, and 'flash', and intent on impressing other people all the time, also they are regarded as untrustworthy, and always ready to cheat the coloured person.

Some Aboriginal families already living in towns, and their town-based organisations, were initially more favourable to the aims of assimilation. From 1942 Aborigines could apply for State Housing Commission homes through local Tenancy Advisory Committees and between 1942 and 1965, 250 Aboriginal families were housed in this way. However, town housing brought its own problems and pressures. Tenancy Boards often refused housing on the grounds of Aboriginal standards of home care and maintenance, and, where it was not refused, spiralling housing problems could lead to official intervention. Housing applicants sharing overcrowded state homes faced rejection as 'undesirable tenants' by Tenancy Committees and threats from the AWB that if they did not find alternative accommodation their children would be removed. There was also greater control and surveillance of families, as one woman put it: the AWB 'laid down the law ... you don't go here, you don't go there, you don't do this, and you don't do that.'[82] In 1962 there were thirteen AWB welfare officers in the field working from a family-based casework model — and assessment against white middle-class criteria could prompt further interventions. Goodall[83] describes a draconian system of inspection where these officers would:

test the income of both men and women;

test that income was spent on furnishing for the individual, nuclear home rather than on assisting relations, on travel to maintain kin contact, on gambling;

measure time spent on and in the home;

measure interest in home [and by implication, 'husband and children,' i.e. in nuclear family relations];

measure interest in hygiene;

test interest in 'morality' and in kin relations [by finding out who and how many people lived in a house and who slept with whom].

These practices contributed to increased removal of children from their families. Removals and committals increased across the 1950s, peaking in 1957 at ninety-nine. In 1951 a total of one hundred and seventy children were in the AWB's system; in 1961 there were three hundred.[84] Estimates indicate that fifty-seven percent of the 5625 children removed in New South Wales between 1883 and 1969 were taken after 1940.[85] The growing number of children requiring institutional accommodation presented a considerable problem and the AWB began to push for funding to expand its institutional facilities. It also sought closer cooperation with state child welfare authorities to further its policies of Aboriginal assimilation. Existing legislation encouraged a cooperative relationship. Under the *Child Welfare Act 1939* a child could only be removed from his or her parents if it had been found to be 'neglected' by a court. 'Neglected' was defined broadly to include children who were destitute, failed to attend school regularly or had 'unfit' parents. Under the *Aborigines Protection (Amendment) Act 1940* Aboriginal children deemed to be 'neglected' or 'uncontrollable' by a court were made wards of the AWB. In theory, at least if not always in practice, the AWB dealt only with children who were 'half-caste' or more and 'lighter' children were dealt with by the Child Welfare Department (CWD). This cemented a relationship of overlapping interests and duties and at times a doubling up of interventions. It also stopped summary removals of children and confined the AWB to committing them as state wards through the Children's Court. In keeping with broader community concerns, there was a new interest in 'the control of aboriginal delinquent children' who could now be deemed 'uncontrollable' under the 1939 Act. In 1955 control of Aboriginal juvenile offenders was placed in the hands of the police. The AWB and CWD cooperated in transporting the mainly country children to children's courts in the city where their cases were typically heard in the absence of their parents.[86] The range of placements for Aboriginal wards also broadened from AWB Homes and indentured employment under its control to include CWD institutions such as Boystown, Parramatta Girls Home and Mount Penang, and fostering with white families. Skin colour determined placement so that 'lighter' children were generally placed by the CWD. There was also a shift towards increased institutionalisation of Aboriginal boys during the 1950s. Goodall links this to broader changes in public perceptions of youth and crime. New theories of developmental psychology and concern about growing youth populations combined to generate anxieties about juvenile delinquency that targeted 'young men as the greatest threat'. In a parallel development, AWB reports in the early 1960s began to present Aboriginal youths as 'the main cause for Board concern'.[87]

While the AWB persistently lobbied without success for more facilities, it also developed its own system of fostering children with non-Aboriginal families. Its official position was clearly spelled out in 1953:

> The Board recognises the generally accepted principle that a child's natural heritage is to be brought up in its own home, under the care of its natural parents. There is no wholly satisfactory substitute for this. Unfortunately, some parents, despite all efforts on their behalf, prove themselves incapable or unsuitable to be entrusted with this important duty, and the Board is forced to take necessary action for the removal of the child. The best substitute for its own home is a foster home, with competent and sympathetic foster parents. Failing this the only alternative is a Home under management of the Board's own officers.[88]

A foster program required the cooperation of families willing to take in the children, and in 1947 the AWB complained of the 'disinclination of white persons to act as foster parents of aborigines' children and the general unsuitability of aboriginal foster parents'.[89] In 1957 it advertised in the press for foster parents to take in one hundred and fifty Aboriginal children from babies to teenagers. Readers were told, 'We have several fine institutions where we care for these children, but no institution can give the security, love and happiness of a good home.' Economically disadvantaged Aboriginal families may well have wondered at the offer to foster families at rates of up to twenty-five shillings a week plus child endowment, free medical and dental care, outfits of clothes and payment of school fees and uniforms.[90]

There was a strong public response to the advertisements and in 1958, the AWB had 116 children in foster families, ninety with non-Aboriginal families.[91] Within a few years more children were in foster care than were living in the Kinchela and Cootamundra homes combined.[92] In the rush to place the children AWB officials looked for the trappings of the middle-class suburban family home. Read notes that while many of the children were 'treated kindly' they were also pressured to 'behave like Europeans' by foster parents imbued with 'racist assumptions'. Read quotes from the letter of a foster mother who had just taken control of a young ward:

The wee girlie has settled down with us very well. She is a charming girl and we are already much attached … I was very pleased to note how modest she is about her person. She is saying her prayers also. She wanted Him to make her 'my colour' (i.e. white). Poor little girl. I explained that God had made men in lots of colours and she seemed much happier then.[93]

White foster parents had little understanding of the complexity of the task they had taken on or of the consequnces for the children as borne out in the subsequent events in this young girl's life:

at the age of eleven [she] began to exhibit the usual behaviour of a child only partially accepted into a foster home and already aware of rejection by the wider society. By the age of twelve her foster mother had rejected her, and at thirteen … she was an inmate of the Cootamundra home.[94]

Quoted in an ABC radio program in 1997, former AWB Chairman, Gerard Kingsmill, spoke of 'managed' removals monitored closely by the Board, to rescue children from disadvantaged living conditions. A former reserve manager stated on the same program that the majority of children taken were neglected — 'If you judged by our standards you could take half the children, it just depended on your standards.'[95] However, AWB records suggest that a major reason was to socialise children away from Aboriginal culture and identity and that strenuous efforts were made to prevent even young adults from having *any* contact with their families. In 1953 the Board wrote to the Bishop of Armidale in response to his offer to take Aboriginal children into the Armidale Girls Home:

It is the policy of the Aborigines Welfare Board to place children committed to its care and control by the Children's Court, with suitable foster parents rather than institutions. When, however, suitable foster parents are not available, the Board arranges for their care in a Children's Home.

… During this period [of control] every effort is made by the Board's Welfare Officers to wean these young people from their old way of life, but it is unfortunate that when they reach the age beyond which the Board's control does not extend, some return to their old environment.

The Board's interest in the young aboriginal people does not cease when they reach their eighteenth birthday. A system of after-care by the Board's Officers has operated with very satisfying results and, despite disappointments occasioned by some young people who will choose to return to conditions which can only be described as most unsatisfactory, the Board will not relax its efforts in the direction of educating the aborigines to a better way of life.[96]

When in 1967 the Matron of Cootamundra Aboriginal Girls Home told a joint parliamentary committee that Aboriginal children were better removed from their parents, she repeated negative perceptions of Aboriginal families:

Q: It has been suggested to us in another sphere that all aboriginal children, to help them for greater assimilation, should be placed in homes of this description [Cootamundra]. Do you agree with this?

W[itness]: I do not think that any institution can equal the natural home life. But these children are not getting a natural home life, because dark people naturally only live unto the day; they do not look after tomorrow even, and very often they would be hungry and they would not get a natural life in that respect. I think they are very much better off in an institution than they would be in some of their home lives.[97]

AWB records contain many heartbreaking letters from parents begging for the return of their children which were routinely refused — there was no notion of family rehabilitation and reconciliation for Aboriginal families.

During the late 1950s educational opportunity (rather than for civilising and training) was a significant rationale for removals, although the AWB was no longer responsible for Aboriginal education. Welfare officers and others pressured parents to send their children away to environments they considered more suited to learning. The following record of one such effort also spoke of the enduring negative effects of a parent's own experiences of removal:

the mother was not convinced of the necessity, but spoke instead of the injustice of her childhood years when children were 'taken away to be apprenticed and never paid.' [The Welfare officer] reported the mother's feelings to be so strong as to 'colour her whole attitude towards official interference' and that she would accept no financial help and have her son educated elsewhere. L believed on the contrary that the child needed a boarding education so that he could 'learn a trade.' At length [the Welfare officer] 'got around her objection that he was being taken away to a home' with the promise that he could return for the summer holidays.[98]

AWB meetings reiterated the imperative to remove Aboriginal children from family environments, regardless of living standards or neglect. During a Board discussion on the proposal to develop hostels for Aboriginal students, one member stated that nothing could be done with adults and young people and the Board must:

> concentrate on the very young child, and concentration on education would give a better standard of living. The Board should gradually use more money on residential education so as to take the children out of their environment.[99]

In 1963 most remaining legislative restrictions were lifted although powers to expel Aborigines from reserves were retained. Following the 1965 meeting of the Native Welfare Council, the AWB moved to 'integrate' education and housing: segregated schools were closed — they had decreased from twenty-six in 1950 to twelve in 1960[100] — forcing families to move to town to send their children to school or face their removal for non-attendance, and no further houses were to be built on reserves.[101] In the same year a New South Wales government Joint Committee Report endorsed the policy of assimilation despite strong Aboriginal opposition, and called for accelerated clearing of reserves:

> To convince people living on reserves that, in their own interest, they should move to centres where employment is available will not be an easy task. These people live in a community of their own where all are of the same standard of living, where few have any great ambition to get on in the world, where worldly goods are shared, and most important, where the stresses of modern living are not experienced ... They are apparently quite content to remain as they are. Because there are no high levels to which they might aspire, the lowest level becomes the norm ... The older generation would find it most difficult to leave reserves and settle happily into the city. But the Committee is convinced that many of the younger generations could and should make the move.[102]

With forty-seven percent of Aborigines still living on stations and reserves, the AWB began in earnest to expedite removals. Managers were instructed to supervise the relocation of residents to town and to inspect homes, collect rent and enforce school attendance and employment.[103] From 1968 a 'more aggressive assimilation' was imposed: all discriminatory legislation was removed, the AWB was dismantled in 1969 and its functions (notably child welfare) were transferred to mainstream departments. Funding, including a home loan scheme, was provided by the new Office of Aboriginal Affairs to rehouse Aboriginal families, and managers were removed from most stations and reserves. In the same year Cootamundra and Kinchela Homes were closed after an earlier Interdepartmental Committee found that they 'tended to perpetuate segregation',[104] and the children were transferred to state children's homes. Aborigines lobbied government to make the sites available for Aboriginal tenancy.[105] At the same time the placement of Aboriginal children from the Australian Capital Territory by New South Wales welfare authorities ceased and, rather than sending them interstate to live in foster families, they were placed in local residential care with the aim of eventual family reunion. Aboriginal people were now to be under surveillance from many more mainstream authorities, each demanding compliance with 'white standards'. Their land base had also been severely reduced with the closure of the reserves and when the New South Wales *Lands Rights Act 1983* was passed the area that could be returned was barely a thousand hectares.[106]

Western Australia and Queensland had the largest Aboriginal populations of all the states. In 1947 Western Australia's Aboriginal population was estimated at 21,000 (although in 1950 it was counted at only 11,498), with twenty percent under direct control of the Department of Native Affairs (DNA) and the remainder still subject to legislative controls. An increase in the proportion of children in the Aboriginal population from forty-four percent in 1950 to fifty-seven percent by 1955 should have alerted administrators determined to create economically viable family units to the very real problems of families in supporting their offspring.[107] In 1947, after fourteen continuous years of Labor government, the new Liberal government determined to act on its frequent criticisms of the handling of

511

Aboriginal issues and, encouraged by the 1948 Premiers Conference and advice from Elkin, it set out to sweep away the cobwebs of the past. The resulting administrative reforms led to a refreshing new outlook. On the eve of debate on the 1954 Native Administration Bill, under a Labor government, Commissioner Middleton condemned the existing legislation on the grounds that it:

> approved of [Aborigines'] pauperisation on the one hand and on the other directed a form of control which bordered on unwarranted interference with personal liberty unparalleled in the legislative treatment of any other people of the Commonwealth or Pacific territories ... We, who are charged with the unpleasant duty of administering it, regard it as repugnant to basic humanitarian and welfare principles, devoid of any common ground with the people we are trying to help and creative of more misunderstanding, dissatisfaction and abuse than any other piece of similar legislation known to the free world today.[108]

However, conservative politicians remained more circumspect. The acting Liberal Premier (later Sir) Charles Court told a Perth radio audience in 1961 that continued tutelage and legislative controls 'relieve our native people of some of their responsibilities and exercise some controls over them in their own interests'.[109]

The Western Australian Commissioner of Native Welfare, S Middleton, with young women from Alvan House Girls' Hostel, Perth, 1953.
(Courtesy of Battye Library, BA368/6/220)

Funding levels increased and for the first time reached the level of one percent of consolidated revenue originally stipulated in the *Constitution Act 1889*. While the first real steps towards legal equality began with the passing of the *Native Welfare Act 1954* and the establishment of the new Department of Native Welfare (DNW) it was to be nine years before the *Native Welfare*

Act 1963 made substantial changes by repealing the powers to forcibly remove Aborigines to reserves and otherwise restrict their movement; automatic guardianship of illegitimate children from birth to the age of twenty-one; controls over Aboriginal earnings and property; and penalties for interracial sex. Aborigines in 'proclaimed areas' would now be granted 'drinking rights'. The definition of 'native' (any person of more than quarter Aboriginal descent) remained unchanged, and the DNW retained the right to intervene in Aboriginal families through its duty of providing for the 'custody, maintenance and education of the children of natives'.[110] In 1972 all remaining discriminatory measures — including interventions in families outside of mainstream family welfare channels — were repealed and the transfer of all services to relevant government departments was completed with the amalgamation of the departments of Native Welfare and Child Welfare.

Nyungar 'mixed race' populations in the south were the initial focus of the assimilation program. Elsewhere the process lagged, reflecting pastoral employers' resistance to change, town residents' determination to keep Aborigines out, enduring stereotypes of 'full-blood' Aborigines as unable to adapt to or even survive change, and the sheer scale and expense of managing the task in areas remote from Perth. The dramatic social upheavals following the introduction of award wages for Aboriginal pastoral workers (1967), equal access to unemployment benefits (1972–73) and sackings by employers and Aboriginal walk-offs, would finally force the Department's hand. Administrators envisaged that they would have an easier task working with the southern 'outcasts [of] white Australia'.[111] However, Nyungar families were not 'empty slates' or impoverished 'would be' whites. Within limits imposed by 'economic and political constraints', they had forged accommodations based on negotiations with local employers; persistence of Nyungar skills, values and strong family networks, and a form of 'social invisibility' to circumvent outside intervention in family life. Anthropologist Sally Hodson[112] writes that they had 'insisted on working in the way that suited them best', which left them to determine 'when, how and with whom they worked'. Their preferred option was to work under contract with local farmers, an arrangement which paid better than salaried work and allowed them to live in their traditional 'runs' and in mobile family groups with their children working and learning skills on the side. In between jobs they lived in town fringe camps in the company of wider kin networks and

513

without costly overheads such as rent. Prior to the 1950s some families had managed to survive largely outside the net of government control. The growing intervention by DNW field staff pressuring families to assimilate coincided with their marginalisation in the rural economy which prompted new adaptations such as moving to the city. Nyungar lifestyles contrasted markedly with DNW aims and staff soon realised that the families would not easily bend to their will. This was true across the generations and Commissioner Middleton informed his minister in 1960 that 'many of the teenagers do not want post primary education or training or being submitted to any restriction of their liberty in any shape or form'.[113]

Western Australia did not follow the Northern Territory practice of using settlements to train families for assimilation. This reflected Western Australian experience that such community 'clearing houses' simply did not work. Instead it announced that the settlements would no longer be used 'as harbours for a displaced, unwanted and industrially incapable people'[114] and that they would be closed down or converted to children's homes. Adults were sent out to fend for themselves in the wider community. Large missions in remote areas would be developed as ongoing communities. There was increasing intervention in Nyungar families through a bevy of government officers and 'experts' — Native Welfare patrol officers, school truancy officers, Child Welfare workers and 'visitors' to assess the condition of the family, the home, family expenditure and measures needed to reshape it into a model nuclear family. DNW field staff were required to:

> maintain close and regular contact with natives in their homes, at work, in schools, etc., and to assist or advise them in any problem of general, social, economic or family welfare that might arise.[115]

This created an ironic situation in which families were rigidly policed and penalised to enable them to become independent and responsible. There was little real attention to assisting families in finding work, and in a shrinking rural employment market the DNW opened four agricultural training schools for youth.

Again the focus was on enforcing education of children and conventional housing. In 1948, after thirty years of official exclusion from state schools and seventy-eight years after compulsory education was introduced for white children, schooling became compulsory for

Aboriginal children with the exception of those living more than three miles from a school or a transport service. This effectively excluded children on pastoral stations. The focus was to be on 'detribalised' children living in or close to towns. The push to enrol children was closely linked to initiatives to create conventional home environments. Officers now began to drill parents in the need to improve home conditions and to send their children to school or to a mission to give them 'a better chance' — or face their forced removal. Parents were told the children could return home for holidays but home inspections often meant that permission was refused and the children stayed on at school year after year. Given their own experiences some parents agreed, fearing that otherwise they would lose their children altogether. Others found it impossible to link schooling with their seasonal round of farm work or even to support their children. In 1954 the Education Department introduced a Provisional Curriculum for Coloured Pupils in Caste Schools for missions and government settlements which focused on basic numeracy and literacy, hygiene, morals and religion but the schools increasingly adopted mainstream programs.[116] Hostels and mission boarding schools were also opened around the state. Through these initiatives school attendance was boosted from 700 in 1943 to 5300 (the majority in the south) in 1965.[117]

To encourage post-primary studies the DNW opened two hostels in Perth for secondary students, office and nursing trainees and apprentices — Alvan House Girls' Hostel (1950) and McDonald House for boys (1952). An Anglican hostel was also opened in Geraldton for secondary girls and a junior technical college was set up in Derby. Some children boarded with relatives on Education Department remote boarding allowances. During the 1960s the DNW moved to open up new vocations for Aboriginal youth through trade apprenticeships for boys and nursing, office, shop and factory employment for girls.

In the fifties and sixties, steps were taken to move Nyungar families from their tin and hessian humpies on reserves and camping grounds into suburban homes. In 1953 in consultation with the State Housing Commission the DNA embarked on a 'transitional housing' program based on tutored house use in three stages of dwellings — Stage I houses on reserves had up to three rooms, a verandah and cooking facilities, with communal sanitation, ablution and laundry facilities; Stage II houses were for selected families to 'graduate' from the camps to five-roomed self-contained houses on gazetted reserves or town blocks; and Stage III was conventional state housing under the supervision of field officers or assistance to purchase a suitable family home. Tenants were required to pay rental which varied according to the type of dwelling. In 1964 this ranged from sixty cents a week to normal state housing rates.[118] The program provided the veneer of positive activity while it delivered cheap and inadequate housing for Nyungar families. It began with the building of twenty-five Stage I houses and the first determined state effort to provide adequate services of running water and sanitation on Aboriginal reserves. By 1967, 773 dwellings had been completed — 487 Stage I houses, 251 Stage II houses and 35 conventional houses[119] — a considerable improvement. However, in 1970 one thousand homes were urgently needed across the state and, in southern towns like Moora, Aboriginal people were still living in humpies on the local reserve. Occupation of government housing was accompanied by enforced training in child care, home management and skills in liaison with outside agencies such as schools. Initially provided by patrol officers (renamed welfare officers in 1965) assisted by local Native Welfare Committees, home training and supervision became an increasingly specialised task. In 1970 the Homemaker Service was established with forty 'home-makers', mainly women from the local white community, working 'to improve and maintain domestic standards among Department tenants and to enhance positive family functioning'.[120] Nyungar men were increasingly cast by field officers and circumstance as the sole wage earners for their families; however, in a shrinking rural labour market this became an almost impossible task, forcing many families to relocate to Perth in search of employment. From the early 1950s, as part of a drive to impose conventional notions of fatherhood and to reduce expenditure, the DNW also began to enforce payment of maintenance by Aboriginal fathers not living with their children.

Many white town residents remained opposed to any Aboriginal presence. In 1965 Gnowangerup Aborigines were still barred from the swimming pool, the drive-in and local cafes: while townsfolk recognised that conditions on the local reserve contributed to 'the natives' inability to lift their standard of living,' they were unwilling to accept them in the town.[121] These race barriers attracted the attention of Aboriginal organisations in Perth such as the Coolbaroo League which challenged Western Australian racism through articles in its newspaper, *Coolbaroo News* (later *Westralian Aborigine*), and held regular dances and protest meetings in Perth and southern country towns. Some families refused to leave the reserves and this led some local authorities to the extreme, but not uncommon action, of bulldozing the camps.

Initially the move to assimilation was predicated on continued removal of children from their families as outlined in the 1948 Bateman Report:

> The welfare of the children is the only thing which should be considered and the fact that parents are likely to be heartbroken for a few weeks should not influence the administration any more than the fact that white parents in similar circumstances suffer grief. Those native parents who will not make any effort to improve their conditions and help their children are not fitted to retain them.[122]

However, by the early 1950s the DNA had developed a more progressive outlook. In 1951 Commissioner Middleton wrote in his Annual Report that the Department was now officially opposed to the forcible removal of Aboriginal children on the grounds that it was:

> a fallacy to expect any real advance in the welfare of natives without their co-operation and participation; they are quite as strongly antipathetic to being 'done good to' as any one else and enforced separation of children from parents does little more than arouse the bitterness of adults and children alike.[123]

Forcible removal would only be considered 'where the welfare of the child [was] endangered by palpable neglect or in cases of minor delinquency' and such cases would be dealt with by mainstream child welfare authorities. In 1954 formal arrangements began between the DNW and the Department of Child Welfare for the removal of Aboriginal children through the Children's Courts under the *Child Welfare Act 1947*. However, the DNW continued to use its powers of legal guardianship to remove children, and the arrangement was further complicated when it set up its own fostering and adoption services. This would in the long run restrict the grounds for child removal; however, initially the doubling up of services between the departments ensured ongoing high rates of removal. The following account from a Nyungar mother presented to the National Inquiry into the Separation of Aboriginal and Torres Strait Islander Children from their Families suggests that established inhumane ways of removing children also continued:

... all of a sudden the Welfare just came and took [the children], they didn't say anything to me, just picked up the boys coming home from the shop and the Welfare made them wards of the state. I used to work at the hospital nursing, keeping my little family together. If the Welfare wanted to help they could have given me money every fortnight like they do now ... they weren't helping taking [them] away or splitting us up, that was the most terrible thing they done to my family, my sons and myself.[124]

The DNW also adopted a program of 'assimilation through education' where children were to be sent to special Aboriginal children's institutions, preferably with parental permission. The Department's field officers were to assess home environments and persuade parents to voluntarily surrender their children to enhance their 'prospects of future assimilation'[125] — or face forced removals. Officers brought considerable emotional pressure to bear on parents:

When refusing to send their children to a well conducted Christian Mission parents have been advised to give their children the opportunity they have not had themselves. In nearly every case they have put aside their sorrow for the sake of the children and sent them away.[126]

A consequence was that, despite official renunciation of forcible removal, families continued to be broken up and removals and institutionalisation of children actually increased. The institutionalisation of Aboriginal children in contradistinction to trends in child welfare practice at the time reflected the continued official commitment to institutions as the optimum environments for re-forming Aboriginal children, as well as the heavy investment over the years in creating an institutional network, and deeply ingrained negative perceptions of Aboriginal parents and family environments. Writing in 1949 the Superintendent of Moola Bulla, C L McBeath, who had just reopened the settlement school after nine years, stated that successful change only came by removing children from the influence of the adults:

This same influence, although often arising from the love of the parents, and others, for the child is completely undesirable from our standards and can only delay the progress of the child to such an extent that it becomes retrogression. Nomadic habits and tendencies must be eliminated if the child is to be given a sense of responsibility sufficient to take its place in the community.[127]

The plan to continue to institutionalise the children also reflected an urgency to get moving after decades of official exclusion of Aboriginal children from schooling. Institutionalisation appeared to provide a way to avoid obstacles created by the children's families and home conditions and the continuing power of white racism and opposition to Aboriginal children in the classrooms.

In 1948 Middleton anounced a 'State-wide plan for the provision of new institutions for native education and welfare, particularly in the case of children, both full blood and half-caste, as may be thought desirable', which he estimated would cost the government 372,600 pounds over a five-year period.[128] Reversing A O Neville's twenty-five-year blitz on missions, Middleton announced three years later that they would become 'valuable and important administrative adjuncts to this department' and 'vitally essential for the welfare of the native race'.[124] The integral role of missions reflected the influence of Papua New Guinean models of providing education through subsidised missions, as well as economic expediency. The state's sixteen missions expanded over the next twenty years into a comprehensive network of over thirty children's mission homes and, in remote areas, mission communities, thereby making missions, under DNW guidance, into the state's major educating and assimilating agents.

In 1951 Moore River Native Settlement was converted into a children's mission — Mogumber Methodist Mission — and in 1952 Carrolup became Marribank Farm School[129] for boys aged fourteen to eighteen and state wards. Moore River boys over fourteen were sent to Marribank while Carrolup boys and girls were transferred, according to their religious denomination, to Wandering Mission (opened by the Catholic Pallottine Order in 1946) or to the interdenominational Roelands Children's Home. These relocations were very upsetting to the children and their parents. Parents 'virtually attacked' the new Marribank Superintendent and told field officers that they would not send their sons to a former 'penal settlement' and that they wanted to train them themselves.[130] In 1955 Moola Bulla pastoral settlement in the east Kimberley was sold to private interests and residents were evicted to Halls Creek and Fitzroy Crossing and most of the children were transferred to Beagle Bay. New community missions, including Balgo and Jigalong, were opened in desert areas. Some Kimberley missions were relocated to make them more 'viable': Kunmunya was moved from the remote north-west Kimberley coast to Mowanjum near Derby, and Forrest River to Wyndham. Attractive land grants and increased financial assistance were offered to the missions. State government capital grants for buildings and facilities were boosted and the subsidy for Aboriginal children increased from seven to nine shillings per week per child. Child endowment payments of five shillings a week were also paid for each mission child. In 1962 alone child endowment payments totalling £31,480 were distributed to missions for 1703 children.[131] These payments were still being made during the 1970s. Over the years they amounted to hundreds of thousands of dollars which could have gone directly to keeping families together.

Mission institutions began to move away from the 'old ways' of caring for children. The practice of locking them in dormitories overnight was abandoned; schools were now required to meet Education Department standards and qualified teachers were appointed and efforts were made to appoint Aboriginal staff to positions of responsibility. An exception was New Norcia Mission where 'rigid conservatism' and 'fixed ideas' had prevented the introduction of a new school curriculum, and although work had begun on a new school building the girls remained 'gloomy' and 'obstinate' and the boys absconded repeatedly.[132] While Sister Kate's, transferred to Methodist control in the early 1950s (Sister Kate died in 1946), and Roelands remained committed to cottage homes, the new institutional model was now the religious children's 'boarding school'.

Tardun Children's Mission and St Joseph's Farm, opened in the Murchison region in 1949, was regarded as the foremost example by authorities and its 1956 Annual Report provides useful insights into this new way of institutionalising Aboriginal children.[133] The mission was conducted as a 'boarding school for native and half-caste children similar to those for white children in cities and towns throughout Australia', while the farm provided employment for older boys and girls. The overall aim was to teach all the children to 'be fit to receive citizenship rights'. The report claimed that every effort was being made to create a family atmosphere for the children. Eighty boys and girls were cared for by three priests, five brothers and four sisters, and staff continuity and stability were a priority. Most of the children had come directly from their families. With the exception of state wards, parental permission was generally required for acceptance into the mission and parents were free to visit and children were allowed go home for holidays. In 1956 seventy-two children were enrolled in grades I to VI, and five working boys and three girls aged fourteen to sixteen were engaged in farm and domestic duties. The report claimed that on arrival the children demonstrated a strong resentment against whites and a lack of appreciation of home life, in particular, the care of property and devotion to parents and siblings. For this reason care was taken to provide a strong religious and educational foundation to help them to eventually 'take their place as equals'. Classes followed the state school curriculum, with additional daily instruction in 'religion, honesty, cleanliness, good conduct, fair play, purity of life and respect for authority'. Assigned daily tasks reinforced this learning. Following the example of educators working with juvenile delinquents, there was a strong focus on teaching the children about family life 'for their own advancement'. This also reflected the imperatives of assimilation and its focus on the nuclear family. Particular emphasis was placed on shaping the children into Christian parents and it was hoped that through their example they would influence their own families to appreciate the benefits of education and a settled home life. Outlining the school curriculum for upper primary children the headmaster wrote:

... the boys are taught the responsibility that devolves on them when once they marry. They must provide for the wife and children; they must work to do this. Before the girls is laid the ideal of motherhood as the natural completion of their desires. On quite a number of girls this has a strong effect and they really manifest a desire to be the mother of a real family.[134]

The working boys and girls were taught about:

The nobility of parenthood of both husband and wife ... for, in fact, parenthood means for most of them co-habitation and nothing else. The unity and indissolubility of marriage is pressed home, namely that when once married they are married for life to procreate and educate their children. The early education of the child is in the hands of the mother. She it is who should first teach matters of hygiene, honesty, fair play etc. The father plays his role by providing, and in a suitable way, for his wife and children. Around this principle are built instructions on drinking, work, the payment of debts, respect of law and authority.[135]

Hostels for Aboriginal children in Western Australia reflected earlier institutional models in design and vocational training programs.
(Courtesy of Battye Library, BA/368/311; BA/368/279)

From the late 1950s, in an effort to bring assimilation through education to remote areas as well, the DNW began to establish a network of town based children's hostels. The limited educational opportunities available to children in remote areas was highlighted during the 1958 royal visit when the southern press reported that a young 'half-caste' girl sent south from Halls Creek to meet the Queen Mother could not finish her schooling and would be sent to become a 'chattel in a sordid native camp on a station'. Offers to adopt the girl followed and even the Queen Mother enquired after her future prospects.[136] By 1961 there were six remote hostels housing three hundred children. Ten years later there were twenty-one government hostels in the state with more planned. The remote hostels were in part a compromise for pastoral employers. Few were willing to set up schools for their workers' children — exceptions in the Kimberley were Gogo (1957) and Christmas Creek (1962) — nor did they want their workers moving off after their children to distant missions. Hostels provided an alternative where children remained in the region where, it was believed, they could keep in touch with their parents and be trained for local employment needs while they lived in environments that were conducive to school learning. Hostels were set up by the Department in cooperation with mission bodies or through committees of prominent townspeople and employers. Children attended local state schools and the committees directed their learning 'to fit them into the work force in the area to which they belong'.[137] Initially this was simply pastoral work for the boys and domestic science for the girls but a new view was that the children's experiences in town would broaden their horizons and lead to a wider range of vocational training and work opportunities. The committees also supervised the general management of the hostels, ensured that overall aims were implemented, conducted regular inspections, decided on the children's diet, clothing, discipline and leisure activities, and raised funds and decided on parents' contributions. Parents whose wages were pegged at two pounds a week could be required to contribute as much as ten shillings weekly to their children's support as 'part of social training in the responsibilities of parenthood'.[138] Nevertheless, field officers reported that in the eastern goldfields and Pilbara many parents were 'very desirous' of educating their children. This may have reflected in part their intention to safeguard their children against removal to far distant places and out of their control.[139]

In 1969 the Aborigines Advancement League in Melbourne alleged that hostels and missions in Western Australia were there:

to break up families. Young children feel lost and alone when they are taken from their families. The purpose of placing them in missions for education is defeated, because they lose the desire to learn.[140]

DNW authorities responded that the children were:

not taken from their parents. We are trying to insist that the parents remain on the properties where the children came from. We do not want to see a shift in population. At the end of the school term the children go back to the homes they came from just as our white children return home from boarding school.[141]

In practice there was little chance for many children to return home. Parents were required to cover their fares, while their dwellings, which employers persistently refused to improve, were often rejected as unsuitable for their holidaying children. In some cases these home conditions led to children being declared wards of the state. The result was that many children stayed in the hostels until their schooling was completed. Some never returned.[142] The role of the hostels declined from the early 1970s with the move of families from stations into towns.

Removals of children, both forced and voluntary, kept pace with this expansion of institutions. In 1961 over 1691 Aboriginal children were living in more than thirty institutions in Western Australia[143]. Forty-five percent of known Kimberley children were in missions or hostels and in the south twenty-five percent were in missions. The government's program of assimilation had served to increase the incidence of separation of children from their families to levels which would never have been tolerated for white families and which continued despite the fact that it was not in the children's best interests as defined by contemporary practice and values. Indeed, removals had continued despite official DNW objectives to reduce levels of separation. Official correspondence indicates that the appointment of field staff to focus on family welfare had contributed to this through increased surveillance and control of families.[144] Nor could officials abandon established models of removing and institutionalising children. After scrutinising removal practices, and expressing alarm that institutionalisation was shattering the children's pride in their Aboriginality and creating distrust of white ways, the 1958 Special Committee on Native Matters[145] could offer only a conservative solution — leave children with their parents to the age of six, if possible; make institutions 'friendlier' and more tolerant of Aboriginal culture; and allow parental visits. In the following year the DNW announced a new focus on the intact family. The practice of 'encouraging and assisting native parents to put their children in missions for educational purposes' would cease and, instead, field officers would work to keep families together in 'better environmental circumstances'.[146] Children whose parents could care for them would be returned from the missions.

A DNW circular in 1960 instructed field officers that they were no longer to deal with children as 'a separate entity' and 'the only part of the Aboriginal race worth saving', but were to deal with *family* welfare in accordance with the principle that children were best reared with their parents under 'normal circumstances'.[147] The only grounds for separation were to meet educational needs of children in remote areas, for medical care or on the basis of 'neglect or deprivation' proved through the Children's Court. Even then 'committal action must be regarded as a last resort.'[148] These pronouncements promised a departure from existing practice. The family would be retained as 'a composite unit, even in accommodation that may be sub-standard in many ways by modern yard-sticks' and considered preferable in many ways to the 'artificiality of the best institutions available'.[149] The shift from institutional to family welfare was also motivated by official alarm at the growing expense of the institutions — they were consuming twenty-seven percent of the DNW annual vote although their populations did not constitute twenty percent of the state's Aboriginal population. Furthermore, officials argued, parents were not contributing to maintenance of their children.

It was a terrible irony that, having 'persuaded' parents to send their children to mission homes, the DNW now turned around and attacked them. 'In many instances', it was claimed, the homes were 'grossly and blatantly exploited by native parents who could and should be maintaining their children.' While the new policy of 'family welfare' envisaged 'the return to the family from missions of those children whose parents could and should provide satisfactorily for their progeny',[150] this was conditional on their having suitable homes and being able to carry out their parental responsibilities. Field officers were instructed to encourage them to improve conditions so they could be reunited with their children. This proved to be problematic. The Welfare Inspector for the Moora sub-district complained in 1960 that 'home conditions and the ability of parents to care for children' were 'rather relative matters' and there were no 'specific standards' to judge them by. He noted that in his sub-district 'in *no case* has the home or economical position been found to be particularly good' with the result that continued institutionalisation of the children was considered to be 'more or less warranted.' Furthermore, he suspected that staff at nearby New Norcia Mission were convincing 'parents that they cannot look after a child and that it is in the child's best interests to be admitted to the institution'. He concluded that 'housing remains the major problem' and that numbers in missions would only be reduced 'with the installation of better housing in the various centres'.[151] With limited housing and an obstinate culture of removal within the DNW, removals continued. A welfare officer reported following an inspection in 1968:

A thorough examination was not made as the father was not present. From what I saw however, I am satisfied that the children are 'neglected', if for no other reason than the shack they live in.[152]

At the same time the DNW had been developing its own system of fostering and adoption in consultation with the Department of Child Welfare (DChW). In 1962 it was conducting its own selection, placement and inspection of families and children and had placed eighty-one children in forty-eight foster homes, thirteen adoptions had been completed, twelve were pending, and four were awaiting placement. Overall a net increase of forty-eight children had been dealt with since the previous year. Children were also declared wards under the Child Welfare Act and placed with foster families by the DChW. The consequences for the entire family are evident in the tragic story of Fred and Joan Dickerson, as recorded by their daughter Coral Suzanne and historian Darren Foster[153] — a story reflected in the experiences of many Aboriginal people recounted to the Inquiry into the Separation of Aboriginal and Torres Strait Islander Children in Perth in 1996. In 1959 eight-year-old Coral Suzanne Dickerson and four of her siblings were taken from their poverty-stricken Aboriginal father and non-Aboriginal mother in Geraldton, committed to the care of the DChW and placed with white foster families in Perth. As was the case for many other Aboriginal fathers at the time, Coral Suzanne's father was obliged to contribute to the costs of maintaining his children in state custody and was subsequently imprisoned for being in arrears with his payments, thereby seriously jeopardising the family's chances of being reunited. In Perth Coral Suzanne and her sister lived with a family who proved to be 'devoted and dedicated'; however, the little girl grew up with an 'underlying sense of insecurity about the life and the foster family' and she longed to return to her natural mother. This in turn was reflected in behavioural problems as she grew up. Coral Suzanne established intermittent contact with her mother but at the age of forty her mother died, filled with 'grief and deep shame over the removal of her children'. It was at this time that Coral Suzanne learned that Fred Dickerson was not her natural father and that her father was a white man. In one swoop she had lost her mother, her father and her Aboriginal identity.

With the passing of the *Native Welfare Act 1963* the Director of Child Welfare assumed responsibility for Aboriginal children committed by the courts, although Native Welfare continued to handle cases in the north until 1970. In 1964 the DNW reported that removals had continued to increase in tandem with appointments of further field officers (who had unrestricted access to 'native' dwellings under new regulations) and improved funding to missions. Twenty-five percent of its annual grant continued to go to missions compared to only thirty percent on improving conditions on reserves.[154] In 1966, 2784 Aboriginal children were living in government or mission institutions.[155] In 1968, 1295 committals of Aboriginal children were in force and two years later DChW noted that twenty percent of children in its institutions were Aboriginal, despite efforts by its officers to stop removals and to rehabilitate families. Aboriginal youths were now dealt with by the courts rather than being sent to Aboriginal institutions: in 1966 and 1967 seventy-one were charged and convicted by the courts. In 1967 Justices of the Peace in the small wheatbelt town of Pingelly announced their intention to whip an Aboriginal youth as it was 'the only way to stop them drinking'.[156] Family unity was also threatened by discriminatory treatment of adult males by the law. Eggleston[157] found in a study of ten Western Australian rural towns in 1965 that of a total of 553 charges laid, 500 were against Aborigines. The charges were for offences against Native Welfare legislation and sections of the Licensing Act dealing with 'natives'. Eggleston found no evidence that alcoholism was more frequent in the Aboriginal community than in white society, rather charge rates reflected public drinking patterns and special legislative prohibitions still in force in the state.

In 1972 the DNW and DChW were amalgamated, forming a large powerful department, the Department of Community Welfare (DCW) with an extensive network of children's institutions inherited from the DNW. Separation of Aboriginal children from their families through mainstream child welfare and juvenile justice processes continued at rates far higher than for the white community. This despite the DCW's statement to the Furnell Royal Commission into Aboriginal Affairs in Western Australia in 1974 that it had 'enough experience to be familiar with the results of parental deprivation on young children and [was] consequently extremely reluctant to remove any child from its parents'.[158]

QUEENSLAND

At the end of the Second World War Queensland had an Aboriginal population of 19,500 along with several thousand Torres Strait Islanders. Like Western Australia it had a legacy of complex legislation and regulations embodying sweeping controls and encompassing powers. The focus of the Director of Native Affairs Office (DNAO) was the management of a network of segregated community institutions (nine missions and five government settlements) which housed over forty percent of Queensland's Aboriginal population in notoriously impoverished conditions. Queensland had greater financial and bureaucratic investments in its institutions than any other state — in

1961 two-thirds of departmental revenue (the highest of the states totalling 1.6 million pounds in 1960) went to settlements and missions, and its only field staff were employed there.[159] Enforced deductions from Aboriginal wages to government trust accounts provided a significant funding source for developing and maintaining institutions and allowed for more rapid expansion than in the other states which had to rely on the annual grant for their funds.[160] It was perhaps not surprising then that Queensland only reluctantly began to contemplate genuine reform through the repeal of legislation and a new role for its institutions to train and then disperse Aboriginal families. Kidd[161] remains sceptical of Queensland government motives and notes that the 'rhetoric of assimilation while philosophically "progressive", also accorded neatly with Queensland's "economic imperatives".' Comments in annual reports suggest that the Queensland government considered that families living outside the institutions were assimilating into the general community, the children attending state schools and the families supporting themselves through steady employment.[162] Nevertheless many lived in desperate conditions and they remained under constant surveillance. The Director of Native Affairs stated in 1959: 'we know the name, family history and living conditions of every aboriginal in the State.'[163] Meanwhile, the Department argued, the settlements offered 'refuge to any coloured person who for some reason or other fail[ed] to maintain his standard of citizenship and desires to return to the settlement township'.[164]

It was only in the late 1950s that Queensland began to express a commitment to a 'clear and purposeful' policy of assimilation based on 'a strong educational foundation and suitable housing' to ensure that 'Aboriginal children [were] ultimately to be assimilated into the white community as useful citizens of the State'.[165] By 1963 this had developed into a firm policy based on:

Preparation of the native people for assimilation through education in all its aspects — academic, industrial, health and hygiene.

Building up within the native people a feeling of pride of race and self-reliance.

Fostering within the white community an awareness of the difficult situations which confront coloured families battling the hard road towards independent outlook and self-support.[166]

This was touted as a two-pronged project of assimilating communities through the existing institutional apparatus and expanding social welfare programs for Aborigines throughout the state. Legislation to implement the policy was not passed until 1965.[167] In the previous year the Queensland Council for the Advancement of Aborigines and Torres Strait Islanders had issued a statement condemning existing legislation on the grounds that it was 'discriminatory and violate[d] fundamental human rights as laid down in the United Nations Charter of Human Rights'. The Council advocated:

> *Freedom for the Family* as for all other citizens. *Because*: Aborigines must now get permission to marry. Children may be taken from their parents without neglect or cruelty being proved. The 'age of consent' for an Aboriginal girl is at puberty.[168]

The *Aborigines and Torres Strait Islander Affairs Act 1965* repealed many oppressive administrative controls, including legal guardianship of children and prohibitions on alcohol, although powers to remove Aborigines to reserves were retained and superintendents' powers to control and discipline inmates were increased.

Queensland's initial approach to assimilation was to endeavour to remove certain residents from the institutions while at the same time maintaining the institutional apparatus. One proposal was to arrange for 'almost white children' on the settlements to be adopted or fostered by white families. A memo of the Director of Native Affairs Office written in 1959 asked:

> Are the circumstances of our beneficial control of children such that we are encouraging the growth of a virtually white population on our settlements who will never be assimilated while their parents desire to retain them and because the parents are incapable or unwilling to leave the settlement?[169]

Settlement superintendents were requested to draw up lists of names of orphans and children who 'appear to be unwanted by their parents' and whose parents would sign adoption papers.[170] However no names were forthcoming. From Cherbourg, Matron Carew reported that the mothers were 'all very definite that they would not consider parting with their children. Three mothers ... whom she felt would be most likely to accept such a suggestion, were also very averse to the idea.'[171] Five years later the DNAO was still promoting the idea but nevertheless responded sanctimoniously to a public inquiry about the availability of children for adoption:

You may be surprised that the number of children available for adoption is very small, Aboriginal parents are just as attached to their children as other people and the few children who can be offered for adoption are mostly orphans.[172]

Conditions on many settlements and missions at this time were potentially explosive. Sickness, death, insanitary conditions, over-crowding and food shortages were rampant and legitimate protests by Aboriginal residents at these conditions evoked only patronising 'dressing-downs' or threats from officials — Palm Island men calling for appropriate pay for their work were told by the Director of Native Affairs 'to get off the Settlement and stay off it.'[173] In this atmosphere, a Conference of Managers of Aboriginal settlements was called in 1960 to devise ways to cut back on expenditure on the settlements, claimed by DNAO officials to total one thousand pounds per year on each resident family.[174] Cabinet policy dictated that:

there shall be a reassessing of the policy that is adopted on our settlements and which we shall say maintains that some of the people should care for themselves ... we have ... given these people every opportunity by tuition, education and so on, and it is up to them to put something back into the work.[175]

This was in response to broader government cutbacks as well as departmental claims that the increased expenditure involved in its new policy of Aboriginal advancement necessitated an 'exacting examination of the whole financial position'.[176] Subsequent comments by the Minister for Health and Home Affairs that Cabinet had directed him to 'lessen the indigence of our native people' suggested where the pressure for change would lie. Changes proposed by the managers[177] involved retaining institutions while engaging in activities that appeared to reduce populations — after all, few would have deliber-ately plotted their own unemployment. Ideas of enforced tutelage in institutions with greater Aboriginal financial contributions were dominant. In practice, plans to teach Aboriginal men to take more 'responsibility' and to promote feelings of pride in 'self, wife and family' in order to encourage the families to enter the wider community, actually meant forcing the men to contribute more to family maintenance, even though they were paid below award wages for their work. It was also suggested that Cherbourg could specialise as a clearing centre for Aborigines from institutions across the state, deemed capable of assimilation. There was a general view that Aborigines would be unwilling to leave the settlements, not because of an emotional attachment to place and community, but because they were 'too timid' and were capitalising on the 'material benefits provided by this Department'. There was also concern that outside they would be 'preyed' upon by whites. The Superintendent of Cherbourg later wrote that it was futile to set up 'modern' settlements and then send Aborigines out to poor conditions and unemployment and that the policy should be to provide supervision and assistance over the next decade for maintaining families on the settlements before settling them into the wider community.[178] In 1965 nine mission and five government institutions were still operating in Queensland with a total population of 8467 Aborigines.[179] While the government claimed that advances had been made through improvements in education,[180] vocational training, housing, infant and maternal health, standards still lagged far behind those acceptable in the wider community. Some three hundred children were still separated from their families in dormitories at Aurukun, Doomadgee, Cherbourg, Woorabinda and Palm Island.[181]

Assimilation through the institutional apparatus was the focus of change in Queensland. Despite a stated commitment to improving social welfare services for families on the outside, little in fact was done. In 1967 liaison officers were appointed to inspect and monitor conditions in Aboriginal homes, to police truancy and to negotiate with police and child welfare authorities in relation to cases of child neglect or juvenile crime. Meanwhile, low wages and destitute living conditions left many families vulnerable to poor health, arbitrary actions of local authorities (for example, the bulldozing of camps to disperse families) and removal.

Removals of children by the DNAO decreased markedly from a total of 376 during the 1950s to fifty-eight during the 1960s, with no removals in 1971. Only twenty-three percent of the total removals from 1908 occurred after 1946.[182] In presenting these figures to the National Inquiry into the Separation of Aboriginal Children from their Families, the Queensland government provided no explanation for this surprising shift. Assuming that these figures are correct, it may be that the DNAO had decided, in accordance with its determination to stop the expansion of settlement populations, to put an end to the cycle of removing children to settlements where they grew up, settled and established new families. Initially at least, it did not expand its system of removal nor did it develop a strong cooperative relationship with child welfare authorities, who refused to process adoptions and dealt reluctantly with a small number of placements of wards in foster homes and institutions. Furthermore, there was no strong impetus to remove children for education since the majority were already enrolled in state schools. The low numbers also reflected changing legal responsibilities. With the repeal of legal guardianship of Aboriginal children in 1965, the primary power for removals became the new *Children's Services Act 1965* which allowed Aboriginal children to be removed through the courts by child welfare and juvenile justice authorities. The following comment during debate on the Bill pointed to the sector of the Aboriginal population to be targeted by this new legislation:

> No group of children is more neglected than those who are living with their parents in the fringe-dwelling areas of many of our country towns.
> I want that unfortunate group of people to be included in the children and youth of the State whose well-being it is proposed to promote, safeguard and protect by the introduction of this Bill.[183]

Several existing missions and settlements were registered as institutions under the 1965 Act to receive Aboriginal children sent in by the DNAO or the State Children's Department. While numbers of removals by the latter are unavailable, the fact that by 1970 half the children in welfare institutions were Aboriginal indicates that removals continued as families were subjected to mainstream processes.

In the face of mounting protest by Aborigines and their supporters in Queensland and across the country, and federal threats to *force* states to 'scrap all discriminatory laws',[184] the Bjelke-Petersen National Party government passed the *Aborigines Act 1971* while protesters filled Brisbane streets demanding change. The Act repealed the bulk of remaining discriminatory laws, in particular powers to forcibly remove and detain Aborigines on reserves. An expanded system of community elected councils and the appointment of a statewide Aboriginal

Advisory Council promised greater Aboriginal control, although opposition members noted the retention of wide-ranging powers to pass regulations and continued government controls over reserve lands which constituted over two percent of state land. Paternalistic protection and management of Aborigines in settlements and missions continued in contravention, government critics claimed, of the United Nations Declaration of Human Rights. Many questioned whether the Act represented a true move away from paternalism or the handing over to Aborigines of a difficult problem without the necessary resources and expertise to deal with it.

SOUTH AUSTRALIA

In 1951 South Australia formally adopted the 'assimilation package' for its 5000-strong Aboriginal population. At the same time it began to relocate Aborigines from its stations at Point Pearce and Point McLeay and smaller town reserves to Adelaide and country towns where some families in search of work had already settled. Families could only return to the stations with official permission. Many were unprepared for the move, or for their reception from white neighbours. Mary Cooper recalled the pain of her move from Point Pearce to town:

> [They] persuaded me to leave ... because there was no future ... for my children ... And so we became outcasts on the fringe of white man's society and not permitted to go back to our Aboriginal society, unless we had a permit from the management ... We didn't fully realise what was going on, we didn't fully understand [in 1972]. It is now, ten years later, that we understand fully just how desolate we were then, and how hard the fight we had to put up to survive, how hard it must have been for our children, to fight the continual slur of 'you're a blackfella, you're an Aboriginal. Ha-ha!' ... The mothers tended to stay inside, because they was frightened of whitefellas looking at them. They were shy people. The children were kept in their backyard, because the white kids made fun of them ... Our children were suffering loneliness; they were suffering poverty; they were suffering fear. The parents was afraid to do something about it, they was afraid to go out and talk about it. We had come away from this great big family that we had on the reservation, whereby we were all brothers and sisters ... We'd lost that and now we were lonely people, and our children were lonely people.[185]

Despite some community support — the Aborigines Advancement League in Adelaide raised funds to set up hostel accommodation for Aborigines visiting Adelaide to work or study — there was public protest at the Aborigines' presence from town residents. In 1962 the Adelaide *Advertiser* reported that sixty Port Pirie residents had petitioned the Point Pearce Mission Council over plans to purchase housing to relocate families in town. They claimed that this would lower the value of their properties and they asked, 'Would you like an Aboriginal family next door?' The Council responded that there were 'good and bad people everywhere' and that Aborigines could fit in and, following a meeting in the town, residents voted to welcome the families. Despite this positive precedent the Aborigines Department then failed to purchase the houses.[186] Children had been enrolled in state schools in South Australia from the First World War, although many attended segregated schools on missions and stations. Now the focus was on encouraging secondary education and the Aborigines Protection Board (APB) contributed to costs and accommodation in hostels. Preschool education was introduced in 1959.

The South Australian government announced the *Aboriginal Affairs Act 1962* as a 'New Deal' for Aborigines which would serve to:

abolish all restrictions and restraints on Aborigines and persons of Aboriginal blood as citizens and to provide the Department with machinery for rendering special assistance to Aborigines and persons of Aboriginal blood during their developmental years and to promote their assimilation into the community.[187]

To achieve this it repealed all remaining discriminatory legislation, including removal powers over children and adults, and created an Aboriginal Affairs Advisory Board and a Department of Aboriginal Affairs. The Department was to focus on providing 'real welfare' and 'help and encouragement to Aborigines ... to accept their full responsibleness and thus promote their social, economic and political development until their assimilation into the community'.[188] To this end welfare officers, including female workers, were appointed in regions with significant Aboriginal populations. South Australia followed the Northern Territory model in proposing the use of institutions in remote areas as 'training centres' in housekeeping and farming. In 1963, in response to growing Aboriginal unrest at Koonibba Lutheran Mission, the Department rated fifty-two resident couples according to 'suitability for assimilation' and proposed to introduce staged training at the mission for the couples and the 'semi-tribal Aborigines at Yalata [Mission]' and to gradually depopulate the missions with the ultimate 'goal of assimilation'. Koonibba Mission was handed over to the government in the same year.[189] Reporting on the 1962 changes, the *Advertiser* reminded its readers that, 'The people of the State have their own part to play by accepting the Aboriginal into their midst as he becomes fitted for life in a predominantly white community'.[190] In the following year geographer Fay Gale[191] wrote that 'probably half of the part-Aboriginal population of this State is segregated from the white community.'

The election of a Labor government in 1965 brought real positive changes and for the first time South Australia began to set the trend for the other states. The new Minister for Aboriginal Affairs Don Dunstan proposed a new policy of self-determination and the Board reported in that year:

Policy objectives are centred on positive welfare ... to promote self-help, self-reliance, and self-determination so that Aborigines may assume more and more responsibility for the management of their own affairs.[192]

The government also promised 'a stepping up of essential services in education, transitional housing, employment, vocational training and education in diet and hygiene'.[193] The Dunstan Labor government elected in 1967 went even further by introducing anti-discrimination and land rights legislation. By 1973 all special functions had been transferred to relevant federal and state authorities and the Department of Aboriginal Affairs filled only a policy formulation and coordination role.

Earlier, numbers of Aboriginal children in care had increased, doubling from 199 in 1957 to 412 in 1959.[194] During the 1950s and 1960s the placement of children was undertaken by several government and voluntary agencies and this uncoordinated approach no doubt contributed to the increase.[195] The problems faced by families in adjusting to town life also were a contributory factor. Like its predecessor, the Department of Aboriginal Affairs was also convinced that the children were socially, economically and educationally disadvantaged by their home life.[196] Although the Chief Protector of Aborigines and local protectors were legal guardians[197] of Aboriginal children to the age of twenty-one, and had powers of summary removal as in the Northern Territory and Western Australia which were not repealed until 1962, these powers do not seem to have been used extensively. While the Aborigines Protection Board claimed that some removals were made with parental consent, Fay Gale[198] identified parents who claimed they had signed up:

> without knowing what they [were] signing. Their regrets later [were] heart breaking. During field work in this state mothers have poured out pathetic stories of what it has meant to realise that they will never see their children again.

Gale also found instances of summary removal including one police officer acting on behalf of the APB who collected together all children lighter than their parents and sent them to institutions, after which their mothers never saw them again. Gale commented that 'legally no individual has the right to make this quite crucial decision. But it happens.' In another case where two children were removed there was a reported 'influx of parents' to the nearby Umeewarra Mission requesting the admission of their children. The parents explained that they wanted to 'get in first' to avoid the threat of their children being removed to far distant institutions where they could lose contact with them forever.[199]

Despite cooperative arrangements between the Board and child welfare authorities earlier in the century, and a provision in the *Aborigines Act 1934–39* specifying that Aboriginal children could be committed to child welfare institutions, the move to mainstreaming in South Australia was frustrated by the initial refusal by the Child Welfare and Public Relief Board (CWPRB) to take in Aboriginal children. It was not until the passing of the *Aboriginal Affairs Act 1962* that the move towards cooperation and liaison between APB and CWPRB began so that *all* neglected, uncontrolled or destitute children would be dealt with in the same manner through the normal processes of law. Again this reflected the mainstreaming intent of the assimilation policy. The government claimed to have developed 'a new concept in relation to the care and maintenance of Aboriginal children':

> By cooperation and liaison with the Child Welfare and Public Relief Board, all carers of neglected, uncontrolled or destitute children will be dealt with in the same manner as are all other children in the

State — that is, through the normal processes of law as provided in the Maintenance Act.[200]

Children were now to be removed only through legal action under the Maintenance or Social Welfare Acts. Up to this point, authorities had been 'trying to turn half caste children into white children'[201] and had argued for mainstream placements in white families and institutions, but they were becoming increasingly aware that Aboriginal children reared in foster homes had more problems with offending, mental health and poor family formation. During the mid-1960s practitioners began to talk about children having rights to Aboriginal identity and to argue for institutional forms of care in hostels and cottages incorporating exposure to Aboriginal culture and identity.[202] In 1970 the departments of Social Welfare and Aboriginal Affairs were amalgamated.

During the 1950s Aboriginal children were placed in Aboriginal mission homes and dormitories — Colebrook, Oodnadatta, Gerard, Umeewarra, Koonibba, Finniss Springs and Nepabunna. In 1956, 186 children were accommodated in these institutions.[203] Between 1955 and 1963 the APB also ran the Campbell House Farm School near Meningie to train older Aboriginal boys in agricultural and pastoral skills. Only a few 'lighter' children were taken into government and private homes for non-Aboriginal children.[204] The Board also supervised schooling for children in South Australia's other missions and reserves and assisted with Northern Territory placements in its institutions and foster homes. It subsidised Aboriginal child placements at missions at twenty-five shillings a week.[205] The only institutional expansion during this time was the establishment of two hostels set up for secondary students and vocational trainees — Tanderra Hostel and the Aborigines Advancement League Hostel at Millswood.

In 1955, convinced that fostering of Aboriginal children increased their chances of being absorbed into the white community, the APB initiated its own scheme to foster Aboriginal children with white families. It may have also been influenced by a growing local critique of institutional care for children. Writing in Adelaide in the early 1960s, Gale[206] pointed to the recognition in the United States of America of the failure of Indian residential schools, and moves from the 1930s to leave children with their families and to work through welfare to help the whole family, and to place unwanted children in foster homes. Gale advocated fostering and adoption as preferable alternatives to institutionalisation:

> Research and experience the world over have shown that foster homes can provide a mother substitute and give the unwanted child the security of home, affection of parents and the individual attention which are essential to normal and healthy growth. Such homes have a far better chance of producing happy, well-adjusted, and easily assimilated adults than most institutions can ever hope for.[207]

Above all she argued for children to remain where possible in their families and commented perceptively:

> A study of records of one children's home revealed that adults who had been reared in the home as children were no cleaner, more able to remain in employment or more sober than those reared out in 'humpies' by their parents. In fact some showed greater success at school and more stability in employment amongst those who had remained in 'the camp' with their parents.[208]

As in New South Wales the APB made public appeals to 'Christian families' and offered a subsidy of up to three pounds a week, which was on a par with CWPRB rates.[209] Despite stated difficulties in finding homes to take in the children, 118 children were living in foster homes just four years later. During the 1960s the Board also began to encourage adoption of Aboriginal children and by 1962 five adoptions had been approved.[210]

With the advent of the fostering program, numbers of children in care escalated. Fostering did not stop institutionalisation of children, as was apparently intended, and instead placements in institutions continued alongside the foster program. By 1959, 234 children, the majority of mixed descent, were in institutions and 146 were living with foster families — almost a third of all Aboriginal children in the state.[211] This was double the number of placements in 1957 and figures had not returned to pre-1957 levels by 1965.[212] The reasons for this are not clear although the Board did indicate a reason for *continued* removals in pointing out that children were often removed because there was insufficient staff to implement family welfare programs.

In the 1950s fostering and adoption became increasingly attractive options for administrations faced with rising numbers of Aboriginal children coming into 'care', limited funds to expand, and imperatives to assimilate Aboriginal populations. Both required less capital output than institutionalisation and fitted with broader drives to provide all children with the opportunity of growing up within intact nuclear families. Adoption in particular fitted the agenda of assimilation. The original identity of the child was erased by law and the child provided with 'a permanent and legal home ... Adopted into a white home [the child] becomes a member of their family and automatically a member of the white community.'[213] By contrast, foster arrangements, in principle at least, allowed continuity of the child's identity and contact with their natural families.

The progressive and inclusive nature of the policy of 'assimilation' appealed to and mobilised some white families to cooperate with the state as an alternative to institutions. This created new forms of separation of child and family, with the fostering or adoptive white family considered a distinct improvement on the existing dormitory model. In a process reminiscent of the earlier role of white female employers of young Aboriginal domestic servants, the role of the white mother as agent of assimilation was pivotal:

> In placing Aboriginal children in non-Aboriginal homes, the state sought to counter the cultural reproductive powers of the Aboriginal mothers from whom children were taken and relied implicitly on the same culturally reproductive capacities of non-Aboriginal women — onto whom the major part of the domestic burden, particularly that of child rearing, fell — to further the project of Aboriginal assimilation. Whether or not they were aware of it, these mothers were given Aboriginal babies and charged with the task of de-Aboriginalising them.[214]

It follows that Aboriginal families were rarely considered suitable for fostering or adoption programs. A consequence of these programs as we saw earlier in the case of Louis Johnson (Chapter 1), was that Aboriginal children were further displaced from contact with Aboriginal people and culture, and their Aboriginal identity; at the same time they were brought more closely into a generally

Form No. 2.

QUEENSLAND.

STATE CHILDREN DEPARTMENT.

Consent to Adoption Order.

In the Matter of an Application to the Director, State Children Department, Brisbane for an order authorising him under the provisions of "The Adoption of Children Acts, 1935 to 1952." to adopt   an infant of

the   sex, born   years of age, resident

at

hereinafter called the infant.

I, the undersigned,

of

being—

    (a) The father of the infant;

    (b) The mother of the infant;

    (c) The guardian of the infant;

    (d) A person (acting on behalf of a body) having the actual custody of the infant;

    (e) A person (acting on behalf of a body) being liable to contribute to the support of the infant;

    (f) The spouse of the applicant;

hereby state that I understand the nature and effect of the adoption order for which

application is made

and that in particular I understand that the effect of the order will be to deprive me of

my parental rights; and I hereby consent to the making of an adoption order in favour

of any applicant approved of by the Director, State Children Department.°

In witness whereof I have signed this consent on the   day

of   19

Signature ....

Signed in the presence of..

Address ....

Description ....

° Where consent to adopt to a specified applicant or two spouses is desired, the form should be modified.

S.C. 70.   Govt. Printer, Brisbane. (%)

Consent to Adoption Form, Queensland.

(Courtesy of Queensland Department of Aboriginal and Torres Strait Islander Policy and Development, QSA QS/505/1 Box 96, 1A/451) unwelcoming white society. The strict legal procedures and professional apparatus surrounding adoption also forced administrators to reassess their heavy-handed and frequently slip-shod methods and to work more cooperatively with mainstream child welfare departments. There was also a new cooperation with medical practitioners and hospitals. Aboriginal access to mainstream medical services exposed the alarming state of Aboriginal infant and child health, leading to babies and children being identified by doctors and nurses for removal by the authorities.

Informal 'fostering' and 'adoption' arrangements had long existed in western society. During the late nineteenth century the 'boarding out' movement led to the introduction of legally constituted foster arrangements and this became the dominant mode of substitute care for white children placed under state care unless they were deemed, on the basis of physical or mental disabilities, to require institutionalisation. From the turn of the century, a body of opinion emerged in support of closed legal adoption for babies of single mothers and by the 1920s adoption had become a major component of child welfare practice.[215] This interest in adoption reflected intrinsic moral and social values — the mothers' guilty secrets would be hidden, infanticide reduced, legitimacy provided for the baby, along with the safety and stability of a good home, while infertile couples would have access to children. Strict provisions of secrecy would conceal identities of all parties. Adoption laws were introduced first in Western Australia in 1896 and the other states followed suit in the 1920s.

Fostering and adoption were distinct under the law. Children placed in foster families were wards of the state and remained under the legal guardianship of the Director of Child Welfare until they turned eighteen or an age stipulated by the Children's Court. Foster children maintained their legal identity and, generally speaking, retained their cultural identity as well. Exceptions were Aboriginal and other children from non-Anglo cultural backgrounds placed with Anglo-Australian families. Child welfare departments solicited applications, selected suitable foster families, provided them with subsidies in cash and kind and operated a system of inspection and supervision. Foster parents had no legal controls over the children and, in theory at least, were required to consult with child welfare authorities over major decisions regarding their care. They had no guaranteed security in their relationship with the child and, in the interest of eventual family reunion, children were encouraged to maintain contact with their birth families, although this was not often carried out in the case of Aboriginal children. This system could result in instability for the children when foster placements broke down and they were sent to live with other foster families or even to institutions. By contrast, adoption was 'a package deal; the king hit of family law' that transferred the 'whole bundle of rights and responsibilities away from birth parents to the adoptive parents'.[216] These included rights of guardianship, custody, inheritance and responsibility for maintaining and naming the child. Children were issued with new birth certificates and, until recently, strict privacy provisions covered all information relating to adoptions. The consent of the birth parents, or, in the case of illegitimate children, the birth mother, was required by law for the adoption to proceed, although under certain circumstances, as seen in Chapter One with Dawna Braedon, the courts could waive the mother's consent. While adoption meant the complete severance of ties between the child and its birth parents, the state also forfeited any special rights since, in the interests of privacy, there was to be no further intervention once adoption arrangements had been completed. A strict system of selection of adoptive parents therefore developed to ensure positive placements. The selection process valorised features of conventional middle-class family life — economic and emotional stability, morality and religion, and the physical and mental health of the adoptive mother. In this process the concerns of the state and the adoptive parents were paramount.

Adoptions flourished following the Second World War. An increasingly punitive attitude embedded in middle-class family values and morals emerged in child welfare practice towards unmarried mothers. They were deemed 'immoral deviants' rather than 'victims' and were considered to be less attached to their babies than married mothers.[217] This was often the attitude of the young women's families, who condemned their 'immorality' and forced them to put their babies up for adoption. With adoption it seemed that everyone benefited — children escaped the stigma of illegitimacy and joined comfortable middle-class families, childless parents had the joys of parenthood and single mothers were released from the consequences of their 'pathological ways' and could go on to realise their own life ambitions and eventually marry and have their own legitimate children. Adoptions in Australia peaked in the 1960s; after that, changing community attitudes, the introduction of reliable birth control and the advent of welfare payments to single mothers drastically reduced the numbers of babies available for adoption since the 1970s.[218]

Torres Strait Islander and Aboriginal communities had their own customary ways of providing alternative care for children. The Torres Strait Islander system was closer to western adoption in that it involved the permanent transfer of parental rights and the children were not usually informed of their parentage. However, adoptive and biological parents and family elders did know and, since the children usually went to live with members of their extended family, they remained part of their family of origin. This system guaranteed the child links through inheritance to traditional land and continued use of the family name, and also forged ties of reciprocity and obligation between the parties involved. These arrangements reflected the ideal that couples of all ages should have children with them and that children should be spread equally across family units.[219] Aboriginal societies had no such formal system. Rather they had loose arrangements where the child, following a death or for other family reasons, or even as an act of choice by the child, went to live with a close relative in the proper kin relationship — typically a mother's sister or mother — on terms that could be redefined as conditions changed over time. There was no secrecy about the child's parentage and no guarantee that arrangements would continue. There was little stigma over illegitimacy as long as the child's parents had not contravened accepted tradition and there was a strong, positive desire to keep the children who were cared for by a range of close kin including aunts, grannies and siblings. Children were not the responsibility of their mothers alone but were part of an extended kin network that made decisions about and actively participated in their upbringing.

Although Queensland recognised Torres Strait Islander adoptions and expressed a willingness to formalise some existing Aboriginal arrangements for the 'protection of the guardian and in the interests of the child',[220] customary arrangements were not generally recognised by Australian governments. The Commonwealth government position was made clear in 1955 in response to a request from the Northern Territory Welfare Branch to the Repatriation Commission for a ruling on the eligibility of a Darwin Aboriginal widow for the war pension. Her husband by customary law had died following service in the war, leaving her to support two children adopted according to customary law following their mother's death. Although the widow was employed at the Retta Dixon Home and received child endowment this was not sufficient to cover the costs of board and lodging. The legal response was that the *Repatriation Act 1920–55* did not recognise customary marriage so her situation did not fit its definition of 'widowhood'. Furthermore the Act recognised only those adoptions arranged under the Adoption of Children Ordinance:

> So far as I can ascertain, Aborigines have not been excluded from the operation of the Adoption of Children Ordinance, and therefore, the only way for any person, aboriginal or otherwise, to effect a valid adoption is under the Ordinance. This being so, an adoption according to the tribal usage or custom of the aborigines is not an adoption under the laws of the Northern Territory.[221]

Structural inequalities in the adoption system made it virtually impossible for Aboriginal people to adopt children. Few could meet the criteria of income, home ownership and health set by adoption agencies and authorities remained convinced that placements in Aboriginal families were not in the best interests of Aboriginal children. Meanwhile Aboriginal parents were forced to abide by arrangements made under Australian law for their children. In 1965 in the Northern Territory Supreme Court two former residents of the Channel Island Leprosarium sought the return of three of their four children taken from them at birth between 1947 and 1954 to protect them from possible contagion.[222] Their children were not placed with their parents' community at the Oenpelli Anglican Mission in western Arnhem Land but were fostered by a Tiwi family at the Bathurst Island Catholic Mission. When they were discharged from the leprosarium in 1958 the parents returned to Oenpelli and began their fight for the return of their three younger children, now aged between eleven and fifteen. As the parents were both classified as wards the Director of Welfare had the duty to act on their behalf against the foster parents. It is not clear why the matter had to go through the courts and why the children were not simply restored to their birth parents. In court the lawyers for the foster parents argued that the children would suffer psychological harm if returned to their parents, however Justice Bridge was reported as saying that 'Whatever view he took the case had tragic features'. In the event he ruled to leave the children with the foster family on the grounds that the children were 'indifferent towards their natural parents' and their removal would cause 'detrimental emotional reactions'.[223] He found that:

A deep mutual affection had grown between the children and the foster-parents whom they treated and addressed as mother and father. All the children had become assimilated into the Tiwi tribe and spoke Tiwi as their native tongue. The girls have been promised tribally in marriage to young Tiwi men.[224]

An appeal was lodged with the High Court in the following year on the grounds that due weight had not been given to the rights of the parents. Since they had not 'disentitled themselves by their wrongful conduct' then their wishes and desires were of great importance. The judge seemed to regard the interests of the children as the principal consideration.[225] Furthermore he had judged them on the same basis as European parents, claiming that they had not been active in visiting their children and giving them presents and was satisfied that the parents had acquiesced to the children remaining with the foster parents after a visit to the children in 1962. Despite these arguments the appeal was unanimously dismissed by the Bench.

The confusion of temporary arrangements with permanent quasi-adoption was not unusual in Aboriginal administrations, reflecting their sweeping powers over Aboriginal children and an almost total disregard for the rights of Aboriginal parents. Many members of the public shared these views, as the Queensland Chief Protector of Aborigines, Walter Edmund Roth, had found when he endeavoured to stop exploitative child indenture arrangements in north Queensland in the early 1900s — employers responded by applying to adopt the children to ensure continuation of their services. The Western Australian Aborigines Department arranged a small number of unsupervised informal 'adoptions' of lighter children from the 1920s which, while not legal adoptions, had the 'force of law' in that the Chief Protector was legal guardian of the children. Sister Kate's Children's Home reportedly persuaded some Aboriginal mothers to sign 'adoption consent forms' and their children were then sent out to live with white families.[226] Requests during the 1960s to adopt children sent by the Northern Territory Welfare Branch with families in the south created considerable confusion about the legal steps in interstate adoptions.[227] Initially the Northern Territory appears to have acted on the assumption that, as legal guardian, the Director of the Welfare Branch had the right to permanently place Aboriginal children with white families. However, the Welfare Branch was obliged to seek clarification from the Department of Territories on behalf of social workers in the Department of Social Security intent on advising prospective adoptive parents on proper legal procedure. It was advised that, in the case of children who were not state wards, there were no special legal bars to adoptions, and applications should be processed under the adoption laws of the state in which the adopting parties resided and the consent of the birth mother was required. It was pointed out that some existing Welfare Branch procedures did not fit with adoption laws — neither missionaries nor the Branch had any authority to deal with adoption inquiries, the Director of Welfare had no authority to approve adoptions, even in cases where both parents were deceased, nor could he request reports on adoptive parents. Children who were state wards could only be fostered and parties looking to adoption had to approach the Northern Territory Children's Council which in turn had to seek parental consent.[228]

Correspondence between the Victorian and Queensland authorities, on proposals by the Blair Holiday Project to encourage adoptions of Aboriginal children by Melbourne families, provides interesting insights into difference in practice and ideology between these states. In 1963 the Blair project organisers proposed a twelve-month trial scheme with the option of going on to apply for adoption. The Queensland government looked favourably on the proposal which fitted neatly with its plan to reduce settlement populations by sending out young children. In 1963 the DNAO wrote to settlement superintendents:

In Queensland settlements aborigines are being trained with a view to their assimilation into the white community. However, once they marry and settle down, families naturally are reluctant to leave the security of the settlements. It is therefore felt that more could be achieved by getting people out earlier as children of school age or after the completion of normal schooling … our fundamental policy is … a wish to assimilate children at a young age into the community through the aegis of reputable citizens of Australia.[229]

However, the project organisers and the Queensland government quickly found that the logistics of adoption were quite different from those of organising short-term holidays — there were complex legal conditions to be met, not the least being the consent of the mothers and the roles in arranging adoptions of the relevant departments in the home states of the natural and adoptive parents. This led to a prolonged exchange between the Victorian Aborigines Welfare Board (AWB) and the Queensland DNAO as the AWB expressed its objections to the proposed adoptions and insisted that Victorian child welfare legislation had to be strictly followed in all arrangements and DNAO authorities sought to enforce their precedents of ignoring the rights of Aboriginal families.[230]

In February 1963 the AWB provided the DNAO with a detailed outline of major legal differences between the states that would require immediate resolution and expressed 'serious doubts' about the proposal on the basis of its experience with Northern Territory adoptions. It advised the DNAO that it should make 'very careful consideration of all the issues involved' and added that it could not help financially with any children sent down. Nothing had been resolved by March when the Board sent a formal objection to the DNAO over the handing over of two Aboriginal girls to a Melbourne family without AWB involvement and in the public glare of a women's afternoon television program. In the AWB's opinion this only served to 'parade in public the misfortune of families who were "down on their luck" and treats everything with tearful emotion'.[231] In the same month the AWB wrote that the only children suitable for legal adoption would be infants with a lighter complexion and in May it wrote to the DNAO criticising claims by Blair project organisers that:

for the sake of the children in question they should be transferred from their present hopeless environment into 'white' homes, in Melbourne, where they will develop in a 'normal' way and eventually become 'assimilated'. The group is not unmindful of some of the difficulties but feels that the risk of failure is worth the taking. Their general approach is rather paternal, and they have an outmoded view of what assimilation means.[232]

The AWB pointed to the essential requirement for the children of 'acceptance, security and love within the family group' and to the risk of breakdown of placements, especially at adolescence as the children faced the stress of adjusting to the 'dominant culture' of the Melbourne families. It expressed its preference for children to move to integration 'from within the emotional security of the [Aboriginal] family group'. This view was based on practical experience and anthropological research favouring raising Aboriginal status through 'community development rather than by individual assimilation'. Furthermore, the

AWB knew nothing of the children's backgrounds, why they were being separated from their parents and what efforts had been made to rehabilitate their families.[233] In a further letter in August the AWB attacked the project on the grounds that it was 'based on the false assumption that Aboriginal children should be separated from their neglectful parents; such reasoning is quite out of touch with current thought on child care.'[234] In the same month the issue of interstate adoptions was raised at the Native Welfare Conference in Darwin.

Exasperated by this sustained attack on its plans, the DNAO wrote to the Victorian Department of Family Welfare (DFW) for assistance in making placements. It argued that the DFW would be better placed to provide professional specialist assistance and indicated that the AWB would be informed but otherwise had no need to be involved since the children considered for adoption would be 'very light skinned and need not necessarily be known to be of ... aboriginal extraction hence my approach to you, rather than to the Aboriginal authorities.' The letter concluded that in fact there appeared to be such a vast difference in thinking between the DNAO and the AWB 'as to what constitutes the most beneficial future for a child ... that such intervention [by the Board] would be undesirable.' The DFW promptly responded that the AWB would be more competent in assessing placements for Aboriginal children and should be involved right from the start.[235] In May 1964 the Queensland State Children's Department informed the DNAO that the DFW would not undertake placements, and that this should be performed by the AWB, and recommended that the matter be raised at the next Native Welfare Council conference in Adelaide.[236] Informal 'adoptions' of Queensland children continued regardless: in 1968 Melbourne newspapers carried sensational headlines claiming that over three hundred Aboriginal children — including Queensland children sent down on holidays — had been illegally adopted by white families in Victoria.[237]

ADOPTION PROGRAMS

Children targeted for adoption were typically 'lighter' children who were considered to have 'greater potential for assimilation and were also more deserving of being included within white society'.[238] The intention was that the children should merge into the white community with no knowledge of their Aboriginal ancestry; as the

Queensland government put it in 1959: 'near white children' should have 'the opportunity of entering into the white community as white girls and boys'.[239] In some cases the children's Aboriginality was not disclosed to adoptive parents by officials intent on placing infants who would otherwise be sent to institutions. Some relinquishing mothers did not admit their own or the father's Aboriginality. In a case quoted in the Link-Up submission to the National Inquiry into the Separation of Aboriginal and Torres Strait Islander Children from their Families, a hospital social worker recalled concealing a baby's Aboriginal identity so that the hospital paediatrician would approve it for adoption. The social worker explained this subterfuge:

It didn't matter. You know at that stage … my main anxiety was to ensure that that man didn't exclude this child from adoption by virtue of having a touch of Aboriginality.[240]

A new obstacle for authorities accustomed to removing and placing Aboriginal children without consideration of parental rights or child welfare procedures was that they had to have the mothers' consent for legal adoptions and they had to work with the statutory bodies invested by law with organising adoptions. When it came to the crunch they often could not get the mothers to consent to adoptions.[241] The motives for legal adoptions discussed earlier — concern about illegitimacy, shame, privacy, family condemnation and lack of support, inability to support and care for the child — were not always relevant for Aboriginal women. They did not fit with their family systems and values and the high value placed on babies and children. A consequence was that relatively small numbers of Aboriginal children were placed for adoption at any one time.

How then did authorities obtain babies for adoption? It seems that rarely was it a matter of the woman making an informed decision, negotiating the best position for herself and her baby in terms of arguments presented to her, her marital status and the identity of the father. This was frequently the case for non-Aboriginal relinquishing mothers as well. There were instances where authorities went to court to have the Aboriginal mother's consent waived, although this appears to have been unusual. There are also testimonies from some Aboriginal mothers that they never gave their consent. Some claim they were told by hospital authorities that their babies had died.[242] In a court case in Perth in the early 1970s an illiterate Aboriginal mother claimed that she had been asked to sign a piece of paper by nursing staff, not realising that she was authorising the adoption of her baby. This woman was married according to customary law and had several children already but had given birth outside her home area and nursing staff apparently judged her incapable of looking after her baby. The actions of the Child Welfare Department in removing the baby and adopting it out to a white family were endorsed by the court.[243] Concerns about the adoption process were raised by Aboriginal adoptees in evidence presented to the 1996 National Inquiry into the Separation of Aboriginal and Torres Strait Islander Children from their Families. A man adopted in Victoria during the 1960s denied that his mother had signed the adoption forms claiming that:

> on the adoption forms it's got written there in somebody else's handwriting — not [my mother's], because it just doesn't match her signature and stuff like that.[244]

Another man adopted in Victoria in 1967 queried the way in which the court has dispensed with his mother's consent to his adoption:

> This decision, made under section 67(d) of the Child Welfare Act was purportedly based on an 'inability to locate mother.' Only paltry attempts had been made to locate her. For example, no attempt was made to find her address through the Aborigines Welfare Board.[245]

Of course there were adoptions that were consented to by their birth parent(s) and which followed legal adoption practices of the time. In some cases welfare authorities took control of babies whose parents had broken Aboriginal law and elders had consented to their adoption outside the community. The birth of twins was regarded as unnatural in some traditional communities and elders agreed to place one or both of the babies for adoption.[246] In other cases sensitive personal factors could prompt agreement to adopt. Some young mothers raised in institutions and missions or reared in white families were influenced by the moral standards of their keepers and therefore may have been more open to relinquishing their children. Indeed some believed that it was the best thing for the baby to be adopted into a white family. With no family network to fall back on and unable to return to the institutions, some young women may have had no option but to adopt their babies out in much the same way as many young poverty stricken white single mothers did.

But there were clearly cases which raise serious questions about 'informed consent' and the extraction of consent through 'undue influence' and 'duress'. The young mothers described by Barbara Cummings[247] at the Retta Dixon Home in Darwin were unaware of their rights as mothers and succumbed to official pressure to place their children for adoption. In Queensland the DNAO maintained pressure on individual mothers on the assumption that if they adopted one baby out they would be willing to adopt out the next and so on.[248] In the case of under-age girls, considerable pressure could be brought to bear. Native Welfare officers in Western Australia reportedly told a fifteen-year-old girl on a pastoral station to 'sign consent or else',[249] and Nyungar women recall that girls having babies in King Edward Memorial Hospital in Perth were routinely visited by Native Welfare officers who encouraged them to sign adoption papers.[250] The Department could shift from this hard-line position when it suited its interests. In response to a white father who applied to adopt his Aboriginal son, officers advised that the mother could not decide as she 'lack[ed] sufficient education or sophistication to grasp the significance of legal adoption and her consent, if given, would not be full and free consent made in complete understanding of its implications.'[251] The pain of relinquishing mothers is evident in the following letter from a young woman in Queensland who, for an unknown reason, had been allowed to keep her baby while awaiting placement for adoption:

> I hope you will let me keep her. I didn't know what I was doing at the time I signed the paper. I have grown so fond of her now and watching her grow up I love her even more deeply ...
>
> Please sir I have made a very bad mistake and I hope you will grant my wish in keeping her ...
>
> With my love for my child I'll work my fingers to the bone to give her everything what other white children have.[252]

The official response to this plea is not known.

A further problem for administrators was persuading respectable white families to consider Aboriginal adoptions. Most states undertook publicity campaigns showing smiling Aboriginal children with happy adoptive parents, similar to the press coverage of the Blair holiday project. Despite strict legal prohibitions on identifying and naming parties to adoptions, the newspapers not only showed photos but also named children and adoptive parents. In South Australia from 1954–55 when APB began its foster program and into the 1960s, articles in the local press advocated adoption:

> Adopted into a white home he becomes a member of the family and automatically a member of the white community.[253]

> Family adopts Aborigines.[254]

> She's Mum to them all.[255]

> Pensive ... but she's really glad.[256]

Similar articles appeared in the Western Australian press:

> Sussanna thrives on love.
> Four white children, one half-caste — all happy.
> She's one of the family.[257]

These stories told of the children's background of deprivation and destitution and described their bleak future in institutions if not adopted. The fact that most came from government settlements where they should have been well cared for seemed to be overlooked and indeed the children's institutional settings provided a strong motivation for their 'rescue'. In keeping with their assimilatory intent, the stories also focused on how well the children fitted into their new families although they often hinted at the discrimination they could face as teenagers. Not all readers were convinced of the benefits of adoption:

> I cannot see any happy future for these youngsters. I cannot see complete assimilation. These children are quite adorable at their present age and their adopted sisters and brothers love them as they would any baby. But how will they feel in a few years time? Will they be allowed to marry fair skinned children ... only heart break can follow. American playwright Eugene O'Neill dealt with this problem of a white girl marrying a young negro in 'All God's Chillun Got Wings.'[258]

Despite such reservations there was a rush of applications to adopt. Applicants showed a mix of 'religious inspired or secular philanthropy' and some were intent on 'sensitising their own children to circumstances of those less well off'.[259] Several Queensland applicants were from religious groups such as the Jehovah's Witnesses and the Assemblies of God who had seen Aboriginal children in hospital while visiting their own sick children.[260] Many applicants expressed a heartfelt wish to save the babies from a life of institutionalisation. Others were childless or unable to have more children or had grown-up families of their own. One couple described their motives as 'humanitarian and based on family planning ideas'. They intended to have 'two birth children and adopt two children of the opposite gender from our birth children'.[261] A minority were self-seeking, as in a request for children of '"mixed race" blood of approx. 25% Aboriginal blood, or of Indian or Iranian parentage. We would like to have attractive looking children with straight or softly waving hair and soft tanned skin.'[262] Most applications were heartfelt and well-meaning but deeply paternalistic and assimilationist in intent:

> We can promise this child the love of a happy home and the under-standing that he will need as he grows up. It is our belief that an aboriginal child brought up in a white home is a further step towards total acceptance of the aborigines in our community.[263]

An older country couple with three children were concerned at:

> the lack of friendship and encouragement offered to dark people by most white Australians ... We believe that the barrier is more social than racial and feel that if only those of us who have so much more in both opportunity and worldly goods would offer a helping hand and real friendship without reserve that the gulf would be bridged much sooner and far more happily for all concerned.[264]

While some applicants had worked or grown up with Aboriginal people the majority had no prior contact and were imbued with community racist myths and stereotypes.[265] According to an article in the South Australian press in 1967 on the formation of a support group for Adelaide families caring for adopted and fostered Aboriginal children, most families came from the lower to average income level bracket. The women interviewed stated, 'We are not do-gooders. The children need loving homes — that's all there is to it,' and claimed that some women had lost friends after they adopted an Aboriginal child.

The view of fostering of Aboriginal children as a permanent arrangement was evident in the article which expressed sympathy for families when children had to be returned to their parents.[266]

Some authorities appeared willing to give serious consideration to virtually any application to adopt. In 1951 in Western Australia the DNA actively promoted a request from an elderly wealthy single woman to adopt a boy and girl aged between four and six years to raise and send to university. In a special memo to field staff and mission superintendents, Commissioner Middleton wrote that this

> humanitarian gesture may provide for a couple of neglected or orphaned children a splendid opportunity for educational and social advancement. It may also be an object lesson to many people who need it.[267]

The UAM missionary Reverend Schenk replied from Victoria that he could suggest no children as 'almost every child has some relatives who regard themselves as mother and father to the children and they would certainly ask if children were coming back etc.'[268] As more families applied to adopt, authorities increasingly imposed mainstream selection criteria and in New South Wales alone at least a third of applicants were rejected as unsuitable.[269]

During the 1960s authorities in most states continued the practice of placing children with families with the option of moving on to adoption if the arrangement proved satisfactory. In 1962 in Queensland, the DNAO arranged for a white family to have a child in their home for a twelve-month trial period to see whether the child settled and to give the family the 'actual experience of a coloured child in your home'.[270] This was a form of adoption 'through the family backdoor', so to speak, where parents uncertain about taking the permanent step could become emotionally bonded to the child over time and in this way became committed to adoption. Alternatively, if the arrangement broke down the child could be returned to the authorities. While the system worked smoothly in most cases it was potentially explosive, as authorities found out when the consent of birth mothers was not forthcoming. In Queensland in such cases, intending adoptive parents were urged to seek legal custody of the child through the courts, a highly intrusive step given their limited formal relationship with the child.[271] A by-product of this bungling was that administrations everywhere were forced to become more professional in foster and adoption arrangements. In Western Australia the DNW appointed female social workers to handle placements and moved increasingly towards cooperative arrangements with the Department of Child Welfare (DChW). In 1964 the whole adoption process was handed over to the DChW's Ngala Mothercraft Home and Training Centre and the University Department of Child Health. Ngala was approved by the Maternal and Child Health Committee of the National Health and Medical Research Council of Australia. It investigated the antenatal history of birth mothers, the social history of both birth parents and the social and medical history of adopting couples and undertook rigorous medical checks of the babies. The adoptive mother was required to spend a week living in at Ngala to learn mothercraft and become acquainted with the baby.[272]

Once the children were adopted the state relinquished control and provided no further special assistance or support for the adoptive families. While some adoptive parents joined in creating their own organisations and support networks, most battled on alone, often to the detriment of the children growing up isolated in a white world. Some parents spoke honestly to their children of their Aboriginal origins as one young woman told Coral Edwards and Peter Read in 1989:

My mother always wanted a little Koori [Aboriginal] baby ... I think Mum told me [about the adoption] when I was little, and then when I started to worry about it all, she told me again ... It never really worried me till I was fourteen.[273]

Others, acting on official advice, destroyed documentation of their child's adoption and told them they were of 'Asian or Greek or Italian descent'.[274] Many children were moved interstate and even overseas by their adoptive families and are only now learning of their Aboriginal families. The tragic life of Russell Moore was brought to the attention of the Australian public during his sensational trial in the United States of America in 1989. Adopted in 1963 and renamed James Savage, Russell was taken from Victoria to the United States of America at the age of five. In 1975 his adoptive parents returned to Australia leaving twelve-year-old Russell behind. Over the next twelve years he lived on the streets and was convicted of various juvenile and criminal offences. In 1989 he was charged in Florida and found guilty of first degree murder, rape and sexual battery and sentenced to life imprisonment, later changed to the death penalty by the judge.[275]

It is impossible to know how many Aboriginal children were adopted into non-Aboriginal families, but it seems that numbers remained fairly low over time. In South Australia fourteen children had been adopted out by 1959, along with several lighter skinned children adopted independently through the Children's Welfare Department.[276] In 1964 in Western Australia thirty-six children had been adopted or were awaiting placement.[277] By the late 1970s opposition by Aborigines and their supporters was such that authorities began to look at phasing out adoption of Aboriginal children into white families. Writing about Aboriginal objections to formal legal adoption, Richard Chisholm states that it was not only that Aborigines were opposed to whites adopting their children, or angry that few Aboriginal families had been able to meet the formal selection criteria to adopt children themselves. Rather, adoption was seen as a possessive and intrusive intervention, a form of 'overkill' where parties only commit to children if they can have the 'whole package'. Chisholm concludes:

> [Adoption] treats children as transferable like property. It ought to be possible for children to be brought up with love and commitment without necessarily cutting them off from their birth parents and relatives, transferring their property rights, and all the rest. I think perhaps we have something to learn from the Aborigines in this area, a notion of community responsibility for children, and of accepting a shared role in caring for them.[278]

There are examples of successful outcomes in adoptions of Aboriginal children but in many cases the hostility of white society and the total break with family and country that adoption entailed brought deep heartache and personal damage. For many this began in adolescence, as a young woman explained to Peter Read:

> I think it worries you when you start high school. You feel a bit funny. You feel a bit funny being the only black person in a whole pile of whites. I got called 'you black bitch' and stuff like this ... It makes you feel dirty. Sometimes I'd come home from school and go to my bedroom and I'd cry. I'd think to myself, I wish I could get this skin off me somehow. That's how you feel when the trouble starts.[279]

A group of adoptees transplanted from northern Australia to Tasmania told the Inquiry into the Separation of Aboriginal and Torres Strait Islander Children from their Families how they felt they were not accepted in Tasmania by whites or Aborigines nor were they welcome back home:

all of us lost ones down here from the mainland are all alcoholics, you know, got nothing, you know ... we all love our adopted parents and stuff like that, but you know, we just didn't fit.[280]

Some adoptive mothers in Melbourne participating in research[281] in the wake of the revelations of the Inquiry have, like Louis Johnson's adoptive parents Bill and Pauline Johnson, expressed shock over their unwitting participation in this process of enforced assimilation. They claimed that they were not fully informed at the time of the circumstances surrounding the adoptions that they entered into with the best of intentions, and they now felt deceived and aggrieved.

By the early 1970s, after a lengthy process of tutelage and preparation, Aboriginal people *could be said* to be no longer 'second-class citizens' either under the law or in terms of formal access to wider community services. However, Hasluck's goal of assimilated comfortable nuclear Aboriginal families as depicted in his official pamphlets remained as remote for the majority as ever. The fact that most families remained 'unhealthy, badly housed and unemployed'[282] was borne out in the findings of the first comprehensive national census of Aborigines in 1966.[283] The counted total of 80,207 Aborigines, just 0.7 percent of the total Australian population, was an extremely youthful population with almost half under the age of twenty-one. Seventy-three percent of those counted were not in the work force and Aboriginal unemployment was more than double the national rate of 0.7 percent. Education levels were far below those of the mainstream population — twenty-three percent of school-age children had received no education whatsoever, compared to 0.9 percent for the non-Aboriginal population. Low levels of education were linked to low status occupations and poverty. A study of poverty in Australia in 1966 concluded that 'probably 90 percent of the people of Aboriginal descent in Australia are living in poverty, some to a degree matched only in the most backward of the poverty-stricken areas of Asia, Africa and Latin America.'[284] A study by Rowley five years later found that in non-metropolitan South Australia 28.3 percent of the Aboriginal people surveyed lived in shacks compared to only 4.2 percent of the Australian rural population as a whole.[285] Research by Elizabeth Eggleston identified alarming levels of Aboriginal imprisonment — in Western Australia where Aborigines formed only 2.5 percent of the population they constituted twenty-five percent of the prison population. Eggleston attributed this to discriminatory methods of law enforcement.[286] Equal access to community services remained an elusive dream and Aborigines remained embedded in their own community and family networks. Life in mission or government institutions remained the norm for many Aboriginal people — in 1961 settlement populations around Australia totalled 75,271 or 32.8 percent of the total Aboriginal population.[287]

Australian governments may have rallied to the call to repeal discriminatory legislation and administrative practice, but they had failed in their duty of fiduciary care to provide the means to significantly improve Aboriginal living conditions or to negotiate a suitable niche for them within Australian society as fully participating citizens. To achieve this necessitated levels of radical social and bureaucratic change and provision of funding and resources that no government was prepared to make. In particular, as Rowley argued in the early sixties, Aborigines' lack of property rights in land prevented them from developing a secure economic and social base from which they could engage in meaningful change:

> He needs the confidence which comes from a firmly based community to compete for a stake in the Australian economy; yet until either as a member of his group, or as an individual, he has such a stake, there seems no way in which he may acquire the confidence, or even the incentive. Much of what looks like stubborn adherence to the non-materialistic interest of Aboriginal culture may be due to the lack of opportunity for a choice.[288]

Governments also needed to devise ways of working with Aboriginal people and responding to their needs and aspirations.

Indeed, government neglect of conditions in Aboriginal camps and even settlements and missions over many decades had left families living in conditions which demanded immediate and extreme action over and above anything provided for other citizens. However, despite massive government programs during the 1950s to create healthy environments through government infrastructure and housing for middle-class white families, and various benefits to ensure their economic security, treatment of Aboriginal families remained neglectful. Hasluck's dream of assimilation also required the widespread endorsement and active support of white Australians; in the wider community and across the board in service delivery organisations in both the public and private sector, as well as adherence to its goals by Aboriginal people — but neither scenario had truly eventuated.

Although Australians were exploring new, non-racial ways of understanding Aboriginal difference and disadvantage they seemed to be unable to stumble out of the fog of the past. Discourse remained embedded in white racism, ethnocentrism and an overwhelming sense of white superiority that saw assimilation as the only possible goal for Aborigines. Research conducted by Eggleston during the mid-1960s showed a 'strong sentiment' in the Australian public that Aborigines should have no special rights or benefits and that 'equal rights' meant 'equal responsibilities'.[289] This coexisted with a simplistic, optimistic view of Australian society as homogenous, cohesive and humanitarian, as if, in suburbs around Australia, Aborigines could knock on the doors of white family homes and be invited in, and, following polite chatter, a cup of tea and some good-humoured bantering, differences would be overcome and all would become 'good neighbours'. Not only did this view of Australian society overlook fundamental conflicts and divergences within the dominant society, it ignored the existence of institutionalised racism, as well as the fact that white Australians benefited from racist practices such as the exploitative triangle of pastoralists, government and Aboriginal workers, the rigid caste barriers of country towns and the ongoing adherence to a White Australia. Oppressive pressures to conform ran through this society. The middle-class modern family was not only the model for all to conform to, but it was synonymous, like racism and indeed, individualism, with the values and institutions of the 'Australian way of life'. In consequence, Aboriginal family forms and functions were further marginalised and Aboriginal ways of doing things were brought into direct conflict with the accepted behaviours and procedures of the dominant society.

What of the Aboriginal people at the centre of these processes? Many would have agreed with the Aboriginal elder who told a conference at the University of New England 'we do not want assimilation. We want to be left to ourselves, and to have something of our own.'[290] Even the majority of those who committed themselves to a house in town did not want to abandon their identity, values or codes of behaviour and disappear with their children into the wider community. Paradoxically, this goal was actually unattainable for most. Racialist perceptions of Aboriginal difference continued along with discriminatory and segregative treatment at all levels. Tutelage in settlements, reserves and even town housing encouraged enclaves and did not lead to the adoption of an 'ethical complexion appropriate to Australian citizens' or the minutiae of behaviours that constituted the 'Australian way of life'. In fact, the policy often encouraged a firm adherence to Aboriginal ways. Wage controls and declining employment opportunities as well as obstacles in the employment market prevented Aboriginal workers from moving up the socioeconomic ladder to join the consumerism of white society. Children raised in institutions away from their families, who may have had some schooling and vocational training, were often hindered by their institutional background and unresolved emotional issues, and many of those reared within the bosom of the white family carried the stigma of their Aboriginality before them. Rather than harnessing Aboriginal initiatives and the growing national Aboriginal leadership to their cause, governments drove them into increasingly oppositional grounds.

And what of the administrators? Rowley writes of the 'illusion of training for independence' in colonial contexts:

> the tragedy is that on both sides most are people of goodwill. Perhaps the biggest stake for the officials in the system is their self-respect. For if a substantial part of one's life has been devoted to a cause in which one believes, how can one believe that all one's effort has been pointless or even harmful? The reaction against such doubts supports the colonial illusion that one is *preparing* 'our natives' for independence.[291]

Rather than preparing Aborigines for independent living, the move to assimilation initially broadened special administrative spheres of control over a wider range of Aboriginal people. Administrations expanded as they absorbed more functions and staff increased. This further stigmatised Aboriginal clients as the apparent recipients of vast sums of money, which actually had to cover virtually all Aboriginal needs, attracted criticism from outsiders.[292] This led eventually to the white backlash of the early 1970s.[293] Administrators of ththe 1950s and 1960s found it hard to abandon old habits of control. Hasluck wrote of 'the danger of going on too long and impeding the development of the aboriginal's own character and sense of responsibility',[294] while in Western Australia the DNW had asserted the ongoing need for protection of the 'vast majority' of Aborigines in the south by welfare officers acting as their agents on a daily basis.[295] These interventions consumed expanding funds and resources while there was never enough to really grapple with deplorable Aboriginal living conditions. Administrations needed a total overhaul to escape the influence of precedent and to develop modern processes of management and planning. In the end they simply had to be scrapped. Institutions remained the major vehicle of reform despite overwhelming evidence of their inherent unsuitability to the task of training *any* section of the community for positive life outside. Their unhappy graduates were then pushed out into society where they came under the ambit of a multiplicity of institutions which were geared to work with mainstream Australian families and which judged and treated them accordingly.

And finally what of the families? The mainstreaming of Aboriginal child welfare did not stop removals and Aboriginal children continued to be removed at rates higher than mainstream populations. A major new focus of government intervention in Aboriginal families became the committal of Aboriginal juveniles for reform and punishment in state correctional institutions. Spiralling youth unemployment from the early 1970s compounded this. In 1977 Elizabeth Sommerlad presented a paper on the incarceration of Aboriginal youth to a symposium of representatives from all states and territories, gathered at the invitation of the Commonwealth Minister for Aboriginal Affairs to discuss the institutional care of Aboriginal juveniles. Sommerlad reported a disproportionate number of Aboriginal juveniles in state correctional institutions. They were more likely than other youth to be charged with offences, convicted and committed to an institution, and they had higher rates of recidivism. The following contributory factors were isolated by Sommerlad:

Demographic — 56.5 percent of the Aboriginal population was under twenty compared to 37.5 percent for the rest of the population.

Cultural — young people were living in stressful 'conflict' situations where pressures to conform to white society conflicted with the preferred Aboriginal lifestyle of their families. Mr Justice Muirhead stated that 'in dealing with Aboriginal children one must not overlook the tremendous social pressures they face. They are growing up in an environment of confusion.'

Attitudinal — young people experienced widespread prejudice and discrimination and this was institutionalised in society.

Psychological — children felt alienated, powerless, and unable to change their situation and could see no future other than that of their parents — 'unemployment, dependency on social welfare, inadequate housing, drunkenness and living from day to day.'[296]

The solution offered in a discussion paper on Aboriginal juvenile offenders, prepared for the New South Wales Department of Youth and Community Services cited by Sommerlad, showed how little the living conditions of Aboriginal families had changed after twenty years of assimilation policies:

Long-term we must work vigorously towards fulfilling the goals of rehousing, better education, remedial health programs, creating better job opportunities, all of which will steadily increase the self-esteem of Aboriginals and improve their image and acceptance in the white community ... We cannot hope for any reduction in the over-representation of Aborigines in the Children's Courts, Residential Care and training schools until such time as we narrow the gap between the living standards and acceptance of the white population and the Aboriginals.[297]

Forty years after the introduction of the assimilation policy, the 1991 Royal Commission into Aboriginal Deaths in Custody noted the ongoing legacy of the separation of Aboriginal children from their families during the assimilation years. Of the thirty-two deaths in custody investigated by the Royal Commission, nineteen involved Aborigines who had been institutionalised as children. Commissioner Pat Dodson linked the policy directly to the marginalisation and oppression that many of those removed as children continued to experience as adults.[298]

CHAPTER NINE

A TWILIGHT OF KNOWING[1]

The past is not dead and gone; it isn't even past.

William Faulkner[2]

'I'm sorry, I'm sorry, I just didn't know,' sobs the motherly figure
seated next to me. At the front of the lecture theatre, the speaker, an
Aboriginal woman of the Stolen Generations, is also crying.[3] It is an
emotionally charged moment at the 1997 National Adoption
Conference in Perth. Suddenly, startling us all, a firm European voice
rings out, 'But how could you not know? I only came to this country in
the 1970s but I knew.' The anguished cry and sometimes disingenuous
reply, 'I just didn't know', was repeated by leaders and members of
the public around the country following the publication of the *Bringing
Them Home* report,[4] but none posed that profound question 'How
could we *not* have known?'

In *The Informed Heart* Bruno Bettelheim reminds us that any German
who claimed not to know about the concentration camps also has to
claim not to have read German newspapers where the camps were
reported in glowing propagandist terms from 1938. How then can we
claim not to have known?

In the late 1990s Australia was haunted by the spectre of the
systematic removal of Aboriginal children from their families over
decades by our governments. Few issues have provoked so much
public anguish. Some of us wept openly and publicly, others retreated
into a defensive state of denial. Normally we associate such emotional
outpourings and denials with the announcement of disturbing
revelations. Yet the evidence on this issue has always been before us. A
search through seventy years of our daily newspapers uncovered
hundreds of stories, letters and photographs that deal with it. There

are the familiar celebratory photos of 'mission children' visiting the 'big smoke,' stories of adoptions of 'cuddly black babies' by white families, and reports on removal policies and legislation. There are also heart-rending stories of Aboriginal parents fighting to keep their children as well as editorials and letters condemning removals. Against a backdrop of apparent apathy or active and tacit approval, there is ample evidence in Australian newspapers of public opposition that was not only vocal but that also influenced government removal policies. There was also some public awareness of governments' generally inferior standards of care for Aboriginal children and condemnation of this form of 'special treatment'.

Changing political and social environments in Australia during the 1970s created a climate more favourable to change, and isolated acts of opposition coalesced into a hard-fought national political campaign to stop this intervention into Aboriginal family life. Particular incidents relating to Aboriginal children also attracted widespread media attention and public interest, but they quickly slipped from the national memory. Twenty years later the issue was revived again, and more forcefully, by the events surrounding the 1996 Human Rights Commission Inquiry into the Separation of Aboriginal and Torres Strait Islander Children from their Families. In this context the question 'How could you not know?' takes on a profound importance.

REMEMBERING AND FORGETTING

Historians and psychologists have become increasingly cognisant of the complex factors involved in the processes of remembering and forgetting the past. At the individual level, the connection of events with our lives and their subjective meanings for us are crucial for remembering. Collective memories of shared events at a societal level, especially those of an extreme and intense nature leading to broad institutional change, are typically retained by members of a group, class or nation.[5] Collectively we remember national events that have profoundly shaped our lives and that are actively recalled and publicly debated. Others are ultimately forgotten in the wash of events vying for our attention. Some analysts have characterised the 'temporality' of our postmodern, information-drenched times in terms of a paradoxical 'need for remembering and the fast track for forgetting' and a 'tendency towards amnesia' driven by the demands of 'immediate profit and political expediency'.[6]

The content and form of 'collective recall' are highly political and contested. What is remembered, and how it is remembered, depend on which groups are doing the remembering and this differs across peoples, class and gender:

> different social groups, categories and collectives, each with its own past, will surely have different social memories that shape and are shaped by their own intersubjectivity. Every memory, as personal as it may be ... exists through its relation with what has been shared with others: language, idiom, events, and everything that shapes the society of which individuals are a part.[7]

At different times diverse versions of events circulate 'simultaneously on varying scales and levels'.[8] This remembering is not a unilinear process. Cultural historian Tom Griffiths[9] speaks of 'seasons of memory, periodic surges of wistful story-telling', while historian Inga Clendinnen suggests a generational process in these surges:

> 'remembering' is not a steady state, but rather, as Roland Barthes puts it, a 'frequent waking out of forgetfulness.' The past stands still, but the present moves and every generation must discover the history of its parents' generation for itself.[10]

What emerges is not a monolithic, seamless history but 'shifting histories and memories that exist between a sanctioned narrative of history and personal memory', a record of 'resemblances and similarities' reworked over and over and transmitted through formal and informal means, shaped by power relations in the society.[11] Nations typically do not commemorate ignoble events from their past, events which belie the image of a moral community, and embark instead on a process of institutionalised forgetting. As the prominent Australian writer David Malouf[12] put it in his 1998 Boyer lecture series, *A Spirit of Play: The Making of the Australian Consciousness*, 'we remember the bits that speak well of us ... the dark bits we suppress'. Some events, such as the slaughter of Australian soldiers at Gallipoli in 1915, *can* be transformed and Anzac Day has become a national commemorative event. However, events such as the removal of Aboriginal children cannot be thus transformed — they are irremediably ignoble and dishonourable and must be 'forgotten'.

Collective forgetting and repressing of memories can be a response to traumatic national events. However, these 'silenced events' persist in a multitude of forms and continue to re-emerge in the collective memory.[13] This is so even when the victims themselves set out deliberately to forget the past. Inga Clendinnen writes that Romanies responded to the 'Devouring' — the Romany term for their Holocaust at the hands of Nazi Germany — by choosing to forget, with a 'kind of defiant insouciance — "their peculiar mixture of fatalism and the spirit, or wit, to seize the day" — is the Gypsy way of enduring.' And yet, despite years of 'political national amnesia and persisting scholarly neglect' their experiences are now being documented through the work of historians such as Isabel Fonseca, although, Clendinnen further observes, 'it is unlikely that her Romany friends will much care'.[14] By contrast, the Jews have erected a 'monumental industry of remembrance' to their collective experience of the Holocaust as they seek, in keeping with their cultural imperatives, 'the deeper significance ... in what only appear to be this-worldly events' and in their drive, as Israeli leader David Ben-Gurion put it, to ensure that 'our youth remember what happened to the Jewish people'.[15]

Aboriginal conceptions of the past diverge significantly in form and content from those of mainstream Australians, reflecting their particular cultural, political, historical and psychological contexts. Aboriginal writer and historian Jackie Huggins comments that Aboriginal people have been 'fed on a diet of lies and invisibility about the true history of this country from a very young age'.[16] Nevertheless they have a 'stronger sense of history than their white counterparts'[17] and have maintained a powerful oral tradition that memorialises their tragic history. Anthropologist Michael Jackson states that 'many Aboriginal people express bafflement and dismay at the ease with which Europeans seem to turn their backs on the past.' He points to cultural factors predisposing Aborigines to 'gloss over the boundary between biography and myth [and] the line between the personal and the historical' so that they experience a history that is 'reiterated and embodied in the very condition of their contemporary lives'.[18] Literary analyst Ann Brewster discusses the intersections of oral accounts of colonial violence with ongoing 'conditions of poverty, violence, incarceration and racism' in shaping what anthropologist Debbie Bird Rose calls 'Aboriginal remembrance'. This is a 'living experience of the past, regenerated through stories' and 'as long as the conditions of the past are the conditions of the present ... then the past is not past.'[19]

Historian Peter Burke also reminds us that history is typically written by victors who can 'afford to forget' while 'the losers are unable to accept what happened and are condemned to brood over it, relive it, and reflect how different it might have been.'[20]

Individual silences over personal experiences associated with national traumas are a further aspect of national 'forgetting'. The confessional element when individuals *do* begin to recount these experiences can be profound. Research into personal memories of another facet of Australia's past, the experiences of Australian prisoners of war (POWs) in Asia during the Second World War, revealed:

> enormous trauma — most of the interviewees had not spoken about their experiences for many years, if ever. They had previously been unable to speak even to close relations who had not shared the experience ... Many constantly repeated that, 'I've never told anyone that before.'[21]

Former Prime Minister Paul Keating acknowledged the significance to the nation of this process of remembering during the unveiling of a war memorial to POWs in 1991:

> Australia should know the truth about its history. A nation is stronger for its knowledge of shared experience and the experience of these men should be engraved in the national memory.[22]

In 1992 Keating led a similar charge into the domain of Aboriginal history in his now famous 'Redfern Speech'. He reminded the nation that the 'starting-point' for reconciliation was:

> the act of recognition. Recognition that it was we who did the dispossessing. We took the traditional land and smashed the traditional way of life. We brought the disasters. The alcohol. We committed the murders. We took the children from their mothers. We practised discrimination and exclusion.[23]

In referring to the removal of Aboriginal children from their mothers, Keating acknowledged another painful event in the nation's past. Like the POWs, Aboriginal mothers had been unable to speak of the trauma they had lived through. The Link-Up (New South Wales) submission to the 1996 National Inquiry into the Separation of Aboriginal and Torres Strait Islander Children from their Families stated that:

> ... Aboriginal women were unwilling and unable to speak about the immense pain, grief and anguish that losing their children had caused them. That pain was so strong that we were unable to find a mother who had healed enough to be able to speak, and to share her experience with us and with the Commission.[24]

The 1990s was a period of strong reflective interest in our national history as many Australians endeavoured to come to terms with the darker aspects of our past and debated possible new forms of the nation on the eve of the centenary of Federation and the new millennium. A significant aspect of this national remembering was the acknowledgement of the tragic history of the Stolen Generations. This was expressively outlined in the *Bringing Them Home* report and in the creative works of Aboriginal film makers, song writers, visual artists, dancers and actors; the volumes of Aboriginal history generated from the 1970s; the findings of the 1991 Royal Commission into Aboriginal Deaths in Custody, and in media accounts of political action and legal representation on behalf of the victims.[25] Like a tragic dirge, the experiences of the Stolen Generations were recounted around the country, an Aboriginal way of teaching the nation about its past through oral tradition and a plethora of artistic genres.

There is a strong popular belief in the power of the speaking of formerly unspeakable personal histories to bring about individual and national healing, with everyone's tears helping to wash clean the deep personal wounds. Jackson describes this as part of a 'strategy of actively coping' with individual experiences:

> In translating *my* suffering into the suffering of my people, *I* is transformed into *we* ... This transformation of particular subjective experience into a universalised and trans-subjective category enables one to grasp and control the situation one experienced first in solitude and powerlessness. It is always easier to bear personal suffering if one can experience it as something shared by many others. Through the sense of kinship born of this identification with fellow sufferers one is able to find common cause against a common foe. The belittling sense of having been singled out and persecuted because of some failing in oneself yields to an empowering sense of

being part of a collective tragedy, a shared trauma. No matter what the wound, it is easier to act as one of many who have been victims of a historical wrong than it is to act as the isolated and sole victim of a personal slight.[26]

In confessional models in other countries, such as the Truth and Reconciliation Commission in South Africa, survivors' memories have proved integral in the process of reconstructing the 'truth' of traumatic national histories and pointing a way forward out of the impasse of pain, grief and bitterness. Chileans grappling with the task of recording the horrors of the Pinochet regime found that:

The most important material for the reconstruction of truth was the memory of the survivors. Although truth is insufficient, it is an essential aspect of the social and political process implying a public acknowledgment of the victims' suffering. If this process does not take place, societies are doomed to repeat the past; and the victims are doomed to private heartaches ... society cannot decree loss of memory, even if it will not support its validation. Those who need to remember will find a way, even if it is stored, to sustain it.[27]

The heartfelt call in the *Bringing Them Home* report for a national apology to the Stolen Generations was in line with recent reconciliatory apologies for past inhumanities by leaders in Britain, the United States of America and the Vatican. In Switzerland the government apologised for the removal of Romany children between 1926 and 1972 and awarded compensation to the families. In 1998 the Canadian federal government offered a formal apology to its First Nation citizens and committed 350 million dollars to a 'Healing Fund' to support communities in their efforts to address 'the legacy of physical and sexual abuse at residential schools'.[28] The United States government has not yet issued a formal apology to Native-American people, although President Clinton has officially apologised for the past mistreatment of African-Americans.[29] The *Bringing Them Home* report was grounded in the belief that 'remembering — in a symbolic way is a sharing of pain, a joint acknowledgment of past wrongs and a sign of hope for a different and renewed future.'[30] However, the Howard federal government refused to offer a national apology, despite the many apologies issued by state and territory government and church and community organisations, offering instead the compromise of a 'statement of regret' and a plan to provide sixty-three million dollars over a four-year period aimed at addressing 'family separation and its consequences'.[31] Indeed, many conservative politicians and community leaders went on to condemn the report for its reliance on 'fallible memory' and for promulgating a 'black armband' version of Australia's past. They naively and patronisingly instructed *all* Australians, including members of the Stolen Generations, to forget the past and look to the future.

Discussing Australians' limited awareness of the Holocaust, political commentator Robert Manne spoke of a national 'culture of forgetting' and a 'provincial naivety, historical ignorance and sentimental multiculturalism'.[32] Similarly, with our indigenous history, it is alarming to note just how much we have forgotten, even of our recent past. This is the case for particular events during the 1960s and 1970s which brought the issue of Aboriginal families and child removal forcefully to the attention of the Australian public and generated heated community debate. The concerted political struggle of activists over three decades to return control of Aboriginal children to Aboriginal families, culminating in the 1996 Inquiry into the Separation of Aboriginal Children from their Families, has also been largely forgotten. This was evident in the many claims in letters published in newspapers such as the *West Australian* that the Inquiry was another example of preferential treatment of Aborigines over other groups such as the 'Empire Children,' although their push for recognition and redress had only begun in the late 1980s.

WINDOWS OF OPPORTUNITY

During the 1970s new 'windows of opportunity' provided openings for Aboriginal activists around Australia to push for full political, social and economic equality and formal recognition of the right to choose to live according to Aboriginal ways. Along with land rights, intervention into Aboriginal families through the removal of children hit the headlines across the country. This marked the beginning of a long and hard-fought political struggle which left many personal tragedies and casualties in its wake.

At the time there was considerable optimism and many believed that the scene in Australia was set for real positive change. The Aboriginal movement, like many social movements amongst oppressed peoples around the world at the time, was replacing an all-pervading self-fulfilling sense of powerlessness with 'self-awareness, pride and assertion ... progress, self-determination, and power', and a new pride in cultural diversity.[33] There emerged, for the first time in our history, a national indigenous perspective and a united front in national and international forums. In 1970 Aboriginal leaders addressed the United Nations and accused the Australian government of 'systematically exterminating the aboriginal people by neglect' and demanded $6000 million compensation for 'illegal confiscation of aboriginal land'.[34] Indeed, indigenous rights were on the United Nations agenda during the 1970s leading to the establishment in 1982 of the Working Group of Indigenous Peoples.

In style and strategy the Aboriginal movement was influenced, but certainly not determined by, United States models such as the American civil rights movement and 'Black Power'. It became increasingly separatist and in 1970 the peak national organisation, the Federal Council for the Advancement of Aborigines and Torres Strait Islanders (FCAATSI), split over the issue of non-Aboriginal involvement. The breakaways formed the National Tribal Council with an Indigenous-only membership and a manifesto of bi-culturalism, abolition of the policy of assimilation and the establishment of a national indigenous administration. On Australia Day in 1972 Aboriginal activists unfurled a beach umbrella with the sign 'Aboriginal Embassy' on the lawns of Parliament House in Canberra and the Aboriginal Tent Embassy, now an emblem of Aboriginal protest, came into being. With Aboriginal artist Harold Thomas' black, yellow and red Aboriginal flag flying proudly above, the Embassy encapsulated, for hundreds of thousands of Australians, Aboriginal demands for a shift from 'native problem' to 'Indigenous nation'.[35] The Embassy was violently removed six months later on the orders of the Liberal government, but not before the Leader of the Opposition and soon to be Labor Prime Minister, Gough Whitlam, had met there with Aboriginal leaders and formulated what was to become his government's goal to 'restore to the Aboriginal people of Australia their lost power of self-determination in economic, social and political affairs.' This reflected a dual concern — to genuinely improve Aboriginal conditions while also defusing and encapsulating what appeared to be an escalating militancy in the Aboriginal movement.[36]

The popular election of the Whitlam Labor government in 1972 with its slogan 'It's Time' suggested that Australians were ready to emerge from the chrysalis of the cold war era into a vigorous new period of change. Under Whitlam the nation moved away from the policies of White Australia and Aboriginal assimilation and the foundations of a multicultural nation were forged. The pace of change in Aboriginal affairs ushered in by the 1967 referendum was accelerated, and directions were laid down which continued with some challenges into the 1990s. Labor's Aboriginal platform set an exciting new agenda for reform — a policy of self-determination (changed to self-management under the Fraser Coalition government), the establishment of a federal Department of Aboriginal Affairs (DAA) with key Aboriginal appointments, an innovative federal definition of Aboriginality, imperatives to consult with Aboriginal communities in all matters, and promotion of national research and collection of Aboriginal social indicators. Unprecedented levels of federal funding (with significant flow-ons to the states) were allocated to bring Aboriginal housing, education, welfare, health, employment and legal aid in line with community standards.[37] Aborigines were now guaranteed equal access to all government services and benefits, including unemployment benefits and the supporting mothers benefits for sole parents. As part of this process of endeavouring to ensure equity across the board, the federal government insisted on the repeal of all remaining discriminatory state legislation. In 1975 it passed the Racial Discrimination Act to override remaining discriminatory Queensland legislation, to ratify Aboriginal civil and political rights and to prevent acts of racial discrimination. Land rights legislation was introduced in the Northern Territory and all states with the exception of Western Australia and Queensland. The issue of state rights and federal intervention remained a niggling problem which could always flare up into a blazing row and, in the case of Queensland, into a dogged refusal to change. Administrative reform continued to be plagued by the old problems of bureaucratic 'accommodation to change'[38] and the deadening effect of 'recycled' staff steeped in old ways of working, many now in key positions in policy and management.

This managed change through control was evident in government action to develop an Aboriginal organisational structure to advise government and link services and the community. Fostered by the federal government through its policy of self-determination, generous funding and the work of DAA officers, the process of change also owed much to the networks and pools of experience of the Aboriginal movement. Incorporated under federal legislation, the mushrooming infrastructure grew from dependent community management councils into self-managing organisations dealing with a range of issues — health, legal aid, community management, land and welfare services — with national umbrella organisations operating to coordinate activities and to lobby as a unified front. The major national body was the National Aboriginal Consultative Committee (NACC) consisting of elected Aboriginal members, set up in 1973 to provide an advisory and consultative function to government. The fate of the NACC demonstrates the government's determination to contain Aboriginal political action to the point of terminating those organisations not following its objectives. From its inception the NACC declared its commitment to becoming an independent congress in charge of Aboriginal affairs, despite repeated government warnings that its funding would be terminated if it did not stick to its advisory role. In 1976, on the recommendation of a federal Committee of Inquiry, the Fraser Coalition government dissolved the NACC. Its replacement, the National Aboriginal Conference, was disbanded under similar circumstances in 1984 by the Hawke Labor government. Despite such 'Big Brother' tactics, these organisations managed to significantly improve Aboriginal people's ability to negotiate change and development, to put funding agencies and mainstream welfare institutions at one remove, and to have more control over processes and decisions affecting Aboriginal people, while at the same time weathering the storms of internal dissent which typically riddle any community organisation. This new-found muscle was also expressed in more formal participation in the growing international movement for recognition of indigenous rights.

While the helping professions remained conservative overall, there was a heartening move amongst the new wave of university-trained social workers towards new ways of working with Aboriginal people within the context of new federal initiatives and Aboriginal endeavours. A radical social worker of the time, John Tomlinson, recalled the influence of a heady jumble of new writings by feminists, black and decolonised people (in particular Fanon), psychologists (Laing and Szasz), anthropologists (Beckett's studies of urban Aboriginal communities), historians (Rowley), community development (Alinsky) and sociologists (conflict models of society) that shaped his view of social work practice as a radical process of change working to shift existing power relations in society, to redistribute wealth and to wage war on poverty. From this perspective

Tomlinson concluded that, despite talk of change, Aboriginal affairs remained locked in a welfare model while most governments continued to 'regard Aboriginal affairs as an area of cheap charity'.[39] This meant that Aborigines were denied opportunity, remained separate and dependent and were unable to develop initiative. Calling for 'rights not welfare', Tomlinson wrote:

> The institutionalisation of so many people in the welfare-rehabilitation style rather than the engaging of people in the producer-consumer struggle of the wider society has had the effect of mortgaging future generations. This is particularly so when the standard of living on welfare is as low as it is in Aboriginal life. [Nugget] Coombs has suggested the present policies are producing a race of cripples.[40]

There was also a growing critique in welfare circles of state intervention in the care of children generally, and of fostering and adoption in particular, with implications for Aboriginal children who were now dealt with by mainstream child and family services in all states and territories. In fact, Aboriginal children and families formed the largest client group in most administrations. At a time when these departments were becoming larger and more bureaucratic, their critics, influenced by human rights, black power and self-help movements of the period, demanded a more humane face, the sharing of control with the community, recognition of the significance of cultural and other forms of difference, and the lifting of the veil of secrecy over fostering and adoption arrangements. Central to this was a profound faith in the importance of stable family life for the healthy emotional growth of the child. In 1982 a workshop of social work professionals delineated the special contributions of family life over substitute care: recognition of the uniqueness of the child, commitment to continuity of care, a two-way flow of love between parent and child, time to listen and be together and a sense of belonging and trust.[41] Broader social changes impacting on family and child welfare services included the greater availability of abortion, contraceptives and family planning advice; more relaxed attitudes to single mothers; and the introduction of supporting parents benefits. Despite more enlightened concepts, language, policies and legislation, much welfare practice remained resistant to change. This reflected the inhibitory effect of the perennial problem in child welfare of having to meet two opposing sets of duties

— to provide care, protection and support services for children and families *and* to enforce social control and social order through the control and correction of deviant children from any background.[42]

In his analysis of the shaping of public debate about Aboriginal policy and political status since the 1960s, media analyst Steve Mickler notes that the years immediately following the 1967 referendum showed:

a remarkable transformation in both the issues constituting Aboriginal affairs and the configuration of relations between readers, the state and Aborigines as organised and made available for public consumption in the news.[43]

A host of new experts vied for media attention along with Aboriginal spokespeople representing organisations, government, political parties and churches, or speaking out as individuals — some in unison with white voices, but the majority from increasingly separatist platforms. Aboriginal *and* non-Aboriginal audiences were absorbing new images of Aborigines as rational actors surviving as best they could, often in circumstances more commonly associated with the 'Third World'. While the media covered a broad range of Aboriginal issues, the sheer number of stories and images about the removal of Aboriginal children and their placement with white families through fostering and adoption suggested a growing public obsession with this particular issue. Opinions of the professionals and experts canvassed — medical doctors, social workers, anthropologists, statisticians, administrators, politicians and Aborigines — indicated a new plurality of opinion and appreciation of Aboriginal difference. The emotional reporting of contentious events involving removal of Aboriginal children in the late 1960s and early 1970s brought several fundamental questions into the public forum. What constituted the 'best interests' of Aboriginal children? When should the state intervene in Aboriginal families? What rights did Aboriginal parents and children have? How could the families' desperate living conditions be improved? What recognition should there be of Aboriginal cultural difference in child welfare services? Were white families and institutions appropriate for Aboriginal children? Despite heated public debate and national attention to these issues there was no simple progression towards enlightened opinion, but, rather, a few lurching moves forward, numerous grinding halts, several reversals, and, in the long run, a profound public inertia and forgetting.

ADOPTION IN VICTORIA

In June 1968 in the midst of media fascination in Victoria with Lionel Rose's flagging boxing career, the recently appointed director of the new Department of Aboriginal Affairs, Reg Worthy, orchestrated another media event with startling claims of widespread 'trafficking' in Aboriginal children. Worthy told the press that his department had identified over three hundred Aboriginal children 'illegally adopted' into white families in Victoria. Many lived in deplorable conditions — some in families with as many as fifteen Aboriginal children in addition to their own — and had been passed between families so that their parents had lost track of them. He claimed that 'the idea of taking away from Aboriginal women the responsibility of caring for their own children [was] unbelievably prevalent in Victoria.'[44] Pregnant Aboriginal women had been approached in the street by white women seeking to adopt their babies and some mothers

Native baby 'bleached'
— Department chief's claim

A European woman had used a mild solution of household bleach on a 19-months-old aboriginal baby she wanted to keep, the Director of Aboriginal Affairs, Mr Worthy, said today.

"We assume she was trying to bleach the child white," he said.

"It was a weak solution and a weak attempt. The child was not burned in any way.

"But it's an indication of the kind of thinking that exists."

Last night Mr Worthy said that in a week's investigation, an officer of his department had discovered that 300 aboriginal children in Victoria were not living with their parents.

White people had taken the children away to look after them.

Mr Worthy was speaking at a quarterly meeting of the Victorian Council of Social Service.

Today he said that a welfare officer had investigated the case of the woman who used bleach on a baby, earlier this year.

'PREVALENT'

"This idea of taking away from aboriginal women the responsibility of caring for their own children is unbelievably prevalent in Victoria," he said.

"I intend to do all I can to stop it. But the only action my department can take is to encourage the natural parents to demand their children back.

"We will tell them that if the foster parents refuse then they should immediately contact the police."

Mr Worthy said that one white woman had "reached double figures" in swapping aboriginal children with other white families.

People who unofficially adopted aboriginal children ranged from the poverty-stricken to those on high income levels.

"For some of these people it's a matter of 'do-gooding' but it is very misguided goodwill," Mr Worthy said.

"For others fostering an aboriginal child is a status symbol, like owning a poodle."

Mr Worthy said hundreds of aboriginal children are being "passed around" among white families throughout the metropolitan area and in some country centres.

Bewildered aboriginal mothers asking white foster parents for the return of their children had been told the children are no longer with them.

(Courtesy Herald & Weekly Times, *Herald* [Melbourne], 25.6.1968)

576

complied because they had been conditioned to 'think that white people always know best. You can always get a "yes" from aboriginals, because they want no trouble.'[45] Some children were from interstate and had been left behind with host families by organisers of holiday schemes. Worthy demanded the immediate return of the children and encouraged Aboriginal parents to 'assert their rights, go to the police and, if necessary, start prosecutions ... It is no good talking about Aboriginal rights if you are not aware of the responsibilities entailed.'[46] When most carers refused to hand over the children — it was claimed that one woman took the drastic step of drenching a baby in household bleach to avoid detection[47] — Worthy threatened to

ABORIGINALS 'ARE NOT CURIOSITIES'

THE Victorian director of Aboriginal Affairs, Mr R. Worthy, charged last night that Australians "generally speaking, overlook the fact that aboriginals are people."

"I know it sounds crazy, but it's true," he said.

"We look at and consider them as aboriginals, and forget that they are people."

This led, he said, to people visiting the Lake Tyers settlement "to look at the aboriginals."

It also led to people wanting to adopt aboriginal foster-children because of their race.

"We should stop putting aboriginals under the microscope and treat them instead as people like ourselves," Mr Worthy said.

"The aboriginal people at Lake Tyers object strongly to being treated as curiosities."

"They have asked that they be left alone and that people stop coming to look at them."

Mr Worthy said: "On the question of adoptions, I believe that children should be taken into foster homes because they are children in need of a home and not because they happen to be aboriginals."

"The sooner we stop treating aboriginals as curiosities and leave them alone the better."

At a meeting in Geelong on Wednesday night, Mr Worthy commended "those people who are performing an essential service for children who need foster homes or adoptive parents."

But he attacked people who travelled interstate to isolated reserves where aboriginals lived and offered to take over the care of aboriginal children.

Misunderstanding on remarks

Mr Worthy said last night there had been a misunderstanding about his remarks, and some people had gained the impression that he disapproved of schemes under which aboriginal children spent holidays with white families.

"Nothing could be farther from the truth," he said. "We do approve of these schemes.

"In fact, the Government provides funds for these children to travel from the country to the families with whom they are staying."

'Don't adopt them'

GEELONG.—People who adopted, or fostered, aboriginal children were "do-gooding busy bodies depriving the children's original parents of a responsibility they could ill-afford to lose."

The Director of Aboriginal Affairs, Mr Reg Worthy, said this here last night.

Speaking on adoption at a discussion night organised by the Geelong branch of the Aborigines' Advancement League, Mr Worthy said some individuals were interfering with the work of the department.

'Accustomed to handouts'

"Aboriginal parents are becoming accustomed to expect handouts from the 'whites.'

"This is undermining the whole program for their assimilation into the local community," Mr Worthy said.

"In the same way, parents who offered to adopt foster aboriginal children are also providing a handout.

"They are relieving the parents of their responsibility towards the child and this can have disastrous effects.

"The humiliation expressed by these children when they see parents holding their hands out for offerings is a pitiful sight."

Mr Worthy said the Government faced a tremendous problem with the aboriginals, and it asked the public to stop giving and let them make a living independently.

(Courtesy of Herald & Weekly Times, *Sun* [Melbourne], 22.8.1968; 23.8.1968)

legislate to get the children back and to stop the movement of Aboriginal children across borders into Victoria.[48]

What motivated this outburst? It was, in part, the action of a new administration flexing its fledgling muscles and endeavouring to bring Aboriginal adoptions under new legal guidelines to defuse a potentially volatile situation. In a community accustomed to positive media coverage of holiday, fostering and adoption schemes for Aboriginal children, Worthy's hard-line comments were meant to shock. He had to shake the public out of its general acceptance of the practice of removing Aboriginal children to live in white families. Worthy emphasised that it was also an official campaign to enforce the 'responsibility side' of assimilation and citizenship. He told a meeting of the Aborigines Advancement League (AAL) that relieving Aboriginal parents of their children was another form of 'handout' and he wanted the public to 'stop giving and let them live independently ... This is the only way we can introduce some of them to responsible citizenship.' Assimilated citizenship was the only future for the state's five thousand Aborigines because 'as far as this State was concerned, Aboriginal culture was dead.'[49] Worthy also questioned the motives of white carers operating outside any formal system of selection and control and expressed concern about the possible harmful effects on the children:

> I'm afraid it's almost become fashionable for a family to have an Aboriginal child. There is a big risk the child might come to regard himself on the same level as a family pet ... well-intentioned people have allowed their sentimentality to run away with them ... They see an appealing child and decide to give him a 'good chance' in life. The chance of success of such an impulse adoption is extremely low ... The child is the worst sufferer. I know of cases of children being brought to Melbourne from North Queensland. They couldn't adapt to the big city and the different climate. Some have drifted back and they can't settle down in their old community.[50]

Worthy's attack fitted with criticisms of Aboriginal child removal by Koori activists Bruce McGuiness and Molly Dyer, and the AAL. AAL Secretary E Bacon told the press:

> Many people with very good intentions take Aboriginal children hoping to assist them and their families. But it does not always work out this way, for when the adopted child grows up and finds itself isolated in a community of Europeans problems develop. The adopted child becomes self-conscious of its colour and racial difference leading to a feeling of inferiority. If one is aware of these problems that will occur as the child grows older, and is able to offer a good home as well as love and understanding, adoption can be successful in some cases. But these are not very many ... it is important for any child to grow up with others with similar families to have the necessary pride in its own race. This is essential, and if

the feeling of identity with its own people is there it will not grow to feel inferior.[51]

The AAL advocated placement of children with Aboriginal families, with fostering in white families as a last resort.[52] An editorial in the *Portland Observer and Guardian* added the following comments to the debate:

> The day it is both *fashionable* and *sensible* to adopt an aboriginal child into a white home and environment will be the day when it is *fashionable* and *acceptable* to take an aboriginal as a husband or wife with the full blessing of the white party's parents and friends.
> Until that day, the adoption of aboriginals by whites, no matter how well intentioned, can lead only to cruel disillusionment.[53]

AAL liaison officer S Murray stated that adoptions and intermarriage 'would mean genocide to the Aboriginal people'.[54] The story was even taken up in the Canadian press. AAL President Stan Davey was reported as saying that Aboriginal children were 'the "in" thing in Australia. Having an Aboriginal baby in the house is fashionable. Some whites adopt black babies and treat them like poodles.'[55]

Aboriginal activist Charles Perkins, then Manager of the Foundation for Aboriginal Affairs, claimed that in New South Wales unofficial adoptions were 'as common as the common cold':

> White people go out to the reserves and shanty towns in the country and because the aboriginal people are mainly uneducated and inarticulate and live in deplorable conditions they are easily persuaded to let their children be adopted. Many agree to let their children go for a month or so, but are unable to get them back.[56]

The New South Wales Deputy Director of Child Welfare, W Langshaw, denied Perkins' claims, stating that his officers were not aware of any illegal adoptions and that his Department had difficulty 'getting people to take these children legitimately so there is no need for people to go under cover to try and get hold of a child.'[57] This reply was shown to be disingenuous by evidence that some Aboriginal children sent from New South Wales to Melbourne on organised holidays had been kept there by their 'hosts'.[58]

Worthy's allegations were hotly debated in the Victorian press. An editorial in the Melbourne *Age* argued that the controversy demonstrated how far Australia had to go to recognise that all citizens have basic rights:

Whatever their colour, whatever the circumstances of their birth, children must be protected against people who would treat them as chattels and for display purposes or as instruments for working out their frustrations.[59]

A letter to the Melbourne *Sun* outlined the unprofessional practice of the Northern Territory Welfare Branch which had asked one family to foster a girl sent down on a holiday scheme:

They were prepared to send her to us without any attempt at matching the foster parents and the child … There was no investigation. It would never be done with a white child. Our impression was that it seemed to be policy to try and get anyone to take aboriginal children.[60]

Melbourne families with Aboriginal children legally in their care retorted that the children were not 'status symbols' and denied that they experienced problems because of their 'colour'. Their comments reflect their commitment to assimilation's rhetoric of social rather than racial explanations as the cause of Aboriginal disadvantage:

[Colour's] just a physical fact — not a disadvantage or defect.

When we go shopping, or something like that, no one ever says anything or pays attention.

His black skin is just a factor in his appearance like the colour of the hair of one of the other children. I think people exaggerate the problems.[61]

A letter to the press signed 'Interested parent' raised several questions that had 'received little public expression' and that would 'need answering before the public is persuaded'. What was to happen to children from 'broken' Aboriginal families and those made wards of the state 'because their parents could not or would not care for them?' Would they be 'restricted to life in an institution and denied the possibility of life and love in a normal family?' Who would they turn to when they left the institutions? What 'more constructive suggestion towards assimilation could the critics of adoption and fostering make for the already disrupted Aboriginal homes (and there are many)?'[62] These were questions being addressed by administrators around Australia and in the context of existing policy, practice and perceptions of Aboriginal families there seemed to be no satisfactory answers. What was required was the radical shift in thinking advocated by Stan Davey in a letter to the *Herald* newspaper in 1967:

> Victorians who are really concerned for these children should rather channel their energies into having the Queensland and Northern Territory authorities change their racially-destructive policies, to enable aboriginal communities to repossess and care for their own children.[63]

What were the immediate outcomes of Worthy's media blitz? The federal Minister for Aboriginal Affairs, Bill Wentworth, threatened to investigate the alleged illegal adoptions, but no official inquiry eventuated. The South Australian government assured its citizens that children were only placed with foster parents licensed by the Department of Social Welfare and that Aboriginal children were placed with Aboriginal foster parents if possible or with 'culturally sensitive' families. Despite these assurances, Maude Tangerie, Vice-President of the Council for Aboriginal Women, called for an immediate investigation into the fostering of Aboriginal children in the state.[64] While it is not clear how many children were returned to their parents, Worthy's actions did have the effect of increasing government surveillance and promoting Aboriginal parents' awareness of their rights. A clampdown on holiday schemes effectively stopped further drift of Aboriginal children from interstate into informal adoptions in Victoria. The issue also provoked discussion on what constituted the 'best interests' of Aboriginal children, and on an embryonic form of what was to become known as the Aboriginal Child Placement Principle.

Meanwhile the press had found similar contentious and popular news items which it continued to exploit. In October 1968 sensational headlines across the country reported one man's failed attempt to reach Europe by stowing away on the *Galileo* in order to retrieve the young son of a Western Australian Aboriginal woman. In 1963, her two-year-old son and another boy were taken to Russia by two female teachers to be educated to become 'leader[s] of [their] people'. One boy had been smuggled back into Australia but the other was not located until 1970 when Australian authorities found him living in East Germany, his name changed to Patrice in honour of the murdered African leader Patrice Lumumba, and speaking fluent German. Interviewed by the press on his return, his mother recalled that the teachers had claimed her son had 'no chance' if he stayed in Australia to which she retorted, 'It may not be good for the child — but it's good for me. Why should I be deprived of my son?'[65]

The newsworthiness of such cases was also evident in the flurry of headlines and heart-wrenching photos devoted by newspapers in Melbourne, country Victoria and nationally over a two-year period, to a relatively minor ongoing custody battle in Melbourne. This involved an Aboriginal girl whose mother had privately placed her with a white family during a period of personal crisis. A major point of debate in the press reports was whether Aboriginal children were better placed with their mothers to shield them from the effects of white racism or with white foster parents who generally could provide superior material comforts. Despite the fact that it was a private placement and not a case of legal fostering or adoption, the case for custody was heard before the Victorian Supreme Court in 1971. Giving evidence for the Aboriginal mother, Reg Worthy told the judge he feared for the child if she was not returned to her mother:

> About 80% of *ad hoc* placements with non Aboriginal families have broken down — either in the early years, or more often, at adolescence ... I believe it is very important that Aboriginal people should recognise and appreciate, as they do, their blackness. I have never known of an Aboriginal in this State who has been rejected by an Aboriginal or Aboriginal group ... Any foster parent who takes on an Aboriginal child and does not visualise difficulties is in for trouble.[66]

Lawyers for the white family argued that returning the girl to her mother would condemn her to 'a childhood of awful unhappiness and deprivation'. However, Mr Justice Stephen ruled that the girl should be returned to her mother on the grounds that she would 'be better able to resist the effects on her of this racial prejudice if she grows up with her own mother ... This is a factor of very special significance in this case and one which weighs heavily in its favour.' He also noted the similar financial situations of both families (the white carers had fourteen children, nine of them living with them in a three-bedroom home) and commented that with her own family the girl would always have access to the 'particular financial benevolence' the state demonstrated towards Aborigines. The girl was made a ward of the court to allow judicial supervision until she turned sixteen.[67]

However the struggle over the girl continued in the courts alongside a welter of emotional press headlines flagging the 'rights and wrongs' of fostering Aboriginal children in white families:

Natives adopt racial line[68]

Doreen[69] — a sad, happy day[70]

Doreen starts off afresh with mum[71]

Doreen better with mother — judge[72]

Court returns Doreen to her mother[73]

Doreen goes back to her mother[74]

Judge gives Doreen to her mother[75]

The agony of a foster mother as Doreen goes to a new life[76]

Mother best for Doreen — Judge[77]

Doreen's back — they're all happy[78]

New fight over baby Doreen[79]

A kind of loving … One foster mother's deeply moving story of her struggles with an Aboriginal child[80]

The long wait is over — Doreen is back[81]

Court to decide their future[82]

We've given them the only home they know[83]

Mother gives up daughters[84]

Mother to give up baby again[85]

Such headlines provided a public voice for the white foster mothers; however, there were few accounts of the feelings of the children's natural parents and families. Instead they were often publicly condemned for their children coming into care, as in the following comment:

ABORIGINAL GIRL ABDUCTED FROM FOSTER PARENTS

Registered for posting as a newspaper —Category "A"

Est. 1904   'Phone: 67-5133

Aust. Press Cuttings Agency
Melbourne, Victoria

From

"NEWS"

Darwin, N.T.

21 SEP 1973

News

Tel: 816582 28 MITCHELL ST., DARWIN Price 10c
Air Delivery Oore 13c

Vol. 22, No. 191
DARWIN, FRIDAY, SEPTEMBER 21, 1973

RETURNED TO TRIBAL HOME

A major investigation is under way to discover why a seven-year-old Aboriginal girl was returned to her natural parents at Maningrida without the knowledge of her Rapid Creek foster parents.

The transfer was made by the Department of Aboriginal Affairs and the Aboriginal Legal Aid Service without the knowledge of Aboriginal Affairs Minister, Mr Gordon Bryant, who was studying the case.

Mr Bryant said last night the Government could not intervene in the case and any further action between the natural and foster parents would have to be by civil legal proceedings.

The child, named Nola, was reported yesterday to have settled in "very happily" with her natural family for her first experience of Aboriginal and bush life.

She is living with her parents, ████ and ████ and two brothers at Cadell Gardens, about 20 miles from the main Maningrida settlement, 260 miles from Darwin.

She went there on Saturday, September 8, after having lived with Mr ████, ████ his wife ████, 45, and their children for nearly seven years.

On Saturday she was taken by welfare officers from the ████'s Rapid

They knew she'd go

Creek home to 'see her brother Leo, 13, and her natural father, at Bagot settlement.

The welfare officers left Nola, her father and her brother at Bagot settlement.

When they returned they found the three had left for Maningrida on a plane chartered the previous day by the Aboriginal legal aid service.

Nola was born at Maningrida on September 19, 1966, and weighed only 2 lb. 6 oz at birth.

She was taken to Darwin Hospital for special premature baby care and became one of several Aboriginal babies for whom the then Welfare Branch of Administration sought foster parents.

Nola was allocated to the ████ who had six

children of their own but she did not leave the hospital and go to them until she was eight months old.

The ████ signed a form acknowledging that they realised Nola eventually would have to return to her natural parents and they had several visits from Welfare officers during the next two years.

The visits practically stopped and the ████ applied to adopt Nola about three years ago. Their application was not acknowledged.

Visits by welfare officers resumed about a year ago and early this year the ████ were reminded that Nola would have to return to her natural parents.

On August 23 they wrote to Mr Bryant asking him to investigate the case on the grounds that Nola had been with them more than six years, was doing well in first grade at school and could return to an Aboriginal environment later by attending Kormilda College.

They told Mr Bryant Nola could speak only English and had no real knowledge of her natural parents or their way of life.

When Mr Bryant received the letter he sent a telegram saying he would investigate the case.

Nola's natural brother Leo, 13, in second grade at Maningrida school, was then brought to Darwin by the Department of Aboriginal Affairs for meetings with Nola, to get her accustomed to her real family.

They had several meetings at Dundee House. When Nola became reluctant to go there, Leo was taken to spend several hours a day with the ████

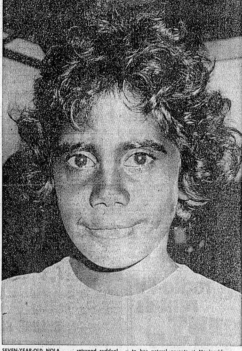

SEVEN-YEAR-OLD NOLA . . . returned suddenly to her natural parents at Maningrida.

He speaks some English but his mother cannot speak it and her father has only a limited command of the language.

Her father also came to Darwin early in September and Nola was taken by the social worker to see him on September 8.

The social worker told the ████ that Nola would be home for lunch, about three hours after leaving.

But he returned at 12.15 p.m. to tell the

████ he had lost contact with Nola, her father and brother.

Some hours later the ████ found the family had gone to Maningrida on the legal aid charter plane.

'Brutal action'

Mr ████ who works with the Taxation De-

partment in Darwin, said last night: "We have always realised Nola may have to go back.

"But after so long it seems unfair to take her, without warning, to a completely strange environment.

"The manner of taking her away was brutal. Probably she won't come back but I would like regular and unbiased reports for several months to ensure that she is settling down happily and is

in good health.

"I sent Mr Bryant a telegram after Nola was taken on September 8 and received a reply saying that the move was not his decision and he was investigating.

"There seems no real likelihood Nola will come back to us but we want to be assured that she is being well-cared for."

● Continued Page 2
● Nola Could Become An Outcast — Page 2

MR BRYANT . . . "We will hold an inquiry."

(Courtesy *NT News* [Darwin], 21.9.1973)

When Ellie went to pick him up from the hospital she was filled
with anger towards the Aboriginal parents who had neglected him
to the point where he became desperately ill with gastro-enteritis
and pneumonia.[86]

THE NUMBER OF SMALL GRAVES[87]

Simplistic perceptions of 'rights and wrongs' were challenged in the
late 1960s by media exposure of the desperate conditions of many
Aboriginal parents battling to care for their children against insurmountable deprivations and disadvantages. In August 1969 Australian
audiences were shocked by revelations of blatant 'legal and medical
inadequacy and small town racism' and neglect of Aboriginal maternal
rights in the ABC television Four Corners documentary, 'Out of Sight
Out of Mind,' which covered the events surrounding the conviction of
a twenty-nine-year-old Queensland Aboriginal mother, Mrs Jones,[88] for
the manslaughter of her baby daughter.[89] Mrs Jones lived in a fringe
camp on the outskirts of Cunnamulla, the prosperous rural centre of
Queensland's richest beef and cattle region. She had ten children, five
in state care and the remainder living with her in a small tin shack
which housed four adults and ten children, and she supported herself
and her children on a meagre wage of six dollars a week. The fringe
camp was located next to the town sewerage outlet and had only one
communal bore water tap and a block of unsewered earth closets. It
was home to swarms of flies and mosquitoes, and widespread
infection and disease contributed to an Aboriginal death rate three
times higher than the town average. The town Health Inspector told
Four Corners journalists that the situation was 'in many respects worse
than the conditions which exist in refugee villages in Vietnam'.[90]
    During the early months of 1968, Mrs Jones had sought treatment
for her baby at Cunnamulla Hospital on several occasions. While
Aborigines could now access mainstream rural hospital services,
professional treatment and advice were often negligent and discrim
inatory, with limited follow-up of cases or awareness of the cultural
and economic constraints faced by Aboriginal families. When the baby
was hospitalised for eight days at the age of six weeks with gastroenteritis, hospital staff advised a diet of 'vegetables, potato, and
pumpkin', an inappropriate diet for an ailing baby, and no one
checked whether her mother could actually afford it. Like many other

babies at the time, often with the active encouragement of Infant Welfare Centres, the baby was bottle fed on Sunshine milk, a dried and unmodified form of cow's milk lacking the extra vitamins and nutrients of commercial baby formulas and insufficient to sustain infant life over an extended period.[91] In July, aged four and a half months, the baby was admitted to hospital again and given the standard treatment of a 'clean bed', a glucose drip and antibiotics. Two days later she was dead. At the inquest the cause of death was given as pneumonia with malnutrition as a contributing factor. Following discussions with the hospital doctor, local detectives suggested to Mrs Jones that bruising to the baby's body was due to 'gross malnutrition and neglect' but no action was taken against her. Four months elapsed until, following a visit to the hospital with another sick child, Mrs Jones was arrested for manslaughter. With bail set at the impossible figure of $1000 she waited in the local jail until April 1969 when, at her own expense, she was put on the train for Roma, two hundred and fifty miles away, for her trial before an all male, all white jury.

Looking back on the trial, Dr Archivides Kalokerinos, a major defence witness and Medical Superintendent at Collarenebri District Hospital in New South Wales from 1957, described the verdict of 'guilty' as 'inevitable'. He recalled that the judge 'did not seem impressed' by his admittedly controversial evidence. On the basis of his own medical work with Aboriginal infants, Kalokerinos advanced the theory, angrily disputed by his colleagues, that sudden Aboriginal infant deaths were due to traumatic Vitamin C deficiency. This caused the onset of scurvy with bruising to the body and dramatic dehydration and weight loss leading to death, unless, as he advocated, the baby was administered massive doses of Vitamin C.[92] He argued that Mrs Jones could not possibly have been aware of the true nature of her baby's condition and should not be held responsible; instead the nurses and doctors should be on trial for seriously mismanaging the case. Kalokerinos also recalled that the judge negatively construed the defence lawyer's decision not to put Mrs Jones in the witness box and instructed the jury to consider this as a matter which could infer guilt. Mrs Jones was sentenced to three years hard labour in Boggo Road Jail in Brisbane where her mother had died twenty-four years earlier.

In a moving report on ABC television's This Day Tonight following the announcement of the verdict, journalist Frank Bennett presented to his viewers an impassioned story of medical negligence and miscarriage of justice. This stirred several organisations into action, including FCAATSI and the Queensland Council for Civil Liberties and students at the Sydney University Law School. An unsuccessful appeal in the Supreme Court, based on the expert evidence of Queensland's leading paediatrician, Dr Felix Arden, was followed by moves for an appeal to the High Court and a petition for pardon was despatched to the Governor.[93] Writing in 1970, Sydney solicitor Geoffrey Robertson and law student John Carrick recalled that the 'turning point' in the unfolding drama was the screening of 'Out of Sight, Out of Mind' which graphically portrayed:

the local hospital's failure to provide prompt treatment for [the baby], exposed the town's racism in a series of interviews, pictured the abject squalor at the reserve with devastating effect, and concluded with a table of Aboriginal infant mortality, superimposed on a close up of [the baby's] rough grave. So ugly was the impression it gave of the Australian treatment of Aborigines that the sale of a colour copy of the film to the BBC was prohibited.[94]

The Queensland government reacted promptly to the screening and before the case could come before the High Court, the Governor had referred the petition for pardon back to a newly constituted bench of judges in the Supreme Court who unanimously quashed the conviction on the grounds of 'fresh' medical evidence. Robertson, Carrick and Kalokerinos all questioned how 'fresh' this evidence was, finding strong parallels with that provided earlier by expert medical witnesses.

These events exposed for public scrutiny and national shame a 'total pattern of attitudes' mirrored in outback towns across Australia which had left Aboriginal families 'locked in a vicious circle of under-privilege and discrimination':

White townspeople come to believe that the Aborigine lives like that simply *because* he is an Aborigine ... Aborigines are seen as 'that way' *because* they are Aborigines, not because of their history of subjection.[95]

It was also evident that after twenty years of assimilation policy, fringe dwellers in towns like Cunnamulla continued to live in Third World conditions, that discrimination was still countenanced at all levels and that white racism remained palpably present. Public sympathy was also directed at the mother and the very fact that her case was taken up at all suggested a shift away from the simplistic solution of attributing blame to Aboriginal mothers and then removing their children. However, overall this brought little change for Mrs Jones and for Aboriginal families living in similar circumstances. Reviewing the case, Robertson and Carrick tagged it another example of:

> 'expiation by *cause celebre.*' An obvious injustice is located, spotlighted by the media, publicly protested, and finally remedied by an establishment device, such as a Royal Commission, or re-appeal with 'fresh evidence' which fails to come to grips with the real cause of the original injustice. [Mrs Jones] was set free. But the manner of her liberation left unsolved, even untouched, the intractable social problems which brought about her prosecution.[96]

Mrs Jones' painful experiences may have provided a personal and emotional interface for a public endeavouring to come to grips with the devastating findings of new medical research on Aboriginal infant and child health and broader social indicators revealing the extent of Aboriginal poverty and disadvantage. The availability of federal funding for research and growing international medical interest in links between health and environment in developing countries had contributed to a burst of research into Aboriginal health by prestigious medical bodies and government departments from the late 1960s. Infant mortality rates across the country were found to be significantly higher than those for non-Aboriginal Australians and other indigenous populations around the world. These findings were widely reported in the Australian press in the early 1970s, with particular attention devoted to the alarming statistics on infant and child mortality:

> Dr P M Moodie, School of Public Medicine, University of Sydney: Aboriginal infant deaths represented ten percent of all such deaths in Australia when Aborigines constituted only one percent of the national population. In the Northern Territory in 1965–67 infant mortality was six times the general Australian rate and higher than for Maori and Native American Indian populations. The main causes of infant death were listed as dysentery, gastroenteritis, flu and pneumonia, neonatal disease, premature birth, post-natal asphyxia and injury during birth. The causal factors were poor living conditions, malnutrition and low standards of child care and personal hygiene.[97]

> The Department of Health, Alice Springs: a medical survey in 1968 that weighed and measured 870 'full-blood' children under the age

of five years found a large percentage between six months and two years were well below half the normal height and weight for their age. Babies under six months were found to be normal. This anomaly reflected a combination of malnutrition, starvation and susceptibility to infection, especially gastro and respiratory illnesses, and increasing rates of admissions to hospital, due to Aboriginal living conditions, community hygiene standards and endemic disease.[98]

Medical Journal of Australia: infant mortality rates in the Northern Territory were one in ten but until recently Central Australia had the highest rates in the world, that is one out of every four babies died. This was due to the effects of malnutrition, over-crowded and unhygienic living conditions, distance from hospitals and cultural and language barriers. In December 1969 a federal and state government health conference in Sydney announced a nationwide survey on Aboriginal health and nutrition. The Director of Medical Services in the Northern Territory advocated education of Aborigines in community living and financing of communities to become economically viable.[99]

Medical Journal of Australia: malnutrition amongst Aboriginal children was 'an Australian health scandal' resembling health profiles of developing countries and while 'several causes have been suggested for Aboriginal malnutrition ... lack of food is the likeliest.'[100]

Federal Minister for Health, Dr Forbes: reported findings that the infant death rate in some parts of Northern Australia was twenty times that of white infants.[101]

Federal Labor member, Senator Keefe: told Federal Parliament that a baby had died in Townsville General Hospital after being fed on a diet of powdered milk and water. The family lived on wages that were below the subsistence level. He stated, 'This monstrous system of dealing with human beings must end, but a thousand more children will die in similar circumstances to those which surround the death of [X], while the Queensland Department pontificates and denies human justice.'[102]

Federal Health Department: one in five babies in the southern division of the Northern Territory died before they reached twelve months.[103]

Dr Jean McFarlane, Queensland Director of Maternal and Child Services: the Aboriginal infant mortality rate may be ten times the national average. The rate for ages from one to four years was seventeen times the national average. The greatest risk to infants was during the period from six months to three years as the supply of breast milk decreased causing 'protein calorie malnutrition syndrome' resulting in retarded growth.[104]

Institutional profiles were equally alarming. A two-year study of 1500 children in twelve major Queensland mission and government settlements by the Queensland Institute of Medical Research, published in 1969, found that child death rates were seven times greater than for the general Australian population. This was due to malnutrition, gastroenteritis and respiratory and bowel infections. The study also found evidence of severely retarded growth and seventy percent of the children had chronic respiratory or ear infections. The study concluded that this reflected poor living conditions and inadequate techniques of child care and infant feeding.[105]

The major diseases linked by medical authorities to Aboriginal infant mortality were upper respiratory infections, gastroenteritis, pneumonia and chronic infections caused by overcrowded and unhygienic living conditions, low standards of personal hygiene, incorrect techniques of child care and infant feeding and widespread malnutrition — all areas that the 'assimilation package' had promised to remedy. However, many medical experts and government officials continued to blame alleged inadequacies of Aborigines as parents, reflecting continued negative perceptions of Aboriginal families. In doing so they followed a well-used ploy of earlier Aboriginal administrations. Blaming Aboriginal families shifted attention away from the wide-ranging social and environmental factors contributing to Aboriginal poor health which could only begin to be remedied through the injection of substantial levels of government funding and expensive medical expertise. Other explanations of the high infant mortality rates in Central Australia were more controversial. In particular, the upwardly spiralling Aboriginal birth-rate in the Northern Territory, which was outstripping available health support services, was linked to the many infant deaths. However, instead of demands for the immediate expansion of services and improved living conditions there were calls for family planning programs for Aboriginal women and even, allegedly, compulsory sterilisation. In

1969 the Federal Minister for Aboriginal Affairs, Bill Wentworth, accused Northern Territory member, Dr Everingham, of advocating 'a publicity campaign to get aboriginals to submit themselves to sterilisation in order to reduce their numbers,' a charge denied by Everingham who claimed that he only wanted to teach Aborigines 'such things as hygiene.'[106] Two years later the Federal Minister for the Interior announced that the federal government was considering a family planning campaign for Aboriginal women in the Northern Territory on the grounds that 'unless Aboriginal women spaced their children better the high infant mortality rate among Aboriginal babies would continue.'[107] In the same year the Minister for Environment, Aborigines and the Arts, Peter Howson, endorsed the need to introduce family planning to prevent a further deterioration in Aboriginal living conditions.[108] In 1972 the Northern Territory Medical Officer told a Senate Committee that the Aboriginal population boom was responsible in part for the ill-health amongst Aboriginal children.[109]

Dr Kalokerinos linked the deaths in Central Australia to recent immunisation programs which, he claimed, increased infant susceptibility to infection in the short term. Some commentators drew attention to the contributory role of discriminatory medical and hospital practice. Dr Kalokerinos condemned the 'straight line thinking of medicine' and the ingrained racial prejudices in country hospitals which hindered professional treatment of Aboriginal patients and simplistically apportioned blame to the 'neglect, stupidity and ignorance ... of the mothers'.[110] Alice Springs community development worker Reverend Downing described hospital treatment of Aboriginal children there as 'deplorable' with contagion, disease and death spread between the children to such an extent that Aboriginal mothers only felt 'fear and hostility towards the hospital ... They were told that babies are doing well, only to be told later, sometimes in a very short space of time, that the baby has died.'[111] The Melbourne *Age* looked for more inclusive explanations of Aboriginal health:

[Aborigines were] a dispossessed people. The health problem is part of a social, economic and cultural problem. What motivation will people have for health, hygiene and better housing when their past has been destroyed, their present is lived in squalor and their future holds little hope? ... the white society as a whole must accept responsibility for the wider plight of Aboriginal people ... Aboriginal babies must not be allowed to die; their parents must not be forced to live without pride, prospects and self-respect.[112]

The differential treatment of Aboriginal health was pointed out by Peter Scott-Young, President of the Aboriginal Children's Advancement Society:

There is no doubt at all that if the babies who are dying were from white parents, there would be a national outcry for urgent action ... Only a massive and determined effort will ensure that the major problems are going to be solved before the end of the century.[113]

Improvements in Aboriginal health *were* possible. Between 1961 and 1970 the Queensland government reduced the rate of Aboriginal maternal deaths from twenty-eight to eight per thousand live births, although this was still higher than for the non-Aboriginal population, which remained steady at three.[114] However, most governments were slow to respond to the magnitude of the task. The federal government initiated further research and investigations into infant health, set aside funding to improve conditions at Alice Springs Hospital, and increased 'feeding' programs and training in hygiene in Aboriginal communities.[115] However, when Whitlam came to power in 1972, little had changed, and his first Minister for Aboriginal Affairs, Gordon Bryant, expended considerable energy and, on occasion, frustrated fury, on the task of reducing infant mortality.

THE WISDOM OF SOLOMON

In 1973 the acrimonious events surrounding the custody of a young Aboriginal girl in the Northern Territory, reported in the press across Australia and overseas, raised public sentiments to a fever pitch and provoked heated emotional debate about the whole system of fostering of Aboriginal children. The girl, Lorna,[116] was born in 1966 near Maningrida, 350 kilometres east of Darwin. A premature baby, she was flown to Darwin Hospital and then moved to the Welfare Branch's reception facility, Dundas House. At the age of eight months she was sent, with her father's approval, to live with a white family until she was strong enough to return home. Six and a half years later the girl was still with the family despite repeated requests from her parents for her return and the fact that the Department had no legal right to detain her. She was not a ward of the state and her placement was an informal arrangement between the Welfare Branch and the white family. In 1973, following further enquiries from her family about her return, departmental social workers, amongst them John Tomlinson, determined to return the girl to her parents and several visits were arranged between the girl and members of her family to accustom her to the planned move. The proposal was vehemently opposed by her 'foster' father who told the social workers, 'I know Lorna — and she's got no time for the Aboriginal race'. He then wrote to the federal Minister for Aboriginal Affairs, Gordon Bryant, seeking custody of the girl and claiming that she would be 'dead within six months' if she was sent back to her family. On 6 September, the same social workers were instructed by Bryant and their Director to advise Lorna's father to take out an injunction against the Department and in this way to avoid a sudden traumatic termination of the current arrangement. In an action unprecedented in the conservative Northern Territory administration, the social workers resolved not to comply with this advice which they believed could only end up in a drawn-out court case which, in all likelihood, would find in favour of the 'foster' parents. The very next day a social worker picked the girl up for a routine visit to her brother but took her instead to her father at Bagot Aboriginal Reserve where they were met by Bill Ryan, Director of the Northern Territory Aboriginal Legal Aid (NTALA), and then taken by charter plane (paid for by NTALA) back to Maningrida. Tomlinson visited the 'foster' parents and told them he had lost contact with the girl at Bagot Reserve.[117]

The distraught 'foster' parents and the Department soon worked out the chain of events and the scene was set for a bitter battle for custody of the girl. The story burst into the press with extraordinary headlines steeped in negative beliefs about Aboriginal customary marriage law and stereotypes of barbarism and primitivism alleging that this seven-year-old 'civilised miss' had been returned to a 'stone-age' world where she would be forced to marry a middle-aged promised husband and to undergo barbaric sexual rites:

Tribe takes girl, 7, from family to be child bride[118]

Aboriginal girl, 7, dragged off to be bride: Forget her, missionary tells white foster parents[119]

Promised Bride Forced Back To Bush Tribe: She's Only 7[120]

'Mother' to fight for child bride[121]

Aboriginal girl abducted from foster parents returned to tribal home[122]

Lorna could become an 'outcast'[123]

Lorna in humpy at river camp and Scoop pictures amazing story of Lorna's return to the stone age[124]

Foster Mum: [Lorna's] a European[125]

Child bride must obey tribal law[126]

Virginity rites fear for Lorna Tug-of-love girl may have fallen victim to ancient Aboriginal virginity rites[127]

Child Between Two Cultures[128]

As anthropologist Les Hiatt[129] later endeavoured to explain in the press, while Aboriginal girls were 'promised' to older men, marriages were not consummated before puberty and the whole system of betrothal and marriage involved complex and strictly regulated sets of social and ritual relationships conducted over many years which bound all parties in a mesh of overlapping ties and responsibilities. In fact the issue of child betrothal had nothing to do with the imperative to return Lorna to her parents and outside of the media beat-up was entirely irrelevant to the case.

It is a terrible irony that the media was so staunchly on the side of the 'foster' parents, given that the government had no legal right to separate Lorna from her natural parents or to place her with a foster family. The press reported that the 'mother' had been prescribed Valium to cope with the loss of the little girl and that, although the family had been advised by Bryant that they had no legal case, she was prepared to 'fight all the way' for the return of the 'child bride'.[130] The family solicitor's comment that their only chance was for the girl to be charged as a neglected child, prompted some debate on just what 'neglect' would mean in this context. Did the shift from suburban living to life in an Aboriginal community constitute 'neglect'? Could the girl's parents claim she was not neglected since she was living in the manner to which her family was accustomed? Did Lorna step from a normal life to a substandard life or was she returning to normal conditions from abnormally high standards? The wishes of the girl's natural family received less attention in the press although her father was reported in *Woman's Day* as saying, 'My wife ... has always been making a row with me about Lorna being in Darwin.' Her twenty-year-old brother added:

> Dad and the rest of us were upset and worried that we couldn't have Lorna with us. She's our only sister and we always asked for her back and she never came back. We wanted our family together, and now we are all together again and we are happy.[131]

The press directed considerable venom at the Labor government's handling of the case. In the Northern Territory this fitted with strong anti-Labor sentiments and parochial ideas about meddling by 'do-gooders' and 'southern stirrers'. Bryant came in for particular criticism. He and his wife had a long history of Aboriginal activism, having been foundation members of the AAL in Melbourne, and he was unpopular with the old guard of public servants in Darwin. Trapped in a political minefield, Bryant had to stick by his department and take account of the strong public opposition to Lorna's return to her family in planning his strategies. Nevertheless he was attacked repeatedly for inaction by the media despite his continual reiteration that he had no legal recourse to reclaim the girl and that she would remain in Maningrida with her family.

The engineering of the return of the young girl to her parents was an unheard-of action in Aboriginal child welfare in Australia. In direct contravention of ministerial and departmental directives, public servants and the head of a federally funded Aboriginal organisation had cooperated with an Aboriginal family to effect the return of their child. Even though they were acting in accordance with child welfare law and practice, in opposing fostering arrangements that were illegal and contrary to professional social work practice, they were widely condemned for their actions. The principal public servant involved, John Tomlinson, was one of a number of social work graduates from the southern states who took up positions in the Northern Territory from the late 1960s. His colleagues included political activists Colin Clague, a graduate of Sydney University, and his Aboriginal wife, Joyce. Both stood for parliament as Labor candidates in Central Australia and actively encouraged enrolment of Aboriginal voters in the Territory. Like Tomlinson they were regarded by most white Territorians as outsiders, radicals and communists. Clague recalled that at the time Aboriginal child welfare in the Northern Territory was in a state of crisis and that the affair would never have erupted if the system had been 'properly administered and supervised'.[132] The other principal actor in the affair, the Director of NTALA, Bill Ryan, had a strong personal interest in the case. The son of an Aboriginal mother and a white station hand, he was removed as a baby and lived in institutions in Darwin, Alice Springs, Goulburn Island and Croker Island. His memories of removal and institutionalisation were reported in the press and may have been the first personal 'confessions' of this type read by Australian audiences. He recalled severe punishments at the hands of his 'carers', his longing for contact with Aboriginal people and 'the heartbreak of lack of identity'. When he finally met his mother he learned that the missionaries had lied when they said that Aboriginal mothers did not want their babies. Formerly employed by the Northern Territory Welfare Branch, Ryan demanded a Royal Commission into the fostering system and was determined to smash the whole system of removing children. 'It is unfair to all and unreal,' he claimed, and 'dangerously cruel'.[133] Ryan told the *Northern Territory News*:

There has been a frightening history in the Territory of abduction of Aboriginal children from their families and placing them in white families and institutions.

These white homes are not able to prepare Aboriginal children for their future life.

This has meant that many Aboriginal children suffered a loss of identity which has affected their whole lives.

White authoritarians have been throughout the history of this country, trying to create white Aboriginals.

While the control of the Aboriginal Affairs Department remains in white hands, there will be no chance for Aboriginals to control their own destiny.[134]

Ryan was supported by his southern Aboriginal colleagues with the catchcry 'Aboriginal children should be left for Aborigines.'[135]

Although there was little that Bryant could do to remedy the situation, he was determined to prevent a repeat of the case. In September he told federal parliament:

the effects of this policy on the child could only be guessed, but there were outstanding examples of Aboriginal men and women who had overcome this trauma without losing their cultural identity. But we should not impose this burden on one more child, or parent or foster parent. New procedures must be developed to care for children in these situations.[136]

He pointed to the urgent need for a 'vigorous policy of developing educational and medical and other services' to stop removals:

Aboriginal children in the Northern Territory will be returned to their natural parents where this is possible ... [Lorna] was one of the many Aboriginal children who because of inadequate medical and educational facilities, had been taken away from their natural parents and reared in missions, orphanages, hospitals, institutions or private foster homes ... There are perhaps hundreds of children in orphanages and such institutions throughout Australia as well as those with foster parents who should be reconciled with their parents ... The grief that this policy has caused to Aboriginal parents is only equalled by the grief of foster parents who have been called to surrender a child they have reared as their own.[137]

Bryant also directed his department to begin programs to reunite all removed children with their parents and to set up a board of inquiry into the Northern Territory fostering scheme and a separate inquiry into how Lorna had been taken from her foster family. He announced that he would not interfere in Aboriginal customs since he believed that 'Aboriginal people are at least as wise in respect of their own affairs as we are in ours.'[138] By the end of September rumours were rife that Bryant was to be removed as minister because of criticisms of his handling of the Lorna affair, inadequate departmental controls over expenditure and his damaging off-the-cuff remarks to the press. In October Senator Cavanagh was appointed Minister of Aboriginal Affairs in his place. Cavanagh had no previous experience in the area, and, together with Aboriginal disillusionment over government actions in relation to land rights, his appointment provoked noisy protests at Parliament House and the re-erection of the Tent Embassy. Under Cavanagh stricter guidelines were introduced by the DAA to control expenditure and administration generally, and Bryant's proposed changes for Aboriginal children and his inquiries were all shelved.

Ryan and Tomlinson were also casualties of the affair. In October Ryan was dismissed from his position as Director of NTALA and offered the position of field officer instead. Disgusted he went to work with the Northern Territory Council for the Rights of Aborigines and Torres Strait Islanders. In the same month Tomlinson was suspended from office, charged with disobedience and misconduct, and demoted. In January 1974 social workers in the Territory went out on strike in his support and in protest against the government's failure to clean up child welfare. A subsequent report in the *National Times* described a system where Aboriginal children were taken without due court process from their parents, often because medical or educational facilities were lacking in their communities, and many subsequently became 'administratively lost'. The report stated that one hundred of the four hundred Aboriginal children in foster families or institutions in the Territory in 1973 fitted this category.[139] Colin Clague was president of the Alice Springs branch of the Union of Australian Social Workers and he lobbied for broader union support. He recalled that the Lorna affair acted as 'a fuse':

> We had detonated their discontent with a generally unsatisfactory situation ... the department's total lack of understanding of what social work is all about [and] major under-staffing with nine social workers doing the work of nineteen positions.[140]

In 1974 the Territory Branch of the Union called for an immediate solution to the 'generally unsatisfactory situation' that existed in the Northern Territory due to understaffing, repressive practices and the 'critical deficiences' in the handling of adoptions of Aboriginal children and welfare services generally.[141]

Progressive social workers outside the Territory linked the issue into a broader ongoing debate on the proper functioning of foster systems in Australia. Many believed that the system was breaking down and noted serious differences in understanding between the public and the profession. In an article in the *Australian*, E R Chamberlain, Head of the Social Work Department at the University of Queensland,[142] reminded readers that fostering was a 'process in which the child is cared for by another family until he is able to return to his own natural family. The child ... is never the sole responsibility of the foster parents.' It was the duty of agencies and professionals to maintain 'the overall interest of the child' and 'to re-establish the natural family'. Serious structural problems in the system had already been pointed out in articles in the *Sydney Morning Herald*.[143] There was a general lack of professionally trained workers, staff levels were inadequate to deal with the numbers of children coming into care, and there was an urgent need to review the entire process of selection, preparation of foster parents and counselling to ensure that all parties understood the 'terms of agreement', especially the ongoing responsibilities of the natural parents. According to Chamberlain the main issue raised by the Lorna affair was how to serve the best interests of Aboriginal children from families needing 'supportive services'. To date the Australian community had endorsed a process of removal and placement in institutions or with white families which ignored Aboriginal children's right 'to continuity and involvement with [their] cultural heritage'. The Northern Territory social workers' efforts to act in the 'deepest interests' of the child had provoked a 'hostile response' shaped by the desire to retain a 'system of care which is expedient but neither just nor humane'. Chamberlain continued that the primary aim should always be to keep Aboriginal families together, that a range of Aboriginal-directed services should be provided to maintain families, and that, if fostering was essential, then Aboriginal foster parents should be recruited using Aboriginal welfare staff in arrangements attractive to Aboriginal families. In conclusion he reminded readers that 'the distress of the foster family in this case should not blind us to the inalienable right of the Aboriginal child and her own parents to live together.'

Many members of the public continued to endorse policies of assimilation and negative stereotypes of Aboriginal families and saw the Lorna affair as a 'black day for assimilation'.[144] However, they could no longer rest comfortably with these assumptions which were increasingly criticised in the press. The Melbourne *Age* positioned Lorna's situation as 'symbolic of the future of all Aboriginal tribal people who are being encouraged by the federal government to decide for themselves, from within, on the pace, direction, and progress of their community development.'[145] In the Darwin press Aboriginal spokesperson and President of FCAATSI, Joe McGinness, attacked the equating of Aboriginal families with neglect in newspaper commentary as 'an absolute insult to the Aboriginal people of Australia'. He added that:

While our sympathy goes out to [the 'foster' parents] for the loss of the child in these circumstances, we should also realise the heartbreak the Aboriginal people have gone through over the years when they have their children removed from them.[146]

In May 1974 the issue was taken up by the National Aboriginal Consultative Council which called for a federal inquiry into the fostering of Aboriginal children by white families in the Northern Territory and South Australia. The NACC also demanded the opening of all holiday scheme files and the immediate return of any children kept illegally in the south.[147] Nevertheless, in all this public debate there was little informed discussion of the crux of the problem — the desperate need for major improvements to Aboriginal living conditions and services which would in the long run obviate the bureaucratic rationalisations for most removals. There was also white Australia's continuing failure to understand and respect 'the human dignity and moral rights of the Aboriginal people'.[148]

FIGHTING FOR A PRINCIPLE

Through Aboriginal and government agency pressure, significant changes in policy and practice — to attend to cultural and economic difference — occurred from the mid-1970s. This represented a new phase in the battle over the children which was fought out primarily between state and federal governments and newly formed Aboriginal organisations against a backdrop of official policies of self-determination and self-management. Although there was less media interest in this grinding struggle for change there was nevertheless growing public support for its essential aim of returning control of Aboriginal children to Aboriginal families and communities, especially in the context of the build up to the 1979 International Year of the Child. However, while the process of reform of Aboriginal child welfare had begun, the impact was proving limited. The 1974 Furnell Royal Commission into Aboriginal Affairs in Western Australia, for example, found that levels of institutionalisation of Aboriginal children were seven times higher than would be expected statistically.

The new militancy and politicisation of the issue of removal of Aboriginal children reflected a growing Aboriginal awareness and alarm at the extent of the system and its devastating effects on families and children. For many this came through involvement with the new Aboriginal legal services. Molly Dyer was the daughter of Aboriginal activist Margaret Tucker, whose autobiography, *If Everyone Cared,* provides a devastating and often quoted account of her own removal, and Dyer herself fostered many Aboriginal children as well as raising her own family. Yet it was her work at the Victorian Aboriginal Legal Service (VALS) in Melbourne that opened her eyes to the connection between child removal and adult incarceration, the high incidence of relationship breakdowns in child placements with white families — up to ninety percent before 1977[149] — and the devastating effects for the children as reflected in VALS statistics, client profiles and the increasing number of requests from young people for assistance in finding their Aboriginal families. Some parents who had lost contact with their children were also seeking legal assistance to get them back. Beginning with an initial desire simply to stop removals and placements with white families, Dyer and her counterparts elsewhere in Australia quickly broadened their platform to demand the abandonment of culturally inappropriate child welfare practices, the development of self-determining Aboriginal services to arrange placements of Aboriginal children with Aboriginal families, and the establishment of programs to encourage family maintenance and to assist with tracing family members and arranging family reunions. At the same time embryonic organisational bases were being established in most states through the voluntary work of individuals and the support of funded Aboriginal organisations. These were to develop into the state-based network of Aboriginal Child Care Agencies and the organisation, Link-Up,[150] established in 1980 in New South Wales to reunite people with their families, culture and land. Communication between these groups reinforced Aboriginal welfare workers' appreciation of commonalities in removal systems across Australia and the long-term effects on individuals.

The National Adoption Conferences, held every two years from 1976, provided an important initial forum for Aboriginal speakers where they could share ideas with professionals and link in to the general critique of adoption of the time, while maintaining Aboriginal control of the issue. Western-style adoption was unacceptable to most Aboriginal people and many saw adoption into white families as the ultimate step in the process of assimilation leading to permanent loss of the children from the Aboriginal community. The 1976 Conference was preceded by a series of Aboriginal workshops in New South Wales, Victoria, South Australia and the Northern Territory to determine issues for discussion at the Conference and to select representatives. Addressing the Conference, Molly Dyer gained unanimous support for her call for an end to 'black adoptions' and for services to keep Aboriginal children in their families and communities. She argued that to develop a strong identity and to learn to cope with racism Aboriginal children had to grow up within their own communities. Non-Aboriginal parents, selected according to criteria of mainstream family service bureaucracies, could not understand the problems of identity the children faced during adolescence and this was causing the present high incidence of placement breakdowns. The solution lay in placing children who could not remain with their own families with other Aboriginal families through the agency of self-managing Aboriginal organisations.[151]

The federal government was sympathetic to these new directions. As a member nation of the United Nations it was actively involved in the drafting of the Convention of the Rights of the Child 1978 and in preparations for the International Year of the Child. On the basis of the 1976 Adoption Conference proceedings, the federal Department of Aboriginal Affairs (DAA) was called on to draw up policy guidelines for Aboriginal adoption and fostering. The resulting policy and action plan, known as the Aboriginal Child Placement Principle, mapped out bold new directions for the care of Aboriginal children.[152] Its central premises were that Aboriginal children were to remain with their families, removals were to be a last resort and children were not to be placed in white families or institutions. When removal was deemed essential, according to criteria determined by Aboriginal practices and values, then the children were to be placed with a member of their extended family or their own community in accordance with Aboriginal customary law, or with other Aboriginal families living in close proximity. The guidelines also insisted that indigenous customs relating to child care were to be recognised and treated as paramount. Aboriginal family support programs were to be implemented to enable families to stay together, processes for Aboriginal advice to governments on issues relating to Aboriginal children were to be formalised, and Aboriginal services for families and child placement agencies should be established in all states. The desperate need for far-reaching improvements in Aboriginal family living conditions across the board was also acknowledged. In framing these principles the DAA was also influenced by the 1977 federal Royal Commission on Human Relationships, which recognised the serious problems resulting from adoption of Aboriginal children into non-Aboriginal homes. It proposed as a legislative model the Indian Child Welfare Act

1978 introduced in the United States of America following prolonged lobbying by Native Americans to bring a stop to child removals and to support indigenous child-rearing practices. The legislation returned jurisdiction over children to Native American communities and set down requirements of state agencies dealing with their children.

In 1976 the federal government established the Office of Child Care[153] (OCC) with a strong pro-active position on Aboriginal child welfare. The OCC played an important supportive role in transforming the embryonic Aboriginal voluntary organisations into a national network of Aboriginal Child Care Agencies (ACCAs) delivering professional Aboriginal foster care and link-up programs. To this end the OCC provided funding in cooperation with the states (with the exception of the Bjelke-Petersen regime in Queensland), negotiated with state instrumentalities to generate support for the transfer of services, created an organisational infrastructure and offered relevant staff training. In 1979 it organised the first national Aboriginal Child Survival Seminar in Melbourne. The OCC also funded visits between Aboriginal and other indigenous groups in the United States of America and Canada to encourage sharing of ideas and solutions in what was, after all, a new area of endeavour for all parties. Molly Dyer visited Canada and the United States of America in 1976 and embraced as a role model for Australia a project run by the Yakima Indian Nation, which had stopped the loss of up to forty children a year to non-Indian families through adoption and fostering. This project provided culturally appropriate support mechanisms to maintain family units in crisis and worked cooperatively with families who had children removed to bring about family reunion.

The combined influence of these support mechanisms and evolving Aboriginal activism in the area were evident in Dyer's expanding philosophical and tactical position as enunciated at the 1978 National Adoption Conference. Dyer's demands may have seemed radical to some in her audience but they fitted with the federal Liberal government's policy of self-management and with what Aboriginal spokespersons had been demanding for decades. Dyer told the Conference:

We are seeking quantitative changes in fundamental concepts on which ... administrators have operated for decades ... the minimum starting point to effect change is to maximise control of our own destiny.[154]

Through their 'new-found voice' in the media, Aborigines were drawing public attention to the widespread 'deprivation and the effect of our deprivation on our children' and generating public support for a 'better deal'. Nevertheless, Dyer expressed concern that pressure for change was running ahead of what administrators — constrained by departmental directives, limited resources, lack of cultural knowledge and their inability to negotiate the barriers Aborigines had erected against white interference — could hope to achieve and she was critical of the tactic adopted by some of her colleagues of forcing change 'through an angry refusal to compromise'. This could lead to a complete breakdown in communication and tensions which made 'a sham' of meetings. Ongoing negotiation to ensure sufficient resources and funding was essential for change. Already, Dyer pointed out, the Victorian Aboriginal Child Care Agency (VACCA), now acknowledged by the Victorian government as the contact point for Aboriginal child welfare matters, was overburdened and under-resourced. How could it continue without government support?[155]

The concept of a national umbrella organisation to represent the ACCAs and the interests of Aboriginal children took shape in the late 1970s. Advocated in 1979 by the First Aboriginal Child Survival Seminar in Melbourne and the National Committee for the Intenational Year of the Child, the Secretariat of National Aboriginal and Islander Child Care (SNAICC) was founded during a national conference in 1981 with the brief to 'ensure the survival of present generations and the well-being of future generations of Aboriginal and Torres Strait Islander children'. Its major platform was to lobby for the acceptance nationally of the Aboriginal Child Placement Principle and the introduction of uniform national legislation modelled on the Indian Child Welfare Act 1978. Located in Melbourne and operating initially through VACCA, SNAICC worked across a range of issues of concern to Aboriginal children and parents — removals, law, health, domestic violence, child poverty, child abuse, family neglect — to ensure that families were not subject to discriminatory or culturally inappropriate practices in the child welfare and juvenile justice systems.[156]

Brian Butler was the public face and driving force behind SNAICC. Chairperson from 1981 to 1997, Butler was also long-term director of the South Australian ACCA and a charismatic spokesperson at conferences in Australia and overseas. Born in the 1940s, he grew up in Alice Springs where his grandmother, mother and aunt had all been residents of the notorious Bungalow, giving him an early awareness of the effects of removal and institutionalisation. Like many local Aboriginal boys at that time he was sent south to school at St Francis Home and there, and in the streets of Adelaide, his understanding of the tragic legacy of removal deepened. Butler went on to attend the University of Adelaide but it was his involvement with the Aboriginal community at Port Augusta in the 1960s, assisting with family searches, reuniting lost children with their families, and developing family support services and informal substitute care programs, that determined his future as an activist. Butler was personally committed to a national approach to Aboriginal child care. This reflected in part his grave concerns about the treatment of Aboriginal families by South Australian welfare agencies as recounted to SNAICC administrator, Nigel de Souza:

> ... the mainstream welfare services were further destroying the fabric of Aboriginal families in South Australia rather than improving the quality of life for Aboriginal families, particularly the children ... That was the basic reason for wanting to wrest away from the State ... the responsibility for our kids and therefore our families. In those days we were in conflict with the DCW and all of their practices and procedures in regard to Aboriginal families and Aboriginal children.[157]

There was also the diversity in policy, legislation and practice between the states and territories that could act against the interests of Aboriginal children. His position was also tactical, demanding the acknowledgment of the 'enormous task' which required the power of national unity and the support of other Aboriginal organisations. Furthermore, it was a valuable sniping point from which to embarrass the Australian government at a time of international scrutiny by showing the extent to which it was 'being very hypocritical in [the] treatment of our people and our kids in this country'.[158] But above all, Butler believed that national control was a moral and legal obligation on the federal government that would finally bring about real change:

> All of the constitutions, aims and objectives of all the Agencies are pointing us in that direction, which demands that the Commonwealth take responsibility. They have been given the responsibility throughout the '67 Referendum to put into place appropriate pieces of legislation that would enhance the quality of

life for Aboriginal people in their country, particularly our kids. I don't see why we can't demand from the federal government that they put in place national legislation — the legislation that would put so much pressure on state and territory governments to support the principle of Aboriginal autonomy in children's programs.[159]

During the 1980s family welfare departments, often working closely with Aboriginal organisations around Australia, energetically supported the Aboriginal Child Placement Principle. In 1982 the New South Wales Aboriginal Children's Research Project Report on Aboriginal Children in Substitute Care endorsed the principle and the primary 'right of Aboriginal people to care for all their children'.[160] At the same time SNAICC lobbied hard for the principle to be enshrined in federal legislation and culturally appropriate processes put in place to safeguard the rights of Aboriginal communities for 'the care, custody and control of Aboriginal children'.[161] SNAICC had some powerful allies in this cause. In 1980 the final report of non-government organisations to the National Committee of the International Year of the Child endorsed the Principle and an overall national thrust:

the highest priority for IYC should be given to devising and imple-menting ongoing national programs to bring the well-being of Aboriginal children up to the same level as that of other children in Australia.[162]

The report noted that the Aboriginal Child Sub-committee had dubbed Aboriginal infant mortality rates as 'genocide' and demanded immediate action to reduce them. Following visits to Aboriginal communities around Australia in 1981, the World Council of Churches issued a statement that Aboriginal communities wanted:

their self-development through social justice, self-reliance and economic well-being and not through permanent dependency as the price for survival, and alienation from their people and history as a price for decent housing, proper medical facilities and white Australian educational models.[163]

In an interim report in 1982 on Aboriginal customary law, the Australian Law Reform Commission (ALRC) advocated the introduction of a federally based set of child care principles similar to the Indian Child Welfare Act 1978. In the same year the Social Welfare Administrators Conference discussed but did not endorse this proposal, despite almost unanimous Aboriginal support.[164] In 1984 the National Committee of Non-Government Organisations called for mechanisms to ensure placement of Aboriginal children with Aboriginal families. Also in 1984, in a promising move, the national Council of Social Welfare Ministers endorsed recommendations based on the Aboriginal Child Placement Principle. Two years later the ALRC made a similar recommendation in its groundbreaking report, *The Recognition of Aboriginal Customary Laws*. Significantly it recommended the introduction of federal legislation to create uniform standards in relation to Aboriginal children and it also recognised the central role of the Aboriginal extended family and the impact of past policies of removal:

> In Aboriginal societies, the role of the extended family, based on kinship relationships and obligations, is of fundamental importance in bringing up children. A child growing up in an Aboriginal community is surrounded by relatives who have responsibilities towards that child and play a meaningful role in child rearing. If, for any reason the biological parents are unable to take care of the child other arrangements will be made for care within the extended family.
>
> The fact remains that deliberate policies of assimilation in the past, together with the emphasis which sometimes tends to be placed on material comfort in determining child placements, have resulted in large numbers of Aboriginal children being removed from their families and placed within non Aboriginal families and in institutions.[165]

These outcomes were the result of tremendous effort by Aboriginal people determined to bring about positive change along directions they had laid out with the active backing and support of many non-Aboriginal professionals and members of the public. *Real* changes *were* achieved — old draconian systems of removal were finally routed, placements of Aboriginal children in substitute care with white families were reduced and the rights and practices of Aboriginal families were finally being acknowledged. However, despite these positive outcomes and a decade of concerted political action, many Aboriginal demands still had not been met. SNAICC's platform of national policy and legislation was rejected and Aboriginal child welfare remained a state and territory responsibility. Despite Aboriginal insistence that the Aboriginal Child Placement Principle be made a statutory obligation in all jurisdictions, it was only incorporated into legislation in the Northern Territory (1983), Victoria (1984), New South Wales (1987) and South Australia (1988). At the turn of the twenty-first century in Western Australia, Queensland and Tasmania it remained enshrined in policy only.

Aboriginal Child Care Agencies around Australia continued to struggle to provide professional services with limited funding and resources and, while often loaded down with crisis cases involving Aboriginal families and children referred from state child welfare services, they continued to be sidelined in government policy and decision-making processes. Many family and child welfare departments continued to work predominantly through non-Aboriginal staff, many of whom found it difficult to abandon assimilatory models and paradigms which treated Aboriginal children in terms of economic and social disadvantage rather than cultural difference, and which stressed functions of social order and control rather than attending to the children's best interests.[166] Of particular concern was the mounting evidence from the early 1970s of a new wave of separation of Aboriginal children from their families through the combined actions of the police, family and community welfare authorities, and the juvenile justice system.[167] Nor had parity of Aboriginal living conditions with the wider community been achieved.[168]

Why was this so? Why did Aboriginal people have to struggle so hard to achieve what other Australians assumed to be their natural rights? And what of the official policies of self-determination and self-management which fitted neatly with Aboriginal demands? There are no simple answers. Plans to improve Aboriginal living conditions were undermined by the sheer scale of Aboriginal deprivation and the vast gap between Aboriginal and mainstream living standards. Federal and state governments seemed to be unable to channel the vast resources of money and time required to bring about real improvements. Instead, they tinkered around the edges and then left Aborigines to defend themselves in the face of a growing white backlash which claimed that Aborigines were receiving and squandering undeserved privileges and resources. At the same time positive gains were eroded by the devastating effects of broader socioeconomic change on Aboriginal communities — the high levels of unemployment and forced migration to urban areas generated by the introduction of equal pay in the pastoral industry, the rural recession and changes in pastoral and farming methods and technology, and the worldwide economic crisis which laid the foundations for a new phenomenon of mass youth unemployment.[169] There were other problems — continuing high birth rates and a gradual lowering of infant mortality rates left families with many dependants to support on shrinking incomes, and there was continuing mistrust of Aboriginal families towards police, welfare officers and other outsiders and resistance to their interventions. To many middle-class white Australians, Aboriginal families continued to represent the scenario of deprivation, chaos and sullen rebelliousness from which children had to rescued 'for their own good'.

At another level the issue of Aboriginal child welfare had become entwined in a tug of war over state rights as governments sorted out jurisdictions in relation to Aboriginal affairs. Aboriginal child welfare, with the exception of the Northern Territory, had always been a state matter and the states were unwilling to relinquish control. There are a host of possible reasons for this resistance — the lure of ongoing federal grants, the economic self-interest of departments whose major clientele was now Aboriginal children and families, and continuing adherence to processes of social order where state instrumentalities endeavoured to control Aboriginal families through their children. There was also considerable state resistance to transferring responsibilities to Aboriginal organisations and families. Former Director of the federal Office of Child Care (OCC) Marie Coleman recalled hostility from some authorities to handing children over to what they considered were 'second class' Aboriginal organisations lacking professional skills and training.[170] There was also resistance to appointing Aboriginal staff to key internal policy and decision-making positions. Furthermore, the more conservative states had never fully abandoned the policy of assimilation and were mistrustful of new federal policy directions. Brian Butler sums up the states' response as follows:

[the states] argue like mad and resist any form of national legislation that is going to prevent them from introducing legislation that would undermine what Aboriginal and Islander people really want from the national legislation. I think that the States still would want to have that control, whereas we understand that they don't want to relinquish any control over any aspects to the Federal Government. We know that autonomy for Aboriginal programs, whether it be

ACCAs or housing or health or education programs is never going to have an easy ride because there is always going to be resistance from the States.[171]

Coleman also recalled conflicts within and between federal departments that thwarted the work of the OCC: elements within the Department of Social Security opposed OCC initiatives in Aboriginal child welfare as untraditional and too radical; the DAA wanted to take over control of the issue from the OCC; and the Department of Prime Minister and Cabinet expressed concerns over OCC procedures of accounting for Aboriginal expenditure.[172] Writing in the 1970s about the administration of Aboriginal affairs, activist A Pittock stated that all advance was blunted by the bureaucracy with its 'vested interests, conservatism and inertia' and that divisions between administrators and politicians 'made the administration of Aboriginal affairs chaotic and inefficient and ... stifled and frustrated numerous Aboriginal initiatives.'[173]

It was also increasingly evident that while former draconian systems of removal *may* have been abandoned, associated procedures and practices had simply been transferred in the flurry of departmental renaming and restructuring. Indeed, they had become institutionalised in the 'new' culture of Aboriginal family welfare which remained committed to the strategy of removing and resocialising Aboriginal children in the interests of maintaining social order and social control. This was borne out in research by Fay Gale into incarceration of Aboriginal juveniles in Adelaide in 1987. Like Elizabeth Sommerlad in the late 1970s, Gale[174] found that Aboriginal juveniles continued to be incarcerated at far higher rates than juveniles from any other background. She attributed this to a set of practices institutionalised at all levels in a remorseless system involving police, child welfare and juvenile justice staff and authorities. This system discriminated against Aboriginal juveniles at each stage, from the point of pick up by the police, through the various stages of assessment by social workers to the eventual sentencing by the courts, with the inevitable outcome that they were far more likely to be placed in the protection of the state and separated from their families. Research in the 1980s also showed continuing high levels of placement of Aboriginal children by welfare authorities in substitute care.[175] In Western Australia in 1989, for example, Aboriginal children made up forty-four percent of children in substitute care although Aborigines constituted only 2.5 percent of the state population. The 1991 Royal Commission into Aboriginal Deaths in Custody concluded that such figures 'lend weight to claims that an institutionalisation process is still being experienced by Aboriginal people'.[176] The 1997 *Bringing Them Home* report similarly found alarming rates of separation of Aboriginal children from their families in the mid-1990s through the agency of child welfare authorities and the juvenile justice system. Many of the recommendations from these national inquiries have yet to adopted or to be implemented in a satisfactory manner.

In the midst of the national and international attention on the Stolen Generations issue, Australia also faced criticisms about its treatment of British child migrants exposed in television programs such as 'Leaving of Liverpool'[177] screened in 1989 and in government inquiries here and in Britain during the 1990s.[178] In 1996, as a signatory to the United Nations Convention on the Rights of the Child, Australia submitted a report to the United Nations Committee on the Rights of the Child which showed significant 'transgressions' between the Convention and Australian law. Clearly Australians still have much to do to ensure the proper care and protection of the rights of *all* children.

NAN AND POP AND THE KIDS

While debates raged in the public arena, hidden away from the public gaze were the thousands of seriously disadvantaged Aboriginal families striving to remain together in the face of rapid social change. Faced by growing unemployment, many were only able to survive through the support of family networks and their new access to the benefits and services enjoyed for many years by the rest of the Australian community, as well as top-up assistance in education, health and housing. The *Regional Report of the Inquiry into Underlying Issues in Western Australia* by the Royal Commission into Aboriginal Deaths in Custody provides a very moving history of the struggles of one extended family to make ends meet from the 1970s into the present. First published in 1991, this account is re-presented here in an abridged form with additional comments from a family member.[179] It provides invaluable insights into the private battles waged by Aboriginal families trapped in the same nexus of poverty, cultural dislocation, discrimination and despair all over Australia. It seriously challenges the view that Aboriginal people 'get heaps'. It also highlights significant differences between Aboriginal and mainstream Australian families, in particular, the pivotal role of Aboriginal grandparents in maintaining family cohesion. The driving imperative in Aboriginal families to do all that one can to help one's family members and to keep them within the protective circle of the family is also powerfully evoked.

Nan and Pop, the principal actors in this story both passed away in the early 1990s. They were raised in the rural south-west where they and their parents worked as casual farm labourers. Pop eventually found regular employment as a council road worker and purchased a small block of land in town. In 1970 the family moved to Perth for the following reasons:

> Pop went on long-service leave from the Shire and returned to find his job given to a white man;

> Many other relatives had moved to Perth when it became difficult to find farm jobs due to the rural recession;

> To secure employment, their sons moved to Perth and were residing in a working boys hostel in Perth controlled by the Native Welfare Department;

> Pop thought he might secure permanent employment in the city to maintain his family.

Through family contacts Pop eventually found work as a wharfie on the Fremantle docks and the family moved into a small State Housing Commission (later Homeswest) home nearby. When Pop retired in the late 1970s due to ill health, the family moved to a suburb closer to Perth.

Nan and Pop had six sons who were aged thirty-six to forty-three in 1991. In that year they had twenty-three grandchildren ranging in age from seven to twenty-two and four great-grandchildren with a further one expected. One son had died aged twenty-four leaving two small children for whom Nan and Pop assumed responsibility after their mother developed a dependency on alcohol, considered by family to be detrimental to the children's welfare. Another son had five children from his first marriage — his wife died in a car accident — and three children from his second marriage which ended in divorce. Nan and Pop also reared seven of these children from an early age. This son had also developed a dependency on alcohol, which once again was considered by family to be to the detriment of the children's welfare. In addition to their grandchildren, Nan and Pop also raised a niece, two nephews and a non-Aboriginal girl. This made a total of twenty children reared by Nan and Pop. There were also innumerable stays by young relatives needing short-term accommodation.

Nan and Pop were determined to look after these children and that no one in their extended family would be taken away into state care. Although their commitment saved the government thousands of dollars over the years they received little in the way of financial support. As a result they had to make many personal sacrifices, although they do not see it this way. They never begrudged their decision and felt they gained untold joy and love in caring for their family.

Nan and Pop's other four sons married and had families and were in regular employment. Only two completed Year Ten and the rest left school at Year Eight. One son subsequently gained a university degree at the age of thirty-six via an employer sponsorship and presently occupies a management position. Another son became a qualified house painter, the eldest is a clerk and the youngest a labourer. Of the six sons, four have been arrested with two being sentenced to terms of imprisonment. From when they started work at the age of fifteen, the sons willingly helped to 'top up' Nan and Pop's family budget from their meagre wages.

In 1991 fourteen of their twenty-three grandchildren were still at school. The nine that had left school ranged from fifteen to twenty-two years in age. One left early due to an intellectual handicap, two were expelled, another left after Year Nine, and another due to an early pregnancy. Four completed Year Ten. Of the nine, one earned a salary as an Aboriginal education worker, two received supporting parents benefits, and six received unemployment benefits. Apart from the two sole parents, five grandchildren were in de facto relationships. One had her own Homeswest accommodation, the other two were transient between relatives. Three, including the handicapped grand-daughter with two dependent children, resided with Nan and Pop. Two others lived with their parents and one with his de facto wife.

Low income and the sheer volume of basic needs brought about by family, social, cultural, and technological factors ensured that Nan and Pop had little choice about such lifestyle matters as locality, enterprise, health and education. In 1991 their fortnightly household budget was as follows:

Income:		Expenses:	
Nan (aged pension)	$335	Rent	$105
Pop (aged pension)	$245	Food	$300
Board	$200	Electricity/gas	$ 50
2 dependants	$ 34	Phone	$ 50
		Transport	$ 50
		Schooling	$ 70
		Clothing	$ 70
		Medication	$ 20
		Hire purchase	$ 50
		Entertainment	$ 40
Total	$814	Total	$785

Balance $29

This budget did not allow for unplanned contingencies such as funerals, transient relatives, school excursions and activities, extended family crises and credit payments. These expenses from time to time prevented, or delayed, regular financial commitments being met. Insufficient income forced a continuous reliance on relatives and welfare organisations to provide a 'top up' in order to survive from pay day to pay day or to meet any other necessities. Generally, final days leading up to pay day meant a diet of cheap bread and meat.

Social Security payments to two young adult grandchildren were received on the alternate week to that when Nan and Pop received their pension. Within two days of that payment being received, the total was spent on food, clothes, taxis (Nan and Pop had no car) or entertainment. A heavy reliance was then placed upon the financial resources of Nan and Pop during the period between when they became broke and the next pay day, a period of ten or more days. In addition, Nan and Pop provided food and support to the friends and peer relatives of the grandchildren who stayed from time to time. There was a chronic lack of money to acquire basic household necessities such as furniture so there was a heavy reliance on welfare organisations for these things.

Nan had to learn her way around the welfare and charity network. People from the church dropped off cheap groceries and fruit and the kids were sent out to get damaged and day old bread from the bakery. They did the rounds of the secondhand shops, and charitable groups sometimes gave them blankets and furniture. Occasionally family members brought bush food — mainly kangaroo — which was cooked up with damper. It was a matter of surviving and making do.

A foster allowance was paid to Nan and Pop for two grandchildren up to 1982. However, when Nan informed the Department for Community Services in an interview that their father had been working (albeit casual employment) and that he had given her a little money towards the keep of the children, the Department cut off the payments. Repeated approaches by Nan were to no avail. Ironically, early in 1991 she was advised to reapply but was so disillusioned by the whole process that she did not feel like going through it all again. This sort of response was not unusual amongst Aboriginal people like Nan for whom approaches to welfare authorities were often restrained.

In 1991 Nan and Pop had been living in their current Homeswest house for over thirteen years. It was in a dilapidated condition. For several years from the commencement of tenancy the dwelling received only a replacement door handle for which Homeswest demanded payment. Unsealed eaves allowed cold air to penetrate through the rooms. The shower leaked through the wall into the adjoining bedroom. Brick mortar had become chalky causing bricks to become loose. The roof was sagging due to drainage malfunction. The internal walls required painting and plaster work. Floor coverings were worn and had to be removed in some rooms leaving bare boards. As a consequence the house did not provide much protection from the elements. This was particularly so during the winter months, and family members suffered from chronic illnesses such as asthma, arthritis and bronchitis. Nan and Pop's bedroom was virtually an icebox. With only a small one-bar heater, they had to keep warm by sitting very close to the heater or remaining fully covered up in bed. The other alternative was to sit next to a wood fireplace in the lounge room amongst the noise of television and children, a fireplace that generated little warmth because of the unsealed eaves and that was frequently unused because of problems accessing a regular wood supply. When no wood was available, the small bar heater served the whole household. When Homeswest finally agreed to install a gas heater Pop was unable to benefit from it because the gas aggravated his asthma.

Both Nan and Pop suffered from chronic diabetes and should have been on special diets to minimise sugar levels. However, limited finances dictated a diet that could accommodate all members of the household, basically, one that consisted of plenty of red meat.

Approaches by the Aboriginal Medical Service for government assistance were rejected. Some government authorities did recognise that Nan and Pop required help. The Home and Community Care program provided assistance in some household duties one day a week. Organisations like the Aboriginal Medical Service and Southcare also helped.

Despite these handicaps Nan and Pop continued to care for their family. Their grand-daughter with the intellectual handicap was frequently in trouble with the police but they always stepped in and brought her back home so that she and her two sons could be properly cared for. One of the boys had a speech impediment and required therapy twice a week. Nan and Pop made sure that he attended these sessions and payed the $10 for transport. They received no additional financial assistance for this.

Nan and Pop's home became a point for surveillance by police. From time to time teenage and young adult grandchildren would come home drunk with others and become boisterous and aggressive and often fight amongst themselves. Sometimes Nan was forced to call in the police which could lead to arrests. Police labelled the grandchildren as 'troublemakers'. One afternoon, four plain clothes officers raided the home. They did not knock and identify themselves but simply walked in through the open front and rear doors. They caught Nan and Pop in the kitchen having a snack. They asked for one of the grandchildren and took him to his room and searched it for goods he was supposed to have stolen. No search warrant was produced. They then took him to the police station for questioning. Nan and Pop were not requested to accompany him or to be present while he was questioned. At the station the youth was punched and asked to own up to a number of break and enter offences. He admitted to one and signed a confession prepared by police so that he could get away from the beatings. The Aboriginal Legal Service advised him to plead guilty. No follow-up action was taken by the family.

Whenever a grandchild was arrested Nan and Pop assisted with matters such as bail. They had an active sense of justice and fair play and used their personal strength to fight for their loved ones. Each time a grandchild was due for a court appearance they were reminded by Nan and Pop and both grandparents would be present in court to provide support.

It would appear that for the grandchildren little had changed since Nan and Pop's days in terms of skills, literacy, living conditions and employment opportunities. The family's difficulties in accessing government services in housing, employment, aged care, handicapped care, legal aid and so on, were indicative of both limited advocacy skills within the family and incompetence, flavoured with racial prejudice, on the part of service providers. The family was reduced to a day-to-day existence with no hopes for the future. Pop often observed that he had worked hard all his life and that surely he was now entitled to government assistance with some obvious needs for his family without being forced to continually justify himself. He stated that the constant need to heckle and hassle for basic services and entitlements was making him 'bitter'. In these circumstances it was often Nan and Pop's great sense of humour that kept them going. Pop especially was able to transform hurtful experiences at the hands of government officers into hilarious stories that entertained his grandchildren and also taught them about how Nyungar people could be treated by the world outside the circle of their family and community.

There were many times when Nan and Pop felt that if things kept going the way they were there was not much hope for the future. Through their own personal encounters with non-Aboriginal people and government systems they adopted a pessimistic outlook. When Homeswest finally agreed to paint the inside of the house, they were afraid to move away fearing that they would not be 'let back in'. This fear was due to Homeswest pressuring them to move into a pensioner unit, an offer they refused on the grounds that if they couldn't house their grandchildren they would end up homeless and on the streets and they were not to prepared to let that happen.

And what of the grandchildren? Despite the material hardships of their daily lives these children grew up surrounded by love and support. They heard from other Nyungar children how different life could be in an institution or foster family. At Nan and Pop's they knew they could go to the fridge at any time, they had a room and a warm bed and they had lots of other children to play with. Nan and Pop were there to keep them in line and to make sure they went to school. They were always there on the sideline to cheer them on when they played sport. As Nyungar children growing up in an often hostile racist environment they learned how to deal with taunts and ridicule and the very real threat of violence on the streets of Perth. They had the safety and warmth of their family to comfort their hurts and the certainty of the back-up, not only of Nan and Pop, but of a wide range of relatives in the case of trouble. They knew where they came from and who they belonged to. There were always visitors coming and going who were interested in them and who cared about them, and older relatives who told them stories about their family. They were part of their extended family network and of the broader Nyungar community.

Nan and Pop gained a lot of respect for the way they cared for their family. In the late 1980s Nan was chosen as the South Perth City Council Citizen of the Year. She was nominated by the primary school that many of her grandchildren had attended. They were also greatly loved and respected by the Nyungar community. Thousands of Nyungars and wadjelas (white people) attended their funerals. Nan died in her eldest son's home surrounded by the children she had devoted her life to caring for. It was a profoundly sad but also strengthening experience to see their deep love for this old dying woman.

Most of the grandchildren are now grown up and have settled down with their own families and are in employment or studying. One grandson is buying his own home. They say they owe this all to the love and care they received from Nan and Pop and wonder how things would have turned out if they had not been there to care for them. There are now twenty-nine great-grandchildren. A son has since passed away and the alcoholic son has stopped drinking. The way of family life cherished by Nan and Pop and Nyungar families generally, of providing a home where all the children and other family members are unconditionally welcome and loved, lives on in the homes of their sons and grown-up grandchildren.

Aboriginal children living with white families or in institutions grow up outside this family-based 'safety zone'. They may have been fortunate — like Louis Johnson — to experience deep love from their adoptive families and the benefits of a comfortable life and educational opportunities that are out of the reach of most Aboriginal families, but they do not experience the deep emotional bonds that come from growing up within this wide circle of family. They do not become part of the kaleidoscope of events that binds family members together and that builds up living family histories over the years. Nor do they learn who they truly are by knowing how they fit into Aboriginal society and culture. Many grow up feeling alienated from white *and* black Australians and, as adults, spend years trying to locate their Aboriginal families and then struggling to learn how to fit in with their way of life.[180] It is a sobering fact of life that the experience of growing up in an Aboriginal family also acts as a form of 'life insurance' for young people living in a racist society. Drawing on a wealth of experiences, Aboriginal families teach their children how to survive racism — how to feel strong about their Aboriginal identity in the face of racist taunts and slurs, and teaching them that there are whole networks of relatives who will unconditionally back them up if trouble breaks out. Children learn the 'numbers game' at an early age — the importance in a potentially hostile world of moving within the 'safety zone' of groups of relatives who can protect them from harm. The tragic murder of Louis Johnson bears out the significance of this survival strategy. Nan and Pop's grandchildren were walking the 'unsafe streets' of Perth in the early 1990s when demonstrators demanding the punishment of Aboriginal youth involved in high speed car chases held up nooses to cheering crowds. They walked together and they survived. Louis Johnson, walking home alone from a party late at night was murdered. This terrible outcome and the interventions that shaped Louis' short life cannot be forgotten. They must be remembered in our hearts. At the same time we must act to ensure that such tragedies never happen again.

Maps

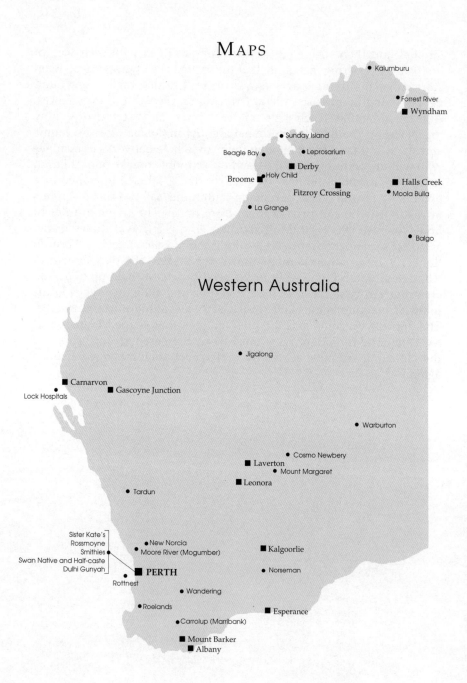

Kalumburu

Forrest River
■ Wyndham

Sunday Island

Beagle Bay
Leprosarium
■ Derby
Broome Holy Child
Fitzroy Crossing ■ Halls Creek
Moola Bulla

La Grange

Balgo

Western Australia

Jigalong

■ Carnarvon
Lock Hospitals
■ Gascoyne Junction

Warburton

Cosmo Newbery
■ Laverton
Mount Margaret
■ Leonora

Tardun

Sister Kate's
Rossmoyne
Smithies
Swan Native and Half-caste
Dulhi Gunyah

New Norcia
Moore River (Mogumber)
■ Kalgoorlie

■ PERTH
Rottnest

Norseman

Wandering

Roelands

Carrolup (Marribank)

Esperance

■ Mount Barker
■ Albany

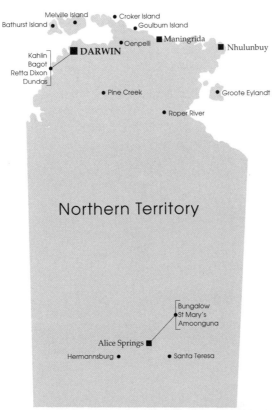

Melville Island
Croker Island
Bathurst Island
Goulburn Island
Oenpelli
Maningrida
Nhulunbuy
Kahlin
Bagot
Retta Dixon
Dundas
DARWIN
Pine Creek
Groote Eylandt
Roper River

Northern Territory

Bungalow
St Mary's
Amoonguna
Alice Springs
Hermannsburg
Santa Teresa

Oodnadatta

South Australia

Yalata
Koonibba
Colebrook (Quorn)
Umeewarra
Port Augusta
Poonindie
Point Pearce
Gerard
Port Augusta
Swan Reach
ADELAIDE
St Francis
Point McLeay

- Cape York
- Mapoon
- Weipa
- Lockhart
- Aurukun
- Hope Vale (Cape Bedford)
- Mitchell River
- Bloomfield
- Cairns
- Normanton
- Yarrabah
- Cardwell
- Doomadgee
- Fantome Island
- Palm Island

Queensland

- Woorabinda
- Fraser Island
- Taroom
- Cherbourg (Barambah)
- Ipswich
- Cunnamulla
- Deebing Creek
- BRISBANE
- Purga
- Myora

- Armidale
- Kinchela

New South Wales

- Parramatta
- SYDNEY
- Warangesda
- Cootamundra Home
- Bomaderry
- Cumeroongunja

Victoria

■ Mooroopna

● Coranderrk
■ **MELBOURNE**

● Lake Tyers

● Lake Condah

● Wybalenna

Badger Island ■
● Cape Barren Island

■ La Trobe
■ Launceston

Tasmania

Orphan School ■
■ **HOBART**

Oyster Cove ●
● Bruny Island
■ Port Arthur

CHRONOLOGY

1814/15
Native Institution for Aboriginal children at Parramatta (NSW)

1830
Orphan School (government, Tas)

1833
Wybalenna (government, Tas)

1834
Poor Laws (Britain)

Abolition of slavery in British colonies

1836
G A Robinson appointed Commandant of Wybalenna

1837
Report of the British House of Commons Select Committee Inquiry into Conditions of Aboriginal Peoples of British Colonies

1841
Rottnest Island Prison (WA)

1842
Smithies Wesleyan Mission (WA)

1844
An Ordinance for the Protection, Maintenance and Upbringing of Orphans and other Destitute Children and Aborigines (SA)

An Act to prevent the enticing of girls of the Aboriginal race away from school, or from any service in which they are employed (WA)

1846
New Norcia Mission (Catholic, WA)

1847
Oyster Cove (Tas)

1850
Poonindie Mission (SA)

1859
Point McLeay Mission (Aborigines Friends' Association, SA)

1860
Board for the Protection of Aborigines to supervise mission and government stations Ebenezer (1859–1904), Lake Hindmarsh (1859–1904), Lake Tyers (1861–1908), Ramahyuck (1862–1905), Framlingham (1865–1890), Lake Condah (1867–1917), Coranderrk (1863–1923) (Vic)

1864
Neglected and Criminal Children's Act (Vic)

South Australia responsible for Aborigines in the Northern Territory

1865
Industrial and Reformatory Schools Act (Qld)

1867
Industrial Schools Act (Tas)

1868
Point Pearce Mission (Yorke Peninsula Aborigines Mission, SA)

1869
Aborigines Protection Act (Vic)

1870
Swan Native and Half-caste Mission (Anglican, WA)

1874
Industrial Schools Act (WA)

Neglected and Criminal Children's (Amendment) Act (Vic)

1876
Indian Act (USA)

1877
Hermannsburg Mission (Lutheran, NT)
Durundur Mission (Catholic, Qld)

1879
Orphanages Act (Qld)

1880
Warangesda Aboriginal Station (Association for the Protection of Aborigines, NSW)

1881
State Children's Relief Act (NSW)

1882
Daly River Mission (Catholic, NT)

1883
Aborigines Protection Board (NSW, 1883–1940)

1886
Aborigines Protection Act (Vic)

Aborigines Protection Act (WA)

Aborigines Protection Board (WA, 1886–1940)

Cape Bedford (renamed Hopevale Mission, Lutheran, Qld)

1887
Neglected Children's Act (Vic)

1889
Constitution Act (WA)

1890
Beagle Bay Mission (Catholic, WA)

1891
Mapoon Mission (Presbyterian, Qld)

1892
Deebing Creek (Presbyterian, Qld)
Yarrabah Mission (Anglican, Qld)

1893
Girls Training Home, Warangesda Aboriginal Station (NSW)

1895
State Children's Act (SA, NT)

Myora on Stradbroke Island (government, Qld)

1896
Report on Aborigines of Queensland
Children's Protection Act
Adoption Act (WA)

1897
Aboriginal Protection and Restriction on the Sale of Opium Act (Qld)

Aborigines Department (Qld, 1897–1939)

W E Roth appointed Northern Protector, Chief Protector 1904–6 (Qld)

Aborigines Act (WA)

Aborigines Department (WA, 1897–1905)

Fraser Island (government then Anglican 1900–1904, Qld)

1898
Koonibba Mission (Lutheran, SA)

Sunday Island Mission (private, WA)

1899
Aborigines Regulations (Vic)

1901
Aboriginal Protection and Restriction on the Sale of Opium (Amendment) Act (Qld)

Constitution Act (C'wth)

State Children Relief Act (NSW)

1902
Electoral Act (C'wth)

1904
Aurukun Mission (Presbyterian, Qld)

Barambah Home (1932 renamed Cherbourg Settlement, government, Qld)

Mitchell River Mission (Anglican, Qld)

Weipa Mission (Presbyterian, Qld)

1905
Neglected Children and Juvenile Offenders Act (NSW)

Roth Royal Commission (WA)

Aborigines Act (WA)

Aborigines Department (WA, 1905–36)

1906
Children's Court Act (Vic)

1907
State Children Act (WA)

1908
Roper River Mission (Christian Missionary Society, NT)

Lock Hospitals (WA)

Drysdale River Mission (renamed Kalumburu, Catholic, WA)

Lake Tyers (the only official government station in Victoria)

Bomaderry Children's Home (NSW)

1909
Aborigines Protection Act (NSW)

Dulhi Gunyah Orphanage (Australian Aborigines Mission, Perth, WA)

1910
Aborigines Act (Vic)

Aboriginals Act (SA, NT)

Melville Island Mission (Catholic, NT)

Lombadina Mission (Catholic, WA)

Walcott Inlet Mission (renamed Kunmunya, Presbyterian, WA)

1911
Northern Territory Aboriginal affairs transferred from South Australia to the Commonwealth.

Aboriginals Ordinance (C'wth)

Aboriginals Department (C'wth, 1911–53)

Aboriginals Act (SA)

Aborigines Department (SA, 1911–18)

Aborigines Act Amendment Act (WA)

State Children's Act (Qld)

Bathurst Island Mission (Catholic, NT)

Cootamundra Aboriginal Girls Home (NSW)

Taroom Aboriginal Settlement (moved and renamed Woorabinda, government, Qld)

Moola Bulla Station (WA)

1912
Cape Barren Island Reserve Act (Tas)

1913
Royal Commission on the Aborigines (SA)

Darwin Half-caste Home (government, NT)

Mona Mona Mission (Seventh Day Adventists, Qld)

Forrest River Mission (Anglican, WA)

1914
J W Bleakley appointed Chief Protector of Aborigines (retired 1942, Qld)

Bungalow Children's Home (government, NT)

Koonibba Children's Home (Lutheran, SA)

1915
Aborigines Protection Amending Act (NSW)

A O Neville appointed Chief Protector of Aborigines (retired 1940, WA)

Neglected Children's Act (Vic)

Carrolup Native Settlement (government, WA)

Purga Mission (Salvation Army, government, Qld)

1916
Goulburn Island Mission (Methodist, NT)

1918
Aborigines Protection (Amendment) Act (NSW)

Advisory Council of Aborigines (SA, 1918–39)

Aboriginals Ordinance (NT)

Children of the State Act (Tas)

Kinchela Aboriginal Boy's Home (government, NSW)

Lock Hospitals closed (WA)

Moore River Native Settlement (government, WA)

Palm Island (government, Qld)

1919
Children's Maintenance Act (Vic)

1920
Adoption of Children Act (Tas)

Oenpelli (government, Christian Missionary Society from 1925, NT)

1921
Emerald River Mission (Christian Missionary Society, NT)

Elcho Island Mission (Methodist, NT)

Mount Margaret Mission (United Aborigines Mission, WA)

1923
South Australia Aborigines (Training of Children) Act

Child Welfare Act (NSW)

1924
Lockhart River Mission (Anglican, Qld)

Aboriginals Ordinance (NT)

Oodnadatta Children's Home (United Aborigines Mission, SA)

1925
Adoption of Children Act (SA)

1926
Maintenance Act (SA)

1927
Dr C Cook appointed Chief Protector (resigned 1939, NT)

Wood Royal Commission (WA)

Colebrook Children's Training Home (United Aborigines Mission, SA)

1928
Aborigines Act (Vic)

Adoption of Children Act (Vic)

1929
Bleakley Report (NT)

1931
Pine Creek Boys Home (government, NT)

Doomadgee Mission (Brethren Assemblies, Qld)

1933
Warburton Ranges Mission (United Aborigines Mission, WA)

1934
Aborigines Act (SA)

Protection of Aborigines and Restriction on the Sale of Opium Amendment Act (Qld)

Moseley Royal Commission (WA)

Sister Kate's Children's Home (government, WA)

1935
Adoption of Children Ordinance (C'wth, NT)

Infant's Welfare Act (Tas)

Port Keats Mission (Catholic, NT)

Santa Teresa Mission (Catholic, NT)

Yirrkala Mission (Methodist, NT)

Adoption of Children Act (Qld)

1936
Aborigines Protection (Amendment) Act (NSW)

Aboriginals Ordinance (NT)

Native Administration Act (WA)

Department of Native Affairs (WA, 1936–54)

Children's Protection Act (SA)

1937
National meeting of Ministers and Heads of Native Affairs Departments

Umeewarra Mission (Open Brethren Assemblies, SA)

1938
Carrolup Settlement reopened (WA)

1939
Aboriginals Ordinance (NT)

Aboriginals Preservation and Protection Act (Qld)

Director of Native Affairs Office (Qld)

Torres Strait Islanders Act (Qld)

Aborigines Act Amendment Act (SA)

Aboriginal Protection Board (SA, 1939–62)

Child Welfare Act (NSW)

1940
Aborigines Protection (Amendment) Act (NSW)

Aborigines Welfare Board (NSW, 1940–69)

Balgo Hills Mission (Catholic, WA)

Cosmo Newbery (government, United Aborigines Mission, WA)

1941

Aboriginal Ordinance (NT)

Child Welfare Ordinance (C'wth, NT)

Social Services Act (C'wth)

Child Endowment Act (C'wth)

Garden Point (Catholic, NT)

Melville Island (Catholic, NT)

Croker Island (Methodist, NT)

Groote Eyelandt (Anglican, NT)

Roelands Children's Home
(Interdenominational, WA)

Holy Child Orphanage (Catholic, WA)

1942

Social Services Amendment Act (C'wth)

1943

Aborigines Protection (Amendment) Act (NSW)

1944

Natives (Citizenship Rights) Act (WA)

Wandering Mission (Catholic, WA)

Social Services Amendment Act (C'wth)

1945

Cape Barren Island Reserve Act (Tas)
Jigalong Mission (Apostolic Church, WA)

1946

St Mary's Home for Aboriginal Children
(Australian Aborigines Mission, NT)

Retta Dixon Home (Australian Inland Mission,
NT)

Gerard (United Aborigines Mission, SA)

1947

Child Welfare Act (WA)

Social Services Act (C'wth)

Oodnadatta Mission reopened (United
Aborigines Mission, SA)

1948

United Nations Convention on the Prevention
and Punishment of the Crime of Genocide

United Nations Declaration of Human Rights

Nationality and Citizenship Act (C'wth)

Bateman Report (WA)

S G Middleton appointed Director of Native
Affairs (WA)

1949

Tardun Children's Mission and St Joseph's Farm
(Catholic, WA)

1951

Conference of State and Federal Ministers of
Aboriginal Affairs (C'wth)

(Sir) Paul Hasluck appointed Minister for
Territories

Mogumber Methodist Mission (formerly Moore
River Native Settlement, WA)

Marribank Farm School (formerly Carrolup
Native Settlement, Baptist from 1952, WA)

Alvan House Hostel for Girls (government, WA)

1952

Conference of State and Federal Ministers for
Aboriginal Affairs (C'wth)

Cosmo Newbery (government, WA)

McDonald House Hostel for Native Boys
(government, WA)

1953

Aboriginals Ordinance (C'wth, NT)

Welfare Ordinance (C'wth, NT)

Welfare Branch (C'wth, NT, 1953–64)

1954

Native Welfare Act (WA)

Department of Native Welfare (WA, 1954–72)

Child Welfare Act (Vic)

Aborigines Welfare Ordinance (C'wth, NT)

H Giese appointed Director of Welfare (NT)

1957

Child Welfare Ordinance (C'wth, NT)

McLean Inquiry into the Operation of the 1928
Aborigines Act (Vic)

Aborigines Act (Vic)

Aborigines Welfare Board (Vic, 1957–68)

Katakuta Aboriginal Home for Young Men
(government, WA)

1958
Child Welfare Ordinance (C'wth, NT)

Special Committee on Native Matters (WA)

1959
Social Services Act (C'wth)

Wards Employment Ordinance (C'wth, NT)

1960
Native Welfare Act Amendment (WA)

Social Welfare Act (Vic)

Child Welfare Act (Tas)

1961
Native Welfare Council (C'wth)

Select Committee on Voting Rights (C'wth)

Welfare Ordinance (NT)

1962
Aboriginal Affairs Act (SA)

Department of Aboriginal Affairs, Aboriginal
Advisory Board (SA)

Electoral Act (C'wth)

1963
Native Welfare Act (WA)

Aborigines Protection (Amendment) Act (NSW)

1964
Report of Special Committee of Inquiry into
Legislation for Promotion of Well-being of
Aboriginal and Torres Strait Islanders in
Queensland

Social Welfare Ordinance (C'wth, NT)

Social Welfare Branch (C'wth, NT)

Social Science Research Council (C'wth)

Adoption Act (Qld)

Adoption of Children Act (Vic)

1965
Aborigines and Torres Strait Islander Affairs Act
(Qld)

Children's Services Act (Qld)

1967
Referendum to amend the Constitution (C'wth)
Commonwealth Council and Office of
Aboriginal Affairs established

1968
Aboriginal Affairs Act (Vic)

Department of Aboriginal Affairs (Vic)

1969
Aborigines Protection (Amendment) Act (NSW)

Office of Aboriginal Affairs (NSW)

1970
Community Services Act (Vic)

1971
Aborigines Act (Qld)

Torres Strait Islanders Act (Qld)

1972
Department of Aboriginal Affairs (C'wth)

Community Welfare Act (SA)

Aboriginal Affairs Planning Authority Act (WA)

Aboriginal Affairs Planning Authority (WA)

Community Welfare Act (WA)

1973
National Aboriginal Consultative Committee
(replaced by National Aboriginal Conference
1976, C'wth)

Youth and Community Services Act (NSW)

1974
Furnell Royal Commission into Aboriginal
Affairs (WA)

1975
Racial Discrimination Act (C'wth)

1976
Draft Aboriginal Child Placement Principles
(C'wth)
Victorian Aboriginal Child Care Agency

1978
Indian Child Welfare Act (USA)

United Nations Convention on the Rights of the
Child

1979
Aborigines and Islanders Amendment Act (Qld)

International Year of the Child

1980
Link-Up (NSW)

1981
Secretariat of National Aboriginal and Islander Child Care

1983
Community Welfare Act (NT)

Central Australian Aboriginal Child Care Agency (NT)

1984
Community Services (Aborigines) Act (Qld)

Community Services (Torres Strait Islander) Act (Qld)

Child and Young Persons Act (Vic)

1986
Australian Law Reform Commission Report on Aboriginal Customary Law

1987
Child (Care and Protection) Act (NSW)

Community Welfare Act (NSW)

1990
Aboriginal and Torres Strait Islander Commission (C'wth)

1991
Royal Commission into Aboriginal Deaths in Custody (C'wth)

Mabo (C'wth)

1993
Adoption Act (ACT)

1994
International Year of the Family

Going Home Conference (NT)

1996
Kruger Case in the High Court of Australia

National Inquiry into the Separation of Aboriginal and Torres Strait Islander Children from their Families

1997
Release of *Bringing Them Home* report

1999
Northern Territory Stolen Generations test case — Lorna Cubillo and Peter Gunner v Commonwealth of Australia

Joy Williams judgement (NSW)

Statement of regret (C'wth)

2000
Northern Territory Stolen Generations test case continues

ENDNOTES

ABBREVIATIONS

AA (ACT)	Australian Archives (Australian Capital Territory)
AA (NT)	Australian Archives (Northern Territory)
AA (VIC)	Australian Archives (Victoria)
NSW AWB AR	New South Wales Aborigines Board Annual Report
NT WB AR	Northern Territory Welfare Branch Annual report
Q AD AR	Queensland Aborigines Department Annual Report
Q DNA	Queensland Director of Native Affairs Office
Q NPA AR	Queensland Northern Protector of Aborigines Annual Report
Q PD LA	Queensland Parliamentary Debates Legislative Assembly
Q PD LC	Queensland Parliamentary Debates Legislative Council
QSA	Queensland State Archives
SASA GRG	South Australian State Archives Government Records Group
SA AAAB AR	South Australian Aboriginal Affairs Advisory Board Annual Report
SA AD AR	South Australian Aborigines Department Annual Report
SA APB AR	South Australian Aborigines Protection Board Annual Report
SA DAA AR	South Australian Department of Aboriginal Affairs Annual Report
SA PA AR	South Australian Protector of Aborigines Annual Report
TSA	Tasmanian State Archives Minutes of Orphan School
TSA CSO	Tasmanian State Archives Colonial Secretary's Office
V AWB AR	Victorian Aborigines Welfare Board Annual Report
WA AD AR	Western Australian Aborigines Department Annual Report
WA DNA AR	Western Australian Department of Native Affairs Annual Report
WA DNW AR	Western Australian Department of Native Welfare Annual Report
WA GG	Western Australian Government Gazette
WA PD	Western Australian Parliamentary Debates
WAS	Western Australian Statutes
WASA	Western Australian State Archives

INTRODUCTION
1   Cited by Lira 1989, p 223.
2   Commonwealth Government, Human Rights and Equal Opportunity Commission, 1997.
3   See for example Manne, 1998; Beresford and Omaji, 1998; and Read, 1999.
4   I would like to thank Bain Attwood for compiling this list of questions.
5   See Commonwealth Government, Human Rights and Equal Opportunity Commission 1996, 1997 on the paucity of systematic records of Aboriginal child removal. Read (1999, p 25) also points to the reluctance of governments to release accurate statistical information, the lack of centralised records in states like Victoria and Tasmania where children were sent to mainstream children's homes and the incidence of unrecorded illegal removals. In Western Australia the arbitrary nature of many removals by police meant that details about the children were often not recorded.
6   Read 1999, p 26; Commonwealth Government, Human Rights and Equal Opportunity Commission 1997, p 37.

CHAPTER ONE
1   Rowse 1989.
2   Rowse 1998a, p 9.

3 Commonwealth Government 1929, p 7.
4 Rowse 1998c.
5 Often attributed to Daisy Bates, this phrase has been widely used to refer to policies of Aboriginal protection in the early twentieth century.
6 Cummings 1990, p 39.
7 AA (NT) F1 1952/250.
8 Harvey 1946, p 129.
9 1964, p 16.
10 The Welfare Branch provided for the welfare of wards and others. In relation to wards ('full-blood' Aborigines) this meant essentially operating large settlements, which were the key instruments of the assimilation policy. Non-wards (Aborigines of mixed descent and non-Aborigines) received normal welfare assistance. The Welfare Branch also had responsibility for the care of 'State children'. In cases where the 'State children' were 'full-blood' Aborigines, they remained 'State children' until the age of eighteen, whereafter, not being eligible to vote (because they were 'full-blood'), they became 'wards' indefinitely, or until and if they could qualify for citizenship (Welfare Ordinance 1953; *Child Welfare Ordinance 1958*; Tatz 1964, pp 34–36).
11 Collmann 1979, p 384.
12 ibid., p 389.
13 ibid.
14 Bill Harney cited in Donovan 1988, p 270.
15 NT WB AR 1968–69, p 25.
16 Cummings 1990, p 129.
17 See Collmann 1988 and Rowse 1989, 1998a.
18 See Rowse, 1998a.
19 *Centralian Advocate* (Alice Springs), 16.8.1973, p 12.
20 *Centralian Advocate* (Alice Springs), 4.4.1974, p 1.
21 *Centralian Advocate* (Alice Springs), 1.1.1973, p 3.
22 ibid., p 1.
23 *Centralian Advocate* (Alice Springs), 29.3.1973, p 8; 12.4.1973, p 6; 12.4.1973, p 8.
24 *Centralian Advocate* (Alice Springs), 26.4.1973, p 5.
25 *Centralian Advocate* (Alice Springs), 7.6.1973, p 5.
26 ibid., p 9.
27 *Centralian Advocate* (Alice Springs), 14.6.1973, p 12; 21.6.1973, p 10.
28 *Centralian Advocate* (Alice Springs), 19.7.1973, p 1.
29 *Centralian Advocate* (Alice Springs), 25.10.1973, p 7.
30 *Centralian Advocate* (Alice Springs), 1.11.1973, p 1.
31 *Centralian Advocate* (Alice Springs), 6.12.1973, p 8.
32 *Centralian Advocate* (Alice Springs), 1.1.1974, p 3.
33 Collman 1988, pp 72–3.
34 Heppell and Wigley 1981, p 51.
35 Thornton 1979, point 2.1., p 1; Japanangka and Nathan 1983, p 1.
36 1981, pp 58–63.
37 Cutter 1976, p 6.
38 Heppell and Wigley 1981, p 128.
39 1977, pp 12–13.
40 *Centralian Advocate* (Alice Springs), 16.4.1970, p 8.
41 *Centralian Advocate* (Alice Springs), 25.5.1972, p 1.
42 *Centralian Advocate* (Alice Springs), 16.8.1973, p 12.
43 *Centralian Advocate* (Alice Springs), 13.5.1971, p 10.
44 Faine 1993, p 68.
45 See *Centralian Advocate* (Alice Springs), 10.10.1974 to 6.2.1975.
46 *Age* (Melbourne), 18.11.69.
47 *Centralian Advocate* (Alice Springs), 12.2.1970, p 3.
48 1980, p 2.
49 *Centralian Advocate* (Alice Springs), 19.2.1970, p 11.
50 *Centralian Advocate* (Alice Springs), 12.2.1970, p 3, 19.2.1970, p 11.
51 *Centralian Advocate* (Alice Springs), 1.1.1973, p 1. One possible effect of threats like the federal minister's was that officials involved in child welfare could have felt themselves under increased pressure to remove babies from their mothers. Reprimanding public servants may have looked like concerted government action to some readers, but it could also simply be the minister scapegoating local public servants.

52 Faine 1993, p 30.
53 1988, p 56.
54 1988, p 70.
55 Faine 1993, p 95.
56 ibid., pp 70–1.
57 1988, p 305.
58 ibid., p 336.
59 AA (NT) F1 1968/3320, 5.5.1965.
60 AA (NT) F1 1968/3320, 17.8.1966.
61 AA (NT) F1 1968/3320, 21.5.1969.
62 ibid.
63 ibid.
64 ibid.
65 Kevin Braedon to Bill Johnson, 6.1.2000.
66 Cited in Donovan 1988, p 29.
67 Donovan 1988, p 29.
68 Born 1909, died c. 1992.
69 Born c.1914, deceased.
70 Deceased.
71 Born 1944.
72 Deceased.
73 Deceased.
74 Deceased.
75 Born 1959.
76 Eric Braedon interviewed by Anna Haebich at Little Sisters Camp, Alice Springs, March 1996.
77 Mary Williams interviewed by Anna Haebich at Little Sisters Camp, Alice Springs, March 1996.
78 Eric Braedon to Bill Johnson, 6.1.2000.
79 Tim Rowse personal communication, 1996.
80 Kevin Braedon interviewed by Anna Haebich at Alice Springs, August 1995.
81 Interviewed by Anna Haebich, March 1996.
82 Kevin Braedon interviewed by Anna Haebich at Alice Springs, August 1995.
83 Born 1961.
84 Deceased 1988.
85 Born 1967.
86 Born 1969.
87 Kevin Braedon interviewed by Anna Haebich at Alice Springs, August 1995.
88 Despite requests by Kevin Braedon the Northern Territory Government has yet to release information to enable him to trace the whereabouts of these two siblings. Kevin believes he saw Jaclyn working as a nurse at an alcohol rehabilitation home in New South Wales.
89 Kevin Braedon interviewed by Anna Haebich at Alice Springs, August 1995.
90 ibid.
91 ibid.
92 ibid.
93 ibid.
94 Private correspondence between solicitors Ward and Keller and Bill and Pauline Johnson, 2.5.1974.
95 ibid.
96 The process of having a child declared a 'State child' involved the following steps. A welfare officer could take a child suspected to be 'destitute, neglected, incorrigible or uncontrollable' into custody without warrant and place him or her in an institution or with a 'responsible person'. Within fourteen days this officer was to make application to the Children's Court to have the child declared one of the above. The officer was obliged to 'take all steps' to ensure the child's parents' presence at the hearing of the application. Having declared the child any of the above, the options available to the court were to commit the child to: the care of the Director of Child Welfare; to a person approved by the court; to an institution — until the age of eighteen or otherwise as specified — or to release the child on probation on conditions set by the court. Among the twelve possible definitions of 'neglected child', the following is likely to have been applied in Warren's case: a child who is not provided with necessary food, clothing, lodging, medical aid or nursing; or is neglected, ill-treated or exposed by his parents (*Child Welfare Ordinance 1958*).
97 Kevin Braedon interviewed by Anna Haebich at Alice Springs, August 1995.
98 Mary Williams interviewed by Anna Haebich at Little Sisters Camp, Alice Springs, March 1996.
99 Private correspondence between solicitors Ward and Keller and Bill and Pauline Johnson, 2.5.1974. The

Ordinance stipulated the grounds for dispensing with a parent or guardian's consent as: 'after reasonable inquiry that person could not be found; the person was in such a physical or mental condition as not to be capable of properly considering the question that he [sic] should give his consent; that a person has abandoned, deserted or persistently neglected or ill-treated the child; the person has, for a period of not less than one year, failed, without reasonable cause, to discharge the obligations of a parent or guardian, as the case may be, of the child; or, there are any other special circumstances by reason of which the consent may properly be dispensed with' (Adoption Ordinance 1964).

100 See for example, *Age* (Melbourne), 28.5.1957, AA (ACT) A884 A650 Part 1.

101 For instance, in New South Wales two decades later, only three of twenty-one Aboriginal children placed for adoption were adopted by Aboriginal families (Commonwealth Government, Australian Law Reform Commission 1986, p 234). This was attributed to the scarcity of Aboriginal families approved to adopt.

102 The Director of Child Welfare reported to the Court on applicants' suitability to adopt on the following grounds. Applicants were to be 'of good repute and ... fit and proper persons to fulfil the responsibilities of parents of a child; ... suitable persons to adopt the child having regard to all relevant matters including the age, physical appearance, state of health, education (if any) and religious upbringing or convictions (if any) of the child and the applicants, and any wishes that may have been expressed by a parent or guardian of the child ... with respect to the religious upbringing of the child; and the welfare and interest of the child will be promoted by the adoption (Adoption Ordinance 1964).

103 Northern Territory Government 1996, p 13. The Report of the Martin Inquiry into welfare was tabled in the Northern Territory Legislative Assembley in 1979. This signalled the beginning of a period of legislative and administrative review and reform which continued during the 1980s in the areas of family and children's services in the Northern Territory.

104 This Act was strongly influenced by the United States' Indian Child Welfare Act 1978 (Commonwealth Government, Australian Law Reform Commission 1986, p 250).

105 The Matter of F (an infant) McMillen v Larcombe cited in Commonwealth Government, Australian Law Reform Commission 1986, p 239; McCorquodale 1987, pp 271–4.

106 Commonwealth Government, Australian Law Reform Commission 1986, p 239.

107 McCorquodale 1987, p 272.

108 ibid., p 273.

109 Faine 1993, p 131.

110 Submission by William Johnson to the Human Rights and Equal Opportunity Commission, National Inquiry into the Separation of Aboriginal and Torres Strait Islander Children from their Families, 1996, transcribed from audio tape.

111 Bill and Pauline Johnson to Anna Haebich and Steve Mickler, Perth, 20.1.2000.

112 Submission by William Johnson to the Human Rights and Equal Opportunity Commission, National Inquiry into the Separation of Aboriginal and Torres Strait Islander Children from their Families, 1996, transcribed from audio tape.

113 Bill and Pauline Johnson to Anna Haebich and Steve Mickler, Perth, 20.1.2000.

114 Submission by William Johnson to the Human Rights and Equal Opportunity Commission, National Inquiry into the Separation of Aboriginal and Torres Strait Islander Children from their Families, 1996, transcribed from audio tape.

115 ibid.

116 This heartless scenario was not uncommon in Aboriginal adoptions of this period in the Northern Territory.

117 Private correspondence between solicitors Ward and Keller and Bill and Pauline Johnson, 27.8.1974.

118 Commonwealth Government, Department of Aboriginal Affairs 1984, p.138.

119 Commonwealth Government, Human Rights and Equal Opportunity Commission 1989, p 40.

120 Commonwealth Government, Royal Commission into Aboriginal Deaths in Custody 1991a, p 258; Commonwealth Government, Equal Opportunity Commission 1989, p 40.

121 Commonwealth Government, Department of Aboriginal Affairs 1984, p 131.

122 ibid., p 115.

123 Commonwealth Government, Australian Law Reform Commission 1986, p 236.

124 Commonwealth Government, Department of Aboriginal Affairs 1985b, p 39.

125 Collard and Palmer 1991, p 86.

126 Commonwealth Government, Royal Commission into Aboriginal Deaths in Custody 1991a, p 571.

127 Commonwealth Government, Department of Aboriginal Affairs 1984, p 114.

128 Australian National Opinion Poll Market Research 1985, p 13.

129 ibid., p 58.

130 ibid., p 52.

131 ibid., p 57.

132 'Nyungar' is the term used by Aboriginal people in the south-west of Western Australia to refer to

themselves.
133 Collard and Palmer 1991, p 85.
134 Western Australian Government 1984, p 28.
135 Collard and Palmer, 1991.
136 Commonwealth Government, Royal Commission into Aboriginal Deaths in Custody 1991a, pp 401–2.
137 Submission by William Johnson to the National Inquiry into the Separation of Aboriginal and Torres Strait Islander Children from their Families 1996, transcribed from audio tape.
138 Pauline Johnson interviewed by Anna Haebich at Wattle Grove, Western Australia, October 1995; Bill and Pauline Johnson to Anna Haebich and Steve Mickler, Perth, 20.1.2000.
139 Submission by William Johnson to the National Inquiry into the Separation of Aboriginal and Torres Strait Islander Children from their Families 1996, transcribed from audio tape.
140 ibid; Bill and Pauline Johnson to Anna Haebich and Steve Mickler, Perth, 20.1.2000.
141 Pauline Johnson interviewed by Anna Haebich at Wattle Grove, Western Australia, October 1995.
142 Submission by William Johnson to the National Inquiry into the Separation of Aboriginal and Torres Strait Islander Children from their Families 1996, transcribed from audio tape.
143 Northern Territory Government 1996, p 31. The 1994 Adoption of Children Act provides parties to adoption with access to identifying information. This Act endeavours to balance the need to 'remove secrecy from the process of adoption' and at the same time to 'honour past guarantees of confidentiality'. In respect to adoptions prior to 1994, the release of information to an adoptee over sixteen years of age can apply at any time. Adoptees under sixteen must have their adoptive parents' consent. Relinquishing parents can only apply for information which identifies the adoptee after he or she reaches eighteen. Adoptive parents can only obtain information which does not identify relinquishing parents. Any party, with the exception of the adoptive parents, can lodge a veto on releasing identifying information. (ibid. 1996, pp 49–50.)
144 ibid.
145 ibid.
146 ibid.
147 Bill and Pauline Johnson to Anna Haebich and Steve Mickler, Perth, 20.1.2000.
148 Supreme Court of Western Australia 1993, pp 359–365.
149 Bill and Pauline Johnson to Anna Haebich and Steve Mickler, Perth, 20.1.2000.
150 ibid.
151 Sercombe 1997, p 52.
152 West Australian, 7.3.1992; Sercombe 1997, p 52.
153 Mickler and McHoul, 1997.
154 ibid.
155 ibid.
156 This reconstruction of events by Steve Mickler sources Johnson 1996 and McCann 1994. See also Mickler 1998.
157 As a juvenile at the time, he cannot be named under Western Australian law.
158 In a tragic irony, Louis' middle name was St John, and he was a fully paid-up subscriber to the St John's Ambulance Fund.
159 McCann 1994, p 20; Bill and Pauline Johnson to Anna Haebich and Steve Mickler, Perth, 20.1.2000.
160 Militant, April 1992.
161 McCann 1994, p 31.
162 Saxon 1992, p1, p9.
163 Laurie 1992, pp 16–20, p 45.
164 Notable exceptions to this were a moving award-winning radio feature story, Louis Johnson, by Adrian Shaw and Nellie Green aired on Perth Aboriginal Radio 6AR in 1992, and serious coverage in various human rights, union and left-wing papers.
165 Laurie 1992, pp 16–20, p 45.
166 ibid.
167 Kevin Braedon interviewed by Anna Haebich at Alice Springs, August 1995.
168 Laurie 1992, pp 16–20, p 45.

CHAPTER TWO
1 Cited in Bonwick 1970, p 19.
2 G A Robinson 4.8.1830 cited in Plomley 1966, p 192. Robinson was referring to a violent attack on two women and a child by employees of the Van Diemen's Land Company in 1829.
3 Cited in Pybus 1991, p 38.
4 Irene Schaffer Papers, nd.
5 Palawa is a term used by some Tasmanian Aboriginal people to refer to themselves.

6   1991, p 34.
7   1996, pp 259–60, p 6, p 3.
8   1995.
9   Matson-Green 1995, p 339.
10 Denoon 1979, pp 512–3.
11 William Hull 1858 cited in McGregor 1997, p 14.
12 British Government 1837, pp 44–5.
13 ibid., p 47.
14 ibid., p 83.
15 ibid., p 97.
16 *Scientific American Supplement* 26/8/1893, (921), p 14721.
17 Sir G Murray cited in British Government 1837, p 14.
18 Reynolds 1995. Dr Eric Guiler, retired academic from the University of Tasmania claims that a European sailing expedition charted the Tasmanian coastline in 1521 and that a Chinese expedition had mapped part of the coastline in the thirteenth century. (Julie Gough personal communication, Hobart, 2000.)
19 Plomley and Henley 1990, p 37; Matson-Green 1995, p 65.
20 The Napoleonic Wars prevented regular transportation of convicts to Australia between 1803 and 1815 with the result that Van Diemen's Land languished as a convict colony until 1818. 1818 also marked the beginning of direct transportation of convicts to the colony from Britain. Prior to this they arrived via Sydney. (Lyndall Ryan personal communication, 1998.)
21 Ryan 1996, p 77.
22 Reynolds 1995, p 81.
23 Ryan 1966, p 77.
24 Plomley 1966, p 27.
25 Ryan 1996, p 78.
26 1991, p 43.
27 Cited from *Colonial Times* in Turnbull 1948, p 76.
28 1995, p 82.
29 Cited in Plomley 1991, p 34, p 24.
30 British Government 1837, p 13
31 Plomley 1966, p 28.
32 1970, p 324.
33 Cited in British Government 1837, p 13.
34 ibid., p 13
35 Plomley 1966, pp 1021–2. See also Levy, 1955.
36 1995, p 4.
37 Cited in Davies 1973, p 70.
38 Plomley 1966, p 43 footnote 42.
39 Cited in British Government 1837, p 14.
40 Reynolds 1995, p 4.
41 ibid., p 156
42 Ryan 1996, p 126.
43 Plomley 1966, p 56.
44 Plomley 1987, p 90.
45 Plomley 1966, pp 56–7.
46 Cited in Plomley 1966, p 62.
47 Lindqvist 1997, p 117.
48 Reynolds 1995, p 191.
49 Cited in Reynolds 1995, p 194
50 See Jaggs 1986, 1991; Van Krieken 1991; Kociumbus 1997.
51 Van Krieken 1991, pp 57–8.
52 Walvin 1992, p 43.
53 Lyndall Ryan personal communication, 1998.
54 Wallace Adams, 1995.
55 Reynolds 1990, pp 165–91.
56 G A Robinson 15.10.1830 cited in Mollison and Everitt 1976, np.
57 1996, p 78.
58 1973, p 40.
59 Davies 1973, p 52.
60 Hamilton 1989, p 254.

61 Ryan 1996, p 78.
62 1996, p 78.
63 1970, p 59.
64 Plomley 1966, pp 26–7.
65 Cited in Turnbull 1948, p 47.
66 Plomley 1966, p 42 footnote 40.
67 ibid., p 43.
68 Ryan 1996, p 79.
69 Kociumbus 1997, p 18.
70 Bonwick 1970, p 386.
71 G A Robinson 1831 cited in Aborigines in Tasmania Project Team 1984b, p 47.
72 Bonwick 1970, p 98.
73 Aborigines in Tasmania Project Team 1984c, p 17.
74 Turnbull 1948, pp 94, 96.
75 Cited in Plomley 1966, p 192.
76 Plomley 1966, p 235 footnote 133.
77 Wedge's account in Bonwick (1970, pp 356–7) contrasts with sealer Robert Drew's more violent account of events in Plomley (1966, p 182).
78 Riddett (1998, pp 156–7) provides an example of a young girl captured in the Northern Territory to act as an interpreter for a colonial official.
79 Plomley 1966, p 434 footnote 5.
80 ibid. p 108 footnote 66, p 238 footnote 161.
81 Tasmanian authorities also offered bounties for 'threatened species' such as the thylacine and the emu.
82 Cited in Plomley 1991, p 29.
83 Plomley 1966, p 434 footnote 5.
84 Ryan 1996, p 102.
85 Cited in Plomley 1966, p 92.
86 Cited in Plomley 1966, p 93.
87 This is the title of Henry Reynolds' (1990) publication.
88 G A Robinson 1834 cited in Plomley 1966, p 913 footnote 32.
89 Aborigines in Tasmania Project Team 1984c, p 14.
90 TSA CSO 1/240/5809 1821, p 117.
91 TSA CSO 1/918, 1827.
92 TSA CSO 1/37/658, pp 122–4.
93 Plomley and Henley 1990, p 61–2.
94 TSA CSO 1/918, 1827, 1831.
95 Bonwick 1970, p 357.
96 ibid.
97 Plomley and Henley 1990, p 63.
98 Plomley 1966, p 911 footnote 10.
99 ibid., p 447 footnote 107.
100 Ryan 1996, p 97.
101 Cited in Turnbull 1948, pp 71–2.
102 Cited in Plomley 1966, p 104 footnote 45.
103 1966, p 27.
104 1970, p 349.
105 ibid.
106 1966, p 27.
107 G A Robinson 8.8.1829 cited in Plomley 1966, pp 69–70.
108 Cited in Plomley 1966, p 475 footnote 278.
109 TSA CSO 1/37/658, pp 124–44; Plomley 1966, p 475 footnote 278.
110 Plomley 1966, p 476 footnote 278.
111 CSO 1/37/658 pp 124–44; Plomley 1966, p 476 footnote 278.
112 Plomley 1966, p 109 footnote 69.
113 ibid., p 104 footnote 45.
114 Cted in Plomley 1966, pp 69–70.
115 TSA CSO 1/416/9360.
116 B Field 1825 cited in McGregor 1997, p 11.
117 Tjedboro was taken into John McArthur's home but on reaching adolescence went to live in the bush and took up with bushrangers (Atkinson 1997, p 167). As a young boy and adolescent, Jandamarra worked on

pastoral stations and for the police. However he went on to lead a resistance movement in the Kimberley Leopold Ranges that threatened the spread of the pastoral frontier for several years (Pedersen and Woorunmurra 1995).

118 Aborigines in Tasmania Project Team 1984b, p 11; Plomley 1987, p 11 footnote 9.
119 Bonwick 1970, pp 95–6.
120 Arriving in Tasmania in 1825, Musquito was initially employed as a stockman and in rounding up bushrangers and Aborigines. He went on to become a notorious bushranger and was hanged for murder along with the Tasmanian Aboriginal Jack in 1825. (Plomley 1966, p 314, p 445 footnote 106, p 578 footnote 8.)
121 The records indicate that, following the death of Birch and the remarriage of his wife, Kickerterpoller was treated cruelly by her new husband. (Plomley 1966, p 104 footnote 5; TSA CSO 1/37.658, 1.4.1834, pp 124–44.)
122 Cited in Bonwick 1970, p 83.
123 Plomley 1987, p 29.
124 Plomley 1966, p 109.
125 Aborigines in Tasmania Project 1984a, p 12; Aborigines in Tasmania Project 1984c, p 19.
126 22.8.1831 cited in Mollison and Everitt 1976, np.
127 Aborigines in Tasmania Project 1984c, p 19.
128 British Government 1837, p 46.
129 Davidson 1991, pp xiii–xiv.
130 Van Krieken 1991 cited in Pearce and Doyle 1997, np.
131 Hamilton 1989, p 238.
132 Davidson 1991, p 81.
133 Ryan 1996, p 126.
134 Cited in Ryan 1996, pp 151–2.
135 Ryan 1996, p 151. This bore some similarity to the initial strategy later adopted in dealing with Aborigines in the Port Phillip Protectorate (Victoria) between 1838 and 1849.
136 Ryan 1996, p 103.
137 Cited in Plomley 1966, p 276.
138 Cited in Plomley 1966, p 80.
139 Cited in Plomley 1966, p 93.
140 ibid.
141 Hamilton 1989, p 245.
142 ibid., p 238.
143 Plomley 1966, p 95.
144 ibid., p 1041.
145 ibid., p 448 footnote 18.
146 ibid., p 931.
147 Bonwick 1973, pp xxiv–xxix.
148 ibid., p 199.
149 ibid., p 201, p 196.
150 His mother, Luggernemener (Queen Charlotte), died on Flinders Island in 1837. His father, Rolepa (King George), was 'Chief of the Ben Lomond tribe' and leader of the Piper River people (Aborigines in Tasmania Project Team 1984c, pp 15–16).
151 His mother, Karnebunyer ('Old Sale'), died in Hobart in 1835. His father, Moneneboyerminer, came from the Campbell Town area and belonged to the North Midlands people. Lurnerminer became the husband of Cooneana (Patty) of the Derwent region who was born c. 1805 and died in 1867 (Aborigines in Tasmania Project Team 1984c, p 16; Bonwick 1970, p 283).
152 Cited in Plomley 1966, p 833.
153 TSA CSO 327/1578/ 16, p 160.
154 Cited in Plomley 1966, p 833.
155 Bonwick 1973, pp xxiv–xxix.
156 Plomley 1987, p 678.
157 These measures are detailed in Chapter Three.
158 Ryan 1996, p 71.
159 Plomley 1990, p 56.
160 1991, p 66,
161 G A Robinson 12.11.1830 cited in Mollison and Everitt 1976, np.
162 Similar reports were made across the Australian colonies in relation to 'half-caste' babies.
163 Butlin 1983, p 74.

164 Cited in Rose 1986, p 36
165 Mollison and Everitt 1976, np.
166 Plomley and Henley 1990, p 60.
167 ibid, p 65.
168 Plomley and Henley 1990, p 61.
169 Tindale 1953, p 16; Plomley and Henley 1990, p 63.
170 Cited in Plomley and Henley 1990, p 59.
171 Cited in Mollison and Everitt 1976, np; Plomley 1966, p 256.
172 Emerenna was taken as a child c.1810 from Cape Grim by John Harrington. She had four children to him: Lucy, James, Henry and Jane. Harrington drowned in 1824. Beeton arrived on the islands in the same year. They were one of the families evicted from Gun Carriage Island by Robinson in 1831. Lucy was returned to her husband and in 1848 was still living on the islands with him and their children.
173 Plomley 1966, p 456 footnote 165.
174 Cited in Bonwick 1970, p 83.
175 Plomley and Henley 1990, p 61.
176 *Colonial Times*, 23.4.1839 cited in Pearce and Doyle 1997, np.
177 Plomley 1987, p 992.
178 1987, p 74.
179 Cited in Plomley 1987, p 645 footnote 1.
180 Cited in Mollison and Everitt 1976, np.
181 Pearce and Doyle 1997, np.
182 *Observer*, 1846.
183 Purtscher, 1993.
184 TSA, Kings Orphan School Minutes of the Committee of Management 22.4.1828 to 23.10.1833.
185 There are no records for 'orphaned' children prior to 1828 and the Orphan School Registers end in 1863. Only applications are available from 1858. This figure draws on biographical details collected by Purtscher (1993) and my own research in the Tasmanian State Archives.
186 Admissions were made from Flinders Island in 1832, 1834 and 1835. Of these sixteen were boys and only three were girls. The children were returned to Flinders Island later in 1835. Children were sent in again from Flinders Island in 1847–8 and some were returned to Flinders Island in the early 1850s.
187 See Plomley 1966, 445 footnote 107; TSA CSO 28/3/1842.
188 TSA Minutes of Orphan School 8.8.1832, p 446.
189 Pearce and Doyle 1997, np.
190 ibid.
191 ibid.
192 *Colonial Times*, 23.4.1839 cited in Pearce and Doyle 1997, np.
193 Purtscher 1993, p 4.
194 Lyndall Ryan personal communication, 1998.
195 Pearce and Doyle 1997, np.
196 Purtscher 1993.
197 Purtscher 1993, p 5.
198 ibid, p 4.
199 All the children were raised as Protestants to 1844 when Catholic instruction was allowed following protest from the Catholic Church (Purtscher 1993, p 3).
200 Purtscher 1993, p 4.
201 Pearce and Doyle 1997, np.
202 ibid., np.
203 Plomley and Henley 1990, p 128.
204 Purtscher 1993, p 5.
205 Purtscher 1994.
206 1970, pp 230–1.
207 Cited in Turnbull 1948, p 178.
208 Hamilton 1989, p 238.
209 Plomley 1987, p 99.
210 ibid., p 96.
211 Plomley 1987, p 100 footnote 7.
212 Cited in Plomley 1987, pp 329–30.
213 ibid., p 701, p 720.
214 Ryan 1996, p 184.
215 The Bell system was introduced in schools in Van Diemen's Land in 1821. Children were taught the '3 Rs',

and girls also learned knitting and needlework. Parents had to pay for additional subjects. This marked the beginning of state supported secular education in the colony. By 1850 400 children were attending school in the colony. The Bell system was officially abandoned in 1839 and the British and Foreign System introduced in its place (Aborigines in Tasmania Project Team 1985, p 32).

216 Plomley 1966, p 102 footnote 21.
217 Plomley 1987, p 85.
218 Cited in Turnbull 1948, pp 182–3.
219 Davies 1973, p 198.
220 Cited in Davies 1973, p 198.
221 Cited in Turnbull 1948, pp 190–1.
222 Further editions can be read in Appendix IV C in Plomley 1987, pp 1009–13.
223 Plomley 1987, pp 679–80.
224 ibid., p 643.
225 TSA CSO 1/838/17761, 26.10.1835.
226 Reynolds 1995, p 165.
227 Plomley 1987, p 85.
228 1995, pp 167–8.
229 Lennox 1994, p 9.
230 Bonwick 1970, p 388.
231 Plomey 1987, pp 940–2, pp 946–7.
232 ibid., pp 765–6.
233 ibid., p 108, p 615, p 784.
234 Russell 1997.
235 Plomley 1987, p 537.
236 Cited in Stone 1974, p 43.
237 Cited in Plomley 1987, p 779.
238 Plomley 1987, p 779; Aborigines of Tasmania Project Group 1984c, p 19.
239 Griffiths 1996, p 50.
240 Woodward 1951, p 211.
241 Cited in Davies 1973, p 210.
242 See Plomley 1987, p 786.
243 In 1831 Pevay married Ploonerenernooprener (Plorenemooperner, Wortabowigee, Planobeenna) or Fanny Hardwicke who was born c. 1805. She was baptised by Reverend John Youl at Launceston at the age of eleven when she was living in the household of C B Hardwick of Norfolk Plains. She had then been stolen by sealers and lived with them on the islands in the Bass Strait and on Kangaroo Island. She could navigate schooners and was 'of middle stature, strong and very robust' and of 'quick intellect'. She spoke only English. She was living with Black Baker (John Baker Negro) who was imprisoned in Hobart in 1829. Later in that year she came to Launceston with Robinson and told him how the women were treated by sealers. She then accompanied Robinson on his 'friendly missions' and married Pevay. She died in 1851 or 1854 at Oyster Cove (Ryan 1996, p 82, pp 105–6).
244 Plomley 1987, pp 138–9.
245 Plomley 1966, p 935.
246 Plomley 1987, p 107.
247 Ryan 1996, p 195.
248 Plomley 1987, pp 109–10.
249 Annual expenditure on the settlement included 1573 pounds for rations, bedding and medical care. Twenty-nine staff were employed with their families and eight convicts, making a total of fifty-nine whites. The major staff positions were commandant, chaplain, medical officer, storekeeper and coxswain. Staff salaries cost 1649 pounds (TSA CSO 8/11/266 pp 276–98).
250 1987, p 130.
251 ibid., p 126.
252 Dove to Colonial Secretary 20/7/40, TSA CSO 5/182/4352.
253 The names of these children are not known.
254 Ryan 1996, p 196.
255 ibid.
256 ibid.
257 Ryan 1996, p 196; Plomley 1987, p 134.
258 Plomley 1987, p 136.
259 TSA CSO 8/72/1642.
260 Plomley 1987, p 144.

261 The petition was signed by Walter George Arthur, John Allen, Dave Bruney, Neptune, King Alexander, Augustus, King Tippoo and Washington (Plomley 1987, pp 148 ff).
262 Reynolds 1995, p 9.
263 ibid., p 18.
264 Cited in Bonwick 1970, p 355.
265 Reynolds 1995, p 19.
266 1995, p 26.
267 Cited in Attwood and Markus 1999, p 39.
268 Plomley 1987, pp 154–5.
269 TSA CSO 24/7/101.
270 Plomley 1987, p 159.
271 TSA CSO 24/7/101, pp 30, 45, 161, 251–3, 292–316.
272 Mary Ann Arthur cited in Bonwick 1970, p 276.
273 Plomley 1987, p 169 footnote 97.
274 ibid., p 173.
275 ibid., p 172.
276 TSA CSO 24/7/101, p 189.
277 See Lennox, 1984.
278 TSA CSO Government Notice no. 109, 4/11/1847.
279 Plomley 1987, pp 180, 181.
280 Ryan 1996, pp 209–10.
281 Plomley 1987, p 183.
282 Ryan 1996, pp 186, 212.
283 1869 cited in Bonwick 1970, p 283.
284 A thorough history of the scramble to collect human remains in Van Diemen's Land remains to be written. Plomley (1987, p 188) and Petrow (1997) provide accounts of the mutilation of William Lanne's corpse in 1869, and Plomley (1987, p 190) describes the desecration of Truganini's body in 1878. It has only been after concerted pressure from Palawa people and their supporters from the 1970s that some of these remains have been returned and respectfully laid to rest.
285 Lennox 1984, pp 29–30.
286 McGrath 1997, pp 50–1.
287 Pybus 1991, p 180–1.
288 Horton 1994, pp 1104–5.
289 Clifford 1988, p 16.
290 Ryan 1996, p 223.
291 Calder 1875.
292 Tindale 1953.
293 Cited in Plomley and Henley 1990, p 60.
294 Matson-Green and Harper 1995, p 67.
295 Aborigines in Tasmania Project Team 1984b, p39
296 Cited in Mollison and Everitt 1976, np.
297 ibid.
298 Cited in Roth 1899, p 177.

CHAPTER THREE
1 From the Manifesto of the Day of Mourning organised by Aboriginal people in Sydney in 1938. Cited in Markus 1990, pp 178-9.
2 Kidd 1997, p xx.
3 Karl Pierson cited in McGregor 1997, p 58.
4 Stoler 1995, p 27.
5 Evans, Saunders, Moore and Jamison 1997, p 25.
6 Evans 1999, p 144.
7 ibid.
8 Cited in Stone 1974, p 69.
9 Loos 1970, p 193.
10 Evans 1982, p 12.
11 Stoler 1995, pp 46-7.
12 Evans 1982, p 18.
13 Young 1995, pp 18, 19, 99 ff.
14 *Bulletin* 1901 cited in Broome 1982, p 93.

15 WA AD AR 1902, p 3.
16 Rudolph, farm manager, Koonibba 1916, p 7; Frederick Linke, teacher, p 9; William Garnett Southern Chief Protector of Aborigines, South Australia, 1913, p 11; Dalton, p 21; South, p 11; Hackett, p 2; George John, Daisy Bates, p 34 (South Australian Government, 1913).
17 See Bourke, Bourke and Edwards (1994) for an introduction to family and kinship in Aboriginal societies.
18 Radzinowicz and Hood 1986, p 343.
19 Evans 1999, p 144.
20 Meston 1900 cited in Evans 1999, p 132. The 'Law of Atavism' was a theory — now discredited — which held that physical traits such as dark skin colour possessed by an ancestor could suddenly reappear ('throwback') in offspring after several generations of race mixing.
21 Southern Chief Protector of Aborigines William Garnett in South Australian Government, 1913.
22 Parry 1995.
23 Rowse 1986, p 183.
24 Day 1996; Armitage 1995, p 29.
25 Butlin 1983.
26 Armitage 1995, Table 2.2.
27 Haebich 1986, pp 33–4.
28 Gale 1969.
29 'Koori' is the term used by Aboriginal people in New South Wales and Victoria to refer to themselves.
30 Barwick 1971.
31 Meston was born in Scotland and migrated to Australia with his family as a child in 1859. The family settled on the Clarence River in northern New South Wales where the photographer J W Lindt made many well-known studies of traditional Aboriginal life during the 1870s. Meston mixed freely with local Aborigines and learned to speak at least one Aboriginal language and was initiated into the 'penultimate stage' of the bora ceremony. As an adult he travelled extensively throughout Queensland working in various positions including owner-manager of a sugar plantation, magistrate, amateur scientist and leader of expeditions in the Cairns district and member of Parliament. In the 1890s he was working as a journalist with Henry Lawson on the 'liberal humanist journal' *The Boomerang*. He was a well-known figure in the colony. While he was informed on Aboriginal life and customs his knowledge was based on 'grabs' or 'glimpses' of practices rather than a holistic view of social life. (Thorpe, 1984; King and McHoul, 1996)
32 Meston 1895.
33 Queensland Government 1896, p 1.
34 ibid., p 2.
35 ibid., p 4.
36 Meston subsequently drafted them off to reserves at Durundur and Fraser Island and later to Barambah further eroding lines of kin and locality. (Raymond Evans, personal communication, 1998)
37 Queensland Government 1896, p 5.
38 ibid., p 12.
39 ibid., p 10.
40 Queensland Government 1897, pp 2–3.
41 Evans 1999a, pp 39–40.
42 Queensland Government 1896, p 10.
43 Q AD AR 1905, p 12.
44 Q AD AR 1902, pp 28–31.
45 Haebich 1998a, p129.
46 See Haebich 1984.
47 Haebich 1998a, p 132.
48 WA AD AR 1902.
49 Cited in Gale 1964, p 83.
50 QSA Aboriginal Protection Commisioners Correspondence 1875 p 161; Cryle 1989.
51 Evans 1999, p 114.
52 Attwood 1989, p 86.
53 Walvin 1992, p 235.
54 ibid., p 331.
55 Ware 1992, p 119.
56 Cited in Foxcroft 1941, p 74.
57 Donzelot 1980; Van Krieken 1991.
58 Radzinowicz and Hood (1986) note that this distinction was not always maintained and the children of the 'perishing' and 'criminal' classes were increasingly domiciled together.
59 Finnane 1997, p 94.

60 L Rose 1991, p 48; Jaggs 1986, 1991; Finnane 1997, pp 93 ff.
61 Jamrozik 1983, p 71.
62 Miller 1997, pp 184–5.
63 Armitage 1995, p 113.
64 Goodall 1990, p 6.
65 Evans 1976.
66 See Long 1970, p 178 and Haebich 1998a, p 166.
67 Cited in Davidson 1991, p 209.
68 Stawell Commission on Penal and Prison Discipline 3rd Report, 1872 cited in Jaggs 1986, p 36.
69 Jaggs 1986, p 36.
70 ibid., p 38.
71 L Rose 1991, p 46.
72 Jaggs 1986, p 38.
73 Cited in Davidson 1991, p 209.
74 Barnardo and Marchant 1907. For revisionist histories of the Empire children in Australia see Bean and Melville 1989, Blackburn 1993, Coldrey 1998, Wesern Australian Government The Select Committee of the Legislative Assembly (1996).
75 Cited in Radzinowicz and Hood 1986, p 223.
76 Cited in Dickey 1985, p 332.
77 Cited in New South Wales Government 1914, pp 17–18.
78 ibid.
79 Goodall 1990, p 6.
80 WA AD AR 1915.
81 ibid., p 8.
82 Bauman 1991, p 20.
83 Dandeker 1990, pp 26–7.
84 This follows T H Marshall's widely used definition of citizenship. See Chesterman and Galligan 1997, pp 4–5; Peterson and Sanders 1998, p 2.
85 Chesterman and Galligan 1997, p 88.
86 Grimshaw 1994, p 11.
87 Bauman 1991, p 28.
88 Sider 1987 cited in Beckett 1988, p 3.
89 Donzelot, 1980.
90 Johnson 1993, p 30.
91 Bacchi 1980, p 201.
92 New South Wales Government 1904 cited in McGrath 1993, p 42.
93 McGrath 1993, p 42.
94 Anderson 1996, p 114.
95 Hunter 1994.
96 Van Krieken 1991.
97 Garton 1986, Evans 1976. In Tasmania teenage girls continued to be sent out as domestic servants as the state did not pay foster families to keep them once they turned thirteen or fourteen and most families refused to maintain them under these conditions (Evans 1994, p 96).
98 Donzelot 1980, p 103.
99 Carter 1983, p 9.
100 Wood 1997, p 111.
101 Armitage 1995, p 29.
102 1996, p 9.
103 1989, p 99.
104 Wood 1997, p 111.
105 Chesterman and Galligan 1997, pp 4–5.
106 ibid.
107 ibid., p 120.
108 ibid., p 41.
109 Brock 1995, p 102.
110 Title of Chesterman and Galligan's 1997 publication.
111 Butlin 1983, p 121; Commonwealth Government, Human Rights and Equal Opportunity Commission 1997, p 58.
112 Christie 1979.
113 1997, pp 19–20.

114 1989, pp 97–8.
115 Christie 1979, pp 91, 92, 196.
116 Attwood 1989, pp 93–4.
117 ibid., p 195.
118 Victorian Government, Department of Human Services 1996, p 38.
119 Commonwealth Government, Human Rights and Equal Opportunity Commission 1997, p 59.
120 Cited in Christie 1979, p 202.
121 Chesterman and Galligan 1997, p 30.
122 Regulations passed in 1899 allowed any Aboriginal child to be placed by the Governor under the control of the Department for Neglected Children or the Department for Industrial Schools.
123 Cited in Chesterman and Galligan 1997, p 26.
124 ibid.
125 Christie 1979, p 204. Claiming that they had no Aboriginal population, the Tasmanian and Victorian governments exempted themselves from participation in federal conferences on Aboriginal affairs in 1937 (Victoria attended as an observer), the 1950s and on into the 1960s.
126 Renkin 1996, p 17.
127 Q AD AR 1905, p 12.
128 Fitzgerald 1986, p 213.
129 Queensland Government 1896, p 14.
130 Meston 1895, p 25.
131 Queensland Government 1897, p 23. Parry-Okeden was formerly a customs officer, visiting police magistrate, immigration agent, head of the Labour Bureau, member of the Royal Commission into Queensland Gaols 1887 and district magistrate (Kidd 1994a, p 166 footnote 254).
132 Guthrie 1976, p 9.
133 QPD LA 1897, pp 1541–3.
134 Section 4 of the 1897 Act.
135 Section 3 of the 1897 Act.
136 This is clearly evident in a circular prepared by Roth in 1904 clarifying legal controls over 'half-caste' men and women (QSA 58751 1672/1905).
137 From 1908 the Government Resident supervised matters relating to the protection of Torres Strait Islanders. In 1917 reponsibility was transferred to the Office of the Chief Protector of Aborigines through a local Protector on Thursday Island. From 1939 the people were administered separately under the *Torres Strait Islanders Act 1939*. Official powers to remove the children mirrored those of the *Aboriginals Preservation and Protection Act 1939* (Queensland Government 1996, p 15; Queensland Government 1997, point 17, p 6 and Attachment 12).
138 Reynolds and May 1995, p 192.
139 See Evans and Scott 1995; Kidd 1997.
140 Reynolds and May 1995.
141 Kidd 1997.
142 Queensland Government 1996, pp 33–4.
143 Queensland Government 1997, p 6.
144 South Australian Government 1913, p 94.
145 Q NPA AR 1903, pp 11–12.
146 ibid., p 94.
146 ibid., p 98.
147 QSA 5A/80.
148 ibid., p 95.
150 Q AD AR 1905, p 12.
151 Q NPA AR 1902, p 10.
152 Queensland Government 1997, Attachment 3.
153 ibid.
154 QSA 10428/1900, 7.7.1902.
155 There were at least twenty-one such church and state institutions in Brisbane and the country (Kath Frankland personal communication, 1998).
156 Q NPA AR 1902, p 18; Q NPA AR 1903, p 18.
157 Q AD AR 1905.
158 Queensland Government 1996, p 20.
159 Q AD AR 1905, p 12.
160 1bid.
161 South Australian Government 1913, p 105.

162 Queensland Government 1997, sub-point 3.
163 See Huggins 1987/8, 1995 and Huggins and Blake 1992 on the experiences of Aboriginal domestic servants in Queensland.
164 Queensland Government 1996, p 21.
165 Kidd 1994a, p 273.
166 Cited in Tasmanian Government 1908.
167 ibid.
168 Mollison and Everitt 1976, p 86.
169 Cited in Commonwealth Government, Human Rights and Equal Opportunity Commission 1997, p 94.
170 Mollison and Everitt 1976, p 87
171 ibid., p 86.
172 Goodall 1995b.
173 Butlin 1983, p 121.
174 ibid., p 77.
175 A ruling by the 1902 Director of Public Instruction allowed the establishment of racially segregated schools. Until 1973 Aboriginal children could be temporarily suspended from state schools if they were considered to be suffering from a contagious disease.
176 Gungil Jindibah Centre 1994, p 15.
177 Cited in Commonwealth Government, Human Rights and Equal Opportunity Commission 1997, p 41.
178 Read 1999, p 33.
179 Read 1981, p 9.
180 Goodall 1995a, p 77.
181 Goodall 1990, p 7.
182 Walden 1995, p 12.
183 See Rose 1998.
184 Goodall 1995b, p 75.
185 New South Wales Government 1910, p 4.
186 Maynard 1997, pp 5–8.
187 Goodall 1995a.
188 Smith 1992, p 93.
189 Dickey 1985, p 360; Roder 1987.
190 Haebich 1998a, p 52.
191 Biskup 1973, p 178.
192 See Read 1995; Read and Read 1993.
193 Austin 1997, p 8.
194 ibid., p 27.
195 D B Rose 1991, p 221.
196 ibid., p 149.
197 Austin 1997, p 5.
198 ibid., p 72.
199 Cited in Austin 1997, p 73.
200 Commonwealth Government 1929, pp 20–21.
201 ibid., p 21.
202 ibid., p 4.
203 ibid., p 7.
204 Austin 1990, p 113.
205 Long 1992, p 81.
206 Austin 1997, p 196.
207 ibid., p 195.
208 AA (ACT) A1 1937/70.
209 Cited in Austin 1990, pp 112–3.
210 Austin 1997, p 198.
211 AA (ACT) A431 1934/6800.
212 D B Rose 1991, pp 211–3.
213 ibid.
214 Austin 1997, p 304.
215 Gale 1964, pp 109–10.
216 SASA GRG 52/7.
217 Cited in Mattingley and Hampton 1988, p 159.
218 Cited in Roder 1987, p 55.

219 Hall 1997, p 7.
220 SA PA AR 1912, p 5.
221 ibid., p 41.
222 Cited in Hall 1997, p 12.
223 SASA GRG 52/7.
224 South Australian Government 1913, p 121.
225 ibid., pp 121–2.
226 ibid., p 16.
227 ibid., p 37.
228 The loneliness and the often abusive treatment of most children in care is evident in Carrington 1993.
229 Hall 1997, p. 11.
230 South Australian Government 1913, pp 121–2.
231 SA PA AR 1912, p 4.
232 SA PA AR 1913, p 3.
233 South Australian Government 1913 and 1916.
234 South Australian Government 1913, p 8.
235 Mission work with Aboriginal communities also commenced at Swan Reach (1925) and Nepabunna (1929).
236 Cited in Commonwealth Government, Human Rights and Equal Opportunity Commission 1997, p 212.
237 1997, p 36.
238 McGregor 1997, p 121.
239 Bock 1991.
240 *Australian*, 21.5.1997.
241 Cited in Commonwealth Government, Human Rights and Equal Opportunity Commission 1997, p 270.
242 Tatz 1999, p 49.
243 Harris 1990; Swain and Rose 1988; Hale 1889; Hall 1996, 1997; Mattingley and Hampton 1988; Brock 1993; McNair and Rumley 1981; Haebich and Delroy 1999; Kidd 1997; Brook and Kohen 1991; Read 1981; Goodall 1996; Woolmington 1988; Massola 1970; Attwood 1989; Christie 1979; Reynolds 1995; Ryan 1996.

CHAPTER FOUR

1   The title of a film on Aboriginal youth by Smith Street Films 1991 and of a song by Australian singer-songwriter Paul Kelly; Kelly 1993, pp 77-8..
2   Stannage 1979, p 249.
3   1995, p 62.
4   Biskup 1973, p 36.
5   Finnane 1997, p 35.
6   ibid., pp 35–6.
7   Western Australian Government 1905, p 15.
8   Gribble 1987, pp 1–2.
9   ibid.
10   The *Aborigines Protection Act 1886* set out conditions for contracts binding employers to provide minimum conditions for Aboriginal apprentices who could be signed up from the age of six to twenty-one. Employers and apprentices faced penalties for breaching the contracts.
11   Western Australian Government 1905, p 9.
12   Green 1995, pp 69–70.
13   Reynolds 1998, p 140.
14   Cited in Hunter 1993, p 43.
15   Haebich 1998a, pp 56–7.
16   Cited in Jebb 1987, p 30.
17   ibid., p 41.
18   Western Australian Government 1905, p 40.
19   WASA 255/122/1902.
20   ibid.
21   WA AD AR 1902, p 14.
22   Cited in Haebich 1998a, p 67.
23   Howard 1982, p 2.
24   Ironically these breastplates have now become valued collector items and the subject of historical research and museum exhibitions.
25   Turner and Hulme 1997, pp 85–6.
26   ibid., p 67.
27   Rose 1996b, p 42.

28 ibid.
29 Michel Foucault 1991 cited in Kidd 1997, p xx.
30 Ripley and Franklin 1986, pp 9–29.
31 WAS, *Aborigines Act 1905.*
32 Haebich 1998a, p 78.
33 *Morning Herald* (Perth), 8.2.1906, 9.2.1906; Haebich 1998a, pp 78–9.
34 I would like to thank Rosie Kerr who is writing a PhD on the history of the State Children's Department in Western Australia for her insights into these contrasts.
35 *West Australian*, 26.5.1996.
36 WA AD AR 1902, 1911, 1918 and WA DNA AR 1943.
37 Commonwealth Government, Human Rights and Equal Opportunity Commission 1997, p 37.
38 In its submission to the Senate Legal and Constitutional References Committee Inquiry into Government Response to the Recommendations of the Report, *Bringing Them Home*, the Commonwealth government stated that one 'basic flaw' in the 'stolen generation concept' was that 'the evidence that a proportion of those removed fitted within the stereotype of "forcible removal" is only anecdotal and has not been subject to proper scrutiny' (Commonwealth Government 2000, p 2.).
39 Turner and Hulme 1997, p 81.
40 ibid., p 77.
41 Rose 1996a, p 35.
42 Hunter 1993, p 43.
43 Cited in Haebich 1998a, p 97.
44 Haebich 1998a, p 97.
45 Isdell was member for the Pilbara in the WA Legislative Assembly from 1903 to 1906.
46 WA PD, 28, 1905, p 427.
47 Cited Haebich 1998a, p 82.
48 *West Australian*, 14.6.1934.
49 WASA 652/213/1909.
50 WASA 652/1433/1909.
51 WASA 653/213/1909.
52 ibid.
53 WASA 652/1312/1909.
54 WASA 653/213/1909.
55 Jebb 1987, p 215.
56 Rumley and Toussaint 1990; Kimberley Language Resource Centre 1996.
57 WASA 653/213/1909.
58 Green 1995, pp 73–4.
59 Jebb 1987, p 33.
60 Cited in Jebb 1987, p 47.
61 WASA 652/213/1909.
62 WASA 652/1309A/1909.
63 Cited in Green 1995, p 202.
64 Choo 1997, p 15.
65 Western Australian Government 1905, p 601.
66 WASA AD AR 1907, p12.
67 WASA AD AR 1909, p 9.
68 Choo 1997, pp 22–3.
69 WASA 652/444/1909.
70 WASA 652/1434/1909.
71 WASA 652/213/1909.
72 WASA 653/16/1920. File includes material from later than file date.
73 Green 1988, p 44.
74 WASA 653/16/1920. File includes material from later than file date.
75 ibid.
76 WASA 653/16/1920.
77 Kimberley Land Council 1996, p 52.
78 WASA 653/16/1920. File includes material from later than file date.
79 ibid.
80 ibid.
81 Western Australian Government 1905, pp 116–18, pp 118–121.
82 WASA 652/991/1910.

83   WASA 652/352/1910.
84   Stannage 1979, p 250.
85   ibid.
86   Haebich 1998a, p 138.
87   ibid.
88   Opened in 1909 in Perth by the Melbourne-based interdenominational faith mission, the Australian Aborigines Mission, Dulhi Gunyah took in babies and children who were supported by charitable donations or a subsidy of ten pence a day if sent in by the Aborigines Department. Following white parents' objections to the children attending Victoria Park School, the Education Department agreed to provide a teacher at the Home (Bishop 1991, p 139).
89   Telfer 1939, p 156.
90   Bishop 1991; Haebich 1998a.
91   Lock personal correspondence 1912 cited in Bishop 1991, p 184.
92   *Great Southern Herald* (Katanning), 29.6.1912.
93   Lock personal correspondence 1914 cited in Bishop 1991, p 184.
94   ibid., p 188.
95   ibid., p 77.
96   Harney 1961, p 52–3.
97   Lock 1916 ibid., p 52–3.
98   Lock personal correspondence 1916 ibid., p 196.
99   Lock personal correspondence 1913 ibid., p 186.
100 Lock personal correspondence 1929 ibid., p 81.
101 Lock personal correspondence 1914 ibid., p 76.
102 Lock personal correspondence 1913 ibid., p117.
103 ibid., p 116.
104 ibid., p 98.
105 Lock personal correspondence 1914 ibid., p 188.
106 ibid., p 117.
107 Cited in Haebich 1998a, p 145.
108 Lock personal correspondence 1914 cited in Bishop 1991, p 118.
109 *Southern Districts Advocate* (Katanning), 28.3.14.
110 Cited in Haebich 1998a, pp 145–6.
111 1981, p 135.
112 1933, p 20.
113 Haebich 1998a, p 146.
114 See Davis 1979; Jacobs 1990; Haebich 1998a; Beresford and Omaji 1998.
115 1947, p 80.
116 Neville 1947, p 176.
117 ibid., p 119.
118 For further background on the settlements see Haebich 1982, 1998a; Bowden and Bunbury 1990; Nannup, Marsh and Kinnane 1992; Maushart 1993; Van den Berg 1994.
119 *Geraldton Express*, 3.10.1919; WASA 24/850/1919.
120 WASA 993/169/1927. File includes material from later than file date.
121 *Southern Districts Advocate* (Katanning), 4.9.22.
122 WA AD AR 1936, p 18.
123 Haebich 1998a, p 340.
124 'Wongi' is the term used by Aboriginal people of Western Australia's eastern goldfields area to refer to themselves.
125 Stanton 1998, p 292.
126 Morgan 1986, p 9.
127 ibid., p 5.
128 Wadley Dowley 2000.
129 Morgan 1986, p 84.
130 Rajowski 1995, pp 64, 123.
131 Morgan 1986, p 94.
132 ibid., p 106.
133 ibid., p 102.
134 Stanton 1979, p 120.
135 Stanton 1988, p 294.
136 Morgan 1986, p 83.

137 ibid., p 85.
138 ibid., p 168.
139 Morgan 1986, p 158.
140 Haebich 1998a, p 333.
141 Morgan 1986, p 159.
142 Cited in Morgan 1986, p 161.
143 Cited in Morgan 1986, p 164.
144 Cited in Morgan 1986, p 165.
145 Cited in Morgan 1986, p 163.
146 Morgan 1986, p 166.
147 ibid., p 197.
148 ibid., pp 214, 223.
149 WASA 993/1025/1940. File includes material from later than file date.
150 ibid.
151 WA AD AR 1926, 1932; Haebich 1998, pp 287–8.
152 Western Australian Government 1934, pp 552–5.
153 Cited in WA PD 1936, pp 2167–8.
154 Haebich 1998a, p 317.
155 Bock 1991.
156 Clay and Leapman 1995.
157 Skidmore 1993, p 76.
158 ibid.
159 ibid.
160 Ambery 1998, p 93.
161 Fitzpatrick 1988.
162 Haebich 1998a, pp 316–17.
163 Neville 1947, p 54.
164 Haebich 1992, p 317.
165 McGregor 1993, p 57.
166 AA (ACT) A1 96/6595.
167 Western Australian Government 1934, p 358.
168 See Morgan 1987; Boladeras 1996; Scott 1999.
169 Haebich 1998, p 96. I would like to thank Alan Charlton for this reference.
170 WASA 993/304/1932.
171 Western Australian Government 1934, np.
172 ibid.
173 Cited in Haebich 1998a, p 335.
174 ibid., p 347.
175 WA PD 1936, p 2897.
176 ibid., p 822.
177 Haebich 1998a, p 351.
178 ibid., p 352.
179 Aboriginal Legal Service of Western Australia, 1995.
180 Whittington, 1999.
181 WASA 993/269/1933. File includes material from later than file date.
182 Uniting Church MN 957/3179A/53.
183 Leaming 1986, p 26.
184 WASA 993/279/1933.
185 Cited in Aboriginal Legal Service of Western Australia 1995, p 173.
186 WASA 993/279/1933. File includes material from later than file date.
187 Western Australian Museum papers, nd.
188 Leaming 1986, p 25.
189 WASA 993/445/1936. File includes material from later than file date.
190 Uniting Church papers.
191 Leaming 1986, p 50.
192 WASA 993/240/1934.
193 Leaming 1986, p 83.
194 Uniting Church MN 957/3179A/53.
195 WASA 993/269/1937.
196 Aboriginal Legal Service of Western Australia 1995, p 40.

197 ibid., p 94.
198 WASA 993/305/1938. File includes material from later than file date.
199 ibid.
200 Cited in Leaming 1986, p 476.
201 ibid 1986, p 45.
202 Leaming 1986, p 52.
203 Glass and Weller 1987, p 70.
204 Leaming 1986, p 49–50.
205 Cited in Leaming 1986, p 42.
206 Aboriginal Legal Service of Western Australia 1995, p 40.
207 Leaming 1986, p 52.
208 ibid., pp 55–6.
209 Leaming 1986; Aboriginal Legal Service of Western Australia 1995.

CHAPTER FIVE
1   Lindqvist 1997, pp 171–2.
2   Cited in Read 1999, p 32.
3   Darryl Kickett personal communication, 1999.
4   QSA A58751.
5   Evans 1991; Q NPA AR 1902 p 8, 1903 p 11.
6   Cited in the *Daily Mail* (Brisbane), 24.10.1905 from a letter in the *Independent* (Cooktown), QSA A58914.
7   QSA A58750, 6.11.1902.
8   QSA A58750, 30.10.1903.
9   QSA A58751.
10   QSA COL/143 in letter 11354/1899.
11   QSA A58751.
12   ibid.
13   Reynolds 1990, p 182.
14   ibid., pp 165–91.
15   Trigger 1991, pp 42 ff.
16   Cited by Trigger 1991, p 47.
17   Austin 1992, pp 86, 76.
18   Evans 1984, p 184; Holland 1995, p 153.
19   In 1897, encouraged by Police Commissioner W E Parry-Okeden who gained government backing for the endeavour, Roth published the first of several works on Aboriginal culture, *Ethnological Studies Among North-West Central Queensland Aborigines*. He was an active member of anthropological societies in Australia and abroad.
20   Roth developed an interest in the history of British Guyana and when he retired in 1928 was appointed curator and government archivist at the Georgetown Museum. He died in 1933. The Anthropology Museum in Georgetown was named after Roth and he is represented in museum collections there and in Australia, Britain, Sweden and the United States (Reynolds 1988, pp 463–4).
21   Q AD AR 1904, p 20.
22   ibid., p 7.
23   *Courier Mail* (Brisbane), 31.5.1904.
24   Cited in Johnston 1988, p 123.
25   ibid., p 127.
26   Q NPA AR 1899, p 1.
27   *Queenslander*, 19.10.1901.
28   Roth was supported by Foxton and Meston who were equally outraged at government inaction. While the Chinese were widely blamed for Aborigines' opium addiction and this was frequently cited as the reason why they should not be allowed to employ Aborigines, the Queensland government and its agents stood to gain the most. The opium trade was worth 30,000 pounds annually in customs duties to the Queensland government which refused to forego these duties by banning importation of opium. Efforts to stop the trade locally were sabotaged by agents serving their own interests. The trade was effectively stopped by federal legislation passed in 1906 (Q PD LC p 1422; Kidd 1997, pp 52–3, p 58).
29   May 1994, p 76.
30   Cited in Pohlner 1986, p 84.
31   *Register* (Adelaide), 17.8.1904.
32   Lees 1902, np.
33   Waterson 1981, p 570.

34   Q NPA AR 1899, p 4. See Evans (1969) for further discussion.
35   Cited in Reynolds 1990, pp 169–70.
36   Ruby de Satge cited in May 1994, p 96.
37   Gribble 1933, pp 73–4.
38   Cited in Kidd 1994a, p 246.
39   Cited in Reynolds 1990, p 173.
40   Q NPA AR 1903, p 11.
41   Reynolds 1990, p 175.
42   1899 cited in Kidd 1994a, pp 190–1.
43   Bardsley cited in Reynolds 1990, p 178.
44   Evans 1965, pp 78–9.
45   ibid.
46   Evans 1991, pp 26–7.
47   ibid.
48   Q PD LA 1901, pp 223–4.
49   Reynolds 1990, p 181.
50   ibid, p 180.
51   See Q NPA AR 1899, p 110; Kidd 1994a, p 193. Under the Queensland Criminal Code carnal knowledge of a
     girl under the age of fourteen carried a sentence of two years hard labour. Kidd (1994a, p 193) notes that
     Judith Allen found low conviction rates for cases involving white girls.
52   Kidd 1994a, p 246.
53   Q NPA AR 1899, p 10.
54   Commonwealth Government, Human Rights and Equal Opportunity Commission 1997, p 72.
55   Kidd 1997, p 58.
56   See police records in the Queensland State Archives. Raymond Evans personal communication, 1998.
57   Q NPA AR 1902, p 2.
58   Cited in Halse 1996, p 235.
59   Q NPA AR 1899, p 6.
60   Cairns Morning Post cited in Halse 1996, p 236.
61   Johnston 1988, p 289.
66   D B Rose 1991, pp 22, 34.
67   Lees 1902, np.
64   May 1994, p 74.
65   Trigger 1991, p 31.
66   QSA A/58752.
67   ibid.
68   ibid.
69   Register (Adelaide), 17.8.1904.
70   Q PD LC 1901, p 1139.
71   Q PD 1901, pp 1136, 1340.
72   Q PD LA 1901, p 213.
73   SASA GRG 2/13.
74   QSA A/58751 21787/1903.
75   QSA A/58750, A/58751.
76   Q NPA AR 1902, p 12.
77   Cited in Johnston 1988, pp 124–5.
78   Raymond Evans personal communication, 1998.
79   North Queensland Register, 13.11.1905.
80   Q PD LA 1905, p 1801.
81   Q PD LA 1905, p 1337.
82   Cited in Q PD LA 1905, p 1340.
83   Q PD LA 1905, p 1803. There was no mention of Roth's presentation of over 300 objects to the Brisbane
     Museum in 1904 and the only reference to a sale of similar artefacts by Meston was to claim that his were
     worthless and that Roth's were valuable. The allegations continued after Roth's departure with continuing
     demands for a public inquiry (Q PD LA 1906, pp 1656 ff).
84   Bolton 1963, p 254.
85   Q PD LA 1905, p 1808.
86   See Kidd, 1994a.
87   Trigger 1991, p 48; May 1994, pp 74, 79.
88   Winton Herald, 8.4.1907.

89 Markus 1990, pp 158–9.
90 Goodall 1996, p 233.
91 Paisley 1995, p 211.
92 ibid, p 230.
93 Cited in Read 1999, p 167.
94 ibid.
95 Barber nd, p 4.
96 Mattingley and Hampton 1988, p 111.
97 ibid, p 7.
98 ibid, p 23.
99 Roder 1987, p 42.
100 See Tindale 1941. Ironically, Tindale's research, which includes genealogies and photographs of Aboriginal people from various states in Australia, has become an invaluable tool for Aboriginal family historians.
101 Haebich, 1998c.
102 Davey 1956, p 113.
103 SA AD AR 1923, p 3.
104 South Australian Government 1913, p 37.
105 ibid., p 121–2.
106 Cited in Mattingley and Hampton 1988, p 119.
107 South Australian Government, 1913.
108 Cited in Hall 1996, pp 10–11.
109 Register (Adelaide), 21.12.1923.
110 South Australian Government, Department of Aboriginal Affairs 1963, p 19.
111 Register (Adelaide), 21.12.1923.
112 Sun (Adelaide), 12.4.1924.
113 ibid.
114 ibid.
115 Sport (Adelaide), 18.4.24
116 Register (Adelaide), 6.6.24.
117 Martin left no autobiographical writings so little is known of the details of her life and the origins of this story apart from the fact that she was an avid traveller and her brothers owned pastoral stations in Western Australia (Allen 1987, p x).
118 Cited in Allen 1987, p x.
119 Allen 1987, p xii.
120 ibid.
121 Martin 1987, p 14.
122 ibid., p 152.
123 SASA GRG 52/32/15. A press clipping contained in the file, includes date but no source identified.
124 AA (ACT) A1 1927/2982.
125 Advertiser (Adelaide), 3.11.1924.
126 SASA GRG 52/32/15. A press clipping contained in the file, includes date but no source identified.
127 ibid.
128 SASA GRG 52/8.
129 Commonwealth Government 1929, p 21.
130 AA (ACT) A452 1961/ 7809.
131 Commonwealth Government, Human Rights and Equal Opportunity Commission, nd.
132 Harmstorf 1979, pp 202–3; McGregor 1997, p 69.
133 McGregor 1997, p. 69.
134 1997, p 119.
135 SASA GRG 52/32/5.
136 Dr H Basedow, Reverend John Blacket, Mrs T R Bowman, Mrs C T Cooke, C F Fryer, Mrs A K Goode, Reverend J Jennison, Jas Lamb, Mrs J Carlile-McDonnell, Miss M Matthews, Mrs J A McKay, Professor Darnley Naylor, Reverend R C Nicholson, N A Richardson, Reverend Dr Seymour, Dr W Ramsay-Smith, John Snell, Reverend A C Stevens, C E Taplin, Miss A L Tomkinson, David Unaipon, Mrs K H Weston, Capt S A White, J Chas Genders (SASA GRG 52/31/5).
137 From a poem 'Daughters of the Ancient Eve, We know the gifts ye gave and give, Who knows the gifts which you shall give, Daughters of the Newer Eve' cited in the Catholic Citizen 1936, 22 (2), p 9.
138 Paisley 1998, p 252.
139 Rischbieth 1964, p 59.
140 Paisley 1995, p 253; 1998, p 255.

141 Article 23 of the League of Nations Covenant cited in Holland 1995, p 55.
142 Paisley 1995, p 257.
143 Also known as the Declaration of Geneva. In 1959 the United Nations prepared its own Declaration of the Rights of the Child and in 1978 began drawing up the Convention on the Rights of the Child.
144 AA [NT] A10664/4 1C45/61/128.
145 Paisley 1998, pp 252–3.
146 Paisley 1995, pp 258–9.
147 Lock to Bennett 1929, SASA GRG 52/53/31.
148 Lock to Cooke 1932, SASA GRG 52/32/49.
149 Bennett to Cooke 1929, SASA GRG 52/32/25.
150 Jacobs 1990, p 201.
151 Bennett 1927, p 259.
152 Bennett 1930, pp 118–19.
153 SASA GRG 52/32/52.
154 Bennett 1930, p 119.
155 SASA GRG 52/32/52. The quotes from Radcliffe-Brown were published in *Oceania*.
156 *West Australian*, 17.5.1932.
157 Cited in Lake 1998, p 96.
158 Cited in Jacobs 1990, p 211.
159 Cited in Daniels and Murnane 1980, p 89.
160 Cited in Western Australian Government 1934, p 225.
161 ibid.
162 ibid., p 225.
163 ibid., p 228.
164 ibid., p 227.
165 ibid., p 229.
166 Western Australian Government 1934, pp 299, 807, 307.
167 Cited in Jacobs 1990, p 235.
168 Western Australian Government 1934, p 553.
169 ibid., p 225.
170 ibid., p 573.
171 ibid., p 335.
172 ibid., p 575.
173 Other Board members included the Commissioner of Public Works, Professor Cleland, Dr Duguid, Alice Johnston, Reverend Canon S T C Best and Leonard J Cook.
174 *Advertiser* (Adelaide), 25.10.57, 13.6.64.
175 SASA GRG 52/32/45.
176 SASA GRG 52/32/8.
177 SASA GRG 52/32/45.
178 Roe 1986, p 201.
179 ibid., p 282.
180 See Roe 1986; Lutton 1988.
181 Western Australian Government 1934, p 539; Paisley 1995, p 266.
182 Paisley 1998, p 265.
183 Paisley 1997a.
184 Cited in Daniels and Murnane 1980, p 89.
185 Bennett 1957, p 34.
186 Neville 1947, p 39.
187 Paisley 1997b, p 4.
188 ibid.
189 ibid.

CHAPTER SIX
1 See Kidd 1994a, p 94.
2 Rintoul 1993, p 241.
3 Ibid., pp 85–86.
4 Commonwealth Government, Human Rights and Equal Opportunity Commission 1997, p 155.
5 Hume 1989, p 93.
6 Nailon (1997, pp 38–9) states that early baptismal records at Beagle Bay Mission contain no information of family names or place of origin. Children were given baptismal names and thereby many lost their

Aboriginal names, reflecting their entry into a new Christian life, also symbolised in their new Christian names.

7   Froh 1998, p 359.
8   See McHoul (1991) for a discussion of photographs taken in the nineteenth century for the Dr Barnardo Homes in Britain.
9   Cited in Harris 1990, p 583.
10 Rowley 1978, p 162.
11 Commonwealth Government, Human Rights and Equal Opportunity Commission, 1997.
12 Parbury 1986, p 121.
13 See Tonkinson 1974 and Long 1970.
14 1989, p 26.
15 Wright 1997, p 20.
16 Cited in Watson 1993, p 29.
17 Wallace Adams 1995.
18 Choo 1997, p 15.
19 Commonwealth Government 1929, p 24.
20 Cited in Austin 1997, p 188.
21 Neville 1947, pp 98–9.
22 Cited in Jacobs 1990, p 80.
23 Cited in Marks 1960, p 90.
24 Rowley 1978, p 173.
25 Jayawardena 1995, p 13.
26 Cited in Harris 1990, p 586. Church support began to increase during the 1950s and 1960s in part due to government efforts to persuade white Australians to actively support the policy of assimilation.
27 See Ware 1992 on the civilising role of white women in mission work around the world.
28 Ware 1992, pp 129, 24.
29 Cited in Bowie, Kirkwood and Ardener 1993, pp 10–11.
30 Bell 1988, p 341–2.
31 Thomson 1989, p 9.
32 ibid., pp 268–9.
33 Young 1989, p 117.
34 Gribble 1933; Halse 1996.
35 *Perth Mail*, 19.8.1948.
36 1996, p 124.
37 Trigger 1991, p 64–67.
38 Watson 1993, p 230
39 Carter 1981, p 22.
40 See Maushart 1993, pp 207–8.
41 ibid., pp 174–5.
42 Biedelman 1982 cited in Tonkinson 1988, p 63.
43 Young 1989, p 89.
44 'For God so loved the world, that he gave his only begotten Son, that whosoever believeth in him should not perish, but have eternal life.'
45 Lock in Bishop 1991, p 84.
46 Australian Board of Missions 1909, np.
47 Cited in Bowden and Bunbury 1990, p 73.
48 Cited in Blake 1992, p 84.
49 Yarrabah Mission Annual Report 1909, np.
50 Maushart 1993, p 52.
51 Cited in Morris 1988, pp 36–7.
52 1990, p 583.
53 Cited in Mattingley and Hampton 1988, p 215.
54 Attwood, Burridge, Burridge and Stokes 1994, p 32.
55 ibid., p 11
56 Cited in Chesson 1988, pp 27–8.
57 Blake 1992, pp 92–3, 100–102.
58 Austin 1997, p 309.
59 Cited in Halse 1996, p 234.
60 Green 1995, p 207. Following his sacking from Forrest River Mission, Jack Gribble was appointed town inspector in Darwin and then acting Superintendent at Bagot Reserve and later patrolled the coast around Melville Island.

61 Read 1999, p 57–8.
62 Cited in Harris 1990, p 572.
63 Cited in Bowden and Bunbury 1990, p 71.
64 This reflected practices in missions in other British colonies. See Jayawardena 1995.
65 Jebb and Haebich 1992, p 34.
66 Cole 1972, pp 56–7.
67 Mattingley and Hampton 1988, p 213.
68 McDonald 1996, p 111.
69 Monica Mushiwun in *Ngoonjook* 1992, p 21.
70 Agnes Palmer in Rintoul 1993, p 128.
71 Pohlner 1986, p 84.
72 Goffman 1961.
73 1993, p 131.
74 Blake 1992, p 88.
75 Bennett 1930, pp 117–8.
76 McDonald 1996, p 17.
77 Lock cited in Bishop 1991, p 73.
78 Attwood, Burridge, Burridge and Stokes 1994, p 100.
79 1995.
80 Young 1989, p 132.
81 Cited in Bishop 1991, p 73.
82 McDonald 1996, p 58.
83 Gsell 1955, p 35.
84 Cited in Bishop 1991, p 70.
85 Bishop 1991, p 87.
86 Cited in Bishop 1991, p 76.
87 ibid, p 102.
88 Cited in Jacobs 1990, p 226.
89 Miller 1985, p 128.
90 West, nd.
91 Austin 1997, p 186.
92 Cited in Watson 1993, p 222.
93 Cited in Watson 1993, p 221.
94 1992, p 118.
95 Maushart 1993, p 61.
96 ibid., p 126.
97 Long 1970, p 181.
98 Watson 1993, p 192.
99 West nd, pp 9–15.
100 Gertie Sambo in Rintoul 1993, p 91.
101 Cited in Mattingley and Hampton 1988, p 215.
102 Cited in Wallace Adams 1995, p 93.
103 Kennedy 1990, p 10; Watson 1993, p 12. The incident is also the subject of a novel by Thea Astley, *The Multiple Effects of Rain Shadow.*
104 Prior 1993, p 27.
105 Kennedy 1990, pp 12–14.
106 Miller 1996, pp 328 ff.
107 Anderson 1988.
108 Pastor Claude Wiebusch personal communication Adelaide, 1997.
109 Mondalmi speaking to Catherine Berndt cited in Scanlon 1986, p 99.
110 Cited in Scanlon 1986, p 99.
111 Arthur Malcolm in Thomson 1989, p 20.
112 Cited in Scanlon 1986, p 99.
113 Blake 1992, p 148.
114 Cited in Young 1989, p 117.
115 Scarry 1985, p 109.
116 Cited in Scarry 1985, pp 110–11.
117 Cited in Nailon 1997, p 194.
118 Spindler cited in Wallace Adams 1995, pp 223–4.
119 Wallace Adams 1995, p 135.
120 Cairns 1996, pp 60–1.

121 Miller 1986, p 163.
122 Cited in Cairns 1996, p 33.
123 This discussion draws on Attwood (1989), Blake (1991) and Rowse (1998a).
124 1997, p 51.
125 This quote is used with permission. Ruth Hegarty won the 1998 David Unaipon Award and her autobiography *Is That You Ruthie?* was published by the University of Queensland Press in 1999.
126 Cited in Blake 1992, p 150.
127 Wadjularbinna in Rintoul 1993, p 142.
128 Poad, West and Miller 1985, p 174.
129 Rintoul 1993, p 242.
130 Blake 1992, pp 141 ff.
131 WASA 752/743/1922.
132 McDonald 1996, pp 23–4.
133 Cited in Chesson 1988, pp 25–26.
134 ibid., pp 24–5.
135 Elsie Roughsey in Huffer 1980, p 3.
136 Cited in Bowden and Bunbury 1990.
137 Kimberley Language Resource Centre 1996.
138 Fred Clay cited in Rosser 1987, p 130.
139 Blake 1992, p 159.
140 Broome 1982, p 106.
141 Blake 1992, pp 348–9.
142 Wadjularbinna in Rintoul 1993, pp 140–1.
143 Cited in Blake 1992, p 153.
144 Poad, West and Miller 1985, p 178.
145 1996, p 39.
146 Maushart 1993, p 103.
147 ibid.
148 Cited in Maushart 1993, p 105.
149 Cummings 1990, p 23.
150 Cited in Maushart 1993, p 103.
151 Carter 1981, p 23.
152 Hume 1989, p 100.
153 Ruth Hegarty cited in Blake 1992, p 203
154 Jack Davis cited in Chesson 1988, p 26.
155 May Smith in Thomson 1989, p 34.
156 Blake 1992, p 158.
157 Hume 1989, p 99.
158 Cited in Rintoul 1993, p 238.
159 WASA 993/169/1927.
160 Maushart 1993, p 86.
161 ibid., p 95.
162 Blake 1992, p 202.
163 Maushart 1993, p 89.
164 Cited in Poad, West and Miller 1985, p 130.
165 Haebich 1998a, p 343.
166 Chi and Kuckles 1991, p 7.
167 ibid., p 13.
168 Harrison 1975, p 20.
169 Wadjularbinna in Rintoul 1993, pp 142–3.
170 McDonald 1996, p 15.
171 Maushart 1993, p 122.
172 Cited in Blake 1992, p 139.
173 Wallace Adams 1995, p 142.
174 Read 1999, p 35.
175 Mathews 1977, pp 56–7.
176 Cited in Reynolds 1989, p 120.
177 Cited in Reynolds 1989, p 121.
178 At first white children studied by correspondence but with sufficient numbers their parents lobbied for a separate school which was opened in 1932 with fourteen white children in attendance (Blake 1992, p 140).

179 Blake 1992, p 134.
180 Cited in Bowden and Bunbury 1990, p 69.
181 Maushart 1993, p 60.
182 Cited in Bowden and Bunbury 1990, p 69.
183 WASA 993/97/1927.
184 Stanton 1988, pp 294, 297.
185 Cited in Stanton 1988, p 297.
186 Morris 1988, p 41.
187 Australian Board of Missions 1909, np.
188 Victoria Archibald in Rintoul 1993, pp 155–6.
189 ibid.
190 Wright 1997, pp 64–5.
191 Bruce Ellis in *Ngoonjook* 1992, p 84.
192 Cited in Chesson 1988, pp 26–7.
193 Read 1999, p 58.
194 Bruce Ellis in *Ngoonjook* 1992, p 84.
195 Richard Murray in Read 1984, p 98.
196 Halse 1996, p 239.
197 Watson 1993, p 216.
198 1997.
199 Watson, 1993.
200 Personal communication Mary Ann Jebb, 1997.
201 All cultures have their own body practices, rules of hygiene and ideals concerning physical appearance and personal manners. See Burke (1996) for an analysis of traditional practices in Zimbabwe and colonial efforts to replace them with 'modern' standards of hygiene, cleanliness and appearance.
202 Kennedy 1990, p 17.
203 Beresford and Omaji 1998, pp 137–8.
204 1991, pp 208–9.
205 Cited in Blake 1991, p 205.
206 Blake 1991, p 210.
207 Calculated by the author using court records of deaths at Moore River Settlement cocollected by the Mogumber Data Base Project (1997).
208 Bartky 1990; Gilchrist 1993.
209 Pastor Kaibel of Hermannsburg cited in Bell 1988, p 343.
210 Read 1999, p 35–6.
211 1997, pp 20–1.
212 Blake 1992, p 155.
213 Nellie Sheridan in Rintoul 1993, p 199.
214 There is a significant literature on the experiences of Aboriginal female domestic servants. See for example Haebich 1982; Edwards 1982; Huggins 1987/8, 1992, 1995; Ward 1987, 1991; Nannup, Marsh and Kinnane 1992; Walden 1995; Goodall 1990, 1995a; Evans and Scott 1996; Rose 1998.
215 Chi and Kuckles 1991, p 10.
216 Burridge 1988, p 28.
217 Cited in Reynolds 1989, p 173.
218 Gribble 1930, pp 99–100.
219 Capps 1995, p 56.
220 Cited in Miller 1985, p 162.
221 ibid.
222 Wadjularbinna in Rintoul 1993, p 141.
223 1990, p 591.
224 Poad, West and Miller 1985, p 177.
225 Cited in Stanton 1988, pp 294, 296.
226 Gsell, 1955.
227 1988, p 342.
228 Scarry 1985, 109.
229 1993a, p 104.
230 ibid., pp 107, 105.
231 WA GG 12/5/1918.
232 *Great Southern Herald* (Katanning), 6.7.1918.
233 Gilchrist 1993, p 67.

234 Watson 1993, p 192.
235 Cited in Watson 1993, p 192.
236 Kennedy 1990, p 9.
237 Cited in Bowden and Bunbury 1990, p 70.
238 Cited in Poad, West and Miller 1985, p 175.
239 Gilchrist 1993, p 70.
240 Kennedy 1990, p 9.
241 Western Australian Museum: Anthropology Collection.
242 Trigger 1988, p 222.
243 Cited in Poad, West and Miller 1985, p 175.
244 Bain Attwood personal communication, 1999.
245 Head shaving was a standard punishment for humiliating female inmates, dating in Australia from the convict period (Damousi 1997).
246 Thomson 1989, p 57.
247 Haebich 1998a, p 182.
248 Cited in Bowden and Bunbury 1990, p 70.
249 ibid.
250 1988, p 49.
251 Matron's Log for the Senior Girls' Home at Yarrabah 1908 cited in Gilchrist 1993, p 68.
252 Aboriginal Legal Service of WA 1995, p 40.
253 1997, pp 187–92.
254 Jackson 1995, p 12.
255 Cited in Maushart 1993, p 69.
256 Mattingley and Hampton 1988, p 170.
257 ibid., p 163.
258 McDonald 1996, p 65.
259 Cited in Blake 1992, p 348
250 Cited from her autobiography, *The Divided Kingdom*, in Blake 1992, p 348.

CHAPTER SEVEN
1   Murphy and Smart 1997, p 1.
2   White 1979, 1981.
3   See McDonald, 1996.
4   Tom Sampey 1947 cited in Attwood and Markus 1999, p 138.
5   Jaggs 1991, p 187.
6   Mickler 1998, p 121.
7   See Haebich 1999b.
8   See also Mickler's analysis of these pamphlets (1998, pp 94–5).
9   MacDonald 1995, pp 53, 57.
10   Haebich 1998b.
11   Hasluck 1953.
12   Hasluck cited in Rowse 1998b, p 124.
13   Tim Rowse personal communication, 1998.
14   Beckett cited in Rowse 1998a, p 107.
15   Tim Rowse personal communication, 1999.
16   WA DNA AR, 1952, p 5.
17   AA (NT) FI 1954/1013.
18   Bridge 1998, p 134.
19   Bain Attwood personal communication, 1999.
20   Taffe 1995, p 156.
21   ibid.
22   ibid.
23   AA (ACT) A1838 929/5/3 Part 1. Referred to in this file.
24   SASA GRG 57/18.
25   AA (ACT) A1838 929/5/3 Part 1. Referred to in this file.
26   Taffe 1995, p 167.
27   Commonwealth Government, Minister for Territories 1959, p 29.
28   ibid., p 30.
29   Commonwealth Government, Federal Minister for Territories 1963, pp 31–3.
30   Looking Through Photographs Conference, Queensland Museum, Brisbane, 1997.

31 Cited in Gungil Jindibah Centre 1994, p 27.
32 WA DNW AR 1964, p 8.
33 Western Australia Government, Department of Native Welfare, nd.
34 *Come On to My House*, Wave Productions for the Department of Native Welfare, nd, held at the Aboriginal Affairs Department, Perth. I would like to thank Steven Kinnane and Lauren Marsh for drawing my attention to this film.
35 Tim Rowse personal communication, 1999.
36 Western Australian Government, Department of Native Welfare 1967, p 49.
37 *Herald* (Melbourne), 22.3.1965.
38 The film has no title. A copy remains in the possession of Bill Grayden.
39 *Sunday Times* (Perth), 1941.
40 Grayden 1957, p 1.
41 ibid., p 5.
42 WA PD 1956, p 144; reprinted in Grayden 1957, pp 2–10.
43 Article 12: No one shall be subjected to arbitrary interference with his privacy, family, home or correspondence, nor to attacks upon his honour and reputation. Everyone has the right to the protection of the law against such interference or attacks.
 Article 25 Clause (2): Motherhood and childhood are entitled to special care and assistance. All children, whether born in or out of wedlock, shall enjoy the same social protection.
 Article 26 Clause (3): Parents have a prior right to choose the kind of education that shall be given to their children.
44 1952.
45 Cited in Clay and Leapman 1995, p 159.
46 Cited in Taffe 1995, p 163.
47 Grayden 1957, pp 29, 41.
48 Western Australian Government 1956; reprinted in Grayden 1957, pp 11–43.
49 ibid., pp 30–33, 41, 47.
50 ibid., pp 171–2.
51 Cited in Grayden 1957, p 82.
52 ibid.
53 WASA 993/384/1957.
54 Cited in Grayden 1957, pp 59, 124.
55 ibid.
56 WASA 993/384/1957.
57 Bill Grayden personal communication Perth, 1997.
58 Goodall 1996, p 274. Public protests against the Woomera Rocket Range included pamphlets published by Dr Charles Duguid and anthropologist Dr Donald Thompson (McGinness 1991, p 57).
59 *Sunday Times* (Perth), 31.3.1957.
60 Kidd 1997, p 201.
61 Cited in Grayden 1957, p 72.
62 ibid., p 110.
63 *Narrogin Observer*, 20.6.1957.
64 McGinness 1991, p 58.
65 AA (VIC) CA 3333 B408.
66 Bauml Duberman 1989, p 490.
67 ibid., p 61.
68 Newspaper cutting held in Council for Aboriginal Rights Papers, La Trobe Collection, State Library of Victoria, MS 12913, Box 2 Folder 9. I would like to thank Bain Attwood for this reference.
69 Read 1990, p 73.
70 Attwood and Markus 1999, p 170.
71 ibid., p 171.
72 Davey 1963, p 6. I would like to thank John McClinton of La Trobe University for providing me with a copy of this pamphlet.
73 WASA 1724/29/1958.
74 WASA 1733/705/1950. File includes material from later than file date.
75 Western Australian Government 1958.
76 Cited in Western Australian Government 1958, p 10.
77 ibid., p 16.
78 Rowse 1998a, p 8.
79 *Smoke Signals* August–September 1958, p 3. I would like to thank Bain Attwood for this reference.

80 ibid.
81 Cited in Western Australian Government 1958, p 35.
82 ibid., p 20.
83 ibid.
84 ibid., p 15.
85 Cited in MacDonald 1995, p 58. Name of film footage provided by Bain Attwood. Deutscher was commissioned by the Council for Aboriginal Rights to make a film on Western Australia, to expose racial discrimination. The film was never completed (Bain Attwood personal communication, 1999).
86 Harold Blair Aboriginal Children's Project brochure in QSA 1A/587 Box 107 505/1.
87 *Standard* (Frankston, Vic), 7.1.1971.
88 *Herald* (Melbourne), 16.7.1968.
89 *Star* (Altona, Vic), 2.6.1971.
90 *Age* (Melbourne), 21.1.1972.
91 *Herald* (Melbourne), 2.12.1971.
92 QSA 1A/587 Box 107 505/1.
93 Harrison 1975, p 233.
94 ibid., p 233.
95 *Age* (Melbourne), 22.12.1970.
96 *Sun* (Melborne), 21.12. 1967.
97 ibid., 10.7.1970.
98 *Australian* 21.10.1971.
99 Tim Rowse personal communication 1999.
100 Sanders 1986, p 267.
101 Gray 1998, pp 56–7.
102 Cited in Sanders 1986, p 268.
103 Commonwealth Government, Department of Territories 1951, np.
104 Cited in Taffe 1995, p.155.
105 Rowley 1961–2, pp 255–9.
106 Organisations invited were as follows: from Western Australia the State Native Welfare Council, the Native Welfare Association, Pindan Pty Ltd and the Aboriginal Advancement League; from South Australia the Aborigines Advancement League; from Victoria the Council for Aboriginal Rights, the Aborigines Advancement League and the Australian Aborigines League; and from New South Wales the Aboriginal Australian Fellowship (McGinness 1991, p 69).
107 Cited in Attwood and Markus 1999, p 176.
108 ibid.
109 Tim Rowse personal communication 1999.
110 McGinness 1991, p 77.
111 See Stretton and Finnimore (1993) for a historical background on the Commonwealth franchise and Aboriginal people.
112 Initially in both states voting was not made compulsory. In Western Australia property qualifications excluded most Aboriginal people from voting in local government elections.
113 For example, prior to 1960 pension benefits were denied to Aborigines living on reserves serviced by government or subsidised institutions. From 1960 Aborigines in institutions were eligible for the maternity allowance and aged, invalid and widow pensions but not for sickness or unemployment benefits. In 1969 Aborigines in institutions in the Northern Territory were paid training allowances rather than unemployment benefits (Sanders, 1986; Rowse 1998a, p 109).
114 1974, p 158.
115 Kidd 1998, p 43; WA DNW AR 1960, p 8.
116 Tatz 1964, p 106.
117 *Social Services Journal* 1960, 13, p 3.
118 Cited in Murphy 1995, p 233.
119 *West Australian*, 20.6.1950.
120 WASA 993/932/1943.
121 ibid.
122 WASA 993/745/1942.
123 WASA 993/932/1943. File includes material from later than file date.
124 WASA SD 332.
125 WA DNA AR 1950, p 75.
126 Cited in McGinness 1991, p 94.
127 WASA 1733/705/1950. File includes material from later than file date.

128 Tatz 1964, Appendix 23.
129 AA (ACT) A431 1949/383.
130 AA (ACT) A431 1949/383.
131 AA (ACT) A431 1949/383.
132 1998, p 42.
133 1998.
134 Attwood and Markus 1998, p 126.
135 ibid., p 123.
136 ibid., p 126.
137 ibid.
138 Attwood and Markus 1999, pp 184–6.
139 ibid., p 190.
140 Coombs 1976.
141 Atwood and Markus 1998, p 131.
142 1998a, p 111.
143 Rowley 1961–2, p 251.
144 Elkin wrote extensively on assimilation policy but his seminal work is the 1944 pamphlet, *Citizenship for Aborigines. A National Aboriginal Policy*. See Wise (1985) on Elkin's life work.
145 Gray 1998, p 199.
146 See Rowse (1998b) for a detailed comparative analysis of the views of Elkin and Hasluck. Hasluck also published extensively on his views of the policy of assimilation and its implementation. See Hasluck 1963, 1988.
147 Gray 1998, p 58.
148 Cited in Wise 1985, pp 230–1.
149 SASA GRG 52/18.
150 Cited in Taffe 1995, p 163.
151 AA (ACT) A/1 1927/2982. File includes material from later than file date.
152 Cited in Rowse 1998b, p 107.
153 Bill McGregor, paper presented at the Australian Historical Association Conference, Sydney, 1998.
154 WA DNA AR 1956, p 27. File includes material from later than file date.
155 Rowley 1961–2, pp 252–4.
156 Rowse 1998a, pp 8–9.
157 Rowley 1961–2, p 250.
158 1991, pp 122, 141.
159 Rowley 1961–2; Berndt 1962–3.
160 Chairman of Northern Territory Housing Commission 1961 cited in Rowse 1998a, p 184.
161 ibid.
162 Tatz 1964, p 141.
163 Jaggs 1986, pp 145–6.
164 Cited in Japanangka and Nathan, 1983.
165 AA (VIC) B2015/0.
166 WA DNA AR 1953, p 4.
167 AA (ACT) A1838 929/5/3 Part 1.
168 Yardi and Stokes 1998, pp 59–60.
169 Rowse 1998a, p. 8.
170 Beckett 1988 cited in Rowse 1998a, p 107.
171 Cummings 1990, p 105.
172 Collmann 1979, p 383.
173 Austin 1993, p 217; Sanders 1986, p 259.
174 Macleod 1997, pp 27–8.
175 AA (CRS) A6119/78, 1091. I would like to thank Bain Attwood for this reference.
176 Porter 1993, p 198.
177 Collmann 1979, p 384.
178 Cummings 1990, p 102.
179 Tatz 1964, p 56.
180 ibid.
181 Donovan 1988, p 202.
182 The system was set up under E W P Chinnery, Director of Native Affairs and former high-ranking official in Papua New Guinea.
183 Long 1992, p xv.

184 ibid., p 90.
185 Evans 1990, p 2.
186 Long 1992, pp xiv, xv.
187 Tatz 1964, p 194.
188 *Age* (Melbourne), 5.6.1964.
189 Collman 1979; Rowse 1998a.
190 Rowse 1998a, p 148.
191 Rowley 1972c, p 118.
192 Rowse 1998a, pp 8–9.
193 ibid., p 10.
194 1998a.
195 Rowse 1998a, p 6.
196 ibid., p 162.
197 ibid., p 160.
198 ibid., p 161.
199 Pittock 1975.
200 Hipsley and Corden report cited in Rowse 1998a, p 163–4.
201 Rowse 1998a, p 108.
202 ibid., p 180.
203 Tatz 1964, p 270.
204 Rowse 1998a, p 151.
205 Cited in Rowse 1998a, p 150.
206 ibid.
207 ibid., p 151.
208 Collmann 1979, p 383.
209 ibid.
210 ibid., p 390.
211 Dr Charles Duguid, *Herald* (Melbourne) 23.10.1951.
212 Cummings 1990, p 79; Armitage 1995, p 59.
213 Long 1992, p 81.
214 ibid.
215 Macleod 1997, p 167.
216 Cited in Macdonald 1995, p 56.
217 Cited in Long 1992, p 83.
218 Long 1992, p 83.
219 ibid.; AA (ACT) A 452/1 1961/7809.
220 AA (ACT) A 452/1 1961/7809.
221 ibid.
222 ibid.
223· ibid.
224 Long 1992, p 83; *Herald* (Melbourne), 23.10.1951; *Sun* (Melbourne), 25.10.1951.
225 AA 452/1 1961/7809.
226 Cited in Long 1992, p 84.
227 ibid.
228 Macleod 1997, pp 167–8.
229 Long 1992, p 84.
230 Macleod 1997, p 166.
231 ibid., p 248.
232 AA (ACT) A452/1 1961/7809.
233 ibid.; AA (NT) F1 1953/659. File includes material from later than file date.
234 AA (NT) F1 1953/659 Part 2.
235 AA (ACT) A452/1 1961/7809.
236 The Ordinance introduced measures for the operation and administration of children's institutions, a Children's Court, affiliation proceedings, committal of deprived children, offences in respect of children and employment of children. The Director of Welfare was made legal guardian of State wards to the age of eighteen. The Child Welfare Council replaced the SCC to advise the Director (Cummings 1990, p 110).
237 AA (ACT) A452/1 1961/7809; Macleod 1997, pp 239–44.
238 Macleod 1997, p 171.
239 The Australian Inland Mission opened the Retta Dixon Home at Bagot Aboriginal Compound in 1946.
240 AA (ACT) A452/1 1961/7809.

241 1990, p 116.
242 1991.
243 *National Times*, 28.5.1974.
244 AA (ACT) A431/1 1959/3487.
245 ibid.
246 AA (ACT) A452/1 1961/7809.
247 AA (ACT) A452/1 1961/7809.
248 AA (ACT) A432/1 1959/3487; AA (ACT) A452/1 1961/7809.
249 AA (ACT) A452/1 1961/7809.
250 ibid
251 *Sun* (Melbourne), 28.5.1974.
252 Cummings 1990, p 98.
253 ibid., p 99.
254 ibid., p 123.
255 AA (ACT) A452/1 1959/ 4025.
256 AA (ACT) A 451/1 1961/7809.
257 QSA 1A/587 Box 107 505/1.
258 Of these children, nine were receiving medical attention, nineteen were living in boarding institutions and eleven had been recommended for adoption. The medical and boarding institutions accommodating the children included: Magill Methodist Children's Home, St Francis Home, the Warrawee Far North Children's Home (for children with long-term illnesses), the Spastic Centre at Woodville, Kate Cock's Babies Home, Farr House (for orphans), St Mary's Baby's Home, Cabra Convent, Home of the Good Shepherd, Kent Town Boy's Home, the Aborigines Hostel and the Central Missions Children's Home (AA (ACT) A431/1 1959/3487).
259 AA (ACT) A431/1 1959/3487.
260 ibid.
261 ibid.
262 Cummings 1990, p 95.
263 ibid., p 98.
264 ibid., p 112.
265 AA (ACT) A452/1 1961/7809.

CHAPTER EIGHT
1 Australian Broadcasting Corporation, 1997.
2 Aborigines Welfare Board cited in New South Wales Government 1996, p 44.
3 Under the *Native (Citizenship Rights) Act* 1944 applicants had to prove that they had ceased all association with Aborigines except their immediate family for two years; had either served in the armed forces or were otherwise 'fit and proper' persons; were fluent in English; and free from any communicable diseases such as leprosy or venereal disease. Referees were required to provide proof that the applicants were hard working, respectable and capable of living independently of the Department of Native Affairs.
4 Eggleston 1976, p 201.
5 Queensland Government 1997b, Attachment 11.
6 Police protectors decreased from seventy-seven in 1950 to twenty-nine in 1956. The majority were located in towns in the south (Biskup 1973, p 233).
7 1999, p 190.
8 McGrath 1993a. See also Haebich 1991; Beresford and Omaji 1996.
9 1976, p 220.
10 Goodall 1995a, p 85.
11 Rowley 1961–2, p 255.
12 Australian Broadcasting Corporation, 1997.
13 Kociumbus 1997, p 212.
14 Rowley 1961–2, p 255.
15 Western Australian Government 1948, p 17.
16 Goodall 1995a pp 85, 87.
17 Bessant 1991, p 13.
18 ibid., pp 8, 26.
19 Gare 1966, p 70.
20 ibid.; p 257.
21 Barwick 1962–3, pp 19–20.
22 Goodall 1996, p 276.

23 Woolmington 1991, p 37.
24 Western Australia Government ndb, p 26.
25 *Sun* (Melbourne), 10.9.1968.
26 *Argus* 14.3.1956; *Maryborough Advertiser*, 27.6.1956; David Bird personal communication, Albany, 1997.
27 David Bird, Albany, personal communication, 1997.
28 ibid.
29 Cited in Woolmington 1991, p 30.
30 A verbal statement from an unidentified Aboriginal woman 1990 cited in Woolmington 1991, p 37.
31 Fink 1957–8, p 110.
32 Commonwealth Government, Human Rights and Equal Opportunity Commission 1997, p 95.
33 *Truth* (Melbourne), 9.1.2.1947.
34 Daniels 1995, p 8.
35 Medcraft and Gee 1995, p xii.
36 Denis Daniels, Hobart, personal communication, 1997.
37 *Infants Welfare Act 1935; Child Welfare Act 1960.*
38 Commonwealth Government, Human Rights and Equal Opportunity Commission 1997, p 96.
39 ibid., p 97.
40 Daniels 1995, pp 9–10.
41 Denis Daniels, Hobart, personal communication, 1997.
42 Cited in Mollison and Everitt 1976, np.
43 Cited in Daniels 1995, p 14.
44 ibid.
45 Tasmanian Government 1995a, p 15.
46 ibid., pp iv–v.
47 Tasmanian Government 1995b, p 10.
48 Tasmanian Aboriginal Centre 1996, p 114.
49 Victorian Government 1957, p 6; V AWB AR 1961, p 5.
50 Also known as the McLean Report.
51 Victorian Government 1957, p 6.
52 ibid., p 9.
53 ibid., p 16.
54 V AWB AR 1960, p 4; Victorian Government, Department of Health and Community Services, Legislation and Legal Branch, 1996.
55 AA (VIC) B 408 item 4, Box 1.
56 Barwick 1962–3 p19, p 22.
57 V AWB AR, 1959.
58 Commonwealth Government, Human Rights and Equal Opportunity Commission 1997, p 63.
59 Cited in Victorian Government 1996b, p 58.
60 *Observer* (Melbourne), 2.12.1973.
61 V AWB AR 1966, p 9.
62 Linda Briskman personal communication, 1997.
63 V AWB AR 1966, p 9.
64 Cited in Victorian Government 1996b, p 61.
65 Victorian Government, Department of Human Services, nd; Felton, 1997.
66 V AWB AR, 1964, p 5.
67 Iredale, 1965.
68 Read 1983, p 29.
69 ibid.
70 Cited in New South Wales Government 1996, p 43.
71 NSW AWB AR, 1958, p 5.
72 Commonwealth Government, Human Rights and Equal Opportunity Commission 1997, p 53.
73 Iredale 1965, p 114.
74 ibid., p 115.
75 ibid., p 113.
76 ibid.
77 Cited in Gungil Jindibah Centre 1994, p 25.
78 Iredale 1965, 115.
79 ibid., p 149.
80 ibid., p 151.
81 Reay 1965, pp 106–7.

82   Gungil Jindibah Centre 1994, p 23.
83   Goodall 1995a, p 87.
84   Goodall 1990, p 9.
85   New South Wales Government 1996, p 14; based on figures collected by Read, 1981.
86   Link-Up and Wilson 1997, p 62.
87   Goodall 1990, p 9.
88   Cited in New South Wales Government 1996, p 52.
89   ibid
90   *Advertiser* (Adelaide), 21.11.57.
91   Read 1983, p 34.
92   Read 1999, p 63.
93   ibid., p 63.
94   ibid., p 64.
95   Eddie Cockburn Manager of Brewarinna Station in 1965 cited in Australian Broadcasting Corporation, 1997.
96   Cited in Link-Up and Wilson, 1997, p 72.
97   ibid.
98   Read 1983, p 34.
99   Cited in Link-Up and Wilson 1997, p 76.
100 NSW AWB AR 1950, 1960.
101 New South Wales Government 1996, p 6.
102 Cited in Goodall 1996, p 329.
103 Eddie Cockburn cited in Australian Broadcasting Corporation, 1997.
104 New South Wales Government 1996, p 53.
105 Kinchela was handed over to a local Aboriginal group and Cootamundra is now an Aboriginal Bible College.
106 Rowse, nd.
107 WA DNA AR 1947; WA DNW AR 1955.
108 WA DNA AR, 1953.
109 WASA 1733/803/1945. File includes material from later than file date.
110 WAS *Native Title Act 1963*.
111 From the title of Rowley's 1972 publication, *Outcasts in White Australia*.
112 Hodson 1993, p 85.
113 Cited in Hodson 1993, p 84.
114 WA DNA AR 1951, p 10.
115 Western Australian Government, Department of Native Welfare, nd.
116 WA DNA AR 1943; WA DNW AR 1965.
117 WA DNW AR 1964, p 10.
118 Western Australian Government, Department of Native Welfare, nd, p 26.
119 WA DNW AR, 1970.
120 Mickler 1998, pp 110–11.
121 Western Australian Government 1948, p 26.
122 WA DNA AR 1951, p 9.
123 Commonwealth Government, Human Rights and Equal Opportunity Commission 1997, p 112.
124 WA DNA AR 1950, p 8.
125 ibid., pp 8–9.
126 ibid., p 40.
127 WA DNA AR 1948.
128 WA DNA AR 1951, p 21.
129 Control of Marribank was transferred to the Baptist Church in 1952.
130 WA DNA 1950, p 34.
131 WA DNW 1962.
132 WASA 1667/528/1946.
133 WA DNW AR 1956, pp 27–8.
134 ibid., p 28.
135 ibid.
136 *Daily News* (Perth), 25.3.1958.
137 WASA 993/ 476/1960.
138 ibid.
139 ibid.
140 *Sun* (Melbourne), 2.4.69.

141 ibid.
142 Kimberley Land Council 1996, p 22.
143 WA DNW AR 1961.
144 WASA NDG1/1/1a, Circular no. 93, 1.7.1960.
145 Western Australian Government, 1958.
146 WASA 993/476/1960.
147 WASA NDG1/1/1a, Circular no.93, 1.7.1960.
148 WASA 1667/118/1963, CNA circular 142.
149 Berndt 1962–63, p 82.
150 WASA 993/476/1960.
151 WASA 1667/528/1946. File includes material from later than file date.
152 Cited in Aboriginal Legal Service of Western Australia 1995, p 80.
153 Foster 1998.
154 WA DNW AR 1964.
155 WA DNW AR 1966.
156 *Australian*, 9.5.1967.
157 1976, pp 211–13.
158 Western Australian Government 1974, p 259.
159 Long 1970; Rowley 1972c.
160 Kidd 1994b.
161 1998, p 240.
162 Queensland Government 1996, p 28.
163 Cited in Kidd 1994a, p 525.
164 Director of Native Affairs 1951 cited in Queensland Government 1997b, Attachment 11.
165 Q DNA AR 1956, p 5.
166 Q DNA AR 1963, p 4.
167 *Aborigines and Torres Strait Islander Affairs Act 1965*.
168 Cited in Attwood and Markus 1999, p 206.
169 Cited in Queensland Government 1997, point 6.
170 QSA R254 1A/ 451 Box 96 DNA to Superintendents, September 1958.
171 QSA R254 1A/ 451 Box 96 Matron to DNA, September 1958.
172 QSA R254 1A/ 451 Box 96 October 1963.
173 Commonwealth Government, Human Rights and Equal Opportunity Commission 1997, p 78.
174 QSA 1A/519, 21/9/1960.
175 ibid.
176 QSA 1A/ 519 14/9/1960. DNA memo to Superintendents of missions and settlements.
177 QSA 1A/ 519 2/12/1960.
178 ibid.
179 Long 1970, p 91.
180 In 1962 the Department of Public Instruction took over responsibility for schools in all institutions.
181 Long 1970 cited in Commonwealth Government, Human Rights and Equal Opportunity Commission 1997, p 75.
182 Queensland Government, 1996.
183 Cited in Commonwealth Government, Human Rights and Equal Opportunity Commission 1997, p 80.
184 WASA 1724/29/1958.
185 Cited in Mattingley and Hampton 1988, pp 53–4.
186 *Advertiser* (Adelaide), 30.7.1962, 17.10.62; Point Pearce Mission News, 12.12.62.
187 Mattingley and Hampton 1988, p 54.
188 SA AAAB AR 1963, p 6.
189 Brock 1993, p 117.
190 *Advertiser* (Adelaide), 1.2.63.
191 1964, p 189.
192 Cited in Mattingley and Hampton 1988, p 54.
193 ibid.
194 SA APB AR 1957, 1959.
195 Hall 1997, p 15.
196 SA DAA AR 1964, p 6.
197 *Aborigines Act 1934–9*.
198 Gale 1964, p 216.
199 ibid.

200 Cited in Hall 1997, p. 16.
201 ibid., p 17.
202 ibid.
203 SA APB AR 1956, p 5.
204 Semaphore, Salvation Army and the Magill Children's Homes.
205 SA GRG 52/32/89 Minutes of Aborigines Protection Board 20/6/56.
206 1964, p 214.
207 Gale 1964, p 222–3.
208 ibid., p 212.
209 SA GRG 52/32/91.
210 SA AAAB AR 1962.
211 SA APB AR 1959.
212 SA APB and AAD AR 1957–65.
213 Gale 1964, p 224.
214 Cuthbert 1998, p 44.
215 Jaggs 1986, p 119.
216 Chisholm 1982, p 87.
217 Spensky 1992.
218 See papers in Picton (1978) and Oxenberry (1982) for background on and critique of systems of adoption.
219 Ban and Zoltan 1993.
220 QSA 1A/ 451 25.9.1945.
221 AA (ACT) A432 1955/3798.
222 *Sun* (Melbourne), 4.11.1965.
223 ibid., 17.11.1965
224 *Australian*, 16.11.1965.
225 *Herald* (Melbourne), 11.3.1966.
226 Daphne Cross, Family and Children's Services, Perth, personal communication, 1997.
227 AA (NT) F1 1962/ 2994.
228 AA (ACT) A452 61/7809.
229 QSA 1A/587 Box 107 505/1.
230 While all Aboriginal children may have been wards of the Queensland DNAO, outside of the state their parents were their legal guardians. The AWB had no similar system of wardship and children could only be declared wards of the Department of Family Welfare by Court order. Furthermore there was no provision for interstate transfer of wardship under the Child Welfare Act. In the case of a child under the age of five sent to a person not its guardian the Department of Family Welfare would have to be notified.
231 QSA 1A/587 Box 107 505/1.
232 ibid.
233 ibid.
234 ibid.
235 ibid.
236 ibid.
237 ibid.
238 Cuthbert 1998, p 43.
239 QSA 1A/474.
240 Link-Up and Wilson 1997, p 83.
241 *Australian*, 3.6.1972.
242 Cuthbert 1998.
243 National Inquiry into the Separation of Aboriginal and Torres Strait Islander Children from their Families hearings Perth, 1997. Similar allegations have been made recently by non-Aboriginal mothers in Tasmania.
244 Commonwealth Government, Human Rights and Equal Opportunity Commission 1997, p 65.
245 ibid., p 69.
246 Bruce Alcorn personal communication, 1997.
247 1990, p 123.
248 QSA 1A/451 September 1958.
249 WASA 993/17/1963.
250 Names withheld, personal communication 1996.
251 ibid.
252 QSA 1A/451 505/1.
253 *Advertiser* (Adelaide), 30.1.1957.
254 *Advertiser* (Adelaide), 20.9.1962.

255 *News* (Adelaide), 1.2.1962.
256 *News* (Adelaide), 30.1.1964.
257 *Weekend Mail* (Perth), 1.2.1956.
258 *Truth* (Brisbane), 23.11,1958.
259 Cuthbert 1998, p 44.
260 QSA 1A/451 12.10.1969.
261 personal communication, name witheld.
262 QSA 1A/ 451 6/9/1974.
263 QSA 1A/ 451 October 1961.
264 QSA 1A/ 451 October 1963.
265 Cuthbert 1998, p 48.
266 *News* (Adelaide), 1.5.67
267 WASA 933/958/1950. File includes material from later than file date.
268 ibid.
269 Australian Broadcasting Corporation 1997.
270 QSA 1A/451.
271 ibid.
272 WASA 993/17/1963. File includes material from later than file date.
273 Cited in Read 1999, p 38.
274 ibid., p 37.
275 ibid., pp 191ff.
276 Gale 1964.
277 WA DNW AR 1964.
278 1982, p 87.
279 Read 1999, p 38.
280 Tasmanian Government 1995b, p 140.
281 Cuthbert 1998.
282 Rowse 1987, p 135.
283 Commonwealth Government, Australian Bureau of Statistics, 1966.
284 Cited in Eggleston 1976, p 7.
285 ibid.
286 ibid., p 236.
287 Long 1970, p 5.
288 Rowley 1961–2, p 253.
289 Eggleston 1976, p 224.
290 ibid., p 257.
291 Rowley 1978, p 141.
292 Tatz 1964, p 295.
293 See Mickler 1998.
294 Cited in Rowse 1998b, p 120.
295 WA DNW AR 1955, p 6.
296 Cited in Sommerlad 1978, p 43–4.
297 ibid., p 45.
298 Commonwealth Government, Royal Commission into Aboriginal Deaths in Custody 1991a, p 491.

CHAPTER NINE
1 Sereny 1995, p 667.
2 William Faulkner cited in Shriver 1995, p 4.
3 This introduction is based on Haebich, 1998c.
4 Commonwealth Government, Human Rights and Equal Opportunity Commission, 1997.
5 Halbwachs cited in Paez, Basabe and Gonzales 1997, p 150.
6 Huyssen 1994 cited in Brewster 1995, p 2.
7 Iniguez, Valencia and Vazquez 1997, p 250.
8 Kammen cited in Darian-Smith and Hamilton 1994, p 23.
9 Griffiths 1996, p 197.
10 Clendinnen 1998, p 203.
11 Sturken in Darian-Smith and Hamilton 1994, p 20.
12 Malouf 1998.
13 Marques, Paez and Serra 1997, p 255.
14 Clendinnen 1998, p 11.

15 ibid., pp 11, 203.
16 Huggins 1998, p 120.
17 Cited in Brewster 1995, p 3.
18 Jackson 1995, pp 139–40.
19 Rose 1992 cited in Brewster 1995, p 3.
20 Burke 1989 cited in Brewster 1995, p 3.
21 Research by Hank Nelson and Tim Bowden cited in Darian-Smith and Hamilton 1994, p 22.
22 Cited in Darian-Smith and Hamilton 1994, p 23.
23 Speech cited in Australians for Native Title and Reconciliation email list, 4.3.1998.
24 Cited in Commonwealth Government, Human Rights Equal Opportunity Commission 1997, p 212.
25 In 1995 in the High Court of Australia the Northern Territory Stolen Generations challenged the constitutional validity of the *Aboriginals Ordinance 1918–1957* under which children in the Northern Territory had been forcibly removed. The case was dismissed. In August 1999 Joy Williams' long-running case for compensation against the New South Wales government for losses and damages suffered due to removal from her mother under assimilationist policies was dismissed by the court on the grounds that she was not a member of the Stolen Generations — that is, that she had not been forcibly removed from her mother. In the same month the federal government issued its 'statement of regret' for past removals of Aboriginal children. Also in 1999 a legal test case involving three lead plaintiffs seeking compensation for 2000 members of the Stolen Generations began in Darwin.
26 Jackson 1995, pp 141–2.
27 Lira 1997, p 233.
28 Tony Buti personal communication, 1999. Tony Buti, Louis Johnson Memorial Trust Research Fellow at Murdoch University, is working on a comparative analysis of systems of removal and institutionalisation of indigenous children in Australia, Canada and the United States of America.
29 ibid.
30 Human Rights and Equal Opportunity Commission press release cited in the *Times Literary Supplement* October 1997, p 5.
31 Tony Buti personal communication, 1999.
32 Manne in Clendinnen 1998, p 6.
33 Pittock 1975, p 44.
34 *Telegraph* (Brisbane), 8.10.1970.
35 Mickler 1998, p 139.
36 Jones and Hill-Burnett 1982, p 223.
37 Federal funding increased from $53 million in 1971–72 to $185.8 million in 1975–76.
38 Jamrozik 1983, p 75.
39 Tomlinson 1977, p 174.
40 ibid., p 192.
41 Fitzgerald 1982, p 12.
42 Jamrozik 1983, p 75.
43 Mickler 1998, p 141. See also Jakubowicz, 1994.
44 *Sun* (Melbourne), 25.6.1968.
45 ibid.
46 *Australian*, 25.6.1968.
47 *Sun* (Melbourne), 25.6.1968.
48 *Age* (Melbourne), 26.6.1968.
49 *Geelong Advertiser*, 22.8.1968.
50 *Herald* (Melbourne), 25.6.1968.
51 *Advertiser* (Geelong), 22.8.1968.
52 *Northern (Suburbs) Progress* (Melbourne), 10.7.1968.
53 *Portland Observer and Guardian* (Victoria), 26.6.1968.
54 *Australian*, 5.10.1971.
55 *Gazette* (Ottawa, Canada), 17.7.1968.
56 *Sun* (Melbourne), 27.6.1968.
57 *Sydney Morning Herald*, 27.7.1968.
58 QSA 1A/587 Box 107 505/1.
59 *Age* (Melbourne), 27.6.1968.
60 AA (VIC) B2292, nd. Unsourced press clipping held in file.
61 *Sun* (Melbourne), 11.7.1968.
62 *Advertiser* (Geelong), 29.6.1968.
63 *Herald* (Melbourne), 5/12/1967; AA A6119/90, 2590. I would like to thank Bain Attwood for this reference.

64 *Advertiser* (Geelong), 27.6.1968
65 *Age* (Melbourne), 20.5.1964, 21.5.1964; *Herald* (Melbourne), 5.10.1968; *Sun* (Melbourne), 11.12.1969, 7.9.1970.
66 *Age* (Melbourne), 6.10.1971.
67 *Age* (Melbourne), 2.10.1971, 5.10.1971, 6.10.1971, 7.10.1971, 12.10.1971, 13.10.1971.
68 *Australian*, 5.10.1971.
69 The girl's name has been changed to protect her privacy.
70 *Sun* (Melbourne), 12.10.1971.
71 ibid.
72 *Age* (Melbourne), 12.10.1971.
73 *Advertiser* (Bendigo), 12.10.1971.
74 *Courier* (Ballarat), 12.10.1971.
75 *Standard* (Warnambool), 12.10.1971.
76 *Age* (Melbourne), 12.10.1971
77 *Sun* (Melbourne), 12.10.1971.
78 *Sun* (Melbourne), 8.1.1972.
79 *Herald* (Melbourne), 2.5.1972
80 *Telegraph* (Sydney), 29.11.1972.
81 *Age* (Melbourne), 29.3.1973.
82 *Herald* (Melbourne), 28.3.1973
83 *Australian*, 29.3.1973.
84 *Age* (Melbourne), 28.3.1973.
85 *Australian*, 28.3.1973.
86 *Telegraph* (Sydney), 29.11.1972.
87 Kalokerinos cited in the *Age* (Melbourne), 27.9.1969.
88 Names have been changed to protect privacy.
89 Robertson and Carrick 1970, p 34.
90 ibid., 1970, p 35.
91 Kalokerinos 1974, pp 71, 66.
92 *Sun* (Melbourne), 24.4.1969.
93 *Australian*, 9.10.1969.
94 Robertson and Carrick 1970, p 41.
95 ibid., p 45.
96 ibid., p 34.
97 *Age* (Melbourne), 27.6.1969.
98 *Sunday Observer*, 16.11.1969
99 *Age* (Melbourne), 18.11.1969.
100 *Sun* (Melbourne), 2.2.1970.
101 *Age* (Melbourne), 19.8.1970.
102 *Sun* (Melbourne), 24.2.1971.
103 *Age* (Melbourne), 25.8.1971.
104 *Sunday Mail*, 18.6.1972.
105 *Age* (Melbourne), 16.10.1969.
106 *Sun* (Melbourne), 5.3.1969.
107 *Age* (Melbourne), 2.3.1971.
108 *Age* (Melbourne), 13.9.1971.
109 *Australian*, 28.4.1972.
110 *Age* (Melbourne), 27.8.1971.
111 *Age* (Melbourne), 31.7.1971.
112 *Age* (Melbourne), 23.9.1971.
113 *Age* (Melbourne), 20.5.1972.
114 *Australian*, 3.4.1971.
115 In 1971 the federal government announced several major initiatives in relation to Aboriginal child health. This included a four year survey of the health of all Aboriginal children aged from six months to sixteen years (*Sunday Mail*, 3.1.1971). $275 000 would be provided for an Aboriginal child care centre in Alice Springs to combat high infant mortality rates there (*Age*, 1.10.1971). The Federal Health Department would launch an investigation into the Alice Springs Hospital and the alleged contribution of cross-infection to high infant death rates (*Age*, 25.8.1971). The Senate Standing Committee would study all federal and state laws which discriminated against Aborigines and Aboriginal environmental conditions (*Age*, 8.10.1971).

116 The names of the girl's natural and foster families have been changed to protect their privacy.
117 *Woman's Day*, 12.11.1973; *Northern Territory News* (Darwin), 17.10.1973; *Times* (Canberra), 15.2.1973.
118 *Australian*, 20.9.1973.
119 *Age* (Melbourne), 20.9.1973.
120 *Sun* (Melbourne), 20.9.1973.
121 *Telegraph* (Brisbane), 20.9.1973.
122 *Northern Territory News* (Darwin), 21.9.1973.
123 ibid.
124 *Telegraph* (Sydney), 22.9.1973.
125 *Sun* (Melbourne), 24.9.1973.
126 *Age* (Melbourne), 24.9.1973.
127 *Observer* (Melbourne), 27.9.1973.
128 *Times* (Canberra), 21.9.1973.
129 *Age* (Melbourne), 25.9.1973.
130 *Mirror* (Sydney), 21.9.1973.
131 *Woman's Day*, 12.11.1973.
132 *National Times*, 28.1.1974; Colin Clague personal communication, 1997; *Times* (Canberra), 15.2.1974.
133 *Sunday Mail*, 14.10 73; *Advertiser* (Adelaide), 1.11.1973.
134 *Northern Territory News* (Darwin), 24.9.1973.
135 *Age* (Melbourne), 21.9.1973.
136 *Telegraph* (Brisbane), 25.9.1973.
137 *Australian*, 2.9.1973, 6.9.1973.
138 *Northern Territory News* (Darwin), 27.9.1973.
139 *National Times*, 28.1.1974.
140 Colin Clague personal communication, 1997.
141 *Times* (Canberra), 15.2.1974.
142 *Australian*, 25.10.1973.
143 12.4.1973.
144 AA (VIC) B4088, Adoption Folder. Unsourced press clipping held in this file.
145 *Age* (Melbourne), 25.9.1973.
146 *Northern Territory News* (Darwin), 22.10.1973.
147 *Mercury* (Hobart), 28.5.1974.
148 *Times* (Canberra), 21.9.1973.
149 Freedman 1989, p 36 footnote 142.
150 See Link-Up and Wilson, 1997; Read, 1999.
151 *Age* (Melbourne), 21.2.1976.
152 Commonwealth Government, Department of Aboriginal Affairs, 1980.
153 The Minister for Social Services was Senator Margaret Guilfoyle and the Director of the Office of Child Care was Marie Coleman.
154 Dyer 1978, p 182.
155 ibid., pp 181–3.
156 De Souza 1994, pp 142–52; Freedman 1989, pp 141–2; Briskman, 1998.
157 Butler cited in De Souza 1994, p 134.
158 ibid., p 136.
159 ibid., pp 140–1.
160 New South Wales Government, Aboriginal Children's Research Project 1982.
161 Freedman 1989, p 201.
162 Commonwealth Government, National Committee of Non-Government Organisations 1980, p 50.
163 Cited in Freedman 1989, p 154.
164 ibid., p 196.
165 1986, pp 233, 240.
166 Tilbury, 1998; Muriel Cadd personal communication, Melbourne, 1998.
167 See White and Wilson, 1991; Cunneen and Libesman, 1995; Cunneen and White, 1995; Luke and Cunneen, 1995; Beresford and Omaji, 1996.
168 See Commonwealth Government, Australian Bureau of Statistics 1966.
169 White and Wilson, 1991; Collard and Palmer, 1991.
170 Linda Briskman personal communication 1998. Linda Briskman is completing a doctoral thesis on the history of SWALAA.
171 Butler cited in de Souza 1994, p 41.
172 Linda Briskman personal communication, 1998.

173 Pittock 1975, p 45.
174 Gale 1987, pp 92–5.
175 See for example Western Australian Government, Department of Community Welfare 1981.
176 Commonwealth Government, Royal Commission into Aboriginal Deaths in Custody 1991a, p 508.
177 Jenkins 1992.
178 Western Australian Government Select Committee of the Legislative Assembly (1996); British Government House of Commons Select Committee (1998).
179 This account was written with my partner Darryl Kickett and is the story of his parents Fraser and Rhoda Kickett. It is reproduced with the permission of the family. A shorter version was included in Commonwealth Government, Royal Commission into Aboriginal Deaths in Custody 1991a.
180 See Read and Edwards 1989; Commonwealth Government, Human Rights and Equal Opportunity Commission 1997; Link-Up (New South Wales) Aboriginal Corporation and Wilson (1997); Read 1999.

BIBLIOGRAPHY

BOOKS, REPORTS AND THESES

Aboriginal Legal Service of Western Australia (1995). *Telling Our Story: A Report by the Aboriginal Legal Service (Inc.) on the Removal of Aboriginal Children from their Families in Western Australia.* Perth, Aboriginal Legal Service of Western Australia.

Aborigines in Tasmania Project Team (1984a). *On Being Aboriginal. Book One.* Hobart, Education Department.

Aborigines in Tasmania Project Team (1984b). *Living on the Land: Adapting and Resisting. Book Five.* Hobart, Education Department.

Aborigines in Tasmania Project Team (1984c). *Continuity and Change. Book Six.* Hobart, Education Department.

Aborigines in Tasmania Project Team (1985). *On Being Aboriginal: Interim Handbook for Teachers.* Hobart, Education Department.

Allen, M (1987). 'Introduction.' In C Martin, *The Incredible Journey.* London, Pandora Press.

Ambery, D (1998). 'The Hopewood Experiment.' In R Nile (ed) and A Haebich and J Huggins (editorial advisers), *Who Will Look After The Children? Steal Away Hide Away. Journal of Australian Studies* (59).

Anderson, B (1996). *Imagined Communities. Reflections on the Origin and Spread of Nationalism.* London, Verso.

Anderson, C (1988). 'Kuku-Yalanji and the Lutherans at Bloomfield River, 1887-1902.' In T Swain and D B Rose (eds). Adelaide, Australian Association for the Study of Religion

Armitage, A (1995). *Comparing the Policy of Aboriginal Assimilation: Australia, Canada, and New Zealand.* Vancouver, University of British Columbia Press.

Astley, T (1996). *The Multiple Effects of Rain Shadow.* Ringwood, Victoria, Viking.

Atkinson, A (1997). *The Europeans in Australia: A History. Volume One: The Beginning.* Melbourne, Oxford University Press.

Attwood, B (1989). *The Making of the Aborigines.* Sydney, Allen & Unwin.

Attwood, B, W Burridge, A Burridge and E Stokes (1994). *A Life Together, A Life Apart: A History of Relations Between Europeans and Aborigines.* Carlton, Melbourne University Press.

Attwood, B and A Markus (1998). 'Representation Matters: the 1967 Referendum and Citzenship.' In N Peterson and W Saunders (eds), *Citizenship and Indigenous Australians. Changing Conceptions and Possibilities.* Cambridge, Cambridge University Press.

Attwood, B and A Markus (1999). *The Struggle for Aboriginal Rights: A Documentary History.* Sydney, Allen & Unwin.

Austin, T (1990). 'Cecil Cook, Scientific Thought and "Half-Castes" in the Northern Territory 1927–1939.' *Aboriginal History*, 14 (1).

Austin, T (1992). *Simply the Survival of the Fittest.* Darwin, History Society of the Northern Territory.

Austin, T (1993). *I Can Picture the Old Home So Clearly. The Commonwealth and 'Half Caste' Youth in the Northern Territory 1911–1939.* Canberra, Aboriginal Studies Press.

Austin, T (1997). *Never Trust a Government Man. Northern Territory Aboriginal Policy 1911–1939.* Darwin, Northern Territory University Press.

Australian Board of Missions (1909). *Annual Report of the Yarrabah Mission to the Aborigines.* Australian Board of Missions.

Australian Broadcasting Commission (1969). *Out of Sight, Out of Mind.* Video.

Australian Broadcasting Corporation (1997). *We Took the Children.* ABC Radio National.

Australian National Opinion Poll Market Research (1985). *Land Rights. Winning Middle Australia: An Attitude and Communications Research Study.* Presented to the Department of Aboriginal Affairs January 1985. ANOP Market Research for Government and Industry, Crows Nest, New South Wales.

Bacchi, C (1980). 'Evolution, Eugenics and Women: The Impact of Scientific Theories on Attitudes Towards Women, 1870–1920.' In E Windschuttle (ed), *Women, Class and History: Feminist Perspectives on Australia 1788–1978.* Melbourne, Fontana Collins.

Ban, P and P Zoltan (1993). *Report to the Queensland Government on Legal Recognition of Torres Strait Islander*

Customary Adoption. Fortitude Valley, Queensland, Ilna Torres Strait Islander Corporation.
Barnardo, S L and Marchant, J (1907). *Memoirs of the late Dr. Barnardo*. London, Hodder and Stoughton,
Barbelet, M (1983). *Far From a Low Gutter Girl: The Forgotten World of State Wards, South Australia, 1887–1940*. Melbourne, Oxford University Press.
Barber, J (nd). *Women's Movement: South Australia*. St Peters, South Australia, Experimental Art Foundation.
Bartky, S L (1990). *Femininity and Domination. Studies in the Phenomenology of Oppression*. New York, Routledge.
Barwick, D (1962–3). 'Economic Absorption Without Assimilation: The Case of Some Melbourne Part-Aboriginal Families.' *Oceania*, 32, (2).
Barwick, D (1971). 'Changes in the Aboriginal Population of Victoria, 1867–1966.' In Mulvaney, D and J Golson (eds) *Aboriginal Man and Environment in Australia*. Canberra, Australian National University Press.
Barwick, D (1978). 'The Aboriginal Family in South Eastern Australia.' In J Krupinski and A Stoller (eds) *The Family in Australia*. Sydney, Pergamon.
Bauman, Z (1991). *Modernity and Ambivalence*. Cambridge, Polity Press.
Bauml Duberman, M (1989). *Paul Robeson*. New York, Ballantyne Books.
Bean, P and J Melville (1989). *Lost Children of the Empire*. Sydney, Allen & Unwin.
Beckett, J (1988). 'Aboriginality, Citizenship and the Nation State.' *Social Analysis*, 24.
Bell, D (1988). 'Choose Your Mission Wisely.' In T Swain and D B Rose (eds), *Aboriginal Australians and Christian Missions. Ethnographic and Historical Studies*. Adelaide, Australian Association for the Study of Religions.
Bennett, M M (1927). *Christenson of Lammermoor*. London, Alston Rivers.
Bennett, M M (1930). *The Australian Aboriginal as a Human Being*. London, Alston Rivers.
Bennett, M M (1957). *Human Rights for Australian Aborigines: How Can They Learn Without a Teacher?* Brisbane, the author.
Beresford, Q and P Omaji (1996). *Rites of Passage: Aboriginal Youth, Crime and Justice*. Fremantle, Fremantle Arts Centre Press.
Beresford, Q and P Omaji (1998). *Our State of Mind: Racial Planning and the Stolen Generations*. Fremantle, Fremantle Arts Centre Press.
Berndt, C H (1962–3). 'Mateship or Success: An Assimilation Dilemma.' *Oceania*, 32 (2).
Bettelheim, B (1970). *The Informed Heart: The Condition in Mass Society*. London, Paladin.
Bessant, J (1991). 'Described, Measured and Labelled: Eugenics, Youth Policy and Moral Panic in Victoria in the 1950s.' In R White and B Wilson (eds), *For Your Own Good: Young People and State Intervention in Australia. Special Edition of the Journal of Australian Studies*. Bundoora, Victoria, La Trobe University Press.
Bishop, C (1991). 'A Woman Missionary Living Amongst Naked Blacks': Annie Lock, 1876–1943. MA Thesis, Australian National University.
Biskup, P (1973). *Not Slaves. Not Citizens*. St Lucia, University of Queensland Press.
Blackburn, G (1993). *The Children's Friends Society: Juvenile Emigrants to Western Australia, South Africa and Canada, 1834–42*. Northbridge, Western Australia, Access Press.
Blake, T (1991). A Dumping Ground: Barambah Aboriginal Settlement 1900–1940. PhD Thesis. University of Queensland.
Bock, G (1991). 'Antinatalism, Maternity and Paternity in National Socialist Racism.' in G Bock and P Thane (eds), *Maternity and Gender Politics. Women and the Rise of the European Welfare States, 1880s–1950s*. London and New York, Routledge.
Boladeras, J (1996). Yindolan's Story. Perth. Typescript, Battye Library.
Bolton, G (1963). *A Thousand Miles Away: A History Of North Queensland to 1920*. Canberra, Australian National University Press.
Bolton, G (1981). 'Black and White after 1897.' In C T Stannage (ed). *A New History of Western Australia*. Nedlands, University of Western Australia Press.
Bonwick, J (1970). *The Last of the Tasmanians or, the Black War of Van Diemen's Land*. New York, Johnson Reprint Corp. First published 1870, London, Sampson Low & Son & Marston.
Bonwick, J (1973). *John Batman the Founder of Victoria*. Melbourne, Wren Publishing. First published 1867, Melbourne, S Mutton.
Bourke, C, E Bourke and B Edwards (1994). *Aboriginal Australia. An Introductory Reader in Aboriginal Studies*. St Lucia, University of Queensland Press.
Bowden, R and B Bunbury (1990). *Being Aboriginal: Comments, Observations and Stories from Aboriginal Australians*. Crows Nest, New South Wales, ABC Books.
Bowie, F, D Kirkwood and S Ardener (eds) (1993). *Women and Missions, Past and Present Anthropological and Historical Perceptions*. Providence, Rhode Island, Berg.
Bowlby, J (1952). *Maternal Care and Mental Health: A Report on Behalf of the World Health Organization as a Contribution to the United Nations Programme for the Welfare of Homeless Children*. Geneva, World Health Organization.
Brewster, A (1995). *Literary Formations. Post-colonialism, Nationalism, Globalism*. Melbourne, Melbourne University Press

Brewster, A (1996). *Reading Aboriginal Women's Autobiography*. Melbourne, Sydney University Press in Association with Oxford University Press.

Bridge, C (1998). 'Diplomat.' In T Stannage, K Saunders and R Nile (eds), *Paul Hasluck in Australian History: Civic Personality and Public Life*. St Lucia, University of Queensland Press.

Briskman, L (1998). 'The Stolen Generations in Australia. Recording Aboriginal Activism.' Paper presented at the Oral History Association Conference, Buffalo, New York.

British Government (1837). *Report of the 1837 Select Committee Appointed to Consider What Measures Ought to be Adopted with Regard to the Native Inhabitants of Countries Where British Settlements are Made*. London, House of Commons, British Parliament.

British Government. House of Commons Select Committee(1998). The Welfare of Former British Child Migrants. Chairman David Hinchcliffe. London, The Stationary Office.

Brock, P (1993). *Outback Ghettos: Aborigines, Institutionalisation and Survival*. Cambridge, Cambridge University Press.

Brock, P (1995). 'South Australia.' In A McGrath (ed) *Contested Ground. Australian Aborigines Under the British Crown*. St Leonards, New South Wales, Allen & Unwin.

Brook, J and J L Kohen (1991). *The Parramatta Native Institution and the Black Town: A History*. Kensington, University of New South Wales Press.

Broome, R (1982). *Aboriginal Australians*. Sydney, Allen & Unwin.

Burke, P (1989). 'History as Social Memory.' In T Butler (ed). *Memory: History, Culture and the Mind*. Oxford, Basil Blackwell.

Burke, T (1996). *Lifebuoy Men, Lux Women. Commodification, Consumption and Cleanliness in Modern Zimbabwe*. London, Leicester University Press.

Burridge, K (1988). 'Aborigines and Christianity: An Overview.' In T Swain and D B Rose (eds) *Aboriginal Australians and Christian Missions. Ethnographic and Historical Studies*. Adelaide, Australian Association for the Study of Religions.

Butlin, N (1983). *Our Original Aggression. Aboriginal Populations of Southeastern Australia 1788–1850*. Sydney, Allen & Unwin.

Cairns, E (1996). *Children and Political Violence*. Cambridge, Massachusetts, Blackwell.

Calder, J E (1875). *Some Account of the Wars, Extirpation, Habits, etc. of the Native Tribes of Tasmania*. Hobart Town, Henn & Co.

Capps, D (1995). *The Child's Song. The Religious Abuse of Children*. Louisville, Kentucky, Westminster John Knox Press.

Carrington, K (1993). *Offending Girls. Sex, Youth and Justice*. St Leonards, New South Wales, Allen & Unwin.

Carter, J (1981). *Nothing to Spare: Recollections of Australian Pioneering Women*. Ringwood, Victoria, Penguin.

Carter, J (1983). *Protection to Prevention: Child Welfare Policies*. Kensington, Social Welfare Research Centre, University of New South Wales.

Chesson, K (1988). *Jack Davis: A Life Story*. Melbourne, Dent.

Chesterman, B and B Galligan (1997). *Citizens Without Rights: Aborigines and Australian Citizenship*. Cambridge, Cambridge University Press.

Chi, J and Kuckles (1991). *Bran Nue Day*. Paddington, New South Wales, Currency Press; Broome, Western Australia, Magabala Books.

Chisholm, R (1982). 'Child Care, Aboriginal Children and Permanency Planning: A Sceptical View.' In R Oxenberry (ed), *Changing Families: Proceedings of the Third Conference on Adoption*. Adelaide, University of Adelaide.

Choo, C (1996). Aboriginal Women on Catholic Missions in the Kimberley, 1900–1950. PhD Thesis, University of Western Australia.

Choo, C (1997). 'The role of the Catholic missionaries at Beagle Bay in the Removal of Aboriginal Children from their Families in the Kimberley region from the 1890s.' *Aboriginal History*, 21.

Christie, M (1979). *Aborigines in Colonial Victoria 1835–1886*. Sydney, University of Sydney Press.

Clay, C and M Leapman (1995). *Master Race: The Lebensborn Experiment in Nazi Germany*. London, Hodder & Stoughton.

Clendinnen, I (1998). *Reading the Holocaust*. Melbourne, The Text Publishing Company.

Clifford, J (1988). *The Predicament of Culture: Twentieth Century Ethnography, Literature and Art*. Cambridge, Massachusetts, Harvard University Press.

Coldrey, B M (1998). *The Scheme: the Christian Brothers and Childcare in Western Australia*. O'Connor, Western Australia, Argyle-Pacific.

Cole, K (1972). *Oenpelli Pioneer. A Biography of the Reverend Alfred John Dyer*. Church Missionary Historical Publications Trust.

Collard, L and D Palmer (1991). 'Aboriginal Young People in the Southwest of Western Australia: Implications for Youth Policy.' In R White and B Wilson (eds), *For Your Own Good: Young People and State Intervention in*

Australia. Special Edition of Journal of Australian Studies. Bundoora, Victoria, La Trobe University Press.

Collmann, J (1979). 'Women, Children, and the Significance of the Domestic Group to Urban Aborigines in Central Australia.' *Ethnology*, 18 (4).

Collman, J (1988). *Fringe-dwellers and Welfare. The Aboriginal Response to Bureaucracy.* St Lucia, University of Queensland Press.

Commonwealth Government (1929). *The Aboriginals and Half-Castes of Central Australia and North Australia.* J Bleakley. Government Printer, Canberra.

Commonwealth Government (1937). *Aboriginal Welfare: Initial Conference of the Commonwealth and State Aboriginal Authorities Held in Canberra 21–23 April 1937.* Government Printer, Canberra.

Commonwealth Government, (2000). 'Senate Legal and Constitutional References Committee Inquiry into Government Response to the Recommendations of the Report, *Bringing Them Home* – Federal Government Submission'. http://www.aph.gov.au/senate/committee/submissions/lc_stolen.htm

Commonwealth Government, Department of Territories (1951). 'Commonwealth and States Native Welfare Conference. Education.' Canberra. Typescript.

Commonwealth Governmeht, Federal Minister for Territories (1957). *Our Aborigines.* Canberra, Commonwealth Government Printer.

Commonwealth Government, Federal Minister for Territories (1958). *Assimilation of Our Aborigines.* Canberra, Commonwealth Government Printer.

Commonwealth Government, Federal Minister for Territories (1959). *Fringe Dwellers.* Canberra, Commonwealth Government Printer.

Commonwealth Government, Federal Minister for Territories (1960). *The Skills of Our Aborigines.* Canberra, Commonwealth Government Printer.

Commonwealth Government, Federal Minister for Territories (1961). *One People.* Canberra, Commonwealth Government Printer.

Commonwealth Government, Federal Minister for Territories (1963). *The Aborigines and You.* Canberra, Commonwealth Government Printer.

Commonwealth Government, Australian Bureau of Census and Statistics (1966). *Census of the Commonwealth of Australia 30 June 1966: The Aboriginal Population of Australia — Summary of Characteristics.* Canberra, Commonwealth Government Printer.

Commonwealth Government, Department of Aboriginal Affairs (1980). 'Aboriginal Adoption and Fostering Policy Guidelines.' Canberra.

Commonwealth Government, National Committee of Non-Government Organisations, Australia (1980). *International Year of the Child Final Report.* Canberra, Australian Government Publishing Service.

Commonwealth Government, Australian Law Reform Commission (1982). 'Reference on Aboriginal Customary Law Research Paper No. 4. Aboriginal Customary Law: Child Custody, Fostering and Adoption.' Sydney. Typescript, Murdoch University.

Commonwealth Government, Department of Aboriginal Affairs (1984). *Aboriginal Social Indicators 1984.* Canberra, Australian Government Publishing Service.

Commonwealth Government, Department of Aboriginal Affairs (1985a). *Department of Aboriginal Affairs Annual Report 1984–85.* Canberra, Australian Government Publishing Service.

Commonwealth Government, Department of Aboriginal Affairs (1985b). *Aboriginal Statistics 1985.* Canberra, Australian Government Publishing Service.

Commonwealth Government, Australian Law Reform Commission (1986). *The Recognition of Aboriginal Customary Laws. Volume 1.* Canberra, Australian Government Publishing Service.

Commonwealth Government, Human Rights and Equal Opportunity Commission (1989). *Our Homeless Children: Report of the National Inquiry into Homeless Children.* Canberra, Australian Government Publishing Service.

Commonwealth Government, Royal Commission into Aboriginal Deaths in Custody (1991a). *Regional Report of Inquiry into Underlying Issues in Western Australia of the Royal Commission into Aboriginal Deaths in Custody. Volume 1.* Commissioner P L Dodson. Canberra, Australian Government Publishing Service.

Commonwealth Government, Royal Commission into Aboriginal Deaths in Custody (1991b). *Regional Report of Inquiry into Individual Deaths in Custody in Western Australia of the Royal Commission into Aboriginal Deaths in Custody. Volume 1.* Commissioner D J O O'Dea. Canberra, Australian Government Publishing Service.

Commonwealth Government (1993). *Aboriginal and Torres Strait Islander People in Commonwealth Records. A Guide to Records in the Australian Archives Australian Capital Territory Regional Office.* R Fraser. Canberra, Australian Government Publishing Service.

Commonwealth Government, Human Rights and Equal Opportunity Commission (1996). *Longing to Return Home. Information for People Giving Submissions to the National Inquiry into the Separation of Aboriginal and Torres Strait Islander Children from their Families.* Darwin, Green Ant Research Arts and Publishing.

Commonwealth Government, Human Rights and Equal Opportunity Commission (1996). 'Families on File:

Laws, Practices and Policies for Access to Personal Records by Aboriginal and Torres Strait Islander People: Paper Prepared for the National Inquiry into the Separation of Aboriginal and Torres Strait Islander People Separated from their Families.' Canberra, Privacy Commissioner. Typescript.

Commonwealth Government, Human Rights and Equal Opportunity Commission (1997). *Bringing Them Home: A Report of the National Inquiry into the Separation of Aboriginal and Torres Strait Islander Children from their Families.* Sydney, Human Rights and Equal Opportunity Commission.

Commonwealth Government, Human Rights and Equal Opportunity Commission (n.d.). *Stolen Children Inquiry. Who Spoke Out at the Time?* Sydney, Human Rights and Equal Opportunity Commission.

Coombs, H C (1976). *Aborginal Australians 1967–76. A Decade of Progress? The Third Walter Murdoch Lecture delivered at Murdoch University on 19 October 1976.* Murdoch, Western Australia, Murdoch University.

Cryle, M (1989). *Duncan McNab's Mission to the Queensland Aborigines, 1875–1880.* St Lucia, University of Queensland Press.

Cummings, B (1990). *Take This Child. From Kahlin Compound to the Retta Dixon Children's Home.* Canberra, Aboriginal Studies Press.

Cunneen, C and T Libesman (1995). *Indigenous People and the Law in Australia.* Sydney, Butterworths.

Cunneen, C and R White (1995). *Juvenile Justice: an Australian Perspective.* Melbourne, Oxford University Press.

Cuthbert, D (1998). 'Adoptive Mothers.' In R Nile (ed) and A Haebich and J Huggins (editorial advisers), *Who Will Look After The Children? Steal Away Hide Away. Journal of Australian Studies* (59).

Cutter, T N (1976). *Report on Alice Springs Fringe Camps.* Alice Springs, Central Australian Aboriginal Congress.

Damousi, J (1997). 'What Punishment will be Sufficient for these Rebellious Hussies? Headshaving and Convict Women in the Female Factories 1820s–1840s.' In J Duffield and J Bradley (eds), *Representing Convicts: New Perspectives on Convict Forced Labour Migration.* London, Leicester University Press.

Dandeker, C (1990). *Surveillance, Power and Modernity: Bureaucracy and Discipline from 1700 to the Present Day.* Cambridge, Polity.

Daniels, D W (1995). 'The Assertion of Tasmanian Aboriginality from the 1967 Referendum to Mabo.' MA thesis, Department of Social Welfare, University of Tasmania.

Daniels, K and M Murnane (1980). *Uphill All the Way: A Documentary History of Women in Australia.* St Lucia, University of Queensland Press.

Darian-Smith, K and P Hamilton (eds) (1994). *Memory and History in Twentieth Century Australia.* Melbourne, Oxford University Press.

Davey, C (1956). *Children and their Law-Makers: Social-Historical Survey of the Growth and Development from 1836 to 1950 of South Australian Laws Relating to Children.* Adelaide, Griffin.

Davey, S (1963). *Genesis or Genocide? The Aboriginal Assimilation Policy.* Aborigines Advancement Council, Melbourne.

Davidson, A (1991). *The Invisible State: The Formation of the Australian State 1788–1901.* Cambridge, Cambridge University Press.

Davies, D (1973). *The Last of the Tasmanians.* Sydney, Shakespeare Head Press.

Davis, J (1986). *No Sugar.* Sydney, Currency Press.

Davis, J (1991). *A Boy's Life.* Broome, Western Australia, Magabala Books.

Day, D (1996). *Claiming a Continent. A History of Australia.* Sydney, Angus & Robertson.

Denoon, D (1979). 'Understanding Settler Societies.' *Historical Studies,* 18.

DeSouza, N (1994). Indigenous Child Welfare or Institutionalised Colonialism? Rethinking Policy in Relation to Aboriginal Children in Australia. MA Thesis, Royal Melbourne Institute of Technology.

Dickey, B (1985). *Family Law.* Sydney, Law Book Co.

Donovan, P (1988). *Alice Springs: Its History and the People Who Made It.* Alice Springs, Alice Springs Town Council.

Donzelot, J (1980). *The Policing of Families.* London, Hutchinson.

Dyer, M (1978). 'Victorian Aboriginal Child Care Agency.' In C Picton (ed), *Proceedings of Second Australian Conference on Adoption. Current Concerns and Alternatives for Child Placement and Parenting.* Melbourne, Committee of the Second Australian Conference on Adoption.

Edwards, C (1982). 'Is the ward clean?' In B Gammage and A Markus (eds), *All That Dirt. Aborigines 1938.* Canberra, Research School of Social Sciences, Australian National University.

Eggleston, E M (1970). Aborigines and the Administration of Justice: A Critical Analysis of the Application of Criminal Law to Aborigines. PhD Thesis. Monash University.

Eggleston, E M (1972). *Aboriginal Children and the Law. Seminars 1971, Monash Centre for Research into Aboriginal Affairs.* Clayton, Monash Centre for Research into Aboriginal Affairs.

Eggleston, E M (1976). *Fear, Favour or Affection: Aborigines and the Criminal Law in Victoria, South Australia and Western Australia.* Canberra, Australian National University Press.

Elkin, A P (1944). *Citizenship for Aborigines. A National Aboriginal Policy.* Sydney, Australasian Publishing Co.

Evans, C (1994). 'State girls: their lives as apprentices.' *Tasmanian Historical Research Association,* 41 (2).

Evans, R (1965). European-Aboriginal Relations in Queensland, 1880–1910. BA (Hons) Thesis, University of Queensland.

Evans, R (1993). '"Keep White the Strain" Race Relations in a Colonial Setting.' In R Evans, K Saunders and K Cronin, *Race Relations in Colonial Queensland. A History of Exclusion, Exploitation and Extermination.* St Lucia, University of Queensland Press.

Evans, R (1976). 'The Hidden Colonists' in J Roe (ed) *Social Policy in Australia. Some Perspectives 1901–1975.* Stanmore, NSW, Cassell Australia.

Evans, R (1982). '"Don't You Remember Black Alice, Sam Holt?" Aboriginal Women in Queensland History.' *Hecate*, 8 (2).

Evans, R (1984). '"Kings in Brass Crescents." Defining Aboriginal Labour Patterns in Colonial Queensland.' In K Saunders (ed), *Indentured Labour in the British Empire 1834–1920.* Canberra, Croom Helm.

Evans, R (1991). 'A Permanent Precedent': Dispossession, Social Control, and the Fraser Island Reserve and Missions, 1897-1904. *The Ngulag Monograph, no. 5.* Aboriginal and Torres Strait Islander Study Unit, University of Queensland, St Lucia.

Evans, R (1999). '"A Permanent Precedent": Dispossession, Social control and the Fraser Island Reserve and Mission, 1897–1904.' In R Evans, *Fighting Words. Writing About Race.* St Lucia, University of Queensland Press.

Evans, R (1999). *Fighting Words. Writing About Race.* St Lucia, University of Queensland Press.

Evans, R (1999a). '"The Owl and the Eagle" The Significance of Race in Colonial Queensland.' In R Evans. *Fighting Words. Writing About Race.* St Lucia, University of Queensland Press.

Evans, R, K Saunders, C Moore and B Jamison (1997). '1901 Our Future's Past.' *Weekend Australian Magazine,* 26–27.4.1997.

Evans, R and J Scott (1995). '"Fallen Among Thieves": Aboriginal Labour and State Control in Inter-War Queensland.' In A McGrath, K Saunders and J Huggins (eds), *Aboriginal Workers. Special Issue of Labour History* (69).

Evans, R and J Scott (1996). 'The Moulding of Menials: the Making of the Aboriginal Female Domestic Servant in Early Twentieth Century Queensland.' *Hecate*, 22 (1).

Evans, T (1990). *Arnhem Land: A Personal History.* Darwin, Northern Territory Library Service.

Faine, J (1993). *Lawyers in Alice. Aboriginal and Whitefella's Law.* Annandale, Sydney, Federation Press.

Felton, P (1997). 'Placement of Aboriginal Children in Victoria. Overview and Chronology.' Melbourne. Typescript, held by the author.

Fink, R (1957–58). 'The Caste Barrier: An Obstacle to the Assimilation of Part-Aborigines in North West New South Wales.' *Oceania*, 28.

Finnane, M (1997). *Punishment in Australian Society.* Melbourne, Oxford University Press.

Fitzgerald, J F (1982). 'Changing directions changing families'. In R Oxenberry (ed), *Changing Families. Proceedings of Third Australian Conference on Adoption, Adelaide.* Adelaide : Department of Continuing Education, University of Adelaide for the Organising Committee of the Third Australian Conference on Adoption.

Fitzgerald, R (1986). *A History of Queensland. From Dreaming to 1915.* St Lucia, University of Queensland Press.

Fitzpatrick, M (1988). 'Preventing the unfit from breeding: the Mental Deficiency Bill in Western Australia, 1929.' In R Nile (ed), *Childhood and Society in Western Australia.* Nedlands, University of Western Australia Press with the Centre for Western Australian History, University of Western Australia.

Fonseca, I (1995). *Bury Me Standing: The Gypsies and Their Journey.* London, Chatto and Windus.

Foster, D (1998). 'She Called her Coral because it was "a Perfect Pink Day": The Neglecting of Coral Suzanne Dickerson.' In R Nile (ed) and A Haebich and J Huggins (editorial advisers), *Who Will Look After The Children? Steal Away Hide Away. Journal of Australian Studies* (59).

Foxcroft, E J B (1941). *Australian Native Policy.* Melbourne, Melbourne University Press.

Freedman, L (1989). The Pursuit of Aboriginal Control of Child Welfare. Master of Social Work Thesis, University of Melbourne.

Frow, J (1998). 'A Politics of Stolen Time.' *Meanjin*, 57.

Gale, F (1964). A Study of Assimilation. Part-Aborigines in South Australia. PhD Thesis, University of Adelaide.

Gale, F (1969). 'A Changing Aboriginal Population.' In A Grenfell Price, F Gale and G Lawton (eds), *Settlement and Encounter. Geographical Studies.* Melbourne, Oxford University Press.

Gale, F (1972). *Urban Aborigines.* Canberra, Australian National University Press.

Gale, F (1987). 'Aboriginal Youth: A History of Inequity in the Delivery of Australian Justice.' *Aboriginal History*, 11 (1–2).

Gare, N (1966). *The Fringe Dwellers.* Melbourne, Sun Books.

Garton, S (1986). 'Sir Charles Mackellar: Psychiatry, Eugenics and Child Welfare in New South Wales, 1900–1914.' *Historical Studies*, 22 (86).

Gilchrist, A (1993). The Dormitory System. Female Relations at the Yarrabah Mission 1892–1910. BA Hons Thesis, Griffith University.

Glass, C and A Weller (1987). *Us Fellas: An Anthology of Aboriginal Writing.* Perth, Artlook Books.

Goffman, E (1961). *Asylums.* New York, Anchor Books.

Goodall, H (1990). '"Saving the Children": Gender and the Colonisation of Aboriginal Children 1788–1990.' *Aboriginal Law Bulletin,* 2 (44).

Goodall, H (1995a). '"Assimilation Begins In The Home": The State and Aboriginal Women's Work as Mothers in New South Wales 1900s to 1960s.' In A McGrath, K Saunders and J Huggins (eds), *Aboriginal Workers. Special Issue of Labour History,* (69).

Goodall, H (1995b). 'New South Wales.' In A Mc Grath (ed). *Contested Ground: Australian Aborigines Under the British Crown.* St Leonards, New South Wales, Allen & Unwin.

Goodall, H (1996). *From Invasion to Embassy. Land in Aboriginal Politics in New South Wales from 1780 to 1972.* St Leonards, New South Wales, Allen & Unwin.

Gray, G (1998). 'From Nomadism to Citizenship. A P Elkin and Aboriginal Advancement.' In N Peterson and W Saunders (eds), *Citizenship and Indigenous Australians. Changing Conceptions and Possibilities.* Cambridge, Cambridge University Press.

Grayden, W (1957). *Adam and Atoms.* Perth, Frank Daniels.

Green, N (ed) (1988). *The Oombulgurri Story. A Pictorial History of the People of Oombulgurri, 1884–1988.* Cottesloe, Western Australia, Focus Education Services.

Green, N (1995). *The Forrest River Massacres.* Fremantle, Fremantle Arts Centre Press.

Gribble, E R (1930). *Forty Years with the Aborigines.* Sydney, Angus & Robertson.

Gribble, E R (1933). *A Despised Race. The Vanishing Aboriginals of Australia.* Sydney, Australian Board of Missions.

Gribble, J B (1987). *Dark Deeds in a Sunny Land, or Blacks and Whites in North West Australia.* Nedlands, University of Western Australia Press; Mount. Lawley, Western Australian Institute of Applied Aboriginal Studies, Western Australian College of Advanced Education. First published 1905, Perth, Daily News.

Griffiths, T (1996). *Hunters and Collectors. The Antiquarian Imagination in Australia.* Cambridge, Cambridge University Press.

Grimshaw, P (1994). *Colonialism, Gender and Representations of Race. Issues in Writing Women's History in Australia and the Pacific.* History Department, University of Melbourne.

Gsell, F X (1955). *'The Bishop with 150 Wives.' Fifty Years as a Missionary.* London, Angus & Robertson.

Gungil Jindibah Centre (1994). *Learning from the Past: Aboriginal Perspectives on the Effects and Implications of Welfare Policy and Practices on Aboriginal Families in New South Wales.* Lismore, Southern Cross University.

Guthrie, G (1976). 'Cherbourg: A Queensland Aboriginal Reserve.' Research paper, Armidale, Department of Geography, University of New England.

Haebich, A (1982). 'On the Inside: Moore River Native Settlement in the 1930s.' In B Gammage and A Markus (eds), *All That Dirt. Aborigines 1938.* Canberra, Research School of Social Sciences, Australian National University.

Haebich, A (1984). 'European Farmers and Aboriginal Farmers in South-Western Australia Mid-1890s to 1914'. In R Reece and T Stannage (eds), *Studies in Western Australian History. European Aboriginal Relations in Western Australian History,* VIII.

Haebich, A (1986). 'A Buch of Castoffs.' Trends in Aboriginal History of Western Australia 1900–1936. PhD Thesis, Murdoch University.

Haebich, A (1991). 'The Imprisonment of Aboriginal Women in Fremantle Prison, 1888–1970.' Community Services Unit of the Centre for Aboriginal Studies, Curtin University. Typescript, held by author.

Haebich, A (1998a). *For Their Own Good. Aborigines and Government in the South West of Western Australia 1900–1940,* 3rd ed. Nedlands, University of Western Australia Press.

Haebich. A (1998b). 'The Formative Years: Paul Hasluck and Aboriginal Issues During the 1930s.' In T Stannage, K Saunders and R Nile (eds), *Paul Hasluck in Australian History: Civic Personality and Public Life.* St Lucia, University of Queensland Press.

Haebich, A (1998c). 'Grim Facts We've Known.' *Adelaide Review,* February.

Haebich, A (1999). 'Irresistible Journeys and Imaginings. Boyd's Bride Series Revisited.' In R Nile and M Williams (eds), *Imaginary Homelands. The Dubious Cartographies of Australian Identity. Journal of Australian Studies* (61).

Haebich, A and A Delroy (1999). *The Stolen Generations. Separation of Aboriginal Children from their Families.* Perth, Western Australian Museum.

Hale, M B (1889). *The Aborigines of Australia: Being the Account of the Institution for their Education at Poonindie in South Australia.* London, Society for Promoting Christian Knowledge.

Hall, A (1996). *'We Took the Children': A Contribution to Reconciliation.* Adelaide, Department for Family and Community Services.

Hall, S (1997). *A Brief History of the Laws, Policies and Practices in South Australia which Led to the Removal of Many Children.* Adelaide, Department of Human Services.

Halse, C (1996). 'The Reverend Ernest Gribble: Successful Missionary?' in B J Dalton (ed). *Lectures on North*

Queensland History, 5. Townsville, Department of History and Politics, James Cook University.

Hamilton, A (1981). *Nature and Nurture. Aboriginal Child-Rearing in North-Central Arnhem Land*. Canberra, Australian Institute of Aboriginal Studies.

Hamilton, A (1989). 'Bond Slaves of Satan: Aboriginal Women and the Missionary Dilemma.' In M Jolly and M Macintyre (eds), *Family and Gender in the Pacific. Domestic Contradictions and the Colonial Impact*. Cambridge, Cambridge University Press.

Hammond, J E H (1933). *Winjan's People. The Story of the South-Western Aborigines, edited by Paul Hasluck*. Perth, Imperial Print Co.

Hampton, K and C Mattingley (1988). *Survival in Our Own Land: Aboriginal Experiences in South Australia Since 1836*. Adelaide, Wakefield Press.

Harmstorf, I (1979). 'Basedow, Herbert.' In B Nairn and G Serle (eds), *Australian Dictionary of Bibliography, 1891–1939 Volume 7*. Melbourne, Melbourne University Press.

Harney, W E (1961). *Grief, Gaiety and Aborigines*. London, Robert Hale Ltd.

Harris, J (1990). *One Blood. 200 Years of Aboriginal Encounter with Christianity: A Story of Hope*. Sutherland, New South Wales, Albatross Books.

Harrison, K (1975). *Dark Man, White World. A Portrait of Tenor Harold Blair*. Cheltenham, Victoria, Novalit Australia.

Harvey, A (1946). 'Ethnic and Sociological Study of an Australian Mixed Blood Group in Alice Springs, Northern Territory with reference to Ethnic Assimilation and Interaction of Groups.' Elkin Papers. University of Sydney.

Hasluck, P (1953). *Native Welfare in Australia. Speeches and Addresses by the Hon. Paul Hasluck, M.P., Minister for Territories*. Perth, Paterson Brokensha.

Hasluck, P (1963). *Assimilation in Action*. Box Hill, The Dominion Press.

Hasluck, P (1988). *Shades of Darkness. Aboriginal Affairs 1925–1965*. Collingwood, Melbourne University Press.

Hausfield, R G (1960). Aspects of Aboriginal Station Management. BA Thesis, Sydney University.

Hegarty, R (1999). *Is That You Ruthie?* St Lucia, University of Queensland Press.

Henriques, F (1974). *Children of Calaban. Miscegenation*. London, Secker & Warburg.

Heppell, M and Wigley, J (1981). *Black Out in Alice. A History of the Establishment and Development of Town Camps in Alice Springs*. Development Studies Centre, Monograph no. 26. Canberra, Australian National University.

Herbert, X (1938). *Capricornia: a Novel*. Sydney, The Publicist.

Herbert, X. (1975). *Poor Fellow: My Country*. Sydney, Collins.

Hipsley, E H and M W Corden (1973). 'Some Observations on the Diets and Nutrition of Aboriginal People in Central Australia. Commonwealth Department of Health.' Typescript. In authors' possession.

Hodson, S (1993). 'Nyungars and Work: Aboriginal Experiences in the Rural Economy of the Great Southern Region of Western Australia.' *Aboriginal History*, 17 (Part 2).

Holland, A (1995). 'Feminism, Colonialism and Aboriginal Workers: An Anti-Slavery Crusade.' In A McGrath, K Saunders and J Huggins (eds), *Aboriginal Workers. Special Issue of Labour History* (69).

Horton, D (ed) (1994). *The Encyclopedia of Aboriginal Australia. Aboriginal and Torres Strait Islander History, Society and Culture*. Canberra, Aboriginal Studies Press for the Institute of Aboriginal and Torres Strait Islander Studies.

Howard, M (ed) (1982). *Aboriginal Power in Australian Society*. St Lucia, University of Queensland Press.

Huffer,V with the collaboration of Elsie Roughey and other women of Mornington Island (1980). *The Sweetness of the Fig: Aboriginal Women in Transition*. Kensington, New South Wales University Press; Seattle and London, University of Washington Press.

Huggins, J (1987/8). '"Firing on in the mind": Aboriginal Women Domestic Servants in the Inter-war Years.' *Hecate*, 13 (2).

Huggins, J (1992). 'Towards a biography of Rita Huggins'. In S Magarey, C Guerin and P Hamilton (eds), *Writing Lives : Feminist Biography and Autobiography. Australian Feminist Studies*, (16), Summer.

Huggins, J (1995). 'White Aprons, Black Hands: Aboriginal Women Domestic Servants in Queensland.' In A McGrath and K Saunders (eds), *Aboriginal Workers. Special Issue of Labour History* (69).

Huggins, J (1998). *Sister Girl: The Writings of Aboriginal Activist and Historian Jackie Huggins*. St Lucia, University of Queensland Press.

Huggins, J and T Blake (1992). 'Protection or Persecution? Gender Relations in the Era of Racial Segregation.' In K Saunders and R Evans (eds), *Gender Relations in Australia. Domination and Negotiation*. Sydney, Harcourt Brace Jovanovich.

Hume, L (1989). 'Yarrabah: Christian Phoenix.' Christianity and Social Change on an Australian Aboriginal Reserve. PhD Thesis, University of Queensland.

Hunter, E (1993). *Aboriginal Health and History. Power and Prejudice in Remote Australia*. Cambridge, Cambridge University Press.

Hunter, I (1994). *Re-thinking the School: Subjectivity, Bureaucracy, Criticism*. St Leonards, New South Wales, Allen & Unwin.

Hyssen, A (1994). 'Monument and memory in a post-modern age.' In J E Young (ed). *The Art of Memory. Holocaust Memorials in History.* New York, The Jewish Museum.

Iniguez, L, J Valencia and F Vazquez (1997). 'The Construction of Remembering and Forgetfulness: Memories and Histories of the Spanish Civil War.' In J Pennebaker, D Paez and B Rime (eds), *Collective Memory of Political Events: Social Psychological Perspectives.* Mahwah, New Jersey, Lawrence Erlbaum Associates.

Iredale, R R (1965). 'The Enigma of Assimilation and the Protection of the Part-Aborigines in New South Wales.' Research paper, Geography Department, University of Sydney.

Jackson, M (1995). *At Home in the World.* Pymble, New South Wales, Harper Perennnial.

Jacobs, P (1990). *Mister Neville.* Fremantle, Fremantle Arts Centre Press.

Jaggs, D (1986). *Neglected and Criminal: Foundations of Child Welfare Legislation in Victoria.* Melbourne, Centre for Youth and Community Studies, Phillip Institute of Technology.

Jaggs, D (1991). *Asylum to Action. Family Action 1851–1991. A History of Services and Policy Development for Families in Times of Vulnerability.* Oakleigh East, Victoria, Family Action.

Jakubowicz, A (ed) (1994). *Racism, Ethnicity and the Media.* St Leonards, New South Wales, Allen & Unwin.

Jamrozik, A (1983). 'Changing Concepts and Practices in Child Welfare and Options for the Future.' *Child Welfare: Current Issues and Future Directions. Social Welfare Research Centre Seminar, 6 July 1983.* Kensington, Social Welfare Research Centre, University of New South Wales.

Japanangka, D Leichleitner and P Nathan (1983). *Settle Down Country.* Alice Springs, Central Australian Aboriginal Congress.

Jayawardena, K (1995). *The White Woman's Other Burden: Western Women and South Asia During British Rule.* New York, Routledge.

Jebb, M A (1987). 'Isolating the Problem.' Venereal Disease and Aborigines in Western Australia 1898–1924. BA (Hons) Thesis, Murdoch University.

Jebb, M A and A Haebich (1992). 'Across the Great Divide. Gender Relations on Australian Frontiers.' In K Saunders and R Evans (eds), *Gender Relations in Australia: Domination and Negotiation.* Sydney, Harcourt Brace Jovanovich.

Jenkins, M (director) (1992). *Leaving of Liverpool.* Australian Broadcasting Commission television production in association with the British Broadcasting Corporation. Murdoch University.

Johnson, L (1993). *The Modern Girl: Girlhood and Growing Up.* St Leonards, New South Wales, Allen & Unwin.

Johnston, W R (1988). *A Documentary History of Queensland.* St Lucia, University of Queensland Press.

Jones, Delmos J and J Hill-Burnett (1982). 'The Political Context of Ethnogenesis.' In M Howard (ed). *Aboriginal Power in Australian Society.* St Lucia, University of Queensland Press.

Kalokerinos, A (1974). *Every Second Child.* Melbourne, Thomas Nelson.

Kammen, M (1991). *Mystic Cords of Memory. The Transformation of Tradition in American Culture.* New York, Alfred A Knopf.

Kelly, Paul (1993) *Lyrics.* Pymble, NSW, Angus and Robertson.

Kennedy, M (1990). *Born a Half Caste.* Canberra, Aboriginal Studies Press.

Kidd, R (1994a). 'Regulating Bodies. Administrations and Aborigines in Queensland 1840–1988.' PhD Thesis, Griffith University.

Kidd, R (1994b) 'You Can Trust Me — I'm With the Government.' Paper delivered to *One Family, Many Histories: A National Conference for Aboriginal and Torres Strait Islander Histories.* Brisbane.

Kidd, R (1997). *The Way We Civilise. Aboriginal Affairs — the Untold Story.* St Lucia, University of Queensland Press.

Kidd, R (1998). 'Deficits of the Past or Deceits of the Present? Defining Aboriginal Disadvantage.' *Southern Review,* 31 (1).

Kimberley Land Council (1996). 'Submission to the National Inquiry into the Separation of Aboriginal and Torres Strait Islander Children from their Families.' Derby, Kimberley Land Council.

Kimberley Language Resource Centre (1996). *Moola Bulla. In the Shadow of the Mountain.* Broome, Western Australia, Magabala Books.

King, D A and A W McHoul (1996). 'The Discursive Production of the Queensland Aborigine as Subject: Meston's Proposal 1895.' *Social Analysis* (19).

Kociumbus, J (1997). *Australian Childhood: A History.* St Leonards, New South Wales, Allen & Unwin.

Lake, M (1998). 'Feminism and the Gendered Politics of Antiracism, Australia 1927–1957.' *Australian Historical Studies* (110).

Laurie, V (1992). 'Victims, Crime and Prejudice in the West.' *Australian Magazine,* 7.11.1992.

Leaming, J (1986). '"Nearly White" Assimilation Policies in Practice in Western Australia at Sister Kate's Children's Home from 1933–1964.' BA (Hons) Thesis. University of Western Australia.

Lees, W (1902). *The Aboriginal Problem in Queensland: How it is Being Dealt With. A Story of Life and Work under the New Acts.* Brisbane, City Printing Works.

Lehman, G (1991). The Ships and the Shapes: A Discussion of Aborigines, Politics and Art. *Press Press,* June.

Lennox, G (1984). 'Oyster Cove Historic Site: A Resource Document. Occasional Paper No 9.' Hobart, National Parks and Wildlife Service.

Levy, M C J (1955). *Governor George Arthur: A Colonial Benevolent Despot.* Melbourne, Georgian House.

Lindqvist, S (1997). *Exterminate All the Brutes.* London, Granta Books.

Link-Up (New South Wales) Aboriginal Corporation and T J Wilson (1997). *In the Best Interests of the Child? Stolen Children: Aboriginal Pain, White Shame.* Canberra, Aboriginal History Incorporated.

Lira, E (1997). 'Remembering: Passing Back Through the Heart.' In J Pennebaker, D Paez and B Rime (eds), *Collective Memory of Political Events: Social Psychological Perspectives.* Mahwah, New Jersey, Lawrence Erlbaum Associates.

Long, J P M (1970). *Aboriginal Settlements.* Canberra, Australian National University Press.

Long, J (1992). *The Go-betweens. Patrol Officers in Aboriginal Affairs Administration in the Northern Territory 1936–74.* Canberra, North Australia Research Unit, Australian National University.

Loos, N (1970). Frontier Conflict in the Bowen District, 1861–1874. MA Thesis, James Cook University.

Luke, G and C Cunneen (1995). *Aboriginal Over-Representation and Discretionary Decisions in the NSW Juvenile Justice System.* Sydney, Juvenile Justice Advisory Council of New South Wales.

Lutton, N (1988). 'Bessie Mabel Rischbieth - biography of a feminist'. In B Nairn and G Serle (eds), *Australian Dictionary of Biography, 1891-1939, Volume 7.* Melbourne, University of Melbourne Press.

MacDonald, R (1995). *Between Two Worlds: The Commonwealth Government and the Removal of Aboriginal Children of Part Descent in the Northern Territory.* Alice Springs, Institute of Aboriginal Development Press.

Macleod, C (1997). *Patrol in the Dreamtime.* Kew, Victoria, Mandarin.

Malouf, D (1998). *A Spirit of Play: The Making of the Australian Consciousness.* Sydney, ABC Books for the Australian Broadcasting Corporation.

Manne, R (1998). 'The Stolen Generations.' *Quadrant,* January–February.

Marks, R S (1960). 'Mission policy in Western Australia 1846–1959.' *University Studies in Western Australian History,* 111 (4).

Markus, A (ed) (1988). *Blood from a Stone: William Cooper and the Australian Aborigines League.* Clayton, Victoria, Monash Publications in History, Department of History, Monash University.

Markus, A (1990). *Governing Savages.* Sydney, Allen & Unwin.

Markus, A (1994). *Australian Race Relations 1788–1991.* St Leonards, New South Wales, Allen & Unwin.

Martin, C (1923, 1987). *The Incredible Journey.* London, Pandora Press.

Massola, A (1970). *Aboriginal Mission Stations in Victoria.* Melbourne, Hawthorn Press.

Mathews, J E (1977). *The Two Worlds of Jimmie Barker: The Life of an Australian Aboriginal 1900–1972.* Canberra, Australian Institute of Aboriginal Studies.

Matson-Green, V Maykutenna and T Harper (1995). 'Palawa Women: Carrying the Burdens and Finding the Solutions.' In A McGrath and K Saunders (eds). *Aboriginal Workers. Special Issue of Labour History* (69).

Mattingley, C and K Hampton (eds) (1988). *Survival in Our Own Land. Aboriginal Experiences in South Australia Since 1836.* Sydney, Hodder & Stoughton.

Maushart, S (1993). *Sort of a Place Like Home: Remembering the Moore River Native Settlement.* Fremantle, Fremantle Arts Centre Press.

May, D (1994). *Aboriginal Labour and the Cattle Industry. Queensland from White Settlement to the Present.* Cambridge, Cambridge University Press.

Maynard, J (1999). 'Fred Maynard and the Australian Aboriginal Progressive Association: One God, One Aim, One Destiny.' *Aboriginal History* (21).

McCann, D (1994). 'Inquest into the Death of Louis St John Johnson, 18.3.1994.' Typescript. Perth Coroners Office.

McCorquodale, J (1987). *Aborigines and the Law: A Digest.* Canberra, Aboriginal Studies Press.

McDonald, C N (1996). *When You Grow Up.* Broome, Western Australia, Magabala Books.

McGrath, A (1993a). 'Colonialism, Crime and Civilisation.' In D Walker (ed) with S Garton and J Horne, *Crimes and Trials. Australian Cultural History* (12).

McGrath, A (1993b). '"Beneath the Skin": Australian Citizenship, Rights and Aboriginal Women.' *Women and the State. Australian Perspectives, Journal of Australian Studies* (37).

McGregor, R (1993). 'Representations of the "Half-Caste" in the Australian Scientific Literature of the 1930s.' *Journal of Australian Studies* (36).

McGregor, R (1997). *Imagined Destinies. Aboriginal Australians and the Doomed Race Theory, 1880–1939.* Melbourne, Melbourne University Press.

McGinness, J (1991). *Son of Alyandabu: My Fights for Aboriginal Rights.* St Lucia, University of Queensland Press.

McHoul, A (1991). 'Taking the Children; Some Reflections at a Distance on the Camera and Dr Barnado.' *Continuum. Media/Discourse,* 5 (1).

McNair, W and H Rumley (1981). *Pioneer Aboriginal Mission: The Work of Wesleyan Missionary John Smithies in the Swan River Colony 1840–1855.* Nedlands, University of Western Australia Press.

Medcraft, R and V Gee (1995). *The Sausage Tree*. St Lucia, University of Queensland Press.

Meston, A (1895). 'Queensland Aboriginals: A Proposed System For Their Improvement And Preservation Addressed To The Hon. Horace Tozer, Colonial Secretary.' Brisbane, Government Printer.

Mickler, S (1992). *Gambling on the First Race: A Comment on Racism and Talk-back Radio — 6PR, the TAB and the Western Australian Government*. Murdoch, Centre for Research in Culture and Communication, Murdoch University and the Louis St John Johnson Memorial Trust.

Mickler, S (1998). *The Myth of Privilege*. Fremantle, Fremantle Arts Centre Press.

Mickler, S and A McHoul (1997). 'Sourcing the Wave: Crime Reporting, Aboriginal Youth and the Perth Press.' *Media International Australia*, 85.

Miller, J (1985). *Koori: A Will to Win. The Heroic Resistance, Survival and Triumph of Black Australia*. North Ryde, Angus & Robertson.

Miller, J R (1996). *Shingwauk's Vision: A History of Native Residential Schools*. Toronto, University of Toronto Press.

Milloy, J S (1999). *'A National Crime.' The Canadian Government and the Residential School System, 1879 to 1986*. Winnipeg, University of Manitoba Press.

Mogumber Data Base Project (1997). 'Moora Court House Records relating to Aboriginal Residents of Moore River Native Settlement.' Canberra, Australian Institute of Aboriginal and Torres Strait Islander Studies. Typescript.

Mollison, B C and C Everitt (1976). 'A Chronology of Events Affecting Tasmanian Aboriginal People Since Contact with Whites (1772–1976).' Psychology Department, University of Tasmania. Typescript, Hobart, State Library of Tasmania.

Mollison, B C and C Everitt (1978). 'The Tasmanian Aboriginals and their Descendants.' Hobart. Typescript, Hobart, State Library of Tasmania.

Morgan, M (1985). *A Drop in the Bucket: The Mount Margaret Story*. Box Hill, Victoria, United Aborigines Mission.

Morgan, S (1987). *My Place*. Fremantle, Fremantle Arts Centre Press.

Morris, B (1988). 'Dhan gadi resistance to assimilation.' In I Keen (ed) *Being Black. Aboriginal Cultures in Settled Australia*. Canberra, Aboriginal Studies Press for Australian Institute of Aboriginal Studies.

Murphy, J (1995). 'Social Policy for Families.' In S Prasser, J R Nethercote and J Warhurst (eds) (1995). *The Menzies Era: A Reappraisal of Government, Politics and Policy*. Sydney, Hale & Iremonger.

Murphy J and J Smart (eds) (1997). 'The Forgotten Fifties: Aspects of Australian Society and Culture in the 1950s.' *Australian Historical Studies* (109).

Nailon, D (1997). Encounter between Catholicism and Aboriginal Peoples in the Kimberley Region of Western Australia with Special Emphasis on the Experiences of Women on Both Sides of the Encounter,1884–1990. PhD Thesis, La Trobe University.

Nannup, A, L Marsh and S Kinnane (1992). *When the Pelican Laughed*. Fremantle, Fremantle Arts Centre Press.

Nelson, H (1985). *Prisoners of War: Australians Under Nippon*. Australian Broadcasting Commission Radio Series.

Neville, A O (1947). *Australia's Coloured Minority: Its Place in the Community*. Sydney, Currawong.

New South Wales Government (1904). 'Report of the Royal Commission on the Decline of the Birth Rate and on the Mortality of Infants in New South Wales. Volume 1.' Sydney, Government Printer.

New South Wales Government (1910). *Forms and Regulations*. Sydney, Government Printer.

New South Wales Government (1914). 'Report of the Royal Commission on Neglected and Delinquent and Mentally Deficient Children.' *New South Wales Parliamentary Papers, 4*. Sydney, Government Printer.

New South Wales Government, Aboriginal Children's Research Project (1982). *Aboriginal Children in Substitute Care. Principal Report*. Sydney, Department of Family and Children's Services.

New South Wales Government (1996). 'New South Wales Government Submission to the Human Rights and Equal Opportunity Commission National Inquiry into the Separation of Aboriginal and Torres Strait Islander Children from their Families.' Typescript, Sydney, Human Rights and Equal Opportunity Commission.

Northern Territory Government (1996). 'National Inquiry into the Separation of Aboriginal and Torres Strait Islander Children from their Families: Northern Territory Government Interim Submission.' Darwin. Typescript, Sydney, Human Rights and Equal Opportunity Commission.

Oxenberry, R (1982). *Changing Families. Proceedings of Third Australian Conference on Adoption, Adelaide*. Adelaide : Department of Continuing Education, University of Adelaide for the Organising Committee of the Third Australian Conference on Adoption.

Paez, D, N Basabe and J L Gonzales (1989). 'Social Processes and Collective Memory: a Cross-Cultural Approach to Remembering Political Events.' In J Pennebaker, D Paez and B Rime (eds), *Collective Memory of Political Events: Social Psychological Perspectives*. Mahwah, New Jersey, Lawrence Erlbaum Associates.

Paisley, F (1995). 'Feminist Challenges to White Australia, 1900–1930s.' In D Kirby (ed), *Sex, Power and Justice. Historical Perspectives on Law in Australia*. Oxford, Oxford University Press.

Paisley, F (1997a). 'Assimilation: a Protest as Old as the Policy.' *Australian*. 5.6.1997.

Paisley, F (1997b). 'Race and Rememberance: Contesting Aboriginal Child Removal in the Inter War Years.'

Australian Humanities Review, November. URL http://www.lamp.ac.uk/ahr/archive/ Issue–November–1997/paisley.html.

Paisley, F (1998). 'Federalising the Aborigines? Constitutional Reform in the Late 1920s.' *Australian Historical Studies*, 29 (111).

Palmer, D (1995). From Kaat Wara to Moorditj Nyidiyang: Youth Work, Change and the Constitution of the Wadjela Self. MPhil Thesis, Murdoch University.

Parbury, N. (1986). *Survival. A History of Aboriginal Life in New South Wales*. Sydney, Ministry of Aboriginal Affairs.

Parry, S (1995). 'Identifying the Process: The Removal of "Half-Caste" Children from Aboriginal Mothers.' *Aboriginal History*, 19 (2).

Pearce, K and S Doyle (1997). 'New Town Historical Research.' Hobart. Typescript, held by author.

Pederson, H and B Woorunmurra (1995). *Jandamarra and the Bunuba Resistance*. Broome, Western Australia, Magabala Books.

Peterson, N and W Sanders (eds) (1998). *Citizenship and Indigenous Australians. Changing Conceptions and Possibilities*. Cambridge, Cambridge University Press.

Petrow, S (1997). 'The Last Man: the Mutilation of William Lanne in 1869 and its aftermath.' *Aboriginal History* 21.

Picton, C (1978). *Current Concerns and Alternatives for Child Placement and Parenting. Proceedings of Second Australian Conference on Adoption*, Melbourne. Melbourne, The Committee of the Second Australian Conference on Adoption, 1978.

Pittock, A B (1975). *Beyond White Australia; A Short History of Race Relations in Australia*. Surry Hills, New South Wales, Race Relations Committee of the Religious Society of Friends (Quakers) in Australia.

Plomley, N J B (ed) (1966). *Friendly Mission. The Tasmanian Journals and Papers of George Augustus Robinson 1829–1834*. Kingsgrove, New South Wales, Halstad Press.

Plomley, N J B (ed) (1987). *Weep in Silence. A History of the Flinders Island Aboriginal Settlement with the Flinders Island Journal of George Augustus Robinson 1835–1839*. Hobart, Blubber Head Press.

Plomley, N J B (ed) (1991). *Jorgen Jorgenson and the Aborigines of Van Diemen's Land*. Hobart, Blubber Head Press.

Plomley, N J B and K A Henley (1990). 'The Sealers of Bass Strait and the Cape Barren Island Community.' *Tasmanian Historical Research Association*, 37 (2–3).

Poad, D, A West and R Miller (1985). *Contact: An Australian History*. Richmond, Victoria, Heinemann Educational Australia.

Pohlner, H (1986). *Gangurru*. Milton, Queensland, Hope Vale Mission Branch.

Porter, R (1993). *Paul Hasluck: A Political Biography*. Nedlands, University of Western Australia Press.

Prior, Peter (nd). *Straight From the Yudaman's Mouth: the Life Story of Peter Prior Before, During and After the Robert Curry Days*. Townsville. Brisbane, John Oxley Library.

Purtscher, J C (1993). *Children in Queen's Orphanage Hobart Town 1828–1863*. New Town, Tasmania, I. Schaffer.

Purtscher, J C (1994). *Apprentices and Absconders from Queen's Orphanage 1860–1883*. New Town, Tasmania, I. Schaffer.

Pybus, C. (1991). *Community of Thieves*. Port Melbourne, William Heinemann.

Queensland Government (1896). 'Report on the Aboriginals of Queensland by Archibald Meston, Special Commissioner under Instructions from the Queensland Government.' Brisbane, Government Printer.

Queensland Government (1897). 'Report on the North Queensland Aborigines and the Native Police.' *Queensland, Votes and Proceedings*, 10.

Queensland Government (1994). *Records Guide Volume One. A Guide to Queensland Government Records Relating to Aboriginal and Torres Strait Islander Peoples*. K Frankland. Brisbane, Queensland State Archives and Department of Family Services and Aboriginal and Islander Affairs.

Queensland Government (1996). 'Interim Submission to the Human Rights and Equal Opportunity Commission Inquiry into the Separation of Aboriginal and Torres Strait Islander Children from their Families.' Typescript, Brisbane, Department of Family Services and Aboriginal and Islander Affairs.

Queensland Government (1997a). 'Final Submission to the Human Rights and Equal Opportunity Commission Inquiry into the Separation of Aboriginal and Torres Strait Islander Children from their Families.' Typescript., Brisbane, Department of Family Services and Aboriginal and Islander Affairs

Queensland Government (1997b). 'Responses to Questions from the Human Rights and Equal Opportunity Commission Inquiry into the Separation of Aboriginal and Torres Strait Islander Children from their Families.' Typescript, Brisbane, Department of Family Services and Aboriginal and Islander Affairs.

Radzinowicz, L and R Hood (1986). *A History of English Criminal Law and its Administration from 1750. Volume 5, The Emergence of Penal Policy*. London, Stevens & Sons.

Rajowski, P (1995). *Linden Girl*. Nedlands, University Of Western Australia Press.

Read, P (1981). *The Stolen Generations: The Removal of Aboriginal Children in New South Wales 1833–1969*. Sydney, Government Printer.

Read, P (1983). '"A Rape of the Soul so Profound": Some Reflections on the Dispersal Policy in New South Wales.' *Aboriginal History*, 7 (1).

Read, P (ed) (1984). *Down There with Me on the Cowra Mission*. Sydney, Pergamon.

Read, P (1990). '"Cheeky, Insolent and Anti-White": The Split in the Federal Council for the Advancement of Aboriginal and Torres Strait Islanders, Easter 1970.' *Australian Journal of Politics and History*, 36 (1).

Read, P (1995). 'Northern Territory.' In A McGrath (ed), *Contested Ground. Australian Aborigines Under the British Crown*. St Leonards, New South Wales, Allen & Unwin.

Read, P (1999). *A Rape of the Soul So Profound: The Return of the Stolen Generations*. Sydney, Allen & Unwin.

Read, P and C Edwards (eds) (1989). *The Lost Children: Thirteen Australians Taken from their Families Tell of the Struggle to Find their Native Parents*. Sydney, Doubleday.

Read, P and J Read (eds) (1993). *Long Time Olden Time: Aboriginal Accounts of Northern Territory History*. Alice Springs, Institute for Aboriginal Development.

Reay, M (1965). 'The Background of Alien Impact.' In R M Berndt and C H Berndt (eds), *Aboriginal Man in Australia*. Sydney, Angus & Robertson.

Renkin, P (1996). 'A Brief Historical Background Outlining Issues Concerning the Involvement of the Uniting Church in Australia, Synod of Victoria — and its Predecessors — in the Separation of Aboriginal and Islander Children from their Families and Placement in the Care of : (a) State Institutions, or (b) Voluntary Sector (Including Church Based) Child/Youth Welfare Agencies, or (c) Non-Aboriginal/Islander Families.' Paper prepared for the Community Services Consultative Committee Task Force on the Human Rights and Equal Opportunity Commission's Inquiry into the Separation of Aboriginal and Torres Strait Islander Children from their Parents. Melbourne, Uniting Church in Australia, Synod of Victoria, Commission for Mission.

Reynolds, B (1988). 'Walter Edmund Roth.' In G Serle (ed), *Australian Dictionary of Biography, 1891–1939, Volume 11*. Carlton, Melbourne University Press.

Reynolds, H (1989). *Dispossession. Black Australians and White Invaders*. St Leonards, New South Wales, Allen & Unwin.

Reynolds, H (1990). *With the White People. The Crucial Role of Aborigines in the Exploration and Development of Australia*. Ringwood, Victoria, Penguin.

Reynolds, H (1995). *Fate of a Free People. A Radical Re-examination of the Tasmanian Wars*. Ringwood, Victoria, Penguin.

Reynolds, H (1998). *This Whispering in Our Hearts*. St Leonards, New South Wales, Allen & Unwin.

Reynolds, H and D May (1995). 'Queensland.' In A McGrath (ed) *Contested Ground. Australian Aborigines Under the British Crown*. St Leonards, New South Wales, Allen & Unwin.

Riddett, L (1998). 'A Bag of Lollies: Children as Mediators in the Northern Territory.' In T Austin and S Parry (eds), *Connection and Disconnection: Encounters Between Settlers and Indigenous People in the Northern Territory*. Darwin, Northern Territory University Press.

Rintoul, S (1993). *The Wailing: A National Black Oral History*. Port Melbourne, William Heinemann.

Ripley, R and G Franklin (1986). *Policy Implementation and Bureaucracy*. Chicago, Dorsey Press.

Rischbieth, B M (1964). *March of Australian Women: A Record of Fifty Years Struggle for Equal Citizenship*. Perth, Paterson Brokensha.

Robertson, G R and J C Carrick (1970). 'The Trials of Nancy Young.' *Australian Quarterly*, 42, (2).

Roder, A F (1987). Aboriginal Children Under the Law: a History of the Specific Legislative Provisions Relating to Aboriginal Children in South Australia 1836–1972. Bachelor of Laws (Hons), University of Adelaide.

Roe, J (1986). *Beyond Belief. Theosophy in Australia 1879–1939*. Kensington, University of New South Wales Press.

Rose, D B (1991). 'Hidden histories.' In *Island*, 51.

Rose, D B (1991). *Hidden Histories: Black Stories from Victoria River Downs, Humbert River and Wave Hill Stations*. Canberra, Aboriginal Studies Press.

Rose, L (1991). *The Erosion of Childhood. Child Oppression in Britain 1860–1918*. London, Routledge.

Rose, L (1986). *Massacre of the Innocents. Infanticide in Great Britain 1800–1939*. London, Routledge and Kegan Paul.

Rose, N (1996a). *Inventing Our Selves. Psychology, Power and Personhood*. Cambridge, Cambridge University Press.

Rose, N (1996b). 'Governing "Advanced" Liberal Democracies.' In A Barry, T Osborne and N Rose (eds). *Foucault and Political Reason: Liberalism, neo-Liberalism and Rationalities of Government*. London, UCL Press.

Rose, V K (1998). 'My One Bright Spot.' A Personal Insight into Relationships Between White Women and Aboriginal Women Under the New South Wales Aborigines Protection Board Apprenticeship Policy 1920–42. PhD Thesis, University of Sydney.

Rosser, B (1987). *Dreamtime Nightmares*. Ringwood, Penguin.

Roth, L H (1899). *The Aborigines of Tasmania*, 2nd ed. Halifax, F King & Sons.

Roth, W (1897). *Ethnological Studies Among North-West-Central Queensland Aborigines.* Brisbane, Government Printer; London, Queensland Agent General's Office.

Roughsey, E (1984). *An Aboriginal Mother Tells of the Old and the New.* Fitzroy, McPhee Gribble, Penguin.

Rowley, C D (1961–2). 'Aborigines and Other Australians.' *Oceania,* 37 (4).

Rowley, C (1972a). *The Destruction of Aboriginal Society.* Ringwood, Victoria, Penguin Books.

Rowley, C D (1972b). *Outcasts in White Australia.* Ringwood, Victoria, Penguin Books.

Rowley, C (1972c). *The Remote Aborigines.* Ringwood, Victoria, Penguin Books.

Rowley, C (1978). *A Matter of Justice.* Canberra, Australian National University Press.

Rowse, T (nd). *Open Learning. Australia Since the War. Part 5 Aborigines and Citizenship.* Sydney, Australian Broadcasting Corporation.

Rowse, T (1986). 'Aborigines as Historical Actors: Evidence and Inference.' *Historical Studies,* 22, (87).

Rowse, T (1987). 'Assimilation and After.' In A Curthoys, A W Martin and T Rowse (eds), *Australians: From 1939.* Broadway, New South Wales, Fairfax, Syme & Weldon.

Rowse, T (1989). White Flour, White Power? Colonial Authority, Rationing and the Family in Alice Springs. PhD Thesis, University of Sydney.

Rowse, T (1996). *Traditions for Health. Studies in Aboriginal Reconstruction.* Darwin, Northern Australia Research Unit, Australian National University.

Rowse, T (1998a). *White Flour White Power. From Rations to Citizenship in Central Australia.* Cambridge, Cambridge University Press.

Rowse, T (1998b). 'The Modesty of the State: Hasluck and the Anthropological Critics of Assimilation.' In T C Stannage, K Saunders and R Nile (eds), *Paul Hasluck in Australian History: Civic Personality and Public Life.* St Lucia, University of Queensland Press.

Rowse, T (1998c). 'Indigenous Citizenship and Self-determination: The Problem of Shared Responsibilities.' In N Peterson and W Sanders (eds), *Citizenship and Indigenous Australians. Changing Conceptions and Possibilities.* Cambridge, Cambridge University.

Rumley, H and S Toussaint (1990). '"For Their Own Benefit?" A Critical Overview of Aboriginal Policy and Practice at Moola Bulla, East Kimberley, 1910–1955.' *Aboriginal History,* 14 (1–2).

Russell, P (1997). '"Her Excellency": Lady Franklin, Female Convicts and the Problem of Authority in Van Diemen's Land.' In R Nile (ed), *Fatal Shores. Journal of Australian Studies* (53).

Ryan, L (1996). *The Aboriginal Tasmanians,* 2nd ed. St Leonards, New South Wales, Allen & Unwin.

Sanders, W G (1986). *Access, Administration and Politics: The Australian Social Security System and Aborigines.* Canberra, Australian National University.

Saxon, M (1992). 'Murder Case Family to Sue.' *Sunday Times* (Perth), 1.3.1992.

Saxon, M (1992). 'Car Killing No Treatment', 'Long-lost Murdered Teenager Got "Home" Too Late.' *Sunday Times* (Perth), 8.3.1992.

Scanlon, T (1986). '"Pure and Clean and True to Christ": Black Women and White Missionaries in the North.' *Hecate,* 12 (1–2).

Scarry, E (1985). *The Body in Pain, the Making and Unmaking of the World.* New York, Oxford, Oxford University Press.

Scott, K (1999). *Benang: From the Heart.* Fremantle, Fremantle Arts Centre Press.

Schenk, R (1937). *The Educability of the Natives.* Melbourne, United Aborigines Mission.

Sercombe, H (1997). 'Youth Crime and the Economy of News Production'. In J Bessant and R Hill (eds), *Youth Crime and the Media.* Hobart, National Clearing House for Youth Studies.

Sereny, G (1995). *Albert Speer: His Battle With Truth.* New York, Alfred A Knopf.

Shaw, G (1977). 'Fringe camps in the Alice.' *Shelter,* 4.

Shriver, D W (1995). *An Ethic for Enemies. Forgiveness in Politics.* New York, Oxford University Press.

Sider, G M (1987). 'Why parrots learn to talk and why they can't: domination, deception and self-deception in Indian-White relations.' In *Comparative Studies in Anthropology and History,* 29.

Skidmore,T E (1993). *Black into White: Race and Nationality in Brazilian Thought.* Durham and London, Duke University Press.

Smith, J D (1992). *The Eugenic Assault on America. Scenes in Black and White.* Fairfax, Virginia, George Mason University Press.

Smith Street Films (1991). *Special Treatment. Locking Up Aboriginal Children.* Sydney, Smith Street Films.

Sommerlad, E (1976). *Homes for Blacks: Community and Adoption. Proceedings of First Australian Conference on Adoption.* University of New South Wales, Sydney.

Sommerlad, E (1977). 'Aboriginal Juveniles in Custody: Report Arising from a National Symposium on the Care and Treatment of Aboriginal Juveniles in State Corrective Institutions.' Canberra, Australian National University Centre for Continuing Education.

Sommerlad, E (1978). 'Aboriginal Juveniles in Custody — New Community and Institutional Approaches.' *Australian Child Welfare,* 3 (3–4).

South Australian Government (1913). 'Progress Report of the Royal Commission on the Aborigines.' *Parliamentary Papers of South Australia* (26).

South Australian Government (1916). 'Repot of the Royal Commission on the Aborigines.' *Parliamentary Papers of South Australia* (21).

South Australian Government, Department of Aboriginal Affairs (1963). 'A Brief Outline of Aboriginal Affairs in South Australia Since Colonisation.' Typescript.

South Australian Government (1996). 'National Inquiry into Separation of Aboriginal and Torres Strait Islander Children from Their Families: South Australian Government Interim Submission.' Adelaide. Typescript.

Spensky, M. (1992). 'Producers of Legitimacy: Homes for Unmarried Mothers in the 1950s.' In C Smart (ed), *Regulating Womanhood: Historical Essays on Marriage, Motherhood and Sexuality*. London, Routledge.

Stannage, C T (1979). *The People of Perth: A Social History of Western Australia's Capital City*. Perth, Perth City Council.

Stannage, C T (1981). *A New History of Western Australia*. Nedlands, University of Western Australia Press.

Stanton, J E (1979). 'The Mount Margaret Community.' In R Berndt and C Berndt (eds), *Aborigines of the West: Their Past and Their Present*. Nedlands, University of Western Australia Press.

Stanton, J E (1988). 'Mount. Margaret: Missionaries and the Aftermath.' In T Swain and D B Rose (eds), *Aboriginal Australians and Christian Missions. Ethnographic and Historical Studies*. Adelaide, The Australian Association for the Study of Religions.

Stevens, C (1994). *White Man's Dreaming. Killalpaninna Mission 1866–1915*. Melbourne, Oxford University Press.

Stevens, F (1974). *Racism: the Australian Experience: A Study of Race Prejudice in Australia. Volume 1. Prejudice and Xenophobia*. Sydney, Australia & New Zealand Book Co.

Stoler, A L (1995). *Race and the Education of Desire. Foucault's History of Sexuality and the Colonial Order of Things*. Durham and London, Duke University Press.

Stone, S (1974). *Aborigines in White Australia. A Documentary History of the Attitudes Affecting Official Policy and the Australian Aborigine, 1697–1973*. Richmond, Victoria, Heinemann Educational Books.

Strehlow, T G H (1968). *Aranda Traditions*. Melbourne, Melbourne University Press, reprinted with permission of original publisher by Johnson Reprint Corporation, New York

Stretton, P and C Finnimore (1993). 'Black Fellow Citizens: Aborigines and the Commonwealth Franchise.' *Australian Historical Studies* (101).

Supreme Court of Western Australia (1993). 'Johnson vs Lapham.' *Western Australian Law Reports*, 6.

Surken, M (1991). 'The wall, the screen and the image: the Vietnam Veterans' Memorial.' In *Representations*, (35), Spring.

Swain, T and Rose, D B (eds) (1988). Aboriginal Australians and Christian Missions, Ethnographic and Historical Studies. Adelaide, Australian Association for the Study of Religion.

Taffe, S (1995). 'Australian Diplomacy in a Vacuum: Government and Aboriginal Affairs.' *Aboriginal History*, 19 (1–2).

Tasmanian Aboriginal Centre Inc (1996). 'National Inquiry into the Separation of Aboriginal and Torres Strait Islander Children from their Families. Additional Submissions to the Wilson Inquiry.' Hobart. Typescript, Sydney, Human Rights and Equal Opportunity Commission.

Tasmanian Government (1908). *Furneaux Islands: Report Upon the State of the Islands, the Condition and Mode of Living of the Half-castes, the Existing Methods of Regulating the Reserves, and Suggesting Lines for Future Administration*. G E Lord. Hobart, Government Printer.

Tasmanian Government (1995a). 'Interim Submission to the Human Rights and Equal Opportunity Commission Inquiry into the Separation of Aboriginal and Torres Strait Islander Children from their Families.' Hobart. Typescript, Sydney, Human Rights and Equal Opportunity Commission.

Tasmanian Government and the Human Rights and Equal Opportunity Commission (1995b). 'National Inquiry into the Separation of Aboriginal and Torres Strait Islander Children from their Families: Tasmanian Government Oral Submission.' Typescript, Sydney, Human Rights and Equal Opportunity Commission.

Tatz, C (1964). Aboriginal Administration in the Northern Territory of Australia. PhD Thesis, Australian National University.

Tatz, C (1999). *Genocide in Australia. Australian Institute of Aboriginal Studies Research Discussion Paper No 8*. Canberra, Aboriginal Studies Press.

Telfer, E (1939). *Amongst Australian Aborigines: Forty Years of Missionary Work*. Melbourne, Fraser and Morphet.

Thomson, J (ed) (1989). *Reaching Back: Queensland Aboriginal People Recall Early Days at Yarrabah Mission*. Canberra, Aboriginal Studies Press.

Thornton, F F (1980). 'Situation Report: Aboriginal Communities in Alice Springs and Fringe Camps.' Reprinted in D Bell and P Ditton (eds). *Law: the Old and the New*. Canberra, Aboriginal History for Central Australian Aboriginal Legal Aid Service.

Thorpe,W (1984). 'Archibald Meston and Aboriginal Legislation in Colonial Queensland.' *Historical Studies*, 21 (82).

Tilbury, C (1998). 'Child Protection Policy and Practice in Relation to Aboriginal and Torres Strait Islander Children in Queensland in the 1990s.' *Australian Social Work*, 51 (2).
Tindale, N B (1941). 'Survey of the Half-caste Problem in South Australia.' *Proceedings of the Royal Geographical Society of South Australia*, XLII.
Tindale, N B (1953). Growth of a People: Formation and Development of a Hybrid Aboriginal and White Stock in the Islands of the Bass Strait Tasmania, 1815–1949.' *Records of the Queen Victoria Museum, Launceston New Series*, (2).
Tomlinson, J (1977). *Is Band-Aid Social Work Enough?* Darwin, The Wobbly Press.
Tonkinson, R (1974). *The Jigalong Mob: Victors of the Desert Crusade*. Menlo Park, Benjamin & Cummings.
Tonkinson, R (1988). 'Reflections on a Failed Crusade.' In T Swain and D B Rose (eds), *Aboriginal Australians and Christian Missions. Ethnographic and Historical Studies*. Adelaide, The Australian Association for the Study of Religions.
Trigger, D (1988). 'Christianity, Domination and Resistance in Colonial Social Relations: The Case of Doomadgee, Northwest Queensland.' In T Swain and D B Rose (eds). *Aboriginal Australians and Christian Missions. Ethnographic and Historical Studies*. Adelaide, The Australian Association for the Study of Religions.
Trigger, D (1991) *Whitefella Comin'. Aboriginal Responses to Colonialism in Northern Australia*. Cambridge, Cambridge University Press.
Tucker, M (1977). *If Everyone Cared. Autobiography of Margaret Tucker*. Sydney, Ure Smith.
Turnbull, C (1948). *Black War. The Extermination of the Tasmanian Aborigines*. Melbourne and London, F W Cheshire.
Turner, M and Hulme, D (1997). *Governance, Administration and Development. Making the State Work*. London, Macmillan.
Van den Berg, R (1994). *No Options No Choice. The Moore River Experience: My Father Thomas Corbett, an Aboriginal Half-caste*. Broome, Western Australia, Magabala Books.
Van Krieken, R (1991). *Children and the State: Social Control and the Formation of Australian Child Welfare*. St Leonards, New South Wales, Allen & Unwin.
Victorian Government (1957). *Report upon the Operation of the Aborigines Act 1928 and the Regulations and Orders Made Thereunder*. Charles McLean, Melbourne, Government Printer.
Victorian Government and Commonwealth Government (1993). *My Heart is Breaking. A Joint Guide to Records about Aboriginal People in the Public Records Office of Victoria and the Australian Archives, Victorian Regional Office*. Canberra, Australian Government Publishing Service.
Victorian Government (1996a). 'National Inquiry into the Separation of Aboriginal and Torres Strait Islander Children from their Families. Interim Submission.' Melbourne. Typescript, Sydney, Human Rights and Equal Opportunity Commission.
Victorian Government (1996b). 'National Inquiry into the Separation of Aboriginal and Torres Strait Islander Children from their Families. Victorian Government Final Submission: Parts One and Two.' Melbourne. Typescript, Sydney, Human Rights and Equal Opportunity Commission.
Victorian Government, Department of Human Services (nd). 'Children's Institutions, Victoria.' Typescript, Sydney, Human Rights and Equal Opportunity Commission.
Victorian Government, Department of Health and Community Services, Legislation and Legal Branch (1996). 'Victorian Legislation which may be of Relevance to the Inquiry into the Separation of Aboriginal and Torres Strait Islander Children from their Families.' Melbourne. Typescript, Sydney, Human Rights and Equal Opportunity Commission.
Vogan, A J (1890). *The Black Police: A Story of Modern Australia*. London, Hutchinson.
Wadley Dowley, C (2000). *Through Silent Country*. Fremantle, Fremantle Arts Centre Press.
Walden, I (1995). '"To Send Her to Service": Aboriginal Domestic Servants.' *Aboriginal Law Bulletin*, 3 (76).
Wallace Adams, D (1995). *Education for Extinction: American Indians and the Boarding School Experience*. Lawrence, Kansas, University Press of Kansas.
Walvin, J (1992). *Black Ivory. A History of British Slavery*. London, Harper Collins.
Ward, G (1987). *Wandering Girl*. Broome, Western Australia, Magabala Books.
Ward, G (1991). *Unna You Fullas*. Broome, Western Australia, Magabala Books.
Ware, V (1992). *Beyond the Pale: White Women, Racism and History*. London, Verso.
Waterson, D (1981). 'Justin Foxton.' In B Nairn and G Serle (eds), *Australian Dictionary of Biography, 1891–1939 Volume 8*. Carlton, Melbourne University Press.
Watson, J (1993). Becoming Bwgcolman: Exile and Survival on Palm Island Reserve, 1918 to the Present. PhD Thesis, University of Queensland.
West, A L (nd). 'Adjustment of Part Aborigines Trained on a Rural South West Mission.' Perth. Typescript, Perth, Aboriginal Affairs Department.
Western Australian Government (1905). 'Royal Commission on the Condition of the Natives: Report Presented to Both Houses of Parliament by His Excellency's Council, Western Australia.' W E Roth. *Western Australia*,

Votes and Proceedings, 5. Perth, Government Printer.

Western Australian Government (1934). 'Minutes of Evidence, Submissions, Diary of Sittings from the Royal Commission on the treatment of Aborigines.' H D Moseley. Typescript, Perth, State Records Office.

Western Australian Government (1935). 'Report of the Royal Commissioner Appointed to Investigate, Report and Advise Upon Matters in Relation to the Condition and Treatment of Aborigines.' H D Moseley. *Western Australia, Votes and Proceedings*, 2. Perth, Government Printer.

Western Australian Government (1948). 'Report of the Survey of Native Affairs.' F E Bateman. *Western Australia, Votes and Proceedings* (19). Perth, Government Printer.

Western Australian Government (1956). 'Report of Select Committee on Laverton and Warburton.' Western Australia, Votes and Proceedings, 3. Perth, Government Printer.

Western Australian Government (1956). 'Report of the Special Committee Appointed to inquire into Native Conditions in the Laverton–Warburton Range Area.' W L Grayden. *Western Australia, Votes and Proceedings*, 3. Perth, Government Printer.

Western Australian Government (1958). 'Report of Special Committee on Native Affairs.' Western Australia, Votes and Proceedings, 3. Perth, Government Printer.

Western Australian Government (1958). 'Report of the Special Committee on Native Matters (with particular reference to adequate finance).' F Gare. *Western Australia, Votes and Proceedings*, 2. Perth, Government Printer.

Western Australian Government, Department of Native Welfare (1967). *A Place in the Sun*. Perth, Government Printer.

Western Australian Government, Department of Native Welfare (nda). *Western Australian Citizens*. Perth, Government Printer.

Western Australian Government, Department of Native Welfare (ndb). *Department of Native Welfare: Functions and Activities*. Perth, Government Printer.

Western Australian Government (1974). *Report of the Royal Commission into Aboriginal Affairs*. L C Furnell. Perth, Government Printer.

Western Australian Government, Department of Community Welfare (1981). *Children in Limbo*. Perth, Department of Community Welfare.

Western Australian Government (1984). *The Aboriginal Land Inquiry Volume 1*. P Seaman. Perth, Government Printer.

Western Australian Government (1996). 'Human Rights and Equal Opportunity Commission National Inquiry into Separation of Aboriginal and Torres Strait Islander Children from their Families: Submission from the Government of Western Australia.' Perth, Department of Family and Children's Services. Typescript, Sydney, Human Rights and Equal Opportunity Commission.

Western Australian Government. The Select Committee of the Legislative Assembley (1996). Select Committee into Child Migration: Interrim Report. Chairman Mike Barnett.

White, R (1979). 'The Australian Way of Life.' *Historical Studies*, 18 (73).

White, R (1981). *Inventing Australia: Images and Identity 1688–1980*. North Sydney, George Allen & Unwin.

White, R and B Wilson (1991). 'Whose Future on Whose Terms.' In R White and B Wilson (eds), *For Your Own Good: Young People and State Intervention in Australia. Special Edition of Journal of Australian Studies*. Bundoora, Victoria, La Trobe University Press.

Whittington, V (1999). *Sister Kate: A Life Dedicated to Children in Need of Care*. Nedlands, University of Western Australia Press.

Wise, T (1985). *The Self-Made Anthropologist: A Life of A P Elkin*. Sydney, Allen & Unwin.

Wood, M (1997). 'The 'Breelong Blacks' In G Cowlishaw and B Morris (eds), *Race Matters: Indigenous Australians and 'Our' Society*. Canberra, Aboriginal Studies Press.

Woodward, F J (1951). *Portrait of Jane: A Life of Lady Franklin*. London, Hodder & Stoughton.

Woolmington, J (1988). 'Writing on the Sand: The First Missions to Aborigines in Eastern Australia.' In T Swain and D B Rose (eds). *Aboriginal Australians and Christian Missions. Ethnographic and Historical Studies*. Adelaide, The Australian Association for the Study of Religions.

Woolmington, J (1991). 'The "Assimilation" years in a Country Town.' *Aboriginal History*, 15 (1–2).

Wright, A (1997). *Plains of Promise*. St Lucia, University of Queensland Press.

Yardi, R and G Stokes (1998). 'Foundations for Reconciliation in Social Science: the Political Thought of C D Rowley.' *The Reconciliation Issue. Melbourne Journal of Politics*, 25.

Young, M W (1989). 'Suffer the Children: Wesleyans in the d'Entrecasteaux.' In M Jolly and M Macintyre (eds) *Family and Gender in the Pacific: Domestic Contradictions and the Colonial Impact*. Cambridge, Cambridge University Press.

Young, R J C (1995). *Colonial Desire. Hybridity in Theory, Culture and Race*. London, Routledge.

Government Records and Reports

Australian Archives (Australian Capital Territory)
Australian Archives (Northern Territory)
Australian Archives (Victoria)
New South Wales Aborigines Welfare Board Annual Reports
Queensland Aborigines Department Annual Reports
Queensland Northern Protector of Aborigines Annual Reports
Queensland Parliamentary Debates, Legislative Assembly
Queensland Parliamentary Debates, Legislative Council
Queensland State Archives
South Australian Aboriginal Affairs Advisory Board Annual Reports
South Australian Aborigines Department Annual Reports
South Australian Aborigines Protection Board Annual Reports
South Australian Archives
South Australian Protector of Aborigines Annual Reports
South Australian State Archives Government Records Group
Tasmanian State Archives
Tasmanian State Archives Colonial Secretary's Office
Tasmanian State Archives Minutes of Orphan School
Victorian Aborigines Welfare Board Annual Reports
Western Australian Aborigines Department Annual Reports
Western Australian Department of Native Affairs Annual Reports
Western Australian Department of Native Welfare Annual Reports
Western Australian Government Gazette
Western Australian Musuem, Anthropology
Western Australian Parliamentary Debates
Western Australian State Archives

Private Papers

Irene Schaffer Papers, Hobart
Uniting Church, Perth
Correspondence between Ward and Keller and Mr and Mrs W Johnson

Interviews and Submissions

Kevin Braedon interviewed by Anna Haebich at Alice Springs, August 1995
Eric Braedon and Mary Williams interviewed by Anna Haebich at Little Sisters Camp, Alice Springs, 16 March 1996
Pauline Johnson interviewed by Anna Haebich at Wattle Grove, Western Australia, October 1995
Submission by William Johnson to the Human Rights and Equal Opportunity Commission, National Inquiry into the Separation of Aboriginal and Torres Strait Islander Children from their Families, 1996

Newspapers and Magazines

Adelaide Review
Advertiser (Adelaide)
Advertiser (Bendigo)
Age (Melbourne)
Argus
Australian
Australian Aborigines Advocate
Cairns Morning Post
Catholic Citizen
Centralian Advocate (Alice Springs)
Colonial Times (Hobart)
Coolbaroo News (Perth)

Courier (Ballarat)
Courier Mail (Brisbane)
Daily Mail (Brisbane)
Daily Mail (Sydney)
Dawn
Gazette (Ottawa, Canada)
Geelong Advertiser
Geraldton Express
Great Southern Herald (Katanning)
Herald (Melbourne)
Hobart Town Gazette
Independent (Cooktown)
Launceston Examiner
Mail (Footscray)
Maryborough Advertiser
Mercury (Hobart)
Militant
Mirror (Sydney).
Morning Post (Cairns)
Narrogin Observer
National Times
News (Adelaide)
Ngoonjook Batchelor Journal of Aboriginal Education
North Queensland Register
Northern (Suburbs) Progress (Melbourne)
Northern Territory News (Darwin)
Observer (Hobart)
Observer (Melbourne)
Perth Mail
Point Pearce Mission News
Portland Observer and Guardian
Queenslander
Register (Adelaide)
Scientific American Supplement
Smoke Signals
Social Services Journal
Southern Districts Advocate (Katannning)
Sport (Adelaide)
Standard (Frankston)
Standard (Warnambool)
Star (Altona)
Sun (Melbourne)
Sun (Adelaide)
Sunday Mail
Sunday Observer
Sunday Times (Perth)
Sydney Morning Herald
Telegraph (Brisbane)
Telegraph (Sydney)
Times (Canberra)
Times Literary Supplement
Truth (Melbourne)
Truth (Brisbane)
Weekend Mail (Perth)
West Australian (Perth)
Western Mail (Perth)
Westralian Aborigine (Perth)
Winton Herald
Woman's Day

ACADEMIC JOURNALSS

Aboriginal History
Aboriginal Law Bulletin
Australian Child Welfare
Australian Cultural History
Australian Feminist Studies
Australian Historical Studies
Australian Journal Of Politics And History
Australian Quarterly
Australian Social Work
Comparative Studies in Anthropology and History
Continuum. Media/Discourse
Ethnology
Hecate
Historical Studies
Island
Journal of Australian Studies
Labour History
Meanjin
Media International Australia
Oceania
Quadrant
Records of the Queen Victoria Museum, Launceston New Series
Representations
Shelter
Social Analysis
Studies in Western Australia History
Tasmanian Historical Research Association

INDEX

opposition 600
parental consent 105
powers 536
practice, condoned 289
prevention strategies 288
public anguish 563
public opinion 578–580
publicity 576–585
rationale 119, 509
regulations 503
remembering and forgetting 564–570
responsibility 287, 290
reuniting programs 597, 600
South Australia 313–326, 534–538
southern states 312–313
statistics 506
to missions 276–277
to separate state issue 325–326
Western Australia 517, 523–527
see also child removal; full-blood Aborigines;
half-castes; mixed race; separations
Aboriginal Child Survival Seminar 603–604
Aboriginal child welfare
new directions 600–611
state and territory responsibility 608–609
see also child welfare
Aboriginal children *289*
abductions 73, 79–82, 140, 297
for labour 190, 297–298
abusive treatment 210–212, 214, 296, 311
admissions to orphanage 106
on Bass Strait Islands 77
behavior 86–88
best interests debate 581, 599
boys 170, 297
captured 86, 100, 211
in care, statistics 535
care and maintenance, new concept 536–537
in colonists' employ 85–88, 99–100, 211
in colonists' homes 85
committals 526
control returned to Aboriginal families 570,
600
controls 225, 231
experiments in civilising 66, 89–94, 109–117
forced removal 374, 517
a genocide crime 206–207
guardianship 348, 532, 535
inferior standards of care 564
in institutional care 198
in institutions, statistics 477
interests 605
representation 604
left with colonists 78
legal guardian 175, 187, 199, 314
legislation 174, 225

living with white families 618
statistics 477
in missions 240
place in colonial society 99
placements 227, 501, 506–508, 511, 525–526,
535, 537
with Aboriginal families 601–602
breakdowns 601–602
in dormitories 18–19, 98, 108
interstate 501
with white families 440–441
removal from families *see* Aboriginal child
removal
rescued from families 296
rights 326, 328
sent south from Northern Territory 477–481
separation from parents 69–70, 97–98,
202–203, 206
sold by pastoralists 298
Tasmanian 65–130
treatment 13–16, 78–79, 293, 326
uniform standards 607
war casualties 82–84
wards *see* wards of the state
see also children
Aboriginal Children's Advancement Society
592
Aboriginal children's homes 202, 478
Aboriginal children's institutions 13, 183, 192,
229–230, 344–348, 475
Aboriginal Children's Project *see* Blair Holiday
Project
Aboriginal communities
assistance 168
breaking up, explanation 498
Central Australian settlements 465–468
neglected 168
Queensland 434
rights 606
rounded up 174
self-managed organisations 31–32
self-supporting segregated 169, 174
Aboriginal conditions 138, 233, 430, 454, 498,
585, 588–589
deplorable 419–420, 422, 430, 585
improvements 444, 571
inquiry 211, 215, 437–439, 498
Aboriginal cultural performances 355
Aboriginal culture 76, 79, 98, 104, 132, 189, 294,
312, 578
undermined 70, 105
Aboriginal customary law 606–607
Aboriginal customs 96, 375
Aboriginal deaths in custody 51
Aboriginal departments, adoption and fostering
responsibilities 490

infertility 79, 126
living with sealers 101
mortality rates 236
permission to marry non-Aborigines 187
punitive controls 191
removal by Robinson 98–104
    from Bass Strait islands 101–104
rights 328, 332–333
    campaign 315, 326–341
rounded up 104
sexual contacts 321
    controls 18, 194, 232, 236
    legislation 236
sexuality, regulation 173
stereotypes 321
treatment 266, 326
and white station men 239
work in institutions 365
Aboriginal youth 51, 70, 353, 460, 486, 490, 515
captured 84–85
crime 57–59
dealt with by courts 527
incarceration 16, 486, 561
sexual needs 88
Aboriginality 23, 54, 57, 63, 126–127, 137, 166,
    168, 180, 203, 283, 343, 404, 406, 524
breeding out programs 161
concealing 549
definitions 484, 572
erasure measures 284, 285
excluded from education system 500
legal restrictions removal 23
replaced with Christian values and
    traditions 345
views 455
'Aboriginals'
definitions 171–172, 174, 307
Aboriginals Department 18–19
Aboriginals Ordinance 1911 191
Aboriginals Ordinance 1918 18
Aboriginals Ordinance 1939 19
Aborigines 65–130, 179–181
abductions 101
abusive treatment 210, 232, 263
amelioration General Plan 75–76
assimilated future and modern family vision
    418–429
attempts to change 165
Australian treatment, portrayal 587
blackbirding 211, 236
breeding out 497
British subjects 73, 78
brutal treatment 293
captured 96, 73, 84–85
in centralised institutions 197
classifications 219

cleared from colony 98
colonial narratives 89–94
community assistance 492–493
compliance with white standards 511
contact with whites, controls 221
controls 216, 273, 511–513
dealing with, concerns 418
definitions 219
departmental services 222–225
deported to reserves and missions 171
described 337
destitute and diseased 169
destruction attempts 66, 74, 76, 96
disappearance, views 165
disenfranchising 157
dispersal into wider community 498–499
a doomed race 138
a dying race 105, 126, 165, 167, 325
enforced compliance 202
excluded from census counts 222
extermination views 66, 74, 76
federal responsibility 453
feeling about white people 375
forced dispersion into wider community 181
forced from stations and missions 166–167
forced removal 169
to reserves 513
of full descent, doomed to extinction 273
governing *see* Aboriginal populations
kept on island settlements 76, 95–96
killed by settlers 18, 69, 71–74
management 233
of mixed descent, program 273
moved to government and mission
    settlements 22
New South Wales 181–186, 501–511
Northern Territory 190–197
official intervention 172
outcasts 156–164, 420
police controls 242–243
postwar changes 418–421, 423
preferential treatment claims 570
pressures on 25–26, 28
property of captors 190
protectorship systems 68, 69
Queensland 168–179, 289–312, 527–533
reared by whites 89–94
relocated 18
    to reserved areas and missions 18
    to towns 533–534
removal *see* removal
resistance to change 76, 86–89, 95, 98, 114,
    118, 120, 122, 466–468, 499, 504–505, 514
responsibility of the States 161–164
restrictions and restraints, abolished 534
rightful place in Australian society 422

British settlements, dealing with native inhabitants 68–69, 98
British subjects 156
  Australian Aborigines 73, 78
  Australian Nationals 156
Bronham, Ada 269, 335
Bruney, Davy 109, 111, 119
Bruney, Peter 109, 111, 113
Bruney, Thomas 112, 113
Bruny Island 91, 127
  Aboriginal Establishment 96
Brusnahan, Margaret 416
Bryant, Gordon 31, 436, 592–595, 597
Bungalow 18–19, 19, 20–22, 192, 196, 322, 324
bureaucracy, necessary features 218
bush skills 231, 401
Butler, Brian 604–605, 609

Campbell House Farm School 537
Canada 69, 78, 146–147, 152–153, 569, 603
Canadian Indian residential school system 146–147, 372, 485
Cape Barren Island 128, 495–496
  Aboriginal residents 129
  reserve 180
    closure 495
  settlement 129
Cape Barren Island Act 1945 495
Cape Barren Island Reserve Act 1912 180
Carrolup Native Settlement 260, 288, 354, 374, 384, 390, 413
  converted to Marribank Farm School 519
  Regulations 410
Catholic children 179
Catholic, children declared 201
Catholic church 237
Catholic institutions 179
Catholic missions 350
cattle killing 210–211, 232, 237–238
census 454
  Aborigines 557–558
    excluded 452
  colony 138
  counts 222
  national 222, 452, 454, 557
  see also population
Central Australia, assimilation 465–468
Central Australian Aboriginal Child Care Agency 63
Central Australian Aboriginal Congress 27, 31, 34
Central Australian Aboriginal Legal Aid Service 31–33, 46–47
Central Australian Legal Aid Service 29
Central Land Council 31, 32

Central Reserve 430, 432–434, 437
Chief Protector of Aborigines
  legal guardian of Aboriginal children 215, 226
  Northern Territory 325
  Queensland 141
  South Australia 315–317, 320
  legal guardianship 315
  Western Australia 213, 219–222, 225, 243–249
  see also Protector of Aborigines
child capture 211–212
child care 31, 37, 45, 146, 438
  Aboriginal societies 543
  alternative 543
  blueprint 154
  boarding out movement 541
  family-based 151
  fostering and adoption arrangements 541
  inferior standards 564
  new directions 602–611
  public opinion 578–580
  standards, concerns 501
  state 541
    intervention 574
  substitute care statistics 610
  Torres Strait Islander system 543
child emigration 152
child endowment 449, 478
  payments 449–452, 520
Child Endowment Act 451
child labour see labour
child mortality 107–108, 138
child offenders 146, 159
child placement agencies 602
child protection 146, 158, 169
  definition 146
child removal 70, 137, 168, 175–176, 199–200, 202, 249, 311, 460, 468–477
  by Aboriginal administrations 287
  by welfare authorities 33–37, 127, 287
  connection with adult incarceration 601
  different treatment 209–287
  disastrous consequences 130
  for education 532
  from families 146–147
  from Northern Territory 324
  half–castes see half-castes
  and institutionalisation 174, 226–27
    legislation 147, 174–175
    see also institutionalisation; institutions
  legislation 537
  opposition 312–326
  powers 175, 183, 187, 226
  Queensland 531–532
  reason 168
  responsibility 287